THE FOXES ALPHABET

A COMPLETE WHO'S WHO OF LEICESTER CITY FOOTBALL CLUB

By PAUL TAYLOR & DAVE SMITH

Published by
POLAR PRINT GROUP LTD

DEDICATION ONE
To Barbara, for 42 years of support; and to Linda,
for her perverse priorities (loving me and hating the game).
P.T.

DEDICATION TWO
For my wife Helen, with all my love as always; and for Tom,
Jennie, Paul and Sally - the new generation of the Blue Army.
D.S.

First published in Great Britain by
Polar Print Group Ltd
2, Uxbridge Road, Leicester LE4 7ST
England

Text © Copyright 1995 Paul Taylor & Dave Smith
Design © Copyright 1995 Polar Print Group Ltd

ISBN 1 899538 06 2

Edited by
Julian Baskcomb

Designed and Printed by
Polar Print Group Ltd
2, Uxbridge Road, Leicester LE4 7ST
Telephone: (0116) 2610800

Photographs and illustrations are courtesy of:
Leicester City FC, Neville Chadwick Photography, Associated Sports Photography, Empics Ltd,
Colorsport, Leicester Mercury, Raymonds Press Agency, David Munden Photography, Leicester
Records Office, Linda Carruthers-Watt and The National Film & Television Archive.
Many of the photographs reproduced are from original material in the files at Leicester City FC,
who also retain the rights to official photocall pictures from the present era taken by the
appointed Club Photographer. Most remaining photographs are from the private collections of
the authors or from albums owned by various Leicester supporters or former players. We have
been unable to trace the sources of all these pictures, but any photographer involved is cordially
invited to contact the publishers in writing providing proof of copyright.

Cover photographs:
*Front: (Clockwise): Gordon Banks; Jon Sammels, Keith Weller & Alan Birchenall; Gary Lineker;
Jack Froggatt; Gary McAllister; Simon Grayson.*
*Back: (Left to Right by column): Ernie Hine; Peter Shilton; Gene O'Callaghan; Fred Osborn;
John O'Neill; Julian Joachim; Arthur Rowley; Colin Appleton.*

FOREWORD

by Gary Lineker

It is a pleasure for me to contribute to The Foxes Alphabet, which I am sure will prove to be the ultimate guide to the players who have been privileged to play for Leicester City in the club's first 100 years or so.

Having read the pre-publication leaflet, I am truly intrigued to know "which ex-Fossil appeared on stage with Charlie Chaplin and Stan Laurel". My guess is Alan Birchenall - but the pages that follow will provide you with the real answer to that particular nugget.

Leicester is the club that I have always supported and it was a proud day for me when I made my debut on the right wing against Oldham on 1st January 1979. We won 2-0. I remember it well, not least for the bitterly cold conditions. My agent, Jon Holmes, remembers it for other reasons: "Gary was absolute crap, to be honest". Things improved a little bit over the next seven years - it was never quite so cold again. I remember those years as some of the happiest of my playing career.

They were good times for the club but there have clearly been many champagne moments in our history - Cup Finals, titles and more recent play-off success. Whenever there has been a football competition created, City has made its mark.

We have produced some fantastic players as well. Two of the greatest goalkeepers in the history of the sport just happened to follow each other into the Leicester team 25 years ago. The youngest-ever FA Cup Final captain led us out at Wembley in 1969. These are players who have stayed vivid in the memory of all Leicester City supporters; but find out more about Arthur Chandler and Sep Smith - great names for the past whom few today will have seen. It's all here. If you're a true Foxes fan - learn your Alphabet!

Gary Lineker
September 1995

CONTENTS

Tea lady Clarice Laxton makes the London boys feel at home at Filbert Street in February 1973. Pictured are Jon Sammels, Alan Birchenall, Keith Weller, Lenny Glover, Dennis Rofe and manager Jimmy Bloomfield.

INTRODUCTION

Many years ago, there used to be an apocryphal story about Aston Villa and their fans' commitment to the club's cause: centred on the contention that the management could hang out eleven claret-and-blue shirts on a washing line at Villa Park and still attract a five-figure crowd. It's fanciful to think that once the same might smilingly have been said about Leicester City and Filbert Street; though of course half the crowd there would have been giving verbal stick to at least two of the blue shirts for not drying quickly enough ...

The relationship between the Leicester supporter and the men who carry his or her hopes for the club has always been a complex one. The crowd have had their heroes, the 'boo boys' their targets: often a single player will have experienced both reactions to his efforts. An 'unforgettable' may have turned out for less than a season in City blue; an 'unforgivable' may soldier on until a testimonial campaign and still look for a niche in the collective affections of his viewing critics. One player returns to Filbert Street with another club to a warm ovation; one to abuse. One spectator's 'flair' player is another's useless 'fancy-dan'; the cornerstone of one manager's defensive line-up regarded as a mere liability to the bulk of the Blue Army.

Leicester is definitely one of those places where a player can be revered and rubbished at the very same time; where potential can have been betrayed before a player's out of his teens, yet where someone can remain 'a promising youngster' until their mid-20s. City fans won't stand for watching any of their team shirts flapping in the breeze, but they'll also demand that the men who fill those shirts actually earn the privilege.

Logic plays little part in this process of acceptance and admiration of those who play **for** the shirt. One of your authors recalls piping out at the age of ten from the Double Decker that City's on-field problems would be solved at a stroke by feeding the ball more regularly to Billy Hodgson; all the writer remembers now of Billy is the all-action scurrying of a little feller with a propensity for embarrassing defenders who (then) looked twice his size. The same author has, though, probably disgraced himself in more recent years by advising loudly from the back of the Carling Stand that under no circumstances should the ball *ever* be played square on the half-way line to such-and-such a City player.

The other author, incidentally, still thinks that it was Hodgson's successor, Jackie Sinclair, who was the greatest thing since sliced bread; but that's what makes football fans the wonderfully diverse breed we are.

So, it's hoped that we've established that the estimations we've made herein of around 800 Fosse and City men (of whom we've personally watched around 300 in action) aren't necessarily going to be wholly consensual. We would, though, hope you'll accept that the purely factual context we've placed them in represents a decently devoted research effort and a significant advance on the first-draft attempt at this project we published six years ago in our club history *Of Fossils & Foxes*. Every first-team player is here, from the Fossils who washed their own shirts to the mid-90s City men faced with several thousand replica tops in the crowd; from the expensive mistakes to the cost-nothing *maestri*; and from the stalwarts to the single-outing substitutes.

A few of the entries remain wholly or partially unchanged from those in the earlier volume, but the vast majority have been buttressed with extra facts and details, and a substantial number rewritten entirely. All active players have had their records updated to the end of 1994/95. The pioneer Midland League players have been worked into the main Alphabet; and those players who performed exclusively within the context of wartime football given their own appendices. We have also made an attempt at comprehensively illustrating this book: the quality of original pictorial material may vary widely for some early players in particular, but the period glories of certain photos we've unearthed should, we believe, more than compensate. Wherever possible, photos have been selected which relate to each player's time with Fosse or City.

We identified several dark clouds over football when we briefly waxed thoughtful in *OF & F*. With the massive changes in and around the game (not to mention the more parochial Filbert Street fluctuations) during the interim period, it could be deemed fair enough to judge that those clouds have merely changed formation, and remain just as threatening to the game we love. Yet football is just as likely to survive and thrive on the sort of contradictions thrown up in the week or so prior to the penning of this introduction. On the one hand, it is eminently possible to agree with *The Independent's* Phil Shaw when he asserts that 'there is a cash register where the heart of English football used to be'; but what does one then make of sitting amidst the City support at Luton as they break, mid-match, into a spontaneous chant of Mike Galloway's name, while the former City loanee lies dangerously injured in a Leicester hospital following an horrific car crash?

We trust that, for readers as much as ourselves, the heart of the game and of Leicester City Football Club still beats both on the pitch and in the stands, and hope that this particular, personality-oriented perspective on the club's history helps nourish its lifeblood.

Paul Taylor / Dave Smith
September 1995

Ken Leek pressurises the Barnsley defence in the FA Cup Sixth Round replay in 1961. Leek scored in every round as City reached Wembley, but was then dropped for the final.

ACKNOWLEDGEMENTS

The acknowledgments page in *Of Fossils & Foxes* bore lengthy testimony to the authors' profound indebtedness to the assistance and support of numerous individuals and institutions in researching and collating the facts which underpin an exercise such as this in the growing (but still underdeveloped) field of football history.

We would wish to reiterate thanks to all who contributed information or material for that volume; but within the space available here concentrate on expressing our sincere gratitude to those who have helped make the substantial difference between our first-draft 'Who's Who' of Leicester Fosse and City and this version of *The Foxes Alphabet*. Such contributors fall mainly into the camps of club supporters, former players and their families, and our fellow-members of the Association of Football Statisticians, and we salute them all as true collaborators.

The indefatigable football researcher (and Norwich City historian), Mike Davage, has to head the list for the sheer volume and superb value of his regular correspondence and crucial challenges; but we will resort (fittingly!) to the alphabetic in sincerely thanking the following: Charlie Adam, Dr John Batterbee, Reg Beaumont, John G Blackmore, Jill Bocock, Colin Boulter, Phil Brown, Stephen Byrne, Joe Calvert, Colin Cameron, Irene Cave, Gary Chalk, Alan Craft, Jack Curtis, Gareth M Davies, Stuart Farmer, Michael Featherstone, Alan Futter, Ian Garland, Alan Harding, Jimmy Harrison, Stewart Henry, Chris Horner, Bill Hume, Gerald Hutchinson, Trefor Jones, Colin Jose, Ray Kirby, David Kirkby, Douglas Lamming, Rob Lee, Eugene MacBride, Colin Martin, Gerald Mortimer, Martin O'Connor, Mark Osborne, Maurice Scott, Tony Sealy, Ray Spiller, Barbara Taylor, Tise Vahimagi, Lars-Olof Wendler and Ian Wilson. Our gratitude, too, goes to the Library staff at Colindale and Leicester, to Steve England and his staff in the Leicester Mercury Library, to the workers at Leicester City Football Club for their gracious assistance, and to anyone else we have inadvertently overlooked.

We particularly wish to record our thanks to all those who subscribed to or purchased *Of Fossils & Foxes*, and those, named within, who have shown faith in advance in this volume: without you, there would be no book.

There would be no book, either - or certainly not one with such high production values - without the wonderfully supportive relationship we have with our publishers, Polar: our deep gratitude especially goes to Julian Baskcomb and Julia Byrne.

And thanks, finally but fundamentally, to those players logged herein who created the Filbert Street tradition, and to those who will carry it forward ....

NOTES ON THE TEXT

In terms of the main Players' Alphabet, the layout of each entry is fairly self-explanatory. Where all relevant facts are known to us, the entry successively lists the player's full name, his primary positional role while at the club, his birth and death details, a chronology of his senior playing career, his Fosse or City debut details, a biographical portrait or assessment, and a statistical summary of his appearances and goalscoring records for Leicester.

A few players (such as Jamie Durrant and Dick Pudan) were invariably known by non-registered forenames, which are here duly parenthesised; while nicknames or familiar derivatives/diminutives are used as appropriate in the biographical notes.

An attempt has always been made to convey a positional role in the terms of the time the player was active.

For many players we have been unable to track down exact birth or death dates: the abbreviation 'c' (for circa, or about) has occasionally been employed; as has the abbreviation 'qtr' when a death has only been registered as occurring within, say, the April/May/June quarter of a given year.

The career entry features successive transfer or registration changes, dated wherever possible, and relates to senior playing contracts only. Details of schoolboy football have been largely excluded; while the continuation of a football career into coaching, management or other backroom roles is noted in the biographical text. Trials and temporary loan moves are usually parenthesised; though in the case of a loan which concluded with the permanent signing of a player, only the earlier date is given. Where doubts persist as to the exact trajectory of a player's moves (as with, for instance, Jock Paterson), mention is made in the text. Common abbreviations are used for the terms junior (jnr), amateur (am), apprentice (app), trainee (YT) and professional (pro). Club names are given as they were at the time a player signed (eg. Small Heath, Birmingham or Birmingham City as appropriate); and foreign club names rendered in the original language rather than Anglicised.

The debut details given relate solely to the first senior appearance for Fosse or City in recognised competitive fare; ie in those competitions for which appearances and goalscoring records are summarised (see below). Friendlies are discounted in this context; as are such instances as Jon Sammels' bow in the 1971 FA Charity Shield match.

The abbreviations utilised in statistically summarising a player's Leicester record are as follows:

PL: FA Premiership (1994/5)
FL: Football League (1894 - 1994)
ML: Midland League (1891 - 1894)
FAC: Football Association Cup (1890 - 1995)
FLC: Football League Cup (1960 - 1995)
Eur: European Cup Winners' Cup (1961/2)
FMC: Full Members' Cup (1987 - 1992)
AIC: Anglo-Italian Cup (1992 - 1994)
P/O: Football League Play-offs (1992 - 1994)
WW1: Football League - Midland Section (Main & Subsidiary Tournaments) (1915 - 1919)
WW2: Football League (abandoned 1939/40 season); Regional League - Midland Division (1939/40); League War Cup (1939 - 1941); South Regional League (1940/1); Midland Cup (1940/1); Football League - Southern Section (1941/2); Football League North (1942 - 1945); Football League South (1945/6).

The inclusion of games categorised as WW1 or WW2 is a departure from *Of Fossils & Foxes*, integrating non-first class appearances into certain players' records. This process has been undertaken in order that players' full careers can be set in their proper context.

Deliberately excluded from such records are other non-first class fixtures, constituting games played in the United Counties League (1894/5), the Southern Professional Floodlit Cup (1959/60), the FA Charity Shield (1971), the Anglo-Italian Tournament (1972), the Texaco Cup (1972 - 1974) and the Anglo-Scottish Tournament (1975). The 3rd/4th place Play-off game in the FA Cup of 1973/4 has also been discounted. (Players whose sole senior appearances for the club came in these invitational or non-standard competitions are invariably mentioned in the Nearly Men appendix; while separate appendices cover those players whose City outings came exclusively in the context of wartime football).

(As ever, the authors would be delighted to hear, via the publishers, from any readers able to furnish missing facts or extra details on any of the players covered within this volume).

ADAM, Charles

Role: Outside left
b. Glasgow, 22nd March 1919

CAREER: Strathclyde/Sept 1938:CITY/July 1952:Mansfield Town/cs 1955:Corby Town.

Debut (WW2) v Tottenham Hotspur (A) 24.5.41; (postwar) v Chelsea (A) 5.1.46 FAC (scored once)

A pre-war teenage signing from Glaswegian junior football, Charlie made the first official mark on City's postwar record when scoring at Stamford Bridge in the two-legged FA Cup tie which constituted the club's reintroduction to nationally competitive football. In the interim, he had built up a modicum of footballing experience with City, QPR and Leeds United, but had primarily served the war effort with stints in the Building Trades Flying Squad (helping repair blitz damage) and on military service in France and Italy. A conventionally neat and nippy but unusually constructive winger, with a fine understanding with spearhead Jack Lee, Charlie became a regular in the No.11 shirt for five seasons, highlighted by his ever-present status in the 1949 Cup run to Wembley. He then lent his veteran skills to the Stags for a further 98 League and Cup games (9 goals) under the management regimes of ex-Leicester men George Jobey and Stan Mercer. Later he spent some 16 years as manager to the County Youth team (during which spell the FA County Youth Cup came to Leicestershire for the only time), and was also briefly a senior City scout. As evidenced in local press items as recently as 1994, Charlie remains a fine judge of a player, and an astute reader of the game.

> **Appearances:**
> *FL: 158 apps. 22 gls.*
> *FAC: 22 apps. 3 gls.*
> *WW2: 8 apps. 0 gls.*
> **Total:** *188 apps.*
> *25 gls.*

Charlie Adam

ADCOCK, Hugh

Role: Outside right
b. Coalville, Leics, 10th April 1903
d. Coalville, 16th October 1975

CAREER: Coalville Town/Apr 1921: Loughborough Corinthians/ Feb 1923:CITY/July 1935:Bristol Rovers/ Sept 1936:Folkestone/Ibstock Penistone Rovers.

Debut v Hull City (A) 25.8.23

Capped five times for England and once for the Football League in 1929 and 1930, after his direct right-wing play had helped City to runners-up spot in the First Division, Hughie was a fine clubman whose twelve-year service encompassed and helped create City's halcyon days as a major force in League football. His partnerships with inside men Johnny Duncan and Ernie Hine (the latter further developed at international level) were especially fruitful, and his supply to Arthur Chandler immaculate, while his tearaway individualism brought him a fair personal tally of hard-struck goals. Hughie gained a Division Two championship medal in 1924/5, and was still exhibiting undiminished footballing enthusiasm over twenty years later, acting as trainer to Leicestershire Senior League outfits Whitwick Colliery and Coalville Town, while working as a maintenance engineer. On three occasions he appeared in the same national side as his cousin,

AGNEW, Stephen Mark

Role: Midfield
b. Shipley, Yorkshire, 9th November 1965

CAREER: app July 1982/pro Nov 1983: Barnsley/June 1991:Blackburn Rovers/ (Nov 1992-loan-Portsmouth)/Feb 1993: CITY/Jan 1995:Sunderland.
Debut v Portsmouth (A) 20.2.93

Always a thorn in City's side when facing them for Barnsley, whose midfield he ran for 234 League and Cup games (scoring 36 times), balding linkman Steve twice had to overcome severe injury problems before arriving at Filbert Street. A broken leg in 1985/6 only briefly halted his Oakwell progress, but Steve's Blackburn career after a record £700,000 move was completely blighted when long-term injury sidelined him after only four games. He eventually proved his fitness on loan at Fratton Park, then became a £250,000 Brian Little capture

Hughie Adcock

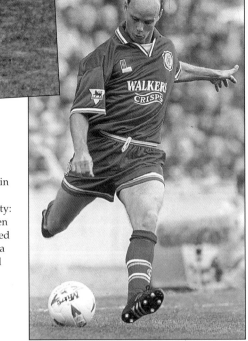

Steve Agnew

Birmingham's Joe Bradford; while, more ironically, he made his Bristol Rovers debut in opposition to Arthur Chandler, himself turning out for the first time for Notts County: the two men had shared a City debut a dozen years before, after Hughie had initially earned plaudits for speed, trickery and pluck (plus a 1922 County Cup-winners medal) at Central Alliance level in Loughborough.

Appearances:
FL: 434 apps. 51 gls.
FAC: 26 apps. 1 gl.
Total: *460 apps. 52 gls.*

to bolster City's promotion bid. Steve appeared at Wembley in the 1993 Play-Off defeat by Swindon, but was missing from the line-up a year later when Derby were dispatched. He became City's acting skipper in Gary Mills' absence, and played a number of fine games as a ball-winner in front of the back line, but he occasionally looked to lack a little of his old flair in more advanced positions, and his once-explosive shooting could tend to the wayward. Steve turned down a mooted move to Stoke in October 1994, but soon became the first departure from Mark McGhee's inherited Premiership squad in a £200,000 transfer to Roker Park.

Appearances:
PL: 7 (4) apps. 0 gls.
FL: 45 apps. 4 gls.
FAC: 2 apps. 0 gls.
LC: 4(1) apps. 0 gls.
P/O: 2 apps. 0 gls.
Total: *60(5) apps. 4 gls.*

AITKEN, Andrew

Role: Centre half
b. Ayr, 27th April 1877
d. Ponteland,
Northumberland,
15th February 1955

CAREER: Annbank/
Ayr FC/1894:Ayr
Parkhouse/July 1895:
Newcastle United/
(Feb 1899-loan-Kilmarnock)/
Nov 1906:Middlesbrough (p/mgr)/
Feb 1909:FOSSE/Apr 1911:Dundee/
June 1912:Kilmarnock/Jan 1913:Gateshead
Town (p/mgr).

Andy
Aitken

Debut v Liverpool (A) 13.2.09

Already a vastly experienced international wing-half/centre-half when signed by Fosse late in their sole First Division campaign, Andy was then handed the position of player-manager in April 1909 (after relegation was confirmed), and went on to reclaim the captaincy of Scotland as he added three caps to his previous tally of eleven. Nicknamed 'Daddler' during his years on Tyneside, he had been part of Newcastle's 1898 promotion side, had won a Championship medal in 1905 and FA Cup runners-up medals in 1905 and

1906, and had skippered that side in many of his 300-plus games; while during his Ayresome spell he had directed the play of such greats as Steve Bloomer and Alf Common. A classily creative defender even as a veteran, Andy led Fosse to 5th and 15th positions in his two full Second Division seasons at the helm, then moved back to Scotland before closing his active career with another player-manager stint in the North Eastern League. He subsequently became a publican in Manchester, and later acted as a Northern scout for Arsenal.

Appearances:
FL: 64 apps. 1 gl.
FAC: 7 apps. 0 gls.
Total: *71 apps. 1 gl.*

ALDERSON, Brian Roderick

Role: Forward
b. Dundee, 5th May 1950

CAREER: Lochee Harp/July 1970:Coventry City/July 1975:CITY/Mar 1978:New England Tea Men/Mar 1980:Atlanta Chiefs.

Debut v Birmingham City (H) 16.8.75 (scored once)

A small but stocky utility forward discovered by Coventry in Scottish junior football, Brian gained one Under-23 cap while playing in successful tandem with Colin Stein at Highfield Road, and cost City a six-figure transfer fee. In two seasons as a Filbert Street regular, however, he failed to reproduce his previously prolific scoring form, and looked uncomfortable when played wide on the right. He eventually faded from the scene during the disastrous 1977/8 relegation

Brian Alderson

season, joining a nine-man transfer and loan exodus to the transatlantic NASL, where he settled for four summer seasons.

Appearances:
FL: 87(3) apps. 9 gls.
FAC: 4 apps. 0 gls.
LC: 4(1) apps. 0 gls.
Total: *95(4) apps. 9 gls.*

ALLEN, Henry

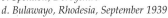

Role: Outside left
b. Spondon, Derbyshire
d. Bulawayo, Rhodesia, September 1939

CAREER: Alvaston/Oct 1898:Derby County/Dec 1899:FOSSE/May 1900: Derby County/1900:Alvaston & Boulton.

Debut v New Brighton Tower (A) 16.12.1899

A 'dainty' outside-left who picked up an FA Cup runners-up medal in his first season at Derby (from the 1-4 defeat by Sheffield United), Harry then surprisingly found himself surplus to the Rams' requirements after only two more appearances in their League side. With Fosse he briefly took the left flank position from Rab King, but failed to make sufficient impact. He was reported to be applying to the FA for reinstatement as an amateur when returning to Derbyshire in April 1900; shortly thereafter emigrated to Rhodesia (now Zimbabwe) to help plan that country's railway system; and was much later heard of in a senior footballing context as vice-president of the Bulawayo FA.

Appearances:
FL: 13 apps. 2 gls.
FAC: 1 app. 0 gls.
Total: *14 apps. 2 gls.*

ALLEYNE, Robert Anthony

Role: Striker
b. Birmingham, 27th September 1968

CAREER: app/pro Sept 1986:CITY/(Oct 1987-loan-Wrexham)/Mar 1988:Chesterfield/Aug 1989:Tielt (Belgium)/Mar 1992:Telford United/1992:Sutton Coldfield Town/

Robert Alleyne

1993: Tamworth/ cs 1994: Matlock Town.
Debut v West Ham United (A) 1.1.87 (sub)

Plucked directly from the youth team ranks to warm the City bench during an injury crisis, Robert got his initial taste of League action without so much as a full reserve game to his credit, and two days later was contributing as a left-sided attacker to one of the relegation season's few highlights - the 6-1 drubbing of Sheffield Wednesday. He materially helped City to the semi-finals of the FA Youth Cup in 1987, then grabbed a chance to add more early experience to his promise with a first-team run at the Racecourse, marked by two goals in ten games. Robert moved on to Saltergate when David Pleat started his initial pruning of the City playing staff, and after a season there was freed into the Belgian Third Division; later returning to the Midland non-league game.

Appearances:
FL: 1 (2) apps. 0 gls.
Total: *1 (2) apps. 0 gls.*

ALLMAN, Messina Wilson (Dick)

Role: Forward
b. Burslem, Staffs, 1883

CAREER: Burslem Higherhave/1903:Burslem Port Vale/cs 1905:Reading/May 1907: Portsmouth/Nov 1907:Plymouth Argyle/July 1908:Liverpool/cs 1909:Wrexham/Ton Pentre/Grantham/Nov 1911:FOSSE/June 1912:Croydon Common.

Debut v Barnsley (H) 18.11.11

A well-travelled inside or centre-forward who

failed to spark a goal-shy Fosse to a single win during his brief first-team tenure, which ended when he was one of six Fossils to leave the field early during the notorious weather-beaten game at Grimsby in January 1912. Before turning professional with his home town club (for whom he scored against Fosse in April 1905), Dick had followed a typical Potteries trade as an earthenware painter. His Southern League career was steady rather than spectacular (17 goals for Reading, 6 for Plymouth's runners-up side); his Anfield experience amounted to a single outing; and probably his best moment in the game was scoring the winning goal for Wrexham in the Welsh Cup Final of 1910. One source places Dick at Maidstone United for a brief post-war stint.

Appearances:
FL: 7 apps. 3 gls.
Total: 7 apps. 3 gls.

ALLSOPP, Thomas Charlesworth

Tommy Allsopp

Role: Outside left
b. Leicester,
18th December 1880
d. Norwich, 7th March 1919

CAREER: Aug 1899:FOSSE/Aug 1902:Luton Town/May 1904:FOSSE/Aug 1905:Brighton & Hove Albion/May 1907:Norwich City.

Debut v Middlesbrough (A) 16.2.01

One of several Fosse players to put in two stints with the club, Tommy was a speedy outside-left who also totted up over 200 appearances for his three (then) Southern League clubs, and a useful cricketing all-rounder for both Leicestershire (1903-5) and Norfolk (1907-12). His goal aided Norwich's celebrated giant-killing of Cup-holders Sheffield Wednesday in 1908, and he was a regular penalty taker for that club. Tommy survived WW1 service as a Labour Battalion sergeant in France, but contracted influenza on the ship home and died shortly afterwards while working as a Norwich licensee.

Appearances:
FL: 64 apps 6 gls.
FAC: 6 apps. 1 gl.
Total: 70 apps. 7 gls.

ANDERSON, Andrew L.

Role: Outside left
b. Glasgow

CAREER:
Ashfield Juniors/
St.Mirren/May
1908:Newcastle
United/May 1912:
Third Lanark/July
1914:FOSSE/1919:
Abercorn.

Debut v Lincoln City (H) 2.9.14

Andy Anderson

Andrew's second spell in English football, as Fosse's regular outside-left during the dire final pre-war League season, was a sharp contrast to his first. His efforts in helping St.Mirren to the 1908 Scottish Cup Final had originally earned him a £350 transfer to Tyneside, a supporting role in Newcastle's 1909 Championship win, and an international trial; but at Filbert Street his left-wing partnership with fellow Glaswegian George Hastie unfortunately failed either to click or to lift Fosse out of the re-election zone.

Appearances:
FL: 25 apps. 1 gl.
FAC: 1 app. 0 gls.
Total: 26 apps. 1 gl.

ANDERSON, John

Role: Goalkeeper
b. Barrhead, Renfrewshire, 8th December 1929

CAREER: St.Charles (Paisley)/
1946:Arthurlie/Dec 1948:CITY/July 1960:
Peterborough United/cs 1961:Nuneaton Borough/Bedworth Town.

Debut v Barnsley (A) 6.4.49

On the short side for a goalkeeper, John nonetheless possessed sharp reflexes and a good sense of anticipatory positioning. Intermittent first team appearances marked his early years at Filbert Street, but he became a regular between the City sticks in 1951/2, and was ever-present in the Division Two championship season of 1954; at the close of

Johnny Anderson

which he won a Scotland 'B' cap and then made his single full international appearance, in a 2-1 win against Finland. Injury sidelined John for the run-in to the 1957 championship, and he subsequently had to battle with Dave MacLaren for the senior jersey; while he suffered even worse luck with Posh when he found himself permanent reserve during their record-breaking initial season in the League, and played in only a single League Cup defeat. During his Arthurlie days, he had been capped in the only Junior international ever to have been staged at Hampden Park (May 1948 versus Republic of Ireland).

Appearances:
FL: 261 apps. 0 gls.
FAC: 16 apps. 0 gls.
Total: *277 apps. 0 gls.*

ANDERSON, Robert

Role: Outside right/left
b. Newton Mearns, Ayrshire, 11th August 1928

CAREER: Mearns Amateurs/am Aug 1944/ pro Jan 1946:CITY/cs 1949:Coalville Town/ 1950:Whitwick Colliery/Sept 1951:Third Lanark/Nov 1951:Kilmarnock/July 1953: Hamilton Academicals/Feb 1954:Forres Mechanics.

Debut (WW2) v Brentford (A) 6.9.45; (postwar) v West Ham United (A) 7.9.46 (scored once)

Having made a handful of appearances as a teenager in the final wartime season of regional football, this nippy Scottish winger then found himself cast in the role of permanent understudy to both Mal Griffiths and Charlie Adam when peaceful combat resumed. His eventual return to Scotland from the North Leicestershire coalfield reintroduced Bob to the senior sphere, and he notched 6 goals in 32 games during his Killie stint.

Appearances:
FL: 19 apps. 2 gls.
WW2: 5 apps. 0 gls.
Total: *24 apps. 2 gls.*

Robert Anderson

ANDREWS, Ian Edmund

Role: Goalkeeper
b. Nottingham, 1st December 1964

CAREER: app 1980: Mansfield Town/Sept 1981:CITY/(Jan 1984-loan-Middlesbrough)/ (Jan 1984-loan-Swindon Town)/July 1988: Celtic/(Dec 1988-loan-Leeds United)/Dec 1989:Southampton/(Aug 1994-loan-Plymouth Argyle)/Sept 1994:Bournemouth.

Debut v Wolverhampton Wanderers (A) 7.5.84

Snapped up by alert City youth coach Dave Richardson while Nottingham Forest (with whom he had been on associate schoolboy forms) and Mansfield (where he had started an apprenticeship) dithered over his potential, Ian was immediately groomed as goalkeeping successor to Mark Wallington. Soon winning England Youth caps, he made prodigious progress to the fringe of the first team, and made an unexpected League bow while on emergency loan to Swindon, only a week after commencing a similar spell at Ayresome. His agility and confidence seemed to mark him as a worthy heir to City's fine goalkeeping tradition and, following Wallington's departure, Ian's deserving candidacy for Under-21 honours was loudly canvassed. He was finally capped at that level as an over-age player in the early months of the 1986/7 season, when showing inspired First Division form. But, as City gradually slid into the danger zone, Ian's own confidence dipped alarmingly, and his comparative lack of experience began to cost the team dearly, with

his sense of positioning coming under rigorous critical scrutiny after several opposition attacks had exploited his habit of wandering from his line. Subsequently, he lost his first-team place to Paul Cooper, but became a prime transfer target for several clubs before City accepted £300,000 from Celtic to allow him briefly to contest the No.1 spot at Parkhead with Irish international (and one-time City trialist) Pat Bonner. Thereafter, reserve status adhered to Ian even following his move to The Dell (where, for instance, he sat out the 1992/3 season as an unused substitute for every fixture), and it was not until he reached Dean Court that he could claim a regular senior place once more.

Appearances:
FL: 126 apps. 0 gls.
FAC: 7 apps. 0 gls.
LC: 6 apps. 0 gls.
Total: *139 apps. 0 gls.*

Ian Andrews

ANSTEY, Brendel

Role: Goalkeeper
b. Bristol, c 1887
d. Wednesbury, December 1933

CAREER: Hanham Juniors/1910:Bristol Rovers/Feb 1911:Aston Villa/Sept 1919:CITY/ cs 1920:Mid-Rhondda/cs 1922:Wednesdbury.

Debut v Wolverhampton Wanderers (A) 6.9.19

A patient understudy to international keeper Sam Hardy for much of his lengthy stay at Villa Park (where he totted up 45 pre-war League appearances), Brendel briefly usurped Herbert Bown's place between the Filbert Street sticks in the early part of 1919/20. However, with a few press criticisms of his susceptibility to low shots, and his failure to leave his line often enough, adding to the pressures on him, he failed to satisfy Peter Hodge's exacting team-building requirements, and soon dropped down to Southern League level. Brendel had additionally guested for Birmingham during WW1.

> **Appearances:**
> *FL: 7 apps. 0 gls.*
> **Total:** *7 apps. 0 gls.*

APPLETON, Colin Harry

Role: Left half
b. Scarborough, 7th March 1936

CAREER: 1951:Scarborough/Mar 1954: CITY/May 1966:Charlton Athletic/ July 1967:Barrow (p/mgr)/ cs 1969:Scarborough (p/mgr).

Debut v Manchester City (H) 4.9.54

Recommended to City by former stalwart Reg Halton (then managing Scarborough), Colin made a rapid first-team break-through, but found his progress in the late 50s hampered both by a stint of National Service and by the competition of successive senior left-halves Eddie Russell, Pat Ward, Don Walker and Ken Keyworth.

ARMSTRONG, George

Role: Outside right
b. Hebburn, Co.Durham, 9th August 1944

CAREER: Hawthorn Leslie/Aug 1961: Arsenal/Sept 1977:CITY/(cs 1978-loan-Philadelphia Fury)/Sept 1978:Stockport County.

Debut v Nottingham Forest (H) 24.9.77

Multiply-honoured with Arsenal (a League and Cup double medallist in 1971, a Fairs Cup winner in 1970, and with runners-up medals from one further FA Cup and two League Cup campaigns), this little Geordie terrier - a rare perpetual-motion winger - was unfortunately past his peak when Frank McLintock laid out £15,000 to bring him to City. The pace that had seen him through over 600 games at Highbury (exactly 500 in the League), and had earned him five England Under-23 caps, was largely

Colin Appleton leads City out, Gordon Banks follows.

gone, and even his renowned spirit waned a little in City's abysmal relegation season. Jock Wallace allowed him to leave early in the 1978/9 campaign, and he retired as a player the following summer. Having subsequently held various coaching positions with Aston Villa, Fulham, Enderby Town, Middlesbrough, QPR and Worcester City, and in both Norway and Kuwait, George returned to Arsenal to look after their reserves in July 1990.

George Armstrong

Appearances:
FL: 14 (1) apps. 0 gls.
FAC: 1 app. 1 gl.
LC: 1 app. 0 gls.
Total: *16 (1) apps. 1 gl.*

ASHBY, Henry Radford

Role: Full back
b. Derby

CAREER: Derby Athletic/cs 1896:Burton Swifts/cs 1899:Brighton United/Nov 1899: not known/cs 1901:Burton United/cs 1904: Plymouth Argyle/July 1905:FOSSE.
Debut v Clapton Orient (H) 2.9.05

A full-back of genuine class, Harry had his career tragically cut short by a serious leg-break, sustained at Hull in March 1907, which necessitated early retirement. At the time of his injury, he had missed only a single Fosse game from the date of his signing, and took a deservedly profitable benefit in recompense from a Midland League game against Hull City reserves in March 1908. Earlier, he

Harry Ashby

From the start of 1959/60, though, Colin missed only eight League games over five seasons, having his coolly forceful defensive half-back play (spiced with occasional forays into the inside-left slot) recognised with a place on the 1961 FA XI tour of New Zealand and the Far East, and a selection for the Football League in 1962. He made two trips with City to Wembley F.A. Cup Finals, skippering the side on the second occasion in 1963, and was also, as captain, the first Leicester player to get his hands on a national knockout trophy when the club won the League Cup in 1964. The same year he took a well-deserved testimonial game, with City facing an All Star XI. A first-leg Final scorer in City's unsuccessful attempt to retain the League Cup in 1965, Colin moved on a year later (to briefly extend his partnership with Ian King at The Valley), and soon turned his experience to coaching and management. He was finally a Wembley

winner with Scarborough in the 1973 FA Challenge Trophy Final (as full-back), and later led his team out there twice more in the same competition: indeed, he was granted a second testimonial game by a grateful Scarborough in 1982. Briefly a coach at Grimsby, Colin subsequently managed Hull City (twice), Swansea City, Exeter City and Bridlington Town. His younger brother David was also on City's professional books in the early 60s.

Appearances:
FL: 277 apps. 19 gls.
FAC: 27 apps. 0 gls.
LC: 20 apps. 2 gls.
Eur: 4 apps. 1 gl.
Total: *328 apps. 22 gls.*

had been tried briefly as an emergency centre-forward by Burton Swifts, and indeed scored a hat-trick against Burnley in his first game as an attacker. Harry skippered Brighton United in their first eight Southern League fixtures of 1899/1900, all of which ended in defeat, but he then disappeared to leave them to their end-of-season fate of the wooden spoon and immediate winding-up.

Appearances:
FL: 66 apps. 0 gls.
FAC: 2 apps. 0 gls.
Total: *68 apps. 0 gls.*

ATHERLEY, R.

Role: Centre forward

CAREER: Nov 1901:FOSSE.
Debut v Blackpool (A) 28.3.02

An otherwise as-yet untraceable centre-forward who was tried out in the above Good Friday defeat, shortly after Fosse forwards Richards and Stevenson had been 'given their papers' for unspecified disciplinary indiscretions.

Appearances:
FL: 1 app. 0 gls.
Total: *1 app. 0 gls.*

ATHERTON, James

Role: Centre half
b. c 1872

CAREER: South Shore/ cs 1894:Blackpool/cs 1895: FOSSE/Aug 1896:Kettering/cs 1898:New Brompton.
Debut v Burton Wanderers (H) 28.9.1895

James Atherton

A promising Lancastrian centre-half - a regular for the Blackpool side who finished as Lancashire League runners-up in 1895, and a member of the South Shore team from that same town which Fosse had removed from the Cup a season earlier - James was unfortunate to find himself understudying the consistent Jack Walker during his year with Fosse. He later, though, gave six years of service (129 senior games) to Southern League New Brompton, during which he featured in a five-game FA Cup marathon against Woolwich

Arsenal - with all the replays coming within 17 days of the original tie.

Appearances:
FL: 2 apps. 0 gls.
Total: *2 apps. 0 gls.*

ATKINS, A.

Role: Outside left

CAREER: Mar 1892:FOSSE/cs 1892:not known/cs 1893:Mansfield Greenhalgh's.
Debut v Derby Junction (A) ML 12.3.1892

A trialist from Hemingfield, near Castle Donington, whom we suspect (so far without confirmation) to have played for Notts Olympic and Heanor Town prior to his single Fosse outing at outside-left. A month later, Atkins left Fosse very much in the lurch at Rotherham Town, where his failure to show up left a 10-man side shipping eleven goals without reply against the Midland League champions-elect.

Appearances:
ML: 1 app. 0 gls.
Total: *1 app. 0 gls.*

ATTER, Charles

Role: Outside right

CAREER: Dec 1891:FOSSE.
Debut v Doncaster Rovers (A) ML 26.12.1891

Jimmy's younger brother took the opposite attacking flank to Fosse's star winger in the above Boxing Day defeat during the initial Midland League wooden-spoon campaign.

Appearances:
ML: 1 app. 0 gls.
Total: *1 app. 0 gls.*

ATTER, James

Role: Outside left
b. Stamford, Lincs, 1870

CAREER: Mill Hill House/1890:FOSSE/ Feb 1892:Crouch End/ Feb 1893:FOSSE/ cs 1893:Crouch End/Melton Town.

Jimmy Atter

Debut (competitive) v Burton Wanderers (H)
FAC 4.10.1890

A star amateur outside-left for Fosse when their fixture list still consisted primarily of friendlies, Jimmy was simultaneously one of the committee men who secured the club's election to the Midland League, and he played in Fosse's inaugural games in both that competition and in the FA Cup, as well as scoring the club's first senior goal at Filbert Street. Business commitments - Jimmy was a

Sep Atterbury

trainee solicitor, eventually settling to practice in Melton Mowbray - led to him playing his football in London for occasional spells, but he regularly returned to lend his all-round skills to both Fosse and Leicestershire CCC (having earlier scored heavily as a local cricketer with Leicester Ivanhoe, Leicester Banks and Egerton Park, he appeared occasionally for the County from 1889-94, just before their recognition as a first-class side). As a teenager, Jimmy had appeared in the first two Finals of the County Cup (1888, 1889) for Mill Hill House (he had been educated at Mill Hill School as well as Oakham); and as a Fossil was a winner in the fourth decider for this trophy. Jimmy's representative honours were various: he featured in inter-county fare for each of Leicestershire, Middlesex and London (being awarded the prestigious cap and badge of the London FA), and also starred for the Midland League select side. Noel Tarbotton's 1948 club history, *'From Fosse To City'*, relates that sandwich-board men used to patrol the city centre on Saturday mornings with placards stating 'Mr.Atter Will Play', such was his drawing power at the gate.

Appearances:
FAC: 2 apps. 0 gls.
ML: 24 apps. 6 gls.
Total: 26 apps. 6 gls.

ATTERBURY, Septimus

Role: Left back
b. Allestree, Derby, 18th October 1880
d. Coalville, Leics, 13th March 1964

CAREER: Jan 1899:Loughborough/
cs 1899:Barnsley/cs 1901:Wellingborough/
Aug 1902:FOSSE/cs 1903:Swindon Town/
May 1907:Plymouth Argyle.

Debut v Gainsborough Trinity (H) 25.12.02

Fosse's steady left-back in the latter half of 1902/3 (and, indeed, again as a regular guest player during WW1), Sep had earlier tasted Southern League football with Wellingborough, but it was his record in that sphere after leaving Filbert Street which is most noteworthy. For after 115 appearances for Swindon, he completed a then-monumental tally of 324 games for Plymouth (champions in 1913), winning Southern League representative honours against the Irish League in 1913 and, as a 40-year-old Argyle reserve, against the Welsh League in 1921; and playing in their first-ever Football League side in 1920. Immediately upon retirement, Sep took up training duties at Home Park, eventually completing 30 years with the club; and indeed took on a further challenge as Chester trainer in August 1938. One unlikely index of how seriously he took the game was his sending-off (in the supposedly more relaxed context of wartime football) for Fosse at Barnsley on Boxing Day 1916. Research by Association of Football Statisticians members indicates that the 17-year gap between Sep's final League game for Fosse and his first for Argyle represents the second longest such hiatus in the history of the game.

Appearances:
FL: 21 apps. 0 gls.
WW1: 50 apps. 3 gls.
Total: *71 apps. 3 gls.*

AYTON, James

Role: Inside left
b. Barrhead, Renfrewshire, 15th October 1923
d. Leicester, 25th August 1988

CAREER: Neilston Victoria/1944:Third Lanark/Oct 1948:CITY/June 1951:Shrewsbury Town/July 1952:Bedford Town.

Debut v Barnsley (H) 30.10.48

A then-record signing for City at £7,750, Jimmy was disappointingly plagued by illness and injury during his Leicester sojourn, initially making five inside-left appearances in succession before succumbing to a bout of debilitating jaundice. In the opening reserve match of 1949/50 he cracked a bone in his jaw, and an injury received on his first-team

comeback resulted in a cartilage operation. Though noted from his Scottish League days as a powerful shot as well as a stylist, Jimmy found it impossible to compete with newcomer Arthur Rowley when he did finally regain fitness. A Shrewsbury history quotes a local press comment that the Shrews' joint-record £4,000 signing rather worryingly displayed 'a tendency for temperamental demonstrations towards his team-mates' during his Division Three (South) season at Gay Meadow. Jimmy had served during the war with the Navy in Ceylon.

Appearances:
FL: 8 apps. 1 gl.
Total: *8 apps. 1 gl.*

Jimmy Ayton

BACON, Ernest Frederick

Role: Right half
b. Leicester, 19th February 1896
d. Aylestone, Leicester, 9th January 1972

CAREER: St.Andrews/Aug 1919:CITY/
May 1920:Watford/July 1921:Charlton
Athletic/May 1923:Nuneaton Town/
1924:Barwell United/1928:Erith & Belvedere/
1929:Callendar Athletic.

Debut v Fulham (H) 13.9.19

A pre-war schoolboy international who
guested for Coventry City in a Filbert Street
friendly during WW1, Ernest was given his
League baptism at right-half by Peter Hodge,
but was largely consigned to reserve football
during his City season (claiming one of the
eleven goals the 'stiffs' scored against Moira
United in the 1920 County Cup Final). He
went on to represent Watford in their first-ever
Football League game, but was primarily
regarded as an occasional stand-in full-back by
his two Third Division clubs, and aggregated
only 21 League outings across his entire senior
career.

> **Appearances:**
> *FL: 4 apps. 0 gls.*
> **Total:** *4 apps. 0 gls.*

BAILEY, Herbert

Role: Centre forward
b. Melton Mowbray, Leics (?)

CAREER: Melton Town/Birmingham
St.Georges/cs 1891:Wolverhampton
Wanderers/Melton Town/Mar 1892:FOSSE.

Debut v Gainsborough Trinity (A) ML 19.3.1892

A brother of Fosse full-back Harry, centre-
forward Herbert was the only Fossil to score
in the final eight fixtures of the club's
disastrous debut campaign in the Midland
League. He also returned for a brief stint
during 1893/4, and that season represented
Leicestershire, scoring twice against
Northamptonshire in a 6-1 win at
Wellingborough. His prior Football League
experience, with Wolves, amounted to a single
outing at Blackburn in October 1891.

> **Appearances:**
> *ML: 5 apps. 1 gl.*
> **Total:** *5 apps. 1 gl.*

BAILEY, Horace Peter

Role: Goalkeeper
b. Derby, 3rd July 1881
d. Biggleswade, Beds, 1st August 1960

CAREER: Sept 1899:Derby County/
1901:Crich/Dec 1902:Ripley Athletic/
1905:Leicester Imperial/Jan 1907:FOSSE/
Apr 1910:Derby County/Nov 1910:Stoke/
Feb 1911:Birmingham.

Debut v Wolverhampton Wanderers (H) 9.9.07

A brilliant amateur goalkeeper who gained
near-immediate full international recognition
for his valuable contribution to Fosse's successful promotion effort - thereby becoming
the club's first England cap - 'H.P.' climaxed
the busy year of 1908 by also appearing for the
victorious United Kingdom XI in the football
Final of the Olympic Games. A year later,
Horace was the blameless last-line during
Fosse's record 0-12 defeat at Nottingham
Forest, and also one of two players to give
satisfactory evidence at the subsequent League
enquiry. His departure, after collecting five
senior and four amateur caps while with

Horace Bailey

Fosse, was solely aimed at helping the Rams out of an injury crisis (he had failed to make a first-team breakthrough for them in his initial, teenage spell) and, after a single outing for Stoke, the bulk of his remaining career was then played out at St.Andrews. Throughout his playing years, Horace was employed by the Midland Railway Company at Derby as a rating official.

Appearances:
FL: 68 apps. 0 gls.
FAC: 2 apps. 0 gls.
Total: *70 apps. 0 gls..*

❏ *FOX FACT: Horace Bailey was the first Fossil to be capped for England while on the club's books; Andy Aitken the first to be so honoured by Scotland; Mick Cochrane the initial Irish international; and Dick Jones and Alf Watkins jointly the first Welsh caps - as well as the club's first internationally recognised players. Following the partition of Ireland and the institution of separate national sides, Tommy Godwin was the first City man to represent the Republic, and Willie Cunningham won the first Northern Ireland call-up. Finland's Jari Rantanen was the first 'overseas' international to be capped while with Leicester.*

BAILEY, William Henry

Role: Left back
b. Melton Mowbray, Leics, 2nd October 1869
d. Leicester, 19th October 1930

CAREER: Melton Rovers/Melton Town/
Birmingham St.Georges/cs 1890:FOSSE.
Debut (competitive) v Derby Junction (H)
ML 12.9.1891

A Fossil from the pre-Midland League days, Harry was a popular, stalwart full-back who became the recipient of the club's first benefit payout - £146 from a friendly against the prestigious London amateurs, Casuals, on Boxing Day 1893. In fact, Harry was at left-back for Fosse's opening games in both the Midland and Football Leagues. It looked as if he had made his final senior appearance in January 1897, but when he turned up to watch Fosse at Walsall in September 1899 (having in the interim reverted to amateur status), he was asked to perform in goal, and was beaten only once as the team notched a rare away win!

Harry Bailey

Such versatility was wholly in character, though, for Harry was also for several years on the books of Leicestershire CCC as a batsman, after initially starring for Egerton Park. His brother Herbert was also briefly a Fossil of Midland League vintage. Harry himself had been a teenage founder member of the Melton Town club, and had played in the Final of the Birmingham Senior Cup while with St.Georges.

Appearances:
FL: 47 apps. 0 gls.
FAC: 17 apps. 0 gls.
ML: 61 apps. 0 gls.
Total: *125 apps. 0 gls.*

BAILLIE, Joseph

Role: Left back
b. Dumfries, 26th February 1929
d. Maryhill, Glasgow, 23rd March 1966

CAREER: St.Roch's/Dec 1945:Celtic/
Nov 1954:Wolverhampton Wanderers/
June 1956:Bristol City/June 1957:CITY/
June 1960:Bradford Park Avenue.
Debut v Preston North End (H) 16.11.57

Joe Baillie

The regular left-back in City's late-50s struggles to survive and establish themselves in the First Division, Joe had initially arrived in England with Scottish League representative honours, a Scotland 'B' cap and a Scottish Cup-winners medal (1951) already to his name. He nonetheless found it impossible to secure a breakthrough at Molineux, making only a single League appearance (in a 6-4 victory over Huddersfield) before rebuilding his confidence at Ashton Gate. Joe's cultured coolness in the No.3 shirt for Leicester was a forceful reminder that he had begun his career in the Parkhead half-back line. His tragic death occurred when his car skidded into the River Kelvin.

Appearances:
FL: 75 apps. 0 gls.
FAC: 5 apps. 0 gls.
Total: *80 apps. 0 gls.*

BAINES, Stanley Norman

Role: Outside left
b. Syston, Leics, 28th July 1920

CAREER: Coalville Town/Nov 1937:CITY/ July 1946:Northampton Town.

Debut v Preston North End (H) 10.9.38

A lightweight teenage left-winger when briefly deputising for Eric Stubbs during the final pre-war season, Stan was noted for his exceptional speed, but nonetheless found himself on the free transfer list in April 1939, after City's relegation had been confirmed. Seemingly he went throughout the war years without a senior club registration (he was turning out for Syston Imperial in 1939/40, when he also briefly represented Northampton, and

Stan Baines

later put together a run of 19 regional games for Watford), but when League football resumed he was able only to add a single selection for the Cobblers to his previous pair of guest outings.

Appearances:
FL: 7 apps. 1 gl.
Total: *7 apps. 1 gl.*

BAIRD, John

Role: Full back
b. Dunbartonshire, c 1870

CAREER:
Vale of Leven/ 1889:Aston Villa/ 1889: Kidderminster Olympic/1890: Kidderminster/ cs 1891:Aston Villa/July 1895:FOSSE.

John Baird

Debut v Burton Swifts (H) 7.9.1895

A versatile defender who had appeared in the last Cup Final to be held at Kennington Oval, as left-half in the 1892 Villa side defeated by West Brom, and had won a League championship medal in 1894, John was unfortunate with injuries during his Fosse season, when he vied for a full-back place with Harry Davy and Harry Bailey. Earlier, John had also assisted an unbeaten Kidderminster Olympic to the inaugural championship of the Birmingham & District League, before that club disappeared in an over-ambitious and short-lived merger with the local Harriers.

Appearances:
FL: 13 apps. 0 gls.
FAC: 1 app. 0 gls.
Total: *14 apps. 0 gls.*

BALDWIN, James

Role: Right half
b. Blackburn, 12th January 1922
d. Blackburn, 13th February 1985

CAREER: Mill Hill St.Peters/am Aug 1943/ pro Dec 1945:Blackburn Rovers/Feb 1950: CITY/Apr 1956:Great Yarmouth (p/mgr).

Debut v Luton Town (H) 25.2.50

Signed from his hometown club for £10,000 by Norman Bullock, Jimmy was the regular right-half, and occasional inside-right, of City's sides of the early 50s. A slight, prematurely balding forager whose stamina belied his physique, and whose unostentatious prompting was the epitome of shrewdness, he earned a championship medal from City's 1953/4 Division Two campaign. After his playing days were over, Jimmy also managed Yeovil for a spell.

Jimmy Baldwin

Appearances:
FL: 180 apps. 4 gls.
FAC: 10 apps. 0 gls.
Total: *190 apps. 4 gls.*

BALL, Alfred B.

Role: Right half
b. Preston, c.1874

CAREER: 1893:Preston North End/1895: Kettering/May 1897:FOSSE/cs 1900:Nelson.

Debut v Luton Town (H) 4.9.1897

An ever-present at right-half in his first two seasons with Fosse, Alf was a model of defensive consistency who had earlier had a brief taste of First Division fare at Deepdale, just as

Alf Ball

Proud Preston were losing their aura of invincibility, and had scored one of the Kettering goals which removed Fosse from the Cup in 1896/7. His Fosse debut (along with those of Dick Jones, Roddy McLeod and Harry Smith) came in opposition to a Luton side playing their first-ever League game.

Appearances:
FL: 75 apps. 3 gls.
FAC: 6 apps. 0 gls.
Total: *81 apps. 3 gls.*

BALLARD, Frank

Role: Full back

CAREER: Long Eaton Rangers/
cs 1898:FOSSE.

Debut v Manchester City (A) 15.10.1898

A full-back recruited from Midland League
football, Frank failed to mount a convincing
challenge to either Jack Walker or George
Swift, and managed only a single senior game
on either flank in place of his vastly more
experienced club-mates.

Appearances:
FL: 2 apps. 0 gls.
Total: *2 apps. 0 gls.*

BAMBER, John

Role: Left half
b. Peasley Cross, Lancs,
11th April 1895
d. Peasley Cross, July qtr 1971

CAREER: St.Helens
Recreational/Alexander Vics/
cs 1914:Heywood United/
St.Helens Town/Dec 1915:
Liverpool/Feb 1924:CITY/
July 1927:Tranmere Rovers/
Aug 1930:Prescot Cables.

Debut v Sheffield Wednesday
(H) 9.2.24

An Anfield regular at half-
back in both wartime and the
first two postwar League
seasons, and then honoured
with an England cap, two
Football League appearances,
and two games for the FA
touring side in South Africa,
Jack missed out (initially
through injury) on the medals
as Liverpool went on to twice
take the League
championship in 1922 and
1923. The move to Filbert
Street revitalised his career,
with Jack a fixture at left-half
as City raced to promotion, an

ever-present in their initial season in the top
flight, and a member of the first team to perch
the club (however briefly) on the League's
pinnacle. Displaced shortly thereafter by
expensive import Sid Bishop, though, Jack
returned to Merseyside to end his career. His
first City goal, against Fulham in November
1924, was scored from a range of one yard,
direct from a referee's bounce-up, after the
goalkeeper had been penalised for lying on
the ball too long!

Appearances:
FL: 113 apps. 7 gls.
FAC: 7 apps. 0 gls.
Total: *120 apps. 7 gls.*

Jack Bamber

*Gordon
Banks*

BANKS, Gordon

Role: Goalkeeper
*b. Sheffield, 30th
December 1938*

CAREER: Millspaugh
Steelworks/Rawmarsh
Welfare/Millspaugh
Steelworks/Sept 1955:
Chesterfield/May
1959: CITY/Apr
1967:Stoke
City/(1971-loan-
Hellenic)/Mar 1977:
Fort Lauderdale
Strikers/(Oct 1977-
loan-St.Patrick's
Athletic).

Debut v Blackpool (H) 9.9.59

First noticed in Chesterfield's unexpected
progress to the FA Youth Cup Final in 1956,
the goalkeeping genius inevitably dubbed
'Banks of England' was, only a decade later, a
national hero for his significant role in his
country's World Cup win. Still a raw
youngster when Matt Gillies signed him for
£7,000 after only 23 League games for the
Spireites, Gordon developed quickly at Filbert
Street, basing his game on an uncanny sense of
positioning and an acute appreciation of the
value of solidity over the gratuitously
spectacular, yet engendering supreme
confidence amongst his defenders that he
could call on superb reflexes and agility when
required. Gordon's second Cup Final
appearance for City in 1963 was the occasion
of a very rare shaky performance, but he'd
already broken Liverpool hearts almost single-
handedly in the semi-final to book
City's Wembley ticket, and had also
by then won the first of his 73 full
England caps (37 earned while on
City's books) to add to two Under-23
and four Football League selections.
The rise to contention of Peter Shilton
spelt a controversially premature end
to Gordon's Leicester career, and when
West Ham dropped their promised
option on his transfer (honourably -
they had in the interim committed to
buy Kilmarnock's Bobby Ferguson), he
moved to Stoke for £50,000. His
England career peaked again during the
1970 World Cup, when a reflex save
from Pele's header became probably
TV's most re-run piece of goalkeeping
action ever, and the civil honour of an
OBE followed. At club level, Gordon
inspired Stoke to their first-ever trophy, the
League Cup (repeating his major City success
for the team he'd helped beat in 1964), and
earned himself the accolade of 1972 Footballer
of the Year, but his world was shattered that
October when a car crash cost him the sight of
one eye. Adherence to his own high standards
precluded a League comeback after recovery,
but stints of coaching at Stoke and Port Vale,
and a spell as manager of Telford United,
bracketed a return to playing in the transatlantic NASL, where he was voted Goalkeeper
of the Year, and a brief stint in Ireland. Gordon,
who returned to Filbert Street in 1986 as chairman of the club's short-lived 'Lifeline' fund-
raising operation, and has subsequently been
involved in the corporate hospitality business,
was the beneficiary of a well-attended testimonial game at Filbert Street in April 1995, and a
suite in the new main stand bears his name.

Appearances:
FL: 293 apps. 0 gls.
FAC: 34 apps. 0 gls.
LC: 25 apps. 0 gls.
Eur: 4 apps. 0 gls.
Total: *356 apps. 0 gls.*

*Banks in action
for England.*

Ian Banks

BANKS, Ian Frederick

Role: Midfield
b. Mexborough, Yorkshire, 9th January 1961

CAREER: Jan 1979:Barnsley/June 1983:CITY/
Sept 1986:Huddersfield Town/July 1988:
Bradford City/Mar 1989:West Bromwich
Albion/July 1989:Barnsley/cs 1992:Rotherham
United/cs 1994:Darlington/cs 1995:Emley.

Debut v Notts County (H) 27.8.83

A stocky but skilful midfielder with an
explosive long-range shot, Ian suffered injury
problems shortly after Gordon Milne paid
£100,000 to bring him to City from Oakwell,
and took time to settle. Never a wholly
automatic choice thereafter, probably because
difficult to motivate to consistent peak
involvement, he nonetheless turned in some
excellent performances on the left, alternating
pinpoint driven crosses with a knack of
shuffling inside for a telling strike. Ian's
penalty goal in the final game of 1985/6
clinched City's First Division survival for
another year, but he moved back to Yorkshire
shortly after Bryan Hamilton's arrival. Ian was

the Terriers' skipper when they nosedived to
Division Three in 1988; earned himself a big-
money transfer back to the Second at Valley
Parade; was the subject of another six-figure
deal during the deadline week of 1989; and
returned to Oakwell for another sizeable fee
after a mere four appearances for the Baggies.
In December 1989, at Bournemouth, Ian was
'sent off' while warming up as a Barnsley
substitute, following some incautious remarks
to a linesman about the validity of a goal; he
was also dismissed on his Darlington debut.

Appearances:
FL: 78 (15) apps. 14 gls.
FAC: 6 apps. 0 gls.
LC: 3 (1) apps. 1 gl.
Total: *87 (16) apps. 15 gls.*

BANNISTER, William

Role: Centre half
b. Burnley, 1879
d. Leicester, 26th March 1942

CAREER: Earley/1899:Burnley/Nov 1901:
Bolton Wanderers/Dec 1902:Woolwich
Arsenal/May 1904:FOSSE/Sept 1910:Burnley/
cs 1912:Crewe Alexandra/1912:Leicester
Imperial.

Debut v Blackpool (A) 3.9.04

Billy Bannister

A tough, towering ex-international centre-half (twice capped for England and twice representing the Football League while with his Lancashire clubs), Billy served Fosse for six seasons after his record £300 transfer from Arsenal, and skippered the side in the promotion season of 1907/8. His attacking instincts, occasionally deemed somewhat reckless for a pivot, were supplemented by a noteworthy long-range shot, and he was awarded a benefit at Christmas 1909 (a reserve fixture with Nottingham Forest), just over a week before his final first-team appearance. In the County Cup Final of 1909, Billy had earned a winner's medal after a full 90 minutes as emergency goalkeeper. He later ran pubs in both Burnley and Leicester, and was mine host at the Woolcomber's Arms at the time of his death.

Appearances:
FL: 149 apps. 15 gls.
FAC: 11 apps. 3 gls.
Total: *160 apps. 18 gls.*

BARACLOUGH, Ian Robert

Role: Striker
b. Leicester, 4th December 1970

CAREER: YT July 1987/pro Dec 1988:CITY/ (Mar 1990-loan-Wigan Athletic)/(Dec 1990-loan-Grimsby Town)/Aug 1991:Grimsby Town/Aug 1992:Lincoln City/ cs 1994:Mansfield Town.

Debut v Charlton Athletic (A) FMC 14.11.89 (sub)

A tall central striker who surprisingly failed to maintain youthful progress at Filbert Street, Ian was chosen alongside Paul Kitson for a Football League Youth XI game in Moscow in 1989, and maintained an initially healthy strike rate on his assumption of a regular Central League slot. His senior bow at Selhurst in the closing minutes of City's Zenith Cup exit was a brief affair, but he shouldered a difficult responsibility well in acting as emergency target-man when Barnsley delivered another first-hurdle FA Cup disappointment a couple of months later, and got off the scoring mark at League level while on loan at Springfield Park. A generally downbeat 1990/1 campaign at reserve level followed, though, and Ian was released as incoming manager Brian Little began trimming his squad. Ian's loan spell with

Ian Baraclough

Grimsby actually yielded more senior football than did his later year on their books, but he found a regular place in midfield with Lincoln, and in defence for the Stags.

Appearances:
FAC: 1 app. 0 gls.
FMC: 0 (1) app. 0 gls.
Total: *1 (1) apps. 0 gls.*

BARLOW, Herbert

Role: Inside forward
b. Kilnhurst, Yorkshire,
22nd July 1916   *Bert Barlow*

CAREER: Silverwood Colliery/July 1935: Barnsley/June 1938:Wolverhampton Wanderers/Feb 1939:Portsmouth/Dec 1949: CITY/June 1952:Colchester United/cs 1954: Crittall's Athletic/cs 1956:Long Melford (p/coach).

Debut v Sheffield Wednesday (H) 17.12.49

A creative inside-forward who also knocked in over 70 League goals during his near-20-year senior career, Bert first hit the headlines in

1939. Jettisoned after only three first-team games at Molineux, he moved to Fratton Park on the 'never-never', scored a Cup semi-final goal to take otherwise struggling Pompey to Wembley, and there struck again in the 31st minute to help his underdog team to a shock 4-1 win - over Wolves! Ten years later, Bert again had Wembley (and a possible Cup/League double) in his sights as champions Portsmouth expected a Highbury semi-final cakewalk - only to find their calculations upset by an inspired, giant-killing City side. Joining Leicester only a matter of months later, Bert lent his wily experience for three Second Division campaigns, and did not leave the League sphere until, at the age of 38, he'd given two further seasons of all-out effort to Colchester. During WW2, Bert had turned out as a guest for Barnsley, Chelsea and Rotherham United.

Appearances:
FL: 42 apps. 9 gls.
FAC: 2 apps. 0 gls.
Total: *44 apps. 9 gls.*

BARLOW, John

Role: Forward
b. Prescot, Lancashire, 1876

CAREER:
Prescot/1897:Everton/
1899:Reading/
cs 1901:Tottenham Hotspur/
Feb 1903:Reading/May 1903:FOSSE.

John Barlow

Debut v Barnsley (A) 5.9.03

A Lancastrian wanderer who totted up only four League appearances in two seasons at Goodison, and then sampled Southern League fare at Elm Park and White Hart Lane, John appeared without conspicuous success at both inside- and outside-left in Fosse's appalling 1903/4 campaign, which ended with the club seeking re-election for the first time.

Appearances:
FL: 22 apps. 2 gls.
FAC: 5 apps. 1 gl.
Total: *27 apps. 3 gls.*

The only known photograph featuring goalkeeper Charles Barnett (see below) and defender Charles Barron (see page 31/32) is a still frame taken from brief newsreel footage of Fosse's final league game, away to Clapton Orient. The historic moment captured shows the last league goal conceded by Fosse - an own goal credited to the unfortunate Barron who is seen vainly attempting to clear his lines.

BARNETT, Charles

Role: Goalkeeper
b. Derby

CAREER: Newark Town/Feb 1913:FOSSE/cs 1920:Mansfield Town/Oct 1921:Alfreton Town.

Debut v Hull City (A) 26.4.13

The goalkeeping understudy to both Brebner and Bown, Charles was recruited from Derbyshire League junior football, and also briefly helped out Derby County as a guest player in 1915/16. He was only seven times in total on a winning side with Fosse, and failed to appear in a single postwar senior game for City, though he took winners' medals from the County Cup Finals of both 1914 and 1920.

Appearances:
FL: 20 apps. 0 gls.
WW1: 5 apps. 0 gls.
Total: *25 apps. 0 gls.*

BARRATT, Alfred E.

Role: Outside left
b. Oadby, Leicester

CAREER: Aug 1914:FOSSE.
Debut v Lincoln City (A) 2.4.15

A local outside-left whose sole senior appearance (in a 3-2 win which failed to lift his club out of the Second Division re-election zone) lent him the rather marginal distinction of being the last player to make a League debut for the Fosse, prior to the upheavals of war and reconstruction. Alfred did, however, make a slightly bigger splash as a rugby player, notching three tries in eight games for the Tigers in 1920.

Appearances:
FL: 1 app. 0 gls.
Total: 1 app. 0 gls.

Alf G. Barratt

BARRATT, Alfred George

Role: Defender
b. Corby, Northamptonshire, 13th April 1920

CAREER: Weldon/Kettering Town/July 1938: Northampton Town/Sept 1939:Stewart & Lloyds (Corby)/Sept 1946:CITY/July 1950:Grimsby Town/July 1951:Southport.

Debut v West Ham United (H) 17.4.48

Having played a single League game as a youngster with the Cobblers, Alf returned from WW2 action as a Marine Commando to become a reserve-team fixture in his four post war seasons at Filbert Street, yet missed the 1947/8 Combination Cup Final victory (over

Bournemouth) while making his third appearance in a week as senior centre-half. Only one further City run-out followed, at right-back the following season, but this tall, well-built stopper finally came into his own at Southport, totting up over 200 senior games for the Third Division (North) side.

Appearances:
FL: 4 apps. 0 gls.
Total: 4 apps. 0 gls.

BARRETT, William Henry

Role: Right back
b. Nuneaton, Warwickshire, July qtr 1893

CAREER: 1910:Stockingford Congregationals/ 1912:Bromsgrove Rovers/1912:Nuneaton Town/Army football/1918:Hinckley United/ Apr 1919:CITY/July 1925:Derby County/ Apr 1927:Hinckley United.

Debut v Wolverhampton Wanderers (H) 30.8.19

Noted by Fosse in the pre-war days as a likely prospect, right-back Billy proved he had lost none of his pluck, speed or first-time tackling power in a short spell with Hinckley, and was snapped up for the resumption of League competition. He gave fine service across five seasons, but was only a covering reserve when

Billy Barrett

City finally secured promotion, and sadly failed to get a first-team look-in at Derby as the Rams followed them up the next year. Billy's only goals for City came from penalties - in the final games he played in each senior competition.

Appearances:
FL: 143 apps. 1 gl.
FAC: 9 apps. 1 gl.
Total: 152 apps. 2 gls.

BARRON, Charles W.

Role: Right back

CAREER: Durham City/ Sept 1914:FOSSE/ cs 1919:Scotswood.

Debut v Birmingham (A) 2.1.15

A right-back introduced to Fosse's hapless struggle of the final pre-war season, when the defence had been shipping goals in sixes and sevens, Charles helped stave off all but the final embarrassment of the club having to go to the re-election vote. One minor personal embarrassment accrued to the club record, however - for his own goal in the final fixture at Clapton Orient proved to be the last strike ever conceded by Fosse at League level (and is preserved on celluloid in a Topical Budget newsreel of the time). Noted as 'a North Country lad', Charles also managed a half-dozen wartime games for Fosse, returning in April 1919 after having 'kept fit playing for a team in the Newcastle area'.

Appearances:
FL: 16 apps. 0 gls.
WW1: 6 apps. 0 gls.
Total: *22 apps. 0 gls.*

BARRY,
Leonard James

Role: Outside left
b. Sneinton, Notts,
27th October 1901
d. Mapperley, Notts,
17th April 1970

CAREER: RAF
Cranwell/ May
1920:Notts County/ Sept
1927:CITY/
Aug 1933:Nottingham
Forest.

Debut v Manchester United (H) 1.10.27

Initially an amateur with the Magpies, while he completed RAF service at Cranwell, Len was capped at that level (v Ireland in 1923/4) before turning professional.

Len Barry

However, it was his consistent cleverness as an old-fashioned dribbling left-winger in the City side that finished successively third and second in Division One which earned him five full England honours in 1928 and 1929, after a £3,500 move from Meadow Lane. His lengthy and profitable partnership with Arthur Lochhead provided an object lesson in the effective employment of complementary ball-control skills, and while Len's personal contributions to the scoresheet were often of a spectacular nature, he is at least as well remembered for his unselfish service to the more prolific Chandler and Hine. He was approaching the veteran stage when Danny Liddle inherited his role, and featured only briefly in Forest's struggling Second Division side.

Appearances:
FL: 203 apps. 25 gls.
FAC: 11 apps. 1 gl.
Total: *214 apps. 26 gls.*

BAUCHOP, William Fotheringham

Role: Outside left
b. Alloa, Clackmannan, 18th January 1882
d. USA, 1948

CAREER: Abercorn/June 1901:East Stirling/ Apr 1903:Alloa Athletic/Sep 1905:Plymouth Argyle/May 1906:Heart of Midlothian/ June 1907:Carlisle United/ May 1909:Stockport County/Aug 1911:FOSSE/ Aug 1912:Norwich City/ July 1913:Fulham/ Jan 1914: Grimsby Town.

Debut v Gainsborough Trinity (A) 2.9.11

A jinky Scottish outside-left signed to partner Frank Rollinson (after playing the last of his 41 Second Division games for Stockport against Fosse), Willie was soon displaced by the youthful promise of George Harrison. He then followed belated-ly in the Norwich-bound bootprints of his more successful younger brother Jimmy, who had been at The Nest during 1907/8, early in a career which also took him to Alloa, Celtic, Crystal Palace, Derby County, Tottenham Hotspur, Bradford, Doncaster and Lincoln. Willie himself had briefly tasted the big time, as one of the Hearts side beaten 0-3 by Celtic in the 1907 Scottish

Willie Bauchop

Cup Final, and would be noted later as one of the Canaries who embarrassed Fosse in the Cup in 1912/13. He played first-team football for neither of his last two clubs, however.

Appearances:
FL: 18 apps. 1 gl.
FAC: 3 apps. 0 gls.
Total: *21 apps. 1 gl.*

BAXTER, James

Role: Wing half
b. Glasgow

CAREER: Parkhead/
Aug 1925:CITY/
June 1929:Reading/
Nov 1930:Torquay
United.

Debut v Bury (A)
24.4.26

A patient reserve wing-half whose half-dozen senior appearances were spread across four seasons when City were at their strongest as a consistent First Division force, Jimmy failed to make the first team at all during his Elm Park period. He had earned Scottish Junior Cup-winners honours (1924, scoring in the initial drawn game with Baillieston) before joining City in a joint deal with team-mate John Allen, and curiously was joined by two more former Parkhead men on the Filbert Street free-transfer list of 1929: Harry Callachan and Dr.Tom Gibson.

Appearances:
FL: 6 apps. 1 gl.
Total: *6 apps. 1 gl.*

Jimmy Baxter

BEADSWORTH, Arthur

Role: Forward
b. Leicester, 1876
d. France, November 1917

CAREER: Aug 1894:Leicester YMCA/
(trials-Notts County, FOSSE)/Hinckley Town/
May 1900:FOSSE/cs 1901:Coventry City/
Oct 1902:Manchester United/cs 1903:Swindon
Town/cs 1905:New Brompton/Aug 1906:
Burton United.

Debut v Newton Heath (H) 29.9.1900

A utility forward with both Fosse and the newly-rechristened Manchester United - his right-wing debut against his future club was followed by three games in the inside-left berth - Arthur had his best spell with Swindon, where he made 54 Southern League appearances (11 goals) while earning the then-substantial wage of £2 per week. There were one or two oddities to his transfer record: Arthur was reported as having signed for Preston North End just before his season in the Birmingham & District League with Coventry, and was actually suspended early in his New Brompton days when it was discovered that he'd also registered for Penrith in the interim. Burton United were set for their final Football League season when Arthur joined them, and his own fate (scoreless in 18 games as a forward) rather accurately mirrored theirs. On retiring from the game, he entered the boot and shoe trade in Hinckley, and was serving as a sergeant in the Leicesters when he succumbed to gas poisoning on a French battlefield.

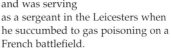

Arthur Beadsworth

Appearances:
FL: 4 apps. 0 gls.
Total: *4 apps. 0 gls.*

BEARDSLEY, Godfrey Leonard

Role: Goalkeeper
b. Barrow-on-Soar, Leics, 1879
d. Erpingham, Norfolk, June 1912

CAREER: Rossal School/Dec 1896:
Loughborough/Sept 1898:FOSSE/
(1903:Corinthians).

Debut v Woolwich Arsenal (A) 10.9.1898

A gentleman goalkeeper from a sporting
family, Godfrey interrupted his law studies to
turn professional and was soon, ironically, at
the centre of a major row between
Loughborough and Leicester over the legality
of his transfer. Eventually the FA found Fosse
guilty of 'poaching' the player, fined the club
£50, and suspended secretary/manager
W.D.Clark *sine die*, yet allowed Godfrey to
continue as a Fossil. He distinguished himself
between the Filbert Street sticks until
December 1900 (once saving a thrice-taken
penalty at Small Heath in March 1899), then
resumed his law practice and reverted to
amateur status, occasionally assisting the
Corinthians before his early death. One of his
brothers was a founder of Loughborough
Corinthians; but we are still unable to
establish whether Godfrey was also in any
way related to Fred Beardsley, the former
Forest goalkeeper who went on to found
Arsenal in 1886.

Appearances:
FL: 69 apps. 0 gls.
FAC: 7 apps. 0 gls.
Total: *76 apps. 0 gls.*

*Godfrey
Beardsley*

BEBY, John Victor

Role: Goalkeeper
b. Gillingham, Kent, 23rd August 1907
d. Rochester, Kent, 8th April 1976

CAREER: Cuxton/am Nov 1924:Charlton
Athletic/Army football/Dec 1929:Gillingham/
Apr 1930:CITY/June 1932:Ashford/Oct 1932:
Bristol Rovers/July 1933:Crystal Palace/
Mar 1934:Darlington/Mar 1936:Exeter City/
May 1936:Ashington/Oct 1936:Vickers
Aviation FC/1945:Shorts Sports.

Debut v Birmingham (A) 3.5.30

A six-foot goalkeeper who had served with
the Grenadier Guards, and appeared in 20
games of Gillingham's re-election zone struggle before signing for City, Jack eventually lost
out in a straight tussle with Jim McLaren for
the First Division green jersey at Leicester. His
two-year spell was almost halved however,
under faintly farcical circumstances: for in
February 1931 he put in a transfer request on
health grounds, reportedly 'as the climate of
Leicester did not agree with him or his wife'!
He also found himself warned by the City
board after a flare-up with Billy Jackson over
dressing room pegs before a reserve fixture at
Brentford in November 1931 had seen the pair
come to blows. Jack then experienced
decidedly mixed fortunes with his Third
Division clubs. An in-and-out choice at
Eastville, he failed to make the League team at
Selhurst (though haplessly appearing in a
sectional Cup-tie against Exeter which ended
in a remarkable 6-11 defeat), then became an
ever-present at Feethams for 1934/5, after
helping Darlington take the Division Three
(North) Cup at the end of the previous season.
For a struggling Grecians side, Jack conceded
27 goals in only 10 games. Long after
retirement, he assisted the Gills in a trio of
1944 wartime fixtures, then commenced a
postwar coaching career, having spells with
AEK Athens and Blida (Algeria) as well as in
Germany and India. Eventually, Jack returned
to take over the Cricketers' pub in Gillingham.

Appearances:
FL: 29 apps. 0 gls.
FAC: 1 app. 0 gls.
Total: *30 apps. 0 gls.*

Right: Jack Beby

BEDFORD, George

Role: Centre half
b. Chesterfield, 12th April 1916
d. Leicester, January 1984

CAREER: Temple Normanton/(trials-Chesterfield)/Jan 1935:CITY/Mar 1941: Northampton Town.

Debut v Barnsley (A) 14.12.35

Though his limited League record might imply otherwise, showing as it does a couple of stopgap appearances in the forward line while new boss Frank Womack negotiated the arrival of Jack Bowers, George was essentially an out-and-out stopper centre-half who proved a stalwart Filbert Street reserve in the late 30s: a fact indexed by his club-record tally of five winner's medals from Leicestershire Senior Cup Finals between 1935-39, and a runner's-up memento from the 1940 Final to boot! War, of course, ruined George's progress, and his final games for City, Northampton, Nottingham Forest and Mansfield were all in regional competitions, before his retirement on medical advice in October 1943. He was a nephew of Harry Bedford, the England centre-forward of the early 20s.

Appearances:
FL: 4 apps. 0 gls.
WW2: 14 apps. 0 gls.
Total: *18 apps. 0 gls.*

BEEBY, Oliver

Role: Right back
b. Leicester,
2nd October 1934

CAREER:
May 1953:CITY/
June 1959:Notts
County/cs 1961:
Oxford United/
cs 1962:Burton
Albion.

Debut v Doncaster Rovers (A) 5.9.55

An England Youth international full-back, local lad Oliver showed admirable patience during his six-year stint with City's

Oliver Beeby

junior and reserve sides, breaking through to senior action only once, in a humbling 2-6 defeat at Belle Vue. Unfortunately, at Meadow Lane he received little better reward, being released after only 13 League outings; while appearances in five straight wins on Oxford's way to the 1962 Southern League championship weren't enough to win him a contract on that club's election to Division Four.

Appearances:
FL: 1 app. 0 gls.
Total: *1 app. 0 gls.*

George Bedford

BELL, John

Role: Centre half
b. Dundee, 1877

CAREER: Dundee Wanderers/Renton/ Bacup/cs 1897: Grimsby Town/June 1899:Chesterfield/ cs 1901:Millwall/ May 1903:FOSSE.

Debut v Barnsley (A) 5.9.03

Jack Bell

Scottish nomad Jack had built a substantial reputation as a constructive pivot by the time he joined Fosse, shortly after Millwall's surprise run to the Cup semi-finals. Yet he was unable to take much pressure off a leaky defence as Leicester found themselves mired in the re-election zone, and he was not retained. (In 'Of Fossils & Foxes' we mistakenly conflated the careers of two players named John Bell who both served Grimsby Town: the forward who signed for the Mariners in 1895 from Wolves later served both Swindon Town and Bedminster).

Appearances:
FL: 21 apps. 0 gls.
FAC: 1 app. 0 gls.
Total: *22 apps. 0 gls.*

BELL, William John

Role: Outside left
b. Backworth, nr.Newcastle upon Tyne, 1906

CAREER: Blyth Spartans/ Chopwell Institute/ (Dec 1923-trials-Aston Villa)/Aug 1924: Lincoln City/May 1925:Mansfield Town/Feb 1926:CITY/ July 1930:Torquay United.

Billy Bell

Debut v West Bromwich Albion (A) 27.2.26

The son of a former Rangers goalkeeper, Billy signed for City in a joint deal with Mansfield full-back Herbert Garner, and proved by far the luckier of the two. Effectively elevated from the Midland League straight into the First Division, he was soon vying earnestly with Harold Wadsworth for City's left-flank attacking role, and indeed held it on merit for some time until Len Barry arrived. He improved on his total City goal tally over the course of a single season at Plainmoor, but failed to impress future City boss Frank Womack sufficiently to earn himself another contract. Billy subsequently opened a grocery business in Torquay.

Appearances:
FL: 41 apps. 5 gls.
Total: *41 apps. 5 gls.*

BELL, William John

Role: Left back
b. Johnstone, Renfrewshire, 3rd September 1937

CAREER: Neilston/1957:Queen's Park/ July 1960:Leeds United/Sept 1967:CITY/ June 1969:Brighton & Hove Albion (p/coach).

Debut v Everton (H) 30.9.67

Already in possession of two Scottish amateur caps from his Hampden Park half-back days, Willie earned a matching pair of full international honours as left-back with Don Revie's Leeds. He also picked up medals from their 1964 Division Two championship campaign, from the 1965 FA Cup Final defeat and as a 1967 Fairs Cup runner-up, before making way for Terry Cooper and being lined up as a £45,000 Filbert Street replacement for Richie Norman. The hefty defender brought solidity rather than flair to his rearguard duties, but failed to survive Matt Gillies' departure, despite being named as temporary first-team coach, and headed for the South Coast after Frank O'Farrell had taken City to Wembley without him. After a spell of coaching at St.Andrews (Blues were fined for employing Willie in this capacity

Willie Bell

while he was still a registered player with Brighton), he became manager of both Birmingham (1975-77) and Lincoln City, but resigned from the latter in October 1978 to join an evangelical religious movement (the Campus Crusade for Christ) in the USA.

Appearances:
FL: 49 apps. 0 gls.
FAC: 6 apps. 0 gls.
LC: 2 apps. 0 gls.
Total: *57 apps. 0 gls.*

BELTON, Thomas

Role: Forward
b. 1879
d. 1944

CAREER: Woodhouse United/Whitwick White Cross/cs 1902:FOSSE/cs 1904:Coventry City/1905:Loughborough Corinthians.

Debut v Small Heath (H) 6.9.02

Fosse were in a sad Second Division tailspin when Tom joined them (after securing the 1902 County Cup for Whitwick with the deciding goal against Hinckley Town), but his efforts from the various inside-forward berths at least delayed the ignominy of a re-election application by a season, for he was second-top scorer in his first campaign, and a spirited trier, whose FA Cup record included a hat-trick in the 10-0 victory over Market Harborough in October 1903. With Coventry he held the leader's role for 15 games (7 goals) of a lowly Birmingham & District League campaign. A decade on, Tom was still appearing regularly as a centre-half for Loughborough Corinthians, alongside his brother Jack, who in fact went on to star for many years for Nottingham Forest.

Appearances:
FL: 49 apps. 12 gls.
FAC: 5 apps. 5 gls.
Total: *54 apps. 17 gls.*

BENFIELD, Thomas Charles

Role: Forward
b. Leicester, 1889
d. France, 10th November 1918

CAREER: Army football/pro July 1910: FOSSE/June 1914:Derby County.

Debut v Hull City (H) 12.11.10

A corporal in the Leicestershire Regiment who had trials with Fosse reserves in February and October 1907 while stationed at Glen Parva barracks, Tommy became in 1909 the first county soldier to take part in the then-prestigious annual Army v. Navy match. He signed for Fosse upon demob, and played in four of the five forward positions over the next four seasons, at a time when such versatility was rare; entering the annals as the very first player to score a goal at Highbury, against Arsenal in their inaugural game there in September 1913. His gradual development as a pacy marksman was noted by the newly-relegated Rams, and he contributed 15 goals as an ever-present inside-right in their 1915 Division Two championship side. With Britain at war, however, he briefly returned to guest for Fosse (as well as Nottingham Forest and

Tom Belton

Grimsby), then found he could not resist a recall to the colours. Tragically, he was killed in action by a sniper's bullet on the day before Armistice Day.

Appearances:
FL: 106 apps. 23 gls.
FAC: 5 apps. 0 gls.
WW1: 36 apps. 9 gls.
Total: *147 apps.*
32 gls.

Tommy Benfield

BENNETT, A.

Role: Centre forward

CAREER: Notts Mapperley/cs 1891:FOSSE.

Debut v Derby Junction (H) ML 12.9.1891

Signed with his club-mate, goalkeeper George Old, to help Fosse make the transition from local friendly fare to their first season of Midland League competition, Bennett was an attack leader who spent more time on the injury list than in action during his eight months on the club's books.

Appearances:
FAC: 1 app. 0 gls.
ML: 5 apps. 2 gls.
Total: *6 apps. 2 gls.*

BENNETT, John William

Role: Right back
b. Liverpool,
29th November 1879

CAREER: Wavertree/ 1899:Wellingborough/ May 1900:Lincoln City/cs 1901: Northampton Town/ cs 1903:Luton Town/ May 1904:FOSSE/Apr 1905:Blackburn Rovers.

Jack Bennett

Debut v Blackpool (A) 3.9.04

A fine right-back who had faced Fosse in the Cup for Wellingborough, then rebuilt his career in the Southern League after being

released by Lincoln on disciplinary grounds, Jack joined Fosse's concerted attempt to bounce back from the re-election reprieve of 1904, and impressed so much that he earned himself a move to First Division Blackburn before season's end. His role there, though, was primarily to understudy international Bob Crompton, and he won but a single senior selection.

Appearances:
FL: 27 apps. 1 gl.
FAC: 7 apps. 0 gls.
Total: *34 apps. 1 gl.*

BENSKIN, F.S.

Role: Forward
b. Leicester

CAREER: Leicester Old Boys/Apr 1902: FOSSE/1904:South Wigston Albion.

Debut v Burnley (A) 24.1.03 (scored once)

FS Benskin

The goalscoring half of the Benskin brothers partnership: an amateur inside- or outside-left who could surely have done with an extended first-team trial. Apart from scoring in his only League game, he also hit a hat-trick in the first of his senior friendlies, at Ripley in April 1902. Both brothers were in the Wigston side which beat Fosse Reserves in the 1905 County Cup Final.

Appearances:
FL: 1 app. 1 gl.
Total: *1 app. 1 gl.*

BENSKIN, William Ewart

Role: Half back
b. Leicester, 8th April 1880
d. Leicester, 1st June 1956

CAREER: Leicester Old Boys/May 1901: FOSSE/1904:South Wigston Albion.

COUNTY CRICKETERS.

W. E. BENSKIN,
LEICESTERSHIRE.

Debut v Burslem Port Vale (H) 25.1.02

A faithful reserve centre- or left-half for Fosse across three seasons of Second Division struggle (culminating in a re-election application), 'Benny' was another to write his name in bolder print across the records of the County cricket club. A fast bowler who had two spells with Leicestershire between 1906 and 1924, bracketing stints representing Perthshire and Scotland and as pro at Ramsbottom, he performed the summer game hat-trick in the very first of his 100 County Championship matches, against Essex at Southend. Renowned as a joker, 'Benny' later worked as an upholsterer at the Royal Infirmary. (We suspect, but have yet to confirm, that he also turned out in the Southern League for Northampton Town in 1906/7).

Appearances:
FL: 11 apps. 0 gls.
Total: *11 apps. 0 gls.*

BERRINGTON, W.A.

Role: Left back
b. 1888

CAREER: Army football/1912:Aberdare/ cs 1913:FOSSE.

Debut v Leeds City (H) 7.2.14

WA Berrington

A former Grenadier Guardsman whom Fosse had spotted during his brief spell of Southern League football in Wales, Berrington played in all five matches of the 1913 Swedish tour, but subsequently was restricted to only two successive Second Division games as left-back deputy for Sam Currie. (It is suspected, but as yet unconfirmed, that this player fell in action at Ypres in June 1915).

Appearances:
FL: 2 apps. 0 gls.
Total: *2 apps. 0 gls.*

BERRY, Arthur

Arthur Berry

Role: Right half
b. Leicester (?)
d. Leicester, October 1940

CAREER: Dec 1900: FOSSE.

Debut v New Brighton Tower (H) 16.3.01

A steady reserve right-half for Fosse across four fairly uninspiring Second Division seasons; Arthur was one of several such Fossils whose careers outside the confines of Filbert Street unfortunately remain a mystery - even the local press was singularly unforthcoming about his life and career when noting his passing.

Appearances:
FL: 24 apps. 0 gls.
Total: *24 apps. 0 gls.*

BETTS, Herbert

Herbert Betts

Role: Left half
b. Leicester

CAREER: Leicester Imperial/(Mar 1902- trials-FOSSE).

Debut v Preston North End (H) 31.3.02

A left-half briefly landed in poverty-stricken Fosse's rather desperate end-of-season trawl of local talent, and soon thrown back to the Imps - despite a win and a draw accruing from the two home fixtures in which he played.

Appearances:
FL: 2 apps. 0 gls.
Total: *2 apps. 0 gls.*

BICKNELL, Stephen John

Role: Outside left
b. Stockton, nr. Rugby, 28th November 1958

CAREER: VS Rugby/app July 1975/
pro Nov 1976:CITY/Aug 1978:Torquay
United/cs 1979:Southam United.

Debut v Newcastle United (A) 9.4.77

Steve Bicknell

A young winger tossed into the First Division deep-end by Jimmy Bloomfield late in his final campaign at the helm (as high hopes of European qualification again receded fast in a plethora of drawn games), Steve failed to impress, and was given no opportunity to rebuild his confidence at senior level as City slithered the following season under Frank McLintock. His Plainmoor record consisted only of three substitute appearances, and he quickly returned to minor-grade football.

Appearances:
FL: 6 (1) apps. 0 gls.
Total: *6 (1) apps. 0 gls.*

BINNEY, John

Role: Inside left

CAREER: Worksop Town/June 1902:FOSSE/
cs 1903:Worksop Town/cs 1904:Denaby
United.

Debut v Small Heath (H) 6.9.02

Impressive in pre-season practice, and chosen for Fosse's opening pair of games for 1902/3 (both heavy defeats), this inside-left then never again made the Filbert Street first team; though he found his level in Midland League football.

Appearances:
FL: 2 apps. 0 gls.
Total: *2 apps. 0 gls.*

BIRCHENALL, Alan John

Role: Striker / Midfield
b. East Ham, London, 22nd August 1945

CAREER: Thorneywood Thistle/June 1963:
Sheffield United/Nov 1967:Chelsea/
June 1970:Crystal Palace/Sept 1971:CITY/
(Mar 1976-loan-Notts County)/(Apr 1977-
loan-San Jose Earthquakes)/Sept 1977:Notts
County/Apr 1978:Memphis Rogues/
Sept 1978:Blackburn Rovers/Mar 1979:Luton
Town/Oct 1979:Hereford United/cs 1980:
Trowbridge (p/mgr).

Debut v Crystal Palace (H) 2.10.71

A recent football book entitled 'The Mavericks', and devoted to personality players of the 70s, aptly features on its cover the famous photo of Alan and Sheffield United's Tony Currie taking time out from match action for a jokey kiss - for many observers this remains the soccer-image antithesis of the well-known shot from a later era of Vinnie Jones and Paul Gascoigne in rather more cynical intimate contact. Times may have changed in this way, but at least at Filbert

Alan Birchenall

Street we have Alan to remind us - through his programme column and his man-with-the-microphone manner - that the game can still be as much about smiles as grimaces and gritted teeth. City's energetic part-time PR man (since 1983) was London-born but Nottingham-raised, and started his playing career as an extrovert blond striker, gaining four England Under-23 caps while figuring as a skilful foil for Mick Jones at Bramall Lane. He became Dave Sexton's initial major purchase at Stamford Bridge, in the first of three six-figure transfers, and Jimmy Bloomfield eventually added him to the rapidly burgeoning community of transplanted Cockneys at Leicester, where Alan gradually assumed a deeper-lying schemer's role as attack-oriented City's fortunes ebbed and flowed entertainingly in the early 70s. Again inclining to the nomadic life, Alan then carried both his boots and his ever-ready smile around the NASL and the lower Divisions for a while (never quite getting his notorious left shooting foot - 'The Claw' - into top gear again!), before returning to Filbert Street. Almost ever since, he's been attempting to rewrite his own substantial legend with his 'Geriatric Megastars', the charity-supporting team of former City favourites. For some time employed in the shoe trade, Alan now runs The Griffin pub in Swithland.

Alan Birchenall

Appearances:
FL: 156 (7) apps. 12 gls.
FAC: 14 apps. 1 gl.
LC: 6 apps. 1 gl.
Total: *176 (7) apps. 14 gls.*

BISHOP, Matthew

Role: Outside left
b. Melton Mowbray, Leics

CAREER: Aug 1895:FOSSE/cs 1897:Warmley/ Feb 1899:FOSSE.

Debut v Hinckley Town (H) FAC 12.10.1895 (scored once)

A young outside-left whose senior progress was initially stymied by the return of old favourite Billy Dorrell, Matt himself became another player to twice sign on to the Fosse payroll, albeit with hardly greater success second time around. His interim spell with Bristol-based Warmley coincided with that club's promotion to the Southern League's First Division, and ended when the club resigned partway through 1898/9. City still enjoy the support of his grandson, albeit from Australia.

Appearances:
FL: 13 apps. 2 gls.
FAC: 6 apps. 2 gls.
Total: *19 apps. 4 gls.*

BISHOP, Sidney Macdonald

Role: Left half
b. Stepney, London, 10th February 1900
d. Chelsea, London, 4th May 1949

CAREER: Ilford/RAF/(trials-Crystal Palace)/May 1920:West Ham United/Nov 1926:CITY/ June 1928:Chelsea.

Debut v Derby County (A) 6.11.26

A former Hammers skipper, a player in the first Wembley FA Cup Final in 1923, and the bearer of the Upton Park nickname 'Sticks' on account of his slender frame, Sid was a cultured, constructive wing-half who fitted in perfectly with City's ascending First Division side, winning himself suitable recognition by way of four England caps (one goal) and one Football League honour. Indeed, only an eve-of-game illness prevented Sid captaining his country against Scotland in March 1928. He was far from keen, however, on living outside London, and was quite prepared to drop a Division to move (for £3,800) to Stamford Bridge; though he actually helped Chelsea to promotion in his second season there. It has recently been discovered that Sid was, in fact, a nephew of Fosse's Matt Bishop.

Appearances:
FL: 49 apps. 7 gls.
FAC: 4 apps. 0 gls.
Total: *53 apps. 7 gls.*

Sid Bishop

Above and right:
Adam Black

BLACK, Adam Hudson

Role: Full back
b. Denny, Stirlingshire, 18th February 1898
d. Leicester, 30th August 1981

CAREER: Govan/Bathgate/Jan 1920:CITY.
Debut v Hull City (H) 24.1.20

Holder of the record for the highest number of League appearances
for City, and second only to Graham Cross in the aggregate reckoning
of senior outings for the club, Adam was ever-present in four of his
sixteen playing seasons, and missed but a single game in each of three
more. His consistent, unostentatious brilliance at full-back - he
alternated for several years between left and right flanks before
settling on the latter side - cried out for international recognition, but
the nearest Adam got to a cap was an appearance for the Anglo-Scots
against the Home Scots in March 1923, the next-to-last time the
Scottish trial took place in that once-popular format. Perhaps his
slight build and stature deceived the selectors, but his resilience
and bravery had already won him the Distinguished Conduct
Medal during his wartime service with the Argyll & Sutherland
Highlanders, and his assured technical mastery had already
been feted even before Peter Hodge swooped for his signature
from little Bathgate (with whom he'd just won a Scottish
Qualifying Cup-winner's medal, and who were themselves
soon to rise from Central League status to join the Scottish

BLACKETT, Joseph

Role: Full back
b. Newcastle upon Tyne, 1875

CAREER: Newcastle United/Gateshead/
June 1896:Loughborough/May 1897:
Wolverhampton Wanderers/Mar 1900:Derby
County/Apr 1901:Sunderland/Oct 1901:
Middlesbrough/May 1905:Luton Town/
July 1906:FOSSE/cs 1909:Rochdale (p/mgr)/
cs 1912:Barrow.

Debut v Burslem Port Vale (A) 1.9.06

Though he started his League career as an
outside-left, and even had the odd game at
centre-forward for Derby, Joe had forged a fair

reputation as an uncompromising full-back by
the time Fosse expended a sizeable £115 fee on
his transfer. (As was the custom then, said fee
was paid to Middlesbrough, who had retained
Joe's League registration, rather than to
Southern League Luton). He gave good value,
too; turning out on either flank as required to
stiffen the Fosse defence and add conviction to
the promotion drive, and then going on to
take part in the club's First Division
(mis)adventure in his final season. Joe represented the English XI in the Players' Union
international at Ibrox in March 1900, and was
selected as travelling reserve for the Football
League's game in Belfast in October 1904. He
first experienced promotion with Boro' in 1902
and, later, in his initial season as player/man-
ager at Rochdale, he led his team into the top
flight of the Lancashire Combination, and to
the championship of that competition a year
later. Joe was a trainer at Reading from 1913,
and enlisted for WW1 service in May 1915.

Appearances:
FL: 78 apps. 0 gls.
FAC: 3 apps. 0 gls.
Total: *81 apps. 0 gls.*

League). Adam won a Second Division
championship medal in 1925 and then
starred for a decade in the top flight before
retiring to run a Leicester newsagent's
shop, having earned three cash benefits for
loyalty from a grateful City. (Ironically, on
the occasion of his first benefit game,
against Southampton in April 1925, he
missed a penalty; having previously that
term claimed three of his eventual total of
four City goals from the spot). Adam's
younger brother Johnny moved from
Denny Hibs to Sunderland in 1921, after
representing Scotland at Junior level, and
eventually played in each Division in the
League as his career subsequently took him
to Nelson, Accrington Stanley, Chesterfield,
Luton Town and Bristol Rovers.

Appearances:
FL: 528 apps. 4 gls.
FAC: 29 apps. 0 gls.
Total: *557 apps. 4 gls.*

Joe Blackett

Mark Blake

BLAKE, Mark Antony

Role: Midfield
b. Nottingham, 16th December 1970

CAREER: YT 1987/pro May 1989:Aston Villa/
(Jan 1991-loan-Wolverhampton Wanderers)/
Aug 1993:Portsmouth/Mar 1994:CITY.

Debut v Notts County (A) 26.3.94

Eight times capped at England Under-21 level
after his breakthrough as a Villa midfielder,
Mark could nonetheless find no regular
guarantee of a senior place in the claret and
blue, and transferred to Fratton in a part-
exchange deal involving Guy Whittingham. A
return to the Midlands suited him fine when
Brian Little swooped for his signature on

deadline day, though the burden of wearing,
for a few months, the tag of City's most
expensive purchase (at £360,000) didn't exactly
aid his integration to the promotion-bound
side. His debut day saw City at their most
inept in a Meadow Lane humiliation, and it
took him some time to catch the pace of the
hectic progress towards the Play-offs, though
he marked that period with a spectacular first
strike at Oxford and an effective spell at full-
back, and was part of the glory line-up which
silenced the Rams in the Wembley decider. In
the Premiership Mark eventually re-emerged
as a shaven-headed middle-line snapper,
bringing a determined ball-winning
dimension to an often under-strength area,
and claiming a memorable goal-double in the
home victory over Southampton; though he
was affected and finally sidelined towards the
end of the term by asthma.

Appearances (to end 1994/5):
PL: 26 (4) apps. 3 gls.
FL: 10 (1) apps. 1 gl.
LC: 2 apps. 0 gls.
P/O: 3 apps. 0 gls.
Total: *41 (5) apps. 4 gls.*

BLESSINGTON, James

Role: Inside forward
b. Linlithgow, West Lothian, 28th February 1874
d. Newton Abbott, Devon, 18th April 1939

CAREER: 1890:Leith Hibernians/1891:Leith
Athletic/(Aug 1892-loan-St.Bernards)/
Aug 1892:Celtic/Feb 1898:Preston North End/
June 1899:Derby County/Oct 1899:Bristol
City/Aug 1900:Luton Town/May 1903:FOSSE.

Debut v Barnsley (A) 5.9.03

The epitome of the tough but thoughtful,
shrewdly skilful Scot whose like did so much
to redefine the face of early English professional football, Jimmy had been a member of
three Celtic championship teams, had picked
up two Scottish Cup runners-up medals, and
earned four full caps and five selections for
the Scottish League side before he crossed the
border to sign on at Deepdale. Curiously, his
spell at Derby was notably short (only two
League games), but he lit up the forward lines
of his two Southern League clubs, and was an
ever-present in the inside-right berth in his
first season at Leicester, having joined the

Jimmy Blessington

BLOCKLEY, Jeffrey Paul

Role: Centre back
b. Leicester, 12th September 1949

CAREER: June 1967:Coventry City/Oct 1972:
Arsenal/Jan 1975:CITY/(Feb 1978-loan-Derby
County)/June 1978:Notts County/
1981:Gloucester City.

Debut v Chelsea (H) 1.2.75

A team-mate of Peter Shilton's in Leicester
Boys' English Schools Trophy-winning team of
1965, Jeff was initially overlooked by his home
town club. His cool, strong centre-half play
soon, however, saw him through the ranks at
Highfield Road, and to the first of his ten
England Under-23 caps; yet it was only after a
£200,000 move to Highbury that he received a
full England call-up. Matters soured somewhat
at Arsenal, with Frank McLintock unready to
relinquish his place, and the crowd
unforgiving after Jeff turned in a below-par
performance in his club's 1973 Cup semi-final
defeat by Sunderland. But what seemed a
desperation £100,000 purchase on Jimmy
Bloomfield's part in fact worked wonders for
both player and club, as City escaped an

remarkably heavy transfer traffic of the time
between Luton and Fosse. Jimmy was still a
valuable playing prompter when he
additionally assumed the onus of becoming
the club's first-ever Team Manager in January
1907 - decades before managers as such were
granted any credit for feats like Fosse's 1908
promotion - and he continued selflessly to
pass on his experience to the Fosse reserves
between his increasingly sporadic League
appearances. He certainly earned the profits
from his benefit match - a Boxing Day 1908
reserve fixture against Leeds City. In 1911,
Jimmy became trainer of Cliftonville, then in
1913 was appointed coach to Belfast Celtic,
and also served as an athletics handicapper in
Ireland. He was about to take up a further
coaching appointment, in Germany, when war
broke out, and he returned to join the
Merchant Navy. Subsequently, Jimmy had a
stint as an electrician in Luton, a spell as
manager of Southern League club Abertillery
(from June 1920), and then became a licensee
in Guernsey and the West Country.

Appearances:
FL: 100 apps. 18 gls.
FAC: 12 apps. 3 gls.
Total: 112 apps. 21 gls.

Jeff Blockley

apparently pre-booked relegation spot thanks to the inspirational successes of Jeff at the back and Chris Garland up front. Injuries unfortunately dogged much of Jeff's subsequent Leicester career, but when he gave up his role as defensive cornerstone, it was only to the high promise of young Steve Sims. Jeff returned to the county on retirement, was briefly manager of Southern League club Leicester United, and in April/May 1989 held the reins at Hinckley Athletic.

Appearances:
FL: 75 (1) apps. 2 gls.
FAC: 7 apps. 0 gls.
LC: 2 (1) apps. 0 gls.
Total: *84 (2) apps. 2 gls.*

BOWERS, John William Anslow

Role: Centre forward
b. Santon, nr. Scunthorpe, 22nd February 1908
d. Allestree, Derby, 4th July 1970

CAREER: Appleby Works/Dec 1927: Scunthorpe United/May 1928:Derby County/ Nov 1936:CITY.

Debut v Swansea Town (A) 21.11.36
(scored once)

A genuine goalscoring giant, of impeccable thrusting bravery, Jack started as he meant to go on - stepping up from the Midland League with Scunthorpe to score on his Derby debut and add a hat-trick in his second game. Record-breaking years followed, with Jack the First Division's top scorer for three consecutive seasons in the early 30s. He notched three goals in his two Football League representative games, and two in his three full England matches, and only a serious knee injury in 1934 brought a hiccup to his exploits. Nonetheless, Jack already had twelve goals in the bag for 1936/7 when Derby accepted struggling City's £7,500 transfer offer - and amazingly he was to add no less than 33 more before the season had ended with City acclaimed as Division Two champions. To talk of hero-worship from the fans in this context is almost to understate Jack's popular status, but there can be no denying his transformational effect on the club. Understandably, his scoring rate decreased a little back

in the top flight, but when the war put an end to Jack's 'official' statistics, he could look back on a career total of 219 goals in only 282 League games. He briefly coached at Notts County from 1940, played a handful of wartime games for City, Forest and Derby, then returned in 1945 to the Baseball Ground as assistant trainer and physiotherapist. His son, John, also made a playing career with the Rams.

Appearances:
FL: 79 apps. 52 gls.
FAC: 5 apps. 4 gls.
WW2: 31 apps. 15 gls.
Total: *115 apps. 71 gls.*

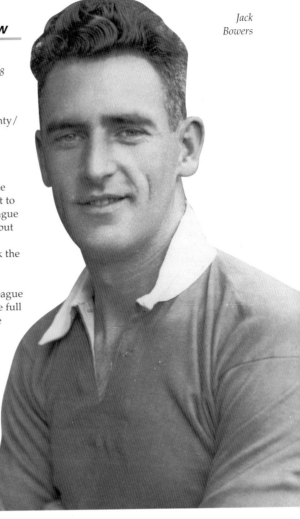

Jack Bowers

BOWN, Herbert Arthur

Role: Goalkeeper
b. East Ham, London, 3rd May 1893
d. Leicester, 11th February 1959

CAREER: Romford Town/(trials-West Ham United)/ Apr 1913:FOSSE/ May 1922:Halifax Town/Jan 1925:Hull City.

Debut v Notts County (H) 8.11.13

A calm, reliable keeper who yet retained a taste for drama - he took a couple of penalties for Fosse during WW1, and also got on the scoresheet for Halifax during his two ever-present seasons in the Third Division (North) - Herbert saw off several challenges for his place between the Fosse sticks before the war and those of City after it. Having represented Essex as an amateur, he only signed professional for Fosse after taking part in their first overseas tour, to Sweden in the summer of 1913. During the first postwar season, Herbert set one City record which still stands: keeping a clean sheet in seven consecutive League games. He had retired to his fish and poultry business in Leicester for several months when Hull called on him for a four-game spell during an injury crisis.

Appearances:
FL: 143 apps. 0 gls.
FAC: 11 apps. 0 gls.
WW1: 112 apps. 1 gl.
Total: *266 apps. 1 gl.*

Herbert Bown

BRACEY, Frederick Cecil

Role: Winger
b. Derby, 20th July 1887
d. Derby, 28th March 1960

CAREER: Small Heath/ Holbrook Swifts/Nov 1905: FOSSE/July 1908:Bradford Park Avenue/cs 1909:Rochdale.

Debut v Hull City (H) 7.12.05

Able to play on both wings, Fred unfortunately couldn't hold down either position for long at Filbert Street, though former team-mate Joe Blackett was sufficiently impressed by his reserve form to take him eventually to Rochdale. In the interim, he made seven appearances for Park Avenue in their initial League season. He is as well remembered as an occasional Derbyshire cricketer, with 77 first-class matches as a bowler to his credit between 1906 and 1914, taking 132 wickets.

Fred Bracey

Appearances:
FL: 10 apps. 0 gls.
Total: *10 apps. 0 gls.*

BRADLEY, Gordon

Role: Goalkeeper
b. Scunthorpe, Lincs, 20th May 1925

CAREER: am:Scunthorpe United/Sept 1942: CITY/Feb 1950:Notts County/Aug 1958: Cambridge City/Glentoran.

Debut (WW2) v Derby County (A) 14.11.42; (postwar) v West Bromwich Albion (A) 21.12.46

Given the nod over the younger Leslie Major

when injury ruled out Ian McGraw, Gordon was City's luckless goalkeeper in the 1949 Cup Final. He had joined City, on Digger Maw's recommendation, during WW2, when he also guested for Grimsby Town, Notts County and Sheffield United, and built a reputation for agility and quick reflexes that may well have been a concomitant of his all-round sporting prowess: he was Leicestershire table-tennis champion and also played lawn tennis professionally. For the Magpies, Gordon totted up 192 League appearances and scored one goal - against City at Filbert Street in September 1956, from an outfield position after he'd injured a hand. He became a coach for the Irish Lawn Tennis Association during the 60s, but was most recently heard of in 1989, back in football as general manager of Washington Stars, in the American Soccer League.

Appearances:
FL: 69 apps. 0 gls.
FAC: 5 apps. 0 gls.
WW2: 6 apps. 0 gls.
Total: *80 apps. 0 gls.*

❏ FOX FACT: *Gordon Bradley is not the only goalkeeper to score against City in senior football, but he's one of a fairly exclusive band. Fulham's Ian Black was similarly playing in an outfield position after injury when he scored a consolation goal in City's 6-1 Second Division home win in August 1952, while Manchester United's Alex Stepney briefly became his side's joint leading scorer when he put a penalty past Peter Shilton during City's 2-1 victory at Old Trafford in September 1973. Shilton himself remains City's only goalkeeping goalscorer at League level, with his long-distance effort in the 5-1 win at Southampton in October 1967, though Herbert Bown registered a successful penalty for Fosse at Hull during WW1. (Incidentally, Bradley's place between the Notts County sticks in the game referred to above was taken by future City player Gordon Wills, who had already also scored in the 6-3 home win).*

BRADSHAW, Thomas Dickinson

Role: Forward
b. Hambleton, Lancs, 15th March 1879

CAREER: Lostock Hall/Apr 1896:Preston North End/Dec 1896:Blackpool/May 1897: Sunderland/Jan 1898:Nottingham Forest/ Mar 1899:FOSSE/cs 1900:New Brighton Tower/cs 1901:Swindon Town/Oct 1901: Reading/cs 1902:Preston North End/ 1903:Wellingborough/Southport Central/ Accrington Stanley/Oct 1905:FOSSE/ May 1907:Glossop.

Debut v Grimsby Town (H)
3.4.1899

A well-travelled outside- or inside-right who had

Right: Tom Bradshaw
Below: Gordon Bradley

two separate spells with Fosse, Tom was also a cricket professional with Preston CC and briefly a summer-game coach at Harrow School. His League bow had come with Blackpool during their initial League season (when Tom had scored against Fosse), and his First Division baptism at Roker, but his wanderlust rather instanced the lack of concentration he was sometimes accused of displaying on the pitch. His temperament was suspect, also; he was briefly suspended during his second Fosse season for 'inattention to training rules', and was said to be under suspension by Glossop (for whom he never played a League game) when criminally charged and found guilty of wife-beating in 1908. Fifteen years later, when City visited Bradford City, Tom appeared in their dressing room, describing himself haplessly as 'down and out', and gratefully departing with the proceeds of a quick whip-round. Then, in December 1924, Tom also dropped in on the City party at Valley Parade, cheerfully relating how he'd used their gift to set himself up successfully as a baker!

Appearances:
FL: 43 apps. 9 gls.
FAC: 5 apps. 1 gl.
Total: *48 apps. 10 gls.*

BRASH, Archibald

Role: Outside right
b. Edinburgh

CAREER: St.Mirren/ cs 1894:Sheffield Wednesday/ cs 1898:Crewe Alexandra/ cs 1899:Sheffield Wednesday/ June 1900:FOSSE/ cs 1901:Aberdeen.

Debut v Stockport County (H) 1.9.1900

A small Scottish right-winger who starred for Wednesday in their 1896 Cup Final victory (his quickly-taken throw-in led to them gaining a first-minute opening goal against Wolves), and returned for their 1900 promotion campaign, Archie did not quite live up to his advance billing with Fosse. Yet he did manage one purple passage, belatedly opening his

Leicester scoring account by netting four times against Burton Swifts in December 1900. The Pittodrie-based club Archie moved to were at the time but one of three leading Aberdonian non-league sides who would amalgamate in 1903 to form the continuing present-day Dons.

Appearances:
FL: 14 apps. 5 gls.
Total: *14 apps. 5 gls.*

BREBNER, Ronald Gilchrist

Role: Goalkeeper
b. Darlington, 23rd September 1881
d. Chiswick, London, 11th November 1914

CAREER: (am - throughout career - Edinburgh University/Northern Nomads/ London Caledonians)/also - 1905:Elgin City/cs 1905:Sunderland/Feb 1906:Rangers/ Oct 1906:Chelsea/1907: Darlington/1907:Elgin City/Aug 1908: Stockton/Feb 1910:Queen's Park/July 1911: Huddersfield Town/ Aug 1912:Chelsea/May 1913:FOSSE.

Debut v Nottingham Forest (A) 3.9.13

Archie Brash

The second of Fosse's multiply-honoured amateur goalkeepers, 'R.G.' won a total of 23 England amateur caps, and had followed Horace Bailey into the United Kingdom Olympic side, matching the latter's achievement by playing in the gold-medal team at the 1912 Stockholm Games. A trained dental surgeon, he also appeared in a full England trial (South v. North, November 1912), and represented the Amateurs v. Professionals in the 1913 Charity Shield match. Having played in all but two of Fosse's first twenty matches in 1913/14 (and having picked up his final pair of caps on the dates of his absences), he

Ron Brebner

was carried off the field at Lincoln with an injury that finished his career and was said to have contributed significantly to his early death ten months later. Back in October 1908, Ronald had saved no less than three York City penalties during a Northern League match which ended in a 7-0 away win for Stockton.

Appearances:
FL: 18 apps. 0 gls.
Total: *18 apps. 0 gls.*

BRIEN, Anthony James

Role: Defender
b. Dublin, 10th February 1969

CAREER: app/pro Feb 1987:CITY/Dec 1988: Chesterfield/Oct 1993:Rotherham United/ July 1995:West Bromwich Albion.

Debut v Ipswich Town (H) 30.9.87 (sub)

The cool, thoughtful central defensive pivot of the City side which fought through to the semi-finals of the FA Youth Cup in 1987, Tony made an impressive early League bow when replacing Phil Horner after only a couple of minutes of the Ipswich game, and was soon adding to his senior experience as a reliable stand-in in both the right-back and centre-back positions. One of the first City players to have his contract extended by the incoming David Pleat, Tony nonetheless soon found himself displaced in the club's 'shadow squad' by Grant Brown; though the £90,000 laid out by Third Division strugglers Chesterfield for the services of the 19 -year-old testified to his evident promise. He was a regular at Saltergate and Millmoor before a recent free transfer to The Hawthorns.

Appearances:
FL: 12 (4) apps. 1 gl.
FAC: 1 app. 0 gls.
LC: 1 app. 0 gls.
FMC: 3 apps. 0 gls.
Total: *17 (4) apps. 1 gl.*

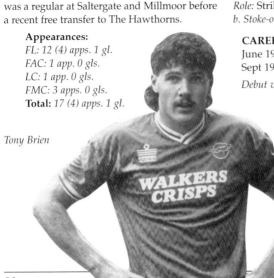

Tony Brien

Mark Bright

BRIGHT, Mark Abraham

Role: Striker
b. Stoke-on-Trent, 6th June 1962

CAREER: Leek Town/1981:Port Vale/ June 1984:CITY/Nov 1986:Crystal Palace/ Sept 1992:Sheffield Wednesday.

Debut v Newcastle United (H) 25.8.84

A late scoring burst for Port Vale at the end of 1983/4 brought Mark to Gordon Milne's attention, and a complex, appearance-related deal, fixed by the League's transfer tribunal and payable in £33,000 instalments, landed the tall striker at Filbert Street. His first season saw him as a regular occupant of the subs' bench -

he had, in fact, claimed each of his first four Vale goals in a No.12 shirt - but unable to add a first-team counter to his fine Central League record of 28 in 27 games. A spectacular brace against champions Everton on the opening day of 1985/6 - when he both replaced and faced the departed Gary Lineker - looked like opening the floodgates, but Mark still struggled to capitalise, and faced a rare degree of hostility (some of it, shamingly, downright racist in character) from the Leicester crowd. After turning down mooted transfers to Hull and Walsall, Mark eventually moved for £75,000 to Selhurst to rebuild his confidence, and soon hit the goal trail in earnest: winning a Golden Boot as the Second Division's top scorer in 1988, helping Palace into the top flight in 1989, picking up an FA Cup runners-up medal with them in 1990, and a Zenith Cup victor's memento in 1991. He had just passed his century of League goals when valued at £875,000 in moving to Hillsborough, and turned out in beaten Wednesday sides at Wembley in the Finals of both major Cup competitions in 1993.

Appearances:
FL: 26(16) apps. 6 gls.
FAC: 1 app. 0 gls.
LC: 3(1) apps. 0 gls.
Total: *30 (17) apps. 6 gls.*

BRODIE, Murray

Role: Striker
b. Glasgow, 26th September 1950

CAREER: Cumbernauld United/Nov 1968:CITY/ Sept 1970:Aldershot/ cs 1983:Basingstoke Town.

Debut v Watford (H) 4.10.69 (scored once)

Murray's first-team career at City was compressed into a single week in October 1969, as the strongly built forward made an unexpected, goal-capped Second Division debut against Watford; scored again, spectacularly, in a midweek

fixture against Middlesbrough; and limped off injured during the following Saturday's match at Preston. Unable to regain a place upon recovery, Murray moved - along with reserve full-back Jimmy Burt - to Aldershot, and set about a successful assault on that club's all-time aggregate appearance record: being eventually freed thirteen years, 461 League games, 84 League goals, and a well-merited testimonial game later.

Appearances:
FL: 3 apps. 2 gls.
Total: *3 apps. 2 gls.*

BROOKS, Joseph Ernest

Role: Outside right
b. Heanor, Derbyshire, 20th November 1892
d. Heanor, April qtr 1975

CAREER: Langley Heanor/May 1919:Grimsby Town/July 1920:Shirebrook/June 1921:CITY/ May 1922:Shirebrook/Kettering Town.

*Murray Brodie (left)
with David Tearse*

Debut v Clapton Orient (H) 9.2.22

A diminutive winger who came probably too late to League football after WW1 - he was almost 27 when making the first of his three appearances for the Mariners - Ernie failed to reproduce at Filbert Street the form which had prompted Peter Hodge to give him a second senior chance, and within months was back at Central Alliance level.

Appearances:
FL: 4 apps. 0 gls.
Total: *4 apps. 0 gls.*

BROWN, Alistair

Role: Striker
b. Musselburgh, Midlothian,
12th April 1951

CAREER: app Oct 1966/ pro Apr 1968:CITY/ Mar 1972: West Bromwich Albion/(May 1981-loan-Portland Timbers)/ Mar 1983:Crystal Palace/ Aug 1983:Walsall/June 1984: Port Vale.

Debut v Sunderland (H) 5.5.69 (scored twice)

The tall, elegant striker who made a teenage dream debut in the tense, relegation-delaying game against Sunderland, Ally went on to become the club's top scorer as City returned to the top flight via the Division Two championship in 1971 (when his goal at Bristol City clinched the title), and earned both Scottish Youth caps and an Under-23 trial appearance while at Filbert Street. Allowed to move for £61,111 by Jimmy Bloomfield (despite having got the 1971/2 First Division campaign off the ground with a goal inside 45 seconds at Huddersfield, and remaining leading marksman that term), he then repeated his experiences of relegation and promotion during an eleven-year stint at the

Hawthorns, in which he made over half of his career total of 495 League appearances (141 goals), and struck a useful partnership with his namesake Tony as Albion sought European glory. Ally had retreated to the middle line by the time he commenced his late wanderings, but helped Port Vale to a 1986 Fourth Division promotion slot in his final season in senior football; later becoming an Aldridge publican.

Appearances:
FL: 93 (8) apps. 32 gls.
FAC: 7 (2) apps. 2 gls.
LC: 10 (1) apps. 1 gl.
Total: *110 (11) apps. 35 gls.*

Ally Brown

Graham Brown

BROWN, Graham Frederick

Role: Striker
b. Leicester, 5th November 1950

CAREER: app June 1967/pro Nov 1968:CITY/
cs 1971:Burton Albion.

Debut v Aston Villa (H) 4.4.70 (sub)

A prolific reserve-team scorer, local lad
Graham earned his senior break after claiming
all four City goals in a testimonial friendly at
Plymouth in March 1970. Having only once,
however, leapt from the sub's bench into the
League fray (replacing John Sjoberg late in the
1-0 victory which helped consign Villa to
Division Three), he now has to share
with Malcolm Clarke, Scott Eustace,
Gary Fitzpatrick and Kevin Reed the
dubious statistical honour of the
most-truncated senior career at
City. Under Richie Norman at
Burton, he was top scorer
for two switchback
Southern League seasons;
the first ending in
promotion and the second in
Premier Division relegation.

    Appearances:
    FL: 0 (1) app. 0 gls.
    Total: *0 (1) app. 0 gls.*

BROWN, Grant Ashley

Role: Centre back
b. Sunderland, 19th November 1969

CAREER: YTS July 1986/pro July 1987:CITY/
(Aug 1989-loan-Lincoln City)/Jan 1990:Lincoln
City.

Debut v Bradford City (A) 30.4.88

One of several members of City's 1986/7
Youth Cup semi-final squad to make an early
senior bow, central defender Grant had a
harsh baptism at Valley Parade as the home
side went full-throttle towards the Play-offs
(winning 4-1), but he impressed David Pleat
sufficiently to be given the nod over
experienced newcomer Steve Thompson (ex-
Charlton) for the opening game of 1988/9,
and gained in poise and pacing during an
extended first-team run in the No.6 shirt over
the next few months. Grant's solid Central
League form and the added grounding of a
successful two-month loan spell at Sincil Bank
were not enough, however, to persuade Pleat
to resist Lincoln's later £60,000 offer. He
became skipper of the Imps in 1992/3, and
had appeared in 221 League games for them
by the end of 1994/5.

    Appearances:
    FL: 14 apps. 0 gls.
    LC: 2 apps. 0 gls.
    Total:
    16 apps. 0 gls.

Grant Brown

BROWN, James

Role: Half back/ Centre forward
b. Renton, Dunbartonshire
d. Leicester, January 1924

CAREER: Renton Union/Renton Thistle/
Renton/cs 1890:Aston Villa/Oct 1893:FOSSE/
Sept 1899:Loughborough.

*Debut v Mansfield
Town (H) FAC
4.11.1893*

A moustachio'd
Scottish 'professor'
who joined Fosse
during their final
Midland League
season as a wing-
half or free-scoring
centre-forward,
Jimmy also gave
stalwart Division
Two service at
centre-half,
skippering the side
for its League bow,
astutely prompting
the attack and
eventually earning

Jimmy Brown

himself a benefit from a friendly with
Southampton in September 1898. A year later
his veteran skills were briefly employed in the
hard-up Luffs' precarious, eventually fatal
struggle to retain League status; while in 1902
he became a League referee, having in the
interim founded a travel agency in Leicester.
Confusion over whether or not Jimmy was a
full Scottish international in his Renton days -
and therefore the first such to represent Fosse -
has deepened over the past couple of years:
several early Fosse team photos show Jimmy
wearing a cap marked 'SFA', and a mid-30's
interview with his son in the local press
mentions him as an international; though the
most highly respected author on Scotland's
players still identifies the J.Brown who
represented his country at inside-right against
Wales in 1890 as a Cambuslang player.

Appearances:
FL: 116 apps. 4 gls.
FAC: 23 apps. 3 gls.
ML: 14 apps. 14 gls.
Total: *153 apps. 21 gls.*

BROWN, John Thomas

Role: Full back
b. Eastwood, Notts, 1901

CAREER: Kirkby Colliery/Aug 1922:CITY/
Aug 1931:Wrexham/July 1934:Nuneaton
Town/Sep 1936:Heanor Town.

Debut v Aston Villa (H) 10.10.25

A patient understudy for either full-back
slot over several seasons, latterly
standing in successfully for both Adam
Black and Reg Osborne, Jack finally
made the left-back slot his own during
the season City made their most
concerted attempt ever for Division One
honours: 1928/9, when they finished
runners-up to Sheffield Wednesday. A
former Notts miner, he presented a
physical and temperamental contrast to
his stylish partner Black, but was no less
effective against First Division wingers.
In 1933 he assisted Wrexham to what
was then also their highest League
placing - runners-up spot in Division
Three (North) - and eventually left the
Racecourse after 99 League and Cup
starts. He also took runners-up medals from
the Welsh Cup Finals of 1932 and 1933.

Appearances:
FL: 114 apps. 0 gls.
FAC: 3 apps. 0 gls.
Total: *117 apps. 0 gls.*

*Jack
Brown*

BROWN, Paul Andrew

Role: Left back
b. Birmingham, 19th September 1964

CAREER: app:Aston Villa/Sept 1982:CITY/
May 1983:Nuneaton Borough/Stourbridge/
Alvechurch/Willenhall Town.

*Debut v Notts County
(H) FAC 8.1.83*

Capped by England
Schools as an
outside-left, Paul had
become an apprentice
left-back with Villa
by the time England
Youth honours came
his way. Signed as a
pro by City after
trials (he scored in
the Final of the pre-
season Bass Charity
Vase tournament at
Burton), Paul was
called up for his
Cup-tie debut in the
wake of Tommy

Paul Brown

Williams' second leg-break, but appeared
overawed as Notts County took City apart,
and suffered a subsequent loss of confidence.
Throughout the 80s he became a nomad on the
West Midlands non-
league scene.

> **Appearances:**
> *FAC: 1 app. 0 gls.*
> **Total:** *1 app. 0 gls.*

BROWN, Thomas

Role: Centre forward
b. Beith, Ayrshire

CAREER: Glenbuck
Cherrypickers/Aug 1899:
FOSSE/Dec 1901:
Chesterfield/cs 1902:
Lanark/Nov 1902:FOSSE
/cs1903:Portsmouth/
Sept 1904:Dundee.

*Debut v Woolwich Arsenal
(A) 2.9.1899 (scored once)*

Tommy Brown

A brother of the goal-hungry Scottish
international Sandy Brown (whose clubs
included Preston, Portsmouth, Spurs,
Middlesbrough and Luton), Tommy was also
a bustling centre-forward. He fell foul of the
Fosse directorate halfway through his third
season, when suspended for breaches of
training discipline, but was forgiven within a
year and returned for a second stint,
before moving on to replace his
brother at Fratton Park. Despite the
hiatus in his Fosse career, Tommy
was the club's top scorer for three
seasons running.

> **Appearances:**
> *FL: 72 apps. 38 gls.*
> *FAC: 5 apps. 3 gls.*
> **Total:** *77 apps. 41 gls.*

BRUCE, David

Role: Outside right
b. Perth, 23rd February 1911
d. Perth, 15th September 1976

CAREER: Perth Thistle/Aug 1930:
East Fife/Apr 1931:Dundee East
Craigie/Aug 1935:CITY/May 1936:Bristol
Rovers/Aug 1937:St.Mirren.

Debut v Burnley (A) 25.4.36

Plucked from
Scottish Junior
football as a full-
back prospect -
his signing indeed
denying him a cap
at that level -
David was briefly
tried out in the
Combination
forward line, then
given a single shot
at Second Division
level as an
outside-right (in
a 2-2 Turf Moor
draw) only days
before being
placed on the free
transfer list.
Moving to
Eastville with
Tommy Mills, he
continued on the

wing, and got on the scoresheet twice in 12 League games before returning north of the border, where he quickly reverted to his original back-line position.

Appearances:
FL: 1 app. 0 gls.
Total:
1 app. 0 gls.

David Bruce

BRUNTON, Matthew

Role: Centre forward
b. Burnley, 20th April 1878
d. Burnley, 29th December 1962

CAREER: Army football (South Lancs Regt.)/ Aug 1899:Preston North End/cs 1900: Accrington Stanley/July 1901:Burnley/ cs 1902:Accrington Stanley/May 1904: FOSSE/ Feb 1905:Nelson/cs 1905:Accrington Stanley/ July 1906:Oldham Athletic/cs 1908:Southport Central/1909:Haslingden/Oct 1910:Darwen/ Nov 1910:Accrington Stanley.

Debut v Blackpool (A) 3.9.04

Though he occupied all five forward positions in making 30 Division Two appearances (8 goals) for Burnley in 1901/2, it was in Lancashire Combination football that Matt excelled. Accrington Stanley became the first non-reserve side to win that championship (in 1903), when Matt scored 40 times from the centre-forward berth; he was back there for the 1906 triumph (following his unsuccessful Fosse spell); and then picked up his third championship medal with Oldham, substantially helping them gain subsequent

Matt Brunton

League election - though Matt himself would appear but once more for the Latics at the higher level. His brief Leicester exile seems a distinct aberration in a career so closely tied to his home county; and when Matt joined the trainer/coach ranks after retirement, it was predictably with Accrington and Burnley. He was a swimming instructor at Burnley Corporation Baths when WW1 broke out, and suffered a serious leg wound while serving as a sergeant in the South Lancashire Regiment; ironically spending his recuperation period in a Leicestershire military hospital.

Appearances:
FL: 5 apps. 0 gls.
FAC: 1 app. 0 gls.
Total: *6 apps. 0 gls.*

BUCHANAN, David

Role: Striker
b. Newcastle upon Tyne, 23rd June 1962

CAREER: app July 1978/pro June 1979:CITY/ (Oct 1982-loan-Northampton Town)/July 1983:Peterborough United/ 1984:North Shields/1984:Blyth Spartans/ July 1986:Sunderland/(Sept 1987-loan-York City)/(Apr 1988-trials-Middlesbrough)/ May 1988:(Norwegian football)/ Aug 1988:Blyth Spartans/1988:Newcastle Blue Star/Bedlington/Whitley Bay.

Debut v Oldham Athletic (H) 1.1.79
(scored once)

City's youngest-ever League player, David made his scoring debut (on the same day as Bobby Smith and Gary Lineker) at the age of 16 years and 192 days, as Jock Wallace turned to the juniors in his efforts to avert the spectre of a second successive relegation. The slender, light-haired striker - a good close dribbler, yet direct - justifiably became an immediate crowd favourite, but a succession of injuries and the club's desire not to rush his development contributed to David suffering a degree of disenchantment and a loss of appetite for the game over the next few seasons. After an unsuccessful spell at London Road, he dropped out of senior football altogether to build a career in

BUCKLEY, *John William*

Role: Winger
b. East Kilbride, Lanarkshire, 18th May 1962

CAREER: Queen's Park/May 1978:Celtic/
Mar 1983:Partick Thistle/July 1984:Doncaster
Rovers/July 1986:Leeds United/
(Mar 1987-loan-CITY)/(Oct 1987-loan-
Doncaster Rovers)/Nov 1987:Rotherham
United/Oct 1990: Partick Thistle/July 1991:
Scunthorpe United/ Feb 1993:Rotherham
United/Dec 1994:Buxton.

Debut v Newcastle United (A) 4.4.87 (sub)

An old-fashioned ball-playing winger of the
unpredictable type, John was twice bought by
Billy Bremner (presumably motivated by
memories of Eddie Gray) after making his
Scottish League mark with Partick, but barely
got a chance to shine at Elland Road, and
came to City on extended loan for the fateful
run-in to eventual relegation in 1987.
Surprisingly, he spent more time on the bench
than in action, for he gave brief, tantalising
glimpses of genuine crowd-pleasing dribbling
talent. John returned to Leeds when it looked
possible that City might face them in the
First/Second Division Play-offs; then started a
second circuit of Yorkshire clubs and a
metamorphosis into a mature midfielder.
At Millmoor, he won a Fourth Division
championship medal in 1989; while he was a

leisure centre management, but his
evident ability and increased maturity
while playing part-time in the Northern
League (and winning England caps at
semi-pro level) nudged Lawrie
McMenemy into offering him another
senior chance at Roker. Nonetheless, by
the age of 28, David had definitively
retired from the game.

Appearances:
FL: 24 (9) apps. 7 gls.
FAC: 4 (1) apps. 1 gl.
Total: *28 (10) apps. 8 gls.*

❏ FOX FACT: *While David Buchanan
holds the club record as the youngest-ever
player to turn out for the club in each of the
Football League and FA Cup (his bow in
this competition coming five days after his
Division Two debut), and Peter Shilton (at
16 yrs, 228 days) was the youngest First
Division debutant, wartime football saw
Gordon Jayes making a senior
breakthrough at only 16 yrs, 46 days in
November 1939. Other under-17s to
feature in senior City line-ups have been
Dennis Cheney (16, 132), Ray Iggleden
(16, 201) and Billy Wright (16, 206)
during WW2; plus David Timson (16,
231) and Neil Grewcock (16, 311)
subsequently.*

John Buckley

Jim Bulling

BULLING, James

Role: Wing half
b. West Bridgford, Nottingham,
12th February 1909
d. Wrexham, 13th October 1992

CAREER: jnr 1926:Nottingham Forest/July
1928:Shirebrook/May 1930:CITY/June 1932:
Wrexham/June 1936:Shrewsbury Town.

Debut v Liverpool (A) 15.11.30

Signed from Shirebrook on the same day as
full-back Charles Gellatly (whose own League
career would start in earnest a year later, at
Gillingham), Jim was a wing-half who had a
couple of brief spells as deputy for George
Ritchie or Billy Findlay, but found his level
more comfortably in the Third Division
(North), with 121 League appearances over
four seasons at the Racecourse, and a runners-
up medal from the 1933 Welsh Cup Final. His
Shrewsbury campaign was that club's last in
the Birmingham League, and Jim helped back

Wembley loser with Scunthorpe in the 1992
Fourth Division Play-Off decider. Then, in
only his fourth game back with Rotherham
after a £10,000 move, John suffered a fractured
skull in an accidental clash of heads with a
Plymouth player, and lay critically ill in a
coma for several days afterwards. Thankfully
surviving, John nonetheless announced his
retirement in July 1993; though he has since
returned to the non-league game.

Appearances:
FL: 1 (4) apps. 0 gls.
Total: *1 (4) apps. 0 gls.*

up Jack Liggins as the Shrews took runners-up spot. He was a nephew of the Forest full-back Harold Bulling, and was presumably also related to Watford's Chris Bulling. Jim served during WW2 with the Royal Engineers, then followed the plumbing trade at Shotton Steelworks until retirement.

Appearances:
FL: 12 apps. 0 gls.
Total: *12 apps. 0 gls.*

BUNCE, Paul Eric

Role: Winger
b. Coalville, Leics, 7th January 1967

CAREER: app July 1983/pro Jan 1985:CITY/ Mar 1987:Northampton Town/cs 1988: Weymouth/cs 1989:Burton Albion/ Feb 1990: Shepshed Charterhouse/ Apr 1992:Hinckley FC.

Paul Bunce

Debut v Nottingham Forest (H) 11.10.86

A teenage winger who progressed through the City ranks to be given a senior break by Bryan Hamilton, Paul failed adequately to assert himself in the First Division, and proved to be no answer to City's desperate need for attacking width in the relegation season of 1986/7. After a £5,000 deadline-day move to Northampton, already booked for the Fourth Division championship, he had to wait until the final games of that season for a look-in, but scored in his first full game. Paul was, however, freed by the Cobblers in 1988.

Appearances:
FL: 5 (1) apps. 0 gls.
Total: *5 (1) apps. 0 gls.*

BURBECK, Ronald Thomas

Role: Outside left
b. Leicester, 27th February 1934

CAREER: May 1952:CITY/Oct 1956: Middlesbrough/Aug 1963:Darlington.

Debut v West Ham United (A) 15.9.52

An England Youth international winger who stood in once for Tom Dryburgh during his first season as a pro (while on National Service in the RAF), and then waited over three and a half years for another brief chance, Ron had to go north to escape the superabundance of experienced flankmen on City's books in the mid-50s. He made 139 League appearances for the Ayresome club, chiefly as provider for the prolific Brian Clough and Alan Peacock.

Appearances:
FL: 3 apps. 0 gls.
Total: *3 apps. 0 gls.*

Ron Burbeck

BURGESS, T.

Role: Forward

CAREER: Leicester Imperial/cs
1901:FOSSE/cs 1902:Leicester Imperial.

*Debut v Stockport County (H) 23.11.01
(scored once)*

A local outside- or inside-right who impressed
in the August trials but found it difficult to
dislodge the then-established Fosse partnership of Webb and Richards during his season
with the professionals.

> **Appearances:**
> *FL: 3 apps. 1 gl.*
> **Total:** *3 apps. 1 gl.*

BURTON, Horace

Role: Wing half
b. Melton Mowbray, Leics, 28th July 1887
d. September 1969

CAREER: Holwell Works/Oct
1910:FOSSE/1919:Loughborough Corinthians.

Debut v Bradford Park Avenue (A) 1.4.11

A burly, two-footed wing-half and loyal clubman for Fosse, never guaranteed a senior place
during his five pre-war seasons, Horace often
forced his way back into the team at the
expense of more experienced imports, and had
taken the captaincy by the time of Fosse's final
peacetime fixture. He was one of Arsenal's
guests in 1963 when they marked the 50th
anniversary of the opening of Highbury and
the first fixture there against the Fosse, in
which Horace played left-half. During the
latter months of World War One, as a Lance-
Corporal in the Leicestershire Regiment, he
was taken as a POW in Germany, and was
actually involved in an 'escape' days after the
Armistice, unaware that peace had been
declared. Prior to this adventure, Horace
had also appeared as a wartime guest
for Notts County.

> **Appearances:**
> *FL: 78 apps. 1 gl.*
> *FAC: 4 apps. 0 gls.*
> **Total:** *82 apps. 1 gl.*

Horace Burton

BUSHELL, William

Role: Outside right
b. Wednesbury, Staffs, 1905

CAREER: 1924:Shrewsbury Town/Darlaston/
Apr 1926:West Bromwich Albion/1927:
Willenhall/May 1928:CITY/Aug 1931:Walsall.
Debut v Birmingham (H) 17.10.29
(scored once)

A luckless understudy to Hughie Adcock
during his three years at Filbert Street, this
right-winger at least set aside his liking for
West Midlands clubs long enough to score the
winning goal against Birmingham on his City
debut, while Hughie was absent on
international duty. Willie had failed to gain a
first-team place in Albion's relegated side
during his season there, but later managed to
notch four goals in his 30 League games at
Fellows Park. City were reported as having
won the race for his signature by only a matter
of minutes from Blackburn Rovers.

Appearances:
FL: 3 apps. 1 gl.
Total: *3 apps. 1 gl.*

BUTLER, Richard

Role: Wing half
b. Shepshed, Leics, 1885

CAREER: Shepshed Albion/cs
1906:Nottingham Forest/Dec 1910:FOSSE/
Loughborough Corinthians.
Debut v Bolton Wanderers (A) 31.12.10

For a couple of seasons one
of Teddy King's chief rivals
for a Fosse wing-half slot,
Dick had previously made
but a single First Division
appearance for Forest,
though he had represented
the Midland League during
his first year as a Trentside
reserve. By 1914/15, he was
skipper of Loughborough's
premier side.

Appearances:
FL: 26 apps. 0 gls.
FAC: 2 apps. 0 gls.
Total: *28 apps. 0 gls.*

Willie Bushell

Right: Richard Butler

BYRNE, Patrick Joseph

Role: Midfield
b. Dublin, 15th May 1956

CAREER: 1974:Bohemians/Mar 1978:
Philadelphia Fury/1978:Shelbourne/
July 1979:CITY/July 1981:Heart of
Midlothian/Aug 1983:Shamrock Rovers/
cs 1988:Shelbourne (p/mgr).

Debut v Rotherham United (H) LC 11.8.79

Already broadly experienced in Irish football (he had played in European competition and in the 1976 FAI Cup final) when Jock Wallace signed him shortly after his brief NASL sojourn, Pat contributed some tenacious midfield performances to City's 1980 promotion push, offering the option of attacking width on the right. In his First Division season he was less able to perk a struggling side, but chose suitably dramatic stages for his rare goals: Anfield and White Hart Lane. Pat helped Hearts to promotion in his second season, by which time he was commuting weekly from Dublin after his wife had failed to settle in Edinburgh, and then he returned with significant success to League of Ireland fare. In his first four years as Shamrock skipper and playmaker, he led them as a virtual ever-present to the championship in 1984 and, remarkably, to the League/FAI Cup double in each of the next three seasons. Then, being named Soccer Personality of the Year for the achievement, he led Shelbourne to the championship in 1992. Pat won his first of eight full caps for the Republic in 1984.

Appearances:
FL: 31 (5) apps. 3 gls.
FAC: 3 apps. 0 gls.
LC: 2 apps. 0 gls.
Total: *36 (5) apps. 3 gls.*

Pat Byrne

CALDER, John

Role: Centre forward
b. Kilbirnie, Ayrshire, 19th October 1913

CAREER: Dalry Thistle/July 1931:CITY/
Aug 1932:Falkirk/cs 1933:St.Johnstone/
Dunfermline Athletic/(1935-trials-Alloa
Athletic)/1935:Morton/Feb 1937:Bolton
Wanderers/May 1938: Barnsley/Jan 1935:
Morton /cs 1941:Albion Rovers/Apr 1942:
Morton.

Debut v Grimsby Town (A) 19.9.31

A rapid, but all-too-brief step up from Scottish
junior football to deputise for Arthur Chandler
(in a 0-3 First Division defeat) was Jack's lot in
his Filbert Street year. Yet later, after a morale-
boosting return north of the border, the record
books beckoned for the tall centre-forward.
For Morton against Raith in April 1936 he
netted no less than eight goals in an 11-2
victory, and a succession of lesser, if still
impressive, goalscoring feats earned him
another crack at the English game. Bolton
were a lowly First Division side at the time,
but Barnsley
became Third
Division champions
with Jack as a
valuable fringe
member of their
squad. Strangely enough, the Alloa trial
mentioned above culminated in a game
against Morton: it was the latter, though, who
signed him!

> **Appearances:**
> *FL: 1 app. 0 gls.*
> **Total:** *1 app. 0 gls.*

CALDER, William Carson

Role: Outside left
*b. Glasgow, 28th
September 1934*

CAREER:
Port Glasgow/
Aug 1955:CITY/
Apr 1959:Bury/Nov
1963:Oxford United/
Nov 1966:Rochdale.

Debut v Everton (H) 23.8.58

Bill Calder

Returning from National Service to understudy Derek Hogg, Bill was given the latter's
vacant No.11 shirt at the start of 1958/9, but
proved unable to hold it against the challenge
of newcomer Gordon Wills. Subsequently,
though, he made a substantial reputation as a
robust, free-scoring right-winger at Bury
(Third Division champions in 1961), switched
to centre-forward duties to assist Oxford's first
promotion from Division Four (1964/5), and
aggregated 96 League goals before retirement.

> **Appearances:**
> *FL: 3 apps. 0 gls.*
> **Total:** *3 apps. 0 gls.*

CALLACHAN, Henry

Role: Left back
b. Madras, India, 9th April 1903
d. Leicester, 11th February 1990

CAREER: Kirkintilloch Rob Roy/Parkhead
Jnrs/Aug 1925:Celtic/(Aug 1925-loan-Alloa
Athletic)/(Aug 1926-loan-Beith)/Sept 1927:
CITY/Aug 1930:Tunbridge Wells Rangers/

Jack Calder

Aug 1931:Burton Town/
Market Harborough Town.

*Debut v Newcastle United (A)
7.4.28*

A tall left-back who could
yet barely see over such
obstacles in his path to the
first team as Reg Osborne
and Jack Brown, Harry was
a soldier's son who learned
his football in Kirkintilloch
before signing professionally
(for a £50 fee) at Celtic,
where his senior chances as
reserve to Willie McStay
were almost as
limited (11 apps) as they
would prove at Filbert
Street. He returned to
Leicester after his senior career ended, and
completed 25 years' service with the Dunlop
Rubber Co., where at various times his work-
mates included Roger Heywood and Jim
McLaren.

Harry Callachan

Appearances:
FL: 3 apps. 0 gls.
Total: *3 apps. 0 gls.*

CALVERT, Joseph William Herbert

Role: Goalkeeper
*b. Beighton, Yorkshire,
3rd February 1907*

CAREER: Owston Park
Rangers/Bullcroft Colliery/
Frickley Colliery/
May 1931:Bristol Rovers/
May 1932:CITY/Jan 1948:
Watford/Apr 1948:Brush
Sports.

*Debut v Sheffield United (H)
27.8.32*

An ever-present in his
Eastville season (conceding
92 goals but performing
heroically), then a fine fifteen-year servant to
City, goalkeeper Joe made only sporadic first-
team appearances in his pre-war Filbert Street
campaigns, briefly displacing one McLaren
(Jim) only to be sidelined by another (Sandy),
but also suffering a broken collarbone on two
occasions in the mid-30s. Neither such injuries
nor advancing years did much to affect his

Joe Calvert (left and inset) in goal for City in 1938.

mobility or near-reckless bravery, though, and after 62 wartime appearances for City (plus guest outings for Northampton Town and numerous RAF representative games in India and Burma) he was the most consistent choice between the sticks in 1946/7 when League soccer resumed. He played his last game for City at the age of 40 years, 313 days, marking him as the club's oldest senior player. Joe then joined the mass transfer-and-loan exodus that took five City players to Watford on the same day, and was still demonstrating true veteran prowess for his final, Loughborough-based team as they lifted the Leicestershire Senior Cup in May 1949.

Appearances:
FL: 72 apps. 0 gls.
FAC: 8 apps. 0 gls.
WW2: 62 apps. 0 gls.
Total: *142 apps. 0 gls.*

CAMPBELL, James

Jim Campbell

Role: Winger
b. Glasgow, 25th November 1918

CAREER: St.Mungo Juveniles/Petershill/ June 1939:Celtic/ (WW2:St.Anthony's)/ Oct 1943:CITY/ Oct 1946:Walsall.

Debut (WW2) v West Bromwich Albion (H) 9.10.43; (postwar) v Chelsea (A) FAC 5.1.46

A wartime signing who claimed eleven goals in regional fare from appearances on either flank, Jim played at outside-right in the Stamford Bridge leg of the first postwar Cup tie, in the only season that the competition operated on a two-leg basis, and was carried off with a cut eye and mild concussion. Previously, he had guested for Chelsea, Aldershot and Reading while serving as a PT instructor, and had seen service in France, Belgium and Germany as a paratrooper. Jim subsequently managed 15 League games in his two seasons at Fellows Park, and scored once.

Appearances:
FAC: 1 app. 0 gls.
WW2: 46 apps. 11 gls.
Total: *47 apps. 11 gls.*

CAMPBELL, John

Role: Centre forward
b. Ardrossan, Ayrshire, 7th March 1910

CAREER: 1930:Dalry Thistle/July 1931:CITY/ Dec 1933:Lincoln City/July 1939:Scunthorpe United/Nov 1946:Lincoln Co-Op.

Debut v Birmingham (H) 17.12.32 (scored once)

Accompanied to Filbert Street by his Scottish junior club-mate Jack Calder, centre-forward Johnny took longer to taste first-team football, but could count himself unlucky not to have had a longer tenure. His goals-per-game ratio was impressive - despite press comment on his 'habit of falling into the offside trap', and a penalty miss in City's first-ever home game against continental opposition (a 1-3 defeat by Rapid Vienna in January 1933) - but competition from Jim Paterson, and the advent of George Dewis, restricted his chances. In compensation - or perhaps to demonstrate to City their mistake in letting him go - Johnny raced to a century of League goals for the Sincil Bank club before the war; during which he returned there as a guest. For four seasons he was Lincoln's top scorer, and claimed seven

Johnny Campbell

hat-tricks on his way to a 104-goal tally for them. Johnny had also used his time at Filbert Street to continue studying: passing exams in Edinburgh that qualified him as a chemist and optician. Indeed he became Superintendent Optician for Lincoln Co-Op before retirement in 1975.

Appearances:
FL: 21 apps. 12 gls.
FAC: 1 app. 2 gls.
Total: *22 apps. 14 gls.*

CAMPBELL, Kenneth

Role: Goalkeeper
b. Cambuslang, Lanarkshire, 6th September 1892
d. Macclesfield, Cheshire, 28th April 1977

CAREER: Clyde Vale/Rutherglen Glencairn/ Cambuslang Rangers/May 1911:Liverpool/ Apr 1920:Partick Thistle/May 1922:New Brighton/Mar 1923:Stoke City/Nov 1925: CITY/Aug 1929:South Shields/Nov 1929: New Brighton.

Debut v Sunderland (H) 14.11.25

A medallist from Cup Finals on both sides of the border (a 1914 loser with Liverpool; a 1921 winner with Partick), and holder of eight post

war caps for Scotland to add to one Scottish League appearance, Kenny maintained his reputation for modesty and quiet efficiency throughout his spell between the City posts. A cool, reliable custodian who was already reaching the veteran stage on his arrival at Leicester to aid First Division consolidation, he managed to stretch his peacetime career out to 370 senior games with two final seasons for the Rakers in the Third Division (North), before opening a sports shop in Wallasey.

Appearances:
FL: 79 apps. 0 gls.
FAC: 2 apps. 0 gls.
Total: *81 apps. 0 gls.*

CAMPBELL, Kevin Joseph

Role: Striker
b. Lambeth, London, 4th February 1970

CAREER: trainee/pro Feb 1988:Arsenal/(Jan 1989-loan-Leyton Orient)/(Nov 1989-loan-CITY)/June 1995:Nottingham Forest.

Debut v Leeds United (H) 11.11.89

A hat-trick hero of Arsenal's 1988 FA Youth Cup triumph, who had made but two brief senior substitute appearances for the

Kenny Campbell

Kevin Campbell

permanent basis, even after success in extending an initial month's loan to the maximum permitted three-month stay, and one had to sympathise with his managerial worries about certain clubs increasingly cornering the market in class players when one realised that Kevin would in the short term be returning to reserve football at Highbury. After his breakthrough there (alongside an unselfish mentor in Alan Smith), he picked up the first of four England Under-21 caps in September 1990, and medals from the Championship win in 1991, FA Cup and League Cup victories in 1993, and the European Cup Winners' Cup triumph of 1994. In the summer of 1995, Kevin became Forest's prospective replacement for Stan Collymore at a £2 million fee.

Appearances:
FL: 11 apps. 5 gls.
FMC: 1 app. 1 gl.
Total: *12 apps. 6 gls.*

CAREY, Brian Patrick

Role: Centre back
b. Cork, 31st May 1968

CAREER: Cork City/Sept 1989:Manchester United/(Jan 1991-loan-Wrexham)/(Dec 1991-loan-Wrexham)/July 1993:CITY.

Debut v Peterborough United (H) 14.8.93

A 6ft.3in Irish central defender who failed to make a senior breakthrough at Old Trafford, Brian nonetheless caught Jack Charlton's eye and won two senior caps for the Republic during 1992 and 1993. He also featured in Wrexham's memorable Cup giant-killing of Arsenal during his second on-loan spell at the Racecourse, and cost City a £250,000 close season fee when added to Brian Little's squad for the third tilt at Play-off-assisted promotion. A plethora of central defensive partnerships (and trios) were tried with varying success during 1993/4, and Brian found it hard to impose himself, coming under criticism for his often wayward distribution, but he shared in Wembley glory alongside Jimmy Willis. His initial Premiership selection brought him dismissal against Wimbledon at Selhurst, and that was his sole outing of the term at the time he asked for a transfer from new manager Mark McGhee in January 1995. He subsequently returned to senior action for a

Highbury club at the time of his loan to Leicester, Kevin soon had City fans reacting with a unique mixture of admiration and envy. The teenage striker's impact on an injury-hit, lightweight City front-line was immense, for despite the sense that he was still learning as he added to his experience, every sign pointed to natural advantages ripe for exploitation: with challenging strength, ball-shielding ability, aerial skill and phenomenal shooting power chief among his attributes. In a previous three-month spell at Brisbane Road, Kevin had claimed nine Division Four goals in 16 games: he was marginally slower off the mark with City, but had become a crowd favourite some time before his rather touchingly emotional Filbert Street farewell. David Pleat was understandably unable to prise Kevin away from his own club on a

Brian Carey

Debut v Birmingham City (A) 20.10.70

A player for whom the once-current journalistic cliche 'pocket dynamo' might have been invented, Willie overcame early disappointments to forge a marvellous motivational career, with City just one of the clubs to benefit from his gee-up presence. Jettisoned by his hometown club after just a single Anfield outing as a diminutive striker, he suffered relegation to the Fourth Division in his first season at The Shay, but soon became Halifax's leading scorer. He then assisted Carlisle to the Third Division championship in 1965, and found himself involved in the Blades' First Division relegation struggles as he made the transition to midfield grafter. A £60,000 Brian Clough cheque imported Willie's pint-sized inspiration to Derby's rise from the Second

Willie Carlin

decent run, but was placed on the open-to-offers list in May, and made his frustration evident when substituted in the final fixture at The Dell.

Appearances (to end 1994/5):
PL: 11 (1) apps. 0 gls.
FL: 24 (3) apps. 0 gls.
FAC: 0 (1) app. 0 gls.
LC: 1 app. 0 gls.
AIC: 1 app. 0 gls.
P/O: 3 apps. 0 gls.
Total: *40 (5) apps. 0 gls.*

CARLIN, William

Role: Midfield
b. Liverpool, 6th October 1940

CAREER: May 1958:Liverpool/Aug 1962: Halifax Town/Oct 1964:Carlisle United/ Sept 1967:Sheffield United/Aug 1968:Derby County/Oct 1970:CITY/Sept 1971:Notts County/Nov 1973:Cardiff City.

Division in 1969, and their fourth placing in the top flight a year later; and it was a real bargain when Frank O'Farrell lured him across the East Midlands for a mere £35,000 to link up with Bobby Kellard and add his all-action, true-grit approach to City's promotion hunt. Jimmy Bloomfield perhaps over-hastily discarded this wily battler after elevation was duly achieved (Willie simply got on with prompting Notts County from Third to Second in 1973), but O'Farrell, at least, was not one to underestimate his infectiously enthusiastic influence, taking him to Cardiff to spark another of that club's then-annual Second Division survival acts before his retirement in May 1974. Willie was most recently heard of running a bar in Majorca.

Appearances:
FL: 31 apps. 1 gl.
FAC: 6 apps. 0 gls.
Total: *37 apps. 1 gl.*

CARNELLY, Albert

Role: Inside forward
b. Nottingham,
29th December 1870
d. Nottingham, August 1920

CAREER: 1889:Notts Mapperley/1890:Notts County/1891:Loughborough/ May 1894:Nottingham Forest/May 1896:FOSSE/ cs 1897:Bristol City/ cs 1898:Ilkeston/ Nov 1898:Bristol City/cs 1899:Thames Ironworks/cs 1900:Millwall/cs 1901:Ilkeston.

Debut v Darwen (H) 5.9.1896

A goalscoring inside-forward who leapt from Midland League to First Division and finished as Forest's top scorer in his first year on Trentside, Albert then only missed two games during his Fosse season, which ended with a 9th-place Second Division finish. He joined Bristol City (along with Harry Davy) for their first Southern League season, and their first under that name, scoring 4 goals in their first-ever FA Cup tie; while Thames Ironworks were in their final season under that name when Albert moved there (the club becoming West Ham United in 1900). Back in his days as a Luffs hero, he had cemented his reputation with an 1891/2 Midland League hat-trick

against Fosse in the two local rivals' first major competitive meeting.

Appearances:
FL: 28 apps. 10 gls.
FAC: 3 apps. 0 gls.
Total: *31 apps. 10 gls.*

CARR, Everton Dale

Role: Full back
b. Antigua, West Indies, 11th January 1961

CAREER: app July 1977/pro Jan 1979: CITY/July 1981:Halifax Town/Mar 1983: Rochdale/Aug 1983:Nuneaton Borough/July 1987:Weymouth/Oct 1987:Bath City/Nov 1987:Barnet/Jan 1988:Nuneaton Borough/ 1988:Oadby Town/1990:Lutterworth Town/1991:North Kilworth.

Debut v Fulham (A) 28.4.79 (sub)

A pacy, harrying full-back who played as an 18-year-old in the final three games of 1978/9, Everton was unfortunate enough to be sent off in the last of them, an ill-refereed farce at Bramall Lane that represented Sheffield United's farewell to the Second

Albert Carnelly

Everton Carr

Division. He stood in once for Dennis Rofe during the following season, and had a brief run of First Division games in 1980/1, but had to move to The Shay for a regular League spot. He later revived his occasional City partnership with Willie Gibson at both Nuneaton and Weymouth; and while with the latter was involved in an amusing incident in a Conference game at Maidstone: entering the fray at half-time as a substitute and failing to report his presence to the referee, who booked him a full 25 minutes later after finally noticing the only black player on the pitch!

Appearances:
FL: 11 (1) apps. 0 gls.
LC: 2 apps. 0 gls.
Total: *13 (1) apps. 0 gls.*

CARR, Franz Alexander

Role: Outside right
b. Preston, 24th September 1966

CAREER: app 1982:Blackburn Rovers/ Aug 1984:Nottingham Forest/(Dec 1989-loan-Sheffield Wednesday)/(Mar 1991-loan-West Ham United)/June 1991:Newcastle United/ Jan 1993:Sheffield United/Sept 1994:CITY/ Feb 1995:Aston Villa.

Debut v Wimbledon (A) 10.9.94

An untried teenage reserve at Ewood when Brian Clough invested in his traditional wing-play promise, Franz soon became a key

Franz Carr

attacker on Trentside, exploiting electrifying pace and fine dribbling skills. He was rewarded with nine England Under-21 caps in 1987 and 1988, and twice appeared at Wembley for Forest, coming on as substitute to lay on the winning goal against Everton in the 1989 Simod Cup Final, and contributing a year later to the League Cup victory over

Oldham. Inconsistency dogged his progress thereafter, though, and he tended to drift through his later clubs, interleaving performances marked either by flashes of high excitement or stretches of utter anonymity. Such a pattern was repeated during Franz's brief Premiership spell with City (which got underway with a nine-man City going under at Selhurst, following the dismissals of Lowe and Carey), and many were surprised that a fairly mundane month's loan spell was converted into a full transfer (at £100,000) by Brian Little. Over-intricacy had largely taken the place of directness in Franz's flank-play, and he made but one appearance in a Mark McGhee line-up before being off-loaded to Little's Villa in the part-exchange deal which brought Garry Parker to Filbert Street.

Appearances:
PL: 12 (1) apps. 1 gl.
Total: *12 (1) apps. 1 gl.*

CARR, George

Role: Inside forward / Centre half
b. South Bank, nr. Middlesbrough,
19th January 1899

CAREER: Nov 1916:Bradford Park Avenue/Jan 1919:Middlesbrough/Feb 1924:CITY/Aug 1932:Stockport County/May 1933:Nuneaton Town (p/mgr).

Debut v Coventry City (H) 23.2.24 (scored once)

A beefy, hard-shooting inside-forward when he came to Leicester - having played First Division football at Ayresome alongside his brothers Jackie and Billy - George scored the goal (against Bradford City) which guaranteed City's 1925 promotion, and proved a splendid linkman between left-winger Wadsworth and spearhead Chandler. It was not long, however, before George's invaluable versatility became apparent, for after recovering from a broken leg he assumed the pivotal position of centre-half as if born to the role (he had, in fact, played there as a teenager for Bradford in wartime football), and provided the solid bedrock from which City's best-ever First Division attack launched its near-miss assaults on the title. George was from 1935-42 manager of Cheltenham Town, helped initiate the experiment of fostering Middlesbrough Swifts as a City nursery team during WW2, and in the immediate postwar period coached both

George Carr

Stockton and South Bank. He then remained for some years a scout for City from the base of his North Ormesby pub. His brother Jackie was an unsuccessful interviewee for the City manager's post taken by Frank Womack in October 1936.

Appearances:
FL: 179 apps. 24 gls.
FAC: 13 apps. 1 gl.
Total: *192 apps. 25 gls.*

CARRIGAN, Patrick

Role: Centre half
b. Cleland, Lanarkshire, 5th July 1898

CAREER: Douglas Water Thistle/
Oct 1923:CITY/Mar 1930:Sheffield United/
(Sept 1933-trials-Southend United)/
Nov 1933:Hinckley United.

Debut v Bury (A) 2.1.24

City's regular first-choice centre-half for only one full season, Pat was nonetheless due a lot of credit for his sturdy efforts towards securing the 1925 Second Division championship. He was a fine successor to Mick O'Brien and, after his year of glory, a

Pat Carrigan

loyal reserve to the likes of Norman Watson and George Carr. Pat then extended his top flight career by three seasons at Bramall Lane, following a £1,750 move.

Appearances:
FL: 75 apps. 3 gls.
FAC: 7 apps. 0 gls.
Total: *82 apps. 3 gls.*

CARROLL, James (Tony)

Role: Outside right
b. Glasgow

CAREER: Strathclyde/Newry Town/
cs 1928:Belfast Celtic/June 1931: Shelbourne/
cs 1933:Clyde/Feb 1935:CITY/June 1938:
Luton Town/Feb 1940:Ayr United.

Debut v Preston North End (A) 23.2.35

A late recruit by Arthur Lochhead to City's eventually futile attempt to avoid relegation in 1935, Tony was a small, nippy outside-right with an eye for goal (15 in 1935/6 alone), whose more orthodox crossing skills also provided Jack Bowers with many an opening as City bounced back up in 1937. Previously having made his mark on both sides of the Irish border (as part of Belfast Celtic's championship squad of 1929, and with Shelbourne's FAI Cup semi-finalists of 1932 and 1933), as well as in the Scottish First Division, Tony was somewhat hindered by injuries in England. His late entry into the promotion side at Leicester was down to recovery from a broken shoulder received in a summer car crash in Scotland, and his Luton debut was curtailed by a broken ankle; but it was later that his luck turned in rather dramatic fashion. For in March 1944, Tony was reported lost at sea as a result of enemy action; and he severely surprised club personnel when he made a postwar visit to Filbert Street, having miraculously survived being marooned on a makeshift raft for some six weeks - losing four stones in weight - before being rescued!

Appearances:
FL: 94 apps. 25 gls.
FAC: 3 apps. 1 gl.
Total: *97 apps. 26 gls.*

CARTER, Alfred Albert

Role: Forward
b. c 1868

CAREER:
Notts Olympic/
Notts Jardine/
Heanor Town/
Aug 1892:FOSSE.

*Debut v Mansfield Town
(A) ML 17.9.1892*

Alf Carter

A hat-trick hero in
Fosse's first pre-season
friendly of 1892/3 (a 10-1 pasting of Coventry
Singers), centre-forward Alf nonetheless took
the brunt of the local Mercury's disdain after
the opening Midland League defeat at
Mansfield: "... he is scarcely worth his place in
the team, and from what transpired in the
game on Saturday it could be seen that he was
not to be trusted too much with the ball." Only
a trio of inside-left outings followed.

> **Appearances:**
> *ML: 4 apps. 1 gl.*
> **Total:** *4 apps. 1 gl.*

CARTER, Roger

Role: Goalkeeper

CAREER: Hugglescote Robin Hoods/Aug
1898: FOSSE.

Debut v Burslem Port Vale (A) 3.2.1900

A local keeper who kept a clean sheet while
standing in for Godfrey Beardsley in the above
match, but then reportedly showed such poor
form for the reserves that only a month later,
when Beardsley again had to drop out, the
Fosse selectors overlooked him and instead
chose inside-forward Lyon as replacement
goalie!

> **Appearances:**
> *FL: 1 app. 0 gls.*
> **Total:** *1 app. 0 gls.*

CHALMERS, Leonard

Role: Right back
b. Corby, Northants, 4th September 1936

CAREER: Corby Town/Jan 1956:CITY/June 1966:Notts County.

Debut v Birmingham City (A) 26.4.58

Forever remembered for two dramatic games - his nervewracking senior debut, when City needed a last-match win at St.Andrews to avoid the drop; and the 1961 Cup Final, when the crippling injury he suffered proved to be the turning point - Len actually gave over a decade's fine service to Leicester. Switching from wing-half to make the right-back slot his own for four seasons, he was an incisive tackler who was tagged with the affectionate nickname 'Chopper' some time before Chelsea's Ron Harris earned a similar dubbing; though Len also showed a compensatory concern for his fellow players' well-being as City's PFA representative, being actively involved in the 1961 maximum-wage negotiations. He went on to make 51 League appearances during his two years at Meadow Lane, and at least one source indicates he was later manager of Dunstable Town.

Appearances:
FL: 171 apps. 4 gls.
FAC: 20 apps. 0 gls.
LC: 9 apps. 0 gls.
Eur: 4 apps. 0 gls.
Total: *204 apps. 4 gls.*

Len Chalmers

CHANDLER, Arthur Clarence Hillier

Role: Centre forward
b. Paddington, London, 27th November 1895
d. Leicester, 18th June 1984

CAREER: Handley Page/Hampstead Town/Sept 1920:Queen's Park Rangers/June 1923:CITY/June 1935:Notts County.

Debut v Hull City (A) 25.8.23

Rivalled only by Arthur Rowley for the title of City's greatest-ever marksman - 'Channy' notched the highest aggregate; the other Arthur had the better scoring ratio - this Cockney centre-forward was an inspired purchase by Peter Hodge, especially as he had a mere 18 senior goals to his credit before arriving at Filbert Street, had been regarded by QPR primarily as a support player, and on grounds of age alone might have been regarded as past his peak. Hard and courageous, but resilient, too - Arthur made a then-record 118 consecutive appearances from the date of his City debut - he bulged nets in both top Divisions with strikes delivered from every angle and distance, though oddly enough for such a sure-shot, never contributed a single penalty goal to his career total. (Against Chelsea in September 1924, he had one saved by B.Howard Baker). He equalled Fred Shinton's long-standing seasonal scoring record for the club in the 1925 promotion drive, and eclipsed it with 34 goals in both 1928 and 1929; also equalled Johnny Duncan's record of six goals in a game (v. Portsmouth in October 1928, while inaugurating the legend of the six swans flying overhead); and clearly deserved the international recognition that was inexplicably denied him. Three times Arthur played in the annual England trial game (once for the North v. South; twice for The Rest v. England) and each time he scored; but a single appearance for the Football League - when they met the Scottish League at Filbert Street in 1927, and when for once 'Channy' failed to register a goal - and a place on the 1929 FA tour of South Africa (which brought him a haul of 33 goals from 16 games, including six in the three 'Test

Matches') were his only tangible honours. There was a shrewd tactical side to Arthur's game as well: it was his eager suggestion that the end-of-season friendly at Port Vale in May 1925 be played under the revised offside rule soon to come into force - he scored a hat-trick in a 5-3 win. A consistently cheery character, Arthur hung up his boots after adding half a dozen goals to his haul as a Magpie, but was then involved in one backroom capacity or another with City until well past retirement age. In this sense, Arthur's true honour was in embodying for successive generations of City players and fans the very best traditions of both the club and the game: a status recognised by the club when it eventually installed in the Filbert Street boardroom a cabinet displaying items of 'Channy' memorabilia.

Appearances:
FL: *393 apps. 259 gls.*
FAC: *26 apps. 14 gls.*
Total: *419 apps. 273 gls.*

❏ FOX FACT: *The record-hogging rivalry of Chandler and Rowley in the City scoring stakes extends further. Chandler scored the most home goals (173 at Filbert Street, against Rowley's 163), while Rowley claimed 102 from away games to pip Channy's 100. Both men take the club laurels for scoring against individual opponents: Chandler scoring 15 times against each of Aston Villa and Newcastle United, and Rowley totalling 15 against Bury. Chandler scored a hat-trick or better on 17 occasions; a feat managed 16 times for City by Rowley.*

CHAPMAN, Vernon William

Role: Forward
b. Leicester, 9th May 1921

CAREER: Aylestone United/Leicester Nomads/Ibstock Penistone Rovers/Bath City/Mar 1941:CITY/July 1947:Leyton Orient/1949:Brush Sports/cs 1951:Burton Albion.

Debut (WW2) v Lincoln City (H) 14.4.41 (scored once); (postwar) v Swansea Town (H) 12.4.47

Initially marked as a teenage rugby prospect (a Wyggeston fly-half), Vernon set one club record during WW2 prior to RAF service, scoring 10 goals for the Colts (ie. reserves) in their 17-0 demolition of Holwell Works in September 1941. His strike rate in senior wartime fare was pretty impressive, too, yet he deputised only once for Mal Griffiths at outside-right after League soccer recommenced. He had slightly better fortune at Brisbane Road, making 31 appearances and scoring seven goals in the Third Division (South) after a £550 move.

Appearances:
FL: 1 app. 0 gls.
WW2: 11 apps. 6 gls.
Total: *12 apps. 6 gls.*

CHARLES, Gary Andrew

Role: Full back
b. Newham, London, 13th April 1970

CAREER: app July 1986/pro 1987: Nottingham Forest/(Mar 1989-loan-CITY)/ July 1993:Derby County/Jan 1995:Aston Villa.
Debut v Birmingham City (H) 25.3.89 (sub)

A young full-back given his initial two-game Trentside break by Brian Clough as an emergency right-winger, Gary joined City on a month's loan as defensive cover when Tony Spearing was facing imminent suspension, and rapidly displayed a surprising amount of mature confidence and coolness both on and off the ball as he earned himself an extension to his Leicester sojourn until the end of the season. Indeed, his form was sufficiently exciting to earn him an England Under-21 squad call-up after only seven weeks at Filbert

Street. Gary eventually won four such honours, and stepped up to full international level on England's 1991 summer tour, by which time he had registered his initial Forest goal in the FA Cup semi-final against West Ham, and earned a runners-up medal from the ensuing Final (when he was the victim of a notorious Paul Gascoigne tackle). He also picked up a Wembley winner's medal from the ZDS Cup Final of 1992 (after Forest had eliminated City at the penultimate stage), but was suffering a severe loss of confidence when involved in Forest's relegation a year later. His first Derby season ended in Play-off defeat at City's hands, and Gary became a transfer target for Brian Little in October 1994, but no deal transpired until Little had decamped to Villa Park, where he took Gary and Tommy Johnson in a joint £2.9 million deal.

Appearances:
FL: 5 (3) apps. 0 gls.
Total: *5 (3) apps. 0 gls.*

Gary Charles breaking clear of Crystal Palace's Ian Wright and former Fox Mark Bright.

CHRISTENSEN, Tommy

Role: Striker
b. Aarhus, Denmark, 20th July 1961

CAREER: AGF (Aarhus)/1979:PSV
Eindhoven/AGF (Aarhus)/Vejle BK/Feb
1985:Elche/(Nov 1985-loan-CITY)/(Nov
1985-loan-Portsmouth)/1986:Brondby/
1987:Vejle BK/July 1988:Eintracht
Braunschweig/1990:(Danish football).

Debut v Southampton (H) 9.11.85 (sub)

Both of Danish international forward Tommy's
loan spells with League clubs were teasingly
inconclusive. With City the compact blond
striker made an immediate impact as he came
on for 30 minutes to bring the best out of Peter
Shilton in the opposing goal, but a week later
he shared in an unconvincing struggle on
Loftus Road's artificial surface. After an
additional three reserve appearances (1 goal),
City tried to extend his loan period, but either
Tommy, his agent or his Spanish club wanted
a definite deal. Then, at Fratton Park, Tommy
knocked in two goals in three League games,
but suffered an injury which shortened his
stay. He later re-emerged from Danish football
for a two-season stint in the German Second
Division ('2 Bundesliga').

Appearances:
FL: 1 (1) apps. 0 gls.
Total: 1 (1) apps. 0 gls.

Trevor Christie

CHRISTIE, Trevor

Role: Striker
b. Newcastle upon Tyne, 28th February 1959

CAREER: app Sept 1975/pro Dec 1976:CITY/
June 1979:Notts County/June 1984:
Nottingham Forest/Feb 1985:Derby County/
Aug 1986:Manchester City/Oct 1986:Walsall/
Mar 1989:Mansfield Town/cs 1991:Kettering
Town/Mar 1992:VS Rugby/cs 1992:Hucknall
Town (p/coach).

Debut v Wolverhampton Wanderers (H) 25.2.78

Given a break by Frank McLintock almost as
an early 19th birthday present, gangling
striker Trevor went on to become City's top
scorer during Jock Wallace's first season in
charge (albeit with only 8 goals). His front-
running, heading and ball-shielding skills only
really developed, though, after his move to
Meadow Lane. A number of his 64 League
goals for the Magpies helped them into the
First Division, while another three harshly
greeted City back into the top flight on the

*Tommy Christensen (centre)
training with City in
November 1985.*

opening day of 1983/4. Brian Clough invested £165,000 to take Trevor across the Trent, but soon off-loaded him to Derby, for whom his 100th aggregate League goal was scored late in the Third Division promotion campaign of 1986. Then surprisingly swapped for Mark Lillis, Trevor had only a short stay at Maine Road before joining Walsall and contributing to both their fine 1987 Cup run and their 1988 promotion. An experienced mentor to David Kelly at Fellows Park, Trevor then went on to perform similarly alongside Steve Wilkinson at Mansfield.

Appearances:
FL: 28 (3) apps. 8 gls.
LC: 1 app. 0 gls.
Total: *29 (3) apps. 8 gls.*

CLARK, William

Willie Clark

Role: Outside right
b. Airdrie, Lanarkshire

CAREER:
Port Glasgow Athletic/May 1904:Bristol Rovers/May 1908:Sunderland/ Oct 1910:Bristol City/Aug 1911: FOSSE.

Debut v Gainsborough Trinity (A) 2.9.11

A Scottish right-winger with considerable English experience (a Southern League championship medal in his first Eastville season, alongside Dick Pudan and Albert Dunkley, on his way to a 133-game, 35-goal record; two terms in the top flight for Sunderland; and a relegation campaign at Ashton Gate), Willie soon lost his Fosse place to Tommy Benfield, and simply had to bow to the younger player's greater consistency and pace.

Appearances:
FL: 6 apps. 1 gl.
Total: *6 apps. 1 gl.*

CLARKE, Allan John

Role: Striker
b. Willenhall, Staffs, 31st July 1946

CAREER: app 1961/pro Aug 1963:Walsall/ Mar 1966:Fulham/June 1968:CITY/June 1969: Leeds United/June 1978:Barnsley (p/mgr).

Debut v Queen's Park Rangers (A) 10.8.68 (scored once)

An instinctive goalscorer whose transfers to and from City both broke the existing British record (at £150,000 and £165,000 respectively), Allan began his Filbert Street year as a tangible symbol of the club's ambition, soon ingratiated himself with the fans with a hat-trick (against Manchester City) among his early goal flow, but increasingly came to look something of a luxury as 1968/9 unexpectedly developed into an earnest relegation struggle. He was clearly a man for the big occasion (scoring the Cup semi-final winner against

Allan Clarke

West Brom; taking the Man of the Match award at Wembley), but his apparently leisurely style seemed at odds with the requirements of a scramble for safety points. The slim striker added one England Under-23 cap to his burgeoning representative tally while with City, but only made the break-through to full international honours after being snapped up by Don Revie. Nicknamed 'Sniffer' at Elland Road in recognition of his clinical penalty-area poaching skills, Allan played in three FA Cup Finals for Leeds (scoring their winner in 1972), won a championship medal in 1974, and was also a scorer in their Fairs Cup victory of 1971. He led Barnsley out of the Fourth Division in his first year of management, then returned to Leeds as boss; subsequently also managing Scunthorpe United, Barnsley again, and Lincoln City. Allan's brothers Frank (who faced him for QPR on his City debut), Derek, Kelvin and Wayne each also carved out football careers at League level, and the latter became another expensive City purchase in June 1989.

Appearances:
FL: 36 apps. 12 gls.
FAC: 8 apps. 1 gl.
LC: 2 apps. 3 gls.
Total: *46 apps. 16 gls.*

CLARKE, Bernard Maurice

Role: Right back
b. Leicester, 2nd March 1891

CAREER: St.Peters/Dec 1919:CITY/July 1921: Halifax Town.

Debut v Clapton Orient (A) 28.8.20

A right-back who spent much of the first post-WW1 season as an amateur in City's reserves, Bernard then signed professional forms and played in the first three matches of 1920/1, only to be permanently sidelined thereafter by a combination of injury (October 1920 to March 1921) and the stronger claims of Billy Barrett and Adam Black. Unfortunately, he made little impact at The Shay, either; apparently failing to win a senior summons to aid Halifax's initial League campaign, and having disappeared from the roll-call there by the time Herbert Bown and Cliff Price arrived. It is believed he may have assisted Barwell United on his return to Leicestershire.

Appearances:
FL: 3 apps. 0 gls.
Total: *3 apps. 0 gls.*

Bernard Clarke

CLARKE, Malcolm McQueen G.

Role: Wing half
b. Clydebank, Dunbartonshire, 29th June 1944

CAREER: Johnstone Burgh/Aug 1964:CITY/ Aug 1967:Cardiff City/July 1969:Bristol City/July 1970:Hartlepool.

Debut v Leeds United (H) 18.9.65 (sub)

Dubiously distinguished by having had the shortest-ever first-team career with City, reserve wing-half Malcolm came on as No.12 in the 89th minute of his sole League game - curiously, as John Sjoberg and Derek Dougan simultaneously left the field injured - and was reliably reported not to have touched the ball during the remainder of play! Partial compensation for such frustration came during Malcolm's two-year Ninian Park spell, when he claimed a goal in the Welsh Cup Final of 1968 (an aggregate victory over Hereford United) and then aided Cardiff's surprising progress to the semi-finals of the European Cup Winners' Cup. His younger brother, Colin, forged a fine 13-year career with Oxford United.

Appearances:
FL: 0 (1) app.
0 gls.
Total: *0 (1) app.*
0 gls.

CLARKE, Patrick

Role: Left back
b. Dundalk

CAREER: Dundalk/May 1934:CITY/
July 1938:Bristol City/1938:Sligo Rovers/
1945:Leicester Frith (p/coach).

Debut v Manchester City (A) 2.2.35

An Irish left-back whose single League chance
came when both Adam Black and Sandy
Wood were unable to turn out in the above
game, a 3-6 Maine Road defeat, Paddy
nonetheless came close to being capped over a
year later when the Irish Free State FA
checked with City on his likely availability for
their European tour of May 1936, but then left
him out of the final party. Slim rewards were
in fact Paddy's lot, for he left City with only
four Leicestershire Senior Cup-winners medals
to show for his reserve-team efforts, and then
failed to make even a single senior breakthrough during his short spell at Ashton Gate.
Eventually, he re-trained as a masseur and
nurse, and returned to Leicester after the war.
(A stray hint that Paddy may have had a brief
loan spell at Clyde while still on City's books
has yet to be substantiated).

Appearances:
FL: 1 app. 0 gls.
Total: *1 app. 0 gls.*

CLARKE, Wayne

Role: Striker
b. Wolverhampton, 28th February 1961

CAREER: app/pro Mar 1978:Wolverhampton
Wanderers/Aug 1984:Birmingham City/
March 1987:Everton/June 1989:CITY/Jan 1990:
Manchester City/(Oct 1990-loan-Shrewsbury
Town)/(March 1991-loan-Stoke City)/
(Sept 1991-loan-Wolverhampton Wanderers)/
July 1992:Walsall/Aug 1993:Shrewsbury
Town/July 1995:Telford United (p/mgr).

Debut v Hull City (A) 19.8.89 (scored once)

The youngest of the five footballing Clarke
brothers, schoolboy and youth cap Wayne
made a top-flight bow for Wolves at the age of
17, and experienced two relegation campaigns
and one promotion while wearing the Old
Gold. An £80,000 move to St.Andrews saw
him become leading scorer in the Blues' 1985
promotion side, but characteristic West
Midlands yo-yo-ing had him poaching against
Second Division defences again before he was
added to Everton's 1987 Championship squad
to contribute tellingly to the title run-in.
Wayne claimed the Wembley winner in the
Charity Shield pipe-opener to the 1987/8
season, but was thereafter never quite certain
of a first-team striking slot at Goodison as
manager Colin Harvey selected his front-men

Paddy Clarke

Wayne Clarke

from amongst Heath, Sharp, Clarke and, latterly, Cottee. Following brother Allan to Leicester at a twenty-year remove, as a £250,000 element of the deal which took Mike Newell to Everton, he showed typical predatory instincts in scoring on his debut, but instilled something of a sad sense of deja vu in older City watchers who saw his leisurely style as inappropriate in the context of the team's unexpected Second Division struggles. The New Year of 1990 saw him returning to fitness after a lengthy injury lay-off, but immediately involved in another part-exchange deal which marked his signing for a second time by Howard Kendall and his replacement by Manchester City's David Oldfield at Filbert Street. Wayne passed his personal 100 League goal milestone early in his Walsall campaign, and later contributed 11 strikes to Shrewsbury's 1994 Division Three title win; ending 1994/5 on an aggregate of 140 League goals.

Appearances:
FL: 10 (1) apps. 1 gl.
LC: 1 app. 1 gl.
Total: *11 (1) apps. 2 gls.*

CLAY, Thomas

Role: Right back
b. Leicester,
19th November 1892
d. Southend,
21st February 1949

CAREER:
Belvoir Sunday School/
Apr 1911:FOSSE/
Jan 1914:Tottenham
Hotspur/June 1929:
Northfleet (p/coach).

Debut v Bradford Park
Avenue (A) 25.11.11

A teenage prodigy as an unflappable full-back in local football circles, Tommy rapidly stepped up to Second Division action when Billy Henry moved to Manchester City. A cultured thinker and passer of the ball in an

Tommy Clay

age of hoof-happy defenders, he shone regularly in Fosse's struggling side, and after the epic FA Cup tussles with Spurs in 1914, he and Harry Sparrow were together snapped up by the victors. At White Hart Lane, Tommy skippered the promotion side of 1920 and starred in the Cup-winning team of 1921, became a sure-shot penalty expert and a fine tactical manipulator of the offside trap, and was even chosen in one game as goalkeeper (keeping a clean sheet at Sunderland in March 1921); while after playing 351 League and Cup games (plus 106 wartime matches) in Spurs' colours, he was entrusted with inspiring the youngsters at their 'nursery' club. Tommy (who also guested for Notts County during WW1) won four full England caps after 1920, and represented the Football League once, but the oft-repeated claim that he was the first Leicester-born man to play for his country is erroneous - that honour had fallen to Small Heath Alliance goalkeeper Christopher Charles Charsley in 1893. Tommy closed his active involvement in football with a spell as coach at St.Albans from July 1931, then worked as a bricklayer.

Appearances:
FL: 63 apps. 0 gls.
FAC: 6 apps. 0 gls.
Total: *69 apps. 0 gls.*

COATSWORTH, Gary

Role: Defender
b. Sunderland, 7th October 1968

CAREER: 1986:Barnsley/cs 1989:Darlington/
Oct 1991:CITY/Apr 1995:Spennymoor United.

Debut v Portsmouth (A) 5.11.91 (sub)

Utterly unceremonious but usually effective, Gary was a tough-tackling, no-frills defender signed initially as cover for broken-leg victim Tony James. He had previously played under Brian Little for Darlington, and entered Quakers folklore when, in but his third appearance of their 1989/90 Conference season, he scored the only goal of the final fixture at Welling to book their return to the League. After only three senior games for City, he faced two successive operations to repair cruciate ligament damage, but came back bravely, marking his 1992/3 return to Oakwell (as City's right-back on the ground where his League career had started) with a joyous two-goal contribution to a 3-2 away win. Where Gary's defensive interventions (also occasionally used to buttress midfield) were often decisive, his distribution skills could just as often appear clumsy, but City still had reason to be grateful for even this aspect of his play when, in what unfortunately turned out to be his final senior outing, his up-and-under cross from the right at Wembley led to Steve Walsh's equaliser in the Play-off Final against Derby. Sadly, further injury problems denied Gary any part in the subsequent Premiership struggle, and he was forced to announce his retirement from senior football early in 1995.

Appearances:
FL: 27 (5) apps. 4 gls.
FAC: 1 app. 0 gls.
FMC: 0 (1) app. 0 gls.
AIC: 0 (1) app. 0 gls.
P/O: 3 apps. 0 gls.
Total: *31 (7) apps. 4 gls.*

COCHRANE, Michael

Role: Right back
b. Belfast

CAREER: Milltown/Distillery/May 1900: FOSSE/Mar 1901:Middlesbrough/cs 1901: Distillery.

Debut v Small Heath (A) 8.9.1900

Coming to Leicester only two years after Glasgow Celtic had failed to tempt Distillery with £200 for his services, Irish international right-back Mick was a Fosse ever-present from the date of his debut to that of his transfer - a period which also saw him win the last of his eight caps (albeit in an horrendous 0-11 mauling in Glasgow). During his first stint in Belfast, he had also represented the Irish League on four occasions; while on his return, Mick took a runners-up medal from the 1902 Irish Cup Final, when a John Mercer-inspired Linfield beat Distillery 5-1.

Appearances:
FL: 27 apps. 0 gls.
FAC: 1 app. 0 gls.
Total: *28 apps. 0 gls.*

CODD, Thomas H.

Role: Outside left

CAREER: Goole Town/Dec 1914:FOSSE.

Debut v Arsenal (A) 26.12.14

A well-respected outside-left in the Midland League, Tommy had anything but a happy introduction to Second Division football - his first two games were both 0-6 defeats. Nonetheless, he retained his position for the bulk of the rest of the ignominious final pre-war season, closing his career in a 5-1 victory! Joining up with the Footballers' Battalion for WW1 service, he lost his left eye in action at Vimy Ridge, but was still pluckily volunteering to turn out for Fosse at Leeds in September 1916, when it briefly looked like they would be unable to raise a full team.

Appearances:
FL: 13 apps. 0 gls.
Total: *13 apps. 0 gls.*

Gary Coatsworth

COLES, Donald Stratton

Role: Right back
b. Plymouth, 1879

CAREER: Ardingly College/cs 1901:Brighton & Hove Albion/Aug 1902:FOSSE/Dec 1902: Brighton & Hove Albion/(Sussex amateur football).

Debut v Chesterfield (A) 13.9.02

A full-back who impressed in pre-season trials, but was given only one chance at League level - in a 0-5 defeat - Donald had previously gained a little experience in the Southern League Second Division under former Fosse trainer John Jackson, and soon rejoined the Goldstone club for a five-game contribution to their 1903 title-winning effort in that sphere. He later regained amateur status and represented his adopted county.

Appearances:
FL: 1 app. 0 gls.
Total: *1 app. 0 gls.*

COLLINS, Arthur

Role: Half back
b. Leicester, 29th May 1882

CAREER: Leicester Old Boys/ Sept 1901:FOSSE/May 1905:Fulham/ May 1914:Norwich City.

Debut v Blackpool (A) 28.3.02

A consistent Fosse performer as an elegantly constructive centre- or left-half, Arthur really made his name in London, where he helped Fulham to two successive Southern League championships and into the Second Division. A popular hero dubbed 'Prince Arthur' by the Craven Cottage crowd, he came close to England honours when playing in the 1906 Professionals v. Amateurs international trial, and by 1909 was on the management committee of the Players Union. After 197 League games for Fulham, he moved back into the Southern League for the 1914/15 season, then returned to play in wartime football for Fosse. Arthur was a son of Fosse director Tom Collins, who served the board for ten years prior to his death in June 1913.

Appearances:
FL: 82 apps. 5 gls.
FAC: 14 apps. 0 gls.
WW1: 47 apps. 0 gls.
Total: *143 apps. 5 gls.*

CONNACHAN, James

Role: Forward
b. Glasgow, 29th August 1874

CAREER: Glasgow Perthshire/Duntocher Hibs/Glasgow Perthshire/Feb 1897:Celtic/ Oct 1898:Airdrieonians/Oct 1898:Newton Heath/Feb 1899:Glossop North End/May 1900:FOSSE/Aug 1901:Nottingham Forest/ Oct 1901:Morton/Aug 1902:Renton/ 1906:Britannia FC (Canada)/Dec 1907: Dumbarton Harp.

Debut v Stockport County (H) 1.9.1900 (scored once)

A roving forward tried everywhere in the front line by Fosse except at outside-left, this Scot was hardly prolific, but at least managed to score against his two previous League clubs during his single season at Leicester. Jamie was noted for his speed - being described as 'a demon in spikes' while with Celtic, for whom he nonetheless made but a single Scottish League start. He certainly didn't let the grass grow under his feet on leaving them: he stayed precisely four days with Airdrie before his move to Manchester!

Appearances:
FL: 29 apps. 6 gls.
Total: *29 apps. 6 gls.*

Arthur Collins

COOPER, Paul David

Role: Goalkeeper
b. Cannock, Staffs, 21st December 1953

CAREER: Sutton Coldfield Town/ (trials-Shrewsbury Town)/app/pro July 1971: Birmingham City/Mar 1974:Ipswich Town/ July 1987:CITY/Mar 1989:Manchester City/ July 1990:Stockport County.

Debut v Crystal Palace (A) 12.9.87

Not the tallest of goalkeepers, but certainly one of the most agile and quick-witted, Paul carved out a thirteen-year career of well over 500 senior games for Ipswich, winning both FA Cup and UEFA Cup winner's medals after initially joining the Suffolk club on loan from Birmingham, and earning en route a testimonial game against Norwich in 1986. Understandably keen to downplay his a car crash sidelined him for a few weeks; his recovery coincided with Hodge's; and he became a deadline-week mover to augment the successful Maine Road promotion challenge. Paul also assisted Stockport's rise from the basement to Division Three in 1991, before an elbow injury enforced his retirement. Curiously, his career had false-started over twenty years earlier with a spell as a Shrewsbury reserve striker!

Appearances:
FL: 56 apps. 0 gls.
FAC: 1 app. 0 gls.
LC: 9 apps. 0 gls.
FMC: 4 apps. 0 gls.
Total: *70 apps. 0 gls.*

CORBETT, William R.

Role: Centre half
b. Falkirk, Stirlingshire, 31st August 1922

CAREER: Dunipace Thistle/Maryhill/May 1941:Celtic/June 1948:Preston North End/Aug 1949:CITY/July 1950: Yeovil Town/Nov 1951:Dunfermline Athletic/ Nov 1952:Morton.

Debut v Bury (A) 1.10.49

'Capped' in the wartime international against England in 1942 (when he formed a middle-line with Bill Shankly and Matt Busby, and

Paul Cooper

long-standing popular reputation as a spectacular penalty-save expert (8 stopped out of 10 faced in 1979/80 alone!), and instead place merited stress on his all-round stability in the six-yard box, Paul joined City as an out-of-contract free agent, and soon renewed his old defensive partnership with Russell Osman after displacing the out-of-sorts Ian Andrews. His rapid, accurate distribution was in fact every bit as noteworthy as his persistent prowess at keeping out spot-kicks, and he soon convinced David Pleat, too, of his right to the senior City berth after the mid-season managerial change. Martin Hodge's early injury allowed Paul another lengthy spell as No.1 during 1988/9, but a shaking received in

Bill Corbett

shackled Tommy Lawton), and a guest player for West Ham, Cardiff City, Swansea Town and Southampton while on military service away from Parkhead, Bill was later bought for £7,000 by Johnny Duncan to challenge Tom McArthur and Norman Plummer for the City centre-half spot. However, he had barely made a breakthrough when the manager departed, and was soon on his way himself after failing to convince Norman Bullock that he could marshall City's defence as well as he had done Celtic's in the immediate postwar period. His older brother Norman was a West Ham stalwart from 1937 to 1951.

Appearances:
FL: 16 apps. 0 gls.
FAC: 1 app. 0 gls.
Total: *17 apps. 0 gls.*

COULSON, Ernest

Role: Outside right

CAREER: Dec 1898:FOSSE/Ratby Swifts/ Nov 1901:Burton United/Nov 1902: Chesterfield/Aug 1903:FOSSE.
Debut v Chesterfield (A) 23.1.04

The outside-right and younger brother of a pair of amateurs with a seemingly strict habit of moving between clubs in tandem, Ernest notched a hat-trick on his Fosse reserve debut, scored the winner in his first senior friendly appearance against Reading four and a half years later, and earned a single shot at League action some seven months after that - in a 0-2 defeat which kept his side rooted to the foot of Division Two.

Appearances:
FL: 1 app. 0 gls.
Total: *1 app. 0 gls.*

COULSON, Henry William

Role: Inside forward

CAREER: Jan 1898:FOSSE/Ratby Swifts/ Nov 1901:Burton United/Nov 1902: Chesterfield/Apr 1903:FOSSE.
Debut v Lincoln City (H) 12.2.1898 (scored once)

Of the nigh-inseparable Coulsons, Henry was first on the Fosse scene with his occasional appearances in the inside-forward berths in friendlies and charity cup games, but could still never improve on his record of a single Second Division selection (when he opened the scoring in a 3-1 win). The pair played together for Fosse reserves on occasions, and presumably did so too at Burton and Chesterfield: for neither played even once at League level at either club!

Appearances:
FL: 1 app. 1 gl.
Total: *1 app. 1 gl.*

COUTTS, William Farquharson

Role: Inside forward / Wing half
b. Gorgie, Edinburgh, 26th June 1909
d. Leicester, July 1991

CAREER: Edinburgh Ashton/Dunbar United/Aug 1930:Heart of Midlothian/(Feb 1932-loan-Leith Athletic)/May 1934:CITY.
Debut v Wolverhampton Wanderers (H) 25.8.34 (scored once)

Billy Coutts

A tricky Scottish inside-forward or wing-half who cost £950 and then made irregular appearances in each of the last five up-and-down seasons before the war, Billy also turned out in regional fare for Northampton Town in 1939/40 and for Nottingham Forest at Filbert Street on Christmas Day 1941. He had been a team-mate of Archie Gardiner with Hearts, for whom he played in the Scottish Cup semi-final of 1932/3. Billy marked the fiftieth anniversary of his City debut by appearing as a still sprightly guest at the club's Centenary celebrations.

Appearances:
FL: 48 apps. 4 gls.
FAC: 2 apps. 0 gls.
WW2: 10 apps. 0 gls.
Total: *60 apps. 4 gls.*

COX, William James

Role: Centre forward

CAREER: Feb 1903:Bury/ May 1904:Plymouth Argyle/ Aug 1905:FOSSE/Oct 1905: Accrington Stanley/ Jan 1906:Preston North End/ May 1906:Dundee/ Apr 1907:Heart of Midlothian/ Nov 1907:Bradford Park Avenue.

Debut v Clapton Orient (H) 2.9.05

Fosse didn't take long to decide that this centre-forward wouldn't fit the bill - he was dropped after the first three games of 1905/6, and within a month was on his way north. His frustrations continued that term: he couldn't displace Matt Brunton from a Stanley side on its way to the Lancashire Combination title, and he failed to get a first-team nod at Deepdale. After his initially successful stint in Scotland (top scoring with 18 League counters at Dundee), William became one of the first players engaged by the newly-formed Bradford club, which had to play its first season, incongruously, in the Southern League, prior to its election to Division Two.

Appearances:
FL: 3 apps. 0 gls.
Total: *3 apps. 0 gls.*

CRAWFORD, James Cherrie

Role: Forward
b. Bellshill, Lanarkshire, 27th September 1930

CAREER: Oct 1947:CITY/March 1954: Plymouth Argyle/cs 1956:Peterborough United.

Debut v Grimsby Town (H) 26.12.50

A ball-playing Scottish inside-forward whose Filbert Street progress was hampered by a spell of National Service, Jimmy made isolated appearances in four forward positions over a four season span, and then found himself similarly cast as a utility reserve at Home Park. His final senior game for Argyle was at Leicester in February 1956, and even Jimmy's contribution to two of Posh's Midland League championship campaigns was sporadic.

Jimmy Crawford

Appearances:
FL: 10 apps. 2 gls.
FAC: 1 app. 0 gls.
Total: *11 apps. 2 gls.*

CREWS, Alexander N.

Role: Centre half
b. Devon

CAREER: Green Waves/cs 1910:Plymouth Argyle/Aug 1912:Chelsea/Sept 1912:FOSSE/ Sept 1913:Stockport County.

Debut v Grimsby Town (A) 12.10.12

Whether unlucky or just unsuitable, this Devonian pivot got only the one chance to impress (in a 0-2 defeat) during a season when Fosse tried six different centre-halves. Records show that Alex had had little more opportunity to shine nearer home, having played only a couple of games for Argyle in the Southern League some two years before, and having lasted only a month in the Stamford Bridge stiffs. There would be no senior breakthrough for him at Edgeley Park, either.

Appearances:
FL: 1 app. 0 gls.
Total: *1 app. 0 gls.*

CROSS, Graham Frederick

Role: Half back / Forward
b. Leicester, 15th November 1943

CAREER: pro Nov 1960:CITY/(Mar 1976-loan-Chesterfield)/June 1976:Brighton & Hove Albion/July 1977:Preston North End/cs 1978: Enderby Town/Mar 1979:Lincoln City/ Aug 1979:Enderby Town.

*Debut v Birmingham City (H) 29.4.61
(scored once)*

Falling just short of Adam Black's club record League appearance total, but bettering his aggregate tally to stand, with 599 senior games for City, as Leicester's most consistent servant ever, Graham also proved himself one of the most versatile over his sixteen seasons. It was often said that his regular switching of position cost him an England place (especially in the days when little premium was put on zonal adaptability), but Graham's failure to add senior international honours to his eleven Under-23 caps nevertheless seemed more a case of culpable oversight on the part of the national team's management. As early as 1962/3, Matt Gillies' tactical interchanging of Graham and Frank McLintock was a match-winning ploy, though a later tendency to shuttle Graham between defence, midfield and the striking line could occasionally be put

down to desperate expediency. Eventually, when the twin centre-back game became the norm, it was in defence that Graham settled - if that's the right word, given his relentless energy and enthusiasm. Four Cup Final appearances, a Second Division championship medal and a 1973 testimonial game were the tangible mementos of his City career but, for supporters, other memories jostle: of the 18-year-old playing like a veteran in City's gallant European exit in Madrid; of the cool back-heel that won a Cup replay at Blackburn; of the 'hat-trick' against Forest, consisting of 'one for them, two for us'; of numerous bustling forays forward, and of countless opposing strikers cowed into frustration by Graham's sturdy shadowing and solid tackle. His football prowess - several times coveted by Brian Clough - probably cost him a much more successful county cricket career than he actually managed (as, naturally, a Leicestershire all-rounder), but the winter game kept a hold on him for some time after his final departure from Filbert Street. He was ever-present in Brighton's runaway rise from Third to Second Division in 1977, and then inspired Preston to take the same promotional route a year later. It was wholly unfitting that when he answered Lincoln's emergency call in 1979, even Graham couldn't save them from relegation. A spell coaching, and then managing Hinckley Athletic marked the final phase of his soccer involvement. Sadly, Graham was back in the news in February 1993, when being jailed for 9 months for theft and false accounting, after utilising Post Office funds in his care to cover serious gambling debts.

Appearances:
FL: 495 (3) apps. 29 gls.
FAC: 59 apps. 6 gls.
LC: 40 apps. 2 gls.
Eur: 2 apps. 0 gls.
Total: *596 (3) apps. 37 gls.*

❑ FOX FACT: *Graham Cross additionally holds City's records for most appearances in each of the two major Cup competitions.*

A rare Graham Cross goal, this in a 1-1 draw at West Ham in October 1971.

Nicky Cross

CROSS, Nicholas Jeremy Roland

Role: Striker
b. Birmingham, 7th February 1961

CAREER: app 1977/pro Feb 1979:West
Bromwich Albion/Aug 1985:Walsall/Jan 1988:
CITY/June 1989:Port Vale/July 1994:Hereford
United.

Debut v Reading (A) 30.1.88

Initially a young rival for an Albion striking
role with the likes of Ally Brown and Peter
Eastoe, Nicky later partnered Trevor Christie
at Fellows Park as he gradually improved his
goals-per-game ratio and developed his
characteristic penalty area control. A well-
balanced, eager bustler, superb at shielding
and turning with the ball in tight positions, he
was an early £65,000 David Pleat buy to play
in support of Mike Newell, and indeed proved
resilient enough to see off the challenge of
Jimmy Quinn during the following season.
Nicky was badly hit by injury at Vale Park,
and had been out of the game for over a year

when returning as substitute against City in
February 1992, after which he shared in both
relegation and promotion campaigns with
Vale. By the end of 1994/5, he had
accumulated 120 League goals.

> **Appearances:**
> *FL: 54 (4) apps. 15 gls.*
> *FAC: 1 app. 0 gls.*
> *LC: 3 (2) apps. 1 gl.*
> *FMC: 1 app. 0 gls.*
> **Total:** *59 (6) apps. 16 gls.*

CUNNINGHAM, Laurence Paul

Role: Winger
b. St. Mary's Archway, London, 8th March 1956
d. Madrid, 15th July 1989

CAREER: app Aug 1972/pro July 1974:Orient/
Mar 1977:West Bromwich Albion/June 1979:
Real Madrid/(Mar 1983-loan-Manchester
United)/Aug 1983:Sporting Gijon/cs 1984:
Olympique Marseille/(Oct 1985-loan-CITY)/
July 1986:Rayo Vallecano/(Aug 1987-trials-
Real Betis)/Oct 1987:RSC Charleroi/Feb 1988:
Wimbledon/July 1988:Rayo Vallecano.

Debut v Manchester United (H) 23.11.85

A superbly skilful, confidently confrontational
winger with six caps at each of Under-21 and
full England levels, Laurie initially moved to

Laurie Cunningham

Spain for just under £1 million, and tasted both sides of the hysterical success ethic on the continent, falling a little from popular favour after helping Real to the Spanish championship, and the European Cup semi-final and Final in his first two years. Later, unsettled in Marseille, he had an extended loan period with City which, despite being injury-strewn, was inspirationally instrumental in keeping them in Division One in 1986. Some of his once-electrifying pace had gone, but little of the ball-juggling cockiness, and Laurie genuinely lit up Filbert Street for a while with his bursts of effective footballing extroversion. In the midst of further continental wanderings, he again briefly returned to London, and appeared at Wembley as substitute for surprise Cup-winners Wimbledon in 1988. He was killed in a car crash in Madrid, only weeks after helping Rayo Vallecano to promotion to the Spanish First Division.

Appearances:
FL: 13 (2) apps. 0 gls.
Total: *13 (2) apps. 0 gls.*

CUNNINGHAM, William Edward

Role: Full back
b. Mallusk, Antrim, 20th February 1930

CAREER: Tranent Juniors/Ardrossan Winton Rovers/1948:St.Mirren/Nov 1954:CITY/ Sept 1960:Dunfermline Athletic.
Debut v Wolverhampton Wanderers (H) 11.12.54

Ironically earning several of his 30 Irish caps while a regular in City's reserves, Willie had learned his football in Scotland, and had already won international recognition for his stylish defensive play with St.Mirren when City laid out £4,750 for him. He settled well initially, shuttling between the two full-back berths, but was then squeezed out by the Stan Milburn/John Ogilvie partnership which saw City through the 1957 promotion year. He returned for three seasons of First Division battling but, again ironically, only ever played twice for City in the centre-half position he held for Northern Ireland throughout the 1958 World Cup. The eventual move to Dunfermline worked well for Willie: he played in the 1961 Scottish Cup victory, and was manager when the Pars returned to Hampden in 1965, having had a spell coaching under Jock Stein in the interim. He sold Jackie Sinclair to City before moving on for further spells of management at Falkirk and St.Mirren, and in 1971 turned down the Scottish FA's offer of the national team manager's post.

Appearances:
FL: 127 apps. 4 gls.
FAC: 11 apps. 0 gls.
Total: *138 apps. 4 gls.*

❏ FOX FACT: *The 23 Irish international appearances made by Willie Cunningham while on City's books made him at the time the club's most-capped player. This honour had successively been held by Alf Watkins (2), Horace Bailey (5), Ernie Hine (6), Dai Jones (7) and Mal Griffiths (11); and has subsequently been taken by Gordon Banks (37) and John O'Neill (39).*

Willie Cunningham

CURRIE, Samuel

Role: Left back
*b. Kilwinning, Ayrshire,
22nd November 1889*

CAREER: 1906:Kilwinning Rangers/May 1909:FOSSE/May 1922:Wigan Borough.

Debut v Birmingham (A) 19.3.10

Fosse's regular left-back for six seasons before the war, and City's for three campaigns after it, Sam displaced Dick Pudan and went on to forge useful partnerships in hard times with Tommy Clay, Billy Barrett and Adam Black: in each case sharing the benefits of his experience with younger players. His signing actually cost him a medal, for Fosse swooped between the drawn final of the Scottish Junior Cup in 1909 and its replay, which Kilwinning won. One of Fosse's several early union activists, Sam played in December 1910 for the Players Union XI against a combined Manchester United/City side - scoring an own goal and being injured badly enough to miss the next eight Fosse games! He took a well-merited club benefit from the League game with North Shields in November 1919, and only dropped into the Third Division (North) at the end of his City career. An older brother was a Bury inside-forward before WW1.

Sam Currie

> **Appearances:**
> *FL: 236 apps. 4 gls.*
> *FAC: 12 apps. 2 gls.*
> *WW1: 123 apps. 7 gls.*
> **Total:** *371 apps. 13 gls.*

CURRIE, Walter Robertson

Role: Wing half
b. Lochgelly, Fife, 5th October 1895

CAREER: East Fife/Dec 1916:Raith Rovers/Dec 1919:CITY/May 1922:Bristol Rovers/1923:Lochgelly United.

Debut v Stockport County (A) 14.2.20

One of several players plucked by City from Starks Park as a result of return visits by former Raith boss Peter Hodge, 'Wattie' had impressed in wartime football as a skilful wing-half. Yet although he played quite a few games in front of his unrelated namesake, he could never secure a regular middle-line place over his three seasons at Leicester. He was, however, an ever-present in his sole Third Division campaign at Eastville.

> **Appearances:**
> *FL: 32 apps. 1 gl.*
> **Total:** *32 apps. 1 gl.*

'Wattie' Currie

CUSACK, Nicholas John

Role: Striker
b. Rotherham, 24th December 1965

CAREER: Birmingham Polytechnic/Long
Eaton United/Alvechurch/June 1987:CITY/
July 1988:Peterborough United/Aug 1989:
Motherwell/Jan 1992:Darlington/July 1992:
Oxford United/(Mar 1994-loan-Wycombe
Wanderers)/Nov 1994:Fulham.

Debut v Shrewsbury Town (H) 15.8.87

As a tall ex-student centre-forward signing
from Alvechurch, young Nick was rather
overburdened from the day of his arrival with
wishful comparisons to the recently-departed
Alan Smith, and not exactly aided by being
plunged straight into the first team on the
season's opening day. His development back
in the reserves was encouraging enough to
earn him an extended contract, but it
promised to be an uphill struggle for Nick to
compete with Newell, Cross, Reid and
newcomer Quinn for a senior slot. Posh were
clearly impressed by his spectacular strike
against them in a testimonial friendly in April
1988, and three months later he moved to
London Road in the deal which brought Alan
Paris to Leicester. After a term as Posh's top
scorer, he was whisked north to make an
instant Premier Division impact (albeit as
much on the disciplinary record - with three
dismissals in his first term - as on the scoring
chart). Nick helped Motherwell reach the 1991
Scottish Cup Final, but missed out on the
medals; moved to Feethams for a club record
£95,000 fee, but couldn't save Darlington from
relegation; and then transferred at equivalent
cost to the Manor Ground. He signed off the
1994/5 campaign with a last-game hat-trick
for Fulham, for whom he has been playing
alongside Simon Morgan.

Nick Cusack

Appearances:
FL: 5 (11) apps. 1 gl.
FAC: 0 (1) app. 0 gls.
FMC: 1 (1) apps. 0 gls.
Total: *6 (13) apps. 1 gl.*

DAINTY, Herbert Charles

Role: Centre half
b. Geddington, Northants, 2nd June 1879
d. Kettering, 10th September 1957

CAREER: Kettering/Aug 1899:FOSSE/May 1900:New Brighton Tower/Aug 1901:FOSSE/cs 1902:Northampton Town/May 1903:Notts County/May 1904: Southampton/May 1905: Dundee/May 1911:Bradford Park Avenue/Oct 1913:Ayr United (p/mgr from May 1914)/Apr 1915:Dundee Hibernian (p/mgr).

Debut v Luton Town (A) 23.9.1899

Herbert Dainty

A sturdy and authoritative Northamptonshire pivot, Herbert had two spells as Fosse's centre-half around the turn of the century (for campaigns in which they finished fifth and fourteenth), and became a noted wanderer around the League and Southern League scene. It was in Scotland, however, that he really distinguished himself. One of four Englishmen in Dundee's first (and only) Scottish Cup-winning team of 1910 (beating Clyde at the third attempt), he also represented the Scottish League that year, enjoyed a testimonial match against Celtic, and eventually became something of a legendary figure on Tayside. He returned to that area as player/manager and even (for a while in 1922) as chairman of the local Hibernians - soon to change their name to Dundee United - and also had his own team, Dainty's XI, which played regularly for charities throughout the WW1 period. After having spent some time coaching in South America, Herbert became Ipswich Town trainer for two years from 1932.

Appearances:
FL: 53 apps. 3 gls.
FAC: 5 apps. 0 gls.
Total: *58 apps. 3 gls.*

DALY, Gerard Anthony

Role: Midfield
b. Cabra, Dublin, 30th April 1954

CAREER: Bohemians/Apr 1973:Manchester United/Mar 1977:Derby County/(May 1978 & May 1979-loans-New England Tea Men)/Aug 1980:Coventry City/(Jan 1983-loan-CITY)/July 1984:Birmingham City/Oct 1985: Shrewsbury Town/Mar 1987:Stoke City/July 1988:Doncaster Rovers/Dec 1989:Telford United (p/coach; p/mgr).

Debut v Carlisle United (A) 5.2.83

A vital midfield cog in Tommy Docherty's mid-70s reconstruction of Manchester United (and an FA Cup runner-up in 1976), Gerry later clashed verbally with the volatile manager at both Old Trafford and the Baseball Ground, and seemed happier with the quieter style of Gordon Milne, who not only signed him for Coventry (for £300,000), but also called on him to contribute to City's 1983 promotion push as a loan player. The slim, multi-capped Eire international responded magnificently, and City only lost once after he joined the fray, with the forwards gratefully latching on to his intelligent promptings and

Gerry Daly

judiciously varied distribution, and Gerry himself showing a fine battling commitment. It was a genuine surprise when Milne decided to face First Division rigours without him, but Gerry knuckled down for one more Sky Blue survival battle, then helped Birmingham out of the Second in his initial St.Andrews campaign.

Appearances:
FL: 17 apps. 1 gl.
Total: *17 apps. 1 gl.*

DARBY, Ernest W.

Role: Goalkeeper

CAREER: Leicester Old Boys/Leicester Nomads/am Oct 1908/am Apr 1910: FOSSE/ cs 1910:Loughborough Corinthians/cs 1911: Belvoir SS/Loughborough Corinthians.

Debut v Hull City (A) 14.4.10

An amateur goalkeeper who continued to play for his first clubs while occasionally assisting Fosse's reserves, Ernest briefly stood in for the absent Jonty Starbuck and Horace Bailey at the tail-end of 1909/10, as Fosse's attempt to bounce back to Division One petered out tamely in a nine-game run without a win. He had previously had trials with Woolwich Arsenal as a teenager.

Appearances:
FL: 4 apps. 0 gls.
Total: *4 apps. 0 gls.*

DAVIES, Benjamin Edward

Role: Goalkeeper
b. Middlesbrough,
9th June 1888
d. Middlesbrough, 1970

CAREER: Middlesbrough United/Feb 1911: Middlesbrough/ May 1920:Cardiff City/ June 1923:CITY/ June 1924:Bradford Park Avenue.

Ben Davies

Debut v South Shields (A) 8.12.23

A tall, slim keeper whose top-flight experience at Ayresome was limited by the form of England international Tim Williamson, Ben joined Cardiff for their initial season in the League, and by the end of it had assisted them to promotion to Division Two. As a Bluebird, he proved an insurmountable barrier to City in their 1922/3 FA Cup exit, yet within less than a year Ben was standing in briefly for George Hebden in the Filbert Street goal: conceding a goal per game, but never on a beaten side. At Park Avenue he failed to win a first-team call, though he had previously kept goal in one WW1 game for them as a guest.

Appearances:
FL: 3 apps. 0 gls.
Total: *3 apps. 0 gls.*

DAVIES, Richard

Role: Forward
b. Hanley, Staffs, c 1876

CAREER: Wrexham/ Nov 1894:Manchester City/1895:Hanley Town/Aug 1895:FOSSE/ June 1896:South Shore/ cs 1897:Glossop North End/ May 1898:Wolverhampton Wanderers/cs 1899:Reading.

Debut v Darwen (A) 21.9.1895

Richard Davies

Signed by Fosse as a youthful centre-forward after he'd joined Hanley's sole season in The Combination from Manchester City's reserves, Richard showed rather more versatility across the Leicester forward line than he did striking success, and after a while his first-team appearances were confined to friendlies. He left Glossop on the eve of their election to the League, and flattered to deceive with Wolves, scoring in his first Division One game, but only once more before his release.

Appearances:
FL: 7 apps. 4 gls.
FAC: 3 apps. 0 gls.
Total: *10 apps. 4 gls.*

DAVIES, Roger

Role: Striker
b. Wolverhampton, 25th October 1950

CAREER: Bridgnorth Town/Worcester City/
Sept 1971:Derby County/(Aug 1972-loan -
Preston North End)/July 1976:Club Brugge/
Dec 1977:CITY/Mar 1979:Tulsa Roughnecks/
Sept 1979:Derby County/Mar 1980:Seattle
Sounders/Apr 1983:Fort Lauderdale Strikers/
(Sept 1983-trials-Burnley)/Nov 1983:
Darlington/Feb 1984:Gresley Rovers/
Nov 1985:Stapenhill/1989:Tutbury Hawthorn.
Debut v Derby County (H) 10.12.77

Frank McLintock's City were already
struggling when Roger returned to Division
One from Bruges with a club record £250,000
transfer fee and high expectations to live up
to. Unfortunately, the lanky striker needed
time to play himself back into the pace of
English football, and that was a commodity
City's predicament (and the crowd's short
patience) excluded. Roger could recover
neither goal touch nor general form, and of the
four efforts that ironically gave him the joint

Roger Davies

top-scorer position for the season, one was a
penalty and another, his first, might less
charitably have been credited as a Norwich
own goal. Even when Jock Wallace took over,
City fans saw little of the razor-sharpness and
awkward unorthodoxy that had marked
Roger's first spell at Derby with some
spectacular goals (all five against Luton in the
Rams' championship season of 1974/5; a
memorable hat-trick in a televised Cup replay
with Spurs) and had won him an England
Under-23 cap. Success had come Roger's way,
too, with Club Brugge, who completed the
Belgian Cup/League double in 1977, and his
four goals in four games in the following
season's European Cup helped them towards
the Final, though Roger was embroiled in
City's plummet by the time they met
Liverpool at Wembley. (Five years earlier, he
had been sent off in Derby's European Cup
semi-final defeat by Juventus). Roger scored
54 goals during his five seasons in the States,
and appeared as a substitute in Soccer Bowl
1982, when Seattle lost 0-1 to New York
Cosmos; while in 1987 he earned a winner's
medal from the Leicestershire Senior Cup in
its Centenary Final, playing for Staffordshire-
based Stapenhill.

Appearances:
FL: 22 (4) apps. 6 gls.
FAC: 2 apps. 0 gls.
LC: 0 (1) app. 0 gls.
Total: *24 (5) apps. 6 gls.*

DAVIES, William McIntosh

Role: Midfield
b. Glasgow, 31st May 1964

CAREER: Pollok United/1980:Rangers/
1986: Jonkoping/1987:IF Elfsborg/
Oct 1987: St.Mirren/July 1990:CITY/
Oct 1990:Dunfermline Athletic/
Mar 1994: Motherwell.
Debut v Bristol Rovers (H) 25.8.90

Unfortunately unable to settle with Leicester
either on or off the pitch, Billy was a scurrying
Scottish midfielder whose £165,000 signing fee
represented David Pleat's first outlay from the
'McAllister Million' of the 1990 close season,
and whose rapid return north was briefly
delayed only by City's desire to break even on
the transfer dealings. Billy actually made his
City bow in a friendly at Love Street, where he

Billy Davies (left) with Ricky Hill.

Bert Davis

Only 5ft.4ins tall, Bert nonetheless posed a rather large threat to opposing defences, who worried far more about his scoring record - remarkably prolific for an orthodox winger - than ever he did about his diminutive stature. He'd won a Third Division (North) championship medal in his first season with his home-town club (after giving up his job as a mill-hand), and was a Roker regular right up until they claimed the First Division title in 1936; arriving at Filbert Street having aggregated 84 League and Cup goals. Yet Bert rather quickly lost his battle with Tony Carroll for the outside-right slot as City rocketed to promotion in 1937, and was not retained for top-flight action. His senior career ended with stints as a wartime guest with York, Huddersfield and back at Park Avenue.

Appearances:
FL: 8 apps. 0 gls.
FAC: 1 app. 0 gls.
Total: *9 apps. 0 gls.*

DAVIS, William

Role: Defender
b. Nantwich, Cheshire

CAREER:
1889:FOSSE/
1893:Hinckley Town.

Debut (competitive) v Burton Wanderers (H) FAC 4.10.1890

Billy Davis

had hitherto been an occasional team-mate of Peter Weir in a struggling Premier Division outfit, but competitive English fare soon showed him short of the inspirational flair it was hoped he would provide. Almost a decade before, Billy had broken into Rangers' senior side as a 17-year-old, but his gradual Ibrox progress (during which he made a substitute appearance in the 1983 Scottish Cup Final) was foreshortened by the policy changes of the Graeme Souness regime, and he chanced his arm thereafter in Swedish football: initially alongside his younger brother John - later of Clydebank - at Jonkoping, then in an Elfsborg side relegated from the Allsvenskan in 1987. His St.Mirren spell was enlivened by a spectacular goal against Rangers, televisually replayed umpteen times thereafter, while with the Pars he suffered a double disappointment in 1991/2, with relegation from the Premier Division following defeat in the Skol Cup Final. Billy was, however, briefly back in European competition with Motherwell during 1994/5.

Appearances:
FL: 5 (1) apps. 0 gls.
Total: *5 (1) apps. 0 gls.*

DAVIS, Herbert

Role: Outside right
b. Bradford, 11th August 1906

CAREER: Guiseley/Nov 1927:Bradford Park Avenue/Apr 1932:Sunderland/Dec 1936: CITY/June 1937:Crystal Palace.
Debut v Chesterfield (A) 12.12.36

An amateur defender who played at left-back in Fosse's initial Cup tie, and at centre-half in their first Midland League game, but spent the bulk of his Leicester career thereafter turning out for the Fosse Rovers. He was, however, a regular representative for Leicestershire in inter-county fare between 1890 and 1895, and was at left-back for Hinckley in the County Cup Final of 1897. 'Unassuming, but very capable', was the verdict of the contemporary local magazine, 'The Wyvern'. Though Jimmy Atter is rightly credited with the first Fosse goal at Filbert Street at senior level, it was in fact Billy who netted the club's initial strike on the ground at reserve level three weeks earlier (equalising Paddy Slawson's goal for Melton Rovers in a 3-2 win on 17th October 1891).

Appearances:
FAC: 1 app. 0 gls.
ML: 5 apps. 0 gls.
Total: *6 apps. 0 gls.*

DAVISON, Robert

Role: Striker
b. South Shields, 17th July 1959

CAREER: Red Duster/Seaham Colliery Welfare/July 1980:Huddersfield Town/ Aug 1981:Halifax Town/Dec 1982:Derby County/Nov 1987:Leeds United/(Sept 1991-loan-Derby County)/(Mar 1992-loan-Sheffield United)/Aug 1992:CITY/Sept 1993:Sheffield United/Oct 1994:Rotherham United.

Debut v Luton Town (H) 15.8.92

A former shipyard welder, who played as a part-timer until he was 21, Bobby first made a striking impact at Halifax, notching that club's first hat-trick in 9 years, and earning an £80,000 move to Derby after scoring against them in the League Cup. For the Rams, he was top scorer in the promotion seasons which took them from

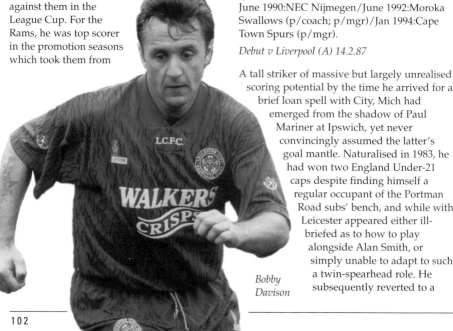

Bobby Davison

Division Three to the top flight, and the effectiveness of his determinedly bustling front-running style had as much to do as inflation with the £350,000 value placed on his next move to Elland Road. Again Bobby made a decent goalscoring contribution to Leeds' promotion back to Division One, and he showed still-predatory form on his loan-outs, leading Brian Little to add him to City's squad as a £50,000 stopgap after new signing David Lowe suffered pre-season injury. A willing, busy performer in his brief Leicester stint, he was soon sidelined by the emergence of Julian Joachim and the conversion of Steve Walsh to a central striking role. A second Bramall Lane loan spell developed into a free transfer in November 1993. By the close of 1994/5, Bobby's career tally of League goals stood at 166.

Appearances:
FL: 21 (4) apps. 6 gls.
LC: 3 apps. 1 gl.
AIC: 2 (1) apps. 2 gls.
Total: *26 (5) apps. 9 gls.*

D'AVRAY, Jean Michel

Role: Striker
b. Johannesburg, South Africa,
19th February 1962

CAREER: Rangers (Johannesburg)/May 1979: Ipswich Town/(Feb 1987-loan-CITY)/ June 1990:NEC Nijmegen/June 1992:Moroka Swallows (p/coach; p/mgr)/Jan 1994:Cape Town Spurs (p/mgr).

Debut v Liverpool (A) 14.2.87

A tall striker of massive but largely unrealised scoring potential by the time he arrived for a brief loan spell with City, Mich had emerged from the shadow of Paul Mariner at Ipswich, yet never convincingly assumed the latter's goal mantle. Naturalised in 1983, he had won two England Under-21 caps despite finding himself a regular occupant of the Portman Road subs' bench, and while with Leicester appeared either ill-briefed as to how to play alongside Alan Smith, or simply unable to adapt to such a twin-spearhead role. He subsequently reverted to a

Mich D'Avray

deeper-lying position at Portman Road, where he took a testimonial before being freed to pick up his career in Holland: unfortunately in a relegation-bound NEC side. Back in South Africa, Mich became a successful player/coach, assuming the reins of the national Under-21 and Olympic sides in September 1994.

Appearances:
FL: 3 apps. 0 gls.
Total: *3 apps. 0 gls.*

DAVY, Harry

Role: Right back
b. Padiham, Lancs, 1872

CAREER: Padiham/ Heywood Central/1892: Blackpool/Apr 1895: FOSSE/cs 1897:Bristol City.

Debut v Burton Swifts (H) 7.9.1895

Signed after accruing substantial Lancashire League experience with his two previous clubs

Harry Davy

(Blackpool were champions in 1894 and runners-up in the seasons before and after), Harry became a sound, strong-kicking right-back for two seasons with Fosse, welding an ever-present partnership with George Swift in 1896/7. He then joined former team-mate Albert Carnelly and Fossil-to-be Jack Hamilton for Bristol City's inaugural Southern League season.

Appearances:
FL: 50 apps. 0 gls.
FAC: 6 apps. 0 gls.
Total: *56 apps. 0 gls.*

DAW, Edwin Charles

Role: Goalkeeper
b. Doncaster, 1876
d. Doncaster, 1944

CAREER: Doncaster Congregationals/ Hexthorpe Wanderers/(trials-Sheffield United)/ Nov 1896:Grimsby Town/cs 1897:Barnsley St.Peters/cs 1898: Rushden/Aug 1899:Luton Town/May 1900: FOSSE/cs 1902:New Brompton/cs 1903: not known/Nov 1904: Doncaster Rovers/Dec 1905:Bradford City/ May 1906:Oldham Athletic (-1907)/ Apr 1910:FOSSE.

Debut v Burton Swifts (A) 1.10.1900

A 6ft-tall goalkeeper who had already packed in quite a bit of experience before joining Fosse for the first time, Teddy had in fact made his League debut for Grimsby against Fosse in 1896/7, then played in Barnsley's last Midland League line-up prior to their Second Division election; for Rushden against Fosse in the Cup; and for Luton in the season they temporarily lost League status. Teddy took over from Godfrey Beardsley for Fosse and was a capable, consistent custodian - staying for the only two-season spell of his career - until his wanderlust reasserted itself, and he moved to the club we now know as Gillingham. At Bradford City, he eventually lost his place to 22-stone

Teddy Daw

giant Willie Foulke (who had kept him out of the Blades first team a decade before), while at Oldham he played in the Lancashire Combination championship team that also earned immediate elevation to the League. Teddy gamely returned to help out Fosse in one match in 1910, but showed his rustiness in conceding six goals to Stockport.

Appearances:
FL: 56 apps. 0 gls.
FAC: 2 apps. 0 gls.
Total: *58 apps. 0 gls.*

DAWKINS, Derek Anthony

Role: Right back
b. Edmonton, London, 29th November 1959

CAREER: pro Oct 1977:CITY/Dec 1978: Mansfield Town/Dec 1981:Bournemouth/ July 1983:Torquay United/Nov 1989:Newport County/Sept 1989:Yeovil Town/Nov 1990: Gloucester City.

Debut v Derby County (A) 22.4.78

Derek Dawkins

Given a run-out at right-back in the final three games of 1977/8 by caretaker boss Ian MacFarlane, as already-relegated City looked for a bit of belated pride and some pointers for the future, Derek was still a teenager when released by Jock Wallace to Mansfield. He subsequently built a lengthy career in the lower Divisions, with 73 League games at Field Mill, 8 at Dean Court and 175 at Plainmoor, where he converted to a midfield

marking role and even popped up with some valuable goals (such as the winner against Spurs in a 1987/8 Littlewoods Cup tie). Derek was one of the last signings Newport made immediately before they wound up, halfway through their initial Conference campaign, and he didn't even get the chance to make his debut for them.

Appearances:
FL: 3 apps. 0 gls.
Total: *3 apps. 0 gls.*

DAWSON, James E.

Role: Outside left / Right half
b. Stoneyburn, West Lothian, 21st December 1927

CAREER: Polkemmet/May 1946:CITY/June 1949:Portsmouth/Sept 1951:Northampton Town/Sept 1952:Southend United.

Debut v Birmingham City (H) 12.9.46

Jimmy Dawson

Signed as a pro by City after leaving the RAF, Jimmy was groomed in the reserves as an outside-left, though two of his limited first team appearances were as an emergency right-half. A move to reigning League champions Portsmouth seemed to promise progress, but Jimmy played only one League game as Pompey repeated their Division One winners act, and failed to make a single senior appearance for either of his two subsequent clubs.

Appearances:
FL: 5 apps. 0 gls.
Total: *5 apps. 0 gls.*

DeVILLE, Thomas

Role: Goalkeeper
b. c 1865

CAREER: Stoke Wanderers/Leicester Town/ 1886:FOSSE/Aug 1888:Loughborough/ Rotherham Town/Jan 1892:FOSSE.

Debut (competitive)
v Long Eaton
Rangers (A) ML
23.1.1892

Tom DeVille

A veteran of the 'Friendly Fossils' era, Tom actually turned out at right-back in the club's first-ever County Cup tie in 1887, but it was as a goal-keeper that he gained a reputation good enough to take him onto the Midland League transfer roundabout, and it was as a last-line that he returned to find Fosse esconced at Filbert Street. He'd initially left the club, along with skipper T.S.Ashmole, when Fosse lost the tenure of the Belgrave Road Grounds in 1888 and had to return to Victoria Park. His former Rotherham team-mates certainly did him no favours in April 1892, when they put eleven past him as their contribution to his 'goals against' total of 27 in only 10 Midland League games. Another of those goals, put across his own line to the credit of Gainsborough Trinity a month earlier, was the first instance of a Fosse own goal at competitive level.

Appearances:
ML: 10 apps. 0 gls.
Total: *10 apps. 0 gls.*

DEWIS, George Renger

Role: Centre forward
b. Burbage, Leics, 22nd January 1913
d. Hinckley, Leics, 23rd October 1994

CAREER: Stoke Golding/1933:Nuneaton Town/Nov 1933:CITY/cs 1950:Yeovil Town.
Debut v West Bromwich Albion (H) 9.12.33

Carefully nurtured as a likely heir to Arthur Chandler after George Carr had overseen his development at Nuneaton, George gave early evidence of his potential centre-forward prowess, based on strength and aerial ability, as City used him sparingly over his first five seasons. He might have known that fate would not always favour him, however, for

his very first City strike, at Birmingham a week after his debut, was voided when fog caused the abandonment of the game after 65 minutes. He was nearing his peak as a bustling leader of the line when war was declared - and George's club record wartime tally of 62 goals, scored in the 81 City games he managed to fit in during Army service (which also featured several representative games for Northern Command, and allowed for a few guest appearances for Chesterfield, Leeds United, Sheffield United and Yeovil Town), instanced both his and the club's loss. George's best years were effectively behind him when peacetime football resumed, even if an aggregate 19 goals in 1946/7 represented City's top individual haul. He gave three more

George Dewis

years' service as a player, and was soon back from his West Country non-league stint to start a second Filbert Street career, initially as assistant coach, then as trainer to the reserve and youth teams. The meticulous dedication and encouragement he lavished on successive waves of City youngsters deserves high tribute - and appropriately drew grateful public testimony from the likes of Peter Shilton. Rather like Arthur Chandler, George wouldn't let even his pension-book keep him away from Filbert Street, where he remained as kit-man until 1983.

Appearances:
FL: 116 apps. 45 gls.
FAC: 13 apps. 6 gls.
WW2: 81 apps. 62 gls.
Total: *210 apps. 113 gls.*

❏ *FOX FACT: Between December 1940 and February 1941, George Dewis scored in ten successive wartime fixtures, totalling 15 goals. The club's peacetime record for a scoring run is held by Arthur Chandler, who scored in seven League and one FA Cup game in succession during 1924/5. Arthur Rowley also twice scored in seven consecutive League games (during 1951/2 and 1956/7). Amongst the thirteen instances of a City player scoring in six successive games, the outstanding feat was Jack Bowers': he did so in his first six games for the club.*

DICKSON, Adam

Role: Goalkeeper
b. Hamilton, Lanarkshire, 4th January 1929

CAREER: Thorniewood United/June 1951: CITY/cs 1955:Peterborough United.

Debut v West Ham United (A) 27.10.51

An understudy to fellow Scottish keeper Johnny Anderson throughout his City career, Adam was a safe-handling, reliable reserve who was unlucky not to find another League club, and more unfortunate

Adam Dickson

still in failing to win the regular first-team jersey with a Posh side steaming to the first two of their five successive Midland League championships. Adam's first five City appearances were in Division Two victories, but his last dozen - spread across both top Divisions and FA Cup fare - brought only one more win bonus.

Appearances:
FL: 16 apps. 0 gls.
FAC: 1 app. 0 gls.
Total: *17 apps. 0 gls.*

DILKS, Thomas Frank

Role: Outside left

CAREER: Daventry Town/1901:Northampton Town/cs 1903:Reading/Oct 1903:FOSSE/cs 1904:not known (possibly Wellingborough)/cs 1905:Northampton Town.

Debut v Grimsby Town (H) 24.10.03

Signed after a mere three-game spell with Southern League Reading, Tom became the third of eight players tried on the left flank by Fosse in the barrel-scraping, rock-bottom season of 1903/4, and fared little better than any other. Twice a Cobbler, he had played alongside Jack Bennett and Herbert Dainty in his first Southern League stint at the County Ground.

Appearances:
FL: 8 apps. 0 gls.
FAC: 1 app. 0 gls.
Total: *9 apps. 0 gls.*

DIXON, Arthur

Role: Inside forward
b. Middleton, Lancs, 17th November 1921

CAREER: Baillieston/May 1940:Queen's Park/cs 1945:Clyde/1947:Heart of Midlothian/Nov 1949:Northampton Town/Oct 1951:CITY/cs 1953:Kettering Town.

Debut v Bury (H) 6.10.51

An English-born, Scottish-raised inside-forward who made a rapid goalscoring impact at Northampton, and earned the nickname 'Rubberneck' from Cobblers' fans impressed by his heading ability, Arthur could only briefly shift Fred Worthington from the first team at Filbert Street, and never got another

Arthur Dixon

look-in after City signed Johnny Morris. He was once chosen for a Scottish representative side during the war (when he scored 86 League and Cup goals for Queen's Park), but dropped out when his birthplace became known. His father, also Arthur, had played for Oldham Athletic, St.Mirren, Rangers and Cowdenbeath between 1912 and 1929, and was later trainer and physiotherapist at both Ibrox and Boundary Park.

Appearances:
FL: 11 apps. 0 gls.
Total: *11 apps. 0 gls.*

DOHERTY, John Peter

Role: Inside forward
b. Manchester, 12th March 1935

CAREER: pro Mar 1952:Manchester United/ Oct 1957:CITY/July 1958:Rugby Town (p/mgr) Sept 1958:Altrincham/Hyde United res trainer.
Debut v Everton (H) 5.10.57

A genuine 'Busby Babe', nurtured through United's junior squads for a League debut at 17, John eventually found competition for an inside-forward place at Old Trafford unbearably intense. He had scored for United on a rare senior outing only two weeks before City swooped for his £6,500 transfer, but it soon became evident that he was carrying an old knee injury, which recurred after a dozen successive First Division games had given City cause for optimism about his progress. John took medical advice to avoid the stresses of the League game, and became the Southern League's youngest player/ manager at the age of 23; though he lasted only two months in post. In the early 80s, he was noted as being Burnley's chief scout; while in the 90s he became Chairman of Manchester United's Former Players Association.

Appearances:
FL: 12 apps. 5 gls.
Total: *12 apps. 5 gls.*

John Doherty

DONNELLY, James

Role: Forward
b. South Bank, 1882

CAREER:
South Bank/Darlington
St.Augustine's/Oct
1902:Sheffield United/
May 1907:FOSSE/
cs 1910:Darlington.

Debut v Leeds City (H)
7.9.07

Jimmy Donnelly

A £150 signing who contributed tellingly to Fosse's only promotion campaign from both right-flank forward positions, Jimmy remains best remembered as the scorer of the club's inaugural First Division goal (in the 1-1 home draw with Sheffield Wednesday which opened 1908/9). Indeed, he finished that unfortunate top-flight campaign as top scorer (with 10), and then turned selfless provider as Fred Shinton raced to a record seasonal goal haul in 1909/10 - his contract for that season showing him to have been one of 573 professionals in England then receiving the maximum wage of £4 per week. Jimmy was a member, as was Ronald Brebner, of the Darlington squad which reached the last 16 of the FA Cup in 1911 (beating his former First Division club Sheffield United along the way) and he was still active when the Quakers took the North Eastern League championship in 1913.

Appearances:
FL: 74 apps. 26 gls.
FAC: 2 apps. 1 gl.
Total: *76 apps. 27 gls.*

DORRELL, William

Role: Outside left
b. Coventry, c 1871

CAREER: 1889:Singers/
cs 1892:FOSSEApr 1894:
Aston Villa/Mar 1896:FOSSE.

Debut v Mansfield Town (A)
ML 17.9.1892

Billy actually made his Fosse bow a fortnight before the above-cited match, in the first friendly of the new season, and contributed a goal to the 10-1 demolition of his former club - the one we now know as Coventry City. He'd been the crowd's hero there, and was to become one (twice!) with Fosse, despite taking the left-wing spot from the popular Jimmy Atter. Speedy and incisive, he was tempted to Villa after scoring Fosse's final Midland League goal, but with England internationals Smith and Athersmith acting as obstacles to him gaining a regular first-team spot on either wing, Billy's chances at Perry Barr were limited. He nonetheless scored five goals in only 11 League appearances, added a brace in his only FA Cup game as Villa progressed towards the 1895 Final, and was chosen for the Football League against the Irish League. The welcome on his return to Fosse was heartfelt - and Billy obliged his fans by scoring in the first League game of his three-year second spell, during which he turned in a number of scintillating displays on both flanks. He even once tested his pace in a 440-yard challenge race with a visiting American athlete, and won, before the kick-off of the home game with Darwen in February 1898. Billy took a benefit from the prestigious friendly against the touring Corinthians in December 1898. He became a Villa scout in the 20s, by which stage his son Arthur was starring both for that club and England; while another son, Billy Jnr (see right), had by then completed a brief City career. One nineteenth-century source credits Billy Snr with a first-XI breakthrough at Small Heath Alliance at the age of 14; but this assertion has yet to be corroborated.

Appearances:
FL: 59 apps. 20 gls.
FAC: 14 app. 11 gls.
ML: 43 apps. 16 gls.
Total: *116 apps. 47 gls.*

❏ FOX FACT: *Billy Dorrell's 11 FA Cup goals for Fosse represent the all-time third-best haul for a Leicester player in the competition. Both Arthur Chandler and Arthur Rowley later claimed 14 goals for City in the premier knock-out competition.*

DORRELL, William Ernest

Role: Outside right
b. Leicester, 9th May 1893
d. Leicester, 17th June 1973

CAREER: Dec 1919:CITY/cs 1920:Hinckley
United/cs 1921:Coalville Swifts/cs 1922:
Loughborough Corinthians/Sept 1923:
Coalville Swifts.

Debut v Rotherham County (H) 6.12.19

Sadly unable to inscribe his family name as
indelibly into the City annals as his father had
into Fosse's, Billy Jnr won from Peter Hodge
only a single opportunity to deputise at
outside right for George Douglas in the initial
post-WW1 season (in a 1-1 home draw).
Happier at a less elevated level of football, he
was twice in County Cup-winning sides: for
City Reserves in 1920, and for Loughborough
Corinthians (where he briefly succeeded
Hughie Adcock) in 1923.

> **Appearances:**
> *FL: 1 app. 0 gls.*
> **Total:** *1 app. 0 gls.*

DOUGAN, Alexander Derek

Role: Centre forward
b. Belfast, 20th January 1939

CAREER: 1955:Distillery/Aug 1957:
Portsmouth/Mar 1959:Blackburn Rovers/
July 1961:Aston Villa/June 1963:Peterborough
United/May 1965:CITY/Mar 1967:
Wolverhampton Wanderers/1975:Kettering
Town (p/chief exec).

Debut v Liverpool (H) 21.8.65

Reversing the usual dynamic by which a
modern 'personality' is constructed, Derek
achieved a remarkable about-turn in his career
and his image midway through his playing
days. A process begun at Peterborough,
accelerated at Leicester and completed at
Wolves actually provided a rare example of a
caricature turning into a genuine character.
Too many of Derek's early energies had been
spent in establishing a rebellious persona as a
joker and wilful controversialist - often to the
detriment of his football - before he found a
mature balance between showmanship and
soccer. He'd been to Wembley with Blackburn
(in 1960, when he'd scored the two semi-final

goals, then posted a transfer request on the
morning of the Cup Final) and his standing as
a Northern Ireland regular seemed assured no
matter what, but the trajectory of his striking
career seemed permanently stalled when Villa
let him go to London Road, after he'd amused
many with his adoption of a shaven head, and
scared more with his propensity for off-field
scrapes. Perhaps a spell in the Third Division
helped restore a sense of perspective, or
perhaps a renewed burst of media interest in
'The Doog' when Posh met Arsenal in the Cup
rekindled ambitions. At any rate, Derek took a
pay cut to join City back in the top flight, and
proceeded to justify Matt Gillies' £25,000 gamble
as he managed both to put a smile back on
City's game and to link with fellow-newcomer
Jackie Sinclair in a lethal finishing partnership.
Brilliant in the air, and with a remarkably sure
and subtle first touch for a tall striker, Derek
led City's forward line with unique flair, and
lapped up the crowd's adulation - not least on
such occasions as when he knocked in a
flamboyant hat-trick against former club Villa,
or when he led a bemused close marker *behind*
the goal while awaiting a City corner! The
Doog's departure was the cause of much ill-
feeling between the club and its supporters,
centred on the belief that City had merely,

Derek Dougan

unimaginatively, cashed in on the first offer to doubly recoup their investment; and City fans were irked even more when Derek (taking over from Hugh McIlmoyle) made an immediate impact at Molineux, where his goals ensured promotion within a couple of months. Settling with Wolves for 310 senior games and 118 goals over almost eight years, Derek also won there his only victor's trophy, for the 1974 League Cup, a year before retirement. Eventually, he finished his career with 222 League goals and 43 Irish caps. An articulate chairman of the PFA, a stimulating author and easeful TV pundit, he surprised few when he later moved into management (albeit with Kettering, where he clashed with the FA over shirt sponsorship before such became the norm), or even when, in 1982, he led a consortium of businessmen in rescuing and reconstructing Wolves after they had fallen into receivership.

Appearances:
FL: 68 apps. 35 gls.
FAC: 5 apps. 1 gl.
LC: 3 apps. 5 gls.
Total: 76 apps. 41 gls.

DOUGAN, Maxwell Spalding

Role: Centre half
b. Stoneyburn, West Lothian, 23rd May 1938

CAREER: cs 1962:Queen's Park/Sept 1963: CITY/Dec 1966:Luton Town.

Debut v Gillingham (H) LC 27.11.63

A Scottish amateur international centre-half, Max made his City debut as an emergency centre-forward, helping the club past one hurdle on their way to League Cup glory, and later being rewarded with a half-back place in the first leg of the Final at Stoke. His Filbert Street chances were severely limited by the consistency of Ian King and John Sjoberg, but it was his occasional experience at full-back which stood Max in good stead for his subsequent years as a rugged, unceremonious No.2 with Luton, who he helped from the Fourth Division basement to the verge of Division Two.

Appearances:
FL: 9 apps. 0 gls.
LC: 2 apps. 0 gls.
Total: 11 apps. 0 gls.

Max Dougan

DOUGLAS, George Harold

Role: Outside right
b. Forest Gate, London, 18th August 1893
d. Tunbridge Wells, Kent, 1979

CAREER: St.Saviours/ Forest Gate/Custom House/Ilford/May 1912: FOSSE/Feb 1921: Burnley/May 1922:Oldham Athletic/Aug 1926:Bristol Rovers/July 1928:Tunbridge Wells Rangers (p/mgr)/Nov 1930:Dover United

Debut v Hull City (H) 21.12.12

Having graduated from West Ham schools football to become an outside-right - and occasional goalscoring centre-forward - in the Isthmian League, George was on the fringe of the amateur international squad when he joined Fosse. Retaining unpaid status for his first season (and winning two England amateur caps during that period), he re-signed in 1913 as a professional and gave fine right-wing service on both sides of WW1 (during which he also guested for Norwich City and Arsenal); though in the final game Fosse ever played under that name, an April 1919 friendly against the B.E.F. (France) XI, George was in the opposing team, and even missed a penalty. Four months later he scored the first League goal attributed to Leicester City (in the 1-2 home defeat by Wolves which inaugurated

George Douglas

1919/20). He took his benefit from the League game against Birmingham in September 1920, then moved on to play First Division football with both his Lancashire clubs; though only appearing twice in Burnley's 1921 Championship run-in. In fact, on the very day of his Clarets bow at Derby, George was summoned in the Police Court at Leicester for desertion of his wife, though the case collapsed when heard a week later. In 1935, George wrote to the national press decrying the amounts of money players were making out of the game compared to the pittance he had accumulated throughout his career.

Appearances:
FL: 127 apps. 10 gls.
FAC: 6 apps. 1 gl.
WW1: 3 apps. 0 gls.
Total: *136 apps. 11 gls.*

DRAPER, Mark Andrew

Role: Midfield
b. Derby, 11th November 1970

CAREER: YT/pro 1988:Notts County/ July 1994:CITY/July 1995:Aston Villa.
Debut v Newcastle United (H) 21.8.94

It took less than a dozen games into City's Premiership misadventure for them to be assailed on all sides by three pieces of consensual wisdom: that they would be relegated, that they had contrived a bargain buy in their new playmaker, and that said quality midfielder would be on his way to a 'big' club either before deadline day or at the end of the season. It took about that time for every professional observer to agree that Mark was the genuine article - which is damning enough comment on the top-flight myopia afflicting football coverage these days; given that the skills and strength Mark brought to that arena had long been evident even in the context of Notts County's regular upheavals. A 17-year-old Meadow Lane debutant in 1988, Mark had played himself into a key prompting role when the Magpies achieved promotion to the old Division One in 1991,

Mark Draper

had tasted relegation the next term, and had top-scored for them from the middle line in 1992/3. He had also won the deserved recognition of three England Under-21 selections; so it was not entirely surprising that Notts valued him at £2.5 million when Brian Little bid for him - the greater shock, perhaps, was that the League's transfer tribunal settled on an initial fee of £1.25 million (by some distance, nonetheless, City's record outlay); while it seemed merely unobjectionably prudent that the player himself insisted on a 'get-out' clause to his contract, potentially operable in the event of relegation. A missed penalty (over-hastily hit towards Pavel Srnicek) clouded Mark's Filbert Street debut - and his overall strike-rate was a disappointment - but there were more than compensatory pleasures aplenty for the City supporter from Mark's mastery of the ball, of the telling angle and of the tight turning circle. The close-cropped Midlander may not have exhibited the sheer elegance of a Gary McAllister, but his knack of finding space around a crowded half-way line, and his dribbling skills, stood out regularly enough in some higher-priced stellar company. Perhaps inevitably, Mark was destined to join the latter at Little's Villa: a £3 million bid was turned down by City in March 1995, but a £3.25 million cheque changed hands less than four months later, with City handing £500,000 over to Notts County as their share of the profit.

Appearances:
PL: 39 apps. 5 gls.
FAC: 2 apps. 0 gls.
LC: 2 apps. 0 gls.
Total: *43 apps. 5 gls.*

DRYBURGH, Thomas James Douglas

Role: Outside left
b. Kirkcaldy, Fife, 23rd April 1923

CAREER: Lochgelly Albert/June 1947: Aldershot/July 1948:Rochdale/Aug 1950: CITY/May 1954:Hull City/July 1955:King's Lynn/Aug 1957:Oldham Athletic/Nov 1957: Rochdale.

Debut v Notts County (H) 4.9.50.

A former ice-hockey star with Kirkcaldy Fliers, and a Scottish Junior international winger in his Lochgelly days, Tom then tasted life in both Sections of the Third Division before

Tom Dryburgh

signing for City at a £6,500 fee. Taking over from Charlie Adam, he became Arthur Rowley's first regular left-wing partner, and maintained a decent scoring rate himself, but lost his place to Peter Small in the 1954 promotion season, and never quite recovered his effective dash with his subsequent League clubs.

Appearances:
FL: 95 apps. 29 gls.
FAC: 4 apps. 1 gl.
Total: *99 apps. 30 gls.*

DUFFY, Christopher Francis

Role: Forward
b. Jarrow, Co.Durham, 1885

CAREER: Jarrow/St.Mary's College
(Hammersmith)/Jan 1905:Brentford/Oct
1905:Middlesbrough/Aug 1906:Newcastle
United/May 1908:Bury/July 1914:North
Shields Athletic/cs 1919:not known/Dec
1919:CITY/Aug 1920:Chester-le-Street.

Debut v Bristol City (H) 6.4.20 (scored once)

Quite a veteran by the time he joined City for
a brief run-out as a left-sided forward late in
the initial post-WW1 season (indeed, regarded
as probably City's oldest debutant until
Lawrie Madden arrived in 1991), Chris had
many years before won a reputation as an athletic sprinter. Certainly he'd used his pace as a
winger to carve a reasonable League career,
which included a 7-game contribution to
Newcastle's 1907 championship campaign,
and a six-year stint at Gigg Lane, where the
bulk of his 122 appearances had been in the
First Division. (Chris had, in fact, been a scorer
in both Bury/Fosse fixtures at that level back
in 1908/9). Trained as a schoolteacher, he took
a headship in Newcastle on retirement from
the game.

> **Appearances:**
> *FL: 4 apps. 1 gl.*
> **Total:** *4 apps. 1 gl.*

DUFFY, Michael Kevin

Role: Striker
b. Leicester, 12th June 1961

CAREER: July 1978:CITY/(1981-trials-Vfb
Stuttgart)/May 1981:Enderby Town/Wigston
Fields/Shepshed Charterhouse/Corby
Town/Oadby Town (p/mgr)/1991:North
Kilworth/Dunton Bassett/July 1992:Oadby
Town (p/mgr).

Debut v Notts County (H) 9.9.78

One of the City youngsters unexpectedly elevated to an early first-team spot by Jock
Wallace, Mick was a busy inside-forward with
a useful junior-team scoring rate, and had a
neat headed 'goal' dubiously disallowed on
his debut. He later provided the 'assist' for
Gary Lineker's initial first team goal in the
return game with the Magpies, and scored

Mick Duffy

himself in the final match of 1978/9, but was
only ever to make one further substitute
appearance in senior football thereafter. Mick's
trial spell in Stuttgart unfortunately led to no
Bundesliga contract; but he has since been a
stalwart of the local non-league scene, most
recently (1995) managing Aylestone Park.

> **Appearances:**
> *FL: 7 (5) apps. 1 gl.*
> **Total:** *7 (5) apps. 1 gl.*

DUMBRELL, George

Role: Left back
b. Catford, London, 23rd September 1906
d. Gravesend, March 1990

CAREER: Botwell Mission/Nunhead/Catford
South End/Cray Wanderers/1927:Dartford/
May 1928:Brentford/May 1930:CITY/
Nov 1933:Bournemouth & Boscombe Athletic/
Aug 1934:Brentford.

Debut v Blackburn Rovers (A) 2.3.31

A reserve full-back in both his Griffin Park spells (retiring in 1938 with an aggregate of only 17 League appearances for the Bees), George nonetheless cost City £1,750 when bought as cover for Reg Osborne. In fact he made light work of bridging the gulf between his background as a Third Division 'stiff' and the exigencies of performing in the top flight whenever he was called upon to partner Adam Black in City's back line. Strangely enough, George had made his name as a goalscorer at Dartford, when he had represented Kent in a friendly 'international' against France.

Appearances:
FL: 37 apps. 0 gls.
FAC: 2 apps. 0 gls.
Total: *39 apps. 0 gls.*

George Dumbrell

DUNCAN, John

Role: Inside forward
b. Lochgelly, Fife, 14th February 1896
d. Leicester, 14th March 1966

CAREER: Denbeath Star/Lochgelly United/1916:Raith Rovers/July 1922:CITY.

Debut v Stockport County (A) 26.8.22 (scored twice)

A scheming but far from shot-shy inside-forward of authentically high class, Johnny had already led Raith to their highest-ever Scottish League placing (3rd) in 1922 when City expended £1,500 to bring him and his brother Tom to Filbert Street. Peter Hodge had overseen his first few wartime appearances for the Kirkcaldy club, and kept close track of his progress, correctly identifying the strongly-built artist who'd been nicknamed 'Tokey' as the potential lynchpin of City's sustained scrap for League honours. Johnny responded with both goals and graft as City missed promotion on goal average at the end of his first season (when he was ever-present for all but the final, crucial defeat at Bury), and was to parade his playmaking skills for five campaigns in the First Division after he'd finally chivvied City up in 1925. That term he'd added 30 League goals to Arthur Chandler's 32, and had become the first scorer of six goals in a single game for the club as they pasted Port Vale 7-0 on Christmas Day. The inevitable, well-merited Scottish cap came in October 1925, with Johnny scoring the opening goal against Wales, but inexplicably it wasn't followed by subsequent selections. The maestro eventually retreated into the half-back line, the better to orchestrate City's championship assaults, and indeed had lost little effectiveness when, in 1930, he found himself at loggerheads with the City directors over their refusal to sanction his running a pub. Over this point of principle, the Turk's Head on Welford Road acquired a genial landlord, and City lost one of their greats - though Johnny's footballing intelligence couldn't be allowed to idle for too long. His pub gained repute

Johnny Duncan

as a football-talk 'academy', Johnny became a founder committee-member of the City Supporters' Club in August 1940, and then, in March 1946, it was to Johnny that City turned for a manager to succeed Tom Bromilow and prepare the club for the return to League football. Three years later, it was he who proudly led out his Second Division team at Wembley. Unfortunately, another argument with the board occurred in October 1949 and, with the same principled abruptness, Johnny returned to his pumps. Something of the man's managerial character is affectionately sketched in Don Revie's 1955 autobiography; but it is in City's cherished reputation over the years as a 'footballing' side wherein resides the best testimony to the influence of Johnny's playing personality. Only one confirmatory quote needs be adduced in support of this contention; from the *Sunday Express*'s 'Man In The Corner' at the end of the 1928/9 season: "The best football team have been Leicester City, who have approached nearer to the pre-war standard than any other in individuality and constructive cleverness. I attribute this largely to the influence of their Scottish captain, John Duncan, who has insisted that the way to success was by expert use of the ball rather than by helter skelter methods."

JOHN DUNCAN
LEICESTER CITY

Appearances:
FL: 279 apps. 88 gls.
FAC: 16 apps. 7 gls.
Total: *295 apps. 95 gls.*

DUNCAN, Thomas Grossett

Role: Outside right
b. Lochgelly, Fife, 1st September 1901
d. Leicester, 9th February 1940

CAREER: Lochgelly United/ 1920:Raith Rovers/July 1922: CITY/Sept 1924:Halifax Town/ May 1926:Bristol Rovers/ cs 1927:Kettering Town.

Debut v Rotherham County (A) 4.9.22

Tom Duncan

For some time the right-flank partner to his elder brother Johnny at both Raith and Leicester, Tom had nothing like as illustrious a career, but was somewhat unlucky to be in direct competition for the City winger's role with Hughie Adcock, and then to find his more delicate skills a little overwhelmed by the harsher rigours of Third Division soccer. Tom nonetheless notched 7 goals in 45 games at that level. His daughter Elsie married Don Revie.

Appearances:
FL: 41 apps. 6 gls.
FAC: 1 app. 0 gls.
Total: *42 apps. 6 gls.*

DUNKLEY, Albert E.

Role: Outside left
b. Northampton, 1877

Albert Dunkley

CAREER: Earls Barton/1897:Northampton Town/May 1900:FOSSE/Feb 1901: Northampton Town/cs 1901:New Brompton/ May 1903:Blackburn Rovers/cs 1904:Bristol Rovers/Aug 1906:Blackpool.

Debut v Stockport County (H) 1.9.1900

Outside-left in the first side ever fielded by Northampton, and top scorer in their initial competitive season (in the Northants League), Albert had only a brief liaison with Fosse, moving back home almost immediately after surrendering his left-wing spot to Tommy Allsopp, and then building quite a reputation as a nomad. He won a Southern League championship medal in his first season with Bristol Rovers, playing alongside future Fossils Willie Clark and Dick Pudan.

Appearances:
FL: 10 apps. 0 gls.
FAC: 1 app. 0 gls.
Total: *11 apps. 0 gls.*

DUNNE, James Peter

Role: Inside left
b. Dublin, 16th March 1935

CAREER: Sept 1953:CITY/cs 1956:St.Patrick's Athletic/July 1959:Peterborough United/cs 1962:Bedford Town/cs 1963:Cambridge United.

Debut v Sheffield Wednesday (A) 16.4.55

A young Irish inside-left who briefly deputised for Arthur Rowley, but never found himself on a winning City side at senior level, Jimmy nonetheless shared in FAI Cup glory with St.Patrick's in 1959. He later managed a further quartet of League outings for Posh after their 1960 election. Some Irish sources claim him as brother to Tommy (see right), but such kinship never seemed to have been commented on in the Leicester press.

Appearances:
FL: 4 apps. 0 gls.
Total: *4 apps. 0 gls.*

Jimmy Dunne

DUNNE, Thomas

Role: Wing half
b. Dublin, 19th March 1927
d. Fazackerley, Lancs, 23rd January 1988

CAREER: Home Farm/St.Patrick's Athletic/1945:Shamrock Rovers/Nov 1949:CITY/July 1954:Exeter City/Aug 1956:Shrewsbury Town/July 1957:Southport.

Debut v Cardiff City (A) 17.2.51

Tommy Dunne

DURRANT, Arthur Francis (Jamie)

Role: Outside right
b. Luton, 1878
d. Luton, 6th April 1927

CAREER: Luton Stanley/Mar 1898:Luton Town/May 1904:FOSSE/Sept 1909:Leyton/cs 1913:Luton Town.

Debut v Blackpool (A) 3.9.04

The epitome of the orthodox outside-right, rarely wandering from his narrow corridor of operation, but patrolling it with pace and a rich repertoire of trickery, Jamie gave Fosse five seasons of valuable service, culminating in the rollercoaster experience of successive promotion and relegation. At Luton, he had learned good footballing habits from Jimmy Blessington, who he followed to Filbert Street, while later, as a senior player at Southern League Leyton, he was in turn mentor to the young Charles Buchan, who acknowledged the debt he owed Jamie in his autobiography. It was another contemporary, however, who came up with the rather fanciful description of how Jamie 'ran with amazing speed in a soft-footed manner reminiscent of a wolf'!

Appearances:
FL: 140 apps. 24 gls.
FAC: 13 apps. 3 gls.
Total: *153 apps. 27 gls.*

Having followed his Shamrock team-mate, international keeper Tommy Godwin, to Leicester, wing-half Tommy had to wait somewhat longer for a first team breakthrough as the City management passed into the hands of Norman Bullock, and had to content himself with becoming the sure-shot penalty expert of the Football Combination. Though he eventually displaced Johnny King to claim the No.6 shirt for a fair run of Second Division games in 1953, he lost out himself to newcomer Eddie Russell midway through the 1954 promotion campaign. A son of the former Sheffield United, Arsenal, Southampton and Ireland goalscorer Jimmy Dunne, Tommy managed a further 61 League outings for his three subsequent clubs (scoring once for Exeter), and later became a Southport licensee.

Appearances:
FL: 33 apps. 0 gls.
FAC: 1 app. 0 gls.
Total: *34 apps. 0 gls.*

EARLE, Stephen John

Role: Striker
b. Feltham, Middlesex, 1st November 1945

CAREER: pro Nov 1963:Fulham/Nov 1973:
CITY/(Nov 1977-loan-Peterborough United)/
Mar 1978:Detroit Express/July 1978:Tulsa
Roughnecks/Oct 1978:Telford United/
Mar 1979:Tulsa Roughnecks/1981:Wichita.

Debut v Tottenham Hotspur (H) 1.12.73
(scored once)

A prolific scorer in three Divisions for Fulham
(his 98 League goals for them included a
hat-trick in the 1966 relegation decider at
Northampton, and a personal nap-hand at
Halifax in September 1969), Steve was also a
one-time striking partner of Allan Clarke, and
was bought for £100,000 by Jimmy Bloomfield
to lift some of the scoring burden from Frank
Worthington. After helping City dispose of his
former club on the way to the 1974 FA Cup
semi-final in his first season, unselfish front-
runner Steve ironically then suffered
something of a goal drought himself, and was
displaced for a spell by Chris Garland, before
returning to hit 13 goals in 1976/7. He took a
belated Craven Cottage testimonial (Fulham
v.City) in October 1975, and in 1979 returned
to Filbert Street with his second NASL club for
a friendly.

Appearances:
FL: 91(8) apps. 20 gls.
FAC: 13 apps. 6 gls.
LC: 3 apps. 0 gls.
Total: *107 (8) apps. 26 gls.*

EASTOE, Peter Robert

Role: Striker
b. Tamworth, Staffs, 2nd August 1953

CAREER: June 1971:Wolverhampton
Wanderers/Nov 1973:Swindon Town/
Mar 1976:Queen's Park Rangers/Mar 1979:
Everton/Aug 1982:West Bromwich Albion/
(Oct 1983-loan-CITY)/(Mar 1984-loan-
Huddersfield Town)/(Aug 1984-loan-Walsall)/
(Oct 1984-loan-CITY)/(Feb 1985-loan-
Wolverhampton Wanderers)/July 1985:
Sporting Farense/1986:not known/cs 1988:
Atherstone United/1989:Bridgnorth Town/
Nov 1991:Alvechurch (p/mgr).

Debut v Norwich City (A) 19.10.83 (scored once)

A much-travelled
striker taken twice
on loan by City
from West Brom,
largely to support
Gary Lineker
during Alan Smith's then-annual slow start to
the season, Peter actually made his Filbert
Street bow in the game with Southampton
which was abandoned during a torrential
downpour. He proceeded to make a good
impression, but then suffered a double fracture
of the jaw in a game against Manchester
United. Adept at shielding and laying off the
ball in attack, Peter had suffered a diminishing
goal rate since his time at Swindon, but his
second goal for City - in the first match of his
second spell, a 5-0 win over Aston Villa - was
the 95th League strike of his career. He had
played in European competitions for three of

Steve Earle

Peter Eastoe

his clubs, and extended his career in Portugal after a remarkable total of five loan-outs from the Hawthorns. In 1993 Peter had a brief spell as assistant manager of Nuneaton Borough.

Appearances:
FL: 11 apps. 2 gls.
LC: 1 app. 0 gls.
Total: *12 apps. 2 gls.*

EATON, Samuel Llewellyn

Role: Forward
b. Derby, 1878

CAREER: Derby St.James/1895:Derby County/ 1897:Hinckley Town/Jan 1898:FOSSE/Aug 1900:Hinckley Town/June 1901:Stockport County/Jan 1902:FOSSE/cs 1903:Luton Town/ May 1905:Watford/cs 1906:Earlestown/ Oct 1906:Accrington Stanley/Dec 1906: Maidstone United.

Debut v Lincoln City (H) 12.2.1898

Unblooded at Derby, where he served a junior

apprenticeship to Steve Bloomer, Sam shuttled between the outside- and inside-right slots for over two seasons after his teenage Fosse debut, and then returned to the squad shortly after revisiting Filbert Street as a Stockport winger. Neither Luton nor Watford were setting alight the upper division of the Southern League when Sam was associated with them, and there is little evidence to indicate that his early promise was borne out in subsequent brief stints in the Lancashire Combination and Kent League.

Sam Eaton

Appearances:
FL: 52 apps. 12 gls.
FAC: 5 apps. 1 gl.
Total: *57 apps. 13 gls.*

ECCLES, Peter Edward

Role: Centre back
b. Dublin, 24th August 1962

CAREER: St.Brendan's (Cabra)/ 1981: Shamrock Rovers/Aug 1988:Kingston Olympic/Oct 1988:Dundalk/Oct 1988:CITY/ (Jan 1989-loan-Stafford Rangers)/ cs 1989: Dundalk/Oct 1989:Shamrock Rovers.

Debut v Blackburn Rovers (A) 8.4.89

Peter Eccles (right), signs for David Pleat.

A tall central defender who had won a fistful of League of Ireland championship and FAI Cup medals with Shamrock, and made an international appearance as substitute for the Republic against Uruguay in 1986 (alongside Gerry Daly, David Langan and clubmate Pat Byrne), Peter joined City on a free transfer shortly after returning from a summer stint in Australian football. He received some fine notices for his Central League performances, and earned a belated senior call-up in place of the injured Steve Walsh, but was unfortunately somewhat embarrassed by the pace of his sole Second Division sortie (being substituted at half-time), and was released by David Pleat in May 1989. Soon back with his beloved Shamrock, he was voted their Player of the Year in 1993.

Appearances:
FL: 1 app. 0 gls.
Total: *1 app. 0 gls.*

EDMUNDS, Paul

Role: Outside right
b. Doncaster, 2nd December 1957

CAREER: Troston Welfare/pro Apr 1979: CITY/May 1981:Bournemouth/cs 1982:Bentley Victoria/Grantham/1985:Burton Albion/ Armthorpe Welfare.

Debut v Sunderland (A) 8.3.80

All but one of Paul's League appearances were made in promotion seasons. The red-haired right winger contributed two cracking individual goals as a latecomer to City's 1980 Second Division championship effort before breaking his wrist at Wrexham, but played again for Jock Wallace only in the initial top-flight game of the following season. Then, at Bournemouth, his fourteen games helped the Cherries out of the Fourth Division in 1982, but failed to gain him a contract renewal. A qualified schoolteacher, Paul continued to play on a part-time basis in non-league football for a while, but has gained greater repute as manager/coach of the successful women's soccer team, Doncaster Belles, for whom his wife has been a squad member.

Appearances:
FL: 8 apps. 2 gls.
Total: *8 apps. 2 gls.*

EDWARDS, Harry Ross

Role: Inside right
b. Coventry, 1870

CAREER: Singers/May 1892:Small Heath/ Aug 1893:Ryton Rovers/Oct 1893:FOSSE/ Aug 1894:Derby County/1895:Wolverton L.& N.W.R./Dec 1898:Watford/cs 1899:Bedford Queens.

Debut v Mansfield Town (H) ML 21.10.1893 (scored once)

Briefly renewing acquaintance with old Singers team-mate Billy Dorrell during Fosse's final Midland League season, Harry was a constructive inside-right who had joined Small Heath for their initial Second Division campaign. At Derby he failed to make a competitive appearance (despite turning out as attack leader against Fosse in the opening friendly of 1894/5), but Wolverton were still a force in Southern League football when he joined them as an attacking centre-half. Watford were in their first season under that title (previously having been known as West Herts) when Harry assisted them.

Appearances:
FAC: 6 apps. 0 gls.
ML: 12 apps. 2 gls.
Total: *18 apps. 2 gls.*

Paul Edmunds

Les Edwards

EDWARDS, Leslie

Role: Right half
b. Nuneaton, Warks, Oct qtr 1910

CAREER: Bradbury's FC (Hinckley)/Dec 1930:CITY/May 1932:Folkestone Town/May 1933:Crystal Palace/May 1936:Newport County/cs 1938:Hinckley United.

Debut v Blackburn Rovers (A) 12.12.31

A right-half who played his trio of City games away from home, and had the misfortune to make his debut in a 0-6 thrashing, Les at least managed to tot up 65 League appearances for his two Third Division (South) clubs; at one point skippering Newport. He also guested during WW2 for Reading, and it is suspected that he may have returned to Folkestone on loan in the middle of his Selhurst stint, and helped them to the Final of the inaugural (1934/5) Southern League Cup. A Football League ledger from the time of his City spell has him listed as Leonard Edwards.

Appearances:
FL: 3 apps. 0 gls.
Total: *3 apps. 0 gls.*

EDWARDS, Walter Thomas

Role: Outside left
b. Llanelli, 13th March 1923

CAREER: Workington/Aug 1946:Fulham/ Mar 1948:Southend United/Dec 1948:CITY/ cs 1949:Bath City/May 1952:Walsall/ cs 1953:Oswestry Town.

Debut v Leeds United (A) 18.12.48 (scored once)

Another hapless pretender to Charlie Adam's first team No.11 shirt, freed by Johnny Duncan after only five months on City's books, Tommy had previously played in only two League games and one Cup-tie for Fulham, and had notched a single goal in eleven outings for Southend. He had barely left Filbert Street before another Walter Edwards, also an outside-left, signed for City from Leeds United; but this latter who had also previously featured for Mansfield Town failed to make a League breakthrough at all during his year with the club.

Appearances:
FL: 3 apps. 1 gl.
Total: *3 apps. 1 gl.*

EGGLESTON, Thomas

Role: Left half
b. Mitcham, Surrey, 21st February 1920

CAREER: am Dec 1936/pro Feb 1937:Derby County/July 1946:CITY/Jan 1948:Watford.

Debut v Manchester City (H) 31.8.46

Though wartime Royal Navy service left him short of senior playing experience (he had guested for Southampton, Coventry and Lincoln, and was an emergency choice for one of the ties which saw Derby through to the 1946 FA Cup Final), Tommy became City's regular left-half in the first postwar League season. He lost his battle for selection against John King, however, early in 1947/8, and became part of the remarkable five-man transfer to Vicarage Road, where he was to make 177 League appearances before retirement. Tommy nonetheless stayed in the game until his pension book became due: coaching at Brentford, Watford, Sheffield Wednesday and Everton; managing Mansfield Town and Greek clubs Ethnikos and Panahaiki; and acting as physiotherapist to

Plymouth Argyle and Ipswich Town. He lives in retirement in Tockwith, Yorkshire.

Appearances:
FL 34 apps. 2 gls.
Total: *34 apps. 2 gls.*

ENGLISH, Thomas Steven

Role: Striker / Midfield
b. Cirencester, Glos, 18th October 1961

CAREER: June 1979:Coventry City/Sept 1982: CITY/Aug 1984:Rochdale/Sept 1984: Plymouth Argyle/Nov 1984:Colchester United/ cs 1985:Canberra City Olympians/Sept 1985: Colchester United/cs 1987:Wealdstone/ cs 1988:Bishops Stortford/Oct 1989:Colchester United/cs 1990:Happy Valley (HK)/Aug 1991: Crawley Town/Oct 1991:Wivenhoe/ 1992:Bishops Stortford.

Debut v Blackburn Rovers (A) 18.9.82

An England Youth international forward upgraded from his Highfield Road apprenticeship by Gordon Milne, Tom struck an early League scoring partnership with Mark Hateley, and managed a hat-trick against City in March 1981. However, he was dogged with domestic troubles which unfortunately continued to distract him after a controversial move to Filbert Street, when Milne acquired him in a straight swap deal for popular Jim

Melrose. Tom failed to impress an accordingly highly critical Leicester crowd, despite his contribution to the 1983 promotion effort, and despite an eventual move from the firing line into a deeper midfield role. Upon his release, he played for three clubs in a season on a

Tommy Eggleston

Tommy English

non-contract basis, spent a summer in Australia, and then returned to Colchester to play regularly alongside his younger brother, Tony. In a rare occurrence in 1985/6, both brothers were sent off during a match at Crewe.

Appearances:
FL: 29 (15) apps. 3 gls.
FAC: 0 (1) app. 0 gls.
LC: 2 (1) apps. 1 gl.
Total: *31 (17) apps. 4 gls.*

ESSOM, Walter

Role: Left back
b. Leicester, Oct qtr 1895
d. Hitchin, Herts, Jan qtr 1966

CAREER: Leicester Imperial/cs 1919:CITY/ cs 1920:Ashby Town.

Debut v Fulham (H) 13.9.19

A local left-back who briefly displaced Sam Currie to play in the successive home and away fixtures with Fulham in 1919/20. Walter, whose family were hoteliers in Ashby, skippered the local Town side to the Leicestershire Senior League championship in 1924 (that club's only such honour).

Appearances:
FL: 2 apps. 0 gls.
Total: *2 apps. 0 gls.*

EUSTACE, Scott Douglas

Role: Defender
b. Leicester, 13th June 1975

CAREER: YT Aug 1991/ pro July 1993:CITY/ (Nov 1994-loan-Shelbourne)/June 1995: Mansfield Town.

Debut v Bristol City (H) 11.12.93 (sub)

A tall central defender who had come through his traineeship to feature in 21 Central League games prior to his short, but utterly composed, debut as substitute for Gary

Scott Eustace

Coatsworth during a 3-0 home win. Scott added to his experience with a month in the League of Ireland, but was a victim of Mark McGhee's evident need to whittle down the size of his professional squad when freed in May 1995.

Appearances:
FL: 0 (1) app. 0 gls.
Total: *0 (1) app. 0 gls.*

EVANS, Allan James

Role: Centre back
b. Polbeth, West Lothian, 12th October 1956

CAREER: Dunfermline United/cs 1973: Dunfermline Athletic/May 1977:Aston Villa/ Aug 1989:CITY/May 1990:Victoria Vistas [Vancouver] (p/coach)/1990:Brisbane United (p/coach)/March 1991:Darlington/May 1991: CITY (p/coach).

Debut v Hull City (A) 19.8.89

Given a free transfer by Villa in recognition of his outstanding twelve-year service, Allan initially joined City to steady the back four, but proved every bit as prone to costly errors as his more junior defensive colleagues while the team plummeted unexpectedly to the Second Division depths. Essentially, and sadly, it was a case of the central defender appearing to have lost the requisite pace by the time he first drew in a blue shirt, and for much of his Filbert Street season he had to take on the less demanding task of anchoring the Central League side, before setting himself up for what looked likely to be a playing swansong in Canada and Australia. Allan's surprising return to the League sphere - albeit for only four minutes of competitive action as a Darlington sub - reunited him with one-time Villa team mate Brian Little as the latter helmed the Feethams

prowess and speedy covering helped inspire Villa to win both the Championship in 1981 and the European Cup the following year. Picking up four Scotland caps (the last in the World Cup Finals of 1982), he later assumed his club's captaincy, and also experienced successive relegation and promotion seasons during his 469-game, 60-goal Villa Park tenure.

Appearances:
FL: 14 apps. 0 gls.
LC: 2 apps. 0 gls.
Total: *16 apps. 0 gls.*

EVENSON, Isaac

Role: Inside left
b. Manchester, November 1882
d. 1954

CAREER: Tonge/Apr 1901:Stockport County/ July 1903:FOSSE/July 1905:Clapton Orient/ Apr 1907:West Bromwich Albion/May 1908: Plymouth Argyle.

Debut v Barnsley (A) 5.9.03

Ike Evenson

Former player Allan Evans had a 100% record as City's caretaker manager.

side to the Division Four championship; and when Little moved to the City boss's chair, Allan became the first recruit to his coaching staff, as well as a buttressing force for the Reserves' successful promotion bid. In November 1994, caught up in the acrimony surrounding Little's departure, he actually took the caretaker manager's role for a midweek Premiership home win over Arsenal, but resigned two days later and was soon, predictably, re-united with Little as Assistant Manager at Villa Park. Allan's top-level career had started in a uniquely unsettling manner back in 1973/4, when, as a 16-year-old amateur, he broke his leg during his Dunfermline debut game against Rangers. He bounced back, however, to star for the Pars as both a central defender and an out-and-out striker and, following his move southwards, he indeed made his delayed League bow for Villa in the No.7 shirt against Leicester, shortly after a 6-goal reserve-team performance. It was from the pivotal defensive berth, though, that Allan's aerial

Signed as a centre-forward by Fosse, but settling at inside-left, Ike was one of the few successes of the disastrous 1903/4 season, finishing as top scorer and remaining to help lift the re-elected club a few rungs up the Second Division ladder the following year. In March 1905 he was, along with Bob Pollock, one of two Fossils sent off at Bolton in a match which 8-man Fosse (Archie Hubbard was stretchered off!) won 1-0. Having previously been Stockport's top scorer in their first season playing at Edgeley Park (1902/3; also a re-election term; as in fact had been County's prior two campaigns!), Ike subsequently moved on to assist Orient in their first-ever League campaign, and even took on the additional responsibility of caretaker team managership of that financially-ailing club for three months in 1906; while on his later travels he became better known as a middle-line schemer than as a spearhead.

Appearances:
FL: 42 apps. 14 gls.
FAC: 10 apps. 6 gls.
Total: *52 apps. 20 gls.*

FARMER, John

Role: Goalkeeper
b. Biddulph, Staffs,
31st August 1947

CAREER: Chatterley BC/
Jan 1965:Stoke City/(July
1972-loan-West Bromwich
Albion)/(Dec 1974-loan-
CITY)/cs 1976:Northwich
Victoria.

Debut v Everton (H) 7.12.74

Despite managing 163 League
games in goal for Stoke and
winning himself England
Under-23 recognition, John
spent much of his Victoria
Ground career in the shadow
of Gordon Banks, and was
just having to come to terms
with the start of another spell
as understudy - this time to
Peter Shilton - when he
answered the call to alleviate
a City goalkeeping emer-
gency. With Mark Wallington
injured and Carl Jayes as yet
inexperienced, John was a

John Farmer

Kevin Farmer

decidedly classy stopgap, but ironically he
was injured himself in his second match (at
Middlesbrough), and returned to Stoke just as
Wallington embarked on his monumental
record of consecutive City appearances. John's
earlier loan spell, at West Brom, had been
somewhat more leisurely: consisting of three
friendly matches on a Swedish tour. He now
manages a crisp factory at Cheadle.

> **Appearances:**
> *FL: 2 apps. 0 gls.*
> **Total:** *2 apps. 0 gls.*

FARMER, Kevin John

Role: Striker
b. Ramsgate, Kent, 24th January 1960

CAREER: app July 1976/pro Oct 1977:CITY/
Aug 1979:Northampton Town/
cs 1982: Bedworth.

Debut v Ipswich Town (A) 17.12.77

City were anchored to the bottom of the First
Division when Frank McLintock threw both

Kevin and Mark Goodwin into the limelight at Ipswich, and for the young striker the 0-1 defeat was his sole opportunity in the first team. Grandson of a QPR director, Kevin was released by Jock Wallace and went on to make 77 League appearances (scoring 12 goals) in three seasons with the Cobblers, whom he represented at centre-back as well as up front. He was later involved with Senior League outfit Kirby Muxloe, and in 1989 assumed the manager's role with Melton Town.

Appearances:
FL: 1 app. 0 gls.
Total: *1 app. 0 gls.*

FARRINGTON, John Robert

Role: Outside right
b. Lynemouth, Northumberland, 19th June 1947

CAREER:
app Sept 1963/pro June 1965: Wolverhampton Wanderers/ Oct 1969:CITY/ Nov 1973:Cardiff City/ Oct 1974:Northampton Town/cs 1980:AP Leamington/Shepshed Charterhouse.

Debut v Bristol City (H) 18.10.69

A direct right-winger who made his Molineux debut whilst still an apprentice, and later laid on several goals there for Derek Dougan, John was a £30,000 Frank O'Farrell purchase who started as he meant to go on, providing a pinpoint centre for Rodney Fern's goal in his first City match, and soon assisting materially in the 1971 Second Division championship campaign. With John on the right and Len Glover on the left, City's quick-break style was based on an attack of genuine width and pace, and the Northumbrian pigeon-fancier's finishing

John Farrington

wasn't bad, either, with some of his best goals reserved for the Cup competitions. O'Farrell called back for John when attempting to keep Cardiff out of the Third Division, and the winger managed a valuable League hat-trick, a Welsh Cup Final appearance and a European game during his short spell at Ninian Park. Then former City coach Bill Dodgin took him to Northampton, where a 232-game spell as schemer ended his 15-year League career. John also briefly managed AP Leamington before that club's demise; while in January 1992, after a long-term coaching spell, he took over the boss's role at Barlestone St.Giles.

Appearances:
FL: 115 (3) apps. 18 gls.
FAC: 16 apps. 6 gls.
LC: 9 (2) apps. 3 gls.
Total:
140 (5) apps. 27 gls.

FEELEY, Andrew James

Role: Midfield / Full back
b. Hereford, 30th September 1961

CAREER: app 1978/ pro Aug 1979:Hereford United/(Mar 1980-loan-Chelsea)/cs 1980: Trowbridge Town/ Jan 1984:CITY/July 1987: Brentford/June 1989: Bury/Aug 1991:Atherton Laburnam Rovers/Nov 1991:Northwich Victoria/ cs 1992:Atherton Laburnam Rovers.

Debut v Manchester United (A) 10.3.84

Andy made his Hereford debut while still an apprentice midfielder, and entered the record books at the age of 17 as the youngest-ever captain of a League team. However, a succession of disciplinary and injury problems led to him dropping into the non-league sphere after 51 games, while still in his 'teens. City were the third League club to offer him another chance - partly on the recommendation of former Trowbridge boss Alan Birchenall - and Andy's Old Trafford baptism showed the value of their investment in his tigerish tackling and committed attitude, which soon led to his establishment as a popular regular at right-back. His uncomplicated spirit and application would have been useful to City's cause in the relegation year of 1987, but injury again sidelined him at a crucial stage, and when he refused new contract terms he was allowed to move on to Griffin Park as a free agent. Later,

Andy Feeley

at Gigg Lane, Andy scored his first League goal in over ten years as Bury made the first of two successive (unsuccessful) forays into the Third Division Play-offs; then in both 1993 and 1994 (while working as a prison officer in a unit for the criminally insane) he was a key member of the Atherton LR championship side in the Bass NW Counties League.

Appearances:
FL: 74 (2) apps. 0 gls.
FAC: 6 apps. 0 gls.
LC: 4 apps. 0 gls.
Total: *84 (2) apps. 0 gls.*

FENWICK, Terence William

Role: Centre back
b. Seaham, Co.Durham, 17th November 1959

CAREER: app/pro Dec 1976:Crystal Palace/ Dec 1980:Queen's Park Rangers/Dec 1987: Tottenham Hotspur/(Oct 1990-loan-CITY)/ Aug 1993:Swindon Town/Feb 1995: Portsmouth (p/mgr).
Debut v Ipswich Town (H) 27.10.90

Out of the Spurs side for a year after breaking his leg, experienced defender Terry was loaned to City both to prove his match fitness and to shore up a regularly crumbling Filbert Street rearguard, and stayed for two months in hardly more secure centre-back pairings with Steve Walsh or Tony James before recall to White Hart Lane. Ironically, he had only then been back in the Spurs starting line-up for a matter of weeks when, in a freak accident, he broke an ankle during the warm-up for a Cup-tie at Portsmouth; while a further setback lay in wait following recovery, for in September 1991 Terry was jailed for motoring offences. Previously, and in contrast, he had been something of a lucky mascot for Terry Venables, who nurtured his early career at Selhurst and then purchased him expensively for each of QPR and Spurs. As a teenager, Terry scored the winning goal in each of the FA Youth Cup Finals of 1977 and 1978; and his later honours list was substantial: playing in Division Two championship sides at both Palace and QPR (where he partnered Bob Hazell and backed up Tony Sealy); featuring in losing Rangers sides at Wembley in each of the FA Cup (when he scored in the first drawn game of 1982) and League Cup; and being capped 20 times at full England level

Terry Fenwick

Debut v Leeds United (H) 3.2.68

A popular utility forward who mixed flashes of creative inspiration with moments of almost endearing clumsiness, Rodney was given his first-team break by coach Bert Johnson (while Matt Gillies was on sick leave), and played out his first season in an unlikely-looking but effective striking partnership with Frank Large. It was Rodney's 44th-minute goal, in only his third game, which prompted City's hoodoo-breaking FA Cup fightback against Manchester City in 1968 (when a 0-2 deficit was turned into 4-3 victory on a night of pulsating drama), and indeed it was the Cup which regularly brought the best out of him. The 6th Round winner at Mansfield helped City towards Wembley in 1969, while his headed 'goal' at Arsenal in 1971 might have opened the way to another medal for Rodney had it not been so controversially disallowed.

following Youth and Under-21 representation. Terry was in the Swindon squad relegated from the Premiership in 1994; while his first managerial appointment came when Jim Smith departed Fratton Park in the wake of Leicester's FA Cup win over Portsmouth.

Appearances:
FL: 8 apps. 1 gl.
FMC: 1 app. 0 gls.
Total: *9 apps. 1 gl.*

FERN, Rodney Alan

Role: Striker
b. Burton-on-Trent, 13th December 1948

CAREER: Measham SW/Dec 1966:CITY/ June 1972:Luton Town/(Jan 1973-loan-Coventry City)/July 1975:Chesterfield/ June 1979: Rotherham United.

Rodney Fern

He was City's top scorer in 1969/70 (when he got off the mark with a spectacular overhead kick in the opening fixture against Birmingham), but it was a superb playmaking performance in the crucial Easter game at Luton in the next promotion campaign which probably earned Rodney his later £45,000 move to Kenilworth Road. He had a mixed time there until the goal ratio increased again at Chesterfield, but it was as a veteran at Rotherham - using his (now-balding) head to save his legs, and still striking regularly - that he enjoyed renewed success: twice embarrassing City in the 1979 League Cup and winning a Third Division championship medal in 1981. He retired in 1983, with a career aggregate of 124 League goals, to concentrate on the running of a pub in Lount, though he has subsequently established himself as a coal merchant back in Measham.

Appearances:
FL: 133 (19) apps. 32 gls.
FAC: 22 (1) apps. 5 gls.
LC: 12 apps. 3 gls.
Total: *167 (20) apps. 40 gls.*

FINCHAM, Gordon Richard

Role: Centre half
b. Peterborough, 8th January 1935

CAREER: Fletton/Nov 1952:CITY/June 1958:Plymouth Argyle/July 1963:Luton Town.
Debut v Rotherham United (A) 6.4.53

Good judges rated Gordon one of the most highly-promising centre-halves City had ever had, but after learning his trade as understudy to Matt Gillies and claiming a regular first-team spot in 1955/6, he was stricken by serious injuries, and only managed one subsequent League appearance for the club, with Tony Knapp and Ian King vaulting over him in the queue. Gordon was able, however, to partially rebuild his career at Plymouth (Third Division champions in his first season), and played many games there alongside former Filbert Street club-mates Dave MacLaren and John Newman. After leaving Luton, he emigrated to South Africa.

Appearances:
FL: 50 apps. 0 gls.
FAC: 4 apps. 0 gls.
Total: *54 apps. 0 gls.*

FINDLAY, William

Role: Wing half
b. Wishaw, Lanarkshire, 17th February 1900
d. Braunstone, Leicester, 11th June 1949

CAREER: 1922:Musselburgh Bruntonians/ June 1923:Third Lanark/Aug 1924:Liverpool/ May 1925:CITY/June 1932:Watford.
Debut v Newcastle United (A) 19.9.25

A Scottish wing-half who provided valuable cover for City over seven First Division seasons, playing in a third of the League games during that period (and representing the London Combination against the London League at Highbury in March 1927, alongside George Carr), Billy doggedly refused to be overawed at the prospect of substituting for the likes of internationals Johnny Duncan, Jack Bamber or Sid Bishop. A member of Musselburgh's Scottish Junior Cup Final side of 1923 (from which City signed match-winning forward Archie Waterston directly), he had been unable to make a first-team breakthrough at Anfield; while on leaving City Billy played for five years at Vicarage Road and then took over the Watford manager's

Gordon Fincham

Billy Findlay

Gary Fitzpatrick

chair for just short of a decade. A qualified physiotherapist and an elder of the Presbyterian Church, he was manager of Edgware Town at the time of his death.

Appearances:
FL: 100 apps. 0 gls.
FAC: 4 apps. 0 gls.
Total: *104 app. 0 gls*

FITZPATRICK, Gary Gerard

Role: Forward
b. Birmingham, 5th August 1971

CAREER: YT 1988/pro Jan 1990:CITY/ cs 1991:VS Rugby/Mar 1993:Moor Green/May 1993:(Swedish football)/Oct 1993:Hednesford Town.

Debut v Sheffield United (H) 5.5.90 (sub)

A fifteen-goal haul for the Youth team during 1989/90 won winger Gary a final-game elevation to the senior bench, and a brief appearance alongside cousin David Kelly in what had already turned into a Blades promotion party. The following term the Irish Youth cap was unable to maintain his progress in a struggling Central League side (even though called up for an eventually-postponed Under-

19 international), and was released in the initial clear-out following City's last-gasp escape from relegation to the Third. Gary made an immediate mark for Rugby, scoring the winner against a Manchester United XI in a pre-season testimonial game, but subsequent interest from League scouts failed to produce a solid offer. At the end of 1994/5, Gary was celebrating Hednesford's promotion to the Conference as Beazer Homes League Champions, and his own feat of scoring for them the final goal at their old Cross Keys ground.

Appearances:
FL: 0 (1) app. 0 gls.
Total: *0 (1) app. 0 gls.*

FITZPATRICK, Paul James

Role: Defender / Midfield
b. Liverpool, 5th October 1965

CAREER: Tranmere Rovers (non-contract)/ Liverpool (n/c)/Preston North End (n/c)/ Mar 1985:Bolton Wanderers/Aug 1986:Bristol City/Oct 1988:Carlisle United/(Dec 1988-loan-Preston North End)/June 1991:CITY/ Jan 1993: Birmingham City/(Mar 1993-loan-Bury)/(July 1993-trials-Shrewsbury Town)/

Sept 1993:Hamilton Academical/Feb 1994:
Northampton Town/1994:(Hong Kong
football)/Dec 1994:Rushden & Diamonds/
Jan 1995:Leicester United.

Debut v Swindon Town (A) 17.8.91

A distinctly versatile performer whose 6ft.4in.
presence was valued in various positional
roles, Paul made his belated League bow as a
Bolton full-back in May 1985, had spells both
in midfield and as a target-man at Ashton
Gate, and shone defensively for Carlisle. Brian
Little's first purchase for City, at a modest
£40,000, Paul continued to have his
adaptability exploited for tactical ends, being
principally utilised as a sweeper or third
centre-back, but demonstrating a cool ease on
the ball when moving forward. Several of his
interventions in the opposition box bore
goalscoring fruit, and his extra-time diving
header at a sodden Meadow Lane in the ZDS
Cup remains especially memorable. Barely
given a break in 1992/3, however, when
competition for rearguard shirts was fierce,
Paul took a free transfer to St.Andrews to bid -
in vain, as it turned out - for regular first-team
football.

Appearances:
FL: 21 (6) apps. 4 gls.
FAC: 1 app. 0 gls.
LC: 2 apps. 0 gls.
FMC: 3 (2) apps. 1 gl.
AIC: 0 (1) app. 0 gls.
Total: *27 (9) apps. 5 gls.*

Paul
Fitzpatrick

FLANAGAN, William

Role: Inside forward
b. Birmingham, c 1876

CAREER: Smethwick Carriage Works/
Oldbury Town/Aston Villa Reserves/
Oct 1896:Burton Wanderers/Aug 1897:FOSSE/
1898:Glentoran/Oct 1900:Morton/1901:Port
Glasgow Athletic.

Debut v Burton Swifts (A) 27.11.1897

An inside-forward who had scored only once
in nine Second Division games at Derby Turn,
in Burton Wanderers' final season in the
League, William got even fewer chances to
impress after joining Fosse, who released him
before the season was out. Glentoran reached
the Irish Cup Final in 1899, but there was no
sign of William in their line-up; and he
appears to have made but a handful of
Scottish League appearances for his two
Clydeside clubs.

Appearances:
FL: 4 apps. 0 gls.
Total: *4 apps. 0 gls.*

FLETCHER, Thomas

Role: Forward
b. Heanor, Derbyshire, 15th June 1881
d. Derby, 29th September 1954

CAREER: Hill's Ivanhoe/Derby Nomads/
Apr 1902:FOSSE/Nov 1904:Derby County.

Debut v Doncaster Rovers (A) 12.4.02
(scored once)

An amateur forward who first turned out for
Fosse, along with his brother, in Billy Dorrell's
testimonial friendly against the Corinthians at
Christmas 1898, Tommy then made sporadic
senior appearances at either inside- or outside-
left over three League seasons from 1901/2,
and with the Rams proceeded to amass a total
of 33 League games in all five forward
positions between 1904-06. He also made one
County Championship appearance as a
cricketing all-rounder for Derbyshire CCC.

Appearances:
FL: 5 apps. 2 gls.
Total: *5 apps. 2 gls.*

J.Flint

FLINT, J.

Role: Outside right

CAREER:
Leicester Teachers/
Sept 1890: FOSSE.

*Debut (competitive)
v Burton Wanderers
(H) FAC 4.10.1890*

One of the amateur
pioneers of Fosse's
pre-league days,
Flint was outside-right in the club's initial
foray into the FA Cup competition, and in the
1891 County Cup-winning side, but made
only the odd appearance in friendly matches
following the club's elevation to the Midland
League.

Appearances:
FAC: 1 app. 0 gls.
Total: *1 app. 0 gls.*

FORD, Gary

Role: Midfield
b. York, 8th February 1961

CAREER: app 1977/pro Feb 1979:York City/
June 1987:CITY/Dec 1987:Port Vale/(Mar
1990 -loan-Walsall)/Mar 1991:Mansfield
Town/Nov 1993:Telford United/Jan 1995:
(Norway - club n/k).

Debut v Shrewsbury Town (H) 15.8.87

Gary Ford

A veteran of 426 senior games for his hometown club (and holder of an ever-present
record in their 1984 Fourth Division
championship season), wide midfielder Gary
was bought by Bryan Hamilton for £25,000 to
play as an out-and-out right winger for City,
and knuckled down to the role with
commendable enthusiasm and energy, despite
an early injury setback. An almost invariable
tendency to drift inside with the ball, though,
evidenced his discomfort at being isolated on
the flank, and Gary became the first player to
depart under the David Pleat regime, to
become immediately involved in Vale's 1988
FA Cup giant-killing of Spurs and, a year later,
their promotion to the Second Division.
Further injury problems then sidelined Gary
for some months, though he proved his fitness
in a relegation-bound Saddlers side, then
unluckily suffered another status-drop the
following season with the Stags. Incidentally,
Gary's trio of strikes for City included the
club's first-ever in the unloved Full Members
(then Simod-sponsored) Cup, the winner
against Huddersfield Town.

Appearances:
FL: 15 (1) apps. 2 gls.
LC: 1 (1) apps. 0 gls.
FMC: 2 apps. 1 gl.
Total: *18 (2) apps. 3 gls.*

FOSTER, James

Role: Half back

CAREER: 1897:Reading/cs 1899:
Northampton Town/May 1900:FOSSE/
cs 1901:Kettering.

Debut v Stockport County (H) 1.9.1900

A half-back signed after one Midland League
season in Northampton's colours, and
originally slated to replace Herbert Dainty,
Foster was allowed to move on when Dainty
returned. 'A heavy but smart player' was the
description he was given during his Kettering
stint. His Fosse debut (shared with fellow
newcomers Brash, Mills, Kyle, Connachan and
Dunkley) was in the 2-2 draw that marked
Stockport's first game as a League club.

Appearances:
FL: 20 apps. 0 gls.
FAC: 1 app. 0 gls.
Total: *21 apps. 0 gls.*

FRAME, William Lammie

Role: Right back
b. Carluke, Lanarkshire, 7th May 1912
d. Nottingham, 9th September 1992

CAREER: Shawfield Juniors/Oct 1933:
CITY/cs 1950:Rugby Town (p/coach).
Debut v Tottenham Hotspur (A) 6.10.34

Signed from Glasgow junior football at the
same time as Johnny Grogan, Billy was
pitched precisely one year later into First
Division action at White Hart Lane in
Adam Black's stead, and promptly netted
an own goal in the 2-2 draw. The right-
back was quick to recover from this
potentially unnerving experience, though,
becoming a regular in time to gain a medal
from City's 1937 promotion campaign, and
going on to give almost 17 years' service
(though never once scoring at the right
end.) Billy played more games in wartime
competitions than any other City player,
and was still an automatic choice when a
Christmas injury sadly robbed him of the
chance to play a major role in City's 1949
Wembley bid. After retiring from the
football scene, he ran the Griffin Inn.

> **Appearances:**
> *FL: 220 apps. 0 gls.*
> *FAC: 19 apps. 0 gls.*
> *WW2: 220 apps. 0 gls.*
> **Total:** *459 apps. 0 gls.*

Willie Freebairn

FREEBAIRN, William

Role: Outside right
b. Glasgow, c 1875

CAREER: 1893:Partick Thistle/cs 1895:
Abercorn/May 1896:FOSSE/cs 1898:East
Stirlingshire/cs 1899:Partick Thistle.
Debut v Darwen (H) 5.9.1896 (scored once)

Willie joined Fosse after helping Paisley-based
Abercorn to the championship of the Scottish
Second Division, and soon made the outside-
right spot his own. Discipline was clearly not
his strongest suit, though: he became the first
Fosse player to be sent off in League football,
for insulting a linesman at Lincoln in April
1897, and was later one of six players
suspended by the club for unspecified (but
probably alcohol-related) offences in February
1898. He never played for Fosse again, and
returned northwards to assist East Stirling to
their 1898/9 Scottish Qualifying Cup win. A
brother, Archie, also played for Partick and
had a long career as a half-back and skipper at
Bolton.

> **Appearances:**
> *FL: 44 apps. 14 gls.*
> *FAC: 4 apps. 3 gls.*
> **Total:** *48 apps. 17 gls.*

FREEMAN, Levi

Role: Inside left
b. Grantham, Lincs, c 1871
d. Grantham, 3rd September 1939

CAREER: 1884:Grantham Rovers/Hyde/
1891:Kettering Town/cs 1892: FOSSE/
cs 1893:Grantham Rovers/Gainsborough
Trinity.

Debut v Mansfield Town (A) ML 17.9.1892

A Grantham first-teamer from the age of 13,
eight years later Levi became the rather
diminutive (5ft.4ins) Fosse inside-left for the
early months of the second Midland League
season; and fared well enough in a front line
whose average height was only
5ft.6ins!

Appearances:
FAC: 4 apps. 2 gls.
ML: 10 apps. 5 gls.
Total: *14 apps. 7 gls.*

FRETTINGHAM, G.

Role: Inside left

CAREER: Newark/(1892-trials-
Nottingham Forest)/(Dec 1892-trials-
FOSSE)/cs 1893:Long Eaton Rangers.

Debut v Wednesbury Old Athletic (A)
ML 24.12.1892

An inside-left who had a distinctly
busy 1892/3 season: after his try-outs
with Forest and Fosse, he also faced
the latter at Midland League level for Newark
on April Fools' Day (scoring once in a 3-3
draw), and a fortnight later lined up for Fosse
in a home friendly against Forest! We presume
him to have been a relative of Jack
Frettingham (John Henry Abel; b. Nottingham,
1871; d. Derby, 17.5.1904), who soon
afterwards signed for Lincoln City from Long
Eaton Rangers (cs 1894) and moved on in 1896
to give seven years' service to New Brompton;
although the unreliability of contemporary
reports (one indeed initials him as 'J') may
mean he was one and the same player.

Appearances:
ML: 1 app. 0 gls.
Total: *1 app. 0 gls.*

FRIAR, John Paul

Role: Right back
b. Govan, Glasgow, 6th June 1963

CAREER: Woodhill BC/app 1979/pro June
1980:CITY/Feb 1983:Rotherham United/(Nov
1983-loan-Motherwell)/July 1984:Charlton
Athletic/(Mar 1986-loan-Northampton
Town)/cs 1986:Aldershot/Oct 1987:Dover/
Nov 1987:Welling United/Dec 1987:Dartford/
1988:Crawley/1988:Aylesbury United/
1988:Enfield/1989:Fisher Athletic/Aug 1990:
Spalding United/Sept 1990:Fisher Athletic/
Oct 1991:Partick Thistle/Feb 1992:East
Stirlingshire/Nov 1993:Albion Rovers.

Debut v Leeds United (H) 17.1.81

Paul Friar

A Scottish Youth
international who got
an early shot at
filling City's
problematic left-back
position, Paul vied
for three seasons
with Willie Gibson
and Norman Leet for
selection, and was
then displaced by
Bobby Smith
through the 1983
promotion season;
quickly moving on.
A competent enough
tackler, willing to mix
it with heftier
opponents, Paul
was also a speedy
overlapper, but his
crossing control was
poor. At the end of
his first Millmoor season, Rotherham dropped
into Division Three, and Paul was out of
favour at Charlton as they rose to Division
One, but in 1987 he helped Aldershot up from
the Fourth via the Play-offs before his
surprising release. After various non-league
travels in southern England, and a single
senior outing for Partick, Paul made a scoring
debut for East Stirling.

Appearances:
FL: 56 (2) apps. 0 gls.
FAC: 6 apps. 0 gls.
LC: 2 apps. 0 gls.
Total: *64 (2) apps. 0 gls.*

FROGGATT, Jack

Role: Centre half / Outside left
b. Sheffield, 17th November 1922
d. Worthing, Sussex, 17th February 1993

CAREER: RAF football/Sept 1945:
Portsmouth/Mar 1954:CITY/Nov 1957:
Kettering Town (p/coach; p/mgr).

Debut v Bury (H) 6.3.54

Capped by England at both outside-left and
centre-half, the masterfully versatile, always
ebullient Jack had twice picked up First
Division championship medals with
Pompey and, after Bert Barlow, was another
of the beaten Portsmouth semi-finalists of
1949 to find his way to Filbert Street. He
became the final link - a virtual insurance
policy against run-in jitters - in the 1954
promotion side, then switched positions
and shirts with effective, unruffled ease

thereafter until settling as ever-present
centre-half and captain for the 1957
Division Two championship season. Utterly
dominant in the air, Jack also continued to
lean on his attacking experience to become
a superb distributor of the ball from the
back. He moved to Kettering for £6,000, and
was player/manager for successive
relegation and promotion teams before
reverting to the playing ranks only. He
retired in 1962, and thereafter ran pubs back
in Portsmouth. Jack's father, Frank, was a
Sheffield Wednesday, Notts County and
Chesterfield player in the 20s; while his
second cousin, Redfern Froggatt of Sheffield
Wednesday, played four times at Jack's side
for England in 1953.

Appearances:
FL: 143 apps. 18 gls.
FAC: 5 apps. 0 gls.
Total: *148 apps. 18 gls.*

FULWOOD, Benjamin

Role: Outside left

CAREER: Long Eaton Rangers/Aug 1898:
FOSSE/cs 1899:Ilkeston.
Debut v Gainsborough Trinity (H) 8.10.1898

A young outside-left who contributed to
Fosse's near-miss promotion effort of 1898/9,
vying for the flank position with Welsh
international Alf Watkins, and occasionally
partnering him. Bennie was later followed
from Long Eaton by a younger brother who
had unsuccessful trials with Fosse reserves in
1906.

> **Appearances:**
> *FL: 11 apps. 3 gls.*
> *FAC: 2 apps. 2 gls.*
> **Total:** *13 apps. 5 gls.*

FURR, Harold Frederick

Role: Goalkeeper
b. Hitchin, Herts, 23rd January 1887
d. 23rd November 1971

CAREER: Hitchin St.Johns/Hitchin Town/
cs 1908:Croydon Common/Oct 1911:
Brentford/May 1912:FOSSE.
Debut v Huddersfield Town (A) 28.9.12

One of two brothers who moved within weeks
of each other from Brentford to Fosse, having

Harold Furr

previously played for manager Jack Bartlett at
Croydon, Harold was a goalkeeper who stood
in for Fred Mearns on several occasions, but
unhappily found himself picking the ball out
of his net 27 times. At Brentford he had understudied former Fosse keeper Archie Ling, and
had also suffered the odd embarrassment:
bowing out of the senior reckoning after an 0-9
defeat at Coventry. In his teenage days, he had
represented Hertfordshire.

> **Appearances:**
> *FL: 8 apps. 0 gls.*
> **Total:** *8 apps. 0 gls.*

FURR, William Stanley

Role: Outside right
b. Hitchin, Herts, Oct qtr 1891

CAREER: Hitchin/(Dec 1911-trials-Everton)
Jan 1912:Brentford/July 1912: FOSSE/(Aug
1913-trials-Luton Town)/1913:not
known/1919:Luton Town.
Debut v Huddersfield Town (A) 28.9.12

Outside-right Willie's League baptism came in
the same game as brother Harold's, but led to
no further chances at Filbert Street. Even when
switched to the left wing in the reserves, he
was unable to get past the ever-present George
Harrison during his Fosse season, and then
failed to win a contract at Luton. He did,
however, make one Southern League
appearance for the Hatters in 1919/20. Two
more of the Furr brothers, Vic and George,
turned out in senior football for Watford, and
the latter was the Croydon Common winger
facing Fosse in the Cup in 1911/12.

> **Appearances:**
> *FL: 1 app. 0 gls.*
> **Total:** *1 app. 0 gls.*

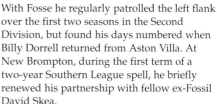

GALBRAITH, Thomas D.

Role: Outside right
b. Vale of Leven, Fife

CAREER: Vale of Leven/Jan 1898:
Sunderland/Aug 1898:FOSSE/cs 1900: not
known/1902:Vale of Leven.

Debut v Lincoln City (H) 3.9.1898

Tommy Galbraith

Whilst he only
contributed briefly
to the Sunderland
campaign that saw
them occupying the
Division One
runners-up spot in
1898, Tommy
became a free-
scoring right-winger
for the Fosse team
that just missed out
on promotion in
1899. However, his
goal touch deserted him the following season,
despite a shift to the inside-right position.

Appearances:
FL: 62 apps. 17 gls.
FAC: 6 apps. 1 gl.
Total: *68 apps. 18 gls.*

GALLACHER, Hugh

Role: Outside left
*b. Girvan, Ayrshire,
11th May 1870*

CAREER: Maybole/
May 1889:Celtic/Sept 1890:
Preston North End/
1892:Lanemark/
Jan 1893:Sheffield United/
Aug 1894:FOSSE/cs 1896:
Rossendale /Nelson/
July 1897:New Brompton.

*Debut v Rotherham Town (H) 8.9.1894
(scored once)*

Hugh Gallacher

A fine outside-left who represented Celtic
once during their initial Scottish League
campaign, Hugh had joined Preston just as
they were losing their 'Invincibles' tag, but
helped them to runners-up spot in the League
for three seasons running. He then moved to
Bramall Lane for the Blades' run-in to
promotion, played in the first Sheffield derby
at League level, and had become noted for the

eccentricity of
chewing his way
through an ounce
of 'twist' tobacco
per game: a half
ounce each half!
With Fosse he regularly patrolled the left flank
over the first two seasons in the Second
Division, but found his days numbered when
Billy Dorrell returned from Aston Villa. At
New Brompton, during the first term of a
two-year Southern League spell, he briefly
renewed his partnership with fellow ex-Fossil
David Skea.

Appearances:
FL: 47 apps. 11 gls.
FAC: 7 apps. 4 gls.
Total: *54 apps. 15 gls.*

GALLOWAY, Michael

Role: Midfield
b. Oswestry, Monmouthshire, 30th May 1965

CAREER: Holyrood Star/Tynecastle BC/am
1981:Berwick Rangers/pro June 1983:
Mansfield Town/Jan 1986:Halifax Town/
Nov 1987:Heart of Midlothian/June
1989:Celtic/(Feb 1995-loan-CITY)/(July
1995-loan-CITY).

Debut v West Ham United (H) 4.2.95

Reputedly turned down by City as a
16-year-old prospect on the grounds of
size, Mike had a convoluted and turbulent
time with the club some 14 years later.
Mark McGhee negotiated a month's loan
deal for the player in January 1995, but he
injured a hamstring during his first training session, and the loan was postponed
pending his fitness. Returning, Mike was
booked during each of his first three City
outings, but impressed with his strength and
energetic commitment both in midfield and at
right back, and exhibited a refreshing and
profitable accuracy with his crossing,
especially in the fightback thrillers at Aston
Villa (4-4) and Coventry (2-4). However, no
sooner had City renegotiated Mike's
temporary registration, with a commitment to
pay £200,000 if the extension to the end of the
season proved successful, than he was struck
once more by injury, and sidelined for the rest
of the term. A further loan spell at the start of
1995/6 produced only the offer of yet another

Mike Galloway

loan extension rather than a permanent move. A disappointed Galloway refused terms and returned to Celtic. Mike's versatility had always been evident throughout his previous career: primarily regarded as a defensive midfielder, he had already essayed excursions to the full-back and striker's roles in the lower reaches of the Football League before his move to Hearts, where he became noted as something of a talismanic goalscoring presence in European competition. A £500,000 move to Parkhead ensued, as did the winning of a couple of Scottish Under-21 caps (as an over-age player, qualified as the son of a Scottish soldier) during 1989/90. Mike was elevated to senior international status in October 1991, when Scotland faced Rumania in Bucharest, while at club level he featured as substitute in Celtic's 1990 Cup Final defeat (on penalties) by Aberdeen, and in the starting line-up for the 1994/5 League Cup Final against Raith Rovers, again lost on spot-kicks.

Appearances:
PL: 4 (1) apps. 0 gls.
FAC: 1 app. 0 gls.
Total: *5 (1) apps. 0 gls.*

GARDINER, Archibald

Role: Centre forward
b. Hamilton, Lanarkshire

CAREER: Burnbank Athletic/Penicuik Athletic/(trials-Clapton Orient)/May 1931: Heart of Midlothian/Feb 1934:CITY/Oct 1934: Wrexham/cs 1936:Hamilton Academicals/ Lille Olympique/cs 1937:Brideville/Dec 1937: Inverness Thistle.

Debut v Portsmouth (A) 21.2.34 (scored four)

The instant impact centre-forward Archie made on his transfer south is unlikely to be bettered in City annals: a four-goal debut in a 5-3 away win (his first strike coming after 90 seconds), followed two matches later by a home hat-trick against champions-to-be Arsenal! Another two games later he was in City's first-ever FA Cup semi-final team, yet after three selections in the following season, he was allowed to move on. The turnaround in fortunes was remarkable, yet Archie was not entirely new to disappointment, having for some time understudied the Scottish international goalscoring legend Barney Battles at Tynecastle, and dropped back into Hearts reserves, no matter how successful, whenever the senior centre-forward returned to the side. With the senior centre-forward at Leicester still being the veteran Arthur Chandler, it was very much a case of 'as you were'. Perhaps predictably, though, Archie managed to mark his Wrexham home debut with a hat-trick. Later, brief stints in France and Ireland spiced the

Archie Gardiner

twilight of his career, which unfortunately ended in ignominy in May 1938 when he was jailed for burglary. Archie's father, Harry, was a former Renton, Bolton Wanderers and Rangers centre-half who had represented the Football League in their first (1892) clash with the Scottish League, despite being Scottish-born himself; while older brothers had been on the books of Motherwell and Hamilton.

Appearances:
FL: 18 apps. 11 gls.
FAC: 1 app. 0 gls
Total: *19 apps. 11 gls.*

GARDINER, William Silcock

Role: Centre forward
b. Larbert, Stirlingshire,
15th August 1929

CAREER: Bo'ness United/ Nov 1950: Rangers/Aug 1955: CITY/Nov 1958:Reading.

Debut v Doncaster Rovers (A) 5.9.55 (scored once)

Another prolific scorer who spent much of his early career in Scottish reserve football (nonetheless claiming one Scotland 'B' cap), Willie moved for £4,000 from Ibrox - as David Halliday's first purchase - to play alongside Arthur Rowley, and even managed the unlikely feat of out-gunning his new partner in his first year: averaging better than a goal a game to end up with 34 Second Division strikes. The tall, fair-haired centre-forward (who certainly made up in effectiveness what he lacked in elegance) lost his place to Derek Hines in the 1957 promotion campaign, but returned to help City survive their first fraught season back in Division One. Unfortunately, a succession of leg injuries, culminating in a bad break, marred Willie's two-year stay at Elm Park.

Appearances:
FL: 69 apps. 48 gls.
FAC: 2 apps. 1 gl.
Total: *71 apps. 49 gls.*

Willie Gardiner

GARDNER, Frank

Role: Left half
b. 1866
d. Leicester, 8th December 1943

CAREER: 1884:FOSSE.

Debut (competitive) v Doncaster Rovers (A) ML 26.12.1891

A genuine founding father of the Fosse (at the age of 18!), Frank was elected secretary and treasurer at the formative meeting of the club in the spring of 1884, and played as a half-back in the very first friendly fixture (on the 1st November 1884, versus Syston Fosse). He was also a leading agitator for the formation of the Leicestershire FA (October 1886), which honoured him with its presidency soon afterwards. Appropriately, he was a scorer in the Final when Fosse secured that body's Senior Cup for the first time in 1890 (with a replay win over Coalville Town), but he was primarily concentrating on his secretarial duties (conducting

Frank Gardner

the club's business from 41 Hinckley Road) by the time he was called upon to make up the Fosse eleven on their Boxing Day 1891 jaunt to Doncaster. A company secretary by profession, Frank was also chairman and treasurer of the old Leicester & District League from 1895, a League referee from 1898, and chair of the Rolleston Charity Cup competition from 1900. Apart from a brief spell on business in Ireland in 1931, Frank spent all his working life in Leicester.

Appearances:
ML: 1 app. 0 gls.
Total: *1 app. 0 gls.*

GARLAND, Christopher Stephen

Role: Striker
b. Bristol, 24th April 1949

CAREER: pro May 1966:Bristol City/Aug 1971:Chelsea/Mar 1975:CITY/Nov 1976: Bristol City/cs 1983:Minehead (p/mgr).
Debut v Coventry City (A) 15.3.75

A teenage local hero at Ashton Gate, blond striker Chris had won one England Under-23 cap when Chelsea laid out a six-figure fee for him, and he appeared for the Blues in their 1972 League Cup Final defeat by Stoke. His £95,000 move to City had an inspirational effect on a struggling side, and his eight goals in ten games at the end of 1974/5 did much to avert the very real threat of relegation. Sent off in the opening game of the following season (when a 9-man City twice equalised to secure an unlikely 3-3 draw against Birmingham City), Chris bounced back in a hard-working support role to Frank Worthington, and had only just lost his first-team place in Jimmy Bloomfield's last campaign when Bristol City's offer to take him home for £110,000 was accepted. Injuries dogged his second spell there, and indeed his contract was twice cancelled (once to help the club from the brink of closure), but Chris refused to lie down, and was still turning out on a non-contract basis in 1982/3, to take his Bristol City appearance record over the 200 mark, and his career aggregate League and Cup scoring record to exactly 100 goals. In 1992, it was revealed that Chris was suffering from Parkinson's Disease, and many of his former playing colleagues rallied round for a series of testimonial events hosted by Minehead FC; while Bristol City played Manchester United on his behalf in May 1993.

Appearances:
FL: 52 (3) apps. 15 gls.
FAC: 3 apps. 3 gls.
LC: 5 apps. 1 gl.
Total: *60 (3) apps. 19 gls.*

Chris Garland

GARRATY, William

Role: Centre forward
b. Saltley, Birmingham, 6th October 1878
d. Birmingham, 6th May 1931

CAREER: Highfield Villa/Aston
Shakespeare/cs 1897:Aston Villa/Sept 1908:
FOSSE/Oct 1908:West Bromwich Albion/
Dec 1910: Lincoln City.

Debut v Bristol City (H) 12.9.08

Billy Garraty

A veteran goalscoring centre-forward who had been capped for England against Wales in 1903, and won both League championship (1900) and FA Cup (1905) medals from his 256-game, 111-goal career with Villa, Billy stayed with Fosse only a matter of some seven weeks when signed to augment their First Division forces. He was hardly over the hill, though - his twenty goals for West Brom over the next two years evidenced that - and the wisdom of Fosse letting him go (at £270, representing £20 profit) has to be questioned in view of their subsequent nosedive to relegation. They had lost only once with Billy in the side, despite his own inability to get off the scoring mark. Back in the early days of his senior career, Billy took part in the notorious ten-and-a-half minute match between Sheffield Wednesday and Villa - the Football League had demanded that a game abandoned in November 1898 had to be completed almost four months later, and Billy, who wasn't in the side for the first 79-and-a-half minutes, had made his break-through in the interim! In later life he was a driver for Ansells Brewery back in Birmingham.

> **Appearances:**
> *FL: 6 apps. 0 gls.*
> **Total:** *6 apps. 0 gls.*

GARVEY, James

Role: Left half / Inside left
b. Paisley, Renfrewshire, 4th June 1919

CAREER: May 1939:Northampton Town/
June 1946:CITY/1949:Corby Town.

Debut v Burnley (H) 24.5.47

Having played in one League game for the Cobblers in the abandoned 1939/40 season - an appearance then expunged from official records - Jim had little more luck after becoming a postwar City signing. The Scottish left-half or inside-left was valued for his constructive approach work, but niggling knee injuries held him back whenever he looked about to make a sustained first-team breakthrough. His final senior outing was in the crucial last game of 1948/9 at Cardiff, when the point gained kept City out of Division Three. Jim did well, though, with Corby in their heyday: sharing in United Counties League championships in 1951 and 1952, and helping them to runners-up spot in the Midland League in their 1953 inaugural campaign at that level.

> **Appearances:**
> *FL: 15 apps. 0 gls.*
> *FAC: 1 app. 0 gls.*
> **Total:** *16 apps. 0 gls.*

Jim Garvey

GAVIN, Patrick John

Role: Striker
b. Hammersmith, London, 5th June 1967

CAREER: Hanwell Town/Mar 1989:
Gillingham/June 1989:CITY/(Sept 1989-loan-
Gillingham)/Mar 1991:Peterborough United/
(Mar 1992-loan-Kettering Town)/(Aug 1992-
loan-Kettering Town)/(Nov 1992-loan-Boston
United)/Feb 1993:Northampton Town/cs
1993:Wigan Athletic/July 1995-trials-Crewe
Alexandra).
Debut v Charlton Athletic (A) 13.10.90 (sub)

The subject of much argument between the
Gills and Leicester when signing on at Filbert
Street - City averred he was a free agent, while
the Kent club for whom he'd scored 7 goals in
13 Third Division appearances claimed he was
under contract to them - young striker Pat was
initially barred from training with either
League club until the wrangle over his
registration had been sorted out. Eventually a
compromise saw City loan Pat back to
Priestfield for the season, where unfortunately
he struggled to consolidate his initial impact
(scoring only one League goal during
1989/90). The former postman fronted City's

Pat Gavin

attack in the Scottish pre-season friendlies of
1990 (scoring at Motherwell), but his total
Second Division experience with Leicester
amounted to only 83 minutes in three games
before he became a £15,000 deadline-day
mover to London Road. Five strikes
immediately helped Posh to Division Four
promotion, but success there was short-lived,
too; and it was not until his final game for
Northampton - in May 1993, when they had to
win at Shrewsbury to be sure of retaining their
Football League status - that Pat again hit the
headlines. The reward for his crucial two-goal
contribution as substitute, however, was the
cancellation of his contract only days later.

> **Appearances:**
> *FL: 1 (2) apps. 0 gls.*
> **Total:** *1 (2) apps. 0 gls.*

GEE, Philip John

Role: Striker
b. Pelsall, Staffs, 19th December 1964

CAREER: Riley Sports/July 1985:Gresley
Rovers/Aug 1985:Derby County/Mar 1992:
CITY/(Jan 1995-loan-Plymouth Argyle).
Debut v Portsmouth (H) 11.3.92

Originally recommended to Derby by David
Nish, in his role at the time of Gresley
chairman, Phil made a significant goalscoring
contribution to the Rams' 1987 Second
Division championship campaign, but was
thereafter regarded more as a useful squad
player than a first-choice striker. He joined
City, along with team-mate Ian Ormondroyd,
as the £200,000 make-weight in the Paul
Kitson package deal, and got off the scoring
mark with a magnificent long-distance strike
at Tranmere, but his efforts in City's qualification for their first Play-off experience weren't
enough to win him the nod over Kevin Russell
when the season's end thrillers were played
(though he did figure as substitute against
Blackburn at Wembley). A remarkable
performance at Filbert Street against his former Derby side (when he scored twice and hit
the post with a brilliant strike during a 3-2
win) was one of the few highlights of the
following term, as Phil gradually faded from
Brian Little's first-team plans; though isolated
games when the front-runner played in a
wider role, and operated a shoot-on-sight
policy, more happily studded his City record.

Phil Gee

Colin Gibson

GIBSON, Colin John

Role: Left back / Midfield
b. Bridport, Dorset, 6th April 1960

CAREER: app July 1976/pro Aug 1978:Aston Villa/Nov 1985:Manchester United/ (Sept 1990-loan-Port Vale)/Dec 1990:CITY/ Aug 1994:Blackpool/Sept 1994:Walsall.

Debut v Watford (H) 23.12.90

Primarily a left-back at Villa, where he won numerous honours in the early years of a subsequently injury-marred career, Colin was also utilised by City in more advanced midfield positions, but had perhaps suffered one too many knocks by the veteran stage to be fully convincing in the increasingly fashionable, but highly demanding, wing-back role. Nonetheless, his contributions to City's

His last-gasp drive against QPR won City their first Premiership point, but Phil never played a full game under Mark McGhee. Indeed, he would have moved to Home Park at the conclusion of his loan period had Argyle been able to raise the £75,000 requested; and he was transfer-listed in May 1995.

Appearances (to end 1994/5):

PL: 3 (4) apps. 2 gls.
FL: 31 (13) apps. 7 gls.
LC: 2 (3) apps. 0 gls.
AIC: 3 apps. 4 gls.
P/O: 2 (1) apps. 0 gls.
Total: *41 (21) apps. 13 gls.*

efforts to raise themselves back to the top flight were patently wholehearted, and it was rather fitting that his final game in a Leicester shirt should have been the promotion-clinching Play Off victory over Derby County. David Pleat's final City purchase at £100,000, Colin showed as much grit as class over his three-and-a-half seasons at Filbert Street, where he was often sidelined by the knee injuries which had first flared at Old Trafford, and enlivened several games with a vicious long-range shot. During 1992/3 he set two minor club records, by becoming the first City substitute to be himself substituted (coming on for Michael Trotter at Watford, and limping off to be replaced by Colin Gordon), and the first City substitute to be sent off (at Luton); and he was actually placed on the free transfer list at the end of that term. Yet he renegotiated a one-year contract with Brian Little, and ended his City days with a Wembley winner's memento and a broad, gap-toothed grin. Eighteen years earlier, he had accepted a Villa apprenticeship despite having been on associate schoolboy forms with Portsmouth, and went on to taste rapid success. An FA Youth Cup Finalist in 1978, he was a regular in Villa's League Championship side of 1981, and played in their European Super Cup side of 1983; though he sat out the 1982 European Cup Final as an unused substitute. Colin also won one cap at each of England B and Under-21 levels while with Villa. During 1994/5 he played a substantial role in Walsall's promotion to Division Two.

Appearances:
FL: 50 (9) apps. 4 gls.
FAC: 1 (1) apps. 0 gls.
LC: 4 apps. 0 gls.
FMC: 2 apps. 0 gls.
AIC: 1 app. 0 gls.
P/O: 4 (1) apps. 0 gls.
Total: *62 (11) apps. 4 gls.*

GIBSON, David Wedderburn

Role: Inside forward
b. Winchburgh, West Lothian,
23rd September 1938

CAREER: Livingston United/ 1955: Hibernian/Jan 1962:CITY/Sept 1970: Aston Villa/Jan 1972:Exeter City.
Debut v Fulham (H) 3.2.62

Davie Gibson

One of the very finest ball-players to have graced Filbert Street since the war, Davie had still to complete his National Service when Matt Gillies paid Hibs £25,000 for his signature, but as soon as he turned full-time to City's cause, he forged an unforgettable early partnership with Mike Stringfellow on the left wing. His elegant control and visionary passing skills were a major prompt to City's Wembley visits in 1963 and 1969, and Davie found the net himself with pleasing regularity, scoring in both legs of the 1964 League Cup Final victory over Stoke, and knocking in three goals in his seven full Scottish international appearances of the early 60s. His artistry - always marbled with a tough resilience - was barely on the wane when he left to give a veteran's course in midfield style at Villa and Exeter, and while with the former club he returned to Wembley as substitute for the 1971 League Cup Final. Davie settled in Leicestershire after bowing out from the playing ranks, working in the postal service and helping run a residential home for the elderly.

Appearances:
FL: 274 (6) apps. 41 gls.
FAC: 29 apps. 5 gls.
LC: 30 apps. 7 gls.
Total: *333 (6) apps. 53 gls.*

GIBSON, George Eardley

Role: Centre forward
b. Biddulph, Staffs, 29th August 1912
d. Blackburn, Lancs, December 1990

CAREER: Kidderminster Harriers/(trials-Stoke City)/Nov 1931:Frickley Colliery/Apr 1932:Sunderland/Nov 1934:CITY/(Aug 1935-loan-Valenciennes)/(Jan 1936-loan-Distillery)/cs 1936:Shelbourne/June 1937:Workington/May 1938:Bradford City.

Debut v Stoke City (H) 10.11.34

Brought down from Roker when City were searching for both short- and long-term replacements for Arthur Chandler in 1934/5, George held a briefer purchase than most on the old goalgetter's centre-forward shirt, only playing in two heavy defeats within ten days of his transfer. A young bustler of the vintage brylcreem-and-centre-parting style, he had indeed only played twice previously in Division One for Sunderland (though he'd netted twice in their first ever floodlit game, an away friendly against Racing Club de Paris), and would eventually taste League fare only three more times in a brief run-out at Valley Parade in 1938. In the interim, though, he had quite an adventuresome time while still nominally on City's books. Playing on loan in France alongside former Chelsea and England defender Peter O'Dowd, he was deemed a great success until wild allegations arose that he and O'Dowd had been bribed to 'throw' a particular match, and in clearing his name with the French FA, he was actually awarded £66 in damages! George then took over Owen McNally's role in Belfast only a fortnight after the latter signed for City.

Appearances:
FL: 2 apps. 0 gls.
Total: *2 apps. 0 gls.*

GIBSON, Dr Thomas M.

Role: Inside forward
b. Dennistoun, Glasgow

CAREER: Parkhead/May 1926:CITY/Dec 1929:Burton Town/Ashby Town.

Debut v West Ham United (A) 12.3.28

The only General Practitioner to have turned out for City in League football, 'Doctor Tom' was an inside-forward who occasionally filled in for Ernie Hine or Arthur Lochhead - though his limited senior career consisted entirely of away matches, and he was never on a winning City side at League level (his only goal coming in a 3-6 Anfield defeat). Still a medical student when he signed (a few days after Peter Hodge, who had set up the deal, left for Manchester City), he qualified through exams taken in September 1926, and then practised in Leicester and Ashby. For many years after release, Tom turned out in local football circles: indeed, he was still taking part in the then-annual Doctors v. Parsons charity fixture at Filbert Street in April 1939. Back in his Parkhead days, Tom had been capped as a Junior.

Appearances:
FL: 4 apps. 1 gl.
Total: *4 apps. 1 gl.*

'Doctor Tom' Gibson

GIBSON, William

Role: Left back
b. Lanark, 24th June 1959

CAREER: Easthouses BC/Mar 1979:CITY/Oct 1982:Nuneaton Borough/cs 1987:Weymouth.

Debut v Ipswich Town (H) 16.8.80

Left-back Willie impressed Jock Wallace on a 1980 close-season tour of Germany and Holland, and surprisingly found himself pitched into City's opening game on their First Division return, holding his place as an enthusiastic harrier for half of that season of struggle against the drop. He lost out, though, in the three-cornered fight with fellow youngsters Paul Friar and Norman Leet early in the next campaign, and was soon to drop out of League football. Willie has skippered Weymouth for several years, was briefly their co-caretaker manager early in 1994/5, and was awarded a testimonial game there in May 1995.

> **Appearances:**
> *FL: 28 apps. 0 gls.*
> *FAC: 1 app. 0 gls.*
> *LC: 3 apps. 0 gls.*
> **Total:** *32 apps. 0 gls.*

Willie Gibson

GILL, Ernest Harry

Role: Left back
b. Mountsorrel, Leics, 1877
d. Hull, 1950

CAREER: Poole White Star/Bridgewater/ (trials-Bristol City)/(Sept 1899-trials-Grimsby Town)/Mar 1900:Southampton/ 1900:Freemantle/May 1901:FOSSE.

Debut v Gainsborough Trinity (A) 26.10.01

Ernest Gill

Best known as a professional right-arm fast-medium bowler with Leicestershire CCC (for whom he played a handful of first-class matches in the summer of 1901, and for whom his brother George also featured), Ernest had previously played football for several years in Dorset, Somerset and Hampshire, and turned out in one Southern League match for Southampton in March 1900. For Fosse he impressed in a couple of friendlies, and replaced George Swift at left-back in the above match, only to have his career abruptly terminated a month later by a serious leg-break suffered in an acrimonious reserve-team 'friendly' at Ilkeston.

> **Appearances:**
> *FL: 1 app. 0 gls.*
> **Total:** *1 app. 0 gls.*

GILLIES, Alexander

Role: Inside forward

CAREER: Lochgelly United/ Oct 1895:Bolton Wanderers/Feb 1896: Manchester City/Aug 1896:Heart of Midlothian/Feb 1897:Sheffield Wednesday/Aug 1897:FOSSE/ cs 1898: Lochgelly United.

Debut v Grimsby Town (A) 18.9.1897

A Scottish forward well and truly bitten by the wandering bug, Alec briefly deposed Johnny McMillan at

Leicester, largely on his record of scoring at least once in each of his six friendly games. Yet, ironically, he contrived to extend throughout his stay with Fosse an unenviable record of failing to notch a single goal for any of his Football League clubs in that competition. He was one of several players whose services were dispensed with as a disciplinary measure in February 1898.

Appearances:
FL: 4 apps. 0 gls.
Total: *4 apps. 0 gls.*

GILLIES, Matthew Muirhead

Role: Centre half
b. Loganlea, West Lothian, 12th August 1921

CAREER: Oct 1942:Bolton Wanderers/ Jan 1952:CITY.

Debut v Doncaster Rovers (H) 26.1.52

A medical student who signed for Bolton while on RAF service during the war and later became their skipper, Matt had previously been on Motherwell's books as an amateur, and also guested for Arsenal, QPR, Chelsea and Chester. He joined City for £9,500 to bolster the central defensive position, and was the regular pivot, thoughtful but solid, in the 1954 Second Division championship season. Despite his on-field influence as a steadying senior pro, however, it was beyond the playing arena that Matt was really to make his mark on City history. Becoming coach in April 1956, he assumed the role of acting manager in November 1958 (on David Halliday's resignation), and was entrusted with the full managerial reins in January 1959. Directing City's generally upbeat fortunes for a decade entirely spent in the top flight, Matt twice led his team out at Wembley, twice took them to the League Cup Final, and thoroughly earned for himself a reputation as both a shrewd market operator and a good judge of character. He became a local Justice of the Peace while still in office at Filbert Street, though his primary commitment to his club's continuing honours-chase even led to him suffering a lengthy spell of stress-related ill-health towards the end of his regime, making something of a nonsense of the occasionally voiced criticism that he was 'too gentlemanly' for the purported rat-race of modern football. Matt was nonetheless quick to pass the lion's share of credit for City's tactical innovations of the 60s to his coach Bert Johnson, and it was little surprise to anyone - least of all, one presumes, to the board - when he immediately resigned in the wake of Johnson's sacking in November 1968. What did surprise many was that he then took another managerial post, at a largely unresponsive Nottingham Forest; but even an apparent 'defection' to City's local rivals failed to diminish Matt's standing for those who recognised his crucial contribution to the process of turning a club with a long-standing 'yo-yo' reputation into one with a sustained 'First Division' image.

Appearances:
FL: 103 apps. 0 gls.
FAC: 8 apps. 0 gls.
Total:
111 apps. 0 gls.

Matt Gillies

GLOVER, Edward Lee

Role: Striker
b. Kettering, Northants, 24th April 1970

CAREER: YT/pro 1987:Nottingham Forest/
(Sept 1989-loan-CITY)/(Jan 1990-loan-
Barnsley)/(Sept 1991-loan-Luton Town)/
cs 1994:Port Vale.

Debut v Bradford City (A) 16.9.89

A League debut-day scorer for Forest as a 17-year-old striker, Lee gained a fair bit of First Division experience during 1987/8, and soon won recognition for the Scotland

Lee Glover

Under-21 side, but was thereafter sidelined by serious injury problems, and had still to win back his place in Brian Clough's front line when David Pleat brought him to Filbert Street on loan. Wayne Clarke and Kevin Russell were removed from contention by injury, and Tommy Wright facing imminent suspension, when Lee arrived to form a teenage spearhead with Paul Kitson, and he at least brightened an otherwise in-and-out month's stay with the only goal of City's belated first win of the season, against Brighton. Lee then had the misfortune to break his leg in a Forest reserve game shortly after returning from his Oakwell loan stint, but he was back to take a runners-up medal from the 1991 FA Cup Final. An unused sub for Forest's two Wembley visits of the following year (in the ZDS and League Cup Finals), Lee has so far failed to develop sufficient goalscoring guile for the game's top level.

Appearances:
FL: 3 (2) apps. 1 gl.
Total: *3 (2) apps. 1 gl.*

GLOVER, Leonard

Role: Outside left
b. Kennington, London, 31st January 1944

CAREER: am May 1959/pro May 1962:Charlton Athletic/Nov 1967:CITY/May 1976:Tampa Bay Rowdies/ Oct 1976:Kettering Town/Apr 1977:Tampa Bay Rowdies/Sept 1977:Kettering Town/ 1978:Earl Shilton Albion (p/mgr) - 1979/ 1994: Harlow Town (p/mgr).

Debut v Arsenal (H) 18.11.67

A series of niggling injuries spoiled both the beginning and end of Lenny's City career, but in the interim seasons his left-wing skills and pace bemused many an opposing full-back, and it was a genuine tribute to both his ability and personality that he became a firm favourite of the usually highly-critical Popular Side supporters, whose anticipatory roar whenever Lenny received the ball must have unnerved many an adversary. He had first faced City as a Charlton teenager in the League Cup during 1962/3, and the £80,000 fee Matt Gillies paid for him five years later represented at the time an English record for a winger. Lenny's goals saw City through the first two rounds of their 1969 Cup run to Wembley (though

Lenny Glover

his fitness to start the Final came down to a gamble), and two years later he regularly ripped Second Division defences apart as City sped to promotion. Back in the top flight he laid on many of Frank Worthington's goals, and when City's entertaining 'nearly' team reached the Cup semi-finals in 1974, Lenny claimed the equalising (though eventually consolational) goal in the replay against Liverpool. After returning from America, he was involved in one last FA Cup campaign, with the oddest of results: having played for Kettering in a First Round victory over Tilbury in November 1977, Lenny had his eligibility officially queried by the losers - and Kettering eventually went out of the Cup after a replay had been ordered by the FA! Subsequently retiring to the role of publican, he made a surprise return to football in the summer of 1994, when taking on the manager's role at Harlow Town; and in fact registered himself as a player in mid-season, making a brief active comeback in January 1995 as the first 50-year-old to appear in the Diadora League, shortly before resigning.

Appearances:
FL: 245 (7) apps. 38 gls.
FAC: 35 (1) apps. 8 gls.
LC: 17 apps. 2 gls.
Total:
297 (8) apps. 48 gls.

Lenny Glover

GODDERIDGE, Albert Edward

Role: Goalkeeper
b. Tamworth, Staffs, 29th May 1902
d. Lichfield, Staffs, Apr qtr 1976

CAREER: Two Gates/(trials-Aston Villa)/
(trials-Preston North End)/May 1922:CITY/
June 1927:Barnsley/Aug 1929:Newark Town/
Nov 1930:Hinckley United/1933:Nuneaton
Town.

Debut v Fulham (H) 29.3.24

Graduating from the backwaters of Trent
Valley League football, and wresting the first
team goalkeeper's jersey from George
Hebden, Albert became the sturdy last line of
defence in City's successful 1925 promotion
push, but found himself back in the reserves
after the squad charged with establishing the
club in the top flight had been augmented by
the arrival of the vastly experienced Kenny
Campbell. Then, at Oakwell, he again had to
knuckle down to being regarded primarily as
an understudy; this time to the consistent
Tommy Gale. Albert used to harbour
goalscoring ambitions with City's seconds: he
took two penalties in the record 22-0 victory

over Ibstock in the 1923/4 County Cup,
netting once, and also missed a spot-kick
against Reading in the London Combination
in 1926/7. His brother was a goalscoring
forward and team-mate with Hinckley United
from November 1931.

Appearances:
FL: 50 apps. 0 gls.
FAC: 6 apps. 0 gls.
Total: *56 apps. 0 gls.*

GODWIN, Thomas Fergus

Role: Goalkeeper
b. Dublin, 20th August 1927

CAREER: Home Farm/Shamrock Rovers/
Sept 1949:CITY/June 1952:Bournemouth &
Boscombe Athletic/June 1963:Dorchester
Town.

Debut v Swansea Town (H) 26.11.49

Signed only days after starring for the
Republic of Ireland in a shock 2-0 win over
England at Goodison Park, Tommy was
another of City's international goalkeepers to
fit the traditional mould of unspectacular

Albert Godderidge

Tommy Godwin

GOLDIE, William Glover

Role: Left half
b. Hurlford, Ayrshire, 22nd January 1878

CAREER: 1895:Hurlford
Thistle/1897:Clyde/
Mar 1898:Liverpool/
Dec 1903:Fulham/
Aug 1908:FOSSE/
1911:Leicester Imperial.
*Debut v Sheffield
Wednesday (H) 1.9.08*

A dour, tough-tackling left-half with a slide-rule pass - "thoroughly reliable under all circumstances" - Billy followed his elder brother Archie (a former Clyde fullback) to Anfield and there, in the middle of one spell of 119 consecutive appearances, became an ever-present in Liverpool's first Championship-winning side of 1901. He helped lift Fulham from the Southern League to the Second Division, and then joined Fosse for their First Division debut, staying three seasons. On leaving he ran a pub, while still turning out occasionally for the local Imps; though how East Midlands patrons coped with his notoriously near-impenetrable Scottish accent is unrecorded: an FA disciplinary committee had once felt the need to employ an interpreter in dealing with Billy during his Liverpool days! Billy's younger brother John became the third of the family to build a career in England, serving Fulham, Glossop and Bury, but was later disgraced in a bribery scandal after moving to Kilmarnock.

Appearances:
FL: 82 apps. 1 gl.
FAC: 6 apps. 0 gls.
Total: *88 apps. 1 gl.*

soundness. A master of the high ball, and no mean shot-stopper, he was nonetheless no stranger to misfortune: a broken leg in an FAI Cup semi-final with Shamrock had cost him both a Final place and more early representative honours, while during his City sojourn his place was constantly under pressure from Scottish international-to-be, Johnny Anderson. Indeed, City's confidence in the younger keeper contributed to Tommy's early departure. He had won four Eire caps while at Filbert Street, and added another four (to take his total to 13) after settling at Dean Court, where he built a total of 357 League appearances over ten seasons. Tommy took a 1962 testimonial there against West Ham, and settled on the South Coast, latterly as a parks supervisor for Bournemouth Corporation.

Appearances:
FL: 45 apps. 0 gls.
FAC: 1 app. 0 gls.
Total: *46 apps. 0 gls.*

GOODFELLOW, James Boyd

Role: Forward
b. Edinburgh, 30th July 1938

CAREER: Third Lanark/May 1963:CITY/Mar 1968:Mansfield Town/cs 1971:Weymouth/ Durban City/Nuneaton Borough/ AP Leamington.
Debut v Stoke City (A) 7.9.63

A nippy, neatly-balanced 'cruiserweight' striker picked up on a free transfer from Thirds when economy measures dictated that the ill-fated Glasgow club divest itself of a superbly skilful forward-line, Jimmy gave excellent inside-forward support to City's mid-60s front line, and notched several useful goals - including one in the first leg of the 1965 League Cup Final, and an 18-yard header in one sweet home win over Forest. He enters the record book indelibly, though, for his 35th League appearance for City - as the club's

Jimmy Goodfellow

GOODWIN, Mark Adrian

Role: Midfield
b. Sheffield, 23rd February 1960

CAREER: app July 1976/pro Oct 1977:CITY/
Mar 1981:Notts County/July 1987:Walsall/
cs 1990:Kettering Town/cs 1991:Eastwood
Town (p/coach; p/mgr)/1992:Arnold Town
(p/coach)/cs 1994:Hucknall Town.

Debut v Ipswich Town (A) 17.12.77

Given a first-team break by Frank McLintock
less than a month after turning professional,
blond midfielder Mark pumped some genuine
enthusiasm into a City side almost resigned to
its relegation fate, and gave a remarkable
display of unrestrained joy on opening his
goal account at Old Trafford. Occasionally
looking a little overwhelmed by the physical
rigours of Second Division struggle, Mark was
often used on the sub's bench by Jock Wallace,
but his spells of service as ball-winner,
distributor and even full-back made him a
suitably versatile understudy for almost any
eventuality. He moved to Meadow Lane as the
last link in County's promotion-winning side
of 1981, alongside Trevor Christie, and passed
the 200 mark in League appearances for the
Magpies early in 1986/7, before once more
rejoining Christie at Fellows Park for,

first-ever official No.12, replacing Graham
Cross against Liverpool on the first day
(21.8.1965) the rules allowed substitutes for
injured players. At Field Mill, Jimmy renewed
an effective partnership with Nick Sharkey
that had first been forged in City's
Combination side, and was a stylish prompter
of Mansfield's 1969 Cup run which City ended
in the Sixth Round. His only senior
representative honour was selection for the
Scottish League against Scotland in February
1962, when Frank McLintock was amongst the
opposition. Jimmy is now a county-based
electrician.

Appearances:
FL: 96 (2) apps. 26 gls.
FAC: 9 apps. 3 gls.
LC: 14 apps. 7 gls.
Total: *119 (2) apps. 36 gls.*

*Mark
Goodwin*

successively, one promotion and two relegation campaigns. In 1994 he and Christie were together again at Hucknall.

Appearances:
FL: 69 (22) apps. 8 gls.
FAC: 4 (1) apps. 0 gls.
LC: 3 apps. 0 gls.
Total: *76 (23) apps. 8 gls.*

GORDON, Colin Kenneth

Role: Striker
b. Stourbridge, Worcs,
17th January 1963

CAREER: Lye Town/ Oldbury United/ Nov 1984:Swindon Town/ July 1986:Wimbledon/ (Feb 1987-loan-Gillingham)/ July 1987:Reading/(Mar 1988-loan-Bristol City)/ Oct 1988:Fulham/June 1989:Birmingham City/ (Sept 1990-loan-Hereford United)/(Dec 1990-loan-Walsall)/(Jan 1991-loan-Bristol Rovers)/ July 1991:CITY/Jan 1993: Kidderminster Harriers (p/coach)/(1993-loan-Gloucester City)/cs 1994:Stourbridge (p/mgr).

Debut v Bristol City (H) 7.9.91 (sub)

A tall, heftily bustling striker who made a fine scoring impact on his belated introduction to the League scene at Swindon, but thereafter found his further wanderings a fairly frustrating affair, Colin had figured in four transfers worth £80,000 or more and a nap hand of loan deals before Brian Little took him on as a free agent in his initial City team-building spree. Always deemed a short-term acquisition, 'Flash' nonetheless proved a useful Second Division target man, even if usually happier when the ball was in the air (efforts with either foot seeming to have a marked affinity for the woodwork!) Colin's otherwise unremarkable St.Andrews sojourn was once disrupted by a possibly unique injury: he contracted blood poisoning after

Colin Gordon

being accidentally bitten on the arm by a Swansea player!

Appearances:
FL: 18 (6) apps. 5 gls.
FAC: 1 app. 0 gls.
LC: 1 app. 0 gls.
FMC: 4 (1) apps. 2 gls.
AIC: 0 (1) app. 0 gls.
Total: *24 (8) apps. 7 gls.*

GORDON, Robert

Role: Centre forward
b. Leith, Edinburgh, 1873

CAREER: 1889:Leith Rangers/Leith Athletic/ 1890:Heart of Midlothian/ 1891:Middlesbrough Ironopolis/July 1893:Heart of Midlothian/May 1894: Aston Villa/Oct 1894: FOSSE/June 1895: Woolwich Arsenal/ cs 1896:Reading.

Debut v Kimberley (H) FAC 3.11.1894
(scored twice)

A well-built bustler of a centre-forward, but none too speedy - the *'Daily Post'* rather harshly described him as 'cumbrous' - Bob was the fifth attack-leader tried by Fosse within the first two months of their initial League season, and the fifth former Ironopolis player to appear in their ranks that term. He'd already notched two goals in four League appearances for Villa that season (plus one in their game against the Football League, played as a benefit for League founder William McGregor), and forged a prolific inside trio partnership with David Skea and Billy McArthur for Fosse before taking his shooting boots to Plumstead for a £30 fee. In February 1897, Bob represented the Southern League against the London FA, scoring twice.

Appearances:
FL: 21 apps. 12 gls.
FAC: 4 apps. 2 gls.
Total: *25 apps. 14 gls.*

GORMAN, James

Role: Centre half
*b. Middlesbrough,
1882*

CAREER: Newport
Celtic/South Bank/
Darlington
St.Augustine's/
Darlington/
Mar 1906:Liverpool/
May 1908:FOSSE/
cs 1909: Hartlepools United.

*James
Gorman*

Debut v Manchester City (A) 3.10.08

A highly-rated centre-half ('zealous and
untiring'), whose Anfield role had been
primarily to understudy Scottish international
Alec Raisbeck, James suffered appalling
fortune with Fosse - being so badly injured on
his debut that he was unable to return until
the club's relegation fate was already settled.
To rub salt into the wound, the second match
of his comeback, and his final Fosse
appearance, was the ignominious 0-12
defeat by Forest.

>**Appearances:**
>*FL: 3 apps. 0 gls.*
>**Total:** *3 apps. 0 gls.*

GOUDIE, A. Peter

Role: Goalkeeper
b. Derby

CAREER: Derby Nomads/Jan 1899:FOSSE/
cs 1899:Derby Nomads.

Debut v Luton Town (A) 14.1.1899

An amateur goalkeeper - in fact a reporter on
a Derby newspaper by profession - who stood
in for Godfrey Beardsley in the above match,
after having faced the Corinthians in a
friendly three weeks previously. There can't
have been many players who've made their
senior bow in a 6-1 away win and never been
picked again, but Peter was one such.
Incidentally, crowd disturbances at this game -
including attempts to assault referee Kingswell
- led to Kenilworth Road being closed for a
fortnight.

>**Appearances:**
>*FL: 1 app. 0 gls.*
>**Total:** *1 app. 0 gls.*

GOULD, William

Role: Inside left
b. Burton-on-Trent

CAREER: 1903:Burton United/June 1905:
FOSSE/ May 1906:Bristol Rovers/May 1907:
Glossop/Sept 1908: Bradford City/May 1909:
Manchester City/1911:Tranmere Rovers.

Debut v Leeds City (H) 16.9.05

Scorer of one of the goals which removed
Fosse from the 1903/4 FA Cup (before he had
even made a League debut), Willie went on to
become top marksman at Peel Croft in 1904/5,
but at Leicester had to vie for his favoured
inside-left spot with fellow newcomer Harry
Moody, and was soon sidelined when he
failed to deliver in the finishing stakes. He
became an ever-present on the
left wing at Eastville, and
remained a useful flank
player for his
subsequent League
clubs. His first half-
dozen Manchester
City apearances were
in the Division Two
championship-
clinching games of
1910; and Willie was
later a stalwart of
Tranmere's Lancashire
Combination title-
winning team of 1914.

*Willie
Gould*

>**Appearances:**
>*FL: 6 apps. 1 gl.*
>**Total:** *6 apps. 1 gl.*

GRAHAM, Harry

Role: Inside forward
b. Edinburgh, 16th December 1887

CAREER: Granton Oakvale/Nov 1908:
St.Bernards/Apr 1910:Bradford City/Oct
1911:Birmingham/Sept 1912:Raith Rovers/
June 1913:Heart of Midlothian/Dec 1920: CITY/
Nov 1924:St.Bernards/July 1925:Reading.

Debut v Stoke (H) 25.12.20

After relatively uneventful spells south of the
border, Harry earned both a runners-up medal
and a move to Hearts from Raith's Scottish
Cup Final appearance in 1913, and starred for

Harry Graham

Alick Grant

the Edinburgh club on both sides of WW1, being chosen for the Scottish League in October 1914. A qualified dentist, he was exempt from military call-up, but volunteered and fought with the Gloucestershire Regiment before returning to football action; latterly alongside Arthur Lochhead at Tynecastle. A creative inside-forward, Harry prompted Jock Paterson to a hat-trick in his City debut match, and held his place in an otherwise regularly changing frontline until the arrival of George Carr. It was slightly ironic that he should eventually return to the Edinburgh-based Scottish League club St.Bernards - that club had attempted to block his move from Birmingham to Raith by petitioning the authorities that they still had a claim on Harry's Scottish registration, and were due a fee.

Appearances:
FL: 110 apps. 14 gls.
FAC: 6 apps. 2 gls.
Total: *116 apps. 16 gls.*

GRANT, Alick Frank

Role: Goalkeeper
b. Peasedown St. John, Somerset, 11th August 1916

CAREER: am:Doncaster Rovers/am:Sheffield United/am Apr 1937/pro Aug 1937:Bury/May 1938:Aldershot/Dec 1941:CITY/Nov 1946:Derby County/Nov 1948:Newport County/Aug 1949:Leeds United/Mar 1950:York City/July 1950:Worksop Town/July 1953:Corby Town.

Debut (WW2) v Walsall (H) 15.11.41;
(postwar) v Manchester City (H) 31.8.46

A dependable reserve keeper for most of his clubs, Alick was probably at his peak during the war years, when he guested for Derby, Nottingham Forest, Notts County, Southport and Mansfield, and represented Western Command, as well as turning out regularly for City. Indeed, his trio of guest appearances for Derby included both legs of the 1944/5 Midland Cup Final against Villa. Alick unfortunately had to pick the ball out of the net seven times in City's first two postwar League games, and soon moved 'officially' to the Baseball Ground, where a unique contract for 1947/8 gave him a 'wage' of threepence per week while he studied at Loughborough for teaching exams he'd missed during the war! A Newport County historian retails the story that Alick used to read poetry and classic literature in the dressing room before games and even at half-time.

Appearances:
FL: 2 apps. 0 gls.
WW2: 97 apps. 0 gls.
Total: *99 apps. 0 gls.*

GRAVER, Andrew Martin

Role: Centre forward
b. Craghead, Co.Durham, 12th September 1927

CAREER: Willington/1947:Annfield Plain/ Sept 1947:Newcastle United/Sept 1950: Lincoln City/Dec 1954:CITY/July 1955: Lincoln City/Nov 1955:Stoke City/Sept 1957: Boston United/Oct 1958:Lincoln City/July 1961:Skegness Town/July 1962:Ilkeston Town.

Debut v Chelsea (A) 18.12.54 (scored once)

Given only one League chance on Tyneside, centre-forward Andy soon made up for lost time at Sincil Bank, knocking in 107 goals in 172 games during his first spell there, including six in one game against Crewe as

Andy Graver

Lincoln raced to the 1952 championship of Division Three (North). City paid a club record fee in the hope that Andy's goal touch would keep them in Division One, but despite scoring in each of his first two games, he failed to spark alongside Arthur Rowley, and returned to Lincoln during the close season, after Derek Hines had reclaimed the City No.9 shirt. Press rumours of the time intimated that City had lost heavily on the deals, but in fact Andy's moves both constituted club records (in the same way that Allan Clarke's and Mark Draper's would later): arriving for £27,000 plus Eric Littler (valued at £600), and departing for £26,000. A further move, however, was definitely to City's detriment: for he scored the Stoke goal which sealed their 1956 FA Cup exit. By the time Andy had finished his third spell with the Imps, he had created (and still holds) that club's aggregate scoring record of 143 League goals; and he later briefly served them as youth coach and scout, while working as a financial consultant. His father, Fred, had played as a forward for Grimsby, Leeds and Southend in the 20s; and a brother, Alf, was a Lincoln reserve.

Appearances:
FL: 11 apps. 3 gls.
FAC: 1 app. 0 gls.
Total: *12 apps. 3 gls.*

GRAYSON, Simon Nicholas

Role: Defender / Midfielder
b. Ripon, Yorks, 16th December 1969

CAREER: YT 1986/pro June 1988:Leeds United/Mar 1992:CITY.

Debut v Ipswich Town (A) 14.3.92

The first City skipper to gleefully raise a trophy at Wembley, Simon was acting captain on the day Derby were vanquished in the 1994 Play-off Final, shortly before being named as the supporters' choice for Player of the Year. One of the trio of central defenders initially fielded for that game, yet also the man whose first-time cross from the right led to Steve Walsh's winning goal, Simon had previously starred in midfield and at right-back since his move from Leeds, and his dogged tenacity in each of those positions has been the most prominent feature of his Filbert Street game. A useful anchorman in his early performances, which included the first Wembley Play-off

Simon Grayson, the first City skipper to lift a trophy at Wembley!

encounter with Blackburn, he has subsequently settled to more overtly defensive roles, working hard to overcome occasional faults in technique and concentration, which were naturally more harshly exposed at Premiership level. Simon, whose brother Paul is a Yorkshire county cricketer, made both his senior outings for Leeds (during 1987/8) while still a trainee; his £50,000 transfer to City came on the same day Ali Mauchlen moved to Elland Road on loan.

Appearances (to end 1994/5):
PL: 34 apps. 0 gls.
FL: 66 (11) apps. 2 gls.
FAC: 4 apps. 0 gls.
LC: 6 (1) apps. 0 gls.
AIC: 4 apps. 0 gls.
P/O: 6 (1) apps. 0 gls.
Total: *120 (13) apps. 2 gls.*

GREATOREX, George Arthur

Role: Inside right
b. Huthwaite, Notts, 4th December 1899
d. Huthwaite, Notts, Oct qtr 1964

CAREER: Sutton Junction/(trials-Derby County)/May 1921:CITY/ cs 1922:Mansfield Town/Sutton Town/ Frickley Colliery/June 1928:Scarborough.
Debut v Bradford Park Avenue (A) 27.8.21

An inside-right who had impressed City while playing Central Alliance football against the reserves, and started the 1921/2 season in support of Jock Paterson, George scored on his first two home appearances. Only 5ft. 5ins tall, yet sturdily-built, he was quickly dubbed 'Baby' by the Leicester crowd, but soon faded from the picture as Peter Hodge sought a promotion-winning combination. His move to Mansfield brought him a 22-goal haul from a season in the Midland League, which was then the Stags' station.

Appearances:
FL: 11 apps. 2 gls.
Total: *11 apps. 2 gls.*

GREENHALGH, Brian Arthur

Role: Striker
b. Chesterfield, 20th February 1947

CAREER: app/pro Feb 1965:Preston North End/Sept 1967:Aston Villa/Feb 1969:CITY/ June 1969:Huddersfield Town/July 1971: Cambridge United/Feb 1974:Bournemouth/ (Aug 1974-loan-Torquay United)/Mar 1975: Watford/cs 1976:Dartford/Staines Town/ Carshalton Athletic (p/mgr)/Wealdstone.
Debut v Coventry City (A) 1.4.69 (sub)

A youthful striking partner for Brian Godfrey at both Deepdale and Villa Park, Brian was brought to Filbert Street by Frank O'Farrell, but barely given a chance to contribute to City's 1969 relegation struggle. He was involved in the crucial incident of the denied penalty on his first substitute appearance in the tense game at Highfield Road (when he was felled in the box, only for the referee to reverse his decision, and give Coventry a free-kick from which they raced away to score the only goal), and was never, in fact, on a winning City side. Brian played fifteen times alongside Frank Worthington as Huddersfield

Brian Greenhalgh - a Frank O'Farrell signing.

rose to the First Division, then rediscovered his long-dormant scoring touch at Cambridge, and commenced a series of southern travels, which also took in coaching spells with Maidenhead United and Chesham United. In November 1990, he was appointed as chief scout at Everton.

Appearances:
FL: 2 (2) apps. 0 gls.
TotaL: *2 (2) apps. 0 gls.*

GREW, Mark Stuart

Role: Goalkeeper
b. Bilston, Staffs, 15th February 1958

CAREER: app 1975/pro June 1976:West Bromwich Albion/(Dec 1978-loan-Wigan Athletic)/(Mar 1979-loan-Notts County)/July 1983:CITY/(Oct 1983-loan-Oldham Athletic)/Mar 1984:Ipswich Town/(Sept 1985-loan-

Mark Grew

Fulham)/(Jan 1986-loan-West Bromwich Albion)/(Mar 1986-loan-Derby County)/June 1986:Port Vale/(Oct 1990-loan-Blackburn Rovers)/July 1992:Cardiff City/cs 1994: Stafford Rangers/Sept 1994:Hednesford Town.

Debut v Notts County (H) 27.8.83

When City laid out £60,000 for goalkeeper Mark while Mark Wallington was in contractual dispute, the newcomer had just completed eight years at the Hawthorns, during which he had patiently aggregated a mere 33 League games. Mark's West Brom debut had, in fact, been a real oddity for the time: coming on as substitute keeper in a 1978/9 UEFA Cup tie against Galatasaray. At Filbert Street, he had an unnerving introduction, being beaten by a succession of long-range power shots as City struggled to find their First Division feet, and giving way to Wallington after five straight defeats and a 14-goal deficit. Mark fared little better at Portman Road, in the shadow of Paul Cooper, but seemed set fair to establish some sort of record for the number of loan deals he had been involved in. He suffered a serious knee injury early in his Port Vale career, but returned to perform heroically in both their 1988 Cup run and their 1989 promotion campaign, going on to complete over 200

League and Cup games for them until being freed following their 1992 relegation. At Cardiff, Mark was briefly a rival with Gavin Ward for first team duties.

Appearances:
FL: 5 apps. 0 gls.
Total: *5 apps. 0 gls.*

GREWCOCK, Neil

Role: Winger
b. Leicester, 26th April 1962

CAREER: app June 1978/pro June 1979:CITY/ Mar 1982:Gillingham/June 1983:Shepshed Charterhouse/Aug 1984:Burnley/(Aug 1991- trials-Cardiff City)/1991:Burnley Bank Hall.

Debut v Cardiff City (H) 3.3.79 (scored once)

Still a 16-year-old apprentice when Jock Wallace gave him a goal-crowned League baptism, Neil had to bide his time for another crack at senior action, having one short spell on either wing near the beginning and end of

Neil Grewcock

the 1980/1 First Division campaign. Short but stocky, Neil didn't quite develop the pace necessary to maintain a flank position, and drifted into a midfield role for Gillingham. He then returned to Leicestershire with his League career seemingly at an end, but was offered a lifeline back by John Bond, which he grasped eagerly. His performances were a rare bright element of Burnley's near-disastrous 1987 cliffhanger, and his goal in the final Fourth Division game of that season helped ward off the prospect of the old club dropping out of the League. When finally freed from Turf Moor, Neil had amassed 202 League appearances for the Clarets, and had claimed 27 goals.

Appearances:
FL: 7 (1) apps. 1 gl.
LC: 0 (1) app. 0 gls.
Total: *7 (2) apps. 1 gl.*

GRIEVE, Robert

Role: Centre forward
b. Greenock, Renfrewshire, 28th March 1884

CAREER: 1903:Morton/Aug 1906:Manchester City/Nov 1909:Accrington Stanley/Dec 1910: FOSSE/cs 1911:Southport Central/1911: Accrington Stanley.

Debut v Wolverhampton Wanderers (H) 7.1.11 (scored twice)

A Scottish centre-forward whose 44 League games for Manchester City had produced 18 goals, Robert had purportedly regained amateur status by the time he was snapped up from Lancashire Combination football by Fosse to replace the departed Jack Hall. He had the ill-fortune, however, to arrive at Filbert Street less than a month before Fred Shinton returned from Bolton, and his first team tenure was accordingly short. It was marked by one oddity, though, which points to the idiosyncracy of then-prevailing registration rules: only a week after his Fosse debut, he played for Accrington in their First Round FA Cup tie against Wolves! Robert's main claim to fame while playing for his local club had been a 4-goal haul from Morton's 1906 Renfrewshire Cup Final win over Arthurlie.

Appearances:
FL: 4 apps. 2 gls.
Total: *4 apps. 2 gls.*

GRIFFITHS, William Malwyn

Role: Outside right
b. Merthyr Tydfil, 8th March 1919
d. Wigston, Leics, 5th April 1969

CAREER: Merthyr Thursday/am Sept 1935/ pro Feb 1937:Arsenal/(May 1936-loan-Margate)/Sept 1938:CITY/cs 1956:Burton Albion.

Debut v Bolton Wanderers (H) 24.9.38

Plucked from Welsh junior football by Arsenal, and then loaned out to their own 'nursery' club for experience, right winger Mal made his senior Highbury bow against City in February 1938, and contributed five goals in nine appearances as the Gunners raced to the First Division title that year. Rivalries for first team shirts at Arsenal were fierce, however, and only a bargain £750 transfer to City opened the door to a regular position - one Mal was still holding some 18 years later. He 'lost' one League appearance and one goal when the 1939/40 season was abandoned after only three fixtures, and after he had become the first senior player to be automatically conscripted (into the Welsh Regiment), City somehow contrived to lose touch with Mal

himself during the war. Given the list of clubs for whom he guested (Cardiff, Aldershot, Fulham, Bournemouth, Chelsea, Brighton and Southampton) this was perhaps not so surprising, but Johnny Duncan (on taking over the managerial reins) had to despatch a City director to Wales to persuade Mal to resume his full-time Leicester career. Thereafter, though, Mal's consistency made him the one automatic choice in an ever-changing City front line, and his steady goalscoring record peaked at two crucial times: when he added to his six counters on City's 1949 Cup run the club's first-ever goal at Wembley, and when he notched his own best seasonal League total of eleven during the 1954 Division Two championship effort. City played an invited International XI at the end of their next promotion campaign in a testimonial match for Mal, who had represented his own country eleven times (scoring twice) between 1947 and 1954. He retired after a season at Wellington Street to run the Queen's Head in Wigston Magna.

Appearances:
FL: 373 apps. 66 gls.
FAC: 36 apps. 10 gls.
WW2: 11 apps. 3 gls.
Total: *420 apps. 79 gls.*

Mal Griffiths taking a corner at Hillsborough

Percy Grosvenor

GROGAN, John

Role: Half back
b. Paisley, Renfrewshire,
30th October 1915

CAREER: Shawfield Juniors/Oct 1933:CITY/Sept 1947:Mansfield Town.

Debut v Newcastle United (A) 19.10.35

Another player who was robbed of his best footballing years by the war, Johnny was Sep Smith's understudy at right-half during the four League seasons before the break, and then had to vie with the same player for the centre-half shirt when League competition resumed. As a trusty reserve, he made several appearances for the London Combination representative XI (indeed, playing for them in front of a 40,000 crowd in Brussels, against Diables Rouges, some seven months before his senior City bow); while as a wartime guest he also turned out for Northampton Town, Crystal Palace, Swansea Town, Luton Town and Grimsby Town. It was suspected that Johnny was nearing retirement when City let him move to Field Mill, but he kept going there for another five years, unfortunately extending his goalless run across 217 League and Cup appearances for the Stags.

Johnny Grogan

> **Appearances:**
> *FL: 46 apps. 0 gls.*
> *FAC: 6 apps. 0 gls.*
> *WW2: 38 apps. 0 gls.*
> **Total:** *90 apps. 0 gls.*

GROSVENOR, Percy

Role: Left half
b. Evesham, Worcs, 17th March 1911

CAREER: Evesham Town/Feb 1933:CITY.

Debut v Aston Villa (H) 30.12.33

A left-half from a footballing family - his father had been on Wolves' books, brother Tom (Birmingham, Sheffield Wednesday, Bolton) was an England international, and younger brother Clifford joined the City reserve roster in August 1937 - Percy had been passed over by West Brom after trials when City took him on as a likely understudy to George Ritchie. He played thirteen League and Cup games during his first season before appearing in a beaten side - that being in the club's first FA Cup semi-final in 1934 - and went on to inherit Ritchie's shirt as a regular from 1935/6 to the outbreak of war, showing both fight and finesse in City's up-and-down travails of the time. Percy also briefly guested for Northampton Town during WW2.

> **Appearances:**
> *FL: 168 apps. 1 gl.*
> *FAC: 12 apps. 0 gls.*
> *WW2: 6 apps. 0 gls.*
> **Total:** *186 apps. 1 gl.*

GROVES, Paul

Role: Midfield
b. Derby, 28th February 1966

CAREER: Belper Town/Nov 1986:Burton
Albion/Apr 1988:CITY/(Aug 1989-loan-
Lincoln City)/Jan 1990:Blackpool/Aug 1992:
Grimsby Town.

Debut v Huddersfield Town (H) 2.5.88
(sub; scored once)

A former part-timer with Burton, whom he
helped to the Wembley Final of the FA Trophy
in 1987 (also scoring their consolation goal in a
replay defeat), Paul was offered the chance to
drop his bricklaying day-job when signed by
David Pleat after the 1988 transfer deadline.
The strongly-built attacking midfielder cost
£12,000 and the promise of a visit from City to
play a friendly under Burton's new
floodlights, and Pleat received Football League
sanction to name him amongst the thirteen
players for the season's penultimate game,
against an already-relegated Huddersfield.
Paul's fine header then made him the first City
substitute to score on his debut; while another
headed goal, in the Littlewoods Cup replay at
Nottingham Forest, proved the high point of
his first full season as a City squad player.
Overall, though, his impact at senior level was
muted and an onward transfer looked likely
from the moment City offered him the chance
to move to Peterborough in March 1989. Paul
soon afterwards accompanied Grant Brown on
loan at Sincil Bank (scoring once in a ten-game
spell), then eventually signed up at Bloomfield
Road for a £60,000 fee. He played at Wembley
again in 1991, when Blackpool failed at the
final Play-off hurdle despite his opening goal,
but finally appeared on a winning side at the
Stadium a year later when the Seasiders sealed
promotion under his captaincy. Back at Filbert
Street with Grimsby in March 1993, Paul
became the first ex-City player ever to notch
an own goal to the credit of his old club at
competitive level. His final goal of 1994/5 was
his 50th League strike at the right end.

Appearances:
FL: 7 (9) apps. 1 gl.
FAC: 0 (1) app. 0 gls.
LC: 1 app. 1 gl.
FMC: 0 (1) app. 0 gls.
Total: *8 (11) apps. 2 gls.*

Paul Groves

GURRY, John William

Role: Right half / Inside right
b. Barking, Essex, 17th July 1907
d. Leicester, 1st October 1983

CAREER: am Dec 1929: West Ham United/
Barking Town/Mar 1930:CITY/July 1935:
Southampton/June 1936:Chester.

Debut v Leeds United (A) 12.11.32

Brought out of the Athenian League by City
(partly with the lure of a job in the Leicester
hosiery trade), Jack was utilised as a reserve
right-half or inside-forward, but suffered like

several players of his era from an inability to dislodge the consistent Sep Smith. He fared little better at either of his subsequent League clubs, but did end his career with three senior goals to his credit: all scored for Chester against Lincoln City in a 7-3 win in November 1936! Strangely enough, Jack also hit one hat-trick for City reserves in spectacular circumstances: on the opening day of 1933/4, when the first of his triple in a 5-1 win was registered after 30 seconds. His first-team debut should have arrived a year earlier than it did: Jack was chosen to replace Ernie Hine for the November 1931 home game with Sheffield United, but went down with 'flu the day before.

Appearances:
FL: 23 apps. 0 gls.
Total: *23 apps. 0 gls.*

GWYNNE, Ernest

Role: Centre forward

CAREER: Aug 1903:FOSSE.
Debut v Woolwich Arsenal (A) 26.10.03

A centre-forward trialist from junior football in the Birmingham area, Ernest could have asked for better luck in making his one and only League appearance for Fosse - the above match ended in a 0-8 defeat.

Appearances:
FL: 1 app. 0 gls.
Total: *1 app. 0 gls.*

*Ernest
Gwynne*

Jack Gurry

HACKETT, A.

Role: Inside left

CAREER: Sept 1901:FOSSE/Leicester
Imperial.

Debut v West Bromwich Albion (A) 6.1.02

An inside-left who played in the last two
pre-season trial matches of August 1901 and
impressed sufficiently to earn a professional
contract, he nonetheless failed to spark his
senior forward colleagues into an effective
scoring response in two away defeats during
1901/2.

Appearances:
FL: 2 apps. 0 gls.
Total: *2 apps. 0 gls.*

HADLEY, Arthur

Role: Outside right
b. 1877

CAREER: cs 1895:Reading/cs 1898:Notts
County/Aug 1902:FOSSE/cs 1904:not known/
Apr 1905:FOSSE/cs 1905:not known/
Dec 1906:Notts County.

Debut v Small Heath (H) 6.9.02

A goalscoring outside-right in both the
Southern and Football Leagues, Arthur was a
member of the first Reading side to play at
Elm Park, and the second Magpies team to
reach third place in the First Division (their

Arthur Hadley

highest position ever). His goal supply,
however, rather dried up as Fosse slithered
towards the Second Division basement, even if
Arthur was a popularly regarded provider. He
was a loyal one, too, for he came back in April
1905 for a 5-game stint to help out the club
which had released him almost a year
previously.

Appearances:
FL: 64 apps. 4 gls.
FAC: 7 apps. 3 gls.
Total: *71 apps. 7 gls.*

HAIG, Paul

Role: Outside left
b. Nottingham

CAREER: Mapperley/cs 1907:Eastwood
Rangers/Feb 1911:FOSSE/cs 1911:Mansfield
Mechanics/cs 1912:Eastwood Rangers/Aug
1913:Notts County/cs 1914:Loughborough
Corinthians.

Debut v Huddersfield Town (H) 25.2.11

An outside-left who briefly stepped up from
Notts & Derbyshire League football at a fee of
£25, and quickly dropped down again to the
Central Alliance, Paul made little impact as
Syd Owen's replacement in a Fosse side which
struggled to 15th place in Division Two. He
later made one League appearance for the
Magpies.

Appearances:
FL: 12 apps. 2 gls.
Total: *12 apps. 2 gls.*

HAINES, John Thomas W.

Role: Inside forward / Wing half
b. Wickhamford, Worcs, 24th April 1920
d. Evesham, Worcs, 19th March 1987

CAREER: Evesham Town/Cheltenham Town/
Nov 1937:Liverpool/June 1939:Swansea Town/
July 1947:CITY/Mar 1948:West Bromwich
Albion/Dec 1949:Bradford Park Avenue/
Oct 1953:Rochdale/July 1955:Chester/cs 1957:
Wellington Town/cs 1958:Kidderminster
Harriers/Oct 1958:Evesham Town.

Debut v Leeds United (A) 23.8.47

His early career stymied by the outbreak of
war, Jack made his long-delayed League debut

Jack Haines

with Swansea in 1946/7 (after having guested for Worcester City, Bradford Park Avenue, Doncaster, Lincoln, Notts County and Wrexham), and impressed Johnny Duncan as a forceful linkman. The City manager seemed unsure of how best to utilise Jack at Filbert Street, however - handing him shirts numbered 4, 6, 8, 9 and 10 in his limited spell with City, before swapping him for Peter McKennan. Jack was used exclusively in the forward line at The Hawthorns, and soon won an England cap, scoring twice against Switzerland. Albion were promoted back to the top flight in 1949, but Jack was tasting more bitter fortunes the next season, as Bradford dropped from the Second to the Third Division (North). Harry Catterick paid a club record of £2,000 to take Jack to Rochdale as he continued to play out his career in the League's lower echelons.

Appearances:
FL: 12 apps. 3 gls.
FAC: 3 apps. 1 gl.
Total: *15 apps. 4 gls.*

HALES, A.

Role: Outside left

CAREER:
Aug 1902:FOSSE.
Debut v Burnley (H) 27.9.02

A.Hales

An outside-left, presumed to have been a local trialist, this Fossil is another whose sole senior game (a 2-1 victory) represents a flicker in a surrounding obscurity our research has failed to penetrate.

Appearances:
FL: 1 app. 0 gls.
Total: *1 app. 0 gls.*

HALL, Benjamin

Role: Centre half
b. Ecclesfield, Yorkshire, 6th March 1881
d. 1963

CAREER: Jan 1900:Grimsby Town/Aug 1903: Derby County/Aug 1911:FOSSE/cs 1912: Hyde/1912:Heywood United (p/coach)/ cs 1913:South Shields.
Debut v Gainsborough Trinity (A) 2.9.11

An inside-right with the Mariners, Ben was taken on by Derby to replace the charismatic Archie Goodall at centre-half, when that role was effectively the midfield lynchpin of the side, and skill and vision were more important requisites than brawn. He made 245 League appearances for the Rams (scoring 11 times), but had lost much of his pace by the time he joined Fosse, and

Ben Hall

could not for long hold off the challenge of the younger Percy Hanger for the pivot's position. He did, though, make a veritable veteran's comeback to Filbert Street during WW1; often assisting Fosse, but almost as regularly making up the numbers for the visitors: Grimsby (twice), Forest, Huddersfield and Lincoln amongst them. He also turned out five times for Derby during this period. Ben became manager of Bristol Rovers in May 1920, later bossed Loughborough Corinthians (May 1929-Jan 1931), briefly contributed a column on local football to the *'Leicester Mail'*, took up an appointment as Leicestershire FA coach in 1935, and was still involved in the game, scouting for Southend United, after WW2. He had three brothers who also played League football: Ellis, Fretwell and Harry.

Appearances:
FL: 14 apps. 0 gls.
WW1: 30 apps. 0 gls.
Total: *44 apps. 0 gls.*

HALL, John Henry

Role: Centre forward
b. Hucknall, Notts,
3rd July 1883
d. Nottingham, 1938 (?)

CAREER: Newark/ (trials-Nottingham Forest)/Oct 1904:Stoke/ May 1906:Brighton & Hove Albion/Apr 1908: Middlesbrough/June 1910: FOSSE/Dec 1910:Birmingham/ 1915:Hucknall Town.

Debut v Bolton Wanderers (H) 3.9.10 (scored twice)

The top scorer for each of his respective clubs from 1905/6 onwards (outshooting even Steve Bloomer during his three years at Ayresome), Jack had only a short spell as leader of Fosse's attack before the directorate accepted a 'substantial' bid from Birmingham for his services. He had certainly engendered high expectations among the Fosse faithful: in the four public trial matches of August 1910, he scored eleven goals, including three hat-tricks! Jack also rewarded Birmingham with a goal in each of his first six League games, scored two for them against Fosse the following season and, in 1912/13, hit a treble against his former

team. (We still harbour suspicions that the Jack Hall who coached extensively in Holland between the wars - for Feyenoord and PSV amongst others - may have been this ex-Fossil, though the oft-quoted date of death would contradict this).

Appearances:
FL: 15 apps. 5 gls.
Total: *15 apps. 5 gls.*

HALTON, Reginald Lloyd

Role: Left half
b. Buxton, Derbyshire, 11th July 1916
d. Buxton, March 1988

CAREER: Cheddington Hospital FC/Oct 1936:Manchester United/June 1937:Notts County/Nov 1937:Bury/Dec 1948: Chesterfield/Sept 1950:CITY/ Feb 1953: Scarborough (p/mgr)/ cs 1954:Goole Town.

Debut v Cardiff City (H) 30.9.50

Starting his career as an outside-left at Old Trafford, Reg soon settled down as a constructive left-half at Gigg Lane, and may well have developed to

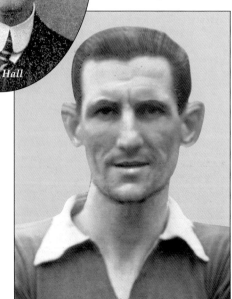

Jack Hall

Reg Halton

international level if the war had not interrupted his career. As it was, he guested for Portsmouth, Aldershot, Millwall, Rochdale, Southampton, York City and Fulham, and also played perhaps his most memorable match before League football resumed - in the Arsenal side which met Moscow Dynamo in a fogbound classic of propaganda and prestige in November 1945. Reg was 34 when former Bury boss Norman Bullock signed him for the second time to add experience to City's middle line, and he gave two seasons' staunch service before taking the reins (and a centre-forward role!) at Scarborough, from where he sent the young Colin Appleton to Filbert Street. As a young cricketing prospect, Reg had undergone trials with both Lancashire and Worcestershire, and he later played at Minor Counties level with Staffordshire.

Appearances:
FL: 64 apps. 3 gls.
FAC: 3 apps. 0 gls.
Total: *67 apps. 3 gls.*

Stewart Hamill

HAMILL, Stewart

Role: Winger
b. Glasgow, 22nd January 1960

CAREER: Anniesland United/Possil YM/ Pollok/Sept 1980:CITY/(Mar 1982-loan-Scunthorpe United)/Sept 1982:Kettering Town/Aug 1983:Nuneaton Borough/Mar 1986: Northampton Town/cs 1986:Altrincham/ Mar 1987:Scarborough/Aug 1988:Boston United/(Summer 1989-tour-Middlesex Wanderers)/1990:not known/Aug 1992: Lutterworth Town/Houghton Rangers.

Debut v Manchester City (H) 8.11.80

Winger or midfielder Stewart made a rapid rise from part-time Scottish junior football - and a job as a Co-Op van driver - to the First Division, and held his place in Jock Wallace's young side for eight games. He didn't then return until the second match of the 1981/2 Second Division season, but was unfortunate to be limited to two games, especially as he scored the winning goal in each of them. Scunthorpe failed to take up their option on Stewart's signature after his 4-game loan spell, and he dropped into non-league football. Former Nuneaton manager Graham Carr gave him a brief chance at a return to the League fray with Northampton, but a contract was not forthcoming despite Stewart scoring after a mere 35 seconds of his Cobblers debut at Tranmere. However, a year later, he joined Scarborough at precisely the time they were overtaking Barnet to become the first side automatically promoted from the top of the non-league pyramid to the Fourth Division; and was part of that club's first-ever League line-up (against Wolves).

Appearances:
FL: 10 apps. 2 gls.
Total: *10 apps. 2 gls.*

HAMILTON, John

Role: Centre half
b. Ayrshire, 1872

CAREER: Ayr/June 1894:Wolverhampton Wanderers/cs 1895:Loughborough/cs 1897: Bristol City/Sept 1900:FOSSE/June 1901: Watford/cs 1902:Wellingborough/cs 1903: Fulham.

Debut v Grimsby Town (H) 15.9.1900

Reportedly leaving Ayr 'in consequence of the dullness of trade', Jack became an early victim of serious injury at Wolves, an ever-present at left-half in Loughborough's inaugural League season,

Jack Hamilton

and the tough-tackling skipper of Bristol City for the last of his Southern League years there, when he played alongside the likes of Harry Davy, Albert Carnelly, Billy Langham and Jimmy Stevenson. He took the pivot's role during his Fosse season, when the failings of the forward line were more marked than those of the defence, and, after further Southern League ramblings, remained at Craven Cottage on the training staff until 1910, then returned to Ashton Gate as reserve trainer and, during WW1, manager. A typical commentary on his game dates from 1902: 'He is endowed with any amount of pluck and endurance, is a champion tackler, and feeds his forwards with wonderful tact and judgment'. (Other players named John Hamilton on the football scene at this time, whose careers have elsewhere been retrospectively conflated with 'our' man, included a winger who turned out successively for Cambuslang, Sunderland, Burton Swifts, Gainsborough Trinity and Millwall; a Derby County forward; and a half-back better known as Jock who served Brentford, Leeds City and Swansea Town).

Appearances:
FL: 28 apps. 0 gls.
FAC: 1 app. 0 gls.
Total: *29 apps. 0 gls.*

HAMILTON, Neville Roy

Role: Midfield
b. Leicester, 19th April 1960

CAREER: app Nov 1976/pro Oct 1977:CITY/ Jan 1979:Mansfield Town/cs 1981:Rochdale/ cs 1984:Wolverhampton Wanderers.

Debut v Manchester United (A) 27.12.77

Nev Hamilton

A teenage midfielder given one game by Frank McLintock and three more by caretaker boss Ian MacFarlane after City's 1978 relegation had become a foregone conclusion, Nev raised £25,000 when sold to Field Mill by Jock Wallace, and went on to play 163 League games for Mansfield and Rochdale before Tommy Docherty took him to Molineux for a shot at Second Division football. Tragically, though, Nev suffered a heart attack during pre-season training with Wolves, and was forced to retire on medical advice before kicking a ball in anger for them. More happily, after recovery, he qualified as a full FA coach in August 1986 and, in the summer of 1989, rejoined City as Community Development Officer. Nev was the beneficiary of a Saffron Lane friendly against an Ex-City All Stars XI in July 1993.

Appearances:
FL: 4 apps. 0 gls.
Total: *4 apps. 0 gls.*

HAMMOND, Walter Henry

Role: Centre forward
b. Chorlton, Lancs, 1868
d. Bolton, December 1921

CAREER: Edgehill/1889:Everton/June 1891: Sheffield United/cs 1897:New Brighton Tower/May 1900:FOSSE.

Debut v Nottingham Forest (A) FAC 9.2.01

Harry Hammond

A centre-forward whose Filbert Street season seemed to be jinxed, Harry had no sooner signed from Fosse's Division Two rivals New Brighton than he was hospitalised with typhoid fever, and when he finally regained fitness some five months later, he had to lead a side in the middle of an eleven-game run without a win. His debut game, a 1-5 defeat, was the only occasion that Leicester and Forest have been drawn together in the FA Cup. Previously, Harry had been a prolific goalscorer for the Blades (representing the Football League once in 1894), and had easily topped New Brighton's scoring charts in his final season there despite spending most of it in the centre-half berth. One amusing story attaches to Harry from his Sheffield days: in becoming the first player from that club to be sent off in a League match, for fighting a Crewe defender, he so incensed the crowd that a panicky flight from the ground seemed the wisest option to him. His teammates eventually found him hiding on Crewe station some time after the match; still wearing his kit!

Appearances:
FL: 4 apps. 1 gl.
FAC: 1 app. 0 gls.
Total: *5 apps. 1 gl.*

HANGER, Percy

Role: Centre half
b. Kettering, Northants, c 1889

CAREER: Kettering St.Mary's/Kettering/ Apr 1910:FOSSE/cs 1913:Kettering.

Debut v Burnley (H) 23.4.10

A centre-half of boundless stamina who understudied both Andy Aitken and Ben Hall before securing a regular first-team slot for himself, Percy had first played trial games for Fosse reserves in December 1908, and was a member of a noted Northamptonshire footballing family,

Percy Hanger

of whom Harry was a half-back with Bradford City and Crystal Palace from 1906 until his death in WW1 action.

Appearances:
FL: 54 apps. 0 gls.
FAC: 3 apps. 1 gl.
Total: *57 apps. 1 gl.*

HARDY, Walter

Role: Forward

CAREER: Aug 1892:Long Eaton Rangers/ Dec 1892:FOSSE.

Debut v Wednesbury Old Athletic (A)
ML 24.12.1892 (scored once)

Described in the local press as a former professional (clubs unknown) who had regained amateur status with Long Eaton, Walter appeared at either outside- or inside-right in eleven consecutive Midland League games for Fosse during their second season in that competition, and also claimed four goals from four friendly outings.

Appearances:
ML: 11 apps. 2 gls.
Total: *11 apps. 2 gls.*

HARPER, Ernest

Role: Full back

CAREER: Hugglescote United/Aug 1904: FOSSE/Mar 1905:Derby County.

Debut v Burton United (A) 21.1.05

An amateur full-back who was elevated from the reserves for Fosse's first away win of 1904/5, Ernest could not thereafter claim a place against the heavy competition of Bennett, Oakes, Robinson and Pollock. He made no League appearances for Derby.

Ernest Harper

Appearances:
FL: 1 app. 0 gls.
Total: *1 app. 0 gls.*

HARPER, William E.

Role: Outside left
b. Nechells, Birmingham, 1876
d. Weston-super-Mare, 1944

CAREER: Smethwick Wesleyan Rovers/Oct 1899:West Bromwich Albion/Sept 1903:FOSSE.

Debut v Chesterfield (H) 26.9.03

Another Fossil who failed to appear on a winning side (unsurprisingly, in the season Fosse first had to go to the re-election vote), Billy was a tall, speedy outside-left with a modicum of previous experience at Albion, having played seven times in their 1902 promotion side, but only once in Division One. He had represented 'England' in 1899 in the little-known series of Junior international matches against Scotland - as there was no precise equivalent south of the border to Scottish Junior football (a non-league set-up that still exists, and confusingly has nothing to do with the ages of the players), the 'national' representative side was then drawn almost wholly from minor West Midland clubs.

Appearances:
FL: 4 apps. 0 gls.
Total: *4 apps. 0 gls.*

HARRIS, W.H.

Role: Goalkeeper

CAREER: Leicester Teachers/1890: Loughborough/Jan 1892:FOSSE.

Debut v Rotherham Town (H) ML 9.1.1892

The goalkeeper in Fosse's best win of their (otherwise dispiriting) inaugural Midland League campaign - and that by 4-1 against the champions-to-be - Harris won subsequent selection only in three friendlies that term.

Appearances:
ML: 1 app. 0 gls.
Total: *1 app. 0 gls.*

HARRISON, Albert

Role: Centre half
b. Leigh, Lancs, 15th February 1904

CAREER: West Leigh/am cs 1921:Wigan Borough/cs 1923:Atherton Colliery/Sept 1925: Chorley/Mar 1927:Nottingham Forest/ Dec 1929:CITY/May 1931:Dundalk/cs 1932: Drumcondra/July 1933:Wigan Athletic.

Debut v Derby County (H) 7.12.29

A tall blond centre-half who took over the pivotal berth from George Carr, Albert had been chosen the summer previously for the FA

Albert Harrison

team touring South Africa, when he played in one 'Test Match' behind Arthur Chandler. His first-team tenure at Filbert Street was not a long one, however - effectively, he carried the can for a 2-8 mauling at Grimsby in November 1930, and then found himself displaced by the up-and-coming Roger Heywood. He was invariably known during his subsequent Irish career as 'Snowy'.

Appearances:
FL: 32 apps. 1 gl.
FAC: 1 app. 0 gls.
Total: *33 apps. 1 gl.*

HARRISON, Derek

Role: Centre half
b. Littlethorpe, Leics, 9th February 1950

CAREER: app Aug 1965/pro Feb 1967:CITY/ Feb 1971:Torquay United/June 1975: Colchester United/cs 1976:Dawlish.

Debut v Bristol City (H) LC 10.9.69

A tall, commanding centre-half and skipper for City reserves, Derek was unlucky to be understudying the consistent John Sjoberg for the bulk of his Filbert Street career, and to be effectively queue-jumped by the more versatile Malcolm Manley. Derek's two League

Derek Harrison

Cup appearances came 13 months apart, and with his chances clearly limited he moved to Plainmoor after a loan spell to tot up 127 League games. Bobby Roberts then took him on at Layer Road, but he failed to make much impression there, and dropped into non-league football.

Appearances:
LC: 2 apps. 0 gls.
Total: *2 apps. 0 gls.*

HARRISON, George

Role: Outside left
b. Church Gresley, Derbyshire, 18th July 1892
d. Derby, 12th March 1939

CAREER: Gresley Rovers/Feb 1911:FOSSE/ Apr 1913:Everton/Dec 1923:Preston North End/Nov 1931:Blackpool.

Debut v Leeds City (H) 22.4.11

George Harrison

A hefty, direct outside-left who soon showed with Fosse that he was worthy of a much higher grade of football, George was ever-present in 1912/13 and then signed for Everton two days after the final game. At Goodison he won a First Division championship medal in 1915, and his continuing reliability as both a provider of quality crosses and a vicious finisher earned him two full England caps after the war; during which he returned to Leicester for a handful of regional games, and also guested for Rangers and West Ham. George's stamina was almost as remarkable as his touchline skill, and he was nearly forty when he retired (having just topped a century of League goals) from the game, initially to run a pub in Preston. He was a licensee back in his native village at the time of his early death. His son, also George and also a winger, signed professional forms for City in October 1931, after trials, but failed to break through to senior level.

Appearances:
FL: 59 apps. 9 gls.
FAC: 1 app. 0 gls.
WW1: 5 apps. 2 gls.
Total: *65 apps. 11 gls.*

HARRISON, James Charles

Role: Full back
b. Leicester, 12th February 1921

CAREER: Wellington Victoria/Dec 1940:
CITY/July 1949:Aston Villa/July 1951:
Coventry City/July 1953:Corby Town.
*Debut (WW2) v Notts County (H) 7.12.40;
(postwar) v Fulham (A) 21.9.46 (scored once)*

A local signing during WW2, Jimmy served in
the forces in India and Burma and guested for
Reading before making his League bow for
City as a centre-forward; a position to which
he occasionally reverted in emergencies from
his more regular slot at full-back. His bulk and
enthusiasm appeared to suit him for forward
forays, but the fact that Jimmy had only ever
added one other first-team counter to his
debut goal made his selection in the No.9 shirt
for City's first Wembley Final something of a
desperate gamble; albeit one partly dictated by
circumstance. The crucial face-saving game at
Cardiff a week after the Cup Final was
Jimmy's last for City, for Villa stepped in with
a £12,000 bid during the close season. He was
only, however, to make eight League
appearances for them (scoring once) before
moving on again to Highfield Road, where a
team with an average age of 31 dropped from
the Second to the Third Division (North), yet

still thrashed City in the FA Cup. Jimmy later
settled to run a successful haulage business
from a Wigston base.

Appearances:
FL: 81 apps. 1 gl.
FAC: 11 apps. 1 gl.
WW2: 15 apps. 3 gls.
Total: *107 apps. 5 gls.*

HARRISON, Walter Edward

Role: Right half
b. Coalville, Leics, 16th January 1923

CAREER: Coalville Town/Navy football/
am June 1945/pro Aug 1945:CITY/Dec 1950:
Chesterfield/1953:Corby Town.

*Walter
Harrison*

Jimmy Harrison

Debut (WW2) v Millwall (H) 2.2.46 (scored once); (postwar) v West Ham United (A) 7.9.46

A tall, wiry right-half who had guested for Kilmarnock (11 games; 4 goals) while on Navy service during the war, Walter soon gained the nickname 'Spider' from the Filbert Street fans, and had his intelligent prompting recognised with two England 'B' caps in May 1949, immediately after helping City to Wembley and picking up a runners-up medal alongside his unrelated namesake. Walter excelled at the wall-pass game, but is still remembered by more senior City supporters for a 50-yard dribble past five men that ended with him scoring a Cup goal against Sheffield Wednesday in 1948. Chesterfield recruited him, for £8,500, to their unsuccessful fight against relegation from the Second Division in 1951, but he went on to make 75 League appearances (13 goals) for the Saltergate side. Curiously, Walter had previously twice completed City games against the Spireites in goal: as City's favoured stand-in, he had to take over the green jersey three times between November 1947 and September 1948, replacing Joe Calvert, Gordon Bradley and Les Major after each had suffered injuries. When his

playing career had finished, Walter qualified as a childcare worker and also acted as trainer to Friar Lane Old Boys.

Appearances:
FL: 125 apps. 3 gls.
FAC: 18 apps. 2 gls.
WW2: 2 apps. 1 gl.
Total: *145 apps. 6 gls.*

HARROLD, Sidney

Sid Harrold

Role: Outside left
b. Stourbridge, Worcs, 5th June 1895

CAREER:
Willenhall Swifts/
1914:Stourbridge/
Wednesbury/
Feb 1919:FOSSE/
May 1920: Nottingham Forest/June 1922: Accrington Stanley.

Debut (WW1) v Nottingham Forest (A) 11.1.19; (postwar) v Wolverhampton Wanderers (H) 30.8.19

HARROLD, James George William

Role: Centre half
b. Poplar, London, 26th March 1892
d. Epsom, Surrey, 7th October 1950

CAREER: 1909:Custom House (Dec 1911-trials-Huddersfield Town)/(1912-am registration-West Ham United)/Feb 1913: FOSSE/July 1923:Millwall/Aug 1925:Clapton Orient.

Debut v Grimsby Town (H) 15.2.13

Fosse were in such a hurry to play this England amateur international centre-half that they were subsequently fined two guineas by the FA for fielding him before the completion of transfer formalities (one week after he'd first appeared for his country, and scored, in Wales, and less than a fortnight before he won his only other

cap, in Paris). The tall Londoner, blessed with brilliant heading ability and a seemingly telescopic tackle, soon proved his worth, and signed as a professional during the 1913 close season. Jim went on to give superb service on both sides of WW1, during which he served with the RAF, and took a benefit from the home game with Blackpool in December 1920. After moving back to London (for, surprisingly, only a two-game, one-goal spell at The Den, and no senior outings at all for Orient), he also started a parallel career with Essex CCC, for whom he played occasional first-class cricket until 1929.

Appearances:
FL: 206 apps. 7 gls.
FAC: 12 apps. 0 gls.
WW1: 13 apps. 0 gls.
Total: *231 apps. 7 gls.*

Unrelated to Jim, Sidney was an outside-left who joined Fosse during the final season of WW1 football, and appeared in the side for City's first League outing after reconstruction, but who found himself out of favour with Peter Hodge before the term was over. He later made 13 appearances in Forest's Second Division championship campaign of 1921/2, but a broken ankle suffered during his sixth game for Accrington brought his career to a sadly premature end. A combined City/Forest XI (featuring Newton, Thomson, Adcock, King and Tompkin) played a Northern selection at Peel Park in a benefit game for Sid in May 1923; while the latter became in turn a cricket pro and a licensee in Wednesbury.

Appearances:
FL: 18 apps. 2 gls.
WW1: 16 apps. 2 gls.
Total: *34 apps. 4 gls.*

HASTIE, George

Role: Inside left
b. Glasgow

CAREER: Govan Glentoran/July 1906:
Ashfield/June 1909:Kilmarnock/June 1910:
Bristol Rovers/Bath City/Nov 1911:
Kilmarnock/Aug 1912:St.Johnstone/
Nov 1912:Abercorn/July 1914:FOSSE/
Oct 1915: Belfast United/cs 1919:Belfast
Celtic/Abercorn/Sept 1920:Johnstone.

Debut v Lincoln City (H) 2.9.14

A Scottish inside-left caught up with understandable bewilderment in Fosse's plummet to the Second Division re-election zone in the war-shadowed season of 1914/15. A Junior international, George had previously claimed six goals in 20 Southern League games for Bristol Rovers, and a Scottish Qualifying Cup winner's medal with Abercorn in 1912/13. He went on to contribute briefly to Belfast Celtic's 1919/20 Irish championship campaign.

Appearances:
FL: 17 apps. 1 gl.
FAC: 1 app. 0 gls.
Total: *18 apps. 1 gl.*

HAZELL, Robert Joseph

Role: Centre half
b. Kingston, Jamaica, 14th June 1959

CAREER: app/pro May 1977:Wolverhampton Wanderers/Sept 1979:Queen's Park Rangers/Sept 1983:CITY/(May 1985-loan-Kilfa AIK)/(Sept 1985-loan-Wolverhampton Wanderers)/Aug 1986-trial-Luton Town/Oct 1986-trial-Leeds United/Nov 1986:Reading/Dec 1986:Port Vale.

Debut v Birmingham City (A) 1.10.83

A valuable and popular contributor to City's First Division survival struggles of 1984 and 1985, Bob came to Leicester after the upward trajectory of his career seemed temporarily to have stalled at Loftus Road. England honours at Youth, Under-21 and 'B' levels had come the way of the big central defender, and he had starred for Rangers in the 1982 FA Cup Final

Bob Hazell

against Spurs, though his disciplinary record was far from unsullied, and Filbert Street regulars had already witnessed one of his dismissals after a clash with Mark Goodwin. There was general approval, though, when Gordon Milne signed Bob for £100,000 to play alongside John O'Neill, and delight in the way he combined an intimidatory presence with some almost delicate ball skills, as well as relish at the sight of him strolling forward with the ball with opponents hesitating over the wisdom of attempting to tackle him. Unfortunately, off the field, Bob soon had disagreements with Milne over both training and tactics, and never played again for the first team after being substituted in a match against Forest in November 1984. A series of injuries then set him back severely, with a ruptured achilles tendon received in the opening game of a loan spell back at Wolves keeping him out for nine months. After City gave him a free transfer in 1986, Bob had a month's trial at Luton again invalidated by injury, but he proved his fitness on a non-contract basis at Reading (where he was sent off on his debut!), and then signed up at Vale Park for just over two more years of Division Three football.

Terry Heath

Appearances:
FL: 41 apps. 2 gls.
FAC: 1 app. 0 gls.
LC: 4 apps. 0 gls.
Total: *46 apps. 2 gls.*

HEATH, Richard Terence

Role: Inside forward
b. Leicester, 17th November 1943

CAREER: app/pro Nov 1961:CITY/May 1964:Hull City/Mar 1968:Scunthorpe United/ Feb 1973:Lincoln City.

Debut v West Ham United (H) 10.11.62

A teenage inside-forward with a good scoring record in the reserves, Terry was a valuable squad member as City mounted their attempt on the Double in 1962/3, when one of his goals proved decisive in separating Leicester and Manchester United at Filbert Street after hat-tricks from Keyworth and Law had cancelled each other out. A first-team place proved more elusive the following season, but Terry left the club on a high note, playing in the first leg of the League Cup Final at Stoke. Gradually withdrawing to a scheming role, he nonetheless scored some important goals for his subsequent clubs, including two for Hull in a memorable Cup giant-killing of Forest, and 50 in 177 League games for Scunthorpe, where he played alongside Kevin Keegan. His career unfortunately ended through injury after two knee operations in less than a year, and, as a technicality prevented compensation being paid, Lincoln very honourably held a testimonial match against Ipswich on Terry's behalf in March 1976. He was last heard of as proprietor of a Newquay guest house.

Appearances:
FL: 8 apps. 2 gls.
LC: 1 app. 0 gls.
Total: *9 apps. 2 gls.*

HEATHCOCK, Joseph Berty

Role: Centre forward
b. Cradley Heath, 5th December 1903
d. Cradley Heath, 21st May 1990

CAREER: Cradley Heath/cs 1923:Leamington Town/Oct 1923:CITY/June 1928:Nottingham Forest/June 1930:Cradley Heath/Sept 1931: Hereford United/cs 1932:Nuneaton Town.

Debut v Sheffield United (A) 19.3.27
(scored twice)

Bert Heathcock

Another City player who could feel justifiably frustrated by his lack of senior breaks, Bert built his reputation in Birmingham Combination football and bided his time in the reserves, but stood in just once at centre-forward for Arthur Chandler, when the latter was representing the Football League against the Scottish League at Filbert Street. Bert scored twice in a 3-0 away win, yet never got another League outing with City after injury in that game necessitated a cartilage operation. His opportunities after a £150 move to Forest were limited, too, even though two spectacular scoring bursts in his first season there brought him a 14-goal haul from 16 games! Bert is thus best remembered for notching nine of City Reserves' record 22 goals against Ibstock Colliery in the Senior Cup during his first Leicester season.

Appearances:
FL: 1 app. 2 gls.
Total: *1 app. 2 gls.*

HEBBERD, Trevor Neal

Role: Midfield
b. Alresford, Essex, 19th June 1958

CAREER: Alresford/app Sept 1974/pro July 1976:Southampton/(Mar 1981-loan-Washington Diplomats)/(Sept 1981-loan-Bolton Wanderers)/(Nov 1981-loan-CITY)/ Mar 1982:Oxford United/Aug 1988:Derby County/Sept 1991:Portsmouth/Nov 1991: Chesterfield/cs 1994:Lincoln City.

Debut v Cambridge United (H) 28.11.81 (scored once)

Often the man to drop out of Southampton's first team whenever one of Lawrie McMenemy's imports arrived, Trevor suffered for his own versatility at The Dell, regularly warming the bench before coming on as striker, wideman or midfield prompter. Jock Wallace brought him to Filbert Street on loan shortly after he'd faced City at Burnden Park, but his elegant, deceptively casual style on the left of midfield failed to impress the boss despite Trevor never being in a losing City line-up. At Oxford, alongside former City reserve Malcolm Shotton, he was a major motive force in the team that raced from Division Three to establish itself in the top flight, and he scored the opening goal at Wembley as United captured the 1986 League Cup. Trevor also took the 'Man of the Match' award from that game. He was still active during 1994/5 in a Lincoln side that occasionally also contained ex-City men Grant Brown, Nicky Platnauer and David Puttnam, plus on-loan keeper Russell Hoult.

Appearances:
FL: 4 apps. 1 gl.
Total: *4 apps. 1 gl.*

Trevor Hebberd

HEBDEN, George Horace Robert

Role: Goalkeeper
b. West Ham, 2nd June 1900
d. Leicester, 16th August 1973

CAREER: Clapton/Barking Town/
May 1920: CITY/May 1925:Queen's Park
Rangers/May 1927:Gillingham/
Nov 1929:Queen's Park Rangers.

Debut v Hull City (H) 9.4.21

A schoolboy international goalkeeper,
whose football future was severely
jeopardised by teenage wartime service
in the Navy and the merchant marine (he
was reportedly torpedoed four times!),
George was later elevated from London
League amateur football to understudy
his fellow East Ender, Herbert Bown, at
Filbert Street. By 1922 he had made the
first team position his own with a string
of instinctively fearless performances
(occasionally criticised for bordering on
the reckless), yet was himself displaced
midway through the 1925 promotion
season by the calmer Albert Godderidge.
Upon retirement from the game - after a
further 130 games for his two Third
Division (South) clubs - he initially ran
his own garage business in Ilford.

> **Appearances:**
> *FL: 101 apps. 0 gls.*
> *FAC: 3 apps. 0 gls.*
> **Total:** *104 apps. 0 gls.*

HEDLEY, George Thomas

Role: Right back
b. Co. Durham, 1882
d. 1937

CAREER: West Stanley/cs 1905:
Middlesbrough/Chester/Jan 1906:Heart of
Midlothian/Mar 1906:Hull City/Apr 1908:
FOSSE/cs 1909:Luton Town.

Debut v Fulham (A) 4.4.08

Bought for £275 to boost Fosse's full-back
strength during the final promotion push of
1908, 'Tot' was the regular right-back in the ill-
fated First Division campaign which followed,
and the only player besides Jim Gorman and
Bob Pollock to make his final appearance in
the infamous 0-12 drubbing by Forest, which
he later helped explain away to the
satisfaction of the League's commission of
enquiry. He had previously tasted League
football with both 'Boro
(3 games) and Hull
(78 apps), and
despite the ruffling
he received while
with Fosse, was
still noted for his
coolness in
clearing his lines
while playing a
season of
Southern League
fare at Luton.

George Hedley

Appearances:
FL: 35 apps. 1 gl.
FAC: 3 apps. 0 gls.
Total: *38 apps. 1 gl.*

HENDERSON, John Neil

Role: Forward
b. Dumfries, c 1874
d. Maxwelltown, Dumfries, 30th August 1930

CAREER: 5th Kirkudbright Rifle Volunteers/
Dumfries/Dec 1895:Celtic/May 1897:Victoria
United (Aberdeen)/May 1898: Lincoln City/
Dec 1900:FOSSE/Mar 1901: Small Heath/
Sept 1902:Maxwelltown Volunteers/Aug 1905:
Carlisle United/ 1906:Maxwelltown
Volunteers (aka Kings Own Scottish Borderers)
/Sept 1910:Annan United/Nov 1910:Nithsdale
Wanderers.

Debut v Woolwich Arsenal (H) 15.12.1900

In a stay of just over three months at Filbert Street, John played five times at outside-left and eight times at inside-right, but failed to perk up a fairly goal-shy Fosse front-line. Perhaps surprisingly, Small Heath still saw him as a likely candidate to buttress their squad in the successful run-in to their 1901 promotion bid, though he only managed four games for them alongside Johnny McMillan. Four senior outings had been his total, too, with Celtic, where he partnered Jimmy Blessington in the infamous 1897 Cup defeat by little Arthurlie, before which many of the regular side declared themselves 'on strike'. Some obituary notes add Notts County and Arsenal to John's list of clubs, but we suspect that the latter reference, at least, had crept in from the career details of his older brother, James, who had also started playing with 5th KRV, and was a member of Woolwich Arsenal's first-ever Football League side. John himself was a Dumfries tobacconist at the time of his death.

Appearances:
FL: 13 apps. 0 gls.
Total: *13 apps. 0 gls.*

HENDERSON, William Martin Melville

Role: Striker
b. Kirkcaldy, Fife, 3rd May 1956

CAREER: 1973:Rangers/ (Oct 1977-loan-Hibernian)/ Apr 1978:Philadelphia Fury/ Oct 1978:CITY/Sept 1981: Chesterfield/Oct 1983: Port Vale (to 1985)/1990:Spalding United/Feb 1991:Leicester United/Mar 1991: Spalding United (p/mgr)/cs 1991: Bourne (p/coach).

Debut v Charlton Athletic (H) 14.10.78 (sub)

One of the few non-internationals in Jock Wallace's Ibrox squad, Martin was a striker with a goal-every-three-games habit and a winner's

medal from the 1976 Scottish Cup Final when he joined the then-annual exodus to the NASL. Wallace brought him back from Philadelphia to Filbert Street and showed remarkable patience with the ever-willing but occasionally clumsy forward as his scoring ratio dropped to less than one-in-six; but it was as foil to his one-time Kirkcaldy schoolboy partner Alan Young that Martin found his most useful support role when City climbed back from Division Two in 1980. Martin later knocked in 23 goals in 87 League games for Chesterfield (relegated to Division Four in 1983), but his League career ended in an acrimonious contract dispute after a second successive relegation season at Port Vale, where he had occasionally partnered Mark Bright. After involvement in a well-publicised fraud case landed Martin with a spell in jail, his rehabilitation included a belated part-time return to the non-league game.

Appearances:
FL: 79 (12) apps. 12 gls.
FAC: 5 apps. 4 gls.
LC: 3 (1) apps. 0 gls.
Total: *87 (13) apps. 16 gls.*

Martin Henderson

Billy Henry

HENRY, William Armstrong

Role: Right back
b. Glasgow, 6th September 1884

CAREER: Blantyre Victoria/cs 1906:Rangers/ cs 1908:Falkirk/June 1909:FOSSE/Nov 1911: Manchester City/July 1920:St Bernards.
Debut v Wolverhampton Wanderers (H) 1.9.09

Missing only a single game during his spell with Fosse of over two seasons, right-back Billy matched consistency with evident class, and came very close to a Scottish cap, appearing for the Anglo-Scots against the Home Scots in the international trial of March 1911. His back-line partnerships with, successively, Dick Pudan and Sam Currie considerably tightened a Fosse defence still smarting from its First Division muggings, and his form soon attracted an irresistible bid from top-flight Manchester City, for whom he made 142 League appearances on both sides of WW1, many of them in front of former Fosse 'keeper Walter Smith. Billy's single League goal was a 40-yard matchwinner for Man. City at Meadow Lane on the opening day of 1912/13. He did gain one 'unofficial' honour during WW1, when Scotland met England at Goodison in a 'Grand Military International' in May 1916; and he also guested for Southampton in that year.

   Appearances:
   FL: 89 apps. 0 gls.
   FAC: 7 apps. 0 gls.
   Total: *96 apps. 0 gls.*

HENRYS, Arthur

Role: Half back
b. Nottingham

CAREER: Notts Jardines/Nottingham Forest/ Gainsborough Trinity/cs 1891:Newton Heath/ Aug 1892:Notts Jardines/Oct 1892:Newton Heath/Mar 1893:FOSSE/June 1896:Notts County.
Debut v Newark (A) ML 1.4.1893

An outside-left in his first Football Alliance season with the team which would later be known as Manchester United, Arthur converted to defensive roles as he played at three different levels over the next three seasons - making 3 First Division appearances for the Heathens in 1892/3 before his move to Leicester; becoming the regular Fosse centre-half (and captain) in the Midland League; and taking the left-half berth in the inaugural Second Division

Arthur Henrys

campaign. After moving on, Arthur found a place in the Magpies' side hard to maintain, dropping out after only seven games of a season that would end with the Second Division championship.

   Appearances:
   FL: 37 apps. 1 gl.
   FAC: 14 apps. 0 gls.
   ML: 23 apps. 1 gl.
   Total: *74 apps. 2 gls.*

HERNON, James

Role: Inside forward
b. Cleland, Lanarkshire, 6th December 1924

CAREER: Mossvale Strollers/Apr 1942:CITY/ Sept 1948:Bolton Wanderers/Aug 1951: Grimsby Town/July 1954:Watford/July 1956: Hastings United.
Debut (WW2) v Northampton Town (A) 16.5.42; (postwar) v Fulham (H) 7.6.47

A teenage signing from Paisley junior football

Jimmy Hernon

A right-sided forward who took the flank position in Fosse's first Midland League game, but faded from the scene shortly after the move from Aylestone Road to Filbert Street. Previously, he had held the left-wing berth in Doncaster's initial competitive fixture, at Midland Alliance level. It is suspected that he may have additionally assisted the strong Nottingham works side, Mellors Ltd, in the late 1880s; while still to be adequately researched is the suggestion that he may also have been associated with Midland League champions Rotherham Town during the latter part of 1891/2.

Appearances:
FAC: 1 app. 1 gl.
ML: 7 apps. 0 gls.
Total: *8 apps. 1 gl.*

HESKEY, Emile William Ivanhoe

Role: Striker
b. Leicester, 11th January 1978

CAREER: YT July 1994:CITY.

Debut v Queen's Park Rangers (A) 8.3.95

Hit by injuries and a 'flu epidemic, City turned out for their midweek Premiership game at Loftus Road with six changes from the side which had drawn with Everton on the previous Saturday, and gave a central striker's debut to 17-year-old first-year trainee Emile, who acquitted himself very well under the circumstances, and would probably have won subsequent selections but for suspension resulting from a County Challenge Cup dismissal against St.Andrews on the interim Monday! A heftily-built 6ft.1in. attacker, Emile won four caps for England's Under-16 schools side, and looks a prospect of immense potential.

Emile Heskey

Appearances (to end 1994/5):
PL: 1 app. 0 gls.
Total: *1 app. 0 gls.*

during the war (when his City record was supplemented by a guest spell with Partick Thistle), Jimmy had to wait until his Army demob in 1947 for a League bow, on the only occasion City's official programme has stretched into June. A lightweight inside-forward who seriously challenged Don Revie for the scheming role at Leicester, he raised the then-highest fee for an outgoing transfer from the club when Bolton invested £14,750 in his late-blossoming talent, but the subtler delicacies of his style of play could, unfortunately, be all too easily nullified by close physical attention. Strangely enough, though, Jimmy claimed a respectable goal tally in the supposedly 'harder' lower divisions with Grimsby and Watford.

Appearances:
FL: 31 apps. 7 gls.
FAC: 3 apps. 0 gls.
WW2: 25 apps. 2 gls.
Total: *59 apps. 9 gls.*

HERROD, E.R.

Role: Forward

CAREER: Derby St.Luke's/Sept 1890: Doncaster Rovers/cs 1891:FOSSE/1892:Derby Town.

Debut v Derby Junction (H) ML. 12.9.1891

HEYWOOD, Roger

Role: Centre half
b. Chorley, Lancs, 4th May 1909
d. Leicester, 30th December 1985

CAREER: Chorley St.James/1927:Chorley/
Nov 1929:CITY/Corby Town.

Debut v Birmingham (A) 3.5.30

Bought for a bargain £575 from the club
which had taken the Lancashire
Combination title two seasons running,
Roger was a towering stopper centre-half
who served City for over twelve years
(latterly as coach to the wartime Colts),
and also appeared as a wartime guest for
Northampton Town shortly before his
retirement in 1941. The bulk of his
appearances came in City's early-30s years
of First Division struggle, and it was
somewhat sadly ironic that
his first-team fortunes
should revive (in a
wing-half slot)
during the final
pre-war relega-
tion season.
Contributing to
a great City
tradition, one
of Roger's rare
goals was an
Anfield
winner. He used
to spend his
summers playing
League cricket back
in Lancashire. (Two
other City defenders of

George Heyes

Roger Heywood   the 20s are occasionally
confused with Roger,
though neither actually
broke through to the first team: Eric
S.Haywood was a centre-half signed in
1924 from Hugglescote Wesleyans, while
fellow back-liner J.B.Heywood was
released in 1926).

Appearances:
FL: 228 apps. 2 gls.
FAC: 12 apps. 0 gls.
WW2: 41 apps. 2 gls.
Total: *281 apps. 4 gls.*

HEYES, George

Role: Goalkeeper
b. Bolton, 16th November 1937

CAREER: Apr 1956:Rochdale/July 1960:
CITY/Sept 1965:Swansea Town/July
1969:Barrow/cs 1970:Hereford United.

Debut v West Bromwich Albion (A) 11.3.61

A reliably unflappable stand-in for Gordon
Banks over six seasons, whenever the
England keeper was either injured or absent
on international duty, George had his
lengthiest first-team run at the start of 1965/6,
as Banks recovered from a broken wrist - yet
moved on within weeks as it became obvious
he'd have to relinquish even his Combination
position to 16-year-old Peter Shilton. George
then played over a hundred senior games for
the Swans (earning a Welsh Cup winner's
medal in 1966) before seeing out his League
career at Holker Street. He clearly passed on
some useful tips to his son Darren, an England
schoolboy keeper who faced City for
Scunthorpe United in the Littlewoods Cup
during 1987/8.

Appearances:
FL: 25 apps. 0 gls.
LC: 2 apps. 0 gls.
Total: *27 apps. 0 gls.*

Roger Heywood

John Hibberd

HILL, Colin Frederick

Role: Centre back
b. Uxbridge, 12th November 1963

CAREER: Glebe Athletic/Park Lane/
Hillingdon/am Dec 1979/pro July 1981:
Arsenal/(Jan 1986-loan-Brighton & Hove
Albion)/cs 1986:CS Maritimo/Oct 1987:
Colchester United/Aug 1989:Sheffield United
(Mar 1992-loan-CITY)/July 1992:CITY.

Debut v Tranmere Rovers (A) 27.3.92

A widely-experienced central defender who
played in the Wembley defeat by Blackburn
Rovers while still on loan with City - his
£200,000 transfer not being negotiated until
two months later - Colin went on to pick up
the club's Player of the Year trophy following

HIBBERD, John Turner

Role: Inside right

CAREER: Oct 1895:FOSSE.

*Debut v Hucknall St.Johns (H) FAC 2.11.1895
(scored once)*

One of the several cases of a 'blink-and-you-
missed-it' senior Fosse career - there's not
even a record of this inside-right playing in
any of the club's then-numerous friendly
matches to supplement the above isolated
appearance against an obscure
Nottinghamshire team of Cup hopefuls. John
did, however, notch the Fosse Rovers' winning
goal in the Leicestershire Senior Cup Final of
the same season; and had represented the
county a year previously.

> **Appearances:**
> *FAC: 1 app. 1 gl.*
> **Total:** *1 app. 1 gl.*

Colin Hill

an ever-present 1992/3, but was sidelined by injury from collecting a hat-trick of successive Play-off Final appearances in 1994. A cool head, a strong tackle and fine anticipation were features of Colin's game under Brian Little, and deservedly won him the captaincy under Mark McGhee. He had initially made an Arsenal breakthrough in 1983/4 at both centre- and right-back, but was deposed by incoming buys Viv Anderson and Tommy Caton; then broadened his repertoire while playing Portuguese First Division football from the offshore base of Funchal, Madeira - and ending up as top scorer in 1986/7! Division Four fare at Layer Road followed, but Colin won his first six caps for Northern Ireland after moving to Bramall Lane. On top form with City, he was oddly overlooked at international level by Billy Bingham, and even when Bryan Hamilton took over the Irish reins, Colin seemed fated - his first three call-ups were each negated by injury. His belated first caps as a City player nonetheless finally came in Spring 1995, when Hamilton selected him as a defensive midfielder against the Republic and in Latvia.

Appearances (to end 1994/5):
PL: 24 apps. 0 gls.
FL: 86 (1) apps. 0 gls.
FAC: 6 apps. 0 gls.
LC: 6 apps. 1 gl.
AIC: 3 apps. 0 gls.
P/O: 6 apps. 0 gls.
Total: *131 (1) apps. 1 gl.*

HILL, John

Role: Outside right
b. Kirkcaldy, Fife, c 1871

CAREER: Leith Rangers/ Leith Athletic/1892: Middlesbrough Ironopolis/ cs 1893:FOSSE/cs 1895: Glossop North End/ Oct 1897:West Herts.

Debut v Burton Wanderers (H) ML 9.9.1893

A 'fast and tricky' team-mate of McArthur and Seymour in the Ironopolis team which reached the quarter-finals of the FA Cup in 1893, outside-right Jacky moved to

Leicester with the latter for what proved to be the final season of Midland League competition, and was soon joined by the former. When Archie Hughes and Bob Gordon then later joined their former fellows, it meant five ex-Nops (all Scotsmen!) were assisting Fosse in their initial assault on the Second Division. A Scottish Junior international (1891), Jacky eventually teamed up with the club we now know as Watford, and indeed became a director of the renamed club in 1909, when he was running a newsagent/ tobacconist business in Watford High Street.

Appearances:
FL: 20 apps. 2 gls.
FAC: 13 apps. 7 gls.
ML: 20 apps. 7 gls.
Total: *53 apps. 16 gls.*

HILL, Ricky Anthony

Role: Midfield
b. Hammersmith, London, 5th March 1959

CAREER: app 1975/pro May 1976:Luton Town/June 1989:Le Havre/Aug 1990:CITY/ (Sept 1991-trials-Oxford United)/1991:Tampa Bay Rowdies/Nov 1992:Hitchin Town/ cs 1993:Chertsey Town.

Debut v Bristol Rovers (H) 25.8.90 (sub)

Rescuing his former Luton playmaker from the French Second Division may have looked to some like an act of sentiment on David Pleat's part, but a City midfield just stripped of the talent of Gary McAllister was clearly in need of added touches of class when the £100,000 deal went through to bring Ricky to Filbert Street. Unfortunately, sporadic flashes of sweet skill were all Ricky could bring to City's anti-relegation battle, in which he was so often harried into ineffectuality by pace-and-power merchants whom he'd have made mugs out of a few years earlier. It was sadly characteristic of Ricky's year with Leicester that perhaps the most overt kudos he received - a virtual

Jacky Hill

Ricky Hill

Kenilworth Road, where he made an immediate impact as a 17-year-old scoring substitute in April 1976, and went on to develop into the powerful creative lynchpin of Pleat's side; eventually amassing 507 senior Luton appearances and scoring 65 goals. At club level his honours came from a Division Two championship in 1982 and from the League Cup Final victory over Arsenal in 1988, while Ricky could count himself distinctly unlucky to have won only three caps for England in the mid-80s. His year in France (alongside Irish international John Byrne) saw Le Havre fail in their promotion bid, and Ricky was replaced there by Cameroonian World Cup star Kana-Biyik; while he belatedly added to his cosmopolitan experience after Brian Little released him with a stint playing and coaching under Rodney Marsh in Stateside soccer.

Appearances:
FL: 19 (7) apps. 0 gls.
FAC: 1 app. 0 gls.
LC: 0 (2) apps. 0 gls.
FMC: 1 app. 0 gls.
Total: *21 (9) apps. 0 gls.*

standing ovation from Plymouth supporters at Home Park, genuinely marvelling at his silky contributions - came during and after another City defeat; while a groin injury curtailed his involvement in the climactic months of the 'Great Escape'. Such disappointments were a far cry from his prime years at

HINE, Ernest William

Role: Inside right
b. Smithy Cross, Yorkshire, 9th April 1901
d. Huddersfield, Apr qtr 1974

CAREER: New Mills/Staincross Station/am:Apr 1921/pro Jan 1922:Barnsley/Jan 1926:CITY/May 1932: Huddersfield Town/Feb 1933: Manchester United/Dec 1934:Barnsley.

Debut v Burnley (H) 16.1.26 (scored twice)

Eventually notching more than 300 senior goals (286 in the League) over a 17-year career span, former miner Ernie was another prolific marksman to announce his intentions early - scoring on his Barnsley debut in a Cup replay at Norwich; averaging the classic ratio of a goal every two games in his first Oakwell stint; then hitting two in his first game in City colours (though also missing a penalty that day!)

Ernie Hine

Ernie Hine (left) and Derek Hines (right).

after a £3,000 move. A First Division regular at inside-right thereafter, he was the only one of City's trio of all-time top scorers to receive halfway decent recognition of his sharpshooting prowess: graduating from Football League honours (5 games; 2 goals) to international trials (4 games and 2 goals in the England v. The Rest series) to the full England side (6 caps; 4 goals). Twice Ernie topped the 30 goals per season mark for City, (saving his best effort for the Division One runners-up season of 1928/9, when he cracked in 32 goals in 35 games), and he was still severely embarrassing top-flight defences when City surprisingly allowed him to move for £4,000 back to Yorkshire. His first goal for the Terriers was actually against City, but neither at Leeds Road nor Old Trafford could Ernie quite recapture his deadly touch, and it took a transfer back 'home' to Oakwell for the veteran to settle back into his old scoring habits (which included a hat-trick against City in a 3-3 draw in December 1935, and another counter in the following season's repeat fixture). With an eventual overall Barnsley total of 123 League goals, he remains that club's record aggregate scorer to date.

Appearances:
FL: 247 apps. 148 gls.
FAC: 12 apps. 8 gls.
Total: *259 apps. 156 gls.*

HINES, Derek Jabez

Role: Centre forward
b. Woodville, Derbyshire, 8th February 1931

CAREER: Moira United/(trials-Southend United)/am June 1947/pro Mar 1948:CITY/Nov 1961:Shrewsbury Town.

Debut v Tottenham Hotspur (A) 27.3.48

A genuine teenage prodigy, tried out in Southend's reserve team at the age of 15, centre-forward Derek was given an early baptism by City and then nursed gradually into regular first-team football while still winning England Youth international caps and, later, Army representative honours. Though his scoring rate was somewhat eclipsed by that of striking partner Arthur Rowley, Derek proved a wonderful forager, and made an inestimable contribution to both the promotion seasons of 1954 and 1957. After winning his first Division Two championship medal, he played and scored for Young England against England in the then-annual eve-of-Cup Final game, but (the next year's repeat fixture apart) was subsequently passed over by the selectors. He was also unlucky in missing out on City's first two Wembley Finals: being regarded as a lucky mascot reserve in 1949 and a veteran calming influence on the 1961 squad. Derek was the last City player to score 4 goals in a League game (in a 6-3 home win over Aston Villa in November 1958). A short while after answering Arthur Rowley's invitation for a brief reunion at Gay Meadow (producing eight goals from 20 League and Cup outings), he returned to Filbert Street as youth team coach.

Appearances:
FL: 299 apps. 116 gls.
FAC: 18 apps. 1 gl.
Total: *317 apps. 117 gls.*

HODGE, Martin John

Role: Goalkeeper
b. Southport, 4th February 1959

CAREER: app Sept 1975/pro Feb 1977: Plymouth Argyle/July 1979:Everton/(Dec 1981-loan-Preston North End)/(July 1982-loan-Oldham Athletic)/(Jan 1983-loan-Gillingham) (Feb 1983-loan-Preston North End)/Aug 1983:Sheffield Wednesday/Aug 1988:CITY/

Martin Hodge

Aug 1991:Hartlepool United/July 1993: Rochdale/Aug 1994:Plymouth Argyle.

Debut v West Bromwich Albion (H) 27.8.88

Though first grabbing the headlines as an expensive Goodison import, goalkeeper Martin nonetheless made and sustained his first real impact at Hillsborough after a bargain £50,000 move. Wednesday were promoted at the end of his first ever-present season, and he went on to break the Owls' record for consecutive appearances (214 in League and Cups) until missing his first game for them in September 1987; having a spell as skipper, and being noted almost as much for the contribution of his kicking to their then-favoured long-ball game as for his penalty area command. David Pleat expended two-thirds of the £300,000 he had recently received for Ian Andrews to bring Martin to Filbert Street in a literally eve-of-season deal; but ironically and sadly, the new No.1 seriously aggravated a stomach muscle injury only minutes into his debut game, and was sidelined for several months. Never thereafter the most consistent of City keepers, Martin was most noteworthy as a courageous master of last-ditch, one-on-one situations; and his best spell for the club came, too, in cliffhanging circumstances, during the final eight instalments of the 1991 survival drama, when last-line inspiration was most needed, and when some of his saves definitely kept crisis from turning to catastrophe. City have rather ungratefully embarrassed Martin since, though: with Ian Ormondroyd chipping him from 35 yards in a Victoria Ground friendly in 1992, and six of the best going past him in the Spotland League Cup tie of 1993/4. Signed by Peter Shilton at the start of the following campaign, Martin finished the term on a career aggregate of 520 League appearances.

Appearances:
FL: 75 apps. 0 gls.
FAC: 1 app. 0 gls.
LC: 4 apps. 0 gls.
FMC: 1 app. 0 gls.
Total: *81 apps. 0 gls.*

HODGKINSON, Albert Victor

Role: Outside left
b. Pembroke Dock,
10th August 1884
d. Shardlow, Derbyshire,
25th November 1939

Albert Hodgkinson

CAREER: Old Normanton/1902:Hinckley Town/May 1903:Derby County/Oct 1903: Grimsby Town/May 1904:Plymouth Argyle/ May 1905:FOSSE/June 1906:Bury/May 1907: Southampton/Aug 1909:Croydon Common/ Mar 1911:Southend United/Nov 1911:Ilkeston United.

Debut v Clapton Orient (H) 2.9.05

Barely 20 when Fosse became his fourth senior club (after much haggling with Grimsby over his League registration and transfer fee), Albert was a clever but 'mercurial' Welsh winger who suffered somewhat at Leicester from the club's inability to settle on a regular inside-left partner for him. He had failed to win a breakthrough at Derby, where his brother William made a brief impact at centre-forward, and instead took his League bow with the Mariners after a trial spell. His outward transfer to Bury - after a Fosse season which saw them fringeing the promotion race until a late tail-off to 7th place - brought about the sort of situation which still mightily

confuses researchers, for he took over there directly from another outside left named Hodgkinson (Joseph, transferred to Crystal Palace); but at least the Welsh selectors knew they had the right man when awarding him a cap against Ireland after he'd helped Southampton to the FA Cup semi-finals in his initial season at The Dell. Albert was also a noted baseball player, and on retirement ran the Rose & Crown at Chellaston in Derbyshire. His father had been a military musketry instructor, who moved to Derby when Albert was only three.

Appearances:
FL: 33 apps. 5 gls.
FAC: 1 app. 0 gls.
Total: *34 apps. 5 gls.*

HODGSON, William

Role: Forward
b. Glasgow, 9th July 1935

CAREER: Dunoon Athletic/cs 1954: St.Johnstone/(1956-loan-Guildford City)/ May 1957:Sheffield United/Sept 1963:CITY/ June 1965:Derby County/Sept 1967:Rotherham United/Dec 1967:York City.

Debut v Bolton Wanderers (A) 14.9.63

Billy Hodgson

A diminutive, enthusiastically industrious and virtually tireless utility forward who wore four different forward shirts at Filbert Street, but made most of his appearances in Howard Riley's right-wing stead, Billy had been an old adversary of City's during his Bramall Lane days, appearing against them in the FA Cup semi-final marathon of 1961. He gained further semi-final experience at Leicester, in the League Cup campaigns of 1964 and 1965, missing out on a winner's tankard in the first season, but taking a runners-up memento from the Finals against Chelsea. Billy also scored the first City goal to be featured on the BBC's 'Match of the Day', when that programme televised the 3-2 home win over Nottingham Forest in October 1964. He became a Baseball Ground regular at outside-left, and a veteran inspiration for York, before taking coaching appointments with both the Blades and the Minstermen. Early in his career, after 21 goals in 80 senior St.Johnstone matches, it had been a National Service posting which drew Billy into the English non-league game.

Appearances:
FL: 46 apps. 10 gls.
FAC: 5 apps. 0 gls.
LC: 13 apps. 5 gls.
Total: *64 apps. 15 gls.*

HOGG, Charles

Role: Inside forward

CAREER: St.Andrews/am Feb 1915/pro Apr 1915:FOSSE.

Debut v Blackpool (H) 27.2.15 (scored once)

In a complaint to the Leicestershire FA, the management of local club St.Andrews claimed that their team were actually getting stripped for a Mutual League game before realising Fosse had spirited away Charlie, their top scorer, for a Filbert Street trial. Apologies ensued, by which time this two-footed inside-forward had made a goal-capped League bow as an amateur. Then, in April 1915, he became the final player to sign as a Fosse professional before the WW1 break; and continued to turn out during the first campaign in the wartime Midland Section.

Appearances:
FL: 7 apps. 2 gls.
WW1: 13 apps. 4 gls.
Total: *20 apps. 6 gls.*

HOGG, Derek

Role: Outside left
b. Stockton Heath, Lancs, 4th November 1930

CAREER: Lostock Hall/(trials-Preston North End)/Chorley/Oct 1952:CITY/Apr 1958:West Bromwich Albion/Oct 1960:Cardiff City/July 1962:Kettering Town.

Debut v Leeds United (H) 14.2.53

Signed from Lancashire Combination football as a potential right-wing successor to Mal Griffiths, Derek claimed a regular first-team spot with City only after switching to the left flank at the start of the 1954/5 First Division season. By October 1955 his usually effective (but occasionally over-elaborate) close-dribbling style had earned him a call-up for the Football League against the Scottish League, and he became a key contributor to City's 1957 Division Two championship effort, working in effective harness with Arthur Rowley. West Brom invested £20,000 in Derek's confident talent to boost their First Division challenge, then he moved on after two full seasons to make a scoring Ninian Park debut against City.

Appearances:
FL: 161 apps. 26 gls.
FAC: 4 apps. 0 gls.
Total: *165 apps. 26 gls.*

Derek Hogg

HOLDEN, Steven Anthony

Role: Centre back
b. Luton, 4th September 1972

CAREER: YT 1989/pro Mar 1991:CITY/(Oct 1992-loan-Carlisle United)/Feb 1993:Carlisle United/Nov 1993:Kettering Town.
Debut v Derby County (H) 22.2.92

A highly regarded prospect as a teenage central defender, Steve had ironically just run into a reserve-team scoring seam before his call-up into the senior back line. A local derby, with promotion rivalry adding to the pressures, represented a fiery baptism; and, in fact, the 1-2 defeat represented Steve's only real chance to impress at Filbert Street. The depth of defensive experience in Brian Little's squad effectively stymied Steve's development, and he moved for a nominal fee to Brunton Park shortly after completing a successful loan spell there. A further loan move, to Kettering, oddly featured a mistaken call-up into the England semi-pro international side in January 1994, duly regularised when Steve then signed permanently for the Poppies. Several caps at that level have ensued.

> **Appearances:**
> *FL: 1 app. 0 gls.*
> **Total:** *1 app. 0 gls.*

Steve Holden

❑ FOX FACT: *Steve Holden is now the fifth ex-City player to have been capped by England at semi-professional level; following David Buchanan and former reserves Paul Culpin, Steve Humphries and Brendan Phillips. Alan Smith was so capped before joining City.*

HOLDING, William

Role: Outside right

CAREER: Castle Donington/Feb 1909:FOSSE.
Debut v Sheffield United (A) 27.2.09

Pitched into the Fosse first team only two weeks after scoring on his reserve debut, this inexperienced outside-right impressed enough to be retained for 1909/10, but dropped out of the picture soon afterwards, never

William Holding

having appeared for a winning Fosse side. Indeed, his 'middle' senior game was the record 0-12 thrashing at Forest.

> **Appearances:**
> *FL: 3 apps. 0 gls.*
> **Total:** *3 apps. 0 gls.*

HOLMES, James Paul

Role: Left back
b. Dublin, 11th November 1953

CAREER: St.John Bosco BC/pro Nov 1970: Coventry City/Mar 1977:Tottenham Hotspur/ Mar 1981:Vancouver Whitecaps/Oct 1982-trials-CITY/Feb 1983-trials-Brentford/Mar 1983:Torquay United/Nov 1983:Peterborough United (p/asst.mgr)/Dec 1985:Nuneaton Borough (p/mgr)/1987:Leicester United/ 1987:Hitchin Town (p/mgr)/Aug 1988: Northampton Town (asst.coach)/ 1989:Bedworth United (p/co-mgr).
Debut v Sheffield Wednesday (H) 30.10.82

The Republic of Ireland's youngest-ever international (at 17 years, 200 days), skilful full-back Jimmy showed precocious class at Highfield Road, playing in a Youth Cup Final

Jimmy Holmes

HOOPER, Harold

Role: Left back
b. Aston, Birmingham, 18th August 1900
d. Birmingham, Jan qtr 1980

CAREER: Brierley Hill Alliance/May 1921:
Southampton/May 1924:CITY/May 1926:
Queen's Park Rangers.

Debut v Manchester United (A) 30.8.24

A dour, resolute defender who arrived in an
exchange deal which saw Fred Price and
Dennis Jones departing for The Dell, Harry
won his personal duel with Reg Osborne for
the City left-back slot for the larger part of the
1925 promotion season, but couldn't keep his
rival out for long once the First Division
campaign got under way. Harry - who was a
cousin of England centre-half Charlie Roberts -
was restricted to Division Three (South) fare
only during his season with QPR: his new club
having forgotten to enter the FA Cup for
1926/7!

Appearances:
FL: 33 apps. 0 gls.
FAC: 6 apps. 0 gls.
Total: *39 apps. 0 gls.*

Harry Hooper

and winning the first of 30 full caps before
making his League bow against Leicester in
December 1971; then going on to attract
numerous bids until Gordon Milne accepted
Spurs' six-figure fee. A horrific leg-break
suffered in an international in Bulgaria
threatened to end Jimmy's career, but after a
year out of the game he returned to the fray
alongside Johnny Giles in Canada. Milne gave
his former charge a brief non-contract trial
with City, when the Second Division pace
seemed too much for him, though Jimmy
managed a total of 78 more League games as
he accomplished a transition to coaching and
managerial roles, ending with a stint as
Coventry Sporting boss before joining the
West Midlands Police. He received a Dublin
testimonial game from the Republic's FA in
August 1985.

Appearances:
FL: 2 apps. 0 gls.
Total: *2 apps. 0 gls.*

Mike Hooper

HOOPER, Michael Dudley

Role: Goalkeeper
b. Bristol, 10th February 1964

CAREER: Mangotsfield United/1983:Bristol City/Feb 1985:Wrexham/Oct 1985:Liverpool/ (Sept 1990-loan-CITY)/Sept 1993:Newcastle United.

Debut v Sheffield Wednesday (H) 22.9.90

Despite being beaten ten times in his first two games, Mike soon joined the line of short-term City signings (after Gary Charles and Kevin Campbell) to prompt the Filbert Street crowd into futile 'Sign him up' chants; and found his initial month-long loan being extended twice as he continued to impress behind a sieve-like defence. Having arrived in Leicester as part of a rare loan-exchange deal (with Carl Muggleton temporarily switching to Anfield), the red-haired 'keeper managed to temper City's Second Division embarrassments by keeping the score down substantially in a couple of virtual whitewashes, and then registering the first clean sheets of the League season: adding to his agile shot-stopping

repertoire the sort of outfield sweeper's vision and covering speed most often associated with his Liverpool mentor, Bruce Grobbelaar. As a teenager, Mike had played but once in each of the League and the FA Cup for his hometown team before a loan move to the Racecourse Ground was made permanent in July 1985; and his form in North Wales quickly attracted the attention of new Anfield boss Kenny Dalglish. A Wembley substitute appearance in the 1986 Charity Shield marked his Liverpool bow, but only 30 League appearances in Grobbelaar's stead had followed by the time of his Leicester stint. Mike was later stricken by injury shortly after winning a regular Anfield selection, and with Newcastle has generally played second string to one-time City trialist Pavel Srnicek - for whom he substituted at Filbert Street after 85 minutes of City's opening Premiership fixture; then conceding City's first goal at that level by way of Julian Joachim's last-minute consolation strike.

Appearances:
FL: 14 apps. 0 gls.
FMC: 1 app. 0 gls.
Total: *15 apps. 0 gls.*

HORNER, Philip Matthew

Role: Centre back
b. Leeds, 10th November 1966

CAREER: app 1983/pro Nov 1984:CITY/
(Mar 1986-loan-Rotherham United)/
July 1988:Halifax Town/Sept 1990:Blackpool.
Debut v Sheffield Wednesday (H) 3.1.87 (sub)

A tall reserve striker for over two seasons,
capped at Youth level and also used up front
in his four League games on loan at
Rotherham, Phil was experimentally
transformed into a central defender just before
his emergency elevation to the first-team
bench, and coolly slotted into that position as
sub for John O'Neill in City's 6-1 win against
the Owls. A couple of his subsequent senior
run-outs proved, however, to be nightmarish
affairs in defensive terms (at Tottenham, and
against Crystal Palace), and Phil failed to
make David Pleat's first retained list in 1988.
He initially took the No.3 shirt at The Shay,
was also noted as sweeper there, and then
moved on again to play alongside Paul Groves
for the Seasiders.

Appearances:
FL: 7 (3) apps. 0 gls.
FAC: 0 (1) app. 0 gls.
LC: 1 app. 0 gls.
Total: *8 (4) apps. 0 gls.*

HOUGHAM, H.

Role: Outside left

CAREER: South Wigston Albion/Apr 1904:
FOSSE.
Debut v Bradford City (H) 16.4.04

A local trialist who played at outside-left in
Fosse's final two defeats of the dismal 1903/4
re-election campaign, but failed to break
through again after being retained for the
following season.

Appearances:
FL: 2 apps. 0 gls.
Total: *2 apps. 0 gls.*

HOUGHTON, William Gascoigne

Role: Left back
b. Hemsworth, Yorks, 20th February 1939

CAREER: Aug 1957:Barnsley/July 1964:
Watford/June 1966:Ipswich Town/July 1969:
CITY/Jan 1970:Rotherham United.
Debut v Birmingham City (H) 9.8.69

A vastly experienced
defender, Billy had the
shortest spell of his
507-game League
career at Filbert Street,
joining Frank
O'Farrell's Second
Division team as a
motorway commuter
after moving house
from Ipswich back to
his native Barnsley. He
had been a schoolboy
prodigy and England
youth international

Billy Houghton

left-half while at Oakwell, and in 1968 had
won a Second Division championship medal
as a left-back at Portman Road, but he was
hard pressed with City to keep out Alan
Woollett, and a small fee took him back to
Yorkshire to play as well as reside.

Appearances:
FL: 6 (1) apps. 0 gls.
LC: 3 apps. 0 gls.
Total: *9 (1) apps. 0 gls.*

Phil Horner

HOULT, Russell

Role: Goalkeeper
b. Leicester, 22nd November 1972

CAREER: Thringstone/Shepshed Amateurs/
YT July 1989/pro Mar 1991:CITY/
(Aug 1991-loan-Lincoln City)/(Dec 1991-loan-
Cheltenham Town)/(Mar 1992-loan-
Blackpool)/(July 1993-loan-Kettering Town)/
(Nov 1993-loan-Bolton Wanderers)/(Aug 1994-
loan-Lincoln City)/(Feb 1995-loan-Derby
County)/June 1995:Derby County.

Debut v Wolverhampton Wanderers (H) 13.9.92

A fine keeper who has had to suffer the now-
common frustrations of featuring youthfully in
a specialist position in which the canniness of
age is often more highly valued (and certainly
one in which players usually soldier on
effectively to a greater age than the footballing
norm), Russell accumulated substantially more
senior experience away from Filbert Street
than between the City sticks; where all his
first-team outings came during 1992/3. City's
Young Player of the Year in 1991, he burst into
the limelight on the occasion of City's first-
ever League game to be televised live, when
Carl Muggleton slipped a disc during the
warm-up kick-in, and Russell had to be
summoned from the stand for an emergency
debut. Immediately (owing to his non-
standard pre-match meal) dubbed 'The Hot
Dog Kid', he went on to perform immaculately
against Wolves; keeping a clean sheet and
earning the Man of the Match kudos. He
conceded only one goal in his first five League

HOWE, Herbert Alexander

Role: Left half / Left back
b. Rugby, 1st April 1916

CAREER: Rugby Town/(Aug 1935-trials-
CITY)/Aug 1935:Market Harborough
Town/ Sept 1935:Leicester Nomads/
(Oct 1936-trials-Northampton Town)/
Feb 1937:CITY/July 1947:Notts County.

Debut v Wolverhampton Wanderers (H) 4.5.39

Forced to mark time in WW2 regional
football between his debut at left-half and
his immediate postwar stint at left-back,
Bert was effectively robbed of the
opportunity to fulfil his evident potential
at Filbert Street. In fact, despite him
playing the odd guest game for
Northampton, only Billy Frame and Sep
Smith won more wartime selections for
City than Bert. Twice in 1946/7 he had to
take over the injured Joe Calvert's
goalkeeping jersey, but such gameness
could not prevent City letting him drop

games, but was rested after the 1-7 League
Cup massacre at Hillsborough; then returned
later with confidence intact, earning particular
admiration for sound handling and his
extensive reach. That admiration turned to
covetous envy on the part of several clubs
who have leaned on his services since: he
conceded only one goal (a penalty) in eight
games for Kettering before breaking a bone in
his hand; he faced a penalty as his first act for
Bolton (substituting for the dismissed Aidan
Davison), then let in only one more goal in
three further starts; and conceded a first-
minute debut goal for Derby yet earned
enquiries about a permanent move before the
end of his impressive 15-game spell.
Curiously, though, it was a new Rams'
manager, Jim Smith, who made Russell his
first capture at £200,000.

Appearances:
FL: 10 apps. 0 gls.
LC: 3 apps. 0 gls.
AIC: 1 app. 0 gls.
Total: *14 apps. 0 gls.*

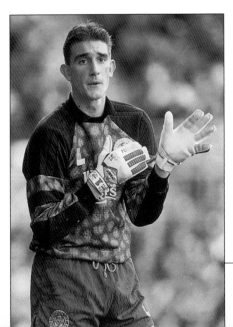

Russell Hoult

into the Third Division. The larger part of his 52-game spell at Meadow Lane, however, was ironically played out before huge crowds and in the full glare of media attention attracted by the presence of his new team-mate Tommy Lawton. Upon retirement through injury, Bert, who had started his amateur career as an inside-forward, became trainer to Rugby Town.

Appearances:
FL: 28 apps. 0 gls.
FAC: 3 apps. 0 gls.
WW2: 209 apps. 7 gls.
Total: *240 apps. 7 gls.*

HOWES, Arthur

Role: Goalkeeper
b. Leicester, c 1876

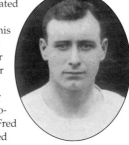

Arthur Howes

CAREER: Sept 1896:FOSSE/ (Mar 1898-trials-Lincoln City)/Mar 1898: Reading/Sept 1898: FOSSE/cs 1899:Brighton United/cs 1900:Dumbarton/cs 1901:Dundee/ cs 1902:Brighton & Hove Albion/cs 1904:Queen's Park Rangers.

Debut v Blackpool (A) 27.2.1897

An alert and agile goalkeeper who loyally played out the bulk of three seasons in the shadows of Jimmy Thraves, Charlie Saer and Godfrey Beardsley, Arthur made his final Fosse appearance in the home victory over Barnsley in January 1899 which put the club on top of the Second Division table for the first time ever (though they were to fall away to 3rd by season's end). He later joined the substantial number of English players (Herbert Dainty and Charles Webb among them) to assist Dundee - a club seemingly intent on single-handedly reversing the usual cross-border flow of football talent around the turn of the century. The lure of the South Coast sea air then exerted itself for a second time (with Brighton's second attempt at a pro-fessional club now esconced at the Goldstone Ground), before Arthur took cap and gloves to QPR's imposing-sounding home of the time: the Agricultural Society Grounds, Park Royal.

Appearances:
FL: 15 apps. 0 gls.
FAC: 1 app. 0 gls.
Total: *16 apps. 0 gls.*

HUBBARD, Archibald

Role: Centre forward
b. Leicester, 7th February 1883
d. Gloucester, 24th September 1967

CAREER: Oct 1901:Humberstone Victoria/ Leicester Imperial/St.Andrews/Aug 1904: FOSSE/May 1907:Fulham/Jan 1908:Watford/ May 1909:Norwich City/Nov 1910:Grimsby Town/Aug 1912:Lincoln City/Sept 1913: Leicester Imperial.

Debut v Gresley Rovers (H) FAC 12.11.04
(scored twice)

Invariably but inexplicably known as 'Ranji' throughout his Fosse career, Archie was switched regularly around the central attacking positions before settling into the centre-forward berth he was to occupy until the advent of the apparently unrelated Shirley Hubbard. A crowd favourite for his dashing enthusiasm, he went on to appear in Fulham's first-ever League team (along-side ex-Fossil Arthur Collins and Fossils-to-be Billy Goldie and Fred Threlfall); then moved through Southern League and Midland League football until Grimsby were re-elected to the League in 1911 - for a season in which Archie was top scorer. He appeared occasionally at wing-half during his 12-game, 3-goal final senior stint at Lincoln.

Archie Hubbard

Appearances:
FL: 58 apps. 21 gls.
FAC: 2 apps. 2 gls.
Total: *60 apps. 23 gls.*

HUBBARD, Shirley

Role: Centre forward
b. Leicester, 18th February 1885
d. Houghton-on-the-Hill, Leics,
22nd February 1963

CAREER: St.Andrews/Army
football/Leicester Imperial/
Feb 1907:FOSSE/May 1913:
Darlington/cs 1914:South
Shields/May 1919:CITY/
cs 1920:Ashby Town (p/coach).

Debut v Burton United (A) 29.3.07

Shirley Hubbard

Still a soldier in the Leicestershire
Regiment when he made his League bow with
Fosse in place of namesake Archie, Shirley had
only recently returned from a couple of years
of service in India. In fact, the two Hubbards
(who also had two local junior teams in
common, but reputedly no close kinship) only
appeared together once in Fosse's first team,
when both scored in the final game of 1906/7
at Lincoln City. Thereafter, Shirley fought off a
series of imported attack leaders, persistently
re-emerging in the forward line as he sampled
promotion, relegation and Second Division
struggle from the sharp end. On Christmas
Day 1912, while his benefit match (a reserve
fixture against Long Eaton St.Helens) was
taking place at Filbert Street, he was being led
off the Clapton Orient pitch with a broken
collarbone; characteristically, though, he was
back in senior action before the season was
out. Even if the Fosse directorate were content
to let him move on in 1913, they were glad to
receive the assistance of Sergeant Hubbard
(back in WW1 khaki from November 1914) in
a few wartime games, and his 5 goals in
1918/19 were enough to earn him a veteran's
contract for Leicester City's inaugural League
season, when he capped a brief comeback with
one last goal. A decade later, Shirley was
described as a dyer's labourer when involved
as the victim of a stabbing incident, but within
months had been taken on as trainer to
Loughborough Corinthians, where his old
team-mate Ben Hall was manager.

Appearances:
FL: 140 apps. 36 gls.
FAC: 14 apps. 3 gls.
WW1: 17 apps. 5 gls.
Total: *171 apps. 44 gls.*

HUFTON, S.

Role: Centre half/Inside forward

CAREER: Aug 1891:FOSSE.
*Debut v Small Heath (H) FAC
3.10.1891*

The hapless pivot when Midland
Leaguers Fosse made their first-
hurdle FA Cup exit to Small
Heath in 1891/2 (losing 2-6 at the
Aylestone Road cricket ground to
the comparative 'giants' from the
Football Alliance), Hufton was
also occasionally thrust into a
more overtly forward role as the club
stumbled through its initial season of regular
competitive fare.

Appearances:
FAC: 1 app. 0 gls.
ML: 16 apps. 1 gl.
Total: *17 apps. 1 gl.*

HUGHES, Archibald

Role: Centre half / Inside forward
b. Arthurlie, Renfrewshire, c 1871

CAREER: Barrhead/Arthurlie/cs 1892:
Middlesbrough Ironopolis/cs 1893:Bolton
Wanderers/Aug 1894:FOSSE/cs 1895:Glossop
North End.

Debut v Grimsby Town (A) 1.9.1894

Preparing for their first tilt at League football,
Fosse signed Archie to assume their
'playmaker' role and, according to the usual
tactical custom of the day, handed him either
the centre-half or inside-forward position from
which to direct midfield operations. He had
built quite a reputation at Bolton, but had
unfortunately spent all but the first five
minutes of their 1894 FA Cup Final defeat by
Notts County as a limping, ineffectual
passenger. His track record with Fosse, however, was interrupted for different reasons, as
Archie twice found himself suspended by the
committee for breaches of training regulations;
and it was little surprise when his registration
was not renewed at the end of the season.

Appearances:
FL: 18 apps. 2 gls.
FAC: 3 apps. 0 gls.
Total: *21 apps. 2 gls.*

HUGHES, Bernard

Role: Right half

CAREER: Aug 1904:FOSSE.
Debut v Hull City (A) 14.4.06

An amateur right-half retained as a professional after impressing in the three trial matches of August 1905 (in the second of which he had to take over from the injured goalkeeper),

Bernard spent almost the whole of his two-year Fosse career in reserve to the experienced William Morgan, and featured only in the above goal-less draw at senior level. A year before he had been in the reserve side beaten by South Wigston Albion in the County Cup Final.

Appearances:
FL: 1 app. 0 gls.
Total: *1 app. 0 gls.*

HUGHES, William

Role: Striker
b. Coatbridge, Lanarkshire, 30th December 1948

CAREER: Coatbridge Jnrs/Dec 1965: Sunderland/Aug 1977:Derby County/Dec 1977:CITY/(Sept 1979-loan-Carlisle United)/ Apr 1980:San Jose Earthquakes/Corby Town.
Debut v Middlesbrough (H) 26.12.77

Despite totting up the years at Roker, Billy had his modest achievements overshadowed for a long time by those of his brother, Celtic's John 'Yogi' Hughes; but eventually righted that particular imbalance when making a valuable contribution to Sunderland's underdog FA Cup-winning side of 1973. The strongly-built forward with the surprisingly subtle touch finally left Roker after 11 seasons and a testimonial game, having won one cap as a substitute for Scotland in 1975; and was hitting his goalscoring stride at Derby when Frank McLintock tempted him to help dig City out of the relegation mire. Understandably, Billy wasn't up to that specific task, but he remained at the club as a utility forward throughout Jock Wallace's first season in charge, before drifting off for a brief taste of Stateside football.

Appearances:
FL: 36 (1) apps, 5 gls.
FAC: 1 app. 0 gls.
LC: 1 app. 0 gls.
Total: *38 (1) apps. 5 gls.*

Billy Hughes

HUMPHREYS, Percy

Role: Centre forward
b. Cambridge, 3rd February 1880
d. Stepney, London, 13th April 1959

CAREER: Cambridge St.Mary's/May 1900:
Queen's Park Rangers/July 1901:Notts
County/June 1907:FOSSE/Feb 1908:Chelsea/
Dec 1909:Tottenham Hotspur/Oct 1911:
FOSSE/cs 1912:Hartlepools United (p/mgr)/
Nov 1914:Norwich City.
Debut v Leeds City (H) 7.9.07

Having represented England and the Football
League once apiece in 1903 (at a time when it
was said that 'his sudden dashes for goal are
not unlike those meteoric spurts which
characterise Bloomer's play'), and having
totalled 66 League goals for the Magpies,
centre-forward Percy made a whirlwind
goalscoring contribution to Fosse's 1907/8
promotion effort. He had no sooner
established himself as seasonal top scorer with
19 goals in 26 games than he was spirited
away to Stamford Bridge before the run-in for
£350 (the precise ceiling for transfer fees then -
briefly - in force between League clubs). His
impressive goal ratio dropped a little in
Division One with Chelsea, then perked up
again with Spurs, but when Percy returned for
a second Filbert Street stint, it was

Don Hutchins

unfortunately with a mediocre side which he
was unable to lift. At the time war was
declared, he was about to take up a three-year
appointment as player/coach with a Swiss
club, but instantly returned home, to make a
three-game adieu to the senior game with
Southern League Norwich. Percy's death was
registered as a suicide.

> **Appearances:**
> *FL: 40 apps. 21 gls.*
> *FAC: 4 apps. 4 gls.*
> **Total:** *44 apps. 25 gls.*

HUTCHINS, Donald

Role: Outside left
b. Middlesbrough, 8th May 1948

CAREER: Stockton Juniors/Feb 1966:CITY/
July 1969:Plymouth Argyle/July 1972:
Blackburn Rovers/June 1974:Bradford City/
1981:Scarborough.
Debut v Burnley (A) 15.4.68

An orthodox outside-left who found it hard to

Percy Humphreys

displace either Len Glover or Mike Stringfellow after being given his break by Matt Gillies, Don got only one chance to impress new manager Frank O'Farrell, who released him after only a few months in charge. Don's natural pace and exuberant skills came to the fore, however, in 96 League games at Plymouth and, two moves later, in Bradford City's 1977 promotion from the Fourth Division. At Valley Parade, in fact, he totalled 256 League appearances, and stretched his career aggregate goals total to a very respectable 74.

Appearances:
FL: 4 apps. 0 gls.
Total: *4 apps. 0 gls.*

HYETT, James

Role: Centre forward

CAREER: Stapleford Town/Jan 1905:FOSSE.

Debut v Liverpool (H) 28.1.05

Another of the elusive 'Fossil-for-a-fortnight' brigade, seemingly destined for obscurity after the briefest of senior try-outs in the centre-forward berth, in a 0-3 defeat at Anfield.

Appearances:
FL: 1 app. 0 gls.
Total: *1 app. 0 gls.*

IGGLEDEN, Horatio

Role: Forward
b. Hull, 17th March 1925

CAREER: am July 1941/pro Mar 1942: CITY/Dec 1948:Leeds United/July 1955: Exeter City/Aug 1956:Goole Town.

Debut (WW2) v Wolverhampton Wanderers (H) 4.10.41; (postwar) v Luton Town (A) 5.10.46

A 16-year-old Hull dock worker when signed by City and handed an early senior debut, Ray later served in the Royal Marines (and guested for Grimsby Town) before returning to the Filbert Street ranks. A versatile forward who made sporadic first team appearances in four attacking positions, he was still looked on as a fine goalscoring prospect when involved in the part-exchange deal with Leeds which brought Ken Chisholm to Leicester. His pace and shooting power brought him exactly 50 League and Cup goals at Elland Road, including a hat-trick against City in January 1954, by which time he was the regular inside-left partner to the great John Charles.

Appearances:
FL: 11 apps. 2 gls.
WW2: 6 apps. 0 gls.
Total: *17 apps. 2 gls.*

Ray Iggleden

JACKSON, Ronald

Role: Left back
b. Crook, Co.Durham, 15th October 1919
d. Althorpe, Lincs, 28th February 1980

CAREER: Sept 1945:Wrexham/Dec 1949:
CITY/July 1955:Kettering Town/Rugby Town.
Debut v Hull City (A) 24.12.49

Norman Bullock's second signing (at a cost of
£9,000), Ron was a left-back noted for his
speed in recovery and a remarkable heading
ability for a man only 5ft.7ins tall. A games
master at a Leicester school (he had been a
science teacher in Wrexham), he appeared to
be on his way out of the first-team reckoning
after a lengthy contract dispute in 1952, but
returned to hold down his position as an
ever-present in the 1954 promotion season.
The highlight of that season for Ron, however,
was in the first game of the Cup quarter-final
marathon with Preston, when he outplayed
Tom Finney and still managed to score his
only City goal; albeit a rather flukey free-kick
from close to the half-way line! His son Roy is
Commercial Manager of Leicester Tigers.

Appearances:
FL: 161 apps. 0 gls.
FAC: 12 apps. 1 gl.
Total: *173 apps. 1 gl.*

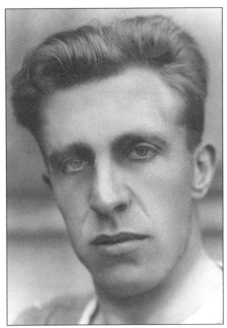

Billy Jackson

JACKSON, William

Role: Winger
b. Farnworth, Lancs, 5th July 1902
d. Blackpool, October qtr 1974

CAREER: Leyland/1922:Altrincham/cs 1923:
Darwen/May 1924:Sunderland/May 1925:
Leeds United/May 1927:West Ham United/
Feb 1928:Chelsea/Apr 1931:CITY/(1932:loan-
Ashford Town)/May 1932:Bristol Rovers/
May 1934:Cardiff City/Jan 1935:Watford/
cs 1935:Chorley/Sept 1936:Netherfield.
Debut v Liverpool (H) 12.9.31

Two-footed winger Billy spent a lot of time in
reserve football with his first five League
clubs, proving unable to make a breakthrough
at all at Roker. He played 38 times (scoring
twice) for Leeds, only twice for the Hammers,
and only 26 times (6 goals) over three and a
half seasons at Stamford Bridge. His spell with
City - which would have started with an end-
of-season debut at Birmingham but for the
death of his father - saw him understudying
Hughie Adcock, and was additionally marked
by the frustration of having his only senior
goal chalked off by the abandonment of the

*Ron
Jackson*

home game with Portsmouth in December 1931. Indeed, his final game for City would come in the following month - in the 3-8 home defeat by Villa which still remains the sole instance of such a scoreline in favour of the away team in League history. Billy found a more regular slot at Eastville after a two-goal start, but his aggregate career figures of only 123 League games across eleven years rather aptly indexed his in-and-out status. His brother Robert was a Bury player.

Appearances:
FL: 4 apps. 0 gls.
Total: *4 apps. 0 gls.*

JAKEMAN, Leslie

Role: Right half
b. Nuneaton, Warks, 14th March 1930

CAREER: Atherstone/June 1947:Derby County/cs 1949:Hinckley Athletic/ May 1951:CITY/cs 1954:Hinckley Athletic/ Sept 1954:CITY/Feb 1955:Coventry City.

Debut v Burnley (A) 6.9.54

A junior released by Derby back to the Midland non-league scene, Les was then nurtured further through the ranks at City as a wing-half or inside-forward, and 'farmed out' to Hinckley to add to his experience. His sudden recall for a surprise First Division bow at Turf Moor in the No.4 shirt (in a 1-3 defeat) caused quite a fuss - City were soon afterwards fined by the League for fielding him while he was still officially registered as a Hinckley player. Les unfortunately then failed to add any further senior appearances during his short spell at Highfield Road.

Appearances:
FL: 1 app. 0 gls.
Total:
1 app. 0 gls.

Les Jakeman

JAMES, Anthony Craig

Role: Centre back
b. Sheffield,
27th June 1967

CAREER: Sheffield FC/1988:Gainsborough Trinity/Aug 1988:Lincoln City/Aug 1989: CITY/July 1994:Hereford United.

Debut v Watford (A) 2.9.89 (sub)

Though too much of his City career was a matter of injury-induced frustration, Tony will never be forgotten for his heroics of 1990/1, when his close-range conversion of a left-wing corner against Oxford United at Filbert Street proved decisive in keeping a severely relegation-threatened City in Division Two. On that same joyous May day, he deservedly received the club's Player of the Year award, though essentially for his defensive contributions. A 6ft 3in gentle giant, blessed with a telescopic tackle and a prodigious long

Tony James

throw, Tony had made a rapid rise from Sheffield amateur football, playing only three times for Gainsborough before joining Lincoln for £6,000 on their return to the League, and learning his centre-back trade in front of Mark Wallington. He cost City £150,000 when David Pleat swooped for him after the first game of 1989/90, and soon became an immensely popular addition to a hard-pressed back line, compensating for a lack of finesse with total enthusiastic commitment, and regularly causing havoc in opposing penalty areas either with his bustling presence or his missile-like throw-ins. A double fracture of the leg during a home win over Wolves in October 1991 was the first of several injuries which marred Tony's progress after his golden goal, and despite a Wembley appearance in the Play-off Final against Blackburn, he never thereafter managed a lengthy first-team run. Tony's cousin Scott James was a youth trainee with City between 1993-95.

Appearances:
FL: 79 (28) apps. 10 gls.
FAC: 2 apps. 1 gl.
LC: 6 apps. 0 gls.
FMC: 0 (1) app. 0 gls.
P/O: 3 apps. 0 gls.
Total: *90 (29) apps. 11 gls.*

JAMES, Robert Mark

Role: Full back
b. Swansea, 23rd March 1957

CAREER: app Mar 1973/pro Apr 1974: Swansea City/July 1983:Stoke City/Oct 1984: Queen's Park Rangers/June 1987:CITY/Jan 1988:Swansea City/Aug 1990:Bradford City/ Aug 1992:Cardiff City/Oct 1993:Merthyr Tydfil (p/mgr)/Sept 1994:Barry Town.

Debut v Shrewsbury Town (H) 15.8.87

A 16-year-old apprentice when he made his Vetch Field debut, Robbie went on to play in all four divisions for his hometown club as they rose to join the elite, and knocked in 110 senior goals as he matured from a hefty front-runner into a powerful Welsh international midfielder. Sizeable fees took him via Stoke to Loftus Road, where he developed another string to his bow by holding down a full-back spot, and where City were reminded of his long-range shooting prowess during their 1987 FA Cup exit. Bryan Hamilton saw in Robbie

Robbie James

the sort of experienced campaigner who could help settle a predominantly youthful Second Division defence, but many of his efforts were negated by a lack of pace, and some of the vigour seemed to leave his game after Wales were eliminated from the European Championships. A couple of particularly lack-lustre performances in front of new City boss David Pleat resulted in a rapid departure for

Robbie, who re-signed for the Swans and immediately assumed their captaincy, leading them to promotion from the Fourth Division via the 1988 Play-offs, and scoring in their Welsh Cup win of 1989. Robbie celebrated a further championship success with Cardiff's Division Three side of 1993, when he also picked up his fifth Welsh Cup-winner's medal. His move to Merthyr prompted the first instance of the FA of Wales convening a transfer tribunal to set the £10,000 fee, and closed his League career on a total of 782 appearances (only ever bettered by Peter Shilton, Terry Paine and Tommy Hutchison).

Appearances:
FL: 21 (2) apps. 0 gls.
LC: 4 apps. 0 gls.
FMC: 1 app. 0 gls.
Total: 26 (2) apps. 0 gls.

JARVIE, John

Role: Goalkeeper
b. Old Monkland, Lanarkshire, 19th October 1900
d. Leicester, 30th January 1985

CAREER: Bellshill Athletic/June 1923: Third Lanark/Aug 1925:CITY/Oct 1926: Portsmouth/Mar 1928:Southend United/(July 1929-trials-Watford)/Aug 1929: Norwich City/Aug 1930:Chester/Aug 1931: Shrewsbury Town/Sep 1933:Solus FC.

John Jarvie

Debut v Manchester United (A) 16.9.25

Compensating for his lack of height through notable agility and clean handling, John impressed City as a likely goalkeeping deputy to Albert Godderidge, and in fact got an early first-team run as the side started its First Division campaign rather shakily. Unfortunately unable to stem a rising goal-deficit column, however, he was edged out definitively by the signing of his international compatriot, Kenny Campbell. At Portsmouth, John's four League games included the demoralising experiences of having seven (Middlesbrough) and eight (Liverpool) goals whizzing past him, but he fared better in Division Three

(South), before curiously leaving Norwich in 1930 despite being an ever-present in League and Cup games during his season there.

Appearances:
FL: 5 apps. 0 gls.
Total: 5 apps. 0 gls.

JAYES, Brian

Role: Right half
b. Leicester, 13th December 1932

CAREER: am/pro July 1954:CITY/July 1956: Mansfield Town/July 1960:Ramsgate.

Debut v Nottingham Forest (A) 31.8.55

Bad timing rather afflicted right-half Brian as he made his first-team bow. The injury crisis that had offered him a Second Division place was in fact quite widespread, and a depleted City side shipped 15 goals in the three successive away defeats in which he played near the beginning of 1955/6. Brian subsequently became a regular at Field Mill, making 115 League appearances and scoring once.

Appearances:
FL: 3 apps. 0 gls.
Total: 3 apps. 0 gls.

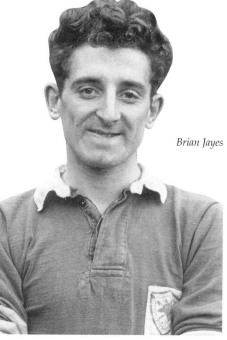

Brian Jayes

JAYES, Carl Geoffrey

Role: Goalkeeper
b. Leicester, 15th March 1954

CAREER: app Mar 1969/pro July 1971:CITY/
Nov 1977:Northampton Town/cs 1980:
AP Leamington.

Debut v Orient (H) FAC 5.2.72

Capped seven times for England schoolboys,
and an occasional City reserve-team
goalkeeper while still at school, Carl looked
set to eventually follow Peter Shilton's route to
the top. His unexpected debut was a
nightmare, however, as City found themselves
in the position of felled giants at the Fourth
Round stage of the Cup, with Carl dropping
Orient's second goal over his head into the
net. He waited patiently for two and a half
years for another chance, briefly but efficiently
deputising for Mark Wallington just prior to
that keeper embarking on his record marathon
run of consecutive appearances. Carl was a
regular for the Cobblers until accompanying
John Farrington to Leamington, and after a
year there hung up his boots to become a
policeman.

Appearances:
FL: 5 apps. 0 gls.
FAC: 1 app. 0 gls.
Total: *6 apps. 0 gls.*

JELLY, Horace Edward

Role: Right back
b. Leicester, 28th August 1921

CAREER: Belgrave United/Navy football/
am Jan 1944/pro May 1946:CITY/Aug 1951:
Plymouth Argyle.

Debut v Southampton (A) 26.5.47

A teenage right-winger who converted to full-
back while on wartime Navy service, Ted first
signed for City while on leave and became a
professional when demobbed. Very much a
reserve for the first two postwar seasons, he
timed his New Year's Day re-entry perfectly in
1949, holding his place in the No.2 shirt
throughout the glory run to Wembley. A
regular in the following campaign, Ted lost
out when City signed Arthur Lever, and spent
an unlucky time at Plymouth: waiting
eighteen months for his senior debut, then
having his 13-game record curtailed by a
cartilage injury. Ted held an FA coaching
badge, but when in 1954 he couldn't find a
senior club, turned his energies to setting up a
thriving electrical business back in Leicester.

Appearances:
FL: 56 apps. 1 gl.
FAC: 9 apps. 0 gls.
Total: *65 apps. 1 gl.*

Above: Carl Jayes   *Right: Ted Jelly*

JOACHIM, Julian Kevin

Role: Striker
b. Peterborough, 20th September 1974

CAREER: YT July 1991/pro Sept 1992:CITY.
Debut v Barnsley (H) 3.10.92

The brilliant 'Crown Jules' of City's recent campaigns, Julian has erected remarkable foundations to his career before reaching the age of 21, and as a genuinely exciting striker has won himself a rare degree of hero-worship from the Filbert Street crowd. Signed professionally only two months into the second year of his trainee contract, having scored ten times in the first five youth games, plus the reserves' only goal to that date, he made an early senior bow, too, following injuries to David Lowe and Phil Gee. His first goal came three days later, in a League Cup tie in the city of his birth, and by the end of the 1992/3 term Julian's was a name noted nationally. For heading the list of his several spectacular strikes was the individualist goal against Barnsley in City's FA Cup exit which took the BBC's Goal of the Month award, and was runner-up in the Goal of the Season rating; while further evidence of his scintillating pace, forceful strength, and controlled, direct dribbling skills had amassed almost weekly. Another solo rampage from the half-way line led to the goal advantage over Portsmouth which eventually saw City to Wembley in 1993, and Julian also led the fightback there against Swindon. His progress was maintained in the following successful promotion campaign, when he came on as sub and prompted the move which led to Steve Walsh's winning goal against Derby at Wembley; and he had claimed both City's first Premiership goal (against Newcastle) and a sparkling double in the opening victory over Spurs before a serious foot injury saw him sidelined for the bulk of the season. At representative level, Julian starred for England in both the 1993 World Youth Championships (scoring against Turkey to put them into the quarter-finals, and against Australia to beat the hosts to third place) and the European Under-18 Championships a few months later, when he collected a winner's medal

after being brought down for the match-winning penalty against Turkey at Nottingham. His Under-21 debut came in March 1994 (hitting the bar after coming on as sub against Denmark), and his first goal at that level (against Malaysia in the Toulon tournament) helped index his eagerly awaited 1995 return to fitness.

Appearances (to end 1994/5):
PL: 11 (4) apps. 3 gls.
FL: 52 (10) apps. 21 gls.
FAC: 3 apps. 1 gl.
LC: 5 (1) apps. 2 gls.
P/O: 4 (2) apps. 2 gls.
Total: *75 (17) apps. 29 gls.*

Julian Joachim

JOBEY, George

Role: Centre forward
/ Right half
*b. Heddon,
Northumberland, 1885
d. Chaddesden,
Derbyshire,
9th March 1962*

George Jobey

CAREER: Morpeth
Harriers/Apr 1906:
Newcastle United/
May 1913:Arsenal/June 1914:Bradford Park
Avenue/Aug 1919:Hartlepools United/
Sept 1919:CITY/May 1920:Northampton Town
(p/mgr).

Debut v Wolverhampton Wanderers (A) 6.9.19

A robust half-back and occasional centre-
forward for his local League club, George
played in the latter position when taking a
runners-up medal from the 1911 FA Cup Final,
and when he made his Arsenal debut (against
Fosse) in the first game at Highbury - an
occasion he also marked by scoring, by being
carried off injured, and by making an
undignified exit from the half-built stadium on
a milk cart! During WW1 he turned out for
Hamilton Academicals, then signed for City
when peace and League football returned
(though he also played for Hartlepools United
in a North Eastern League match a week
before his City debut!). After three games up
front, the veteran resumed his old half-back
position, but was not retained after his loss of
pace had become apparent. It was initially
announced that he had assumed
the player/manager role at Ebbw
Vale, but George disappointed the
Welshmen by changing his mind
and taking the reins at
Northampton, also there adding
another 77 League games to his
considerable appearance
aggregate. In 1922 George became
manager of Wolves, and from
1925 to 1941 was the boss at
Derby County. Renowned there as
a disciplinarian who bought big,
George got the Rams promotion
in 1926, and took them to the
championship runners-up spot
twice in the 30s, but he was
eventually suspended by a joint
FA/League commission for

alleged complicity in the over-payment of
bonuses and signing-on fees. When his ban
was finally lifted, George took charge for
1952/3 at Mansfield, but reportedly his heart
was no longer in the game.

Appearances:
*FL: 30 apps. 0 gls.
FAC: 4 apps. 0 gls.*
Total: *34 apps. 0 gls.*

JOBLING, Kevin Andrew

Role: Midfield
b. Sunderland, 1st January 1968

CAREER: app July 1984/pro Jan 1986:CITY/
Feb 1988:Grimsby Town/(Jan 1994-loan-
Scunthorpe United).

Debut v Newcastle United (A) 4.4.87

A tidy teenage midfielder who seemed to lack
the necessary confidence to express himself
with more flair on his intermittent senior
opportunities with City, Kevin was one of
several players to be given a break by Bryan
Hamilton and then quickly to be assessed as
not meeting David Pleat's standards. Perhaps
unfortunately, Kevin reserved his most
forceful display for the Full Members (Simod)
Cup tie at Charlton in 1987/8, when his match
-winning two-goal performance was watched
by hardly more spectators than he was used to
playing before in City's reserves. It was Bobby
Roberts who snapped up his signature in part-
exchange when City moved for Phil Turner,
but Kevin couldn't keep Grimsby from
slipping into Division
Four by season's end.
He did, however, assist
them to successive
promotions in 1990 and
1991, from a nominal
left-back berth, and had
amassed 222 League
appearances for the
Mariners by the end of
1994/5.

Appearances:
*FL: 4 (5) apps. 0 gls.
FAC: 0 (1) app. 0 gls.
FMC: 3 apps. 2 gls.*
Total: *7 (6) apps. 2 gls.*

Kevin Jobling

Jimmy Johnson

A popular right-half who had taken over the Fosse captaincy in 1889, Jimmy led his men into their first FA Cup foray (played at Mill Lane), and was also involved alongside his brother Teddy in the first two County Cup-winning sides: thus becoming the first Fossil to raise a trophy of any description following the 4-0 replay win over Coalville at Loughborough in April 1890.

Appearances:
FAC: 1 app. 0 gls.
Total: *1 app. 0 gls.*

Teddy Johnson

JOHNSON, Edward A.

Role: Inside left

CAREER: c 1886:FOSSE/1892:Leicester YMCA.

Debut (competitive) v Burton Wanderers (H) FAC 4.10.1890

The inside-left in Fosse's first two FA Cup-tie defeats, Teddy played with the club he had joined around 1886 for the initial Midland League season but, like many of his fellow pioneers, found the regular competitive demands of the club's new station a little too much for him. The YMCA team he joined was Leicester's premier amateur club of the time.

Appearances:
FAC: 2 apps. 0 gls.
ML: 18 apps. 1 gl.
Total: *20 apps. 1 gl.*

JOHNSON, James

Role: Right half

CAREER: 1886:FOSSE/1892:Leicester YMCA.

Debut (competitive) v Burton Wanderers (H) FAC 4.10.1890

JOHNSON, Robert Simon

Role: Full back
b. Bedford, 22nd February 1962

CAREER: Bedford Town/app/pro 1980:Luton Town/(Aug 1983-loan-Lincoln City)/ Aug 1989:CITY/Aug 1991:Barnet/Nov 1991: Hitchin Town/cs 1994:Bedford Town.

Debut v Hull City (A) 19.8.89

A junior full-back under David Pleat at Luton, Rob made his League bow while on loan at Sincil Bank (filling in for Worcestershire

cricketer Phil Neale), but then had his senior development interrupted by a serious knee injury. One of his subsequent stints as a Kenilworth Road regular encompassed a starring role in Luton's 1988 League Cup Final win over Arsenal, though Rob was once more being regarded primarily as a back-up

Rob Johnson

squad player when he was reunited with his former manager at Leicester in the eve-of-season part-exchange deal which took Mick Kennedy down the M1. Such was to become his lot at Filbert Street, too, after early experience on both flanks of City's rather porous Second Division defence had left him looking a little rattled. Rob failed to impress in a handful of midfield outings, either; though a fortnight after being freed by Brian Little he made a last claim to fame as a member of Barnet's first-ever Football League line-up.

Appearances:
FL: 19 (6) apps. 0 gls.
LC: 1 app. 0 gls.
FMC: 1 app. 0 gls.
Total: *21 (6) apps. 0 gls.*

JOHNSTON, James C.

Role: Left half
b. Boddam, Aberdeenshire, 12th April 1923

CAREER: Peterhead/Feb 1947: CITY/May 1950:Reading/Mar 1953: Swindon Town/June 1955:Merthyr Tydfil (p/mgr).

Debut v Brentford (A) 15.9.48

A wiry, tough-tackling left-half signed from the Highland League after trials, Jimmy found his first-team breakthrough delayed by a niggling foot injury, and was then edged out of the Wembley running by Johnny King's consistency. The pair vied for the senior No.6 shirt throughout the following 1949/50 season, but Norman Bullock let Jimmy move on to Elm Park, where he was immovable for three seasons and 120 games. He added 75 more Third Division (South) appearances at Swindon.

Appearances:
FL: 35 apps. 0 gls.
FAC: 1 app. 0 gls.
Total: *36 apps. 0 gls.*

Left: Jimmy Johnston

JONES, David Owen

Role: Full back
b. Cardiff, 28th October 1910
d. Oadby, Leics, 20th May 1971

CAREER: Ely United/1929:Ebbw Vale/(1929-trials-Charlton Athletic)/(May 1930-trials-Millwall)/Aug 1931:Clapton Orient/May 1933:CITY/Oct 1947:Mansfield Town/cs 1949:Hinckley Athletic (p/mgr).

Debut v Aston Villa (A) 26.8.33

A bargain buy from penurious Orient at only £200, and initially signed to partner Adam Black, Dai was an outstanding full-back who soon walked into the Welsh international side, and won a total of seven caps. An ever-present in the 1937 promotion campaign, he went on to play throughout the war for City, Notts County, Wolves and West Ham, and was still a Filbert Street regular throughout the first peacetime season, in which he notched the club's opening goal (at West Ham in the third fixture). Almost 37 years old when he moved to Field Mill, Dai still stamped his authoritative class on another 74 League games before moving down to Birmingham Combination level.

Successively a sawyer and a trawlerman before he became a football professional, on retirement from the game he became a partner in the local firm of Day & Jones (Leather Factors) until the late 60s, and was working as a sales executive in the shoe trade at the time of his death.

Appearances:
FL: 226 apps. 4 gls.
FAC: 12 apps. 0 gls.
WW2: 54 apps. 2 gls.
Total: *292 apps. 6 gls.*

Dai Jones

JONES, Dennis

Role: Right half
b. Shirebrook, Derbyshire,14th May 1894
d. Bolsover, Derbyshire, 7th September 1961

CAREER: Shirebrook/June 1921:CITY/May 1924:Southampton/June 1925:Mansfield Town /Shirebrook/Aug 1927:Sutton Town/Aug 1928:Wombwell.

Debut v Barnsley (H) 5.11.21

A centre-half for his Central Alliance club, Dennis made the bulk of his City appearances on the right of the middle line, deposing the veteran Teddy King and holding the position until Billy Newton arrived, then going south as part of the deal which brought Harry

Dennis Jones

Hooper to Filbert Street. He had only seven Second Division outings for the Saints, though, before commencing a ramble around the Midland League.

Appearances:
FL: 64 apps. 2 gls.
FAC: 3 apps. 0 gls.
Total: *67 apps. 2 gls.*

JONES, Richard

Role: Left half
b. Wales, c 1875

CAREER: Hanley Swifts/Jan 1896:South Shore/May 1897:FOSSE/ Aug 1901:Burton United /Sept 1902:Royston United/1904:Leeds City.

Debut v Luton Town (H) 4.9.1897

Dick Jones

For years football record books (including, unfortunately, the first draft of this tome as it appeared in 'Of Fossils & Foxes'!) conflated the personal details and careers of two separate Welsh international players: the Wrexham-born, Everton and Manchester City defender Robert Samuel Jones, and Fosse's Dick Jones. Thanks to the excellent sleuthing of Welsh historian Ian Garland, we can now at least identify the Fossil capped for Wales against Scotland in March 1898 (alongside club-mate Alfred Watkins) by his given name, though we are still at a loss to place the birth credentials of a man we believe to have been raised in the Stoke-on-Trent area! Dick had well earned his country's recognition with some stalwart Second Division displays at left-half, and when Fosse just missed out on promotion a year later, he was absent only once from a steadfast defence. He had disciplinary problems at Burton (earning a year-long club suspension, ratified by the FA, for some unspecified misdemeanour), and then reappeared in junior football in Yorkshire. But later, when the newly-formed Leeds City embarked on a series of high-class friendlies as a means of angling for League election, the now-veteran Dick was in their side which faced Fosse at Elland Road.

Appearances:
FL: 104 apps. 1 gl.
FAC: 9 apps. 0 gls.
Total: *113 apps. 1 gl.*

JONES, Robert

Role: Striker
b. Coventry,
17th November 1964

CAREER: app June 1981: Manchester City/Sept 1982: CITY/Aug 1986:Walsall/ cs 1987:Kidderminster Harriers/Nov 1989:Burton Albion/July 1991:VS Rugby /Oct 1991:Burton Albion/ Aug 1993:Ravenstone.

Debut v Oldham Athletic (A) 7.5.83 (scored once)

An England schoolboy international who failed to win a contract at Maine Road, Robbie then took

Robbie Jones

freed by Gordon Milne at the end of 1985/6. He appeared in the 1989 Welsh Cup Final for Kidderminster (beaten 0-5 by a Robbie James-led Swansea), and moved to Burton jointly with former City reserve Jon Pearson in the Brewers' then-record purchase deal.

Appearances:
FL: 12 (3) apps. 3 gls.
LC: 2 apps. 0 gls.
Total: *14 (3) apps. 3 gls.*

JOPLING, Joseph

Role: Left back
b. South Shields, 21st April 1951

CAREER: Aug 1969: Aldershot/Sept 1970: CITY/(Jan 1974-loan-Torquay United)/Mar 1974:Aldershot.

Debut v Sunderland (H) 10.10.70

Joe Jopling

advantage of parental links to become the possessor of Welsh youth caps shortly after arriving at Filbert Street as a professional. He made a stunning impact when standing in for Gary Lineker in the crucial, televised promotion tussle at Boundary Park, scoring the first goal as City grabbed an invaluable win. When he next scored to help City to their belated opening First Division point of 1983/4 (against Stoke in the seventh fixture), a rosy future looked assured for the young striker; but despite his close control, willing running and impressive reserve-team scoring ratio, Robbie's diminutive stature eventually told against him at the highest level, and he was

Rejected by Sunderland after youth team trials, but a teenage regular in his first season with the Shots, full-back Joe was regarded by Frank O'Farrell as very much an investment for the future when he arrived in a deal which sent £30,000 plus Murray Brodie and Jimmy Burt south. He made an early bow in place of David Nish, but got few chances to impress Jimmy Bloomfield over the next three seasons, and eventually returned to Aldershot to stay. By the time Joe retired, he had proved his all-round defensive versatility at the Recreation Ground in an aggregate of over 400 League and Cup games.

Appearances:
FL: 2 (1) apps. 0 gls.
Total: *2 (1) apps. 0 gls.*

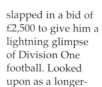

KEECH, William

Role: Centre forward
*b. Irthlingborough,
Northants, 1872*

William Keech

CAREER: Wellingborough/Sept 1894:Barnsley
St.Peters/Oct 1895:Liverpool/cs 1896:
Barnsley/cs 1897:Blackpool/Feb 1898:FOSSE/
Feb 1899:Loughborough/Aug 1899:Queen's
Park Rangers/cs 1902:Brentford/cs 1904:
Kensal Rise United.

Debut v Walsall (A) 26.2.1898

A hat-trick in a friendly against old rivals
Loughborough two days before his League
debut immediately endeared centre-forward
William to the Fosse followers. But after leading the attack for the rest of 1897/8 and the
beginning of the next season, he struggled to
find a first-team place, and ironically became
one more hand to the pumps for the terminally
floundering Luffs. He next turned up at wing-
half, however, in QPR's first professional team
in the Southern League, and remained in the
middle line until finishing his career in that
sphere with the then-lowly Bees. An 1899 profile credited him with honours as both a skater
and a boxer; and also alluded mysteriously to
William holding the gold medal of the Royal
Humane Society. Before WW1, he was on the
training staff back at QPR.

Appearances:
FL: 15 apps. 5 gls.
Total: *15 apps. 5 gls.*

KEELEY, Ernest

Role: Right half
*b. Ellesmere Port, Cheshire,
1st October 1908
d. Little Sutton, Cheshire,
24th May 1974*

CAREER: Ellesmere Port
Town/Aug 1931: Chester/
Feb 1932:CITY.

*Debut v West Ham United
(H) 18.2.32*

A product of Cheshire
junior football, wing-half
Ernie was signed up in time to play in
Chester's first-ever League side, and had barely
had time to adjust to this elevation when City

Ernie Keeley

slapped in a bid of
£2,500 to give him a
lightning glimpse
of Division One
football. Looked
upon as a longer-
term contender for the problematic right-half
position, Ernie unfortunately never got much
chance to lay claim to it, injuring his knee so
badly early the next season that he was forced
to quit the game entirely in 1933; initially
going into the insurance business. His father
had been Chester's goalkeeper when they won
the Welsh Cup in 1908, while Ernie's younger
brother Arthur was truly ill-fated, moving
optimistically up in status as a forward from
Chester to Portsmouth in 1939, but being
killed in action during the war.

Appearances:
FL: 4 apps. 0 gls.
Total: *4 apps. 0 gls.*

KELLARD, Robert Sydney William

Role: Midfield
b. Southend, 1st March 1943

CAREER: am 1958/pro Mar 1960:Southend
United/Dec 1963:Crystal Palace/Nov 1965:
Ipswich Town/Mar 1966:Portsmouth/July
1968:Bristol City/Aug
1970:CITY/Sept 1971:
Crystal Palace/Dec 1972:
Portsmouth/(Jan 1975-
loan-Hereford United)
/Sept 1975:Torquay
United.

*Debut v Cardiff City (H)
15.8.70*

A combative midfielder
with an alert brain to
complement his ball-
winning skills, Bobby
was the mainspring of
City's 1971 promotion
side, and as soon as he
linked with Willie Carlin,
the club's upward
ambitions achieved an
undeniable momentum.
Chipping in with some
valuable goals on the way to that
championship, Bobby was unfortunate not to
consolidate his First Division career with City,

Bobby Kellard

KELLY, Bernard

Role: Inside forward
b. Carfin, Lanarkshire, 21st October 1932

CAREER: Law Hearts/1951:Muirkirk
Juniors/Oct 1951:Raith Rovers/July 1958:
CITY/Apr 1959:Nottingham Forest/Sept
1959:Aberdeen/Aug 1960:Raith Rovers.

Debut v Arsenal (A) 30.8.58

A hefty goalscoring inside-forward who
developed a formidable reputation at Starks
Park and garnered due recognition in 1957 at
Scotland 'B' and Scottish League levels, Bernie
came south as a David Halliday purchase with
a record of 92 League and Cup goals from 207
games. He was soon on the goal trail again at
Filbert Street, sniping successfully during a
typically entrenched rearguard campaign for
the club, but sadly failing to settle off the
pitch. A brief stay on Trentside (featuring two
League outings and a Charity Shield
appearance) did nothing to ameliorate Bernie's
homesickness, but he never quite recaptured

but new boss Jimmy Bloomfield
soon had him crossing paths with
Alan Birchenall as the club's
tactical emphasis changed. His
League career had begun at the age
of 16, and England youth caps had
come his way before he embarked
on his travels; while the alacrity
with which former clubs Palace
and Pompey welcomed the mature
player back for second spells was
testimony to the value placed on
his tenacious talent. At the end of
his playing career, Bobby occupied
the manager's chair at Chelmsford
City for a short time, and then
entered the antiques business. In
1994 he was briefly tempted back
into football in an assistant
manager's role to Len Glover at
Harlow Town, where his son was a
Diadora League player.

Appearances:
FL: 48 apps. 8 gls.
FAC: 6 apps. 0 gls.
LC: 6 apps. 0 gls.
Total: *60 apps. 8 gls.*

Bernie Kelly

former glories after returning to Scotland. He was most recently heard of working in a solar heating business in Canada.

Appearances:
FL: 24 apps. 13 gls.
FAC: 3 apps. 2 gls.
Total: *27 apps. 15 gls.*

KELLY, David Thomas

Role: Striker
b.Birmingham,
25th November 1965

CAREER: Alvechurch/(trials-Wolverhampton Wanderers)/ Dec 1983:Walsall/Aug 1988: West Ham United/Mar 1990: CITY/Dec 1991: Newcastle United/June 1993: Wolverhampton Wanderers.

Debut v Plymouth Argyle (H) 24.3.90

Top scorer for City in his only full campaign - albeit that of the near-disastrous flirtation with the drop to the Third Division - David substantially rehabilitated himself as a fine finisher and supporting attacker during a Filbert Street tenure that promised to last somewhat longer than it did. A £300,000 deadline-week mover from Upton Park, where his goal touch had deserted him during

David Kelly

Hammers' relegation from the top flight, the compact Brummie-Irishman soon realigned his sights at Leicester, and offered reminders of his predatory instinct at every opportunity to Republic boss Jack Charlton, who capped him seven times during his City stint, but whose over-reliance on beanpole target men nonetheless left David sidelined during the 1990 World Cup finals. David's nippiness, control and occasionally impish cheek within the six-yard box gave a contrasting focus to City's attack, and a hat-trick in the 5-4 win over future club Newcastle was a highlight of the doom-threatened season which followed; though strangely only two strikes from David

followed the mid-campaign change of management. He was still the man in possession of the spearhead role throughout the first weeks of Brian Little's regime, but a clash with the new manager led to his listing, and he moved to Tyneside only a few days after turning down Sunderland's advances. David had actually overcome childhood disability to build his footballing career, but was working for Cadbury's and part-timing for Alvechurch at the time he was given his professional Fellows Park break. He scored in each of his first three full appearances for the Saddlers, and then - in tandem with Nicky Cross and Trevor Christie - helped shoot them into the Second Division. A hat-trick on his international debut ensued, as did the big-money move to West Ham which turned into something of a nightmare thanks to a cruelly barracking crowd. In May 1993, David registered yet another hat-trick - in a 7-1 win over City which confirmed him as top scorer for Division One champions Newcastle - to mark his last game on Tyneside prior to a further expensive (£750,000) return to the Midlands. With Wolves he remained a thorn in City's side, and his diving header removed his old club from the 1995 FA Cup at the 5th Round stage. Three days previously, David had scored for his country against England in the notorious abandoned international at a riot-torn Lansdowne Road. At the end of 1994/5 he had aggregated 153 League goals.

Appearances:
FL: 63 (3) apps. 22 gls.
FAC: 1 app. 0 gls.
LC: 6 apps. 2 gls.
FMC: 2 apps. 1 gl.
Total: *72 (3) apps. 25 gls.*

KELLY, Edward Patrick

Role: Midfield
b. Glasgow, 7th February 1951

CAREER: Possilpark YMCA/app 1966/ pro Feb 1968:Arsenal/Sept 1976:Queen's Park Rangers/July 1977:CITY/July 1980:Notts County/Aug 1981:Bournemouth/Dec 1981: CITY/Mar 1983:Kettering Town/Melton Town/Oct 1984:Torquay United.
Debut v Manchester City (A) 20.8.77

Frank McLintock's first and probably most valuable signing at £50,000, Eddie was a former team-mate of his new boss during the glory years at Highbury as well as at Loftus Road. A scorer in the 1970 Fairs Cup Final, Eddie had gone on to contribute mightily to Arsenal's 1971 Double, entering the record books as the first substitute to score in an FA Cup Final, and winning Scotland Under-23 honours. His compact midfield style was somewhat overwhelmed in City's 1978 plummet, but he reacted well as mature anchorman to Jock Wallace's young promotion side, and it was a genuine surprise when greater efforts to retain his services weren't made in 1980, after his contract had expired. Eddie's immediate success in inspiring Notts

County to swap divisions with City seemed a sad irony to Leicester supporters, but it wasn't in fact long before Wallace called him back to the Second Division fray, for Leicester once more to lean a little on his experience. In 1984 David Webb, too, signed Eddie for a second time to add another reviving jolt to his career. Eddie thereafter settled on the South Coast, working in the double-glazing business, and was noted in 1993 firstly as player/coach of Torquay Amateurs Combined 89, then as manager of Devon League side N.T. Paignton.

Appearances:
FL: 119 apps. 3 gls.
FAC: 8 (1) apps. 0 gls.
LC: 5 apps. 0 gls.
Total: *132 (1) apps. 3 gls.*

Eddie Kelly

Robert Kelly

Steve Kember

KELLY, Robert Anthony

Role: Midfield
b. Birmingham, 21st December 1964

CAREER: app Oct 1981/pro Dec 1982:CITY/
(Dec 1984-loan-Tranmere Rovers)/Feb 1987:
Wolverhampton Wanderers/cs 1990:Burton
Albion.

Debut v Sunderland (H) 12.5.84

A Brummie midfielder whose parentage
qualified him to play as an Eire youth
international, Robert clearly possessed useful
ball skills, but occasionally appeared less well
equipped for the robust physical challenge of
top-class football. A loan spell with Bryan
Hamilton's Tranmere (two goals in five games)
seemed to signal City's willingness to jettison
him after only one first team run-out, but
Robert was in Gordon Milne's line-up at the
start of 1985/6, and was also a squad member
under Hamilton the following season,
distinguishing himself with a neatly chipped
goal against Manchester United. With his
Filbert Street development at something of a
standstill, though, the club accepted Wolves'
£30,000 bid for Robert, who helped steer the

Molineux side into the 1987 Third/Fourth
Division Play-offs, but then sustained a
serious back injury which kept him out of
Wolves' successful promotion sides of the
following two years, and sadly resulted in him
being forced to retire from the senior game in
May 1990. Two years later, though Robert
returned to run Wolves' School of Excellence.

Appearances:
FL: 17 (7) apps. 1 gl.
LC: 1 (2) apps. 0 gls.
Total: *18 (9) apps. 1 gl.*

KEMBER, Stephen Dennis

Role: Midfield
b. Croydon, Surrey, 8th December 1948

CAREER: app July 1965/pro Dec 1965:Crystal
Palace/Sept 1971:Chelsea/July 1975:CITY/
(Apr 1978-loan-Vancouver Whitecaps)/
Oct 1978:Crystal Palace/Mar 1980:Vancouver
Whitecaps.

Debut v Birmingham City (H) 16.8.75

A tigerish midfielder who made an early
impression at Selhurst, and was part of the

first Palace side to reach Division One, Steve moved to Chelsea for £170,000 - then a club record - just as Dave Sexton's side were going into decline. By the time he came to Filbert Street for £80,000, on the heels of Chelsea's eventual relegation, Steve had already totted up nearly 350 League games (and had won three England Under-23 caps), but there was no sign of tiredness in his play as he chased and prompted among his fellow London exiles with City. The 1977/8 debacle took much out of him, though, and Steve didn't last long into the Jock Wallace regime. A £50,000 move saw him back at Selhurst for two more playing seasons, and successive stints as youth coach and caretaker manager. In the late 80s, while running a Croydon wine bar which unfortunately later bankrupted him, Steve took on the management of Vauxhall-Opel League side Whyteleafe.

Appearances:
FL: 115 (2) apps. 6 gls.
FAC: 5 apps. 0 gls.
LC: 6 apps. 0 gls.
Total: *126 (2) apps. 6 gls.*

KENNEDY, Michael Francis Martin

Role: Midfield
b. Salford, 9th April 1961

CAREER: app 1977/pro Jan 1979:Halifax Town/Aug 1980:Huddersfield Town/Aug 1982:Middlesbrough/June 1984:Portsmouth/ Jan 1988:Bradford City/Mar 1989:CITY/ Aug 1989:Luton Town/Aug 1990:Stoke City/Aug 1992:Chesterfield/cs 1993:Wigan Athletic.

Debut v Plymouth Argyle (A) 18.3.89

Having brought Halifax their then-record incoming fee of £50,000 as a teenage midfielder, Mick developed his ball-winning skills in several hard-knocks schools throughout the 80s, drawing admiration from many for his drive and commitment (and winning two caps for the Republic of Ireland in May 1986), but also attracting censure during his Pompey days for some ill-judged verbal revelling in his hard-man image. Having helped Portsmouth into Division One in 1987, and Bradford City into the Play-offs in 1988, he arrived at Filbert Street shortly before

the 1989 transfer deadline, in a straight £250,000 rated swap with Jimmy Quinn, and immediately assumed Paul Ramsey's midfield anchoring role. Nonetheless, after showing few signs of matching his combativeness with creativity, Mick was on his way again on the eve of the following season, in a part exchange deal which brought Rob Johnson and some £150,000 to City.

Appearances:
FL: 9 apps. 0 gls.
Total: *9 apps. 0 gls.*

Mick Kennedy

KEOGH, George

Role: Left back

CAREER: Leicester Imperial/Oct 1905:
FOSSE/Sept 1907:Leicester Imperial/
1908:Hinckley United.

Debut v Leeds City (A) 20.1.06

A local left-back who showed promise in trial
and friendly games, but only got a lone crack
at senior level, replacing the injured Billy
Oakes in a 1-4 defeat at Elland Road. George
was in the Hinckley side beaten by City's
reserves in the County Cup Final of 1909.

Appearances:
FL: 1 app. 0 gls.
Total: *1 app. 0 gls.*

KERR, Paul Andrew

Role: Midfield
b. Portsmouth, 9th June 1964

CAREER: app June 1980/
pro May 1982:Aston Villa/
Jan 1987:Middlesbrough/
Mar 1991: Millwall/July
1992:Port Vale/(Mar 1994-
loan-CITY)/Nov 1994:
Wycombe Wanderers/
Mar 1995:Waterlooville.

*Debut v Portsmouth (H)
30.3.94 (sub)*

Brian Little's 1994 deadline-
day exchange of loanees
with Port Vale worked rather
well for both clubs, for
attacking midfielder Paul
contributed impressively to
City's run-in to Play-off
qualification, and David
Lowe added a 5-goal punch
to the Valiants' own
successful promotion quest
from the Division below. A
cool penalty conversion at
Roker and the decisive goal
at Fratton Park were the
most tangible elements of
Paul's brief stay (probably
prompted by the time player

Paul Kerr

and manager spent together at Ayresome
Park), but he definitely buttressed a side
which was relying heavily on reserve strength
to maintain its promotion-bound momentum.
He had made his League bow (as a Villa
substitute) at Filbert Street in April 1984, and
curiously also made his Millwall debut there
during 1990/1; going on to score for the Lions
at Leicester the following term. Indeed, for a
deep-lying player, Paul always
maintained a decent goal-rate, and claimed
one for Port Vale at Wembley in the 1993
Autoglass Trophy Final. He also scored on his
single substitute outing for Wycombe during
1994/5.

Appearances:
FL: 4 (3) apps. 2 gls.
Total: *4 (3) apps. 2 gls.*

KEYWORTH, Kenneth

Role: Left half/
Centre forward
*b. Rotherham,
24th February 1934*

CAREER:
am:Wolverhampton
Wanderers/
Jan 1952:Rotherham
United/May 1958:CITY/
Dec 1964:Coventry City/
Aug 1965:Swindon Town.

Debut v Everton (H) 23.8.58

One risks describing the
cliché Yorkshireman in
attempting to characterise
Ken. Rugged, dour, and an
honest grafter, he gave City
seven seasons of unflashy
commitment as he
developed from left-half to
top-scoring centre-forward,
playing all his Filbert Street
games in the First Division
and capping his career with
the superb diving header
that proved the 1963 side's
only moment of Wembley
glory. Ken almost joined
Wolves as a junior, but
became a hometown
Millmoor regular after

finishing his National Service. His only representative honour was at winghalf for a Sheffield Select team against England 'B', and he cost City a bargain £9,000 a couple of seasons before Matt Gillies and Bert Johnson began experimenting with him up front. Ken wore the No.10 shirt in the 1961 Cup Final, No.9 two years later, and was still the club's central striker in both legs of the 1964 League Cup Final triumph. Injuries received in a car crash severely blunted his effectiveness thereafter, though, and his free-transfer move to Jimmy Hill's Coventry was ironically completed on the same day City slaughtered them 8-1 at Highfield Road on the way to another League Cup Final. After hanging up his boots, Ken returned to his Rotherham roots, becoming in turn a quantity surveyor at a steelworks, and office manager for a building company.

Appearances:
FL: 177 apps. 63 gls.
FAC: 23 apps. 7 gls.
LC: 11 apps. 4 gls.
Eur: 4 apps. 3 gls.
Total: 215 apps. 77 gls.

Ken Keyworth

KING, Edwin

Role: Half back
b. Leicester, 1884
d. Braunstone, Leicester, 7th July 1952

CAREER: Aylestone Swifts/St.Andrews/ Leicester Imperial/May 1906:FOSSE.

Debut v West Bromwich Albion (A) 6.4.07

Serving his sole senior club for eighteen playing seasons until retiring to become City's coach at the age of 40, Teddy was a hard-working worrier of a half-back who would fit in wherever Fosse or City required his wholehearted reliability. He waited longer for a regular first team place than many of his peers, having only 15 appearances to his name before 1910, after which he successively held down the pivotal position, both wing-half spots, and even, in 1914/15, the centre-forward berth, with his ten goals making him Fosse's second-top scorer that season. Teddy's versatility was just as invaluable after the war, and it was at this juncture that he also

KING, George

Role: Left back
b. Coalville, Leics

CAREER: Coalville Town/Aug 1909:FOSSE/ cs 1911:Mansfield Mechanics.

Debut v Gainsborough Trinity (H) 10.12.10

A reserve left-back for two seasons with Fosse, George was described as possessing a 'pretty style' but appearing 'fragile' when making his sole League appearance in a 1-0 Filbert Street victory. His original contract, still on the club's files, gives some insight into a footballer's conditions at the time, with George taking home the princely sum of £1.7s.6d per week from September 1909 to April 1910, with

George King

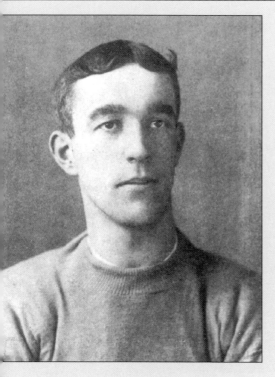

became the regular wicket-keeper for Leicestershire's Second XI, eventually making a belated County breakthrough for two matches in 1925. A distinctly well-earned club benefit came his way from the League game with Stockport County in February 1920, while Teddy also wrote his name indelibly into the City record as coach to the side which came so close to the First Division title in 1929. Three years later he was coaching Leicester Nomads. Incidental entries in the City annals for Teddy include the fact that he was the first City player sent off after reconstruction (at Fulham in September 1919, along with the home side's Johnny McIntyre), and the first to register an own goal against the 'new' club (in the 3-7 Cup defeat by Burnley in January 1921). Before joining Fosse, he had been part of the Imps' 1906 County Cup-winning side.

Appearances:
FL: 227 apps. 26 gls.
FAC: 9 apps. 0 gls.
WW1: 121 apps. 24 gls.
Total: *357 apps. 50 gls.*

no guarantee of any summer wages whatever if his registration wasn't renewed. He switched clubs with John Thorpe on departure.

Appearances:
FL: 1 app. 0 gls.
Total: *1 app. 0 gls.*

KING, Harry Edward

Role: Centre forward
b. Evesham, Worcs

CAREER: Evesham Star/Worcester City/Nov 1907:Birmingham/cs 1910:Crewe Alexandra/June 1911:Northampton Town/Apr 1914:Arsenal/Oct 1919:CITY/Sept 1920:Brentford/cs 1921:Stourbridge.

Debut v Huddersfield Town (A) 18.10.19

A free-scoring centre-forward who came to prominence in the Cobblers' Southern League days, with 67 goals in only 99 games, Harry then continued to hit the net regularly at Highbury, where his tally included a four-goal

haul from the last game Arsenal ever played in the Second Division. He couldn't, however, claim a senior spot there immediately after the war (during which he served with the Royal Garrison Artillery in Italy), and came to Leicester in a package deal with forward partner Billy Spittle. Though both scored in their first home match, neither settled down with City. Yet Harry was to go on to create more goal records at Griffin Park, finishing as top scorer in Brentford's initial League season, and notching their first hat-trick at that level. In retirement, he lived in Worcester.

Appearances:
FL: 8 apps. 1 gl.
Total: *8 apps. 1 gl.*

KING, J.

Role: Forward

CAREER: Feb 1892: FOSSE.

Debut v Gainsborough Trinity (H) ML 13.2.1892

Another Midland League mystery man: a

forward whose outings in the above home defeat and the rearranged April fixture at Port Vale were utterly isolated appearances; for he played in none of the 21 senior friendlies of the 1891/2 term.

Appearances:
ML: 2 apps. 0 gls.
Total: *2 apps. 0 gls.*

KING, John

Role: Inside left
b. Birmingham

CAREER: Hockley St.Georges/Hinckley United/Jan 1922:CITY / July 1924:Halifax Town/Oct 1925: Nuneaton Town.

Debut v Clapton Orient (H) 9.2.22

Jack King

Kept in the reserves primarily by Harry Graham's consistency, £140 purchase Jack was

an inside-left who managed a respectable goal ratio on his sporadic senior appearances during 1921/2 and 1923/4, yet who later lasted less than a season at The Shay after moving with Tommy Duncan and scoring on his Halifax debut (indeed, notching 5 goals in 12 starts).

Appearances:
FL: 7 apps. 4 gls.
Total: *7 apps. 4 gls.*

KING, John Charles

Role: Left half
b. Great Gidding, Cambs, 5th November 1926

CAREER: am Sept 1943/pro Sept 1944:CITY/ July 1955:Kettering Town.

Debut (WW2) v Nottingham Forest (H) 26.2.44; (postwar) v Manchester City (H) 31.8.46

Signed as a part-timer during the war after impressing in Peterborough schools football (and invariably then known as 'Boy' King), Johnny was a left-half and occasional inside-

KING, John Aitken (Ian)

Role: Centre half
b. Loanhead, Midlothian, 27th May 1937

CAREER: Broughton Star/Arniston Rangers/ June 1957:CITY/Mar 1966:Charlton Athletic/ Mar 1968:Burton Albion (p/mgr).

Debut v Sheffield Wednesday (A) 11.9.57

A Scottish schoolboy international surprisingly released from a provisional contract with Hearts, Ian was a Matt Gillies discovery who eventually won a lengthy personal battle with England prospect Tony Knapp for the City No.5 berth. The rugged pivot in all four of City's early 60s Cup Final sides (missing only the second leg of the

League Cup Final against Chelsea), he was notably strong in the air and also a composed distributor who spread the ball forward with some poise and vision. When Ian finally surrendered his position to John Sjoberg, he soon found himself in familiar company at The Valley, playing alongside Colin Appleton, and on leaving Burton at Christmas 1969 he returned to live locally, spending time coaching at Enderby Town and managing Thringstone.

Appearances:
FL: 244 apps. 6 gls.
FAC: 27 apps. 0 gls.
LC: 22 apps. 1 gl.
Eur: 4 apps. 0 gls.
Total: *297 apps. 7 gls.*

Johnny King

forward who maintained the unusual dual professions of footballer and farmer throughout his career. The youngest and smallest player of the 1949 Cup Final team, he couldn't have been further from the rustic stereotype, for his wiry physique was driven by a shrewd footballing intelligence which served City well for nine postwar seasons.

Appearances:
FL: 197 apps. 5 gls.
FAC: 21 apps. 0 gls.
WW2: 40 apps. 2 gls.
Total: *258 apps. 7 gls.*

KING, Robert

Role: Forward

CAREER: 1893:Wishaw Thistle/1895:Airdrieonians/Aug 1897:FOSSE/ Apr 1900:Glossop/Aug 1901:FOSSE/cs 1902: Hamilton Academicals.

Debut v Small Heath (A) 11.9.1897

A versatile forward in both his spells with Fosse, Rab alternated primarily between the outside-left and centre-forward positions, and was top scorer in the season before he first moved on to Second Division rivals Glossop.

One of his meagre two goals for the Derbyshire side was against Fosse, and when Rab returned, he played through 1901/2 as an ever-present. His older brother Alex was a near-contemporaneous Hearts and Celtic hero.

Appearances:
FL: 115 apps. 34 gls.
FAC: 9 apps. 5 gls.
Total: *124 apps. 39 gls.*

KING, William

CAREER: Hull City/Sept 1911:FOSSE/ cs 1912:Goole Town.

Debut v Nottingham Forest (A) 16.9.11

'His only defect was lack of weight', summed up the *Daily Post's* critic when Fosse released young forward Willie after his season's shot at League football - a level he had failed previously to reach with Hull. He joined Goole as they prepared for their first season in the Midland League.

Appearances:
FL: 7 apps. 4 gls.
FAC: 1 app. 0 gls.
Total: *8 apps. 4 gls.*

'Rab' King

KIRKMAN, Norman

Role: Left back
b. Bolton, 6th June 1920

CAREER: May 1939:Burnley/Sept 1946:
Rochdale/Dec 1947:Chesterfield/Aug 1949:
CITY/July 1950:Southampton/Mar 1952:
Exeter City (p/mgr).

Debut v Hull City (H) 27.8.49

Freed by Burnley without playing a peacetime
League game (though his WW2 Turf Moor
outings were supplemented by guest stints
with Bradford City, Fulham, Brighton,
Manchester United and Rochdale, between
duties as an RAF navigator), Norman became
a sought-after full-back at Spotland, and
earned his club its then-record fee from
Second Division Chesterfield. Johnny Duncan
paid £8,500 from the Cup-run profits to bring
him to Leicester but, after breaking his nose
during his debut game and failing to hang on
to the senior No.3 shirt for long, he was soon
asking new manager Norman Bullock for a
transfer. Two seasons at The Dell saw a similar
in-and-out record develop, and Norman's subsequent managerial stints were also of fairly
short duration: a year at Exeter, and just under
two holding the reins at Bradford Park
Avenue. In 1965 he had an unsuccessful 14-
game spell in charge at Northwich Victoria.

> **Appearances:**
> *FL: 12 apps 0 gls.*
> **Total:** *12 apps. 0 gls.*

Norman Kirkman

KITSON, Paul

Role: Striker
b. Easington, Co.Durham, 9th January 1971

CAREER: YT July 1987:CITY/(Mar 1988-loan-
VS Rugby)/pro Dec 1988:CITY/Mar 1992: ·
Derby County/Sept 1994:Newcastle United.

Debut v West Bromwich Albion (H) 9.9.89 (sub)

Rather prematurely and inaccurately dubbed
'the second Lineker' during his brief stint of
effective striking form with City's seniors,

Paul Kitson

Paul became the subject of City's record out-going transfer deal when moving to promotion rivals Derby at a cash-plus-players valuation of £1.35 million. The slender but extremely pacy young striker had won early representative recognition with the League's Youth XI in Moscow, and when David Pleat elevated him to the first team at Leicester, he soon notched a League Cup counter at Selhurst Park. Yet his club progress thereafter was erratic, and it was essentially his scoring impact for England's victorious Under-21 side in the 1991 Toulon tournament that won him a regular place in Brian Little's starting line-up. A burst of quicksilver front-running performances, and a clutch of well-struck goals, then catapulted Paul into the transfer-gossip columns; and unfortunately, before his first full season was out, motivational flaws soon became evident in his play. Accordingly, the 'controversy' that attended his departure was somewhat media-contrived, and despite a fair scoring rate he proved unable to lift an expensively-assembled Rams outfit to their top-flight goal. Nonetheless, Paul's transfer value had soared to £2.25m by the time Kevin Keegan added him to Newcastle's Premiership squad.

Appearances:
FL: 39 (11) apps. 6 gls.
FAC: 1 (1) apps. 1 gl.
LC: 5 apps. 3 gls.
FMC: 5 apps. 1 gl.
Total: 50 (12) apps. 11 gls.

KNAPP, Anthony

Role: Centre half
b. Newstead, Notts,
13th October 1936

CAREER: Newstead Colliery/ am:Nottingham Forest/ Bentinck Jnrs/Dec1953:CITY/ Aug 1961:Southampton/ Aug 1967:Coventry City/ Mar 1968:Los Angeles Wolves/ Mar 1969:Bristol City/ Oct 1969:Tranmere Rovers/ July 1971:Poole Town (p/mgr).

Debut v Stoke City (A) 11.2.56

Tony Knapp

A classy young centre-half who made rapid strides after 1958 and was soon on the fringe of the England side - being once chosen as travelling reserve for the national team, and once appearing for the Football League against the Scottish League in March 1960 - Tony had the ill-fortune to lose his place through injury and find such a capable rival as Ian King barring his way back. The disappointment of missing out on the 1961 Cup run led to an almost inevitable move, but in the course of a 233-game League career for the Saints, Tony's sole tangible honour was to help that club into Division One for the first time in 1966. Coventry sent out a desperate call to Tony to replace broken-leg victim George Curtis after only two games of their first-ever top-flight season, and he eventually saw out his playing days in the Third with Tranmere, before taking up his initial managerial appointment with Poole. It was abroad that Tony made his biggest impact, though; managing the Icelandic national side as well as four leading Norwegian clubs: Viking Stavanger, Fredrikstad, Vidar Stavanger and Brann Bergen.

Appearances:
FL: 86 apps. 0 gls.
FAC: 4 apps. 0 gls.
LC: 2 apps. 0 gls.
Total: 92 apps. 0 gls.

KRUSE, Patrick Karl

Role: Centre back
b. Arlesey, Beds,
30th November 1953

CAREER: Arlesey Town/ app June 1970/pro Feb 1972: CITY/(Sept 1974-loan-Mansfield Town)/Mar 1975:Torquay United/Mar 1977: Brentford/(Feb 1982-loan-Northampton Town)/ cs 1982:Barnet.

Debut v Tottenham Hotspur (A) 27.4.74

Like Derek Harrison, another 'homegrown' centre-half edged out of the first team reckoning by the similar internal promotions of the likes of Munro and Sims, Pat got his only City chances in the final games of 1973/4, then actually replaced Harrison at

Plainmoor. It was towards the end of his 79-game spell with Torquay that Pat unwillingly put himself in the record books - as scorer of the fastest-ever own goal in League history, after only six seconds of the Torquay v Cambridge United game of January 1977. He totalled 186 League games for Brentford after being signed by former City coach Bill Dodgin, scoring 12 goals at the right end, but his experience couldn't help lift Northampton out of the re-election zone during his extended loan spell at the County Ground.

Pat Kruse

Appearances:
FL: 2 apps. 0 gls.
Total: *2 apps. 0 gls.*

KYLE, Peter

Role: Inside forward
b. Rutherglen, Lanarkshire, 1880

CAREER: Oct 1898:Clyde/cs 1899:Liverpool/ May 1900:FOSSE/cs 1901:Wellingborough/ Oct 1901:West Ham United/Dec 1901: Kettering/Sept 1902:Aberdeen/Jan 1903: Cowdenbeath/Apr 1904:Port Glasgow Athletic/Nov 1904:Royal Albert/Apr 1905: Partick Thistle/May 1905:Tottenham Hotspur/ Apr 1906:Woolwich Arsenal/Mar 1908:Aston Villa/Oct 1908:Sheffield United/1909:Royal Albert/Nov 1909:Watford.

Debut v Stockport County (H) 1.9.1900

A merry wanderer of an inside-forward - overly merry for most of his English clubs, as several actually sacked him for alcohol-induced breaches of discipline - Peter proves yet another researcher's nightmare. With official transfer recognition at the time in place only between the Football and Scottish Leagues, it comes as no surprise to find Peter's registration being swapped between Fosse and Port Glasgow some three years after he left Leicester - and when he had played for a trio

of Southern League clubs and two Scottish non-league clubs in the interim. His Anfield record amounted to only four barren League games, and one in the Cup, and Peter had one Fosse season in which his scoring rate was hardly more prolific; though he later gave decent striking service to both Southern League Spurs and First Division Arsenal (a 21-goal return from 52 games for the Gunners), and figured in a Scottish international trial match in March 1907. All too characteristically, however, it was 'disgraceful conduct' which earned him his papers at Watford.

Appearances:
FL: 31 apps. 3 gls.
FAC: 1 app. 1 gl.
Total: *32 apps. 4 gls.*

Peter Kyle

LANE, William Harry Charles

Role: Centre forward
b. Tottenham, London, 23rd October 1903
d. Chelmsford, Essex, 10th November 1985

CAREER: Gnome Athletic/Park Avondale/
Nov 1923:Summerstown/Jan 1924:Barnet/
Northfleet/May 1924:Tottenham Hotspur/
Nov 1926:CITY/May 1928:Reading/
May 1929:Brentford/May 1932:Watford/
Jan 1936:Bristol City/July 1937:Clapton
Orient/cs 1938:Gravesend.

Debut v Derby County (A) 6.11.26 (scored once)

Signed for £2,250 after showing early
goalscoring potential with Spurs (7 goals in
26 games, including a strike against City two
months before his purchase), Billy spent an
almost inevitably frustrating couple of seasons
at Leicester as understudy to Arthur Chandler,
scoring in the first two of his extremely limited
outings in the centre-forward berth. By the
time he got to Griffin Park, though, Billy was
really ready to let loose - notching 84 strikes in
only 114 games for the Bees. 72 more goals
followed at Watford, including a hat-trick
scored inside a three-minute spell in a game
against Clapton Orient - ironically to become
his last club. By 1938, he had amassed a fine
record of 208 goals in 344 League games. Billy
went on to serve a postwar managerial
apprenticeship as assistant at Brentford and,
from 1947-50, in full
charge at Guildford
City; and was
guiding the fortunes
of Brighton & Hove
Albion (1951-61)
when they took the Third Division (South)
championship in 1958. He later managed
Gravesend & Northfleet, and scouted for
Arsenal and Brighton. Watford's Centenary
history mentions Billy's cunning habits of
talking non-stop while on the pitch, and
instructing his wingers always to aim their
first couple of crosses a little nearer the keeper
than usual, to let him know Billy was around;
while it quotes from an interview with him in
later life about his hat-trick record: "I doubt [it]
will ever be beaten. Modern players spend too
much time hugging and kissing to ever get
around to hitting three goals in three minutes."
Billy's German emigre parents had anglicised
their name from Lohn on settling in London.

Appearances:
FL: 5 apps. 2 gls.
Total: *5 apps. 2 gls.*

LANG, John

Role: Outside right / Inside right
b. Kilbirnie, Ayrshire, 16th August 1882

CAREER: Co-Operative United (Glasgow)/
Govan/cs 1902:Barnsley/Feb 1903:Sheffield

Billy Lane

John Lang

United/Sept 1909:FOSSE/cs 1910:Denaby United.

Debut v Lincoln City (A) 18.9.09

The right wing partner of Jimmy Donnelly for several of his early seasons with the Blades, John was a candidate for full international honours when chosen for the Anglo-Scots against the Home Scots in March 1905, having earned Junior caps some years previously. He briefly resumed his old Bramall Lane liaison at Filbert Street, though as often as not the former team-mates were effectively in competition for the outside-right spot during Fosse's highest-scoring season (when 79 goals helped them to 5th place in Division Two). John's transfer itself was a far from straightforward affair: not only was the £75 fee to rise by another £25 should John be retained for a second season; but Fosse's cheque for the lower amount actually bounced on first presentation!

Appearances:
FL: 17 apps. 2 gls.
Total: *17 apps. 2 gls.*

LANGAN, David Francis

Role: Right back
b. Dublin, 15th February 1957

CAREER: Cherry Orchard/app June 1974/pro Feb 1975: Derby County/July 1980: Birmingham City/July 1984: Oxford United/ (Oct 1987-loan-CITY)/ Nov 1987: Bournemouth/July 1988:Peterborough United/1989:Ramsey Town/1989:Holbeach United/Aug 1990: Rothwell Town/ 1990:Mirlees Blackstone.

Debut v Hull City (H) 24.10.87

David Langan

A regular right-back choice for the Republic of Ireland over almost a decade, David played all his football for both the Rams and Blues (for whom he represented a record purchase at £350,000) in the First Division, and aided Oxford's ascent to that status within a year of being freed from St.Andrews; going on to win a Milk Cup victor's medal in 1986. A tenacious tackler with an adventurous streak, he briefly added his experience to Bryan Hamilton's struggling Second Division side, but Oxford's demand for a transfer fee precluded a permanent move to Filbert Street. Within days of his loan spell coming to an end, Second Division rivals Bournemouth invested £25,000 in his defensive acumen.

Appearances:
FL: 5 apps. 0 gls.
Total: *5 apps. 0 gls.*

LANGFORD, Walter

Role: Inside left
b. Wolverhampton, 24th March 1905
d. Wolverhampton, January qtr 1976

CAREER: cs 1924:Sunbeam Motor Works/Wellington Town/May 1928:CITY/ Aug 1933:Queen's Park Rangers/July 1935: Wellington Town.

Debut v Newcastle United (H) 2.2.29

Another of the several City reserves of decent class left champing frustratedly at the bit during the club's First Division heyday of the late 20s, Walter was the deputy for Arthur Lochhead at inside-left, and eventually grabbed the rare first team chance at wing-half, too. Mick O'Brien signed him for QPR, but he had still to score there after a dozen senior games.

Appearances:
FL: 13 apps. 5 gls.
FAC: 2 apps. 1 gl.
Total: *15 apps. 6 gls.*

Walter Langford

LANGHAM, William

Role: Outside right
b. Nottingham, 1876

CAREER: Stapleford/Hucknall Portland/
1894:South Shore/cs 1896:Notts County/
cs 1898:Bristol City/Nov 1900:FOSSE/cs 1901:

Doncaster Rovers/
cs 1903:Gainsborough
Trinity/cs 1906:
Doncaster Rovers/
Mar 1907:Lincoln City.

*Debut v Woolwich Arsenal
(H) 15.12.1900*

A well-travelled outside-
right who spent his
shortest spell with one
club at Filbert Street,

Billy Langham

deposing Archie Brash, Billy moved on to
assist Doncaster in the Midland League, only
to find his new club hurriedly elected to
Division Two alongside Fosse a week after his
debut! Previously he had helped Notts County
to Division One in 1897, scoring the winning
goal in one of the Test Matches that then
decided promotion and relegation issues; and
had played alongside Blessington, Carnelly,
Davy, Hamilton, Pollock and Stevenson in
Bristol. His scoring ratio had certainly
improved by the time he reached Lincoln:
during 1908/9 he had notched 30 goals in only
26 Midland League outings at centre-forward
before injury sidelined him. In 1920, Billy
became trainer and groundsman at Sincil
Bank; and later ran a pub in Gainsborough.

Appearances:
FL: 14 apps. 2 gls.
FAC: 1 app. 0 gls.
Total: *15 apps. 2 gls.*

LARGE, Frank

Role: Striker
b. Leeds, 26th January 1940

CAREER: British Railways (Halifax)/June
1959:Halifax Town/June 1962:Queen's Park
Rangers/Feb 1963:Northampton Town/Mar
1964:Swindon Town/Sept 1964:Carlisle United/
Dec 1965:Oldham Athletic/Dec 1966:
Northampton Town/Nov 1967:CITY/June
1968:Fulham/Aug 1969:Northampton Town/
Nov 1972:Chesterfield/Apr 1974:Baltimore
Comets/Sept 1974:Kettering Town.

Debut v Manchester City (A) 11.11.67

Retiring in 1974 with 209 League goals under
his belt - and presumably an expert
knowledge of the geography of Britain - Frank
was one of the old have-boots-will-travel
brigade: an anachronistically effective bustling
centre-forward who could terrify goalkeepers

Frank Large

LAWRENCE, James Hubert

Role: Winger
b. Balham, London, 8th March 1970

CAREER: Cowes/1993:Sunderland/Mar 1994:
Doncaster Rovers/Jan 1995:CITY.
Debut v Crystal Palace (A) 14.1.95

A late starter in the professional game, after
serving two years in Parkhurst prison for his
part in an armed robbery, Jamie was given a
rehabilitative break at Roker after starring in
Wessex League football on the Isle of Wight,
and shortly before Terry Butcher's sacking as
Sunderland manager. After only a handful of
senior outings, a £20,000 fee took him to Belle
Vue, and his form and flair on the wing there
attracted Mark McGhee's attention to the
extent that he made Jamie his initial City

with nothing more than a smile in their
direction. It looked a desperate measure for
City to give him his first break in the top
flight, but the two-thirds of a season he spent
leading the Filbert Street attack remain utterly
memorable - for his bravery, his unselfish lay
offs, his aerial power, and his sheer infectious
delight that First Division defences were as
susceptible to his barnstorming style as had
been those at lower levels. When City
included Frank in the package deal which
secured Allan Clarke there was a distinct sense
of loss to be set against the excitement of a
record buy - and the club's history might have
been a lot different if Frank had been around
for the relegation battles of 1969. (Matt Gillies
did, in fact, bid to recapture Frank, but Fulham
quoted a distinctly inflated fee). As it was, he
was soon back at the County Ground for a third
stint with the Cobblers. With Northampton,
he had previously won a Third Division
championship medal and had experienced
relegation back, while he had repeated those
contrasting achievements at other junctures
with Carlisle and Fulham respectively. Frank,
originally a railway worker, was last heard of
running a farm in Ireland.

Appearances:
FL: 26 apps. 8 gls.
FAC: 6 apps. 3 gls.
Total: *32 apps. 11 gls.*

Jamie Lawrence

capture (at an appearance-related fee rising from £125,000 to £175,000). Avowedly, the pacy and tricky flank player with the distinctive piled-up dreadlocks was deemed a buy for the future, but he picked up some useful Premiership experience and gave highly encouraging signs of developing for City fans into another cult hero. His cross gave Mark Robins the debut goal at Maine Road which earned City their only top-flight away win, and his own first strike against Wimbledon at home indexed his surprising aerial effectiveness.

Appearances (to end 1994/5):
PL: 9 (8) apps. 1 gl.
Total: *9 (8) apps. 1 gl.*

LEE, Alan Robert

Role: Outside left
b. Wegberg, West Germany, 19th June 1960

CAREER: 1975:Rangers/Apr 1978: Philadelphia Fury/Jan 1979:CITY/cs 1981: Kidderminster Harriers.
Debut v Fulham (A) 28.4.79

Alan Lee

A tall, sandy-haired winger, born on an RAF base in Germany but brought up in Scotland, Alan had been a youth team player under Jock Wallace at Ibrox, and was the third City signing from Philadelphia within a year, following Pat Byrne and Martin Henderson to Filbert Street after a half-dozen NASL selections. Unfortunately, he made minimal impact on his senior outings, at the end of 1978/9 and the opening of the next season, as a left-sided attacker.

Appearances:
FL: 6 apps. 0 gls.
Total: *6 apps. 0 gls.*

LEE, Albert George

Role: Inside left

CAREER: Oxford Victoria (Leicester)/ Aug 1904:FOSSE/ Leicester Imperial.
Debut v Lincoln City (A) 18.3.05

Albert Lee

A local amateur inside-forward who deputised for Arthur Mounteney in the above game, a 1-5 defeat, and whose only other senior game was a friendly against Coventry City a year later. Albert was at centre-forward for the reserves when they lost the 1905 County Cup Final to South Wigston Albion.

Appearances:
FL: 1 app. 0 gls.
Total: *1 app. 0 gls.*

LEE, John

Role: Centre forward
b. Sileby, Leics, 4th November 1920
d. Loughborough, Leics, 15th January 1995

CAREER: Quorn Methodists/am Dec 1940/ pro Feb 1941:CITY/June 1950:Derby County/ Nov 1954:Coventry City.

Debut (WW2) v Northampton Town (H) 25.12.40 (scored once); (postwar) v Luton Town (A) 5.10.46 (scored twice)

City's main marksman in the immediate post-war years, after he returned from RAF service in India (and Forces football alongside Joe

Jack Lee in action (centre) during City's 1949 FA Cup semi-final defeat of Portsmouth at Highbury.

Calvert), Jack overcame a couple of serious injury setbacks to show international-class striking prowess, though it wasn't until he became a Derby player that he actually gained his England cap, scoring in a 4-1 win in Belfast in 1950. Kenilworth Road must have been Jack's favourite away ground - apart from his League debut-game double, he notched four there in the 5-5 Cup-tie of 1949: just half of his striking contribution to City's Wembley progress. Lethal with both head and feet, he was a distinct crowd favourite (his equalising goal in the post-Cup Final game at Cardiff in May 1949 had kept City in Division Two; and there were many who thought City could have even pulled off a Wembley shock if Jack hadn't been shifted to the inside-right berth on the big day), so there was accordingly uproar when the club accepted Derby's £16,000 bid - even if hindsight suggests City got the better of that day's dealings, with Arthur Rowley arriving as replacement on the same date. Jack was second-top scorer in the First Division at the end of his first Baseball Ground season, but soon suffered more injuries which restricted his appearances thereafter. His aggregate League goal total when he finally left Highfield Road was 136 (in 232 games). Also a Leicestershire cricketer, Jack only made one County Championship appearance, in

1947: despite taking a wicket with the first ball he bowled. In later life, he acted as groundsman for VS Rugby.

Appearances:
FL: 123 apps. 74 gls.
FAC: 14 apps. 10 gls.
WW2: 26 apps. 13 gls.
Total: *163 apps. 97 gls.*

LEE, Robert Gordon

Role: Striker
b. Melton Mowbray, Leics, 2nd February 1953

CAREER: app July 1971/pro Feb 1972:CITY/ (Aug 1974-loan-Doncaster Rovers)/Sept 1976: Sunderland/Aug 1980:Bristol Rovers/July 1981:Carlisle United/Mar 1983:Southampton/ Aug 1983:Darlington/Oct 1983:Boston United/ (cs 1984:Hong Kong)/1984:Boston United.

Debut v Derby County (A) 18.3.72 (sub)

Sustained only by the memories of one-and-a-bit senior games for City over almost three years (and probably haunted by recall of a missed 'sitter' on his brief debut appearance), rangy striker Bob might have been forgiven for feeling he was on his way out when loaned to Doncaster at the beginning of 1974/5. Yet a decent run of League football re-invigorated his play, and a two-goal City comeback at Loftus Road on Boxing Day 1974 eased him into a regular support role to Frank Worthington and Chris Garland. In fact, Bob himself headed City's scoring list in 1975/6 as he began to make his powerful physique pay dividends in opposing penalty areas, but he was soon off to Roker in a £200,000 deal after Sunderland had failed to land Worthington. He played through relegation seasons for both Sunderland and Bristol Rovers, and a promotion year for Carlisle, but Bob actually had his proudest moment in non-league football, virtually ending his career at Wembley after scoring two semi-final goals to take Boston United to the FA Trophy Final in 1985. Bob then took a pub in Loughborough.

Appearances:
FL: 55 (8) apps. 17 gls.
FAC: 3 (1) apps. 2 gls.
LC: 4 apps. 0 gls.
Total: *62 (9) apps. 19 gls.*

Bob Lee

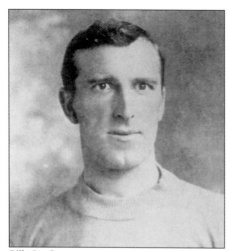

Billy Leech

LEECH, William

Role: Right half
b. Newcastle-under-Lyme, Staffs, 1875
d. Leicester, 24th November 1934

CAREER: Newcastle White Star/Newcastle Swifts/ cs 1898:Tottenham Hotspur/ cs 1899: Burslem Port Vale/ cs 1900:Stoke/cs 1903: Plymouth Argyle/ July 1906:FOSSE.

Debut v Burslem Port Vale (A) 1.9.06

A defensive half-back broadly experienced in Potteries football (after a 'false start' as a Spurs winger, his Port Vale season saw him playing in both Birmingham and Staffordshire Cup Finals as well as the Second Division, while his Stoke years were spent in a side exercising successful top-flight brinkmanship), Billy was tempted south for a second time to feature in Plymouth's inaugural season, and stayed three years in Southern League combat before joining Fosse. Missing only two League games in his first season in Fosse's right-half berth, and an ever-present in the 1908 promotion campaign (when a little grudgingly described by the *Nottingham Post* as 'a bit prone to wander, but feeds his forwards well'), Billy then patiently coaxed along the reserves, occasionally deputising for his successor, Arthur Randle, until re-engaged in 1912 as the senior club trainer; a position he held until WW1. His son Jack signed for City as an amateur on leaving the RAF in August 1926, but failed to make the grade.

Appearances:
FL: 84 apps. 3 gls.
FAC: 3 apps. 0 gls.
Total: *87 apps. 3 gls.*

LEEK, Kenneth

Role: Centre forward
b. Ynysybwl, nr.Pontypridd, 26th July 1935

CAREER: Pontypridd YC/Aug 1952:
Northampton Town/Apr 1958:CITY/June
1961:Newcastle United/Nov 1961:
Birmingham City/Dec 1964:Northampton
Town/Nov 1965:Bradford City/Aug 1968:
Rhyl/Merthyr Tydfil/1970:Ton Pentre.

Debut v Everton (H) 23.8.58 (scored once)

Ken Leek

Ironically best remembered for the game he didn't play for City, Ken was a fine centre-forward who may have developed a truly stellar career if the blow of being dropped on the eve of the 1961 Cup Final hadn't hit him so hard. Already a Welsh Under-23 cap at Fourth Division Northampton, Ken joined City in the top flight initially as an inside- or outside-left (inheriting the recently-departed Arthur Rowley's shirt for his debut), but was soon vying with Derek Hines for the No.9 role, winning the first six of his eventual 17 full Welsh caps, and accelerating his chance-taking ratio - to the point where he had scored in every round of the 1961 FA Cup before City incomprehensibly and controversially took the field at Wembley without him. A move was inevitable after that, and Ken became a noted marksman at St.Andrews following his brief spell on Tyneside, claiming two goals in Blues' League Cup Final win over Villa in 1963. He returned to his first club to help the Cobblers up into the First Division, and fetched a club record £10,000 fee from Bradford City shortly afterwards. By the time he moved back to Wales, Ken had totted up 147 League goals. He later settled in the Daventry area, working for Ford Motors.

Appearances:
FL: 93 apps. 34 gls.
FAC: 17 apps. 9 gls.
LC: 1 app. 0 gls.
Total: *111 apps. 43 gls.*

LEET, Norman David

Role: Left back
b. Leicester, 13th March 1962

CAREER: Shepshed Charterhouse/June 1980:
CITY/Feb 1983:Shepshed Charterhouse/
Oadby Town/British Shoe.

Debut: 2.5.81 v.Norwich City (A) 2.5.81

Norman Leet

A sturdily-built, no-frills defender who had been an England schoolboy international at centre-half, Norman came into senior contention for the game in which already-relegated City contrived to take Norwich down with them, and subsequently held the left-back spot for a couple of spells during 1981/2 under Jock Wallace. He had only one first-team chance to impress Gordon Milne, however, and was soon released; and was then denied, through a combination of injury and employment difficulties, even a decent part-time career in senior non-league football.

Appearances:
FL 19 apps. 0 gls.
LC: 3 apps. 0 gls.
Total: *22 apps. 0 gls.*

LEGGE, A.

Role: Centre forward
b. London

CAREER: Custom House/July 1914:FOSSE/
cs 1915:Croydon Common.

Debut v Glossop (A) 13.3.15

A reserve centre-forward who followed Jim
Harrold's path from London League football
to the Fosse, but met with little success,
finding himself only the sixth selection as
attack leader during the club's last, dismal
pre-war season. In common with City's
Dennis Cheney, he had the odd experience of
appearing only in an away win and a home
defeat. A recently-published history of the
ill-fated Croydon Common club gives Legge's
initial as 'J'; while there is also some evidence
to suggest that he turned out during WW1 for
Millwall.

Appearances:
FL: 2 apps. 0 gls.
Total: *2 apps. 0 gls.*

LEIGHTON, John

Role: Left half

CAREER:
Hibernian/
July 1896:FOSSE.

*Debut v Darwen
(H) 5.9.1896*

Initially vying
with Jack Lord for
the left-half spot
during his Fosse
season, John almost
invariably completed an
all-Scottish half-back line
(with Jimmy Brown and either
Jack Walker or David Proudfoot)
whenever he appeared. He was
reported as returning north of the border in
1897, but no record of him playing
subsequently at Scottish League level is
apparent.

*John
Leighton*

Appearances:
FL: 14 apps. 0 gls.
Total: *14 apps. 0 gls.*

Arthur Lever

LEVER, Arthur Richard

Role: Right back
b. Cardiff, 25th March 1920

CAREER: Machine Products/Cardiff
Corinthians/cs 1943:Cardiff City/Sept
1950:CITY/July 1954:Newport County.

Debut v Sheffield United (H) 9.9.50

Always popularly known as 'Buller',
right-back Arthur was an ever-present
member of the Cardiff side which took
the Third Division (South) title in 1946/7,
and was soon knocking on the door of the
First. A club record buy for City at £15,000,
Arthur was entrusted by Norman Bullock
with the team captaincy, and exhibited a cool
defensive acumen, though for his last two
seasons he had to fight hard with Stan
Milburn for the Filbert Street senior berth.
He won his sole Welsh cap in October 1952,
against Scotland, and later returned to his
homeland to assist Newport for three years.
On retirement from the game, Arthur worked
as a market gardener.

Appearances:
FL: 119 apps. 0 gls.
FAC: 5 apps. 0 gls.
Total: *124 apps. 0 gls.*

LEWIS, Albert Edward Talbot

Role: Goalkeeper
b. Bedminster, Bristol, 20th January 1877
d. Bristol, 22nd February 1956

CAREER: Jan 1896:Bedminster/cs 1897:Bristol City/1898:Everton/1899:Bristol City/cs 1901: Walsall/cs 1902:Sheffield United/Aug 1904: Sunderland/cs 1905:Luton Town/Aug 1906: FOSSE/Oct 1907:Bristol City.

Debut v Burslem Port Vale (A) 1.9.06

Usually known simply as 'Tal', this tall, athletic goalkeeper was an ever-present for Fosse as they narrowly missed out on promotion in 1906/7 - making his career-best unbroken run of first-class games in a term that finished with a placing of 3rd - and it was a major surprise that he was not retained for the following campaign. Certainly, First Division Bristol City had no qualms about re-signing him for a third spell on their books; though, after a season there, 'Tal' retired to concentrate on his parallel career as a Somerset cricketer, going on to score one double-century championship innings, and coaching in India in 1920. Prior to his Fosse sojourn, he had managed 23 League games for

'Tal' Lewis

the Blades (sharing duties with man-mountain Willie Foulke) and four at Roker Park (after signing in a joint deal with Alf Common), but his time at both Everton and Luton had been spent entirely in reserve football; while his Walsall season saw him engaged in Midland League fare (and therefore facing Fosse's reserves). Until the turn of the century, most of his recorded appearances had been as a full-back!

Appearances:
FL: 38 apps. 0 gls.
FAC: 1 app. 0 gls.
Total: *39 apps. 0 gls.*

LEWIS, George

Role: Left back
b. Chasetown, Staffs, 1876

CAREER: Nov 1894:Walsall Town Swifts/ Feb 1897:Notts County/cs 1902:Bristol City/ cs 1903:Stourbridge/Oct 1903:FOSSE.

Debut v Burnley (H) 10.10.03

A left-back who had accumulated a fair amount of First Division experience from his Magpies days (129 games), George came to Leicester via Ashton Gate to contest his defensive berth with Walter Robinson, but showed few signs of being able to reverse the team's

George Lewis

precipitous drop into the re-election zone, and rather too obvious signs of advancing age. As an aside relevant to changing trends in football fashion, George was invariably photographed in team groups with his hands in his shorts pockets! His Walsall stint consisted of two Second Division campaigns bracketing a season in the Midland League.

Appearances:
FL: 10 apps. 0 gls.
FAC: 5 apps. 0 gls,
Total: *15 apps. 0 gls.*

LEWIS,
Neil Anthony

Role: Left back
b. Wolverhampton,
28th June 1974

CAREER: YT July 1990/
pro July 1992:CITY.

Debut v Wolverhampton
Wanderers (H)
13.9.92 (sub)

An orthodox left-winger throughout his successful trainee period, Neil subbed for Richard Smith and slotted in at left-back during City's first 'live' televised League game, and subsequently underwent conversion to that role on a semi-permanent basis. His first start at Cambridge in March 1993 was in the No.3 shirt, and despite the occasional run-out in a wide midfield role, it has been as a newly-defined wing-back that he has made most impact, albeit with maddening inconsistency. At times, his positioning and concentration can be suspect, yet at others he will simply 'pocket' an opponent and give full rein to his attacking flair down the flank. His early-season form in the Premiership was encouraging, though, with his performance at Elland Road probably the highlight; and the only blot on his disciplinary record to date came in excusable circumstances, when his instinctive hand-ball on the line against Forest led to dismissal. A year earlier, he had left the field at Millwall for a few minutes, mistakenly thinking he'd been sent off.

Neil Lewis

Appearances (to end 1994/5):
PL: 13 (3) apps. 0 gls.
FL: 26 (5) apps. 0 gls.
FAC: 2 apps. 0 gls.
LC: 4 apps. 0 gls.
AIC: 2 apps. 0 gls.
Total: *47 (8) apps. 0 gls.*

LEWIS, R.

Role: Centre half

CAREER: Mar 1892:FOSSE.

Debut v Derby Junction (A) ML 12.3.1892

An as-yet untraced centre-half who made his debut in the same goalless Midland League game as Lisle and Atkins, and officially 'lost' a quarter of his appearance total when the April 1892 fixture at Port Vale (refereed by a spectator) was declared void, and was eventually replayed without him.

Appearances:
ML: 3 apps. 0 gls.
Total: *3 apps. 0 gls.*

LEWIS, William Jasper

Role: Centre forward
b. Bordesley Green, Birmingham, 1871

CAREER: Windsor Street Gasworks/Feb 1894: Small Heath/cs 1896:Nechells/Stourbridge/ May 1902:FOSSE/cs 1903: Stourbridge.

Debut v Small Heath (H) 6.9.02 (scored once)

William Lewis

All five members of the Fosse front line were making their club debut when this veteran centre-forward made his scoring bow against his former team, and he was one of only three who saw out the season, albeit at inside-right and with a fairly dismal goal-getting record. Eight years previously, William had scored for the Heathens on each of his League and FA Cup debuts, yet left them with only three senior games in total to his credit!

Appearances:
FL: 30 apps. 3 gls.
FAC: 1 app. 0 gls.
Total: *31 apps. 3 gls.*

LIGGINS, John Granville

Role: Centre forward
b. Altrincham, Cheshire, 26th March 1906
d. Hyde, Cheshire, 22nd February 1976

CAREER: Rotherham YMCA/ Rotherham United/1932: Mossley/cs:1933:Hyde/Dec 1933:CITY/Nov 1935: Burnley/June 1936: Shrewsbury Town/Jan 1937: Wigan Athletic/cs 1938: Worksop Town/Sept 1938:Bridlington Town.

Debut v Leeds United (H) 24.11.34 (scored once)

A former railway worker whose Cheshire League scoring exploits attracted City's envious gaze, Jack became another pretender to the mantle of the ageing Arthur Chandler, and was doubly unfortunate to suffer an early broken collarbone and to be fighting for his place in a relegation-bound team, for his strike rate was good given his limited opportunities. After moving to fellow Second Division team Burnley for £640, he again walked into a difficult situation, with the 16-year-old Tommy Lawton pressing his irresistible claim to the first-team leader's role, and Jack missing out once more after only four selections and a single goal. A fourteen-strike haul before Christmas for Birmingham League high-flyers Shrewsbury indexed his proficiency at lower levels, however.

Appearances:
FL: 8 apps. 5 gls.
Total: *8 apps. 5 gls.*

LIGHTBODY, Thomas

Role: Centre half
b. Motherwell, Lanarkshire

CAREER: Law Volunteers (Motherwell)/ Dec 1911:FOSSE/cs 1913:Peebles Rovers.

Debut v Clapton Orient (H) 9.4.12

'Belies his name, for he turns the scale at nearly twelve and a half stone', remarked the *Nottingham Post Football Guide* of 1912 of this young Scottish centre-half. Tom found himself understudying Percy Hanger at Leicester, and moved on after Jim Harrold had arrived to claim the regular pivotal role, having at least had the satisfaction of contributing to a trio of home victories, as well as to the 1912 County Cup Final victory over Hinckley United.

Appearances:
FL: 3 apps. 0 gls.
Total: *3 apps. 0 gls.*

Jack Liggins

Danny Liddle

LIDDLE, Daniel Hamilton Sneddon

Role: Outside left
b. Bo'ness, West Lothian, 17th February 1912
d. Wigston, Leics, 9th June 1982

CAREER: Bo'ness/Wallyford Bluebell/April 1929:East Fife/May 1932:CITY/July 1946: Mansfield Town.

Debut v Sheffield United (H) 27.8.32

A small, tricky left winger with a fair eye for goal, Danny became the first East Fife player to be capped for his country, and had turned out three times for Scotland in the year before he trekked south to Filbert Street. A remarkably consistent performer for City up to and through the war, and occasionally an electric one, Danny was twice the club's top scorer in the years of First Division struggle, switching to the inside-left berth to accommodate Eric Stubbs in the 1937 Division Two championship effort. He also assisted Northampton, Notts County, Mansfield and Leicester City Police in wartime competition, and after nominally retiring in May 1946, came back for one final League game with the Stags. Danny had originally delayed turning professional with East Fife until completing his carpentry apprenticeship.

Appearances:
FL: 255 apps. 64 gls.
FAC: 19 apps. 7 gls.
WW2: 115 apps. 21 gls.
Total: *389 apps. 92 gls.*

❏ FOX FACT: *In the context of Gary Lineker's deservedly honour-strewn career, it may look unduly trivial, but one minor City record is his: the four goals he aggregated at Loftus Road against QPR made him City's leading scorer on artificial pitches, on which the club totalled only ten strikes in thirteen fixtures while such surfaces were permissible for Football League and FA Cup matches.*

Gary Lineker

LINEKER, Gary Winston

Role: Striker
b. Leicester, 30th November 1960

CAREER: app July 1977/pro Dec 1978:CITY/
June 1985:Everton/July 1986:Barcelona/June
1989:Tottenham Hotspur/June 1992:Nagoya
Grampus Eight.

Debut v Oldham Athletic (H) 1.1.79

Although eventually and justifiably regarded as one of the world's foremost strikers, Gary made a rather stumbling start to his first-team career with City, who initially struggled to harness the youngster's remarkable pace to a coherent tactical role. Indeed, Gary was quite often played wide in his early days, until his alert goal-poaching habit began truly to blossom during 1981/2. There were still distinct gaps in his footballing repertoire when City fought their way back to Division One in 1983, but Gary gradually refined his ball-holding and control skills while leading the Filbert Street scoring list for four seasons running on quick-witted predatory instinct, and became an inevitable England choice up front despite City's lowly status in the top flight. Equally inevitable, perhaps, was a move; and it was to reigning champions Everton that Gary went in return for an £800,000 cheque. Thirty League goals, ten more in Cup competitions (including one at Wembley in the FA Cup Final), and both versions of the Footballer of the Year award made up Gary's individual tally from his Goodison season, when he also emerged as an unexpectedly fine header of the ball; though the Toffees finished as runners-up to Liverpool in both major domestic competitions. Gary's value escalated dramatically again, however, following his summer exploits in the 1986 World Cup, when his hat-trick against Poland made him a national hero and his total of six goals won him the competition's Golden Boot award as top scorer. Terry Venables' Barcelona laid out some £2,750,000 in pesetas for Gary's now globally-famous talent, with City benefiting from a negotiated percentage of Everton's profit (amounting to £250,000), and the quicksilver striker maintained his fine scoring record at both club and international level, though neither of his partnerships with fellow exiles Mark Hughes or Steve Archibald could quite prompt Barcelona higher than second place in the Spanish League in 1987. Gary picked up his first-ever winner's medal from the 1988 Spanish Cup Final, but took the first real knock to his modestly-handled prestige when, suffering from the onset of hepatitis, he shared in England's poor European Championship displays that summer. Perhaps ironically, his rehabilitation at Barcelona under Johan Cruyff's management entailed a return to virtually orthodox wing play; with his cross from the right providing the opening goal in the Catalans' European Cup Winners' Cup victory of 1989. A comeback to characteristic scoring form for England, and a second signing for Terry Venables, then heralded Gary's return to the Football League and, immediately, to the head of the First Division scorers' list. The 1990 World Cup saw him claim another 4 goals as England's campaign reached a semi-final penalty shoot-out before derailing, and Gary picked up the individual FIFA Fair Play award. He earned an FA Cup winner's medal with Spurs in 1991, despite missing a penalty against Nottingham Forest; and eventually another missed spot-kick (against Brazil) proved crucial in leaving his international tally at 48 - one short of Bobby Charlton's England record - when Graham Taylor controversially closed his occasional captain's representative career in 1992 on the 80-cap mark. Gary was named Footballer of the Year again in 1992 by the FWA, by which time he had announced his intention to move to Japan to assist in the 1993 launch of the J-League. His ambassadorial role there was superbly handled, but unfortunately a series of foot injuries marred his on-field contributions to the Grampus Eight cause (including a spell under former City boss Gordon Milne), and Gary announced his retirement from the game in November 1994. Now a newspaper columnist, radio presenter and regular 'Match of the Day' pundit (plus a familiar face from TV advertisements), Gary's previous extra-curricular activities included the co-authorship of a well-received, football-themed novel in Spain, a role as co-creator of the less successful ITV drama series, 'All In The Game', and inspirational status for the long-running play 'An Evening With Gary Lineker'. He returned to the Filbert Street pitch for the last time to feature briefly in Gordon Banks' benefit game in April 1995, on the day before he was honoured as a Freeman of the City of Leicester.

Appearances:
FL: 187 (7) apps. 95 gls.
FAC: 13 apps. 6 gls.
LC: 9 apps. 2 gls.
Total: *209 (7) apps. 103 gls.*

LING, Arthur Samuel (Archie)

Role: Goalkeeper
b. Cambridge

CAREER: Cambridge/June 1902:FOSSE/cs
1905:Swindon Town/cs 1909:Brentford.

Debut v Small Heath (H) 6.9.02

Archie Ling

The regular goalkeeper, over-exposed behind a flimsy defence, during two lowly seasons of Second Division struggle at Fosse, Archie loyally returned in December 1904 to deputise for the injured Walter Smith, despite having been released some months before. At Swindon, he was a Southern League custodian for four years and 140 games, although only a registration wrangle had stopped him moving to Norwich in 1907. With Brentford, in the same competition, Archie also showed commendable consistency, and even a flair for drama: scoring the Bees' initial two goals of 1910/11, both from the penalty spot, in their second and third fixtures, after having saved a spot-kick taken by Exeter's keeper in the opening game! He additionally played a reasonable standard of Minor Counties cricket for Cambridgeshire.

Appearances:
FL: 59 apps. 0 gls.
FAC: 7 apps. 0 gls.
Total: *66 apps. 0 gls.*

LINTON, Desmond Martin

Role: Defender
b. Birmingham,
5th September 1971

CAREER: YT 1988/pro
Jan 1990:CITY/Oct 1991:
Luton Town.

Debut v Portsmouth (H) 14.4.90 (sub)

A leggy young defender who could perform with equal distinction on the flanks or in the centre of the back line, Des was marked early for senior progress, winning several friendly-game run-outs prior to his League debut, and earning the Young Player of the Year award for 1990. Developing his reputation as a reliable cover player under the aegis of each of David Pleat, Gordon Lee and Brian Little, Des was a surprise departure (along with Scott Oakes) when Little and Pleat engineered the exchange deal which saw Steve Thompson arrive at Filbert Street. He was unlucky to suffer a long-term injury only a few games into his Luton career, but was still a useful squad player at Kenilworth Road during 1994/5.

Appearances:
FL: 6 (5) apps. 0 gls.
LC: 0 (1) app. 0 gls.
FMC: 1 app. 0 gls.
Total: *7 (6) apps. 0 gls.*

LISLE, C. R.

Role: Outside right

CAREER: Mar 1892:FOSSE.

Debut v Derby Junction (A)
ML 12.3.1892

C.R.Lisle

Another one-shot Midland Leaguer, an otherwise anonymous outside-right who failed to sparkle in the above goalless draw, and whose 2-goal performance in a friendly later that month against Notts St.Johns failed to earn him a contract. He was also in the Fosse reserve side which fell to Hugglescote Robin Hoods in the County Cup Final replay that April.

Appearances:
ML: 1 app. 0 gls.
Total: *1 app. 0 gls.*

Des Linton

LITTLER, Eric Joseph

Role: Centre forward
b. St.Helens, Lancs, 14th April 1929

CAREER: Stubshaw Cross/May 1951:CITY/
Dec 1954:Lincoln City/June 1955:Wrexham/
Dec 1955:Crewe Alexandra/Aug 1956:Chorley.

Debut v Notts County (H) 26.4.52 (scored once)

Plucked from the lower reaches of Lancashire
Combination football, Eric was a stubborn
trier of a centre-forward who made sporadic
appearances over the course of four seasons as
deputy to Derek Hines, then moved on in part
-exchange for Andy Graver. His inability to
command a regular senior berth (despite, for
instance, notching 39 reserve goals in 1952/3)
was repeated with his three subsequent clubs,
and Eric compiled an aggregate of only 28
League appearances and five goals after
leaving Filbert Street.

Appearances:
FL: 5 apps. 2 gls.
FAC: 1 app. 0 gls.
Total: *6 apps. 2 gls.*

Eric Littler

LOCHHEAD, Andrew Lorimar

Role: Centre forward
b. Milngavie, Dunbartonshire, 9th March 1941

CAREER: Renfrew Juniors/Dec 1958:Burnley/
Oct 1968:CITY/Feb 1970:Aston Villa/
Aug 1973:Oldham Athletic/(Apr 1974-loan-
Denver Dynamo).

Debut v Newcastle United (A) 2.11.68

Andy Lochhead

A six-foot, bullet-
domed central
striker who made
his First Division
mark as a superb
header of the ball,
Andy had won one
Scotland Under-23
cap in 1963 and gone
on to amass more
than a century of
League goals for
Burnley prior to his
£80,000 move to
Leicester. Though
he'd once totally frustrated a City attack when
serving as a stand-in centre-half for the Clarets
at Filbert Street, it was definitely his goal
touch that the soon-to-depart Matt Gillies
coveted as City struggled in 1968/9, and
which would help pave the way to Wembley
during that season of contrasts. Andy gloried
in the headed Fifth Round Anfield winner, but
rather muffed his Cup Final chance of greater
kudos with a miscued shot over the bar from a
fine position. He started the following season
with a quickfire goal spree, but couldn't
maintain the momentum, and after Frank
O'Farrell let him move on to Villa Park, Andy
proved unable to save his new club from their
embarrassing drop into the Third Division. He
did assist them to the League Cup Final in
1971, though, and then to promotion in 1972,
and also prompted Oldham up to the Second
in his initial season at Boundary Park. Andy
later coached the Latics and managed
Padiham, before becoming successively a
licensee and a bowling club steward back in
the Burnley area.

Appearances:
FL: 40 (4) apps. 12 gls.
FAC: 12 (1) apps. 3 gls.
LC: 6 apps. 4 gls.
Total: *58 (5) apps. 19 gls.*

LOCHHEAD, *Arthur William*

Role: Inside left
b. *Busby, Lanarkshire, 8th December 1897*
d. *Edinburgh, 30th December 1966*

CAREER: 1917:Heart of Midlothian/(Jan 1919-loan-Clyde)/June 1921:Manchester United/Oct 1925:CITY.

Debut v West Bromwich Albion (H) 17.10.25 (scored twice)

Another of Peter Hodge's key signings, Arthur was bought from Old Trafford for £3,300 to add his guile in both the scoring and scheming departments to City's initial attempts at First Division consolidation - and the inside-left duly delivered in a nine-year playing span at Filbert Street which ended with his elevation to the manager's chair in October 1934. Arthur had shown sufficient early promise at Hearts (as top scorer in the same team as Harry Graham) to merit a Scottish trial in the Home Scots v. Anglo-Scots fixture in March 1920, and was still displaying consistent high class stealth when chosen to represent the Anglos in the equivalent game eight years later, while simultaneously helping City to their highest-ever top-flight positions. In the interim, he had experienced both relegation and promotion with United (scoring three times against City during 1923/4) while establishing the goal-every-three-games ratio he would maintain at Filbert Street - though the qualified schoolteacher would not again be associated with a relegated side until persuaded by the City board to swap his veteran player status for that of manager following Peter Hodge's death in 1934. A City side whose central figures had aged together went down in 1935 despite Arthur's attempts to turn over the staff, yet it was a surprise when he resigned shortly after the start of the 1936/7 season, as his reshaped team had finished a respectable sixth in the Second Division the term before. Returning to Edinburgh, Arthur was considered a front-runner for the managerial vacancy at Hearts in early 1937, but didn't land the job, and is believed to have had no further football connections thereafter.

Appearances:
FL: 303 apps. 106 gls.
FAC: 17 apps. 8 gls.
Total: *320 apps. 114 gls.*

Tom Lonie

LONIE, Thomas

Role: Centre forward
b. Dundee, c 1872

CAREER: Dundee Harp/Jan 1894:Notts County/July 1894:Darwen/Dundee Wanderers/Dundee/Oct 1895:Stoke/Aug 1896:FOSSE.

Debut v Darwen (H) 5.9.1896 (scored once)

A Fosse centre-forward for a little over two months, Tom claimed a hat-trick in the second public trial match of 1896, and scored each of his Second Division goals against his former Darwen club-mates. He was rather contradictorily described by one local pressman as being 'a plodding player', yet 'at home in a vigorous contest'; while a report on his piqued absence from the reserves in November 1896 had him quoted as returning to Scotland, and not coming back 'until sent for'. This abrupt departure later made its way into the club secretary's report as a 'defection'.

> **Appearances:**
> *FL: 7 apps. 2 gls.*
> **Total:** *7 apps. 2 gls.*

LORD, Jack

Role: Wing half
b. Derby, c 1870

CAREER: 1885:Derby St.Luke's/Derby Junction/cs 1891:FOSSE.

Debut v Derby Junction (H) ML 12.9.1891

A veteran of Fosse's first Midland League fixture, and a stalwart at half-back for all three seasons in that competition, as well as across the first three in the Second Division, Jack was invariably described as a dogged, rather than brilliant player, and praised more for his stickability than for any stylish panache; but was clearly esteemed as the sort of artisanal clubman essential to the temperamental blend of a squad. Accordingly, he took a well-supported benefit (worth £50) from a friendly against Burton Wanderers in September 1897, and was a reliable skipper for Fosse Rovers. He had reputedly first turned out for St.Luke's at the age of 15.

> **Appearances:**
> *FL: 29 apps. 2 gls.*
> *FAC: 16 apps. 2 gls.*
> *ML: 56 apps. 3 gls.*
> **Total:** *101 apps. 7 gls.*

LORNIE, John

Role: Centre forward
b. Aberdeen, 2nd March 1939

CAREER: Banks O'Dee/Mar 1958:CITY/June 1961:Luton Town/June 1963:Carlisle United/June 1964:Tranmere Rovers/Sept 1966:Ross County.

Debut v West Bromwich Albion (A) 7.2.59 (scored once)

A Scottish schoolboy international and holder of a winner's medal from the 1957 Scottish Junior Cup Final (when Banks O'Dee beat Kilsyth Rangers 1-0 in front of almost 31,000 at Hampden), Jack spent three seasons at Filbert Street as reserve centre-forward, getting few chances to shine despite claiming a goal from each of his first two games, and eventually moved to Kenilworth Road without having once appeared in a winning City line-up at senior level. A total of only 13 goals from 58 League games accrued over the following five years, and Jack made his only subsequent faint mark on the record books as Tranmere's first-ever substitute. His brother, Jim, was the St.Mirren goalkeeper in the 1955 Scottish League Cup Final, while his grandfather, James Lamb, had long before found goalkeeping fame of the wrong sort - as the Bon Accord keeper beaten a record 36 times by the Arbroath forwards in the notorious Scottish Cup tie of 1885.

Appearances:
FL: 8 apps. 3 gls.
LC: 1 app. 0 gls.
Total: *9 apps. 3 gls.*

LOVATT, Harold Albert

Role: Centre forward
b. Audley, Staffs, 18th August 1905
d. Halmerend, Stoke-on-Trent, 11th November 1984

Jack Lornie

Harry Lovatt

CAREER: Wood Lane United/Red Street St.Chads/1923:Audley/(trials-Sunderland & Stoke)/Mar 1924:Port Vale/July 1924:Preston North End/Sept 1925:Crewe Alexandra/Mar 1926:Bradford City/Nov 1926:Wrexham/Aug 1927:Scarborough/May 1928:CITY/Dec 1930: Notts County/Nov 1931:Northampton Town/ July 1932:Macclesfield Town/Nov 1934: Stafford Rangers.

Debut v Cardiff City (H) 21.2.29 (scored once)

Centre-forward Harry could hardly have done more to lay claim to a first-team berth at City - at the time of his debut, he had notched 33 goals in only 19 reserve games, and his limited senior outings were marked by two First Division hat-tricks (both against Bolton) - yet there was still no question of him displacing a fit Arthur Chandler for any lengthy spell. Strangely, his Filbert Street stay was the longest of his first-class career, which had effectively started with an impressive goal-rush at Crewe (18 counters in only 33 League and Cup starts). Harry failed to settle at either of his last two League clubs, despite three goals in nine games for the Magpies and eleven in twenty for the Cobblers.

Appearances:
FL: 10 apps. 9 gls.
Total: *10 apps. 9 gls.*

LOWE, David Anthony

Role: Striker
b. Liverpool, 30th August 1965

CAREER: app Aug 1982/pro 1983:Wigan Athletic/June 1987:Ipswich Town/(Mar 1992-loan-Port Vale)/July 1992:CITY/(Feb 1994-loan-Port Vale).

Debut v Brentford (H) 19.9.92 (sub)

A useful penalty-box predator who also likes to drag defensive cover wide, and plays well with his back to goal, David has most recently been used by City under Mark McGhee as a virtual midfielder. The Liverpudlian made his breakthrough at Wigan in October 1982, while still an apprentice, and was a team-mate of Steve Walsh and Mike Newell in the 1985 Freight/Rover Trophy win at Wembley, scoring the final goal in the 3-1 win over Brentford. He top-scored in his initial Ipswich campaign, but had a merely peripheral role by the time of their 1992 Second Division

championship win. A £200,000 Brian Little signing, he shattered his cheekbone in a home pre-season friendly against Borussia Mönchengladbach, but settled well after his delayed League debut, though missing out on the 1993 Play-offs. He then failed to make any impact at all in his second Filbert Street term, but aided Port Vale's promotion after he and Paul Kerr had been swapped temporarily. His Premiership experiences were decidedly mixed: scoring and then being sent off with Vinnie Jones in the away game with Wimbledon, and a week later coming on as sub against Spurs to curl in the strike eventually voted by the supporters as Goal of the Season. He also had to convince incoming manager McGhee of his worth: and a double in the 4-4 draw at Villa Park, again in a substitute's role, definitely helped.

Appearances (to end 1994/5):
PL: 19 (10) apps. 8 gls.
FL: 28 (9) apps. 11 gls.
FAC: 1 (2) apps. 0 gls.
LC: 0 (3) apps. 1 gl.
AIC: 3 apps. 0 gls.
Total: *51 (24) apps. 20 gls.*

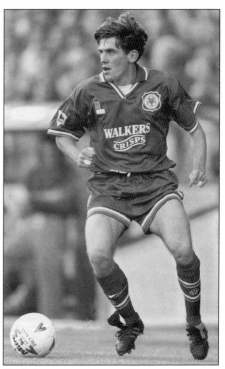

David Lowe

LOWE, William

Role: Forward
b. c 1870

CAREER: Long Eaton Midland/1886:Long Eaton Rangers/Notts Rangers/Oct 1890: Loughborough/ cs 1892:FOSSE/ cs 1893:Long Eaton Rangers/cs 1895: Loughborough.

'Kiddy' Lowe

Debut v Mansfield Town (A) ML 17.9.1892 (scored once)

Known throughout his Fosse spell as 'Kiddy' - though whether in acknowledgement of his youth, his on-field trickery or his sense of humour, we are unsure - this right-sided forward eventually made the first of his three appearances in League football at Filbert Street, albeit in the colours of the Luffs, in October 1895. Earlier, he'd made his Midland League bow for Fosse as emergency goalkeeper, when Jimmy Thraves arrived 35 minutes late for the game at Mansfield, then resumed his place up front and claimed Fosse's consolation goal. 'Kiddy', who had broken into the Long Eaton Rangers side as a 16-year-old for the season in which they won the Birmingham Senior Cup, and at 5ft 10in was the tallest Fosse forward of his era, was also known in the Midlands as a successful amateur sprinter. Shortly after leaving Fosse, he wrote to the local press from a Long Eaton address, offering £20 reward to anyone identifying the 'slanderer' who had started the rumour that he'd just been jailed for theft!

Appearances:
FAC: 4 apps. 2 gls.
ML: 20 apps. 9 gls.
Total: *24 apps. 11 gls.*

LOWERY, Edward

Role: Inside right
b. Walker-on-Tyne, October qtr 1907

CAREER: Walker Park/Usworth Colliery/ Dec 1930:East Fife/May 1932:CITY/(1934-loan-Yeovil Town)/July 1934:Torquay United/ June 1936:Darlington/cs 1937:Frickley Colliery/Burton Town.

Debut v Sheffield United (H) 27.8.32

A Geordie inside-right who had learnt the graces of Scottish style before arriving at Filbert Street in the company of Danny Liddle, Ted was City's first-choice schemer for the first ten games of 1932/3, and looking every inch another of Peter Hodge's subtly effective cross-border purchases, when successive illness and injuries completely ruined his

Ted Lowery

progress. To the extent, in fact, that soon he was only able to parade his talents in a Third Division context, claiming a dozen goals at Plainmoor and three more in a struggling Quakers side.

Appearances:
FL: 14 apps. 1 gl.
Total: *14 apps. 1 gl.*

LYNES, James

Role: Forward
b. Cheltenham, Glos, c 1869

CAREER: Nov 1895:FOSSE/May 1896: Lincoln City.

Debut v Hucknall St.Johns (H) FAC 2.11.1895

Signed from a junior club in the Birmingham area, James rejoiced in the nickname 'Trilby', and made intermittent appearances during 1895/6 at both outside-right and centre-forward. For some unfathomed reason, he utilised his forename as a pseudonymous surname on each of his first three Fosse outings - a friendly at Nottingham Forest, the above Cup-tie and a League game at Anfield. The last of his four Second Division goals for Lincoln proved to be the winner against Fosse in April 1897. James also played cricket for Lincoln Lindum CC. (A recently-published 'Who's Who' of Lincoln City players notes, somewhat dubiously, that James moved on in the 1897 close season to Halifax - as a goalkeeper! However, Halifax Town were not formed until 1911, and we have no record of a previous professional outfit in that town).

Appearances:
FL: 7 apps. 3 gls.
FAC: 3 apps. 0 gls.
Total: *10 apps. 3 gls.*

LYNEX, Stephen Charles

Role: Outside right
b. West Bromwich, 23rd January 1958

CAREER: Sandwell Rangers/app July 1974/pro Jan 1976:West Bromwich

Steve Lynex

Albion/(cs 1977-trials-Sligo Rovers)/Aug 1977: Shamrock Rovers/Apr 1979:Birmingham City/ Feb 1981:CITY/(Oct 1986-loan-Birmingham City)/Mar 1987:West Bromwich Albion/cs 1988:Cardiff City/(Mar 1990-loan-Telford United)/Aug 1990:Trafford Park/Feb 1991: Telford United/Mar 1991:Mitchells & Butlers/ Ansells.

Debut v Sunderland (A) 14.2.81

Despite having only a limited League career at St.Andrews, where he rapidly gained a reputation as 'super-sub', Steve also had two cup-winning medals to his name by the time Jock Wallace paid £60,000 to bring him to Leicester - from West Brom's Youth Cup v ictory in 1976, and from Shamrock's FAI Cup win in 1978. In fact the speedy winger's confidence-building sojourn in Irish football got off to a uniquely unpromising start - with a gunman offering Steve a persuasive reason not to prolong his trial period with Sligo - but Johnny Giles soon gave him a second chance after having been responsible for freeing him from the Hawthorns only weeks before. At Filbert Street, later, he developed quickly with regular top-flight football, soon assuming the mantle of penalty-taker and going on to claim a good proportion (23) of his respectable goal tally from the spot. For most of his City days the only orthodox winger on the club's books (and Player of the Season in 1983/4), Steve suffered occasionally from either instructions or an inclination to make himself more of an all-round midfield player, and sometimes appeared strangely reticent to play to his pacy, dribbling strengths; but the sight of him taking on his marker close to either touchline or by line, and leaving him flailing, brightened many an early-80s afternoon. However, a combined loss of form and, apparently, motivation led to a marked drop in Steve's valuation: he moved back to his hometown club for a merely nominal fee only a year after City had held out for a six-figure price from Albion. Steve hit the headlines again in 1994 in unfortunate circumstances when, as a West Midlands licensee, he was burned in a Firework Night bonfire explosion which proved fatal for one child.

Appearances:
FL: 200 (13) apps. 57 gls.
FAC: 12 apps. 1 gl.
LC: 14 (1) apps. 2 gls.
Total: *226 (14) apps. 60 gls.*

LYON, Herbert Ernest Saxon Bertie Cordey

Role: Inside forward
b. Yorkshire, 1877

CAREER: Sept 1895:Overseal Town/Aug 1898:Gresley Rovers/Jan 1899:FOSSE/cs 1900: Nelson/June 1901:Watford/cs 1902:Reading/ cs 1903:West Ham United/cs 1904:Brighton & Hove Albion/cs 1905:Swindon Town/cs 1906: Carlisle United/cs 1907:Swindon Town/June 1908:Blackpool/cs 1909:Walsall.

Debut v Luton Town (A) 14.1.1899 (scored once)

Primarily an inside-forward, Bertie makes the Leicester record books as the only outfield player actually selected in advance by the club to play a full first-class game as goalkeeper - and he kept a clean sheet against Bolton Wanderers in March 1900, after only three reserve outings between the sticks, before once more reverting to his attacking duties. Otherwise he's renowned for his mouthful of Christian names (almost certainly self-adopted, including the affected corruption of 'coeur-de-lion'), and for his habit of switching clubs on an annual basis. Fosse actually picked up £35 from Blackpool for his League registration eight years after he'd left the club (in a joint transfer with Alf Ball), and immediately after he'd helped the two-year-old Carlisle United club to promotion from the Lancashire Combination's Second Division.

Appearances:
FL: 15 apps. 5 gls.
FAC: 1 app. 2 gls.
Total: *16 apps. 7 gls.*

MABBOTT, C.

Role: Inside right

CAREER: Mellors Ltd FC (Nottingham)/
(1889-trials-Nottingham Forest)/
1891: Kettering/Apr 1892:FOSSE.

Debut v Doncaster Rovers (H) ML 30.4.1892

Making his senior bow (after friendly
outings against Loughborough and Bolton
Wanderers) in the game which confirmed
Fosse as Midland League wooden-
spoonists in their first shot at 'a fixity of
fixtures', this inside-right got one more
(goal-capped) chance the following
term, but then disappeared. The
Saturday Herald columnist's view may
explain why: "He plays the proper
game wonderfully well, but he is a
mere midget". It is suspected that he
may later have assisted Long Eaton
Rangers and Newark, but we have as
yet been unable to unravel confu-
sions around a contemporaneous
player (or, possibly, the same
man) who also briefly turned
out for Notts County at
League level, and has
elsewhere been identified
as John Mabbott.

Appearances:
ML: 2 apps. 1 gl.
Total: *2 apps. 1 gl.*

McALLISTER, Gary

Role: Midfield
b. Motherwell, Lanarkshire, 25th December 1964

CAREER: Fir Park BC/1981:Motherwell/Aug 1985:CITY/
June 1990:Leeds United.

Debut v Ipswich Town (H) 28.9.85

Notionally 'a buy for the future' when included as 'make-weight' in a
joint £250,000 transfer deal with the more experienced Ali Mauchlen,
attacking midfielder Gary very soon displayed a refreshing and
remarkably mature regard for the value of accurate passing to feet, and
rapidly gained confidence to express a pleasingly ambitious range of
skills on the ball as he adapted to regular First Division football. Indeed,
by his second City season he was justifiably attracting the attention of
Scottish international boss Andy Roxburgh - but with mixed results when
it came to being honoured. Gary scored the equaliser on his debut for
Scotland 'B' against France in April 1987, but also picked up the injury
which kept his much-needed talent out of City's vital last three games prior

McARTHUR, Thomas

Role: Centre half
b. Neilston, Renfrewshire, 23rd April 1925
d. Enderby, Leics, 19th April 1994

CAREER: Neilston Thistle/
Neilston Victoria/Jan 1947:CITY/
Jan 1954:Plymouth Argyle/cs
1954:Brush Sports/Enderby Town.

Debut v Chesterfield (A) 17.5.47

*Gary
McAllister*

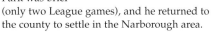

Tom McArthur

on immediately after being given a rare runaround in a 1-7 defeat at Leeds, his stay at Home Park was brief (only two League games), and he returned to the county to settle in the Narborough area.

Appearances:
FL: 97 apps. 0 gls.
FAC: 2 apps. 0 gls.
Total: *99 apps. 0 gls.*

McARTHUR, William

Role: Inside forward
b. Neilston, Renfrewshire, 1871

CAREER: 1889:Renton Union/1890: Sunderland Albion/1890:Middlesbrough Ironopolis/cs 1893:Bolton Wanderers/Apr 1894:FOSSE/Sept 1896:Dundee/May 1898: Brighton United/(Apr 1900:Army service)/ 1901:Worthing.

Debut v Grantham Rovers (A) ML 28.4.1894

A tall, tough, former Scots Guardsman, centre-half Tom made first team appearances across eight Second Division seasons, commanding the position only during 1950/1, yet loyally and reliably understudying Sep Smith, Norman Plummer and Matt Gillies in succession while skippering the reserves (and lifting the Combination Cup in 1948). Moving

Unable to break into Bolton's FA Cup Final side of 1894, centre- or inside-forward Willie joined Fosse in time to play in the club's last match in the Midland League. In fact, a fortnight before that fixture, he won over Fosse supporters with a hat-trick performance in a friendly against old rivals Loughborough, and there was little doubt he would be

to their eventual relegation. Given by Bryan Hamilton the rather backhanded tribute of being expected to function effectively in a variety of midfield and forward roles, Gary found his form suffering for a while, but he perked up under David Pleat's guidance, and his elegant playmaking abilities were soon drawing envious glances from several clubs of higher status. A distinctly erratic successor to Steve Lynex as City's regular penalty taker, he nonetheless boosted his goal tally to respectable levels with a number of blindingly executed strikes from rather less favourable positions. The only ever-present player in 1988/9, Gary remained the nub of constant transfer speculation throughout the following term. A level-headed young man, he was unimpressed by manager Brian Clough's brusque and rude comments to him at a City

Ground interview and memorably turned down a mooted £1.15 million move to Nottingham Forest and saw out his contract with City. But after three full caps had boosted him into Scotland's 1990 World Cup squad, Gary finally silenced the rumour machine by signing for Leeds, at a fee later set by tribunal at £1 million. His sinuous prompting alongside fellow Scot Gordon Strachan was a major component of the 1992 League Championship-winning effort, and his subsequent key role at the hub of midfield has earned him the captaincy of both his club and country.

Appearances:
FL: 199 (2) apps. 46 gls.
FAC: 5 apps. 2 gls.
LC: 14 (1) apps. 3 gls.
FMC: 4 apps. 0 gls.
Total: *222 (3) apps. 51 gls.*

Willie McArthur

re-registered for the first assault on the Second Division - to which he duly contributed as second-top scorer to David Skea, and during which he notched four goals in Fosse's record 13-0 FA Cup win over Notts Olympic. He went one better in 1895/6, as leading goalgetter, but then moved back north of the border. Willie, who appeared in a Scottish Cup semi-final against Kilmarnock in 1898, terminated his stint with Brighton (who withdrew from the Southern League and wound up in March 1900) by signing up with the Royal Sussex Regiment to fight in the Boer War, and was then reinstated as an amateur on his return.

Appearances:
FL: 55 apps. 27 gls.
FAC: 10 apps. 9 gls.
ML: 1 app. 0 gls.
Total: *66 apps. 36 gls.*

MACAULEY, James Lowry

Role: Inside left
b. Portarlington, 1889
d. Preston, 8th October 1945

CAREER: Cloughfion/Cliftonville Olympic/ 1907:Cliftonville/Oct 1910:Huddersfield Town/ Nov 1913:Preston North End/(1918-loan-Belfast Celtic)/July 1919:CITY/June 1920: Grimsby Town/cs 1921:Lancaster Town/ July 1923:Morecambe.

Debut v Wolverhampton Wanderers (H) 30.8.19

Initially capped as an amateur, five times chosen for the Irish League, and then honoured six times as a full Irish international after moving to Huddersfield during that club's initial season in the League (following a registration dispute also involving Glasgow Rangers), James lent his considerable experience to City's first campaign after WW1, plying his artistry in the inside-left position. His goals came in successive home and away fixtures with Grimsby, who were sufficiently impressed to later take him on for a further season of Second Division fare - a sphere in which he had played all his English football to that date, as war had delayed Preston's ascent after they had finished as runners-up in 1914/15.

Appearances:
FL: 19 apps. 2 gls.
FAC: 4 apps. 0 gls.
Total: *23 apps. 2 gls.*

McCULLOCH, David

Role: Centre forward
b. Hamilton, Lanarkshire, 5th October 1911
d. Hamilton, May 1979

CAREER: Hamilton Amateurs/Shotts United/ May 1932:Third Lanark/June 1934:Heart of Midlothian/Nov 1935:Brentford/Oct 1938: Derby County/July 1946:CITY/Dec 1946:Bath City/Aug 1949:Waterford (p/coach)/July 1951:Alloa Athletic (p/mgr).

Debut v Manchester City (H) 31.8.46

Unfortunately looking well past his best when briefly turning out for City in the first postwar League season, Dave had been a centre-forward in the classic mould throughout the 30s, leading the Scottish scorers' list in 1934/5 (with 38 goals) and winning his first honours while averaging a goal per game at Tynecastle. He scored in his

James Macauley

Above: Dave McCulloch

Right: Billy McDerment

McDERMENT, William Stirling

Role: Wing half
b. Paisley, Renfrewshire, 5th January 1943

CAREER: Johnstone Burgh/May 1961:CITY/
July 1967:Luton Town/May 1969:Notts
County/1970:Morton.

Debut v Aston Villa (A) 15.5.63

A reliable reserve half-back who made
sporadic appearances across five First Division
seasons in the mid-60s, Billy could never quite
lay claim to a regular senior berth, and
perhaps the closest he came to a moment of
glory in English football was in getting one
hand on the Football Combination Cup in
1967 as skipper of the City reserves side which
shared that trophy with Spurs. He briefly
partnered Max Dougan in Luton's Fourth
Division promotion side, but fared better back
in Scotland after failing to click at Meadow
Lane. Billy had initially won recognition as a
Scottish amateur international in 1961.

Appearances:
FL: 20 (3) apps. 1 gl.
FAC: 2 apps. 0 gls.
LC: 5 apps. 0 gls.
Total: *27 (3) apps. 1 gl.*

McDONALD, David

Role: Inside right

CAREER: Dundee Wanderers/
cs 1895: Dundee/cs 1896:Everton/
Oct 1896:FOSSE/cs 1897:Dundee/
Feb 1898:Millwall.

Debut v Lincoln City (H) 7.11.1896

Unable to make a Goodison Park
breakthrough, Scottish inside-right Davie was
signed by Fosse as an instant early-season
replacement for his former Dundee team-mate,
Tom Lonie, but lost his goal touch after an
early burst of deadly finishing. He had been
Dundee's top scorer in the Scottish First
Division in 1895/6, but his impact as a whole
in England was muted, with a Millwall record
of one goal in only two Southern League
appearances.

Appearances:
FL: 16 apps. 7 gls.
FAC: 2 apps. 0 gls.
Total: *18 apps. 7 gls.*

only Scottish League
representative game, then
added three goals while
winning seven full caps,
and also played in one
wartime international for
Scotland at a time when
he was guesting regularly
for the likes of Falkirk,
Aldershot, Bath City,
Chelsea, Bournemouth,
Swansea Town and Brentford. The latter club
had originally paid £6,000 for his aerial ability
and all-action foraging, and got 85 First
Division goals in return, out of Dave's pre-war
total of 178. He had been Derby's record
signing at £9,500, and joined City with Tom
Eggleston for a joint fee of £3,100. As a real
veteran, Dave led the League of Ireland
scoring chart at the end of his first season with
Waterford, and in later years worked for Rolls
Royce at East Kilbride.

Appearances:
FL: 4 apps. 2 gls.
Total: *4 apps. 2 gls.*

MacDONALD, Kevin Duncan

Role: Midfield
b. Inverness, 22nd November 1960

CAREER: Inverness Caledonian/May 1980:
CITY/Nov 1984:Liverpool/(Dec 1987-loan-
CITY)/(Nov 1988-loan-Rangers)/July 1989:
Coventry City/(Mar 1991-loan-Cardiff City)/
Aug 1991:Walsall.

Debut v Norwich City (H) 29.11.80 (sub)

Striding into the First Division after only two
seasons of Highland League football,
midfielder Kevin impressed
immediately with his combativeness
and almost cocky confidence. The
latter attribute stuck with him
throughout his City career, from the
moment he stepped up to convert a
crucial penalty in his first full home
game, and was later evidenced by
some memorably cool defensive work
(including a number of heart-
stopping back-headers to Mark
Wallington) when he filled in at
centre-back for Larry May during the
1983 promotion run-in. Indeed, once
Kevin had mastered his occasionally
fiery temper (he was the first City
player to be twice sent off), he proved
himself a genuinely classy operator,
with only a marginal lack of pace
detracting from his repertoire of
control, vision and ball-winning
ability. A £400,000 cheque took him to
Anfield, where injuries cruelly
hampered his progress in a
formidably strong squad. Even so, he
picked up an FA Cup winner's medal
in 1986, before a broken leg once
more heralded a long lay-off. Kevin
had still to return to the senior
Liverpool line-up when he came back
to Filbert Street for a loan spell under
caretaker manager Peter Morris, and
unfortunately showed every sign of
rustiness in the three defeats in which
he played. Eventually freed from
Anfield in 1989, he remained for a
while in First Division contention at
Highfield Road, then turned down a
proffered player/coach role at Cardiff
before moving to Bescot Stadium.

Kevin retired after Walsall's 1993 Play-off exit,
and rejoined City that summer as a youth
coach. In December 1994, in the wake of Brian
Little's departure, he and Tony McAndrew
jointly assumed the club's
caretaker management role for three
Premiership fixtures; but both men resigned in
January 1995.

Appearances:
FL: 136 (5) apps. 8 gls.
FAC: 4 apps. 0 gls.
LC: 10 apps. 0 gls.
Total: *150 (5) apps. 8 gls.*

Kevin MacDonald

McDONALD, Thomas

Role: Outside right
b. Glasgow, 24th May 1930

CAREER: Hibernian/Apr 1954:
Wolverhampton Wanderers/July 1956:CITY/
cs 1960:Dunfermline Athletic/Dec 1962:Raith
Rovers/cs 1963:Queen of the South/Dec 1963:
Stirling Albion.

*Debut v Doncaster Rovers (H) 18.8.56
(scored twice)*

Initially understudy to, and then replacement
for, the great Gordon Smith at Hibs, Tommy
won one Scotland 'B' cap and then found
himself stuck in Wolves' reserves for much of
his Molineux stay. David Halliday paid £6,000
to bring the outside-right to Leicester, and he
got the 1956/7 promotion effort off to a flying
start; though eventually missing out on the
run-in. For three seasons thereafter he battled
Howard Riley for the No.7 shirt, having his
best scoring season (13 League and Cup goals)
just prior to moving back to Scotland. Ill-luck
dogged him there, especially
when he went down with
appendicitis virtually on the
eve of the 1961 Scottish
Cup Final, though he
subsequently played in
European competition
for Dunfermline along
with Willie Cunningham,
and passed on more
than a few tips to the
young Jackie Sinclair.

Appearances:
FL: 113 apps. 27 gls.
FAC: 5 apps. 2 gls.
Total: *118 apps.*
29 gls.

MacFARLANE, Ian

Role: Right back
b. Lanark, 26th November 1933

CAREER: Aberdeen/Aug 1956:Chelsea/
May 1958:CITY/July 1959:Bath City.

Debut v Luton Town (H) 4.10.58

A tough, hefty
full-back who
probably set the
Doug Rougvie
mould at both
Pittodrie and
Stamford Bridge,
yet who only got
one chance to
deputise for
Willie
Cunningham at
Leicester after a
£9,000 transfer,
Ian moved on to
partner Tony
Book in Bath's
1960 Southern
League cham-

Ian MacFarlane

pionship side. He later embarked on a
much more successful coaching career,
which saw him return to Filbert Street
as assistant manager to both Frank
McLintock and Jock Wallace between
1977 and 1982. In the interim, Ian had
fulfilled second-in-command duties at
Middlesbrough, Manchester City and
Sunderland, and had held the full
managerial reins at Carlisle; though
almost invariably tended to be associated
with highly-motivated yet essentially dour
sides. After leaving Leicester, he had a
brief spell as manager of Yeovil
Town, and was later chief scout
for Leeds United.

Appearances:
FL: 1 app. 0 gls.
Total: *1 app. 0 gls.*

*Tommy
McDonald*

McFARLANE, Peter

Role: Left back
b. Motherwell, Lanarkshire

CAREER: Carfin/1894:Motherwell/
Dec 1894:FOSSE.

Debut v Crewe Alexandra (A) 12.1.1895

A 'sturdy' full-back who matched his single
Scottish League appearance for Motherwell
with one senior game south of the border (a
2-2 draw at Gresty Road), Peter was described
as 'too prone to dribble' in an era when the
back line positions were dominated by big
kickers specialising in first-time clearances. He
was listed as available for a £10 fee at the end
of his Fosse term, but we have yet to find
evidence of any club paying it.

Appearances:
FL: 1 app. 0 gls.
Total: 1 app. 0 gls.

McGRAW, Ian

Role: Goalkeeper
*b. Glasgow, 30th
August 1926*

CAREER: Arbroath/
Dec 1948:CITY/
cs 1951:Corby Town.

*Debut v Tottenham
Hotspur (H) 25.12.48*

Ian's was a tragically
truncated City career
following his £4,200
signing by Johnny
Duncan. The
easefully authorita-
tive young Scottish
keeper had really
endeared himself to
City supporters with
his performances in the 1949 Cup run, and
had helped rebuff hot favourites Portsmouth
in the semi-final, when he was seriously
injured a week later in a rough-house League
game with Grimsby. A broken little finger not
only kept him out of the Wembley line-up, but
also developed complications which led to the
necessity of the digit's amputation. At that
stage, Ian had made eight appearances in each
of the League and Cup competitions, and

Ian McGraw

while he bravely came back to add another
five games in 1950/1 despite his handicap, he
could not for long displace internationals
Tommy Godwin or Johnny Anderson. He was,
however, granted a testimonial game in April
1953: a City friendly against Wolves.

Appearances:
FL: 13 apps. 0 gls.
FAC: 8 apps. 0 gls.
Total: 21 apps. 0 gls.

McGREGOR, William

Role: Right back
b. Paisley, Lanarkshire, 1st December 1923

CAREER: Mossvale YMCA/April 1947:CITY/
Sept 1953:Mansfield Town.

Debut v Tottenham Hotspur (A) 27.3.48

A spirited, compact, quick-tackling reserve
right-back for six seasons at Filbert Street,
Willie picked up a medal from the
1948 Combination Cup win, but
got few chances to shine in the
Second Division before joining the
colony of ex-City men at Field
Mill, where in contrast he played
119 League games across three
seasons.

Appearances:
FL: 9 apps. 0 gls.
FAC: 1 app. 0 gls.
Total: 10 apps. 0 gls.

*Willie
McGregor*

McILMOYLE, Hugh

Role: Centre forward
b. Cambuslang, Lanarkshire, 29th January 1940

CAREER: Port Glasgow Juniors/Aug 1959:
CITY/July 1962:Rotherham United/Mar 1963:
Carlisle United/Oct 1964:Wolverhampton
Wanderers/Mar 1967:Bristol City/Sept 1967:
Carlisle United/Sept 1969:Middlesbrough/
July 1971:Preston North End/cs 1973:Morton/
July 1974:Carlisle United/cs 1975:Morton
(p/coach).

Hugh McIlmoyle

Debut v West Ham United (H) 3.4.61
(scored once)

The centre of a major City controversy when
chosen in Ken Leek's No.9 shirt for the 1961
Cup Final, after having played only seven
League games, Hugh was in no way overawed
by the Wembley occasion, assuming an
intelligent deep-lying role and looking City's
most dangerous forward. Nonetheless, he was
then subjected to perhaps over-intense
scrutiny from a sceptical crowd as he
struggled to maintain a first-team striker's role
the following season. The sense of too much
responsibility being heaped upon the slender
youngster too soon was borne out by his
future development into a fine and versatile
servant for a host of other clubs. His first of
three spells at Brunton Park saw Hugh top the
Football League scoring charts with 39 goals in
Carlisle's 1964 rise from the Fourth Division,
and he helped them into the Second Division a
year later. Subsequent moves attracted some
hefty transfer fees, with Hugh's heading
abilities in particular being much in demand,
and he matured eventually into a perceptive
attacking midfielder, bowing out of the senior
game with a career aggregate of 161 League
goals.

Appearances:
FL: 20 apps. 5 gls.
FAC: 1 app. 0 gls.
Eur: 1 app. 1 gl.
Total: *22 apps. 6 gls.*

MACKAY, Robert

Role: Midfield
b. Harthill, Lanarkshire, 6th May 1948

CAREER: Whitburn Bluebells/Harthill
Juniors/Apr 1965:CITY/1970:Burton Albion/
cs 1970:Boston United/cs 1971:Kidderminster
Harriers.

Debut v Manchester City (H) 21.8.68

A versatile defensive midfielder who looked
set for a useful run in City's first team, Bobby
suffered a definitive knock to his progress in
the first game he played for new manager
Frank O'Farrell: being stretchered off in the
Third Round FA Cup tie at Barnsley as City
embarked on their 1969 Wembley run. Only
one League Cup game followed his cartilage
operation, and Bobby's senior career came to a

Bobby Mackay

help Bath to the championship of the Southern League's Western Division in 1933. On his return to Leicestershire football, he additionally acted as honorary secretary to Thursday League club Solus FC, with whom Johnny Duncan also had a lengthy off-field association; and in 1935 turned down terms offered by Lancaster Town.

Appearances:
FL: 1 app. 0 gls.
Total: *1 app. 0 gls.*

McKENNAN, *Peter Stuart*

Role: Inside forward
b. Airdrie, Lanarkshire, 16th July 1918
d. Dundonald, Ayrshire, 28th September 1991

CAREER: Whitburn Juniors/July 1935:Partick Thistle/Oct 1947:West Bromwich Albion/ Mar 1948:CITY/Sept 1948:Brentford/ May 1949:Middlesbrough/July 1951:Oldham Athletic/July 1954:Coleraine (p/coach).

Debut v Cardiff City (A) 13.3.48

A fascinating character who barely settled at Filbert Street at all, inside-forward Peter was known throughout his career by the nickname 'Ma Ba' ('My Ball'), after his habitually confident on-field shout for possession - all the more noticeable for his voice's honing on the wartime parade grounds he'd commanded as a sergeant-major in the Royal Welch Fusiliers. At that period, having already gained near-legendary status at Firhill, he also guested for Wrexham, West Brom, Chelsea and Brentford, and assisted Irish side Glentoran throughout 1941 - winning Irish League representative honours to add to his two pre-war Scottish League selections. Peter came to Leicester as the more highly-valued component of the part-exchange deal that took Jack Haines to the Hawthorns, and left within a month of the new season starting, signing for Brentford for £7,000 on the day City beat them at Griffin Park. As a veteran, he inspired Oldham to the

premature end. At Kidderminster he briefly linked up with former City reserves John and Jim Flanagan.

Appearances:
FL: 6 (1) apps. 1 gl.
FAC: 1 app. 0 gls.
LC: 1 (1) apps. 0 gls.
Total: *8 (2) apps. 1 gl.*

McKENNA, *James Peter*

Role: Goalkeeper
b. Blackpool, 18th April 1910
d. Blackpool, 27th August 1986

CAREER: Great Harwood/ Feb 1930:CITY/cs 1932:Bath City/Sept 1933:Nuneaton Town /Aug 1935:Market Harborough Town.

Debut v Birmingham (H) 26.3.32

Jim McKenna

The third-choice City 'keeper behind Jim McLaren and John Beby, Jim got but one chance to exhibit his prowess at senior level, in the above 3-1 home win, and moved on to

Peter McKennan

Colin Mackleworth

Third Division (North) championship in 1953, then finished his active career back in Ireland. His repute lives on in Glasgow however, where stories still circulate of how the gate for the St.Mirren v. City friendly of April 1948 was boosted by several hundred Partick supporters who made the trip just to see their former hero perform.

Appearances:
FL: 18 apps. 7 gls.
Total: *18 apps. 7 gls.*

MACKIE, Robert

Role: Full back
b. Dalry, Ayrshire,
August 1882

CAREER: Stenhousemuir/ May 1904:Heart of Midlothian/Aug 1905: Chelsea/Nov 1907: FOSSE/ cs 1909:Darlington/ 1909:Airdrieonians.

Debut v Derby County (H) 23.11.07

Bob Mackie

'Ungainly but obstinate', Bob was a full-back signed by Chelsea for their first-ever League campaign, and later became a vital defensive cog in Fosse's promotion season,

before suffering along with his team-mates some of the First Division embarrassments of 1908/9. Returning to Scottish football to settle at Broomfield, he received an Airdrie benefit from a game against Albion Rovers in 1914. Oddly enough, like David Webb, Bob played one full game in goal for Chelsea, standing in for Willie Foulke in an FA Cup preliminary tie against Southern United in October 1905.

Appearances:
FL: 33 apps. 0 gls.
FAC: 3 apps. 0 gls.
Total: *36 apps. 0 gls.*

MACKLEWORTH, Colin

Role: Goalkeeper
b. Bow, London,
24th March 1947

CAREER: app 1962/pro Apr 1964: West Ham United/Nov 1967:CITY/ cs 1971:Kettering Town/Metropolitan Police/Clapton.

Debut v Rotherham United (A) FAC 9.3.68

A capable reserve keeper for both his League

clubs, Colin won a Youth Cup medal with the Hammers in 1963, but only turned out three times for their first team. Brought to Filbert Street as cover for Peter Shilton, he faced a high-pressure debut in the drawn Fifth Round Cup tie at Millmoor, and also saw City through the replay before making his League bow. For another three seasons he bore the frustrations of regular Combination football and highly irregular senior opportunities, then left for Southern League fare before joining the police force.

Appearances:
FL: 6 apps. 0 gls.
FAC: 3 apps. 0 gls.
Total: *9 apps. 0 gls.*

McLAREN, Alexander

Role: Goalkeeper
b. Tibbermore, Perth, 25th December 1910
d. Perth, 5th February 1960

CAREER: am Apr 1927/pro Dec 1927: St.Johnstone/Feb 1933:CITY/Oct 1940: Morton/Oct 1945:St.Johnstone.

Debut v Everton (A) 8.3.33

Taking over the City green jersey from namesake Jim, former blacksmith and Scottish international keeper Sandy must have wondered what had hit him on his debut, as a Dixie Dean hat-trick accounted for only half the Everton goals which flew past him that afternoon. Nonetheless, he went for 102 consecutive games between the City sticks from that date, and was still very much the first-choice custodian when war brought a halt to League football over six years later. Noted particularly for his unflappability and the prodigious strength of his punch, Sandy was unfortunate not to add to his tally of five caps while with City (he'd remarkably won the first at the age of 18), and took a Second Division championship medal in 1937 as the only tangible honour from a superb Leicester career. After wartime spells as a taxi driver and in the Navy, plus stints with Morton and (as a guest) Airdrieonians, he returned to his first senior club for an eight-game farewell.

Appearances:
FL: 239 apps. 0 gls.
FAC: 17 apps. 0 gls.
WW2: 30 apps. 0 gls.
Total: *286 apps. 0 gls.*

MacLAREN, David

Role: Goalkeeper
b. Auchterarder, Perthshire, 12th June 1934

CAREER: 1948:Comrie Athletic/St.Johnstone Jnrs/RAF/Feb 1956:Dundee/Jan 1957:CITY/ May 1960:Plymouth Argyle/June 1965: Wolverhampton Wanderers/Sept 1966: Southampton/July 1967:Worcester City.

Debut v Notts County (A) 2.2.57

Though unrelated to either of City's other goalkeeping McLarens, Dave was clearly destined by kinship for fame as a custodian: brothers Jimmy and Roy both kept goal in League football (the former for Berwick, Chester and Carlisle; the latter for St.Johnstone, Bury and Sheffield Wednesday), and another brother, Monty, was a Liverpool reserve.

Dave MacLaren

An emergency buy from Dundee when Johnny Anderson suffered injury part-way through the 1957 Second Division championship campaign, Dave thereafter shaded the rivalry for the green jersey on a regular basis until the advent of Gordon Banks. His soundness then saw him through five Second Division seasons at Home Park and Molineux, and made him an ideal choice to shore up Southampton's defence in their first-ever Division One season. Way back in 1954, while on RAF service, Dave had won both the 'Sportsman of the Year' award and unofficial representative honours in Malaya, and in 1970 returned there as a coach; going on to manage the Malaysian national team in 1972, and later managing Australian side Hakoah in the New South Wales Federation.

Appearances:
FL: 85 apps. 0 gls.
FAC: 5 apps. 0 gls.
Total: *90 apps. 0 gls.*

Sandy McLaren

Jim McLaren

McLAREN, James

Role: Goalkeeper
b. Falkirk, Stirlingshire, 12th July 1897
d. Leicester, 16th November 1975

CAREER: Bonnybridge Heatherbell/1920:
Stenhousemuir/May 1922:Bradford City/
May 1927:CITY/Oct 1933:Watford.

Debut v Newcastle United (H) 7.5.27

The son of a former Scottish champion racing cyclist, Jim had been, in 1911, the goalkeeper in the first schoolboy international played by Scotland, and the lad from Larbert Central School had then distinguished himself with a penalty save against the English. After WW1 service in France with the Argyll & Sutherland Highlanders, he helped Stenhousemuir into, and through, their first season in the Scottish League, then built a good reputation in a struggling Bradford City side which was relegated from Division Two in 1927 - his transfer to City helping to relieve some of the severe financial embarrassment the Valley Parade outfit were then suffering. At Leicester, Jim displaced fellow-countryman Kenny Campbell as City mounted their most convincing assaults on the First Division title, and held his key position for all but a few games until succeeded in turn by namesake Sandy: like himself, a keeper not averse to using a hefty frame to full advantage when advancing from his line. By the time he retired from Vicarage Road in 1939, Jim had amassed a career total of 519 League games, and had become only the second player in League history to receive five-year benefit payments from three separate clubs. In fact he holds the record as the oldest player to turn out for Watford (at 41 years, 172 days): a feat he shades by a mere matter of months from another former City keeper, Joe Calvert.

Appearances:
FL: 170 apps. 0 gls.
FAC: 10 apps. 0 gls.
Total: *180 apps. 0 gls.*

McLEOD, Roderick

Role: Inside forward
b. Kilsyth, Stirlingshire, February 1872
d. Lambeth, London, December 1931

CAREER: Westburn/Partick Thistle/Jan 1891:
West Bromwich Albion/Aug 1897:FOSSE/
May 1898:Brighton United/Apr 1899:
Southampton/Aug 1900:Brentford.

Debut v Luton Town (H) 4.9.1897

A baby-faced, classy inside-forward whose successful stint with West Brom had brought him 50 League goals and appearances against Aston Villa in both the 1892 and 1895 FA Cup Finals, Roddie was Fosse's leading marksman in his only season, but was soon to join the Southern League roundabout onto which so many early players leapt from Leicester (in this case, accompanying Fosse trainer John Jackson, and initially playing alongside ex-Fossils Willie McArthur and Peter McWhirter). Moving along the coast, Roddie later left Southampton in pique after being dropped from their 1900 Cup Final team, but won a Southern League Division Two medal with the Bees.

Appearances:
FL: 28 apps. 13 gls.
FAC: 1 app. 1 gl.
Total: *29 apps. 14 gls.*

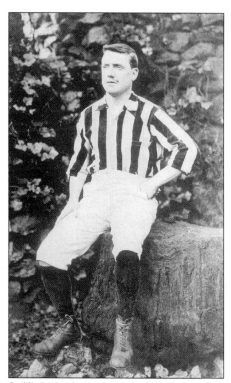

Roddie McLeod

McLINTOCK, Francis

Role: Right half
b. Glasgow, 28th December 1939

CAREER: Shawfield Juniors/Jan 1957:CITY/ Oct 1964:Arsenal/June 1973:Queen's Park Rangers.
Debut v Blackpool (A) 14.9.59

Brought down from the Gorbals and nurtured at Filbert Street as a probing wing-half, Frank possessed the rare combination of toughness and elegance and soon became a key element in City's then-revolutionary midfield strategies of the early 60s. Whether switching wing-half and inside-forward roles in mid-match with Graham Cross or creating crossfield magic with Davie Gibson, he oozed footballing class; and it was no surprise either when he graduated to full Scottish honours or when Billy Wright's Arsenal eventually paid City their then-record outgoing transfer fee of £80,000 for his services. Frank took some time to settle at Highbury, and extended his apparent Wembley hoodoo in the late 60s (following heartbreak FA Cup Final defeats for City in 1961 and 1963 with a pair of losing League Cup Final appearances for Arsenal in

1968 and 1969) even after settling to the role of central defender. Then, though, he experienced a couple of years of genuine glory: skippering the Gunners to their 1970 Fairs Cup win, and to the domestic Double a year later, as well as picking up both the 1971 Footballer of the Year award and a CBE, and re-establishing himself as an influential international. Subsequently, it looked a certain case of Frank being written off too early when he was allowed to move cheaply to QPR, and assisted them to a near-miss title bid in 1976; but it was equally evident that, after 609 League games, he was handed too much backroom responsibility too soon when engaged as City manager in 1977 in succession to Jimmy Bloomfield. Too many of his transfer-market dealings bore the stamp of desperation, too few of his tactical ideas translated effectively to on-field practice, and Frank's unwillingness to commit to living again in Leicester (or to leaving behind his London business interests) hardly helped his cause. His broken-backed City team were already certainties for relegation when he resigned in April 1978, and he returned to the capital as, successively, adviser on the dire soccer-themed movie 'Yesterday's Hero', youth coach at QPR, broadcaster, Brentford manager, assistant boss at Millwall, and part-time players' agent.

Appearances:
FL: 168 apps. 25 gls.
FAC: 20 apps. 0 gls.
LC: 11 apps. 3 gls.
Eur: 1 app. 0 gls.
Total: *200 apps. 28 gls.*

McMAHON, Sam Keiron

Role: Midfield
b. Newark, 10th February 1976

CAREER: YT July 1992/pro July 1994:CITY.
Debut v Wimbledon (H) 1.4.95 (sub)

First noticed for his energetic probing during City's 1994 schedule of pre-season friendlies, Sam had a fine Central League campaign which developed his high promise as an attack-minded midfielder and earned him the club's Young Player of the Year award in 1995; and had graduated to the senior bench by March. Unused at Loftus Road, he finally got his brief Premiership break in the see-saw home game with the Dons: replacing Nicky

Frank McLintock

Sam McMahon

Mohan late in the second half with the scoreline at 1-2, injecting life into the midfield and drawing a fine save out of goalkeeper Sullivan which led to Jimmy Willis equalising from the ensuing corner-kick, and then watching City take and lose the lead in a game which finished, ludicrously, at 3-4.

Appearances (to end 1994/5):
PL: 0 (1) app. 0 gls.
Total: *0 (1) app. 0 gls.*

McMILLAN, John Stuart

Role: Inside forward
b. Port Glasgow, Renfrewshire,
16th February 1871
d. Birkdale, Lancs, 3rd November 1941

CAREER: Port Glasgow Athletic/cs 1890:
St.Bernards/Nov 1890:Derby County/
May 1896:FOSSE/Jan 1901:Small Heath/
May 1903:Bradford City/May 1906:Glossop
(p/mgr).

Debut v Darwen (H) 5.9.1896 (scored once)

A prodigy in Scottish Junior football, appearing regularly from the age of 14, Johnny made only one appearance for his first senior side, leaving the Edinburgh-based St.Bernards in a bitter row over professionalism, but then gave fine service to Derby, scoring 50 League and Cup goals over six seasons (including the late winner in the Test Match against Notts County at Filbert Street which retained top-flight status for the Rams in 1895). With Fosse, the versatile forward led by example, maintaining a high scoring ratio while demonstrating a rare degree of creative flair, and prompting the club to its first serious promotion challenge in 1899, when Fosse finished 3rd. He took a club benefit from a friendly with Notts County in December 1900, and moved to Small Heath only a month later, there to experience promotion, relegation and promotion again during an eventful stay. Johnny was handed the role of captaining Bradford City for their inaugural League season (when still being described as 'an agile player with excellent command over the ball'), and gradually prepared himself for a managerial career, which he picked up again after WW1 with two seasons in charge at Gillingham after their 1920 election to the League. He was later landlord of the Normanton Hotel in Derby. His Leicester-born son, Stuart, was also a player with Derby, Wolves, Chelsea, Clapton Orient and Bradford City, and managed Derby to their 1946 FA Cup win.

Appearances:
FL: 122 apps. 43 gls.
FAC: 9 apps. 5 gls.
Total: *131 apps. 48 gls.*

Johnny McMillan

McNALLY, Owen

Role: Centre forward
b. Denny, Stirlingshire, 20th June 1906

CAREER: Denny Hibs/Feb 1927:Celtic/(Aug 1927-loan-Arthurlie)/(July 1928-loan-Hamilton Academical)/(Feb 1929-loan-Hamilton Academical)/Sept 1930:Bray Unknowns/ cs 1931:Cardiff City/cs 1932:Bray Unknowns/ 1933:Lausanne/cs 1934:Sligo Rovers/cs 1935: Distillery/Jan 1936:CITY/Aug 1937:Racing Club de Calais/cs 1938: Shamrock Rovers.

Debut v Nottingham Forest (A) 30.1.36

Born in the same Scottish town as Adam Black, centre-forward Owen was certainly possessed of rather more wanderlust than his eminently settled City predecessor. A frustrated reserve to record scorer Jimmy McGrory at Celtic (totalling but a dozen League games and a trio of goals for the Bhoys), he once took out his ire in a Scottish Second Division match for Arthurlie against Armadale to the record tune of eight goals (in a 10-0 win on 1st October 1927), and then

Owen McNally

soon started collecting clubs and countries in almost equal proportion. The trek from Scotland through Ireland, Wales and Switzerland might have satisfied many a footballing mercenary, but the 5ft.7ins. Owen maintained his rolling stone status for some years yet; playing again on both sides of the Irish border, and gathering the 'moss' of a scoring appearance for the victorious Irish League against the Football League at Blackpool in September 1935. Shortly there-after, signing for £1,000, he had a spirited bash at solving City's centre-forward problem, at that time being wrestled with by centre-half Fred Sharman, but soon to be comprehensive-ly resolved by the advent of Jack Bowers. Accordingly, nothing daunted, Owen simply got out his passport again ...... It could be additionally noted that Owen's manager at each of Bray, Sligo and Distillery was Scotsman Bob Preston; while his coach at Lausanne was the legendary Jimmy Hogan. He was the 14-goal top-scorer for League of Ireland champions Shamrock in 1938/9.

Appearances:
FL: 16 apps. 7 gls.
FAC: 1 app. 1 gl.
Total: *17 apps. 8 gls.*

McNEILL, Ian McKeand

Role: Inside Forward
b. Bailleston, Glasgow, 24th February 1932

CAREER: Bridgetown Waverley/ 1950: Aberdeen/Mar 1956:CITY/Mar 1959: Brighton & Hove Albion/July 1962: Southend United/ July 1964:Dover.

Debut v Sheffield Wednesday (H) 2.4.56

Signed jointly with Joe O'Neil from City boss David Halliday's former club, inside-forward Ian soon made an impact at Filbert Street, contributing 18 goals to the 1957 Second Division championship campaign. He found goals, and a regular place, somewhat harder to come by in the top flight against the challenges of John Doherty, Jimmy Walsh and Bernie Kelly, but it was nonetheless Ian's invaluable strike at St.Andrews in the final game of 1957/8 which saved City from an immediate drop back. Later, on the South Coast, he adopted a deeper-lying schemer's role in 116 games for

Brighton and 41 for Southend. Ian entered management with Ross County (leading them to their first-ever Highland League championship in 1967); twice held the reins at Wigan Athletic (taking that club into League football in 1978); briefly managed Northwich Victoria; then bracketed a late-80s spell as Shrewsbury Town boss with periods as assistant manager at Chelsea and Millwall.

Appearances:
FL: 72 apps. 26 gls.
FAC: 4 apps. 1 gl.
Total: *76 apps. 27 gls.*

Ian McNeill

McWHIRTER, Douglas S.

Role: Right half
b. Erith, Kent, 13th August 1886
d. Plumstead, London, 14th October 1966

CAREER: Bromley/ Mar 1912:FOSSE/ July 1914:Southend United.

Debut v Bradford Park Avenue (H) 30.3.12

Douglas McWhirter

A valuable right-half during Fosse's pre-war years of steep decline, Douglas was a newly-capped amateur international when Fosse signed him, and went on to add mementos of three more England appearances, plus an Olympic football Final victor's medal (when the United Kingdom beat Denmark in Stockholm in July 1912), to that he had gained from Bromley's 1911 FA Amateur Cup Final win against Bishop Auckland. Having eventually turned professional, though, (and having played an additional four Southern League games for Southend as such), he was refused reinstatement as an amateur by the FA in 1921.

Appearances:
FL: 58 apps. 2 gls.
FAC: 2 apps. 0 gls.
Total: *60 apps. 2 gls.*

McWHIRTER, Peter

Role: Outside right
b. Dumbarton, 1872
d. 1943

CAREER: Toronto Scots/Chicago Thistles/ 1894:Morton/1895:Clyde/Oct 1895:FOSSE/ Aug 1896:Freemantle/cs 1897:Warmley/ cs 1898:Brighton United/Oct 1899:FOSSE.

Debut v Darwen (H) 26.10.1895

An outside-right signed from Scottish reserve-team football, Peter only briefly held his position during Fosse's second season in the League and, after joining a Southampton-based non-league club, was next heard of sailing for Canada in December 1896 to rejoin his emigrant family. He nevertheless swiftly returned, to link up with former Fosse inside-forward partners Manson and McArthur at Southern League Warmley and Brighton respectively. His second stint with Fosse was almost entirely played out in the reserves, and spiced only with an outing in Jack Walker's benefit friendly against Everton.

Appearances:
FL: 17 apps. 1 gl.
FAC: 1 app. 0 gls.
Total: *18 apps. 1 gl.*

MADDEN, Lawrence David

Role: Centre back
b. Bethnal Green, London, 28th September 1955

CAREER: am 1973:Arsenal/Manchester University/1975:Mansfield Town/Boston United/(1977-trials-Tottenham Hotspur)/Dec 1977:Charlton Athletic/Mar 1982:Millwall/Aug 1983:Sheffield Wednesday/(Jan 1991-loan-CITY)/(July 1991-trials-Derby County)/Aug 1991:Wolverhampton Wanderers/Sept 1993:Darlington/Oct 1993:Chesterfield.

Debut v West Ham United (A)
19.1.91

David Pleat's final signing, veteran defender Lawrie arrived on loan to cover for Steve Walsh's absence through suspension; became City's oldest-ever debutant at the age of 35; saw Pleat depart ten days later; was rendered idle for two snowed-off games; and then declined the offer of a month's extension to his stay at crisis-racked Filbert Street. By this time very much a member of Wednesday's shadow squad (having received a profitable testimonial from an Owls/Blades friendly in August 1990), the Londoner had already experienced a lengthy career notable for its stop-start elements. A youth-level team-mate of the likes of Brady, Stapleton and Rostron at Highbury, Lawrie turned down Arsenal's offer of professional terms to take a full-time degree course in Economics & Social Sciences, but impressed so much in university football that he made a League breakthrough as a non-contract player at Field Mill, playing in the final seven games of Mansfield's Division Four championship campaign of 1975. A spell under Howard Wilkinson at Boston was followed by trials at The Valley, and Lawrie's professional career then got underway in earnest. Charlton slipped from Division Two to Three and rose back again during his time there as a central defender (sent off at Filbert Street in 1980) and, following a comparatively uneventful year at The Den (when he nonetheless picked up a winner's medal from the Football League Trophy Final against Lincoln City), he joined the Owls on a free transfer in time to help them up into the top flight in his initial Hillsborough season. While contributing to keeping them in Division One until 1990, he had briefly formed a defensive pairing with Larry May, and also returned to university on a part-time basis to earn an MA degree in Leisure Management in 1988. Following his spell at Filbert Street, Lawrie appeared as substitute in Wednesday's League Cup Final win over Manchester United, and also turned out in the penultimate League match which assured the Owls of promotion, before moving free to Molineux and remarkably earning Player of the Year kudos from the Wolves fans in 1992. Less happily, he was sent off on his Chesterfield debut, but was still an occasional contributor to their Play-off qualification in 1994/5 (featuring in his 500th League game during that term); as well as a *Sheffield Star* columnist.

Appearances:
FL: 3 apps. 0 gls.
Total: *3 apps. 0 gls.*

Lawrie Madden

Les Major

MAJOR, Leslie Dennis

Role: Goalkeeper
b. Yeovil, Somerset, 25th January 1926

CAREER: Loughborough Corinthians/Brush Sports/am June 1943/pro Dec 1944:CITY/ May 1949:Plymouth Argyle.
Debut (WW2) v Aston Villa (H) 18.12.43; (postwar) v Plymouth Argyle (H) 25.8.47

Trained as a PT instructor and based at Loughborough, Les represented the RAF on several occasions as a goalkeeper, as well as playing wartime football for City and Notts County. On demob he became Gordon Bradley's rival for the City's custodianship, having one run of fifteen games at the beginning of 1947/8, and then being pitched into the anti-relegation scuffles of 1949, but being overlooked for the keeper's job at Wembley that year. Almost immediately, Les moved to Home Park for £1,800 and played 75 League games for the Pilgrims across seven seasons, before injury cut short his career. He returned to Leicestershire for a stint as a village publican, and is now living in Madeley, Staffs.

Appearances:
FL: 26 apps. 0 gls.
WW2: 28 apps. 0 gls.
Total: *54 apps. 0 gls.*

MANDY, Leonard Aubrey

Role: Goalkeeper
b. Transvaal, South Africa

CAREER: State Mines Club (Transvaal)/ Oct 1929:CITY/Jan 1930:State Mines Club.
Debut v Grimsby Town (H) 26.12.29

Briefly preferred to Joe Wright as stand-in keeper for Jim McLaren, South African amateur trialist Aubrey kept a clean sheet on his Boxing Day debut, but saw in the New Year with seven Sheffield United goals whistling past him, and left for home a couple of weeks later, citing his 'indifference' to the professional game. An official in the gold-mining industry, he was originally recommended to City by Reg Osborne and Arthur Chandler, who had faced him on the FA tour (representing both Transvaal and the South African national side) the previous summer. At the time of his retirement from football in March 1936, a Reuters report from Johannesburg described him as a motor-racing enthusiast and fine polo player.

Appearances:
FL: 3 apps. 0 gls.
Total: *3 apps. 0 gls.*

MANLEY, Malcolm Richardson

Role: Centre back / Midfield
b. Johnstone, Renfrewshire, 1st December 1949

CAREER: Johnstone Burgh/Jan 1967:CITY/ Dec 1973:Portsmouth.
Debut v Southampton (H) 20.4.68

Equally adept at the centre of the back four or playing just in front of it (and even once utilised as a scoring spearhead), Malcolm had his youthful versatility traded into a fairly regular position on the City substitute's bench - from where he joined the action in three crucial Cup ties in 1969, including the Wembley Final. When he did make the starting line-up on a more regular basis, Malcolm was living testimony to the redundancy of the conventional shirt numbering system, and some of his most useful defensive contributions to the 1971 promotion effort came when he was wearing a No.11. For a couple of First Division seasons he vied strongly with John Sjoberg and Alan Woollett for a pivotal berth, then lost his hard-won place with the advent of Malcolm Munro. A £50,000 move to Fratton Park looked promising, but a serious injury cut short Malcolm's career after only 11 League games for Pompey. Eventually, in April 1976, Portsmouth and City played a testimonial friendly on his behalf.

Appearances:
FL: 109 (11) apps. 5 gls.
FAC: 1 (4) apps. 0 gls.
LC: 11 apps. 1 gl.
Total: *121 (15) apps. 6 gls.*

MANSHIP, E.

Role: Inside left

CAREER: Dec 1902:FOSSE.

Debut v Burton United (H) 28.2.03

A local inside-left, unimpressive in his only senior game (a 0-1 home defeat). Even his main claim to fame for Fosse reserves, his goal in the first game of the 1903 County Cup Final, went for nothing when a dispute over replay dates led to opponents Whitwick White Cross being awarded a walkover.

Appearances:
FL: 1 app. 0 gls.
Total: *1 app. 0 gls.*

Malcolm Manley

David Manson

MANSON, David Garrioch

Role: Forward
b. Glasgow, 20th September 1871

CAREER:
1891:Ayr/Glasgow Thistle/cs 1894: Rotherham Town/ Apr 1895:FOSSE/ Oct 1896: Lincoln City/cs 1897:Warmley/ Feb 1899: Gravesend United/cs 1900:Coalville Town.

Debut v Burton Swifts (H) 7.9.1895

Initially tried by Fosse at outside-right, David met with more success in the inside position, and was re-signed for the 1896/7 season. After only one senior game that term, though, he was suspended as an internal disciplinary measure by the directorate, and swiftly packed his bags - only to find himself plunged into the midst of a Lincoln run of twelve consecutive defeats. He later joined fellow ex-Fossils Bishop and McWhirter for Warmley's brief Southern League honeymoon: promotion, then mid-season disbandment.

Appearances:
FL: 24 apps. 8 gls.
FAC: 1 app. 1 gl.
Total: *25 apps. 9 gls.*

MARSH, John Kirk

Role: Inside left
b. Mansfield, 8th October 1922

CAREER: Mansfield BC/Aug 1942:Notts
County/Sept 1948:Coventry City/
Mar 1950:CITY/Sept 1950:Chesterfield/
Aug 1951:Worksop Town.

Debut v Sheffield United (A) 18.3.50

One of three City acquisitions on the same
transfer-deadline day, Jack figured in the part-
exchange deal which took Ken Chisholm to
Highfield Road, and made his bow in a
reconstructed City front line that also included
Peter Small and Ian Wilson for the first time.
Luckless in front of goal by the end of
1949/50, the inside-left started the following
season with a couple of double strikes, but
then had to drop out to accomodate Arthur
Rowley's shift from the No.9 to the No.10
shirt. Jack had never really been able to
recapture the burst of scoring form he had
found alongside the inspirational Tommy
Lawton at Meadow Lane, and drifted out of
the League game altogether in 1951.

Appearances:
FL: 14 apps. 4 gls.
Total: *14 apps. 4 gls.*

Jack Marsh

MARSHALL, Arthur George

Role: Inside left
b. Liverpool, 1881

CAREER: Crewe Alexandra/May 1901:FOSSE/
Jan 1902:Stockport County/May 1902:
Manchester United/May 1903:Portsmouth/
cs 1904:Hull City.

Debut v Woolwich Arsenal (A) 7.9.01

Arthur Marshall

Reputedly a highly
promising inside-left
with Fosse, Arthur
nonetheless moved
on immediately after
the club signed
Jimmy Stevenson,
then claimed one of
his pair of Stockport
League goals when
City went down to
them at Edgeley
Park in March 1902.
By this time he had
already been tried at
full back, though, and it was as a defender
that he soon joined United, where his record
was restricted to a mere six League outings.
Arthur then made only a solitary appearance
in the Southern League for Pompey before
signing for the newly-formed Hull, who
played only friendlies in the season prior to
their League election, including one on 19th
September against Fosse.

Appearances:
FL: 15 apps. 5 gls.
FAC: 1 app. 0 gls.
Total: *16 apps. 5 gls.*

MATTHEWS, Paul William

Role: Outside right / Midfield
b. Leicester, 30th September 1946

CAREER: app Aug 1963/pro Aug 1964:CITY/
(Sept 1972-loan-Southend United)/Dec 1972:
Mansfield Town/Oct 1977:Rotherham United/
(Mar 1979-loan-Northampton Town)/Heanor
Town/Oadby Town.

Debut v Aston Villa (H) 19.4.65

Deceptively frail-looking, Paul initially
developed as an orthodox outside-right and
stood in several times for Jackie Sinclair before

seeming to drop out of the senior reckoning for a year or so. He returned to the fray, however, in City's desperate late attempts to beat the drop in 1969, and came closest to establishing a regular first team place in midfield during the following season, when Frank O'Farrell asked him to assume the nigh-impossible task of replacing Davie Gibson. His mature playmaking skills were better valued, however, at Field Mill, where in the course of a 124-game stay he helped prompt the Stags from the Fourth to the Second Division. Nonetheless, in retrospect, it is possible to pinpoint a December 1971 knee injury as being the most limiting factor to Paul's career: nowadays he unfortunately has little movement in the joint.

Appearances:
FL: 56 (5) apps. 5 gls.
FAC: 4 apps. 0 gls.
LC: 6 (3) apps. 0 gls.
Total: *66 (8) apps. 5 gls.*

MAUCHLEN, Alister Henry

Role: Midfield
b. Kilwinning, Ayrshire, 29th June 1960

CAREER: Irvine Meadow/ 1978:Kilmarnock/Oct 1982:Motherwell/ Aug 1985:CITY/(Mar 1992-loan-Leeds United)/July 1992:Heart of Midlothian/ Oct 1993:Glenavon/1995:Ballymena United.

Debut v Oxford United (A) 24.8.85 (sub)

A terrier-like, ball-winning midfielder, Ali was originally a Jock Wallace purchase for Motherwell, then, like Gary McAllister, a key member of the 'Well team which won the Scottish First Division championship and took Celtic to a replay in the Scottish Cup semi-final in 1985. The pair moved together for a quarter of a million pounds to Leicester, and neither looked out of place in the English top flight, with Ali settling to

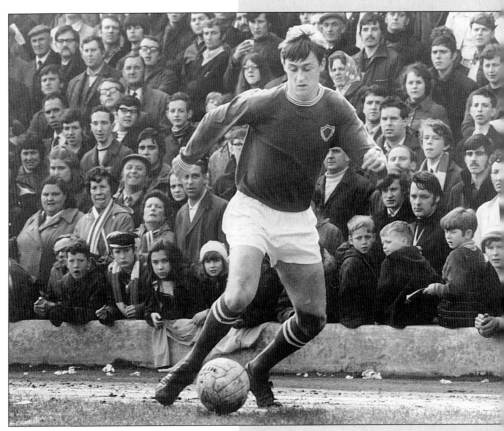

Paul Matthews

the more defensively-inclined role, and linking well with Ian Wilson in a neat, if diminutive, partnership. His goal against Newcastle in the final game of 1985/6 helped keep City up, and he shed a lot of honest sweat in toiling vainly to repeat the feat a year later. Bryan Hamilton had tried him a few times as an emergency full-back, and Ali settled in that position when David Pleat arrived; or at least used it effectively as a starting block for his forays forward. Very much a crowd favourite for his intense commitment, Ali took on player/coach responsibilities under Gordon Lee (figuring in the last-ditch relegation reprieve game against Oxford United), but returned to the ranks on Brian Little's appointment. His loan spell at Leeds was an in-reserve insurance policy for their Championship run-in of 1992, and he didn't actually get a senior game again until being freed to Hearts. Later, on a seven-month loan stint in Ireland, Ali helped inspire Glenavon to within one game of what would have been their first championship win in 34 years; then, a few months into the following season after a full transfer, briefly assumed their caretaker managership.

Appearances:
FL: 228 (11) apps. 11 gls.
FAC: 6 (1) apps. 0 gls.
LC: 17 (1) apps. 1 gl.
FMC: 9 apps. 0 gls.
Total: *260 (13) apps. 12 gls.*

Ali Mauchlen

Arthur Maw

MAW, Arthur

Role: Inside forward
b. Frodingham, nr.Scunthorpe,
29th December 1909
d. Frodingham, 20th April 1964

CAREER: Frodingham Athletic/
Scunthorpe United/Mar 1929:Notts County/
July 1932:CITY/July 1939:Scunthorpe United.
Debut v Wolverhampton Wanderers (H) 7.1.33

Always known as 'Digger', inside-forward
Arthur got off to a good start with City,
topping the 1932/3 scorers' list with 14 goals
from only 18 games, and maintaining his form
at the beginning of the following season at
such a level that he was chosen as travelling
reserve for both the Football League against
the Irish League and England's full
international in Belfast in October. It was poor
reward for his consistently dangerous efforts
during City's mid-30s struggles (top scorer
again in 1936) that he should miss out on the
Second Division championship medals in
1937, his leanest season; but Arthur bounced
back to commit his foraging skills to the club
until just before the outbreak of war - during
which he also guested for Grimsby Town.

> **Appearances:**
> *FL: 179 apps. 58 gls.*
> *FAC: 10 apps. 6 gls.*
> **Total:** *189 apps. 64 gls.*

MAY, Lawrence Charles

Role: Centre back
b. Sutton Coldfield, 26th December 1958

CAREER: app July 1975/pro Sept 1976:CITY/
(Apr 1978-loan-New England Tea Men)/Aug
1983:Barnsley/Feb 1987:Sheffield Wednesday/
Sept 1988:Brighton & Hove Albion.
Debut v Bristol City (H) 26.3.77

Given the briefest of teenage opportunities by
both Jimmy Bloomfield and Frank McLintock,
Larry began to exhibit his central defensive
skills and strength most forcefully under Jock
Wallace's management: supplying the pace in
a fine partnership with John O'Neill, and
getting forward to claim some vital goals in
the promotion seasons of 1980 (including the

Larry May

championship clincher at Brisbane Road) and 1983, and on the Cup semi-final trail of 1982. Larry's aerial prowess and acute reading of the game were much appreciated by a Leicester crowd that was accordingly somewhat baffled when Gordon Milne accepted £110,000 from Barnsley for his talents on the very eve of 1983/4. Three and a half years and 122 League games later, Larry's transfer value had almost doubled as the Owls swooped for his signature and returned him to the First Division stage, and the price was again high when the newly-promoted Seagulls took on Larry to plug their leaky Second Division defence. Sadly, a recurrent knee injury enforced Larry's premature retirement in September 1989, and his stint as cash-strapped Brighton's reserve coach ended in redundancy in November 1993; though he stayed in Sussex as coach to local club Ringmer.

Appearances:
FL: 180 (7) apps. 12 gls.
FAC: 12 apps. 3 gls.
LC: 8 apps. 0 gls.
Total: *200 (7) apps. 15 gls.*

MEARNS, Frederick Charles

Role: Goalkeeper
b. Sunderland, 31st March 1879
d. Sunderland, 21st January 1931

CAREER: Selbourne/Jan 1901:Sunderland/ May 1902:Kettering/Mar 1903:Tottenham Hotspur/May 1904:Bradford City/cs 1905: Barrow/Southern United/Grays United/ May 1906:Bury/cs 1908:Hartlepools United/ cs 1909:Barnsley/Jan 1911:FOSSE/cs 1913: Newcastle City/Oct 1919:Sunderland West End.
Debut v Glossop (H) 11.2.11

A well-travelled goalkeeper who started his senior career as understudy to the long-serving Scottish international Teddy Doig at Roker Park, Fred had sampled the game at numerous levels before joining Fosse in an exchange deal which took forward George Travers to Barnsley. Kettering and Spurs were of equal Southern League status when he assisted them between the sticks (reputedly saving 19 penalties during his Kettering season!), Bradford City utilised him at Second

Division level and Bury in the top flight, while Hartlepools United had just been formed and admitted to the Northern League when Fred signed for them. He was Barnsley's keeper in both games of the 1910 FA Cup Final (lost to Newcastle), and gave Fosse fine service as a hefty last liner for two and a half years, after which he moved homeward into the North Eastern League. He later also acted as trainer to Durham City, but was working as a joiner when he died following a building-site accident. A 1903 testimony read: 'A cool, calculating and level-headed player, wonderfully active, and clears low shots with ease'.

Fred Mearns

Appearances:
FL: 68 apps. 0 gls.
FAC: 2 apps. 0 gls.
Total: *70 apps. 0 gls.*

MEEK, George

Role: Winger
b. Glasgow, 15th February 1934

CAREER: Thorniewood United/Hamilton Academicals/Aug 1952:Leeds United/(Jan 1954-loan-Walsall)/July 1960:CITY/July 1961:Walsall/Mar 1965:Dudley Town/cs 1965:Rushall Olympic.

Debut v Blackpool (H) 20.8.60

Almost invariably described by contemporary commentators as a 'big-hearted little 'un', George wasn't one to let his limited stature in any way diminish his effectiveness as a darting winger, and he was a regular thorn in City's flesh for Leeds throughout the 50s. He had 230 League games under his belt by the time Matt Gillies brought him to Leicester, but he struggled to displace either Howard Riley

or Gordon Wills, and was soon grateful to return for a second spell at Fellows Park, encompassing Walsall's heady Second Division days. George eventually played on in West Midlands football until the age of 50; he was last noted in 1992 as a Walsall postman.

Appearances:
FL: 13 apps. 0 gls.
Total: *13 apps. 0 gls.*

MELROSE, James Millsopp

Role: Striker
b. Glasgow, 7th October 1958

CAREER: Eastercraigs/1975:Partick Thistle/July 1980:CITY/Sept 1982:Coventry City/Aug 1983:Celtic/(Sept 1984-loan-Wolverhampton Wanderers)/Nov 1984: Manchester City/Mar 1986:Charlton Athletic/Sept 1987:Leeds United/Feb 1988:Shrewsbury

George Meek

Jimmy Melrose

tenure. Maintaining a decent scoring record, Jimmy nonetheless subsequently became something of a wanderer, but at Celtic he made substitute appearances in the Finals of both Scottish knockout competitions of 1984, and he assisted both Manchester City and Charlton into the First Division. Indeed, his goals for the latter in the 1987 promotion/relegation Play-offs did a lot to keep them there. While at Shrewsbury (initially on loan), Jimmy was the victim of an on-field assault by Swindon's Chris Kamara that eventually saw the latter player become the first to face legal prosecution for such an act.

Appearances:
FL: 57 (15) apps. 21 gls.
FAC: 2 (6) apps. 4 gls.
LC: 6 apps. 1 gl.
Total: *65 (21) apps. 26 gls.*

MERCER, John Thompson

Role: Outside right
b. Belfast, 1879
d. January 1947

CAREER: Linfield Swifts/Distillery/May 1899:Brighton United/Feb 1900:FOSSE/cs 1900:Linfield/Feb 1903:Distillery/Oct 1903:Derby County.
Debut v Chesterfield 24.2.1900

A 'dashing' Irish international outside-right (capped four times before first sampling English football, and a further seven after leaving Fosse), Johnny had impressed in Brighton United's terminally struggling Southern League line-up, but failed to bolster Fosse's still-viable promotion prospects after his mid-season arrival. Further glory back in Belfast (including two Irish Cup-winning medals from the Finals of 1902 and 1903) encouraged Derby to give him another chance at League level, but a more experienced Johnny was only a little more successful with the Rams in Division One (26 apps; 1 gl), though he did assist them to the 1904 FA Cup semi-finals. He later had lengthy spells as a director at each of Glentoran and Distillery, and was chairman of the Irish League in 1941/2.

Appearances:
FL: 9 apps. 2 gls.
Total: *9 apps. 2 gls.*

Town/Aug 1990:Macclesfield Town/Oct 1990: Curzon Ashton/1991:Halesowen Harriers.
Debut v Ipswich Town (H) 16.8.80

Capped eight times at Scotland Under-21 level, and once for the Scottish League, Jimmy developed a nippy striking profile at Firhill, and became City's third £250,000 buy when Jock Wallace judged him a likely foil for target man Alan Young. He initially struggled to adapt to the pace of the First Division - as did many of his youthful teammates in 1980/1 - but picked up a few useful goals as City belatedly battled against their relegation fate, and signed off his first term with a cheeky hat-trick at Norwich which doomed the Canaries as well. Jimmy developed into a crowd favourite during the next season, and many were critical that his enforced role as 'super-sub' kept him for too long out of the important action (like the FA Cup semi-final against Spurs); while almost all were vocal in their condemnation of the exchange deal involving Tommy English which Gordon Milne engineered early in his Filbert Street

MERCER, Stanley

Role: Centre forward
*b. Birkenhead, 11th
September 1919*

CAREER: Blackpool
Services/am Jan 1944:
Blackpool/am July
1944/pro Nov 1944:
CITY/Jan 1947:
Accrington Stanley/
Oct 1948:Mansfield
Town.

*Debut (WW2) v Walsall
(A) 16.9.44 (scored once);
(competitive) v Chelsea (A)
FAC 5.1.46*

A handily aggressive centre-
forward with a decent wartime strike
rate for City, Stan also guested for
Accrington (for whom he scored a hat-trick to
celebrate his Leicester pro status), Arsenal and
Manchester United while serving as a PT
instructor in the RAF, and at one point

Stan Mercer

represented the RAF
against Portugal in
Lisbon. Despite top-
scoring in the
interim 1945/6
season, he hardly got
a break at Filbert
Street (as Jack Lee's
understudy) when
peace returned, and
moved on for £750.
A total of 46 goals in
84 League and Cup
games followed,
until a knee injury
curtailed his Field
Mill career. He stayed on as Mansfield trainer
and then, between 1953 and 1955, occupied
the manager's chair there, in succession to
George Jobey. Later moving back north to
Lytham, Stan worked as an administrator in
the Premium Bonds office until his retirement.

Appearances:
FL: 1 app. 0 gls.
FAC: 2 apps. 0 gls.
WW2: 27 apps. 13 gls.
Total: *30 apps. 13 gls.*

Robert Messer

MESSER, Robert

Role: Outside right
b. Edinburgh

CAREER:
Broxburn
Shamrock/Kings
Park/Bo'ness/
May 1910:FOSSE
/cs 1911:
Broxburn United.

*Debut v Clapton
Orient (A) 24.9.10*

A tall young
Scottish outside-right,
one of no less than nine
players tried in that
problematic position during
1910/11, and not a conspicuous
success. Strangely, each of Robert's
three known senior clubs over the border
would later (briefly) hold Scottish League
status, though none did at the time he played
for them.

Appearances:
FL: 2 apps. 0 gls.
Total: *2 apps. 0 gls.*

MIDDLETON, Francis

Role: Outside left
b. Whitwick, Leics, c 1881

CAREER: 1896:Whitwick White Cross/
Nov 1901:Derby County/Aug 1906:FOSSE.
*Debut v Burslem Port Vale (A) 1.9.06
(scored once)*

An outstanding outside-left whose top-class
promise was first signalled when Derby paid
£100 to his local Midland League club for his
signature, Frank stepped straight into the
Rams' First Division front line alongside the
near-legendary likes of Steve Bloomer. After
65 League games he had confirmed his chief
role as provider by scoring only three goals,
yet upon moving to Leicester he notched one
counter in each of his first four games before
suffering injury. Frank contributed some fine
wing performances in the first half of Fosse's
promotion season - being described as 'a
capital hand at centring' - but was sorely
distressed by the tragic death of his young

Above: Frank Middleton

Right: Jack Middleton

child in January 1908, and dropped out of contention soon after.

Appearances:
FL: 49 apps. 10 gls.
FAC: 3 apps. 0 gls.
Total: 52 apps. 10 gls.

MIDDLETON, John

Role: Inside right
b. Sunderland, 19th April 1898
d. Aldershot, 16th January 1974

CAREER: Herrington Swifts/Lambton Star/ May 1922:CITY/May 1925:Queen's Park Rangers/July 1927:Aldershot.
Debut v Bury (H) 28.4.23

Elevated from Wearside League football, Jack was a skilful reserve inside-right who deputised for several of City's stars in the early 20s, but could never quite claim a regular Filbert Street role. He was a scorer for the reserves in their 1924 County Cup Final replay win, by 5-1 over Barwell United. With QPR, he occasionally played with former City team-mates George Hebden and Hugh

Richmond, while himself converting to a wing-half role for a 54-game, 9-goal record. Jack returned to Aldershot in the mid-30s as trainer/coach.

Appearances:
FL: 12 apps. 3 gls.
FAC: 1 app. 0 gls.
Total: 13 apps. 3 gls.

MILBURN, Stanley

Role: Right back
b. Ashington, Northumberland,
22nd October 1926

CAREER: Ashington/Jan 1947:Chesterfield/ Feb 1952:CITY/Jan 1959:Rochdale/cs 1965: Spotland Methodists/TBA (Rochdale).
Debut v Sheffield United (A) 22.3.52

A member of the remarkable Geordie footballing dynasty of Milburn's and Charlton's, Stan followed three of his brothers in exhibiting an affinity for the full -back position, and took little time at Saltergate in impressing the various selection panels who honoured him with one England 'B' cap, two Football League

Stan Milburn

appearances, and a place on the FA XI tour of Canada, all in 1950. Norman Bullock expended £10,000 in bringing him to Leicester, where his sterling defensive work was a feature for seven seasons, including the promotion campaigns of 1954 and 1957. Stan was an ever-present in the latter championship season, scoring his only City goal in a 5-4 win at Bury, and keeping Irish international Willie Cunningham sidelined. Then, after bowing out of the First Division fray at an age when many players would be contemplating retirement, he took his boundless enthusiasm to little Rochdale, playing on for seven more seasons, skippering his side to the 1962 League Cup Final, and completing his first-class career with an aggregate of 589 League games. Characteristically, though, Stan was still turning out in local football in Rochdale in the early 80s!

Appearances:
FL: 173 apps. 1 gl.
FAC: 10 apps. 0 gls.
Total: *183 apps. 1 gl.*

❏ FOX FACT: *At Stamford Bridge in December 1954, during City's 1-3 First Division defeat by Chelsea, Stan Milburn and Jack Froggatt contrived, in attempting a clearance, to strike the ball simultaneously into their own net, and were officially credited with a joint own goal: a unique occurrence at League level.*

MILES, Idris

Role: Outside right
b. Neath, 2nd August 1908
d. Dudley, October qtr 1983

CAREER: Radnor Road FC/Nov 1930:Cardiff City/May 1932:Yeovil & Petters United/ Oct 1932:CITY/May 1934:Clapton Orient/ May 1937:Exeter City/cs 1938:Worcester City.
Debut v Everton (H) 22.10.32 (scored once)

A tiny right-winger who had been released by Cardiff after only three League games, Idris briefly assumed Hughie Adcock's position with City, notching a debut goal in a 2-2 draw at Goodison, but suffered appalling fortune in twice breaking his collarbone during the course of his first Filbert Street season. Failing to get another chance, he moved on in the part-exchange deal with Orient that brought fellow-Welshman Tommy Mills to Leicester

Idris Miles

(and which re-united Idris with his ex-Yeovil boss David Pratt), and for the club then playing at Lea Bridge Speedway he totted up 73 League games across three seasons, scoring six times. He was goalless after 10 outings for Exeter; then joined Worcester as they switched from the Birmingham League to the Southern League. Idris's younger brother joined City as an inside-left in August 1935 after two seasons with Ashford, but moved on a year later to Barry Town.

Appearances:
FL: 7 apps. 1 gl.
Total: *7 apps. 1 gl.*

MILLER, William

Role: Forward

CAREER: Derby Junction/Burton Wanderers/ cs 1893:FOSSE/cs 1895:Kettering/cs 1899: Northampton Town.
Debut v Burton Wanderers (H) ML 9.9.1893

An inside- or centre-forward who impressed sufficiently as an ever-present in the final Midland League season to be retained for the first shot at the Second Division. William's goal tally in the latter sphere should have been

William Miller with the 1894 Kettering Charity Cup.

higher: he missed the first penalty awarded to Fosse in the League, against Newcastle in October 1894 - it would have given him a hat-trick! On dropping back into Midland League football, he assisted Kettering to their first-ever championship in 1896, and later continued at this level with the Cobblers.

Appearances:
FL: 10 apps. 2 gls.
FAC: 9 apps. 5 gls.
ML: 20 apps. 7 gls.
Total: *39 apps. 14 gls.*

MILLS, Andrew

Role: Right back
b. Knighton, Radnorshire, 15th December 1877

CAREER: Knighton/May 1897:Blackburn Rovers/cs 1898:Swindon Town/cs 1899:Brighton United/May 1900:FOSSE/cs 1905:Shrewsbury Town.

Debut v Stockport County (H) 1.9.1900

Andy Mills

A versatile defender who settled best in Fosse's right-back position in partnerships with old hands George Swift or Walter Robinson, Andy ironically came closest to international recognition just as he was fading from the first-team picture at Leicester. In fact he was stretchered out of the Welsh trial game of February 1903, and subsequently made only one further Fosse appearance. Two of Andy's goals were penalties; the other a lofted shot from his own half, against Burnley in September 1902! He had originally joined Fosse upon Brighton United's liquidation, and had previously had two outings in the top flight with Blackburn.

Appearances:
FL: 64 apps. 3 gls.
FAC: 3 apps. 0 gls.
Total: *67 apps. 3 gls.*

MILLS, Gary Roland

Role: Midfield / Full back
b. Northampton, 11th November 1961

CAREER: Long Buckby/pro Nov 1978: Nottingham Forest/(Mar 1982-loan-Seattle Sounders)/(Oct 1982-loan-Derby County)/ (Apr 1983-loan-Seattle Sounders)/Aug 1987:Notts County/Mar 1989:CITY/Sept 1994:Notts County.

Debut v Walsall (H) 4.3.89

The son of former Northampton stalwart Roly Mills, Gary was a schoolboy star at both rugby and soccer, whose choice of the latter sport was almost instantly rewarded with a first-team berth at Forest. His prodigious impact on Trentside saw him playing in both the First Division and Europe while still only 16; earning a winner's medal from Forest's second European Cup triumph in 1980 while still a teenager; and picking up two England Under-21 caps to add to his youth international honours. The attacking midfielder later fell foul, however, of the League's attempts to tighten up the regulations regarding loan and transfer deals with American clubs in the NASL (where Gary played in the cumulative

Gary Mills

showpiece Soccer Bowl of 1982, when Seattle finally bowed to New York Cosmos), and a combination of such difficulties and severe injury problems kept him away from the City Ground limelight for some time. By the time he made the short move to Meadow Lane, Gary had been somewhat eclipsed by a new generation of Brian Clough discoveries, but his consistency for the Magpies encouraged David Pleat to regard him as a likely belated replacement for Peter Weir at Filbert Street, and he became a City player in a part-exchange deal involving Phil Turner. After a brief acclimatisation, Gary settled to a key role on City's right, getting forward effectively from either a middle-line or attacking full-back slot, and exciting with both his trademark diagonal dribbles and fine crossing control. Reliability as well as flair marked his mature game, and Gary won the club's Player of the Year award at the end of each of the 1989/90 and 1991/2 campaigns. In the interim he successively assumed the team and club captaincies, and for a time shouldered penalty-taking duties; while his ever-present seasonal tally of 61 appearances in 1991/2 set a new club record. A slight lapse in form and a series of injuries bit into Gary's last two terms with City, though he was a popular choice to lead out the team at Wembley in 1994 in Brian Little's stead, when his radio commentary contributions at the time of Steve Walsh's winner immediately entered Leicester folklore! Unfortunately, Gary's £50,000 departure from City's Premiership struggle only led him into an analogous position with Notts County, duly relegated from Division One in 1995; though he made another playing appearance at Wembley in the Magpies' Anglo-Italian Cup victory over Ascoli in March.

Appearances:
PL: 1 app. 0 gls.
FL: 194 (5) apps. 16 gls.
FAC: 7 apps. 0 gls.
LC: 9 (1) apps. 1 gl.
FMC: 7 apps. 0 gls.
AIC: 2 apps. 0 gls.
P/O: 6 apps. 0 gls.
Total: *226 (6) apps. 17 gls.*

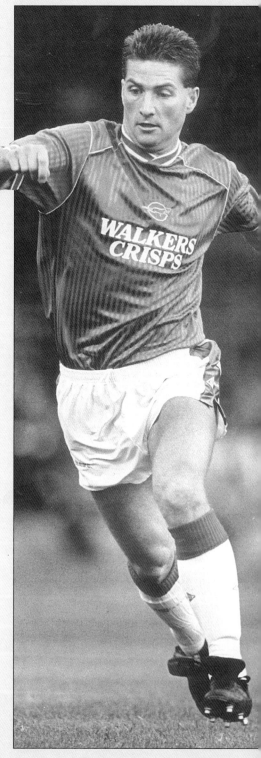

Gary Mills

MILLS, Thomas James

Role: Inside forward
b. Ton Pentre, 28th December 1911
d. Bristol, 15th May 1979

CAREER: Ton Pentre BC/Trocadero
Restaurant/Sept 1929:Clapton Orient/
May 1934: CITY/May 1936:Bristol Rovers/
cs 1939: Chester.

Debut v Everton (H) 3.9.34 (scored once)

The scorer of one of Wales' winning goals
against England at Newcastle in November
1933, creative inside-forward Tommy doubled
his tally of caps to four while on City's books,
but struggled with several less nominally
illustrious rivals for a regular place in the
club's relegation-bound side, and then failed
to make his mark in the initial attempt to
climb back. His £575 move to Eastville, in
company with David Bruce, revived his career
a little, and he managed 99 League games
(17 goals) for Rovers before retirement in 1939.
Though capped as a
schoolboy,
Tommy believed
his footballing
chance had
passed by
when he took
successive
jobs as a
miner and
in a London
hotel, but he
was spotted by
Orient playing

for the Sunday staff team of the latter. His final
games for the O's were played in tandem with
veteran goalscorer David Halliday, later to
manage Leicester. Tommy's death came as a
result of being knocked down by a lorry.

Appearances:
FL: 17 apps. 5 gls.
FAC: 1 app. 0 gls.
Total: *18 apps. 5 gls.*

Billy Mills

MILLS, William

Role: Inside forward
*b. Hackney, London,
1891*

CAREER: Barnet
Alston/Vicar of
Wakefield FC/
Dec 1911:FOSSE.

*Debut v Stockport
County (H) 16.12.11
(scored once)*

An enthusiastic inside-forward who cost Fosse
a £5 signing-on fee from London junior
football, Billy felt the wrath of the game's
hidebound establishment almost as soon as he
arrived -receiving a draconian two months
suspension for the heinous offence of having
played Sunday football in London after
registering with Leicester. Thankfully not
overly discouraged by such pettiness, Billy
continued to assist Fosse regularly until the
outbreak of war (being top scorer in the
disastrous 1914/15 re-election season), and
very occasionally, while on leave, during it.
Unfortunately, he suffered serious wounds -
losing a foot after an aerial bombardment - in
the conflict in France; and City played a
benefit friendly on his behalf in October
1919, against a Select XI, which
raised just over £100.

Appearances:
FL: 77 apps. 20 gls.
FAC: 2 apps. 1 gl.
WW1: 2 apps. 1 gl.
Total: *81 apps. 22 gls.*

Tommy Mills

MILNES, Frederick Houghton

Role: Right back
b. Wortley, Yorkshire, 25th January 1878
d. Leeds, 1st July 1946

CAREER: Sheffield Wycliffe/Sheffield Club/
(May 1902:Sheffield United)/(Oct 1904: West
Ham United)/(Dec 1905:Tottenham Hotspur)/
(Mar 1906:Manchester United)/(1906:
Reading)/(Feb 1907:FOSSE)/(Ilford)/
(Sept 1908:Norwich City).

Debut v Lincoln City (A) 27.4.07

A classy amateur international right-back
(capped in the 15-0 cakewalk over France in
Paris in November 1906), Fred's primary
allegiance was to the long-established
Sheffield Club - for whom he scored a penalty
in their 1904 FA Amateur Cup Final win over
Ealing. Always ready to lend his assistance on
a non-contract basis to almost any senior club
who asked, (after a March 1903 League bow
for the Blades, in what was also Jimmy
Donnelly's debut for that club), he had short
spells with all those mentioned above - and
possibly more besides - and also represented
the combined Sheffield team in their then-
annual inter-city prestige matches against
Glasgow. For Fosse he only turned out in a
home friendly against Stockport County and
in the above League match, yet the local press
reaction to his appearance was little short of
ecstatic. Fred also played at Filbert Street in
1907 as a member of the Pilgrims, an amateur
combination about to tour Canada and the
United States, against a Leicestershire XI.

Appearances:
FL: 1 app. 0 gls.
Total: *1 app. 0 gls.*

MITCHELL, J.

Role: Left half
b. Waterford, November 1890

CAREER: Royal Field Artillery/(Apr 1912:
FOSSE)/(Mar 1913:FOSSE).

Debut v Leeds City (H) 27.4.12

A serving bombardier (in the 47th Brigade,
RFA) who occasionally turned out for Fosse
reserves when stationed nearby, and was
given a senior break at left-half in the final
game of 1911/12, along with fellow squaddie

Sharpley, Mitchell also scored a week later in
the friendly played for the Titanic Disaster
Fund, a 3-3 draw with a Leicestershire XI.
Something of an all-rounder, he also played
football for Aldershot Command against
Southampton (and for Fosse reserves in the
County Cup Final victory over Holwell Works
in April 1914), and had represented the Irish
Army at both rugby and hockey. During
WW1, he wrote as Lieutenant Mitchell to
Fosse secretary Harry Linney, asking for
footballs to be forwarded to his battery at the
front.

Appearances:
FL: 1 app. 0 gls.
Total: *1 app. 0 gls.*

MITTEN, John

Role: Outside left
b. Manchester, 30th March 1941

CAREER: am 1957:Mansfield Town/am 1958/
pro Sept 1960:Newcastle United/Sept 1961:
CITY/(Apr 1963-trials-Manchester United)/
Aug 1963:Coventry City/Jan 1967:Plymouth
Argyle/July 1968:Exeter City/Aug 1971:Bath
City/Tiverton Town.

John Mitten

Debut v West Ham United (A) 30.9.61

The son of former Manchester United and Fulham player Charlie Mitten, and honoured by England at both schoolboy and youth levels, John was managed and blooded by his father at both Mansfield and Newcastle - and hardly endeared himself to a Geordie crowd already whispering of nepotism when he missed a penalty on his Magpies debut as a 17-year-old. He came to Leicester initially on trial, being signed permanently only after his first-team debut at outside-left, playing in four senior competitions in a four-month spell, and then having his City progress comprehensively blocked by the arrival of Mike Stringfellow. In the meantime, John was also making his mark in Leicestershire cricket as a useful wicket-keeper, with 14 first-class matches to his name between 1961 and 1963. Eventually he joined Jimmy Hill's Sky Blue revival at Coventry, and then settled for several seasons of West Country football as a useful midfielder.

Appearances:
FL: 12 apps. 0 gls.
FAC: 1 app. 0 gls.
LC: 1 app. 1 gl.
Eur: 2 apps. 0 gls.
Total: *16 apps. 1 gl.*

MOHAN, Nicholas

Role: Centre back
b. Middlesbrough, 6th October 1970

CAREER: YT/pro Nov 1987: Middlesbrough/(Sept 1992-loan-Hull City)/July 1994:CITY/ July 1995:Bradford City.

Debut v Newcastle United (H) 21.8.94

Primarily a central defender, but also utilised occasionally at full-back by his hometown club, Nicky made his Boro debut during their 1988/9 slide from Division One, and experienced promotion and relegation again during his stint as an Ayresome squad player. He clearly impressed former Boro coach Brian Little during this period, though, for the City boss made

strenuous attempts to sign him before the 1994 deadline day and, having failed, went back with £300,000 for the player after promotion had been sealed. Nicky's immediate impact with City could have been happier: he netted a Filbert Street own goal within two minutes of the start of the pre-season showpiece game against Rapid Bucharest! Indeed, his entire Premiership experience could only be adjudged a disappointment, with a sending-off at Forest interrupting his acclimatisation, and only intermittent selections at the heart of City's shaky five-man defensive line preceding his placing on the open-to-offers list in May 1995, following confirmation of relegation. He subsequently moved to Bradford for £225,000 in the summer.

Appearances:
PL: 23 apps. 0 gls.
FAC: 1 app. 0 gls.
LC: 2 apps. 0 gls.
Total: *26 apps. 0 gls.*

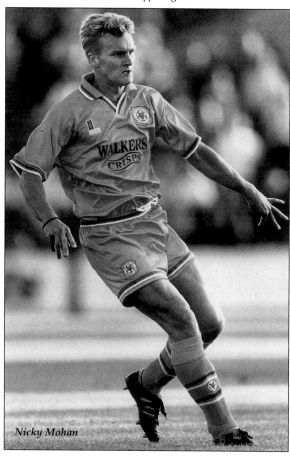

Nicky Mohan

MOODY, Herbert B.

Role: Centre forward
b. Luton, 1880

CAREER: Luton Stanley/
cs 1901:Luton Town/Aug
1905:FOSSE/cs 1907:Luton
Town/June 1912:Millwall.

Debut v Clapton Orient (H)
2.9.05 (scored once)

Six times chosen for the
Southern League represen-
tative side between 1910
and the outbreak of war,
this clever inside- or centre-
forward, seemingly
alternately known as Bert or
Harry, was equally adept at creating and
collecting chances; though his most prolific
scoring days were still in front of him after
two seasons in an improving Fosse side
building towards its promotion challenge. In
both his first spell with Luton and his Fosse
days, he benefited enormously from the
tutelage of Jimmy Blessington, and was also
able to exploit for Fosse his familiarity with
Jamie Durrant's style and strengths. His debut
goal was the first conceded at League level by
Clapton Orient, playing their initial game in
the competition at Filbert Street, and drawing
2-2. He left Millwall just before they became
one of the founder members of Division Three
in 1920, having totalled over 350 Southern
League games in his career, and having
claimed about 125 goals.

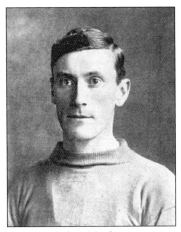
Bert Moody

Appearances:
FL: 54 apps. 11 gls.
FAC: 1 app. 1 gl.
Total: *55 apps. 12 gls.*

MORALEE, Matthew

Role: Inside forward
b. Mexborough, Yorkshire, 21st February 1912
d. Doncaster, Yorkshire, September 1991

CAREER: Ormsby United/Apr 1929:Denaby
United/May 1930:Gainsborough Trinity/
Jan 1931:Grimsby Town/Oct 1936:Aston Villa/
Nov 1937:CITY/July 1939:Shrewsbury Town/
Denaby United.

Debut v Preston North End (H) 13.11.37

An intelligent, prompting
inside-forward who never
quite bore out his initial
promise, Matt came to
Leicester effectively a year
late. His Grimsby boss
Frank Womack, accepting
the Filbert Street
managerial vacancy,
proposed bringing Matt
with him, but only a day
later was ordered by his
old directorate to oversee
the player's sale to Villa
(then suffering the
ignominy of their first-ever
season in Division Two). In
fact, Matt got few breaks as
Villa failed to rebound
immediately, and when he did belatedly
reunite with Womack, it was primarily a
hectic, eventually unsuccessful battle to help
keep City in Division One which he joined.
Despite a few sparkling displays, he was
released into Midland League football on the
eve of war. Appearances as a guest player for
Grimsby, Bradford City, Doncaster Rovers and
Rotherham United followed, before Matt saw
out his active career back at Denaby.˙

Appearances:
FL: 38 apps. 6 gls.
FAC: 5 apps. 0 gls.
Total: *43 apps. 6 gls.*

Matt Moralee

MORAN, Edward

Role: Inside right
*b. Cleland, Lanarkshire,
20th July 1930*

CAREER: Cleland BC/
Sept 1947:CITY/
Oct 1951:Stockport
County/Feb 1957:
Rochdale/Sept 1958:
Crewe Alexandra/
Aug 1959:Flint Town
United/1963:Glossop
(p/coach).

*Debut v Grimsby Town
(H) 2.4.49*

Another of the skilful
young Scots snapped up
in Johnny Duncan's
regular cross-border
raids of the immediate
postwar years
(reputedly from under
the nose of Manchester
United), Eddie was a

Eddie Moran

ball-playing inside-right who was initially
noted for coming unscathed through his
teenage debut game - a veritable battle with
Grimsby in which eight City men suffered
injuries of varying severity. A brief run in Bert
Barlow's shirt in 1950/1 was the pinnacle of
Eddie's senior career at Leicester but, after a
return home and a protracted dispute over
City's transfer valuation (eventually knocked
down by two-thirds to a
Stockport record of £5,000),
the schemer also found his
shooting boots at Edgeley
Park, knocking in 47 goals in
117 League and Cup games,
and then remaining in the
North West to see out his senior
playing days. Eddie, the elder
brother of Jimmy (see right),
settled in Stockport to work for
British Aerospace, Shell, and a
games machine company
amongst others.

Appearances:
FL: 8 apps. 1 gl.
Total: *8 apps. 1 gl.*

Jimmy Moran

MORAN, James

Role: Inside right
*b. Cleland, Lanarkshire,
6th March 1935*

CAREER: Wishaw
Juniors/Dec 1955:
CITY/Nov 1957:
Norwich City/Jan 1961:
Northampton Town/
Aug 1962:Darlington/
July 1963: Workington/
May 1966:Lowestoft
Town (p/coach).

*Debut v Leyton Orient
(A) 19.4.57 (scored once)*

Jimmy's City career
was short but relatively
sweet - his League bow
coming in the 5-1
victory at Brisbane
Road which clinched
the Second Division
championship of 1957.
There seemed little
chance of the inside-right deposing Ian
McNeill for long, however, and his transfer to
Norwich looked merely a wise career move
until the Canaries introduced a note of teasing
mystery to the proceeedings - playing Jimmy
in a floodlit friendly against Aberdeen under
the pseudonym of 'Johnstone' prior to signing
him. After up and down spells with both
Cobblers and Quakers, Jimmy
settled to a century of League
games at Workington, then
returned to East Anglia, where
he also managed Yarmouth
Town. He still lives in Norwich
and until July 1988 ran a local
team, Coltishall HV. Both of
City's Moran brothers finished
their senior careers with
aggregate tallies of just over
50 League goals; while a third
brother, John, made only two
League appearances for
Derby in 1954, before a
homeward move to
St.Mirren.

Appearances:
FL: 3 apps. 1 gl.
Total: *3 apps. 1 gl.*

MORAN, Joseph

Role: Outside left

CAREER: Aston Villa/cs 1903:Doncaster Rovers/Sept 1904:FOSSE.

Debut v Lincoln City (H) 19.11.04

Discarded by Doncaster on their re-election to the Second Division (despite a 12-goal haul from their 1903/4 Midland League campaign), this left-winger proved an unimpressive one-off deputy for Tommy Allsopp on Fosse's flank in a 0-1 home defeat. Joe had previously failed to make the Villa first-team at all.

Appearances:
FL: 1 app. 0 gls.
Total: *1 app. 0 gls.*

MORAN, Paul

Role: Striker
b. Enfield, London, 22nd May 1968

CAREER: YT July 1984/pro July 1985: Tottenham Hotspur/(Jan 1989-loan-Portsmouth)/(Nov 1989-loan-CITY)/(Feb 1991-loan-Newcastle United)/(Mar 1991-loan-Southend United)/(Sept 1992-loan-Cambridge United)/cs 1994:Peterborough United.

Debut v Sheffield United (A) 4.11.89

Having made an early senior bow for Spurs under David Pleat, Paul had fought his way back into the White Hart Lane squad as a utility attacking midfielder under Terry Venables, and arrived at Filbert Street for an initial month-long loan period only a week after he'd laid on a Gary Lineker goal at Old Trafford. With City, following an impressive front-running debut marred only by his penalty-area profligacy, he settled alongside fellow loan striker Kevin Campbell in the fine run which catapulted the side from the basement of the Second Division towards a much more respectable ranking, and was recalled by Spurs only after Pleat attempted earnestly to secure his services for a third month. Pacy, and with a neat and occasionally flamboyant touch on the ball, Paul also claimed a hat-trick in a 10-1 friendly win at Andover during his City spell. Injuries and disciplinary problems later cut severely into Paul's progress - which characteristically featured curtailed single outings for each of

Paul Moran

Newcastle and Southend, and no starts at all at Cambridge. He made little impact, either, during 1994/5 with Posh.

Appearances:
FL: 10 apps. 2 gls.
Total: *10 apps. 2 gls.*

MORAN, Steven James

Role: Striker
b. Croydon, 10th January 1961

CAREER: app/pro Aug 1979:Southampton/ Sept 1986:CITY/Nov 1987:Reading/Aug 1991: Exeter City/cs 1993:Hull City.

Debut v Sheffield Wednesday (A) 13.9.86 (scored once)

Bought for £300,000 to help consolidate City's seemingly well-established First Division position, record signing Steve unfortunately extended a dismal sequence: his predecessors with the 'most expensive' tag, Allan Clarke and Roger Davies, had each arrived for relegation seasons, and Bryan Hamilton's team duly made the drop in 1987 despite Steve's goals. In fact, Steve's City spell has to be adjudged a disappointment overall, for only in sporadic flashes did Filbert Street fans witness the incisive opportunism which had established him at the Dell and won him England Under-21 selection, and he proved unable to strike up an effective partnership with any of the club's other frontmen, as he had previously for the Saints with Mike Channon and Kevin Keegan. Lawrie McMenemy had spotted Steve as a schoolboy, offering him a new pair of boots if he collected a second-half hat-trick in a Sunday junior game, duly coughing up when the feat was

achieved, and signing him shortly afterwards. He made a scoring substitute's debut for Southampton, and his mercurial progress thereafter was hampered only by a couple of lengthy spells on the treatment table. It was, however, inconsistency rather than injury which prompted his in-and-out status at Leicester (where a debut header against Sheffield Wednesday, and a hat-trick in the return fixture stand out most sharply in the memory), and even after a £200,000 move to Reading (a record for that club, too), Steve's frustrations continued: he was cup-tied and therefore sidelined as the Royals took the Simod Cup at Wembley, and was then unable to stop them sliding into Division Three. Steve's first League goal for Hull was his 150th in that sphere.

Appearances:
FL: 35 (8) apps. 14 gls.
FAC: 1 app. 0 gls.
LC: 5 (2) apps. 3 gls.
FMC: 0 (1) app. 0 gls.
Total: *41 (11) apps. 17 gls.*

MORGAN, Simon Charles

Role: Defender
b. Birmingham, 5th September 1966

CAREER: YT July 1983/pro Nov 1984:CITY/ Oct 1990:Fulham.
Debut v Coventry City (A) 6.10.85

A left-back of seemingly unbounded promise when he joined the City defensive ranks as a teenager, Simon settled quickly to his responsibilities in a struggling side, showing the sort of style and spirit which made Under-21 honours for his country an inevitability. Both his anticipation and his tackling skills marked the fair-haired Brummie as the first apparent specialist No.3 to hold a regular City place since Dennis Rofe, but squad-system exigencies soon saw his mettle being tested in roles all across the back four (and even behind it, in Bryan Hamilton's short-lived tactical experiments utilising a sweeper). A degree of inconsistency was an understandable concomitant, and Simon also suffered lengthy injury problems in each of 1987/8 and 1989/90, but his value as a utilitarian defender was buttressed by his unquenchable enthusiasm, and it was surprising that he should be offloaded (for £100,000) at precisely

Steve Moran

the time his motivational qualities might have been deemed most useful to City's Second Division survival campaign. Simon was soon elevated into a popular skipper at Craven Cottage; and was evidencing a fair nose for goal from midfield during 1994/5.

Simon Morgan

Appearances:
FL: 147 (13) apps. 3 gls.
FAC: 4 (1) apps. 0 gls.
LC: 14 apps. 1 gl.
FMC: 3 apps. 0 gls.
Total: 168 (14) apps. 4 gls.

MORGAN, William

Role: Right half / Centre forward

CAREER: 1896:Newton Heath/Mar 1903:Bolton Wanderers/cs 1903:Watford/ Aug 1904:FOSSE/cs 1906: New Brompton.

Debut v Blackpool (A) 3.9.04

William Morgan

A long-serving stalwart of the Manchester club which had been officially re-christened as United before he left them, Billy was retrieved for League football by Fosse from Watford's unbeaten Southern League Second Division championship side, to give two seasons' worth of consistent, grafting effort at either right-half or centre-forward. His veteran skills in each of these roles then had their final outings in a lowly Southern League term for the club later to become Gillingham.

Appearances:
FL: 66 apps. 9 gls.
FAC: 7 apps. 3 gls.
Total: 73 apps. 12 gls.

MORRIS, John

Role: Inside right / Right half
b. Radcliffe, Lancs, 27th September 1924

CAREER: Mujacs/am Aug 1939/pro Mar 1941:Manchester United/Mar 1949:Derby County/Oct 1952:CITY/May 1958:Corby Town (p/mgr)/cs 1961:Kettering Town (p/mgr).

Debut v Plymouth Argyle (H) 4.10.52

On the Old Trafford books as a junior from the age of 15, Johnny made his senior bow in wartime football while still a month short of his 17th birthday, and by the time peace returned he had also guested for Bolton, Wrexham and Charlton while on leave from his Royal Armoured Corps tank crew. A skilful, thoughtful dribbler at inside-forward, and blessed with a thunderous shot, he helped engineer United's 1948 FA Cup victory, and had won the first of his five Football League representative honours when, after disagreeing with Matt Busby on tactics, he attracted a British record fee of £24,500 from Derby. His form with the

Johnny Morris

Rams won him three full England caps (and three international goals to go with them), and his capture by Second Division City (at a club record of £21,500) was regarded with some surprise. A regular at inside-right for four seasons (with a Division Two championship medal from 1954), Johnny then switched to right-half and was an ever-present inspiration to the next table-topping promotion side of 1957. His off-field relations with the club management were not always of the most cordial variety (he was fined for his part in incidents which led to the sacking of Norman Bullock), but Johnny's most notorious brush with authority came when he managed to get himself sent off for insulting the referee during City's public practice match in August 1957, and picked up a 14-day suspension to interrupt the early part of his final Leicester season. Following his Southern League player/manager days (taking over from Jack Froggatt at Kettering), he also held the executive reins at both Great Harwood and Oswestry Town. Johnny's younger brother, William, had a brief League career at Rochdale.

Appearances:
FL: 206 apps. 33 gls.
FAC: 14 apps. 1 gl.
Total: *220 apps. 34 gls.*

MORTIMER, Francis Ernest (Fred)

Role: Centre forward

CAREER: Grenadier Guards/ 1912:Crystal Palace/May 1913: FOSSE/May 1914:Swansea Town/cs 1920:Rugby Town/ 1922:Coalville Swifts.

Debut v Birmingham (A)
20.9.13

A former soldier who proved the goalscoring success of Fosse's tour of Sweden in the summer of 1913, and claimed 29 reserve-team goals in 1913/14 (including the County Cup Final winner in

Fred Mortimer

the 2-1 victory over Holwell Works), Fred also hit a hat-trick in his first senior home game (against Bristol City), but was generally unable to perk up a struggling side, and followed manager Jack Bartlett to Southern League Swansea. Previously in that sphere he had made but a single appearance for Palace. Following the war, during which he appeared for Fosse both before and after receiving a serious arm wound, Fred started a sports out-fitter's business on the Hinckley Road, but in December 1924 was sadly declared bankrupt.

Appearances:
FL: 22 apps. 8 gls.
FAC: 2 apps. 1 gl.
WW1: 14 apps. 5 gls.
Total: *38 apps. 14 gls.*

MOUEL, Ernest Alfred

Role: Outside right
b. Cambridge, c 1872

CAREER: Cambridge Swifts/ Cambridge Rovers/Aug 1891:FOSSE.

Debut v Loughborough (A) ML
14.11.1891
(scored once)

A Cambridge county representative at soccer from the age of 16, Ernest came to Leicestershire as a cricket professional in 1890 (he was loaned in this respect to Ashby-de-la-Zouch CC in 1892), and signed amateur forms for Fosse shortly afterwards. His single campaign was Fosse's first in the Midland League, and his goal-every-three-games return made him second-top scorer. Curiously, he was nicknamed 'The Doctor' by his team-mates.

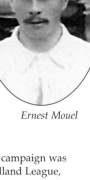

Ernest Mouel

Appearances:
ML: 15 apps. 5 gls.
Total: *15 apps. 5 gls.*

MOUNTAIN, George

Role: Right back
b. Grimsby, 1874
d. Grimsby, 10th July 1936

CAREER: 1889:Grimsby White Star/Waltham Hornets/Aug 1895:Grimsby Town/Grimsby All Saints/(Oct 1897-trials-Swindon Town)/ 1897:Grimsby Town/May 1903:FOSSE/ cs 1904:Grimsby Rangers.

Debut v Barnsley (A) 5.9.03

George Mountain

A hearty, play-anywhere man who eventually settled to the right-back spot after breaking his football career in 1895 to go to sea, 'Bodge' totted up 152 League games for the Mariners, helping them win the Second Division championship in 1901, accepting from them a benefit game against Lincoln City, and only leaving them after their relegation in 1903. Thoughts of frying pans and fires must have crossed his mind, though, as Fosse slumped into the re-election mire, and for all his fighting spirit (literally expressed in the FA Cup defeat by Burton United, when he was sent off - not for the first time in his career!), 'Bodge' was unable to effect a turn-around in their fortunes before he returned to the fishing town. 'As a tackler few can beat him, but he plays with in-and-out judgement' commented a critic at the time of George's move to Leicester, whose cheque would have been passed on directly to the player by Grimsby if the FA hadn't forbidden this fine gesture. Earlier, his one Southern League outing with Swindon had been recorded under the pseudonym 'J.Smith'. His one appearance on the Fosse scoresheet was an own goal conceded in December 1899: to date he remains the only player to have scored for Leicester before actually joining the club!

Appearances:
FL: 26 apps. 0 gls.
FAC: 4 apps. 0 gls.
Total: *30 apps. 0 gls.*

MOUNTENEY, Arthur

Role: Inside forward
b. Belgrave, Leicester, 11th February 1883
d. Leicester, 1st June 1933

CAREER: Belgrave Non-Conformists/ Leicester Imperial/Nov 1903:FOSSE/ Apr 1905:Birmingham/Apr 1909:Preston North End/July 1911:Grimsby Town/ Dec 1912: Portsmouth/cs 1914:Balmoral United/Nov 1914:Hinckley United.

Debut v Bolton Wanderers (H) 30.1.04

Arthur Mounteney, batting for Leicestershire

Joining Fosse when they were at their lowest ebb, 'Pecker' was one of the young local forward prospects on whom the club pinned hopes of a revival, and he didn't let them down, winning a regular place shortly after the start of 1904/5 and ending that season as top scorer. It was, though, his Cup hat-trick which, simultaneously destroying West Brom and alerting top-flight clubs to his potential, made it certain that Fosse couldn't hope to hang on to him. In the First Division with both Birmingham and Preston he developed into a coolly precise all-round forward, with a calculating approach to tactics befitting the son of a county cricket strategist - a status 'Pecker' would soon enjoy himself, appearing for Leicestershire in 144 first-class matches between 1911 and 1924. When his dual playing careers ended, he became cricket coach at Stoneygate School.

Appearances:
FL: 30 apps. 11 gls.
FAC: 4 apps. 10 gls.
Total: *34 apps. 21 gls.*

Davie Moyes

MOYES, David

Role: Left back
b. Cowdenbeath, Fife, 14th November 1895
d. 1984

CAREER: Cardwell FC/Kingseat Juniors/
(Sept 1919-trials-CITY)/Dec 1919:Raith
Rovers/Aug 1926:CITY/Aug 1927:
Cowdenbeath/cs 1930:East Fife.

Debut v Liverpool (A) 23.10.26

Unsuccessful in his initial brief try-out for
Peter Hodge, left-back Davie then built a
substantial career and reputation with the
manager's old club. A stalwart of the Raith
side (also including the Duncan brothers)
which finished third in the Scottish First
Division in 1922, he amassed a 218-game
record for the Starks Park outfit, and was the
beneficiary of a Raith v Darlington friendly in
April 1925. He was also involved in the ship-
wreck that got Raith's 1923 summer friendlies
in the Canary Islands off to a frightening start!
Davie then spent most of his 'official' Filbert
Street season in the shadow of Reg Osborne,
failed to appear in a winning City side, and,
not wishing to serve a belated reserve-team
apprenticeship, was glad to return homeward
to the east of Scotland to extend his senior
career.

   Appearances:
   FL: 3 apps. 0 gls.
   Total: *3 apps. 0 gls.*

MUGGLETON, Carl David

Role: Goalkeeper
b. Leicester, 13th September 1968

CAREER: app cs 1985/pro Sept 1986:CITY/
(Sept 1987-loan-Chesterfield)/(Feb 1988-loan-
Blackpool)/(Oct 1988-loan-Hartlepool
United)/(Mar 1990-loan-Stockport County)/
(Sept 1990-loan-Liverpool)/(Aug 1993-loan-
Stoke City)/(Nov 1993-loan-Sheffield United)/
Jan 1994:Celtic/July 1994:Stoke City.

Debut v West Bromwich Albion (A) 21.1.89

*Carl
Muggleton*

A nerveless, sure-handed goalkeeper who strangely seemed often to impress opposition managers more than his own, Carl never quite commanded possession of the City No.1 jersey in a way that would have borne out his immense promise with his hometown club. Initially denied senior experience by the presence of Ian Andrews and Paul Cooper, he eagerly grasped several on-loan opportunities to prove his early worth at League level and boost confidence (his Chesterfield stint literally ending with a last-minute penalty save at Fulham), before calmly stepping up for his City bow at the Hawthorns. Martin Hodge was the next experienced man to keep Carl sidelined, but summer 1990 saw him nonetheless called up for an England Under-21 cap against France in Toulon. He was involved in a rare loan-exchange (with Mike Hooper) to taste Kenny Dalglish's Anfield set-up, and on his return became the first City keeper to be sent off: a victim of the new 'professional foul' rules when conceding a penalty to Charlton in March 1991. The following season he had a new rival for senior selection in Kevin Poole, but it was Carl who ended the season in relative glory, capping a fine Wembley display in the Play Off Final against Blackburn by saving Mike Newell's second penalty. Injury-hit during the following term, Carl later found himself one of four League-experienced keepers on the books, and the one deemed most dispensable by Brian Little. A loan spell with Lou Macari's Stoke was followed by a surprisingly modest £150,000 move to Macari's Celtic; and a further change of management at Parkhead then saw Carl return to the Potteries at a £200,000 fee.

Appearances:
FL: 46 apps. 0 gls.
FAC: 3 apps. 0 gls.
FMC: 1 app. 0 gls.
AIC: 1 app. 0 gls.
P/O: 3 apps. 0 gls.
Total: *54 apps. 0 gls.*

MUNCIE, William (Paul)

Role: Winger
b. Carluke, Lanarkshire, 28th August 1911
d. Leicester, January 1992

CAREER: Carluke/Shettleston/Aug 1934: CITY/May 1938:Southend United/Aug 1939: Nuneaton Borough/Nov 1939:Hinckley United/Mar 1944:CITY/Oct 1946:Crewe Alexandra.

Debut v Middlesbrough (A) 20.10.34

A reliable stand-in winger on either flank, and the final player signed by Peter Hodge before his death, Willie was unfortunate to be stuck in the queues behind Hughie Adcock and Tony Carroll for the rightwing berth, and Danny Liddle and Eric Stubbs for that on the left. He scored on his Southend debut, but was back in local non-league football when war was declared. He was an Army PT instructor in Northern Ireland in 1943, playing the odd game for Derry City, and additionally able to make only isolated appearances in regional fare for both City and Northampton until discovering that his pace had deserted him

Willie Muncie

when he attempted to make a veteran's League comeback at Crewe. While at Leicester, he was a table-tennis star with the Ashleigh club.

Appearances:
FL: 42 apps. 11 gls.
FAC: 1 app. 0 gls.
WW2: 2 apps. 1 gl.
Total: *45 apps. 12 gls.*

MUNRO, Malcolm George

Role: Centre back
b. Melton Mowbray, Leics, 21st May 1953

CAREER: app July 1968/pro May 1970:CITY.

Debut v Ipswich Town (A) 11.9.71

With only a handful of senior appearances to his name up to that point, young central defender Malcolm assumed the first team No.5 shirt at the beginning of 1973/4 and held it almost solidly until Jeff Blockley arrived a season and a half later, welding a rigid partnership with Graham Cross, and helping secure City's route to the Cup semi-finals. An England cap at school and youth levels, the slender and extremely speedy defender

Malcolm Munro

actually did well to recover from the mishap of scoring an own goal on his 1973 break-through day, but he was less mature about showing patience when Blockley displaced him: walking out on his contract to emigrate to Canada. City retained his registration until July 1980, when it became evident he would not return. He remains perhaps best remembered for the goal-line clearance which saved City from going 0-3 down to little Leatherhead in the 1975 FA Cup-tie.

Appearances:
FL: 69 (1) apps. 1 gl.
FAC: 9 apps. 0 gls.
LC: 5 apps. 1 gl.
Total: *83 (1) apps. 2 gls.*

MURDOCH, James

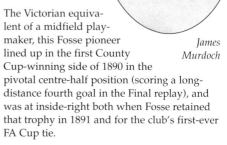

Role: Centre half / Inside right

CAREER:
1888:FOSSE.

Debut (competitive) v Burton Wanderers (H) FAC 4.10.1890

The Victorian equivalent of a midfield playmaker, this Fosse pioneer lined up in the first County Cup-winning side of 1890 in the pivotal centre-half position (scoring a long-distance fourth goal in the Final replay), and was at inside-right both when Fosse retained that trophy in 1891 and for the club's first-ever FA Cup tie.

James Murdoch

Appearances:
FAC: 1 app. 0 gls.
Total: *1 app. 0 gls*

NEWELL, Michael Colin

Role: Striker
b. Liverpool, 27th January 1965

CAREER: am:Liverpool/Sept 1983:Crewe
Alexandra/Dec 1983:Wigan Athletic/
Jan 1986:Luton Town/Sept 1987:CITY/June
1989:Everton/Nov 1991:Blackburn Rovers.
Debut v Oldham Athletic (H) 16.9.87
(scored once)

One of Bryan Hamilton's protégés at Wigan
(and a Wembley scorer in Athletic's 1985
Freight/Rover Trophy victory over Brentford),
Mike became an expensive David Pleat
signing at Luton, and forged a useful striking
partnership with Mick Harford. The tall, slim
forward then swapped the dubious delights of
Kenilworth Road's artificial turf for the Filbert
Street sward in a club record £350,000 deal,
and rapidly headed himself into the good
graces of City fans before succumbing to a
bout of the inertia which spread itself
alarmingly over the struggling Second
Division side in mid-season. Mike experienced
continuing spells of frustration in front of goal
even after Pleat's takeover from Hamilton at
Leicester, and twice let his temper boil over to
earn himself
dismissals; but
when allying his
remarkable ball
control and
mobility to an
admirable work-rate he was awarded the City
captaincy midway through 1988/9: a season
he finished as top scorer, with flashes of form
that earned him a highly-valued move to
Goodison. He made a scoring bow as a
substitute for England B, and took a runners-
up medal from the Full Members Cup Final in
1991 as an Evertonian, before becoming a
£1.1m Kenny Dalglish capture at Ewood.
Mike's first Wembley penalty for Blackburn in
the 1992 Play Off Final (his second was saved
by Carl Muggleton) denied City entry to the
inaugural season of the Premiership; and he
helped establish big-spending Rovers at that
level before being sidelined by injury and the
Shearer/Sutton combination for most of the
1995 championship campaign (which he
ended as he began, on a career aggregate
record of 105 League goals). Mike also showed
early prowess as a cricketer, representing
Lancashire at both Under-18 and Under-25
level.

Appearances:
FL: 81 apps. 21 gls.
FAC: 2 apps. 0 gls.
LC: 9 apps. 5 gls.
FMC: 4 apps. 0 gls.
Total: 96 apps. 26 gls.

NEWMAN, John Henry George

Role: Half back
b. Hereford, 13th December 1933

CAREER: jnr:Hereford United/St.Andrews
Athletic/Mar 1951:Birmingham City/
Nov 1957:CITY/Jan 1960:Plymouth Argyle/
Oct 1967:Exeter City.
Debut v Burnley (A) 9.11.57

Limited to 59 League games with Birmingham
primarily by the rivalry of Trevor Smith, with
whom he shared the No.5 shirt during the
1955 Second Division championship
campaign, Johnny was an emergency choice
at right-half for the Blues in their 1956 FA Cup
Final defeat by Manchester City. He
nonetheless stepped straight into the pivot's
role at Leicester as City fought to establish

*Mike
Newell*

themselves back in the First Division, and must have quickly doubted the wisdom of his £12,000 move as he stood at the centre of a defence which shipped 29 goals in his first eight games, including seven on his debut! He gratefully gave back the No.5 shirt to Ian King after that little whirlwind, but after helping assure top flight survival in the April 1958 crunch match back at his old St.Andrews stamping ground, he was immovable from the right-half position throughout the whole of the next consolidatory term, until finally giving way to the promise of Frank McLintock in September 1959. Johnny amassed almost 300 League appearances as Plymouth skipper, and close to another hundred at Exeter, where he also embarked on a managerial career that

subsequently took in Grimsby Town, Derby County and Hereford United, plus assistant roles at York City, Notts County and Burton Albion, and the chief scout's job at Mansfield Town. It was at Plymouth in November 1964 that he fuelled countless 'fancy that' snippets in the press by actually passing a penalty kick a few feet forward for teammate Mike Trebilcock to score. Back in 1953, while on army service, Johnny had somehow contrived to represent Wales v. Scotland in the 'Junior International' series.

Appearances:
FL: 61 apps. 2 gls.
FAC: 4 apps. 0 gls.
Total: *65 apps. 2 gls.*

John Newman

NEWTON, Robert Arthur

Role: Outside left
*b. Earl Shilton, Leics,
19th January 1946*

CAREER: app Dec
1962/pro Aug 1963:
CITY/July 1965:
Bradford City/
cs 1966:Wellington
Town/cs 1968:
Tamworth.

*Debut v Aldershot (H)
LC 25.9.63 (scored
once)*

Bob Newton

A rangy teenage out-
side-left who briefly
understudied Mike
Stringfellow, Bob took his only real Filbert
Street consolation from firing the opening goal
of City's eventually successful League Cup
campaign of 1963/4 (on the only occasion that
the club ever met the Shots). A season at
Valley Parade (also marked by a debut goal,
and by an occasional partnership with Ken
Leek) closed his League career, and by the
time Bob appeared in little Tamworth's FA
Cup runs of the late 60s and early 70s, he had
been converted to a full-back role.

Appearances:
*FL: 2 apps. 0 gls.
LC: 1 app. 1 gl.*
Total: *3 apps. 1 gl.*

NEWTON, William

Role: Right half
*b. Quebec, Co.Durham, 6th August 1898
d. Stockport, 29th April 1973*

CAREER: Hartford Colliery/Blyth Spartans/
Aug 1919:Newcastle United/Aug 1920:Cardiff
City/May 1922:CITY/May 1926:Grimsby
Town/June 1927:Stockport County/July 1931:
Hull City.

Debut: 13.10.23 v.Bradford City (A) 13.10.23

A tough-tackling Geordie whose senior career
got off to a slow start, Billy showed
remarkable stamina in remaining involved in
football until past pensionable age, returning
to Edgeley Park in 1932 for a 33-year stint on
Stockport's coaching and
training staff. He could hardly
have looked forward to such a
lengthy professional life when
Newcastle released him without
a senior game to his name, but
he made sufficient sporadic
wing-half appearances in Cardiff's
first two seasons in the League to
attract Peter Hodge's attention.
Another reserve team season
followed, but Billy was soon to
displace Dennis Jones from the
City right-half berth, and hold it
through the 1925 promotion
campaign and on into the First
Division. Thereafter, though
Grimsby and Hull each got a
season's commitment out of him,
he devoted his considerable
enthusiasm to Stockport on an almost lifelong
basis.

Appearances:
*FL: 87 apps. 1 gl.
FAC: 8 apps. 0 gls.*
Total: *95 apps. 1 gl.*

Billy Newton

*David
Nish*

NISH, David John

Role: Midfield / Left back
b. Burton-on-Trent, 26th September 1947

CAREER: Measham/am/pro July 1966:
CITY/Aug 1972:Derby County/Feb 1979:
Tulsa Roughnecks/Mar 1980:Seattle
Sounders/Shepshed Charterhouse/June
1982:Gresley Rovers (p/mgr; chairman)/
Stapenhill.
Debut v Stoke City (H) 3.12.66 (scored once)

A teenage prodigy who won numerous
England youth honours and was once
chosen as first-team substitute by City while
still at school, David exhibited amazing
versatility over his first few seasons in
City's senior squad, appearing as a creative
midfielder and a defensive wing-half before
settling as an attacking left-back. By this
time his natural ease and cool authority had
made him ideal material for the team
captaincy, and when City got to Wembley in
1969, David became the youngest-ever Cup
Final skipper at 21. Rarely missing a game,
and amassing ten England Under-23 caps
and several Football League honours in
recognition of his elegant effectiveness, he
led City back to the top flight in 1971 and
looked set for a lengthy Leicester career
when reigning champions Derby came in
with a British record fee of £225,000 to take
him to the Baseball Ground. Five full
England caps and a League championship
medal (1975) deservedly came David's way,
but he subsequently suffered a series of
knee injury problems and left for the less
demanding sphere of NASL football when
he felt he was slipping from his own high
standards of performance. A testimonial
game between current Rams and their
championship-winning predecessors in
December 1979 was Derby's fitting adieu to
him, but he eventually rejoined former
team-mates Bruce Rioch and Colin Todd on
the coaching staff at Middlesbrough in July
1988. David then returned to Filbert Street
in July 1991, twenty five years after his
initial professional signing, as Youth
Development Officer, and additionally
assumed coaching responsibility for the
youth team during 1994/5.

Appearances:
FL: 228 apps. 25 gls.
FAC: 28 apps. 4 gls.
LC: 16 apps. 2 gls.
Total: *272 apps. 31 gls.*

NOBLE, Robert

Role: Inside forward
b. Buckhaven, Fife, 29th September 1891
d. Newcastle on Tyne, 1st May 1975

CAREER: 1908:Bromley/(am 1910:Aston
Villa)/(am Nov 1910:Queen's Park Rangers)/
May 1912:FOSSE/Nov 1912:Millwall/
1921:London Caledonians.

Debut v Nottingham Forest (H) 7.9.12

A Scottish-born civil servant who played as an
amateur in England from the age of 17, Robert
had been a team-mate of Douglas McWhirter
in Bromley's Amateur Cup-winning side of
1911, and represented both London and Kent.
He failed to impress the Fosse directorate in
his brief, early-season try-out at inside-
forward, but was presumably happier anyway
to assist Southern League Millwall and cut
down on the travelling from his capital base.
His postwar career at The Den encompassed a
single Third Division outing in that
competition's inaugural 1920/1 campaign.

Appearances:
FL: 4 apps. 0 gls.
Total: *4 apps. 0 gls.*

NORMAN, Alfred

Role: Outside right

CAREER: Leicester Imperial/Aug 1906:
FOSSE/cs 1907:Leicester Imperial.
Debut v Bradford City (A) 24.11.06

A local outside-right who twice deputised in
League games for Jamie Durrant during
1906/7 (scoring in a 3-0 home win over
Lincoln City), and once in a friendly against
Luton.

Appearances:
FL: 2 apps. 1 gl.
Total: *2 apps. 1 gl.*

NORMAN, Richard

Role: Left back
b. Newcastle on Tyne, 5th September 1935

CAREER: Ferryhill Athletic/cs 1958:Horden Colliery Welfare/Nov 1958:CITY/June 1968: Peterborough United/cs 1969:Burton Albion.

Debut v Newcastle United (A)
23.1.60

A steady, unflamboyant Geordie left-back, overlooked by his hometown League club despite starring for Ferryhill's Northern League championship team of 1958, Richie only needed a couple of chances to deputise for Willie Cunningham to develop an unshakeable grip on City's No.3 shirt. From April 18th 1960

to the end of February 1964 he never missed a match, shattering the then-standing City record for consecutive League and Cup appearances, and matching consistency to fitness through 194 games, including two FA Cup Finals and City's brief European adventure. Richie wasn't to miss many games over the next four seasons, either, playing in both League Cup Finals, and leaving an abiding impression of cheerful sportsmanship. After a brief stint with Posh, Richie joined Ian King at Burton, then succeeded him as player/manager there, and later took on coaching and training duties at Derby County, Northampton Town, Kettering Town and Northamptonshire CCC.

Appearances:
FL: 303 apps. 2 gls.
FAC: 30 apps. 0 gls.
LC: 28 apps. 3 gls.
Eur: 4 apps. 0 gls.
Total: *365 apps. 5 gls.*

NORTH, Marc Victor

Role: Utility
b. Ware, Herts, 25th September 1966

CAREER: app/pro Mar 1984:
Luton Town/(Mar 1985-loan-
Lincoln City)/(Jan 1987-loan-
Scunthorpe United)/(Mar 1987-
loan-Birmingham City)/
Aug 1987:Grimsby Town/
Mar 1989:CITY/(July 1991-trials-
Luton Town)/(Sept 1991-trials-
Grimsby Town)/Oct 1991:
Leicester United/Nov 1991:
Whetstone United/Jan 1992:
Shepshed Albion/(Jan 1992-
trials-Walsall)/Mar 1992:Boston
United/Mar 1992:Kettering
Town/Aug 1992:St. Andrews/
Dec 1993:Desborough Town/
Jan 1994:St.Andrews/Oct 1994:
Corby Town/1995:St.Andrews.

Debut v Birmingham City (H)
25.3.89 (sub)

Marc North

Initially signed as a teenage
goalkeeper by David Pleat at
Luton, and later taken on as a
striker at Blundell Park by Bobby
Roberts, Marc rejoined both as a
£100,000 deadline-day City signing,
just a couple of months after
hitting the goalscoring headlines
in Grimsby's giant-killing Cup
run. Marc had, in fact, taken his
conversion from last-liner to front
man in stages: making his League
debut as a defender while on loan at Lincoln,
before briefly partnering Mike Newell and
Mick Harford at Kenilworth Road. With City,
Marc again found opportunities in each
position (twice, in fact, taking over as an
emergency keeper in mid-match) but became
something of a victim of his own versatility
after a luckless start. His full Leicester debut,
against Crystal Palace, saw him open the
scoring with a fine header, then exit with a
broken shin; while throughout the following
two seasons he was unsettlingly experimented
with as sweeper, fullback, central defender,
midfielder and target-man. Marc's final game
was in the status-saving win over Oxford, but
he was then offloaded as Brian Little set about
slashing the club's wage bill; and
unfortunately neither a Scottish pre-season

tour with Pleat's Luton nor another nostalgic
return to Grimsby earned him a further
contract at League level. Indeed, he actually
served no less than eight clubs during the
1991/2 season alone. Marc's brother Stacey
also came up through the Kenilworth Road
ranks, later playing at centre-back for West
Brom and Fulham.

Appearances:
FL: 51 (20) apps. 9 gls.
LC: 0 (2) apps. 0 gls.
FMC: 1 app. 0 gls.
Total: *52 (22) apps. 9 gls.*

NORTON, Joseph Patrick

Role: Winger
b. Leicester, 1890

CAREER: Leicester Imperial/Atherstone Town/cs 1911:Stockport County/cs 1912: Atherstone Town/cs 1913:Nuneaton Town/ Dec 1913:Manchester United/July 1919:CITY/ May 1920:Bristol Rovers/cs 1922:Swindon Town/June 1923:Kettering Town/Atherstone Town/Hinckley United/Ashby Town.

Debut (WW1) v Coventry City (A) 15.3.19; (postwar) v Tottenham Hotspur (A) 1.9.19

Joe Norton

An elusive little winger who was never the most prolific of scorers, Joe actually opened his League account in December 1911 with an equaliser for Stockport on the ground of his home town club, at a time when claims were being advanced for him as the lightest man in senior football: he weighed precisely 8st.4lbs when signing for County! His second spell in the northwest (after a £195 transfer) saw him as a First Division regular at Old Trafford on the eve of war, but another homeward move saw him turning out in regional fare for both Nottingham Forest and the Fosse while he was serving with the Leicesters, and he signed for the reconstructed City prior to their first League season. Happily working either flank after his debut as an emergency centre-forward, Joe nonetheless seemed to carry a jinx throughout his Filbert Street season - in only three of the twelve games he played did City manage even to score! At Eastville, one of his own rare goals helped Rovers to their first-ever League win. Joe later resettled in the Belgrave area, and worked for the City Corporation.

Appearances:
FL: 11 apps. 0 gls.
FAC: 1 app. 0 gls.
WW1: 7 apps. 0 gls.
Total: *19 apps. 0 gls.*

NUTTALL, Ernest A.

Role: Wing half
b. Leicester, c 1871

CAREER: Mill Hill House/Repton School/ 1889:FOSSE/1894:Crouch End.

Debut (competitive) v Burton Wanderers (H) FAC 4.10.1890

An amateur wing-half signed prior to Fosse's initial foray into the FA Cup, and elected club captain for the first assault on the Midland League, having previously skippered the Leicestershire FA for three seasons in inter-county fare. A law student, always known as 'Snooks', he actually claimed the club's first-ever FA Cup goal (in their second tie, against Small Heath in October 1891) and was still turning out in the occasional Fosse friendly in 1893/4 as the club embraced professionalism ever more firmly. 'Snooks' was also alongside Jimmy Atter in both Mill Hill House's County Cup Final side of 1889 (beaten by Loughborough) and Crouch End's London Senior Cup run (to the semi-finals) in 1894.

Appearances:
FAC: 3 apps. 1 gl.
ML: 35 apps. 2 gls.
Total: *38 apps. 3 gls.*

'Snooks' Nuttall

OAKES, Scott John

Role: Utility
b. Leicester, 5th August 1972

CAREER: YT Aug 1988/pro May 1990:CITY/ Oct 1991:Luton Town.
Debut v Plymouth Argyle (A) 17.10.89 (sub)

Boasting a healthy youth-team scoring rate and a handful of Central League outings, Scott was still a 17-year-old trainee winger when pitched late into the fray at Home Park as City vainly attempted to pull back a three-goal deficit. The son of local rocker Trevor Oakes (of *Showaddywaddy* fame), he was steadily nurtured into the professional ranks, and tried out both at full-back and as sweeper on City's pre-season tour of Scotland in 1990. Indeed, it was at right-back that Scott made a promising breakthrough into Brian Little's line-up a year or so later; though strangely it was to be only a matter of days after his initial League start (at Newcastle) that he rejoined David Pleat as part of the Steve Thompson exchange package. At Kenilworth Road, he was rapidly lauded as the mature-beyond-his-years playmaker of Luton's anti-relegation struggle, but a cartilage injury then kept him out until

his side's fate was virtually sealed. Scott got one brief shot at England Under-21 football in the summer of 1993; while his steadily rising goal tally has included the hat-trick against West Ham which shot the Hatters into the FA Cup semi-finals of 1994. His brother Stefan became a YT signing at Leicester in summer 1995.

Appearances:
FL: 1 (2) apps. 0 gls.
FMC: 1 app. 0 gls.
Total: 2 (2) apps. 0 gls.

OAKES, William H.

Role: Left back
b. Barking, Essex
d. 8th September 1927

CAREER: Barking/Clapton/Feb 1904:West Ham United/May 1904:FOSSE.
Debut v Blackpool (A) 3.9.04

A well-regarded full-back, noted for the length and accuracy of his clearances, Billy signed after 14 Southern League appearances for West Ham, just prior to that club's move to Upton Park. He had three rather injury-hit seasons with Fosse, contesting the left-back position with Walter

Above: Billy Oakes

Left: Scott Oakes

O'BRIEN, Michael Terence

M. O'BRIEN

LEICESTER CITY

Role: Half back
b. Kilcock, Dublin, 10th August 1893
d. Uxbridge, Middlesex,
21st September 1940

CAREER: Walker Celtic/Wallsend/
Blyth Spartans/Newcastle East End/
Celtic/Alloa Athletic/Dec 1914:
Brentford/Aug 1919:Norwich City/
Dec 1919:South Shields/
May 1920:Queen's Park Rangers/
Mar 1922:CITY/June 1924:Hull
City/May 1926:Brooklyn Wanderers/
Dec 1926:Derby County/June 1928:
Walsall/May 1929:Norwich City/
June 1931:Watford.

Debut v Notts County (H) 18.3.22

Mick was a virtually legendary figure in inter-war football, whose itchy feet and love of the blarney could scarcely disguise a genuine talent for classical centre-half play. One of his claims was that he'd never kicked a football until the age of 18, when his family moved from Ireland to the North East, and shortly before he joined the Army. Nonetheless, he quickly became a footballing mercenary before the outbreak of war, served during the hostilities in both the Navy (seeing action at the Battle of Jutland) and the Royal Flying Corps, and then resumed his soccer wanderings in 1919. After almost two seasons easing QPR into the League, and having won both his first Irish cap and selection for the Football League against the Army (November 1921), Mick brought his 6ft.1in. presence and his outsize personality to Leicester. A further four caps came his way as firstly he played alongside Jim Harrold in a daunting defensive pairing, then usurped his partner's pivotal role. Eventually, a £750 cheque took him to Hull, and his subsequent moves even included an inquisitive (but quickly disillusioning) taste of early Stateside soccer. When Mick finally hung up his boots (alongside 10 caps for Ireland and 4 as the Republic's skipper), he moved straight into management: at QPR for two years from 1933, as assistant at Brentford for a season, and then in control at Ipswich Town in their first, championship-winning, season of Southern League football (1936/7). He was coaching in Middlesex for the FA at the time of his death.

Appearances:
FL: 65 apps. 6 gls.
FAC: 2 apps. 0 gls.
Total: 67 apps. 6 gls.

Robinson and Bob Pollock, but being displaced by Joe Blackett for all but one game of the 3rd-place campaign of 1906/7.

Appearances:
FL: 40 apps. 0 gls.
FAC: 1 app. 0 gls.
Total: 41 apps. 0 gls.

O'CALLAGHAN, Eugene

Role: Inside right
b. Ebbw Vale, Monmouthshire, 6th October 1906
d. Fulham, London, 4th July 1956

CAREER: Victoria United/Ebbw Vale
Corries/am 1924:Tottenham Hotspur/
(loan-Barnet)/(loan-Northfleet)/pro Dec
1926:Tottenham Hotspur/Mar 1935:CITY/
Oct 1937:Fulham.

Debut v Middlesbrough (H) 2.3.35

An outstanding Welsh international inside-right who earned eleven caps while scoring 93 League goals in 252 games with Spurs, 'Taffy' had experienced both relegation and promotion at White Hart Lane, and it was ironic that his move to Filbert Street should be a desperate (and unsuccessful) strategy to help City avoid their fate of accompanying Spurs in the big drop to Division Two. Gene nonetheless soon knuckled down to the task of prompting (and skippering) City back up again, and earned his 1937 championship

*Gene
O'Callaghan*

medal as second-top scorer behind Jack Bowers. Reaching the veteran stage, though, he was soon content to join Fulham in the lower echelon, and eventually retired after a few games of wartime football, including a nostalgic return to Tottenham as a guest player, as well as appearances for Aldershot and Brentford. For ten postwar years, until his death, Gene was reserve-team trainer at Craven Cottage. A schoolboy international, he had also as a teenager represented London while on loan at Barnet; and had initially come to the Leicester crowd's attention as the scorer of the first two Spurs goals in the 1928 Cup tie which attracted Filbert Street's all-time record attendance of 47,298.

Appearances:
FL: 84 apps. 30 gls.
FAC: 5 apps. 1 gl.
Total: *89 apps. 31 gls.*

OGDEN'S CIGARETTES

E. O'CALLAGHAN (LEICESTER CITY)

OGILVIE, John Forrest

Role: Left back
b. Motherwell, Lanarkshire,
28th October 1928

CAREER: Thorniewood United/
Hibernian/(Aug 1955-trials-Sheffield
United)/Oct 1955:CITY/Jan 1960:
Mansfield Town.
Debut v Swansea Town (H) 12.11.55

Denied his true share of the glory as a
valuable defensive member of
Hibernian's 1951 Scottish championship
squad - he took a runners-up medal from
that term's League Cup Final and then
broke a leg after 15 minutes of the
Scottish Cup semi-final - John found it
difficult subsequently to pick up the
pieces of his career at Easter Road, and
was freed in 1955. Bramall Lane briefly
beckoned, but it was David Halliday who
offered John a firm contract, and the
left-back settled into sound partnerships
with, first, Willie Cunningham, and then,
throughout the 1957 promotion
campaign, with Stan Milburn. In the years
of First Division consolidation, Ogie's
place was not quite so secure, but even
with an in-and-out senior record and a
series of injuries, he remained the chief
dressing-room joker and morale-booster
among the club's large Scottish
contingent. His two penalty goals came in
his final two senior City games. Back in
Leicester, in the knitwear and then
printing trades, he has for some time
helped manage Alan Birchenall's team of
self-avowedly geriatric ex-City players.

Appearances:
FL: 82 apps. 2 gls.
FAC: 3 apps. 0 gls.
Total: *85 apps. 2 gls.*

John Ogilvie

OLD, George

Role: Goalkeeper

CAREER: Notts Mapperley/Mar 1891:FOSSE/
cs 1892:Ruddington.
Debut v Derby Junction (H) ML 12.9.1891

Fosse's first goalkeeper in the Midland
League, George saw the club through its brief
tenancy of the Aylestone Road cricket ground
(including the 1891 Cup exit to Small Heath),
and on to Filbert Street, but lost his place at
Christmas 1891, and drifted away; returning
only to face Fosse Rovers the following term.

Appearances:
FAC: 1 app. 0 gls.
ML: 7 apps. 0 gls.
Total: *8 apps. 0 gls.*

OLDFIELD, David Charles

Role: Striker / Midfield
b. Perth, Australia, 30th May 1968

CAREER: Almondsbury Rovers/app 1984/
pro June 1986:Luton Town/Mar 1989:
Manchester City/Jan 1990:CITY/(Feb 1995-
loan-Millwall)/July 1995:Luton Town.

Debut v Newcastle United (A) 13.1.90

Nicknamed 'Skippy' by the Filbert Street
crowd on account of his Australian birth
(though he'd grown up in England from the
age of 4), David started his City career as a
gangly, awkwardly unorthodox front-runner,
and gradually retreated into a deeper-lying
role. His persistently individualistic
dribbling style, often involving abrupt changes
of direction and a step-over speciality, has
many times seen him dubbed 'coltish'; though
scrappy distribution occasionally spoiled his
energetic approach work, and his finishing
could be as wildly erratic as it was sometimes
lethally spectacular. Like Marc North and Rob
Johnson, a product of the David Pleat/John
Moore youth set-up at Kenilworth Road,
David made his initial Luton impact with a
goal at Anfield, and had won one England
Under-21 cap prior to his £600,000 move to
boost Manchester City's promotion bid.
Introduced on the pitch to the Maine Road

David
Oldfield

crowd immediately before they beat City 4-2,
he made his biggest mark there in the following season: scoring twice in the 5-1 local derby
slaughter of United. Then involved in the part-
exchange deal that saw Wayne Clarke depart
for Manchester, David made his bow in a
typically crazy Leicester performance at St.
James' Park, which saw City 4-2 up with just
13 minutes left, only to lose 4-5 to a Mark
McGhee-inspired Magpies side. Never a
wholly consistent goalscorer thereafter, he
nonetheless had a knack of opening up
opposing defences to team-mates' benefit with
his unpredictable meanderings and willing
support play, and won fairly regular selections
from each of Pleat, Lee and Little; though the
Swindon Town defeat was the only one of
City's three successive Wembley Play-off dates
in which David appeared. McGhee, too, gave
him a break while assessing his Filbert Street
inheritance, but soon loaned him out for an
unlikely stint with the Lions: David had been
sent off on his previous outing at the New
Den. Six goals from seventeen games resulted,
but no permanent transfer ensued; though a
£150,000 fee took him back to Luton Town
later in the summer.

Appearances:
PL: 8 (6) apps. 1 gl.
FL: 155 (19) apps. 25 gls.
FAC: 7 apps. 3 gls.
LC: 10 (2) apps. 1 gl.
FMC: 5 (1) apps. 1 gl.
AIC: 3 apps. 1 gl.
P/O: 3 (2) apps. 0 gls.
Total: *191 (30) apps. 32 gls.*

O'NEIL, Joseph

Role: Wing half
b. Glasgow, 15th August 1931

CAREER: Bridgeton Waverley/1950:
Aberdeen/(Nov 1952-loan-Southend United)/
Mar 1956:CITY/Oct 1957:Northampton
Town/July 1959:Bath City.

Debut v Manchester United (H) 24.8.57

Never a Pittodrie regular, Joe nonetheless
drew startled admiration from Dons followers
for one particular show of bravery, bordering
on recklessness. Three weeks before the 1954
Scottish Cup semi-final against Rangers, Joe
suffered a depressed skull fracture - yet played
on the big day and contributed a hat-trick to

Joe O'Neil

O'NEILL, John Patrick

Role: Centre back
b. Derry, 11th March 1958

CAREER: Derry BC/non-contract Mar 1976/
pro Feb 1979:CITY/July 1987:Queen's Park
Rangers/Dec 1987:Norwich City.
Debut v Burnley (A) 19.8.78

John was still a Loughborough undergraduate,
playing for City on a non-contract basis while
completing his economics studies, when Jock
Wallace gave him an unexpected first-team
nod for the opening game of 1978/9 at Turf
Moor. The gamble soon paid off, for John
quickly developed into a cool, polished central
defender. Already capped at Under-21 level
for Northern Ireland prior to his League bow,
he soon began adding full caps on a regular
basis as his fine reading of the game brought
him the added responsibility of the City
captaincy. Occasionally criticised for an
apparently over-casual on-field approach, and
sometimes embarrassed by a relative lack of
pace, John nonetheless saved Leicester many a
goal against with his intelligent interventions,
and the experience gained in two World Cup
campaigns for his country stood City's defence

Aberdeen's 6-0 win. Further injury problems
unfortunately ruled the tall forward out of the
Hampden Final line-up. He accompanied
club-mate Ian McNeill to Filbert Street, to
renew acquaintance with former Dons boss
David Halliday, but had to wait over a season
for his first-team bow, briefly figuring at wing-
half during City's shaky start to the 1957/8
First Division campaign, then swiftly moving
to the County Ground (28 apps; 4 gls) before
re-uniting at Bath with another ex-
Aberdonian, Ian MacFarlane. Joe's year-long
Southend stint was related to his National
Service army posting at Shoeburyness: he was
actually withdrawn from one first-team fixture
there to fill sandbags in the wake of severe
Essex flooding.

Appearances:
FL: 5 apps. 2 gls.
Total: *5 apps. 2 gls.*

John O'Neill (above and right)

in good stead during the up and down struggles of the early 80s. In 1986, he surpassed Gordon Banks' record as the most-capped City player (eventually playing 39 times for his country), but a year later was allowed to move on to Loftus Road for £150,000. As QPR enjoyed a brief flurry of Division One success, John was restricted to only two League appearances, and then hit even worse fortune: suffering a crippling knee injury after only 34 minutes of his Norwich debut at Wimbledon, and some months later having to concede his career had come to a sadly premature end. Norwich very honourably held a testimonial match on his behalf in May 1989; and John's subsequent involvement in the game seems to have amounted only to a two-year spell as manager of League of Ireland side Finn Harps from February 1990. Having then concentrated on a wine and spirits business in Derry, he hit the headlines in October 1994 with a High Court action for negligence against John Fashanu and Wimbledon FC (arising from the tackle that put him out of the game), which terminated with an out-of-court settlement of £70,000 in John's favour.

Appearances:
FL: 313 apps. 10 gls.
FAC: 19 apps. 1 gl.
LC: 13 apps. 1 gl.
Total: *345 apps. 12 gls.*

ORMONDROYD, Ian

Role: Striker
b. Bradford, 22nd September 1964

CAREER: Manningham Mills/
Thackley/Sept 1985:Bradford City/
(Mar 1987-loan-Oldham Athletic)/
Feb 1989:Aston Villa/Sept 1991:Derby
County/Mar 1992:CITY/(Jan 1995-loan-
Hull City)/July 1995:Bradford City.

Debut v Portsmouth (H) 11.3.92

A 6ft 4 in attacker who seems to have polarised the opinions of home crowds wherever he has played, Ian could easily be represented as a bundle of contradictions: probably more effective on the ground than in the air, where he sometimes struggles to exploit his natural advantage, he will as happily play wide on the left as in a central striking role,

while his undoubtedly high work-rate and general unselfishness is too often undermined by an ungainly awkwardness on the ball. His ups-and-downs with City were hardly accompanied by a significant goal touch overall, but Ian was a crucial scorer in each of the Play-off semi-finals the club was involved in between 1992 and 1994, and it was his parried header in the Final against Derby which led to Steve Walsh's winning goal. It was subsequently sadly ironic that Ian's only Premiership goal for City, in the home victory over Arsenal, should later have been scrubbed off when the League panel re-assigned it as a Gunners' own goal. A late entrant to the senior game, Ian made unsuccessful Play-off appearances for both Bradford and Oldham before his £650,000 move to join Graham Taylor at Villa Park, but his price had fallen to £300,000 when he signed for Derby after a loan spell. He scored in both 1991/2 fixtures

Ian Ormondroyd

against City prior to his involvement in the deal which took Paul Kitson to the Baseball Ground, and in which his value was estimated at a club record-equalling £350,000. Ian rediscovered a scoring flair when Mark McGhee allowed him out on loan to Boothferry Park, but he was recalled to briefly cover an injury crisis at Filbert Street, and then transferred in July 1995 as part of the £475,000 package that also took Gavin Ward and Nicky Mohan to Bradford City.

Appearances:
PL: 6 apps. 0 gls.
FL: 61 (10) apps. 7 gls.
FAC: 1 (1) apps. 0 gls.
LC: 6 apps. 2 gls.
AIC: 4 apps. 0 gls.
P/O: 7 apps. 3 gls.
Total: *85 (11) apps. 12 gls.*

OSBORN, Frederick

Role: Centre forward
b. Leicester, 10th November 1889
d. Leicester, 11th October 1954

CAREER: Avondale/Hinckley United/ Apr 1910:FOSSE/May 1913:Preston North End/Jan 1921:Nuneaton Town.

Debut v Huddersfield Town (A) 22.10.10

COPE'S
"CLIPS"
CIGARETTES

No. 273—OSBORNE
Leicester Fosse
Noted Footballers

A local inside- or centre-forward who developed a fine reputation for marksmanship (notching 45 goals for Hinckley in 1909/10), Freddie was top scorer for Fosse in 1913, and was soon snapped up for £250 by First Division Preston. At Deepdale he experienced relegation and promotion in his first two seasons, and then attempted to play on in the top flight after the war despite having received a bullet through the thigh while on active service as a driver with the RFA in November 1918. Ironically, it was the form of Fosse's wartime discovery Tom Roberts, transferred to Preston in the 1919 close season and destined to become an England international, which was largely responsible for Freddie failing to hold his place there. Another of Leicester's amazingly numerous breed of footballer/cricketers, Freddie was also a stylish batsman for the County before the war; and for some unfathomable reason rejoiced in the nickname of 'Spoe'.

Appearances:
FL: 67 apps. 28 gls.
FAC: 4 apps. 2 gls.
Total: *71 apps. 30 gls.*

OSBORNE, John

Role: Right half
b. Renfrew, 14th October 1919
d. Leicester, 19th September 1981

CAREER: Linwood Thistle/Sept 1938:CITY/ Jan 1948:Watford/1949:Rugby Town.

Debut (WW2) v Manchester City (H) 26.8.39; (postwar) v Chelsea (A) FAC 5.1.46

A right-half who arrived at Filbert Street from Scottish Junior football on the same day as Charlie Adam, Johnny made his first-team

John Osborne

Reg Osborne

OSBORNE, Reginald

Role: Left back
b. Wynberg, South Africa, 23rd July 1898
d. Hounslow, Middlesex, April qtr 1977

CAREER: Army football/Feb 1923:CITY/
Nov 1933:Folkestone.

Debut v Fulham (H) 2.4.23

A stylish left-back whose football prowess came to light while he was serving in the Army, Reg initially attracted City's attention with two starring roles as a 'neutral' in matches played at Filbert Street in 1921: for RAMC (Aldershot) against the Inniskillen Dragoons in an Army FA Cup tie in February, and in the England v Ireland amateur international in November. When he left the service (into which he had followed his father, an RAMC colonel), the club were instrumental in finding him a job with the Watling Street Boot Company in the city, and deemed him a likely full-back partner for Adam Black. His debut found him in direct opposition to his brother Frank, Fulham's England winger, and it was only four years before Reg himself stepped up to full international status, winning one cap in a home defeat by Wales, and later touring the land of his birth (in the company of Arthur Chandler) with an FA party, when injury unfortunately kept him out of the 'Test Matches'. Nevertheless, he came under pressure for his senior jersey at Leicester on several occasions (from the likes of Harry Hooper and Jack Brown), and there was much to commend in the loyalty which kept him with City for more than a decade. Both his goals were penalties and both were scored against Sunderland in 1931/2; though it was one Reg missed almost seven years earlier that threatened briefly to be his biggest embarrassment, for he failed from the spot in the game against Bradford City which, thanks to George Carr's later goal, sealed City's promotion in 1925. A third Osborne brother, Harold, appeared once at League level for Norwich City.

Appearances:
FL: 240 apps. 2 gls.
FAC: 9 apps. 0 gls.
Total: *249 apps. 2 gls.*

breakthrough on the opening day of the abandoned 1939/40 season, and thus had his only League appearance for City expunged from all official records. Severely wounded in the arm and side while serving in France, he didn't return to Leicester until the transitional year of 1945, but was back in the No.4 shirt for both legs of the FA Cup tie with Chelsea. Johnny later became a component of the extraordinary five-man, £4,750 transfer deal with Watford, for whom he made 34 League appearances, scoring thirteen times.

Appearances:
FAC: 2 apps. 0 gls.
WW2: 13 apps. 1 gl.
Total: *15 apps. 1 gl.*

OSMAN, Russell Charles

Role: Centre back
b. Repton, Derbyshire, 14th February 1959

CAREER: app July 1975/pro Mar 1976:
Ipswich Town/July 1985:CITY/June 1988:
Southampton/Oct 1991:Bristol City/Jan 1995:
Sudbury Town/Apr 1995:Plymouth Argyle
(p/coach).

Debut v Everton (H) 17.8.85

The son of Rex Osman, a Derby County reserve half-back of the 50s, Russell made great strides as an Ipswich youngster, winning an FA Youth Cup-winners medal in 1975 and

Russell Osman

only just missing out on a place in the 1978 FA Cup side. Established at club and eventually England level in a resolute centre-back partnership with Terry Butcher, he was also a member of Bobby Robson's victorious UEFA Cup team of 1981, but his once meteoric career, founded equally on strength and skill, appeared to be standing still during his latter years at Portman Road. Russell cost Gordon Milne a £240,000 fee when arriving to stiffen City's First Division defence, and expressed the hope that he'd hit high enough form to start adding to his personal tally of eleven full caps (which had been preceded by seven Under-21 call-ups). The latter ambition failed to materialise, but Russell's energetic efforts to keep City in the top flight could hardly be faulted. He assumed the captaincy for the beginning of the 1987/8 campaign, and his coolness and comfort on the ball stood out pleasingly against a Second Division backdrop, but his retention of higher ambitions led to him moving to The Dell on the expiry of his contract. Later, Russell was in the Bristol City side which removed City from the FA Cup in 1992, and assumed player/manager duties at Ashton Gate in January 1993, only to be sacked in November 1994. After a brief stint in non-league football, he joined Plymouth Argyle as reserve team player/coach, and was within days elevated to the post of 'football adviser' to that managerless, relegation-haunted club. Indeed, for several of their final league fixtures of 1994/5, Russell was forced to name himself as substitute goalkeeper, though luckily was not called upon.

Appearances:
FL: 108 apps. 8 gls.
FAC: 2 apps. 0 gls.
LC: 8 apps. 0 gls.
FMC: 2 apps. 0 gls.
Total: 120 apps. 8 gls.

OSVOLD, Kjetil

Role: Midfield
b. Aalesund, Norway, 5th June 1961

CAREER: IK Start/Lillestrom/Apr 1987: Nottingham Forest/(Dec 1987-loan-CITY)/Apr 1988: Djurgardens IF/Apr 1989:PAOK Thessalonikis/(Nov 1989-loan-Admira Wacker)/1990:Lillestrom.
Debut v Middlesbrough (H) 5.12.87

One of Bryan Hamilton's last acts as City manager was to bring Norwegian cap Kjetil to Filbert Street on loan, but the blond midfielder looked as unhappy in the left-flank problem position as had most previous candidates, especially as his time in a blue shirt coincided with City's seven-game Second Division goal drought. A few months earlier, Brian Clough had paid £100,000 for 'Ossie', whose 37-game international career had previously peaked in 1986 when he claimed the winning goal for Norway against Argentina; but the Forest boss gave him few first-team opportunities, and soon accepted £70,000 from Sweden for his unsettled import. Further moves to Greece and Austria quickly followed, before a return to the club with whom he'd won Norwegian Cup and Championship medals in 1985 and 1986.

Appearances:
FL: 3 (1) apps. 0 gls.
Total: 3 (1) apps. 0 gls.

❏ FOX FACT: *Kjetil Osvold appeared in City's most cosmopolitan team to date. The thirteen players who featured in the Boxing Day 1988 home fixture (lost 0-1 to Bournemouth)*

Kjetil Osvold

represented seven nationalities: comprising five Englishmen (Andrews, Venus, Morgan, Ford and Cusack), three Scots (Mauchlen, McAllister and MacDonald), a Welshman (James), an Irishman from each of the North (Ramsey) and the Republic (Brien), plus a Finn (Rantanen) and the on-loan Norwegian.

OWEN, Alfred Sydney

Role: Forward
b. Stoke, c 1885
d. Blackpool, 22nd August 1925

CAREER: North Stafford Nomads/Northern Nomads/ Jan 1907:Stoke/July 1907:Stockport County/Apr 1908:Stoke/Sept1908:FOSSE/ (cs 1911:English Wanderers)/July 1911: Blackpool/Nov 1912:Stoke.

Debut v Nottingham Forest (H) 7.11.08

A noted amateur who signed for Fosse just before completing his chartered accountancy examinations, and after Stoke had resigned from the Football League, Syd was one of the few individual successes of Fosse's relegation-bound team of 1909, and continued to turn out for the club as a forceful inside- or outside-left over the next two seasons whenever business commitments - or amateur international fixtures - would permit. Originally he had been a full-back at Stoke, but took to the advanced role so well that he was chosen for the senior England trial match of January 1910, scoring once in the Whites v. Stripes fixture at Anfield but failing subsequently to win a full cap. It was in 1910, too, that Syd was elected to the secretaryship of the Players' Union (rising from the role of membership auditor to a position ex-Fossil Charlie Saer had held 12 years previously), but his tenure would end in controversy following the union's 1912 defeat in the courts in an ill-fated legal challenge to the League's retain and transfer system ('The Kingaby Case'). An intemperate response, by way of a letter to the press assigning qualities

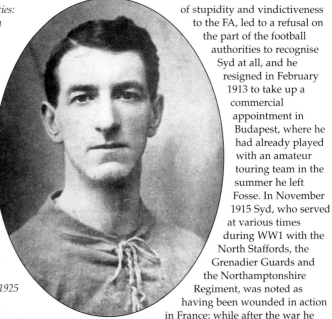

Syd Owen

of stupidity and vindictiveness to the FA, led to a refusal on the part of the football authorities to recognise Syd at all, and he resigned in February 1913 to take up a commercial appointment in Budapest, where he had already played with an amateur touring team in the summer he left Fosse. In November 1915 Syd, who served at various times during WW1 with the North Staffords, the Grenadier Guards and the Northamptonshire Regiment, was noted as having been wounded in action in France; while after the war he returned to business matters in Czechoslovakia.

Appearances:
FL: 43 apps. 12 gls.
FAC: 8 apps. 1 gl.
Total: *51 apps. 13 gls.*

OWEN, James

Role: Right back
b. c 1868

CAREER: Rushden/Dec 1891:FOSSE.

Debut v Wednesbury Old Athletic (A) ML 5.12.1891

A 5ft 4in right-back partner to Harry Bailey during the first two Midland League seasons, James was a former Northamptonshire County representative, having played against the touring Canadian team in 1888. He was also a well-known amateur runner, holding a host of athletics prizes. The columnist 'Half-Back' in the Leicester *'Saturday Herald'* averred that he 'kicks well and with capital judgement'.

Appearances:
FAC: 4 apps. 0 gls.
ML: 18 apps. 0 gls.
Total: *22 apps. 0 gls.*

PARIS, Alan David

Role: Defender
b. Slough, Berkshire, 15th August 1964

CAREER: Slough Town/Nov 1982:Watford/
Aug 1985:Peterborough United/July 1988:
CITY/Jan 1991:Notts County.
Debut v Portsmouth (A) 29.8.88

Never a first-teamer at Watford, Alan built
himself a fine reputation as a footballing full-
back with Posh, and joined City's Second
Division squad in the deal which took Nick
Cusack to London Road. It was as a central
defender that he made his initial Filbert Street
mark, however; allying pace and determination to an evident relish for playing his way
out of trouble whenever possible, and winning
over an initially sceptical crowd which was
soon regularly hailing him with his dressing-
room nickname of 'Delbert'. Inconsistency and
a tendency to self-effacement, though, afflicted
Alan after he had picked up the fans' Player of
the Year trophy in 1989, and sporadic lapses in
concentration and confidence on his part
invariably, if unluckily, seemed to cost his side
dear. An £80,000 fee from higher-placed
Second Division rivals confirmed his reservoir
of ability, however, and within months he had
helped the Magpies into the top flight via the
Wembley Play Off Final. Injury then cruelly
cut short Alan's Meadow Lane career; and in
1994 he was back at Slough Town, coaching
the youth team there.

Appearances:
FL: 80 (8) apps. 3 gls.
FAC: 2 apps. 1 gl.
LC: 7 (2) apps. 1 gl.
FMC: 3 apps. 0 gls.
Total: *92 (10) apps. 5 gls.*

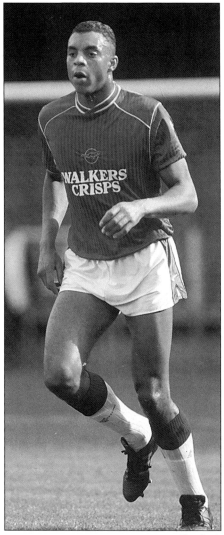

Alan Paris

PARKER, Garry Stuart

Role: Midfield
b. Oxford, 7th September 1965

CAREER: app/pro 1982:Luton Town/
Feb 1986:Hull City/Mar 1988:Nottingham
Forest/Nov 1991:Aston Villa/Feb 1995:CITY.
*Debut v Wolverhampton Wanderers (A)
FAC 18.2.95*

Central to the transfer deal with which City
and Villa nominally settled their (financial and

legalistic) differences over the Brian Little
affair, Garry featured in City's Fifth Round
Cup exit at Molineux, then made his
Premiership bow at Villa Park in the sweet-
tasting 4-4 draw which City contrived from a
1-4 deficit situation. Initially played in a
holding role in front of the back-line (allowing
Mark Draper to advance more through
midfield, while maintaining for the side some
passing vision from deep), Garry soon
exhibited his classy reading of the game, but
seemed for a while reluctant to trust to his
pace. By the end of the relegation term,

however, he was visibly relaxing into his middle-line role, and getting forward himself to greater purpose: a development which culminated in a wonderfully individualistic goal at The Dell in the final fixture. Garry's senior career started under David Pleat at Luton, but it was in an influential stint at Boothferry Park that he first attracted representative interest, winning two of his eventual six England Under-21 caps as a Tiger. A Brian Clough swoop followed; as did a quartet of Wembley appearances in a Forest shirt. Garry scored twice in the 1989 Simod Cup Final win over Everton; took winner's medals from each of the League Cup Finals of 1989 and 1990; and was in the 1991 side beaten in the FA Cup showpiece by Spurs. His Villa days were comparatively uneventful, despite Garry being a regular in the 1992/3 effort which landed his club in the Premiership runners-up slot; and he missed out entirely on the 1994 League Cup triumph. Garry assumed the city captaincy from the start of 1995/6.

Appearances (to end 1994/5):
PL: 14 apps. 2 gls.
FAC: 1 app. 0 gls.
Total: *15 apps. 2 gls.*

Garry Parker

PARKER,
John Francis

Role: Centre forward
b. Ellistown, Leics, 16th January 1896
d. Burton on Trent, 2nd November 1973

CAREER: Midway Athletic/Army football/ Newhall Swifts/(Feb 1919-trials-FOSSE)/ Sept 1919:CITY/May 1920:Norwich City.
Debut v Fulham (A) 20.9.19

A compact centre-forward whose lack of inches counted against him in an era of towering leaders, Jack had to act as understudy to Harry King and Jock Paterson for most of his season with City, and best distinguished himself in the reserve side, scoring six in the 11-2 Leicestershire Senior Cup Final victory over Moira Athletic. After a £50 move, he led Norwich's attack in their inaugural Football League game, but managed only two goals in 20 games for the Canaries. Jack was originally chosen for a Fosse wartime fixture at Coventry in March 1919, but missed his train connection and the game. He was later a painter and decorator in Swadlincote.

Jack Parker

Appearances:
FL: 5 apps. 1 gl.
Total: *5 apps. 1 gl.*

PARRY, Maurice Pryce

Role: Left half
b. Oswestry, 1877
d. Bootle, Lancs, 24th March 1935

CAREER: 1895:Oswestry United/(Sept 1897-trials-Nottingham Forest)/1898:Long Eaton Rangers/Aug 1898:FOSSE/Feb 1899: Loughborough/May 1899:Brighton United/ cs 1900:Liverpool/May 1909:Partick Thistle/ cs 1911:(South Africa)/1913:Oswestry United.
Debut v Woolwich Arsenal (A) 10.9.1898

A half-back from a footballing family (his younger brother Tom won Welsh caps while remaining with Oswestry), Maurice nonetheless came to Leicester primarily to find work in the engineering trade, and had to be persuaded to try his luck as a professional. Unfortunately, he got only one chance with Fosse to displace his countryman Dick Jones (in a 0-4 defeat at Plumstead), and was soon on his way to assist the ailing

Maurice Parry

Luffs. He was a Southern League regular at Brighton before that club withdrew from the competition, then embarked on a fine nine-year career at Anfield, making 207 League appearances as a tough ball-winner, and winning championship medals from both top Divisions (in 1905 and 1906) as well as sixteen Welsh caps. Maurice, an organ-playing advocate of teetotalism, was later a member of the first Partick team to play at Firhill. He suffered the lingering after-effects of wartime gassing, but managed Rotherham County from 1921-23, and later coached Liverpool, Barcelona, Dusseldorf, Frankfurt, Cologne and in Jersey. His son Frank played as a winger for Everton, Grimsby Town, Accrington Stanley and Nelson in the Twenties.

Appearances:
FL: 1 app. 0 gls.
Total: *1 app. 0 gls.*

PARTRIDGE, Malcolm

Role: Striker
b. Calow, nr. Chesterfield, 28th August 1950

CAREER: app/pro Sept 1968:Mansfield Town/Sept 1970:CITY/(Jan 1972-loan-Charlton Athletic)/Mar 1975:Grimsby Town/July 1979:Scunthorpe United/Mar 1982: Skegness Town.

Debut v Charlton Athletic (A) 19.9.70
(scored once)

Malcolm Partridge

A tall striker who impressed Frank O'Farrell as a teenage goalscorer at Field Mill (where he had made his debut in the first game Nick Sharkey and Jimmy Goodfellow played for the Stags), Malcolm cost £50,000 when added to City's 1971 promotion-chasing squad. He was just settling alongside Ally Brown when a broken arm interrupted his progress, and thereafter he struggled to hold down a regular senior place, despite a palpable willingness to draw markers all across the field, and a useful habit of scoring in Cup ties. Malcolm nevertheless worked hard on developing other aspects of his game, and at both Grimsby (in 138 League games) and Scunthorpe (in 97) he was successful as a deeper-lying attacker.

Appearances:
FL: 25 (11) apps. 4 gls.
FAC: 3 (1) apps. 3 gls.
LC: 1 (2) apps. 1 gl.
Total: *29 (14) apps. 8 gls.*

PATERSON, James

Role: Centre forward
b. Stirling, 1907

CAREER: Causewayhead FC/Camelon Juniors/Jan 1927:Everton/Aug 1927: St.Johnstone/cs 1930:Cowdenbeath/May 1932: CITY/July 1935:Reading/July 1938:Clapton Orient.
Debut v Sheffield United (H) 27.8.32 (scored once)

Though he was unable to get a look-in at Goodison, with Dixie Dean blocking his senior chances, Jim rebuilt his confidence quickly back in Scotland, winning three caps in 1931 while notching 53 goals in only 74 games for Cowdenbeath. A comparatively lightweight centre-forward, but blessed with great pace and bravery, Jim wasn't quite so prolific after his second move south of the border, and could never quite shake off the challenge of the veteran Arthur Chandler at Leicester, though he hits the record books for scoring the first goal against continental opposition at Filbert Street (in the 1933 friendly defeat by Rapid Vienna). City experimented with him in different forward positions during the 1935 relegation season, and Jim settled at Reading as an inside-left, claiming 23 goals in 73 League games, before taking his boots to Orient and then bowing out of the senior game.

Appearances:
FL: 48 apps. 17 gls.
FAC: 1 app. 1 gl.
Total: *49 apps. 18 gls.*

Jim Paterson

PATERSON, John

Jock Paterson

Role: Centre forward
b. Dundee,
14th December 1896

CAREER: Fort Hill/ Dundee North End/ Army football/ Dundee/Dec 1919: CITY/Mar 1922: Sunderland/Oct 1924:Preston North End(to 1925)/June 1928:Mansfield Town/Montrose.

Debut v Stoke City (H) 20.12.19 (scored once)

Another of Peter Hodge's shrewd postwar signings, Jock had proven his fitness at Dundee after having been wounded five times while serving with the Black Watch in France, and was soon among the goals at Filbert Street. He claimed the reconstructed club's first League hat-trick (against Lincoln in March 1920) a week before scoring for the Anglo-Scots in the international trial, and was then chosen to face England a month later. Top scorer in each of the following two seasons in the City centre-forward role, Jock attracted an irresistible £3,790 bid from Sunderland, and subsequently led the Roker team to second and third positions in the First Division with

37 goals in 74 games. Preston, however, were relegated at the end of his season there. (Jock's movements between 1925 and 1928 are the subject of so-far unresolved debate between researchers: one source places him at Raith Rovers from September 1925; others from the same date at Southern League club Mid-Rhondda. There is also evidence that 'our' Jock featured for Queen's Park Rangers from January 1926 to late 1927; though this latter man has as often been identified as a later Bristol Rovers player of the same name.)

Appearances:
FL: 81 apps. 34 gls.
FAC: 8 apps. 3 gls.
Total: *89 apps. 37 gls.*

PATERSON, Thomas

Role: Forward
b. Lochore, Fife, 3rd April 1927

CAREER: Raith Rovers/Lochgelly Albert/ Mar 1948:CITY/June 1950:Newcastle United/ July 1952:Watford/July 1955:Berwick Rangers.

Debut v Brentford (A) 15.9.48 (scored once)

Tom Paterson

Tom had a few outings for Raith in wartime football, but had reverted to the Junior ranks when Johnny Duncan spotted him on a trip home. A play-anywhere forward with an expressed preference for the inside-right spot (which he briefly inherited from Peter McKennan), Tom effectively had to settle for becoming Charlie Adam's understudy for the No.11 shirt. He got only two chances to impress on Tyneside after a £2,500 move, but made 45 League appearances (7 goals) for Watford before assisting Berwick in their first assault on the Scottish 'B' Division. Knee injuries ended his career at Shielfield, and he later settled in Gateshead. (Tom should not be confused with his later City namesake, who left Filbert Street without a senior appearance to his name, but played League football in the 70s for Middlesbrough, Bournemouth and Darlington).

Appearances:
FL: 17 apps. 4 gls.
Total: *17 apps. 4 gls.*

PEAKE, Andrew Michael

Role: Midfield
b. Market Harborough, Leics, 1st November 1961

CAREER: app July 1978/pro Jan 1979:CITY/ Aug 1985:Grimsby Town/Sept 1986:Charlton Athletic/Nov 1991:Middlesbrough/Oct 1994: Leicestershire Constabulary FC.

Debut v Norwich City (H) FAC 6.1.79

Another teenager given a deep-end dunking by Jock Wallace, midfielder Andy performed with remarkable maturity on his televised Cup debut and proceeded to establish himself as an exciting linkman of prodigious promise, winning numerous England Youth caps, a Second Division championship medal, and one Under-21 honour (against Poland during 1981/2). A series of injuries, and City's early desire not to rush his development, occasionally kept Andy out of the limelight, but his inventive playmaking and mastery of the accurately flighted and weighted long ball could rarely be suppressed, and his knack of scoring spectacular long-range goals was a valuable feature of City's attacking options in the early 80s. It was regrettable that Andy's departure (for £110,000) seemed to set the seal on growing suspicions that he had failed quite to live up to his immense early potential, but

Andy Peake

PEAKE, Jason William

Role: Midfield
b. Leicester, 29th September 1971

CAREER: YT 1988/pro Jan 1990:CITY/
(Feb 1992-loan-Hartlepool United)/(July 1992-
trials-Newcastle United)/Aug 1992:Halifax
Town/Mar 1994:Rochdale.
Debut v Charlton Athletic (A) FMC 14.11.89

Heavily tipped to inherit Gary McAllister's
midfield role at Leicester, young Jason
appeared well on course for development into
an elegant playmaker as his precocious form
elevated him successively into England squads
at each of Under-18 and Under-19 level.
Sporadic senior selections also seemed
encouraging pointers to the local lad's future -
a lively willingness to take venomous potshots
spicing his neat passing game, and a wind-
assisted free-kick winner against Barnsley
boosting his confidence - but an enigmatic
'standstill' season followed Brian Little's
arrival, and summer 1992 saw Jason released
on a free. Unfortunately, summer 1993 then
saw him reflecting on a term in which the
hapless Shaymen lost their Football League
status; though Jason's starring Conference
performances were to earn him a return to
Division Three before long.

Appearances:
FL: 4 (4) apps. 1 gl.
FMC: 1 (1) apps. 0 gls.
Total: *5 (5) apps. 1 gl.*

at least he was back in top-flight football within a year, battling to keep Charlton there. His
mature lynchpin role was later honoured
when manager Lennie Lawrence signed him a
second time for (successfully) promotion-chasing 'Boro. Andy retired from the professional
game in July 1994, when far from a spent
footballing force, and joined the police.

Appearances:
FL: 141 (6) apps. 13 gls.
FAC: 9 apps. 0 gls.
LC: 5 (1) apps. 0 gls.
Total: *155 (7) apps. 13 gls.*

❑ FOX FACT: *Andy Peake's England Youth
record included an appearance in the Final of the
UEFA Youth tournament in 1980 (a 2-1 victory
over Poland). Two other City players have featured
in this pinnacle of the European 'teenage' game:
Peter Shilton in the 0-1 defeat by the USSR in
1967, and Julian Joachim in the 1-0 win against
Turkey in 1993.*

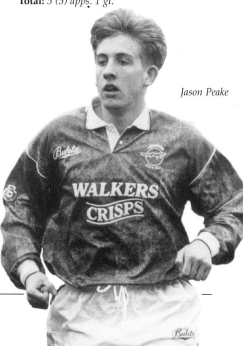

Jason Peake

PEERS, Samuel

Role: Centre half / Outside left

CAREER: Apr 1901:Coventry City/Apr 1902:FOSSE/Nov 1903:Swindon Town/ cs 1904:Coventry City.

Debut v Lincoln City (H) 19.4.02

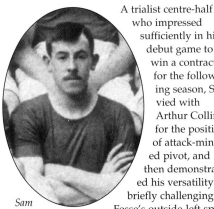

A trialist centre-half who impressed sufficiently in his debut game to win a contract for the following season, Sam vied with Arthur Collins for the position of attack-minded pivot, and then demonstrated his versatility by briefly challenging for Fosse's outside-left spot. Swindon Town accounts show him earning the princely sum of £1.15s. per week for his Southern League season there.

Sam Peers

Appearances:
FL: 14 apps. 1 gl.
FAC: 2 apps. 0 gls.
Total: 16 apps. 1 gl.

PEPPER, William

Role: Goalkeeper

CAREER: Sheppey United/Jan 1913:FOSSE/July 1913:Gillingham.

Debut v Leeds City (A) 8.2.13

A young trialist goalkeeper plucked from the Kent League, Bill kept a clean sheet in a senior friendly at Gillingham, and a week later was given the chance to deputise for Fred Mearns at League level, when unfortunately five goals whistled past him at Elland Road. His subsequent Southern League career with the Gills was equally brief - one outing in a 4-2 home win over Southend.

Appearances:
FL: 1 app. 0 gls.
Total: 1 app. 0 gls.

PERKINS, George

Role: Goalkeeper

CAREER: Market Harborough/May 1904: FOSSE/Hinckley United.

Debut v Lincoln City (H) 19.11.04

George Perkins

In signing this young keeper, Fosse might well have been trying to console him for a recent major embarrassment - he had been the hapless Harborough last-line who'd conceded ten goals when the Fossils removed his Northants League team from the previous season's FA Cup. His Filbert Street role, however, was to understudy the consistent Walter Smith, and he got only a solitary senior chance (in a 0-1 home defeat) to display his capabilities.

Appearances:
FL: 1 app. 0 gls.
Total: 1 app. 0 gls.

PERRY, Richard

Role: Half back

CAREER: 1889:FOSSE/Hinckley Athletic.

Debut (competitive) v Burton Wanderers (H) FAC 4.10.1890

A Fossil from 1889 onwards, Dick played (and was injured) in the first, drawn Final of the 1890 County Cup, and was at centre-half when the club made its FA Cup bow during the following season. He also managed a handful of games during the initial Midland League campaign.

Appearances:
FAC: 1 app. 0 gls.
ML: 5 apps. 0 gls.
Total:
6 apps. 0 gls.

Dick Perry

John Philp

PHILP, John Beveridge

Role: Right half
b. Kelty, Fife, 5th September 1911

CAREER:
Kelty Boys/
Inverkeithing/
May 1932:CITY/
July 1934:Rhyl
Athletic.
*Debut v Tottenham
Hotspur (H) 9.9.33*

Another addition to
the club's solo
appearance ranks, this
Scottish right-half
briefly attempted to fill
Sep Smith's boots in
the above 1-3 home
defeat. After two years
on the Filbert Street
payroll, John moved on
to settle for Birmingham
& District League fare
with his Welsh club (the
notion then of the
Second City's 'district'
being somewhat
flexible).

Appearances:
FL: 1 app. 0 gls.
Total: *1 app. 0 gls.*

PHILPOTT, Lee

Role: Winger
b. Barnet, Herts, 21st February 1970

CAREER: Cambridge Crusaders/(assoc
schoolboy:Luton Town)/YT 1987/pro 1988:
Peterborough United/May 1989:Cambridge
United/Nov 1992:CITY.
Debut v Bristol Rovers (H) 28.11.92

One of the flank players expected to hare after
the long balls from the back which were
Cambridge's trademark tactic as they rose via
successive promotions from the League's
basement to the upper reaches of the Second
Division, Lee was himself the object of a long
chase by Brian Little. Eventually signed for an
appearance-related fee rising to a record-
equalling £350,000 (in time to watch a 2-2
Filbert Street draw between his old and new
clubs), he was soon noted for the quality of his
crosses, but berated for not delivering enough
of them. After possibly his finest moments as
provider in the 1993 Play
Off Final comeback
against Swindon Town,
Lee has virtually defined
inconsistency, whether
employed wide up-front
(in mazy or direct
mode), in midfield, or
even at left-back; and
can appear frustratingly
less than motivated on
occasion. His transfer-
listing in May 1995
came as little surprise;
though he remained a
squad member as
1995/96 got underway.

**Appearances
(to end 1994/5):**
PL: 19 (4) apps. 0 gls.
FL: 37 (9) apps. 3 gls.
FAC: 4 (2) apps. 0 gls.
LC: 2 (1) apps. 0 gls.
AIC: 2 apps. 0 gls.
P/O: 2 (1) apps. 0 gls.
Total:
66 (17) apps. 3 gls.

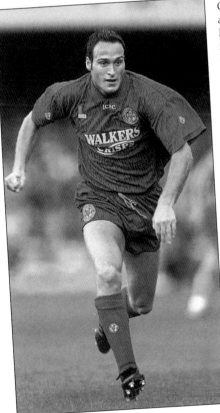

Lee Philpott

John Pickard

PICKARD, John W.

Role: Outside right
b. Syston, Leics

CAREER: am 1894/pro Sept 1895:FOSSE.

Debut v Loughborough (H) 5.10.1895

A young outside-right whose initial senior game was Fosse's first in the Football League against their old local rivals, the newly-elected Luffs. Apparently the 5-0 scoreline here, and that of a 4-0 Cup romp against Hinckley Town the following week, satisfied more than did John's performances, for his only other marks on the Fosse record came in lesser circumstances. At first-team level he could match a single United Counties League outing (1894/5) with one in the Christmas Day 1895 friendly against the club's first Irish guests, Cliftonville; though he was also a scorer in the reserves' capture of the 1895 County Cup, and was again in the line-up when they repeated the feat in 1896.

Appearances:
FL: 1 app. 0 gls.
FAC: 1 app. 0 gls.
Total: *2 apps. 0 gls.*

PILKINGTON, Saville H.

Role: Outside left

CAREER: Loughborough Corinthians/
(Dec 1913-trials-FOSSE).

Debut v Birmingham (H) 17.1.14

An outside-left taken on trial from the reigning champions of the Leicestershire Senior League, Saville played only in the above goalless League game and in an embarrassing 1-5 friendly defeat at Northampton a fortnight later.

Appearances:
FL: 1 app. 0 gls.
Total: *1 app. 0 gls.*

PLATNAUER, Nicholas Robert

Role: Left back
b. Leicester, 10th June 1961

CAREER: Bedford Town/Aug 1982:Bristol Rovers/Aug 1983:Coventry City/Dec 1984: Birmingham City/(Jan 1986-loan-Reading)/ Sept 1986:Cardiff City/Aug 1989:Notts County/(Jan 1991-loan-Port Vale)/July 1991: CITY/Mar 1993:Scunthorpe United/(July 1993-trials-Kettering Town)/Aug 1993: Mansfield Town/Feb 1994:Lincoln City.

Debut v Swindon Town (A) 17.8.91

A multi-club veteran before he joined his hometown team as a free agent, Nicky was

Nicky Platnauer

fondly regarded as 'a supporter in a City shirt' during his stint as a left-back for Brian Little. Not by then the paciest of coverers, he nonetheless exuded an effective enthusiasm and commitment during the near-miss promotion drive of 1992, while both his positional play and distribution were ultra-reliable. Originally a forward with Bedford's 1981 Southern League Cup-winners (a year before the Eagles' demise), Nicky was then signed by Bobby Gould for both his first two League clubs, and on further travels converted through midfield roles to his eventual No.3 berth. He earned a winner's medal from the Welsh Cup Final of 1988, and appeared at Wembley for Notts County in the 1990 Play Off Final as that club rose from the Third Division. A day after leaving City, Nicky scored on his Glanford Park debut.

Appearances:
FL: 32 (3) apps. 0 gls.
LC: 4 (1) apps. 0 gls.
FMC: 2 apps. 0 gls.
Total: *38 (4) apps. 0 gls.*

Norman Plummer

PLUMMER, Norman Leonard

Role: Centre half
b. Leicester, 12th January 1924

CAREER: ATC football/am July 1942/pro Nov 1942:CITY/July 1952:Mansfield Town/ Aug 1956:Kettering Town.

Debut (WW2) v Coventry City (A) 3.11.42 (scored once); (postwar) v Brentford (A) 25.12.47

A former RAF sports officer, and a play-anywhere enthusiast after his wartime signing, Norman made his first and last senior City appearances as a centre-forward, but it was his interim adherence to the central defensive role which was to make his name. He inherited the team captaincy from Sep Smith early in the 1948/9 season of radical contrasts, getting plenty of hard work in City's desperate struggle to avoid the drop into Division Three, and taking appropriate kudos for the qualities of undemonstrative leadership which saw the club through to Wembley. Strangely enough, Norman was soon having to fight for his place with the likes of Tom McArthur and Bill Corbett, and eventually followed the well-worn path from Filbert Street to Field Mill (as a George Jobey signing) shortly after Matt Gillies had arrived to assume the City No.5

shirt. He made 166 League appearances (5 goals) for the Stags, then assisted Kettering to the Southern League championship of 1957; and was later involved in a Leicester haberdashery business for many years.

Appearances:
FL: 66 apps. 1 gl.
FAC: 9 apps. 0 gls.
WW2: 24 apps. 6 gls.
Total: *99 apps. 7 gls.*

POLLOCK, Robert

Role: Defender
b. Wishaw, Lanarkshire

CAREER: Wishaw Thistle/Third Lanark/ Jan 1900:Bristol City/cs 1900:Kettering/ cs 1901:Notts County/Sept 1902:FOSSE/ cs 1909:Leyton/cs 1910:Leicester Imperial.
Debut v Preston North End (A) 4.10.02

A Scottish Junior international, and a veteran of Southern League fare at Bristol and Kettering, Bob failed to make a first-team breakthrough with the First Division Magpies, but proved a remarkably resilient and versatile defender with Fosse over seven seasons. He favoured the wing-half positions and a

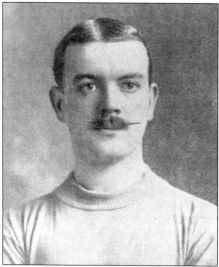

Bob Pollock

passing game, building long runs of appearances on either flank, but could slot into a full-back role whenever the necessity arose. It was fitting that his benefit match - against Grimsby in February 1908; the first time the profits from a League match had been set aside for such a purpose by the Fosse - should have come in the season which climaxed in the promotion he had laboured so hard to secure. His total of senior appearances constituted a Fosse record; as, incidentally, did his aggregate haul of fourteen successful penalties.

Appearances:
FL: 211 apps. 14 gls.
FAC: 19 apps. 5 gls.
Total: *230 apps. 19 gls.*

❏ FOX FACT: *Bob Pollock's record as Fosse's penalty king has been superceded by four City players, and equalled by one. Arthur Rowley heads the list with 41 successful spot-kicks (38 FL, 3 FAC), and is followed by Sep Smith's 26 (13 FL, 1 FAC, 12 WW2), Steve Lynex's 23 (all FL), and Gary McAllister's 15 (12 FL, 2 FAC, 1 LC). David Nish's total of 14 (10 FL, 2 FAC, 2 LC) equated to Pollock's record of 10 FL and 4 FAC counters from the spot; though it must be remembered that all those who've broken the latter's benchmark have done so with the rules demanding that the keeper remains on his line until the ball is kicked - he could advance from the moment of the whistle prior to 1929.*

POOLE, Kevin

Role: Goalkeeper
b. Bromsgrove, Worcs, 21st July 1963

CAREER: app June 1980/pro Aug 1981:Aston Villa/(Nov 1984-loan-Northampton Town)/ Aug 1987:Middlesbrough/(Mar 1991-loan-Hartlepool United)/July 1991:CITY.
Debut v Swindon Town (A) 17.8.91

A decade as a professional had seen 'keeper Kevin amass only 86 League and Cup appearances before his ex-Boro coach Brian Little added him to the Filbert Street roster for £40,000 a day after his 28th birthday. Yet he stepped straight between the sticks for City with Carl Muggleton carrying over a suspension, and has subsequently won the lion's share of senior possession in competition with Muggleton, Russell Hoult and Gavin Ward; though his only Wembley outing in City's trio of Play Off deciders was the 3-4 defeat by Swindon. Not the tallest of last-liners (and occasionally exposed for his concomitant lack of reach), Kevin is nonetheless a fine reflex shot-stopper, and has peppered his City progress with some outstanding performances. One of these, at Tottenham in 1994/5, virtually ensured he would win the club's Player of the

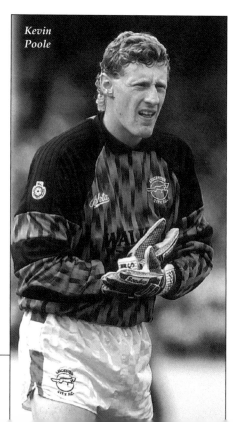

Kevin Poole

Year award for the Premiership campaign
(when he contributed to multiple morning-
after quips as reports spread that he'd
dropped the memento in question)!

Appearances (to end 1994/5):
PL: 36 apps. 0 gls.
FL: 75 apps. 0 gls.
FAC: 6 apps. 0 gls.
LC: 6 apps. 0 gls.
FMC: 5 apps. 0 gls.
AIC: 1 app. 0 gls.
P/O: 3 apps. 0 gls.
Total: *132 apps. 0 gls.*

POTTS, Brian

Role: Right back
b. Sunderland, 3rd September 1948

CAREER: app Aug 1964/pro Sept 1965:CITY/
July 1969:Peterborough United.
Debut v Newcastle United (A) 3.4.68 (sub)

A teenage member of City reserves'
Combination Cup-winning side of 1967, Brian
finally got a substantial first-team chance
during the last months of Matt Gillies'
managerial tenure at Leicester, filling in for
Peter Rodrigues in the right-back spot as City
unfortunately began their slide into the
relegation zone. Frank O'Farrell released him
at the end of the season, but he put together a
50-game career over two years with Posh.

Appearances:
FL: 9 (1) apps. 0 gls.
LC: 1 app. 0 gls.
Total: *10 (1) apps. 0 gls.*

PRICE, Ernest Clifford

Role: Inside left
b. Market Bosworth, Leics,
13th June 1900

CAREER: Coalville Swifts/
am Jan 1917: FOSSE/(Nov
1919-loan-Coalville Swifts)/
pro Oct 1920:CITY/
June 1922:Halifax Town/
Dec 1923:Southampton/
June 1926:Nottingham
Forest/Sept 1928:Loughborough
Corinthians/cs 1929:Nuneaton Town/
Gresley Rovers/Oct 1933:Snibston United.

Brian Potts

Cliff Price

Debut (WW1) v Notts County (H)
13.1.17; (postwar) v Tottenham
Hotspur (H) 11.9.19 (scored twice)

Having claimed 33 goals for the
Fosse in wartime competitions, to
make himself leading scorer for
the period, Cliff was finally
persuaded to turn professional by
Peter Hodge over a year after
making his League bow at inside-
left and hitting three counters in
his first two games. The local lad
didn't, however, find it easy to
compete for a senior slot with
imports like Macauley and Graham,
and eventually moved on to make his mark
elsewhere: as a goalscorer in Division Three,

and as a more studious contributor to the attacks of the Saints and Forest. Cliff was a collier during WW1, and was sent back to pit work only four days after enlisting for active service in the summer of 1918.

Appearances:
FL: 28 apps. 8 gls.
WW1: 75 apps. 33 gls.
Total: *103 apps. 41 gls.*

PRICE, Frederick Thomas

Role: Outside left
b. Ibstock, Leics, 24th October 1901
d. Leicester, November 1985

CAREER: Whitwick Imperial/am Feb 1921/ pro May 1921:CITY/May 1924:Southampton/ May 1925:Wolverhampton Wanderers/June 1927:Chesterfield/Feb 1929:Burton Town/ cs 1929:Nuneaton Town/Sep 1930:Midland Red Sports.

Debut v South Shields (H) 26.2.23

A clever outside-left, Fred was unfortunate to find himself third in line for the City first-team shirt behind Sandy Trotter and Percy Tompkin, and moved to The Dell, along with Dennis

Fred Price

Jones, as part of the deal which brought Harry Hooper to Leicester. His most consistent campaign - and, with 8 goals, his highest-scoring - was his first with Wolves in the Second Division. Fred's brother Jack played as a full-back for City reserves, Bristol Rovers, Swindon Town and Torquay United, while Cliff (see previous page) was his uncle and, briefly, his inside-forward partner with both Southampton and Nuneaton. Fred was also on the Leicestershire CCC ground staff in 1923.

Appearances:
FL: 4 apps. 0 gls.
Total: *4 apps. 0 gls.*

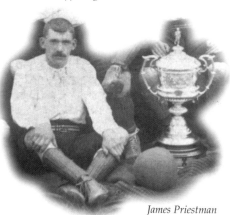

James Priestman

PRIESTMAN, James (Derrick)

Role: Forward
b. Melton Mowbray, Leics, c 1872

CAREER: Melton Town/Mar 1893:FOSSE.

Debut v Long Eaton Rangers (A) ML 11.3.1893

A versatile reserve forward who turned out in all the front-line positions for Fosse across the final two Midland League seasons and the first in the Second Division, James appeared at outside-left in the club's initial League fixture after a mix-up over new signing Hugh Gallacher's registration - and Grimsby keeper Whitehouse later admitted that one of his shots had been clawed back from over the line, unseen by the referee, during the 3-4 defeat. He was also a goalscoring representative for Leicestershire in inter-county fare.

Appearances:
FL: 8 apps. 2 gls.
ML: 7 apps. 3 gls.
Total: *15 apps. 5 gls.*

Steve Prindiville

PRINDIVILLE, Steven Alan

Role: Left back
b. Harlow, Essex, 26th December 1968

CAREER: YT July 1985/pro Jan 1987:CITY/ cs 1988:Chesterfield/cs 1989:Mansfield Town/ Aug 1991:Hinckley Town/Sept 1991:Leicester United/Sept 1991:East Bengal/Feb 1992: Leicester United/Feb 1992:Doncaster Rovers/ (Jan 1994-trials-Wycombe Wanderers)/ Feb 1994:Halifax Town.

Debut v Shrewsbury Town (A) 16.1.88 (sub)

A scorer in City's FA Youth Cup semi-final defeat against Charlton in 1987, full-back Steve made a brief step up to senior level during the early days of David Pleat's management, and looked confidently adventurous in his Simod Cup outing against Stoke, but was freed in the summer of 1988. At Saltergate he was for one season a Third Division regular, linking again at various times with Robert Alleyne and Tony Brien, but relegation saw him move on to Field Mill, and briefly renew on-field acquaintance with Steve Wilkinson, another Filbert Street youth-squad contemporary. A brief return to local football was rather exotically spiced with a three-month playing contract in India, during which Steve played in both the Durand Cup Final and in the quarter-finals of the Asian Cup Winners Cup; and then a non-contract spell at Belle Vue turned into a two-year engagement. At the end of 1994/5, Steve was named as Conference side Halifax's Player of the Year.

Appearances:
FL: 0 (1) app. 0 gls.
FMC: 1 app. 0 gls.
Total: *1 (1) apps. 0 gls.*

PROCTOR, James F.

Role: Inside right
b. London

CAREER: Custom House/cs 1911: Huddersfield Town/Nov 1912:FOSSE.
Debut v Fulham (H) 30.11.12

Briefly one of Dick Pudan's charges during his stint as manager at Leeds Road, this inside-right then played a few games in front of his former boss when the latter resumed his playing career with the Fosse. Proctor had also been a former amateur teammate of Jim Harrold, but made nothing like the same impact at Leicester. However, his sole League goal (a consolation in a 1-5 defeat at Birmingham in January 1913) was the club's 1000th in the competition. His other Fosse counter had come two days earlier, and was even less consoling: lending no respectability to the 1-4 home Cup defeat by Southern League Norwich City.

Appearances:
FL: 7 apps. 1 gl.
FAC: 1 app. 1 gl.
Total: *8 apps. 2 gls.*

James Proctor

PROCTOR, Norman

Role: Inside forward
b. Alnwick, Northumberland, 11th May 1896
d. Winlaton Mill, Co. Durham,
27th February 1947

CAREER: Spen Black & White/Scotswood/ Blyth Spartans/May 1922:Rotherham County/ June 1923:West Ham United/June 1924:CITY/ May 1925:Tranmere Rovers/Aug 1927:Halifax Town/cs 1931:Workington/Oct 1933: Newbiggin West End.

Debut v Manchester United (A) 30.8.24

A deep-lying, scheming inside-forward who first came to notice in the County Durham schools side, Norman found himself unexpectedly elevated in status during the 1923 close season: as the Rotherham team he left had just been relegated from the Second, promoted

Norman Proctor

West Ham were preparing for their initial First Division term. He only managed seven games for the Hammers, though, and then had an even shorter senior career at Filbert Street, definitively losing his place after four of the first five games of 1924/5 had seen City scoreless - and this in a term which nonetheless saw them crowned champions of Division Two. Norman's best spell came with the Shaymen, for whom he made 126 appearances.

Appearances:
FL: 5 apps. 0 gls.
Total: *5 apps. 0 gls.*

PROUDFOOT, David

Role: Centre half
b. c 1873

CAREER: Whiteinch Juniors/ 1893:Partick Thistle/Dec 1896: FOSSE/cs 1898:Bedminster/cs 1899:Partick Thistle.

Debut v Grimsby Town (H) 5.12.1896

A skilful centre-half from a footballing family - his brother John also trekked south from Partick to play for Blackburn, Everton and Watford, then returned to Hamilton Academicals - David failed to complete his second season with Fosse. One of six players suspended by the club as a disciplinary measure in February 1898, he never played again in Leicester colours; though he scored his only goal in English football on his Southern League debut for Bedminster against Spurs.

Appearances:
FL: 25 apps. 0 gls.
FAC: 2 apps. 0 gls.
Total: *27 apps. 0 gls.*

PUDAN, Albert Ernest (Dick)

Role: Left back
b. West Ham, London

CAREER: Clapton/cs 1900:West Ham United/ cs 1902:Bristol Rovers/July 1906:Newcastle United/May 1909:FOSSE/Aug 1910: Huddersfield Town (mgr)/Nov 1912:FOSSE.

Debut v Wolverhampton Wanderers (H) 1.9.09

Universally known throughout his career as Dick, this extremely cultured full-back stood out in an age of hefty kickers by dint of his thoughtful and constructive approach to the game. He joined West Ham as an amateur for their initial Southern League season under that name, and won a championship medal in that sphere in 1905 while totting up 116 appearances for Bristol Rovers. Dick also took an FA Cup runners-up medal from Newcastle's 1908 Final defeat by Wolves. His Fosse full-back partnership with Billy Henry was the classiest the club had fielded, and Dick became a sure-shot penalty taker; but Huddersfield, newly elected to the League, offered him an early chance to preach tactics rather than play, and he directed their fortunes from the sidelines for two seasons before briefly

Dick Pudan

returning to Leicester and donning his boots again to partner the young Tommy Clay. When the club was reconstructed as Leicester City in 1919, Dick - described on registration documents as a hosiery manufacturer - was among the new directors; though as he had been a professional player, it took until March 1921 for the FA to sanction his appointment in that capacity. He remained on the board until February 1940, and briefly (1929-31) took the chair; the only former player so to serve the club. Dick was also regarded as a valid candidate for the City managerial vacancy in June 1939, prior to the appointment of Tom Bromilow.

Appearances:
FL: 46 apps. 7 gls.
FAC: 5 apps. 0 gls.
Total: *51 apps. 7 gls.*

PUTTNAM, David Paul

Role: Outside left
b. Leicester,
3rd February 1967

CAREER: Kirby Muxloe/
cs 1985:Leicester United/
Feb 1989:CITY/Jan 1990:
Lincoln City.

Debut v Barnsley (H)
11.4.89 (sub)

David Puttnam

A reserve-team trialist who scored one goal and made two more on his Central League debut, David soon signed up from City's Blaby-based Southern League neighbours as David Pleat sought to fill the left-wing gap occasioned by Peter Weir's return to Scotland. His willingness to take on his full-back for pace and skill provided some optimistic pointers from the tail-end of 1988/9, but David failed to consolidate his progress during the following term. He rejected a mooted move to Carlisle, but soon signed on at Sincil Bank for £40,000 after impressing during a two-month loan spell, and became Lincoln's Player of the Year for 1992/3.

Appearances:
FL: 4 (3) apps. 0 gls.
LC: 0 (1) app. 0 gls.
Total: *4 (4) apps. 0 gls.*

PYNEGAR, Albert

Role: Inside forward
b. Eastwood, Notts, 24th September 1895
d. Basford, Notts, January qtr 1978

CAREER: 1913:Sutton Town/May 1920: CITY/Jan 1924:Coventry City/July 1925: Oldham Athletic/Jan 1929:Port Vale/Oct 1930: Chesterfield/Aug 1932:Rotherham United.
Debut v Bury (H) 2.9.20 (scored twice)

Almost 25 before he made his League bow, but rapidly regarded as a veritable goal machine, Albert was unfortunate to be edged out of the senior reckoning so often with City by Jock Paterson, George Waite and Arthur Chandler. He could hardly be faulted for the vigour with which he pressed his claims, though: swapping Central Alliance football with Sutton for record-breaking action in the same league with City reserves, he scored six times on his debut and finished 1920/1 with 49 goals from only 25 appearances, to add to his six counters for the first team. A prematurely-balding bustler who actually preferred the inside-forward positions to the leader's role, Albert indexed his goal-knack again in 1922/3, with eleven goals from only fourteen Second Division games, yet still wasn't assured of a regular place.

At Coventry he was top scorer in a relegated team; then twice topped Oldham's Second Division charts before helping both Vale and Chesterfield to the Third Division (North) championship in successive seasons. By the time he left Millmoor, Albert's senior striking tally numbered 173 League goals, plus 8 in the FA Cup.

Appearances:
FL: 44 apps. 20 gls.
FAC: 4 apps. 1 gl.
Total: *48 apps. 21 gls.*

QUINN, James Martin

Role: Striker
b. Belfast, 18th November 1959

CAREER: Whitchurch Alport/Oswestry
Town/Dec 1981:Swindon Town/Aug 1984:
Blackburn Rovers/Dec 1986:Swindon Town/
June 1988:CITY/Mar 1989:Bradford City/
Dec 1989:West Ham United/July 1991:
Bournemouth/July 1992:Reading.

Debut v West Bromwich Albion (H) 27.8.88 (sub)

Often an international team-mate of John
O'Neill and Paul Ramsey, Jimmy had collected
19 Northern Ireland caps
as a striker by the time
City signed him for a
tribunal-set fee of £210,000
(and would add a further
four international
selections as a Leicester
player). A relatively late
entrant to senior football,
he had quickly built a
reputation as an elegant
front-runner, but it was not
until the 1987/8 season,
when he played alongside
hefty target-man Dave
Bamber at Swindon, that
he revealed a really prolific
predatory knack. Three
goals against City had
featured in his sizeable
haul that term but, having
arrived at Filbert Street, he
proved unable to convince
David Pleat that he
merited a regular
spearhead role in lieu of
either Nicky Cross or
Mike Newell.

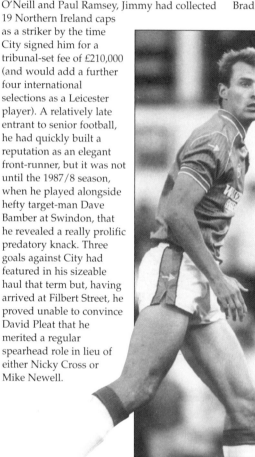

Jimmy Quinn

Jimmy accordingly
suffered much
frustration on the
subs' bench during
his short City spell
(despite three times
coming on and scoring); was able to offer only
tantalising glimpses of his aerial power and
dead-ball accuracy; and soon had to accept
that he was something of a tactical fish out of
water with Leicester, moving on to Valley
Parade in the exchange deal which brought
Mick Kennedy in the opposite direction.
Perhaps predictably, Jimmy claimed
Bradford's late winner against City a month
after, and repeated the
dose the following term,
before re-uniting with
former Swindon boss Lou
Macari at Upton Park.
Jimmy's contribution to
the Hammers' promotion
in 1991 was substantial
(even if it again involved
a fair few outings in shirts
numbered 12 or 14), but a
cut-price £40,000 move to
Dean Court was his only
reward. He led Reading's
Division Two
championship effort of
1993/4 from the front, as
the League's 35-goal top
scorer; and on Mark
McGhee's move from Elm
Park to Filbert Street,
Jimmy became joint
player/manager of the
Royals alongside Mick
Gooding. In fact he led his
side to Wembley and the
Play Off brink of the
Premiership (scoring the
final goal in a 3-4 thriller
shaded by rivals Bolton),
by which point his career
tally of League strikes
alone stood at 171.

Appearances:
FL: 13 (18) apps. 6 gls.
FAC: 0 (1) app. 0 gls.
LC: 2 (1) apps. 0 gls.
FMC: 0 (1) app. 0 gls.
Total: *15 (21) apps. 6 gls.*

RAMSEY, Paul Christopher

Role: Midfield
b. Derry, 3rd September 1962

CAREER: Derry Athletic YC/app 1979/
pro Apr 1980:CITY/Aug 1991:Cardiff City/
Aug 1993:St.Johnstone/(Nov 1994-loan-Cardiff
City).

Debut v Arsenal (H) 7.3.81 (sub)

One of many latter-day City midfielders also
utilised extensively as a full-back, Paul
developed his ball-winning skills during the
club's Second Division stint of the early 80s,
wearing the No.2 shirt throughout the 1983
promotion campaign, and timing his first goal
- in the crucial victory at Oldham - to
perfection. He won the first of 14 Northern
Ireland caps in September 1983, though
injuries and spells of in-and-out form
occasionally left him sidelined from both
domestic and international action.
Probably strongest in a man-marking
role, and least effective as the fulcrum of
a passing game, Paul nonetheless
claimed the City Supporters' 'Goal of the
Season' award for a precise piece of
opportunism against QPR in 1986/7. He
was handed the team captaincy on the
arrival of manager David Pleat, and
granted a testimonial in 1989 (with Spurs
in opposition), yet City were ready to
offload him in a mooted exchange deal
with Walsall's Craig Shakespeare before
that year's transfer deadline. Paul opted
to stay and fight for his place, and
indeed reasserted himself as a middle-
line grafter as City turned around their
disastrous start to the 1989/90 Second
Division campaign, when his two-goal
'super sub' intervention in a 4-3 win
over Leeds marked a vital turning point.
Two dismissals somewhat marred his
final season at Filbert Street, and he
moved on when it became clear there
would be no regular role for him in
Brian Little's selections, to rejoin his one-
time City reserve coach, Eddie May, at
Ninian Park. Two Welsh Cup medals
and a Third Division championship gong
(as skipper) accrued from his initial
Cardiff spell; and Paul would have
returned to Wales in October 1993 after
failing to settle (under the management
of former Irish team-mate John

McClelland) in
Scotland, had not
the Football League
invoked a rule
forbidding a
transfer back
within twelve months. Rules tripped him up
again when, a further year on, he rejoined the
Bluebirds on loan, for he was ineligible to turn
out against Ebbw Vale in the Welsh Cup, and
his team was unceremoniously ejected from
the 1994/5 competition (though legal
arguments eventually won them a
reinstatement).

Appearances:
FL: 278 (12) apps. 13 gls.
FAC: 9 (1) apps. 1 gl.
LC: 19 apps. 1 gl.
FMC: 2 (1) apps. 0 gls.
Total: *308 (14) apps. 15 gls.*

*Paul
Ramsey*

RANDLE, Arthur John

Role: Right half
*b. West Bromwich,
3rd December 1880
d. West Bromwich,
29th September 1913*

CAREER: Lyng Rovers/Oldbury Town/Darlaston/ cs 1901:West Bromwich Albion/ May 1908:FOSSE.

Debut v Sheffield Wednesday (H) 1.9.08

An experienced wing-half who had made 132 League appearances during his seven-year stint as a Throstle, Arthur signed on for Fosse's fateful First Division bow, and shook off the disappointments of that campaign to complete five years'

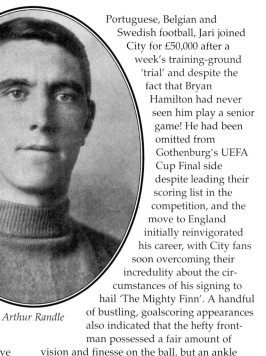

Arthur Randle

service in the right-half berth as a defensive lynchpin. When Fosse released him in 1913, he became licensee of 'The Golden Cup' back in his home town, but within months succumbed to cancer at the age of 32. All proceeds from the South Eastern League game between Fosse and Brentford reserves were donated to Arthur's widow. Arthur was another West Midlander to have been selected early in his career as a 'Junior International'; his hobby during his playing years was beekeeping.

Appearances:
*FL: 123 apps. 2 gls.
FAC: 10 apps. 0 gls.*
Total: *133 apps. 2 gls.*

RANTANEN, Jari Juhani

Role: Striker
b. Helsinki, Finland, 31st December 1961

CAREER: HJK (Helsinki)/Estoril/Beerschot VAV/1986:IFK Gothenburg/Aug 1987:CITY/ (Dec 1988-loan-Belenenses)/July 1989:HJK (Helsinki)/1993:FinnPa.

Debut v Crystal Palace (A) 12.9.87

A peripatetic international striker whose goal earned Finland a draw against England in 1985, and who had gained wide experience in

Portuguese, Belgian and Swedish football, Jari joined City for £50,000 after a week's training-ground 'trial' and despite the fact that Bryan Hamilton had never seen him play a senior game! He had been omitted from Gothenburg's UEFA Cup Final side despite leading their scoring list in the competition, and the move to England initially reinvigorated his career, with City fans soon overcoming their incredulity about the circumstances of his signing to hail 'The Mighty Finn'. A handful of bustling, goalscoring appearances also indicated that the hefty frontman possessed a fair amount of vision and finesse on the ball, but an ankle

Jari Rantanen

injury and subsequent loss of confidence denied Jari the chance to develop his initially promising partnership with Mike Newell, which was never renewed again by David Pleat. The latter's attempts to offload Jari were for a long time frustrated - the terms of his work permit precluded sale or loan to a British club, while the demands of the player's agent scuppered a proposed deal with Bundesliga club Koln. Jari had been out of first-team action for almost a year prior to his unsuccessful trial spell in Lisbon, but continued to add caps to his tally (which eventually totalled 35 games; 8 goals) throughout this unhappy period on Leicester's books. The award of another year's contract to Jari, after he had done much to keep the reserves in the top flight of the Central League in 1989, was soon revealed to be a method of assuring City of a fee (£45,000, in fact) when he did indeed move on. Eventually recovered from further injury setbacks, Jari shared in HJK's 1990 Finnish title win, but hit the headlines for the wrong reasons when sent off in the second leg of the championship play offs. In 1994, he suffered a fractured skull after colliding with a goalkeeper in a Finnish league game.

Appearances:
FL: 10 (3) apps. 3 gls.
LC: 2 (1) apps. 1 gl.
FMC: 2 (1) apps. 0 gls.
Total: 14 (5) apps. 4 gls.

REED, Kevin David

Role: Winger
b. Leicester, 22nd September 1960

CAREER: app July 1977/ pro May 1978:CITY.
Debut v Wrexham (H) 22.11.78 (sub)

A diminutive winger, Kevin made his solitary senior appearance under faintly farcical circumstances. Larry May's car broke down on the way to an evening match, nominated substitute Peter Welsh stepped into the vacant defensive berth, and Kevin was plucked from the stand to wear the No.12 shirt despite having only one reserve game's experience to his credit at the time. The inevitable happened when Trevor Christie suffered injury, and Kevin almost made his bow a scoring one when hitting the Wrexham bar with his first shot. Never again in contention, though, he was released in July 1979.

Appearances:
FL: 0 (1) app. 0 gls.
Total: 0 (1) app. 0 gls.

REEDAY, Maurice J.

Role: Full back
b. Darwen, Lancs, 28th August 1909

CAREER: 1929:Darwen/May 1934:Blackpool/ May 1936:Accrington Stanley/Mar 1937:CITY.
Debut v Arsenal (H) 11.9.37

Kevin Reed (left) with Larry May - the man he had to thank for his one first team appearance.

Maurice Reeday

REID, Paul Robert

Role: Utility
b. Warley, Worcs, 19th January 1968

CAREER: app July 1984/pro Jan 1986:CITY/ (Mar 1992-loan-Bradford City)/July 1992: Bradford City/May 1994:Huddersfield Town.
Debut v Southampton (A) 7.3.87

A competitive, nimble teenage striker when his promise was first recognised by Bryan Hamilton, Paul found his career given a major boost when David Pleat decided to play him as a left-footed right-winger. He thrived initially on this unorthodox tactical switch, especially when able to exploit his penchant for cutting inside and across a defence before unleashing a powerful shot, but the predictability of the manoeuvre eventually diminished its effectiveness. The distinct lull in Paul's progress was barely disguised by his later assumption of alternative roles in midfield and at full-back; though he could for a while be relied upon for a sprinkling of spectacular goals, such as the brilliant solo effort at Blackburn which won the 1988 'Goal of the Season'

The full-back always popularly known as 'the man Stanley Matthews couldn't beat', Maurice was given confirmatory credit as such by his frustrated victim, who never relished the ultra-tight marking that was Maurice's trademark. "He was a grand player. I'd say, 'Haven't you got a home to go to, Maurice?' And he'd say, 'Sure I have, but it won't burn down till the end of this 90 minutes, Stan.'" Though he had never made a senior breakthrough at Bloomfield Road, Maurice showed sufficient promise in his 27 League and Cup games at Accrington to tempt a £900 bid from Frank Womack, and in the final two pre-war seasons regularly displaced either Dai Jones or Billy Frame in showing that his defensive capabilities could be adapted to either flank. Another player to 'lose' three appearances from the abandoned 1939/40 season, Maurice virtually ended his career as a guest player back in Lancashire, for Accrington, Blackburn and Burnley; though he also had a few last games for non-league Darwen after rejoining them as coach in October 1947.

Appearances:
FL: 74 apps. 2 gls.
FAC: 5 apps. 0 gls.
WW2: 4 apps. 0 gls.
Total: *83 apps. 2 gls.*

Paul Reid

award from the supporters. Two disastrous back passes, each costing important goals, ended Paul's final spell as a City defender, and he has subsequently reverted to wide midfield play in Yorkshire; substantially assisting Huddersfield to the Play Offs in 1995, but missing out on the Wembley decider which took them into Division One.

Appearances:
FL: 140 (22) apps. 21 gls.
FAC: 5 (1) apps. 0 gls.
LC: 13 apps. 4 gls.
FMC: 6 (2) apps. 0 gls.
Total: *164 (25) apps. 25 gls.*

RENNIE, David

Role: Defender
b. Edinburgh, 29th August 1964

CAREER: app July 1980/pro May 1982:CITY/Jan 1986:Leeds United/July 1989:Bristol City/Feb 1992:Birmingham City/Mar 1993:Coventry City.

Debut v West Bromwich Albion (A) 3.9.83

An almost automatic choice for Scotland at youth international level in the early 80s, David looked set for a long Filbert Street career as a coolly elegant defender in the Alan Hansen mould. But City's constant need for experience at the back in their First Division rearguard campaigns allowed scant opportunities for him to play himself into the side in his favoured berth, and a series of lacklustre performances when David was experimentally shoe-horned into midfield or full-back roles did little to aid his confidence. His only goal for City, though, was a landmark: his header against Coventry during Filbert Street's first-ever Sunday game in December 1984 being the club's 5,000th in the League. Sold to Elland Road for £45,000, David initially had to get used once more to his versatility being exploited for tactical purposes, though he popped up with Leeds' first goal in their 1987 FA Cup semi-final defeat before successfully claiming central defensive responsibilities there. His move to Ashton Gate involved a £175,000 fee, duly paid off in contributions to Bristol City's Third Division promotion season of 1989/90, but he only briefly partnered Russell

Osman for that club before moving on to aid Birmingham's equivalent 1992 elevation, and then to supplement the Premiership back line at Highfield Road.

Appearances:
FL: 21 apps. 1 gl.
LC: 2 apps. 0 gls.
Total: *23 apps. 1 gl.*

David Rennie

REVIE, Donald George

Role: Inside forward
b. Middlesbrough, 10th July 1927
d. Edinburgh, 26th May 1989

CAREER: Middlesbrough Swifts/ Aug 1944: CITY/Nov 1949:Hull City/Oct 1951:Manchester City/ Nov 1956:Sunderland/Dec 1958: Leeds United.

Debut (WW2) v Wolverhampton Wanderers (H) 26.8.44; (postwar) v Manchester City (H) 31.8.46

Though the controversies of his managerial career seem to have set the tone of posterity's overly harsh judgement on him, Don was no stranger to acrimony even in his early days at Leicester. A teenage signing from City's short-lived North Eastern 'nursery' club, who was taken under Sep Smith's wing and taught the basics of constructive inside-forward play, Don was an early victim of the City crowd's occasional propensity for giving 'stick' to their own players, with his thoughtful style initially deemed ponderous by spectators wanting the ball delivered into the box rather more speedily. He turned City hero, however, with his efforts in the 1949 Cup run, culminating in his two semi-final goals against Portsmouth; and it was a hefty blow to both player and club that he had to miss out on the Wembley showpiece after broken blood vessels in his nose almost cost him his life. Several transfer requests later, a £20,000 fee took him to Hull, to learn more of the game's finer points

Do

alongside player/manager Raich Carter (and, as emergency goalkeeper, to concede an Arthur Rowley special in October 1950); and then at Maine Road he hit the headlines as the tactical architect of the so-called 'Revie Plan', which represented a domestic response to recently rubbed-in lessons from the Hungarians. Don played as a deep-lying centre-forward in both the 1955 and 1956 FA Cup Finals, picked up the 'Footballer of the Year' award for 1955, and won recognition at both Football League (two games, six goals) and full England levels (six caps, four goals). He had rather less playing success at either Roker or Elland Road, but assumed the Leeds player/manager's role in March 1961, dropped the on-field responsibility in May 1963, and thereafter led his uncompromising side through a lengthy catalogue of successes and near-misses in League, Cup and European competitions. He took the England manager's reins in 1974; was honoured with the OBE; shouldered much criticism for his safety-first approach and his legendary dossiers on the national side's opposition; and was then accused of everything short of treason when secretly negotiating himself a more highly-paid coaching job in the United Arab Emirates from July 1977. Tragically, the last few years of Don's life were blighted by motor neurone disease.

Appearances:
FL: 96 apps. 25 gls.
FAC: 14 apps. 4 gls.
WW2: 33 apps. 4 gls.
Total: 143 apps. 33 gls.

❑ FOX FACT: *Don Revie was the first of five former City players to be honoured as Footballer of the Year (named by the Football Writers Association since 1948) or Player of the Year (elected by the Professional Footballers Association since 1974). He has been followed by Frank McLintock (Arsenal, 1971), Gordon Banks (Stoke City, 1972), Peter Shilton (Nottingham Forest, 1978, PFA), and Gary Lineker (Everton, 1986, both awards; Tottenham Hotspur, 1992, FWA).*

REYNOLDS, W.

Role: Outside right
b. Leicester

CAREER: Belvoir SS/Oct 1912:FOSSE/ cs 1913:Leicester Imperial.

Debut v Birmingham (A) 18.1.13

An outside-right from the same local club as Tommy Clay, Reynolds understudied Tommy Benfield and George Douglas for a few months, and made his sole senior appearance in a 1-5 defeat at St.Andrews.

Appearances:
FL: 1 app. 0 gls.
Total: 1 app. 0 gls.

RICHARDS, Charles Henry

Role: Inside right
b. Burton-on-Trent, 9th August 1875

CAREER: Gresley Rovers/July 1895:Notts County/Jan 1896:Nottingham Forest/ Jan 1899:Grimsby Town/June 1901:FOSSE/ Aug 1902:Manchester United/Mar 1903: Doncaster Rovers.

Debut v Woolwich Arsenal (A) 7.9.01

Charles Richards

Though he featured in Fosse's most goal-shy attack ever (1901/2 saw them collectively notch only 38 goals from 34 fixtures), stocky inside-right Charles had a fair scoring record behind him. 1898 had seen him win his sole England cap (in place of Steve Bloomer against Ireland) and help Forest to FA Cup Final victory over Derby, and he had claimed 42 goals in 80 League games at Grimsby, leaving after helping them into Division One. He later notched the first League goal scored by the newly-rechristened Manchester United under that name, but failed in his late bid to save Doncaster from an unsuccessful re-election application. (We suspect - thus far without confirmation - he may have been a printer by trade, taking over the family business which held copyright in both the Notts County and Forest team-sheet 'programmes' of the late Victorian era).

Appearances:
FL: 25 apps. 5 gls.
FAC: 1 app. 0 gls.
Total: *26 apps. 5 gls.*

Percy Richards

RICHARDS, Percy

Role: Outside left
b. Merthyr Tydfil, 1908

CAREER: Merthyr Vale/Aug 1925:Cardiff City/May 1928:Tranmere Rovers/Sept 1929: Newport County/Aug 1930:Merthyr Town/ Jan 1931:CITY/May 1932:Coventry City/ Apr 1934:Bath City/July 1936:Brierley Hill Alliance/July 1937:Hereford United.
Debut v Arsenal (H) 5.2.31

A Welsh outside-left who understudied Len Barry during his City days, and experienced distinct ups and downs: his first two appearances were in a 2-7 defeat and a 6-0 victory! Percy had made a First Division bow as an 18-year-old for Cardiff, but seemed to

have betrayed early promise when finding himself back in the Welsh League with Merthyr. However, his hard-up club came to Filbert Street in January 1931 for a friendly against City's Reserves arranged explicitly as a 'shop window' for their saleable talent, and nine days later Willie Orr offered Percy another top-flight chance. A Highfield Road record of 46 League games (7 goals) followed his release.

Appearances:
FL: 10 apps. 2 gls.
Total: *10 apps. 2 gls.*

RICHARDSON, David

Role: Left half
b. Billingham, 11th March 1932

CAREER: Nov 1949:CITY/June 1955:Grimsby Town/June 1960:Swindon Town/July 1961: Barrow.
Debut v Newcastle United (H) 18.9.54

Recruited from Teesside junior football, Dave developed into a versatile reserve defender who had the misfortune to get his patiently

Dave Richardson

awaited senior break - in a 3-2 home win followed by a remarkable 4-6 defeat at the Hawthorns - while Eddie Russell was still firm favourite for the No.6 shirt, and just after Colin Appleton had given notice of his claim on the same position. In his first season at Grimsby, where he eventually totalled 175 League games, Dave helped the Mariners to the championship of Division Three (North). Despite the coincidence of name and north-eastern origins, he should not be confused with City's youth coach of the 80s.

Appearances:
FL: 2 apps. 0 gls.
Total: *2 apps. 0 gls.*

RICHMOND, Hugh

Role: Inside forward / Centre half
b. Kilmarnock, Ayrshire, 9th March 1893

CAREER: 1911:Kilbirnie Ladeside/July 1913: Kilmarnock/May 1914: Galston/Aug 1916:Arthurlie/ Mar 1919:FOSSE/(Jan 1920-loan-Nuneaton Town)/May 1922: Coventry City/May 1925:Queen's Park Rangers/July 1926:Blyth Spartans (p/coach)/Aug 1929:Spennymoor United.

Debut (WW1) v Notts County (H) 22.3.19 (scored twice); (postwar) v Wolverhampton Wanderers (H) 30.8.19

Signed on a recommendation from regular WW1 Fosse guest Alec Donaldson, who had played with him at Arthurlie, Hugh was initially regarded as a goalscoring inside-forward, but soon demonstrated a natural facility at centre-half, too. Unfortunately, in settling to the latter role, he then had to play second fiddle to Jim Harrold for the bulk of his stay. He skippered the City reserve team in the Central Alliance, then built a more substantial senior reputation at Coventry, where his aerial ability earned him the nickname 'Rubberneck', as well as a 19-goal return from 67 League and Cup games (including a consolation against City in 1924/5). During WW1, Hugh had

Hugh Richmond

served with the Seaforth Highlanders: he never appeared at senior level for Killie.

Appearances:
FL: 24 apps. 2 gls.
WW1: 5 apps. 4 gls.
Total: *29 apps. 6 gls.*

RICKUS, J.

Role: Inside forward

CAREER: West Bromwich Albion/cs 1893: FOSSE/1894:not known/1897:Gravesend United.
Debut v Long Eaton Rangers (H) ML 23.9.1893

A former West Brom reserve who got his Fosse chance at Midland League level a week after scoring in a 4-1 friendly win over Sheffield United, Rickus completed but a trio of scoreless games at inside-forward for the seniors. His stint in the Southern League's top flight with Gravesend was almost as brief. (The mysterious interim period of Rickus's career may possibly have been at least partly spent with Hinckley Town, though their mid-1890s half-back was usually known as Alf).

Appearances:
ML: 3 apps. 0 gls.
Total: *3 apps. 0 gls.*

Fred Ridley

RIDLEY, Frederick

Role: Outside left

CAREER: Barnet Alston/ June 1913: FOSSE.
Debut v Birmingham (A) 20.9.13

One of several outside-lefts tried out following the departure of George Harrison, this experienced amateur had been a squad member when Barnet Alston (forerunners of the current League club) won the London League championship in 1907. Fred's sole Fosse outing ended in a single-goal defeat at St.Andrews.

Appearances:
FL: 1 app. 0 gls.
Total: *1 app. 0 gls.*

RIDLEY, John

Role: Midfield
*b. Consett, Co.Durham,
27th April 1952*

CAREER: Sheffield
University/Aug 1973:Port
Vale/(Apr 1978-loan-Fort
Lauderdale Strikers)/
Oct 1978:CITY/Aug 1979:
Chesterfield/Aug 1982:Port
Vale/Aug 1985: Stafford
Rangers(p/coach)/
Eastwood Hanley/
Rists United.
*Debut v Bristol Rovers (H)
28.10.78*

Signed by Jock Wallace to
stiffen the City midfield
during the manager's first,
crucial 'holding' season in
the Second Division, John
performed his short-term function well, with
some gritty displays in front of the back four,
and exercised a useful calming influence on

John Ridley

the predominantly
younger players around
him. Subsequently, he
helped Chesterfield take
the Anglo-Scottish Cup in
1981, was a valuable
member of Port Vale's
Division Four promotion
side of 1983, and led
Stafford to Bob Lord
Trophy success in 1986. A
maths graduate, John had
originally been signed as
a Vale pro by Gordon Lee;
his NASL stint saw him
playing in front of
Gordon Banks. In the
early 1990s, he was
manager of Eastwood
Hanley, and has
subsequently returned to
playing in minor
Staffordshire football.

Appearances:
FL: 17 (7) apps. 0 gls.
FAC: 2 apps. 0 gls.
Total: *19 (7) apps. 0 gls.*

RILEY, Howard

Role: Outside right
b. Wigston, Leics, 18th August 1938

CAREER: Wigston Old Boys/Aug
1955:CITY/ Dec 1965:Walsall/Apr
1967:Atlanta Chiefs/ July
1968:Barrow/1969:Rugby Town/
cs 1970: Burton Albion/1972:Ibstock
Penistone Rovers/Midland
Athletic/Wigston Old Boys.
Debut v Nottingham Forest (H) 22.8.55

A first-teamer within months of leaving
Kibworth School, Howard came from a fine
local sporting family. His grandfather Edwin
and father Harold had both been County
cricketers, and the latter had been a City
reserve in 1924, as would be Howard's
brother Bob in the 60s. His energetic
performances at outside-right earned him
the crowd's nickname of 'Puffer', as well as
two England Under-23 caps (the first won
while he was a Private in the Royal

Leicestershire Regiment) to add to his youth
international honours, and Howard was the
only county-born player in the 1961 Cup
Final team. He maintained his place as an
orthodox speedy winger throughout the
1963 run to Wembley, and drove home the
winning goal against Stoke in the 1964
League Cup Final, at a time when he was
effectively a part-timer, training for and then
following a parallel schoolteaching career.
Following a brief stint in the FIFA-outlawed
National Professional Soccer League in
America (forerunner of the NASL), his
League days ended with Colin Appleton at
Holker Street, and his senior non-league
career with Richie Norman at Burton.
Howard nonetheless remained active in local
soccer for some years, latterly serving as
manager of Wigston Town.

Appearances:
FL: 193 apps. 38 gls.
FAC: 24 apps. 5 gls.
LC: 12 apps. 4 gls.
Eur: 4 apps. 0 gls.
Total: *233 apps. 47 gls.*

RITCHIE, George Thompson

Role: Left half
b. Maryhill, Glasgow, 16th January 1904
d. Leicester, 10th September 1978

CAREER: Maryhill/Feb 1923:Blackburn
Rovers/Royal Albert/cs 1924:Falkirk/Sept
1928:CITY/Aug 1937:Colchester United.
Debut v Burnley (H) 29.9.28

Having quickly bounced back from an
abortive two-game spell at Ewood as a youthful centre-forward, George developed into a
classy left-half at Falkirk, and never looked in
danger of disappointing on his second sortie
into English football. Signing shortly after he'd
starred for a Scottish League XI in a Filbert
Street friendly for the benefit of Leicestershire
CCC, he soon took a grip on the wing-half
spot vacated by Sid Bishop and forged a fine
triangular link on City's left flank with Arthur
Lochhead and Len Barry as the club rose to
runners-up position in the top flight. Eight
seasons of poised performances followed, with
George captaining the side until his place was
put under pressure by Percy Grosvenor. The

George Ritchie

Howard Riley

promotion campaign of 1937 was his last with City for, ignoring offers from Motherwell and Derby, he joined the newly-formed Colchester United and skippered them to the Southern League Cup and championship in successive seasons. Appointed assistant coach at Ipswich Town on the eve of WW2, George was then to be found on the training staff back at Filbert Street between 1946 and 1950.

Appearances:
FL: 247 apps. 12 gls.
FAC: 14 apps. 1 gl.
Total: *261 apps. 13 gls.*

Iwan Roberts

ROBERTS, Iwan Wyn

Role: Striker
b. Bangor, Caernarvonshire, 26th June 1968

CAREER: app May 1985/pro July 1986: Watford/Aug 1990:Huddersfield Town/ Nov 1993:CITY.
Debut v Wolverhampton Wanderers (H) 27.11.93 (scored twice)

"Iwan is a Welshman..." (as the Kop song has it), indeed. Watford enticed him to join them from school precisely because they had a Welsh-speaking coach in Tom Walley; while Iwan has remained in demand for media work in his native tongue as one of very few contemporary internationals able so to converse. Initially developing as a gangling teenage striker at Vicarage Road, Iwan memorably scored the first of his dozen goals for the Hornets as a substitute against Manchester United, and won his first cap against Holland in 1989. Further national call-ups, though, were delayed until he'd settled as a Terriers regular following a £275,000 move (Huddersfield's record outlay). Iwan's decent strike rate brought him to Brian Little's attention, but it took months of rumour - and a misfiring City experiment to play without a target-man following Steve Walsh's injury - before £300,000 landed him at Filbert Street. Iwan's fine two-goal debut rescued a home point, and his goal-every-two-games ratio was soon lending credibility and substance to City's promotion drive. A 12-minute hat-trick in a 3-3 draw against Derby sealed his place in City folklore (and song!), and both his shooting and heading power recommended that Little should gamble on his return from injury to share the sharp end of the attack against the Rams at Wembley. Iwan made less impact during the following Premiership season, with his first touch too often letting him down, but always a willing workhorse, still ended up as top scorer for the second term running. Iwan has so far added a trio of Welsh caps to his tally while with City.

Appearances (to end 1994/5):
PL: 32 (5) apps. 9 gls.
FL: 26 apps. 13 gls.
FAC: 3 apps. 2 gls.
LC: 2 apps. 0 gls.
P/O: 1 app. 0 gls.
Total: *64 (5) apps. 24 gls.*

Jerry Roberts

ROBERTS, Jeremy

Role: Goalkeeper
b. Middlesbrough, 24th November 1966

CAREER: YT 1983:Hartlepool United/
June 1984:CITY/Oct 1986:Luton Town/
Mar 1987:Darlington/Sept 1988:Brentford/
(Oct 1988-loan-Maidenhead)/cs 1989:
Gillingham/1989:Whitby Town.

Debut v West Bromwich Albion (H) 12.10.85

A non-contract trainee at Hartlepool,
goalkeeper Jerry made his senior bow as a
16-year-old in an FA Cup tie at Rotherham,
and subsequently played in the replay and one
Fourth Division game before being released.
He followed Ian Andrews into the England
Youth team's yellow jersey shortly after
arriving at Filbert Street, and understudied his
international predecessor for the first-team
custodianship after Mark Wallington moved
on; standing in for one draw and two defeats
during the 1985/6 First Division campaign.
His contract was cancelled by mutual consent,
however, in October 1986, and Jerry returned
to the North East to resume his League career
after a spell in Luton's reserves. He briefly
featured in the same Brentford defence as
Andy Feeley, but made no breakthrough at all
with the Gills.

Appearances:
FL: 3 apps. 0 gls.
Total: *3 apps. 0 gls.*

ROBERTS, Robert

Role: Utility
b. Edinburgh, 2nd September 1940

CAREER: Edinburgh Norton/
1958:Motherwell/Sept 1963:CITY/Sept 1970:
Mansfield Town/cs 1972:Coventry City
(coach)/July 1973:Colchester United
(p/coach).
Debut v Fulham (H) 21.9.63

City's record signing at the time, Bobby cost
£41,000 as Matt Gillies outbid Ipswich Town
for his services. Primarily an attacking
linkman, with one appearance for each of
Scotland Under-23 and the Scottish League to
his credit, he struggled initially to justify high
expectations at Filbert Street, especially as City
employed him successively at left-half, inside-
right and centre-forward, and he missed out
on the 1964 League Cup Final despite scoring
in both legs of the semi-final classic against
West Ham. Bobby really clicked, however,
when he inherited Frank McLintock's No.4
shirt, rolling up his sleeves and becoming
City's midfield anchorman throughout the
mid- and late-60s, and finally gaining a
modicum of reward as an ever-present in the

Bobby Roberts

1969 Cup run. Much valued for his 100% effort and skilful prompting, he had one trait that became almost perversely endearing: rarely finishing a game without having endangered the crowd with at least one thunderbolt shot way over the bar! He later gave two seasons and 80 games service to Mansfield, and twice returned to the League fray when coaching at Colchester, where he assumed his first managerial role in June 1975 and met much success. Subsequently, as boss at Wrexham, Bobby was forced to make one last return to action - playing in a Welsh Cup tie as a goalkeeper! (His dubious qualifications for this amounted to the fact that he'd temporarily replaced the injured Peter Shilton at Old Trafford in 1967, and had even earlier guarded the net behind Ian St.John in a trophy-winning Motherwell 5-a-side team!). Bobby later coached the El Shabar side in Kuwait, managed Grimsby Town during their 1987/8 relegation season, and then returned to Leicester in June 1988 for a three-year spell on the City coaching staff. In 1992, he was once more back in Kuwait.

Appearances:
FL: 224 (5) apps. 26 gls.
FAC: 30 apps. 4 gls.
LC: 21 (1) apps. 6 gls.
Total: *275 (6) apps. 36 gls.*

Lammie Robertson

ROBERTSON, Archibald Lamond

Role: Midfield
b. Paisley, Renfrewshire, 27th September 1947

CAREER: Sept 1966:Burnley/June 1968:Bury/ Feb 1969:Halifax Town/Dec 1972:Brighton & Hove Albion/May 1974:Exeter City/(Apr 1976-loan-Chicago Sting)/Sept 1977:CITY/ Sept 1978:Peterborough United/Jan 1979: Bradford City/July 1981:Northwich Victoria (p/mgr)/Oct 1981:Darwen.
Debut v Arsenal (A) 17.9.77

A junior at Turf Moor, midfielder Lammie got his League break with Bury and helped Halifax clinch their first-ever promotion in 1969. He dropped from Division Two to Three in his first season at Brighton, but prompted Exeter to rise from the basement to Division Three in 1977. Then Frank McLintock moved in to bring him to Filbert Street for £8,000 (on a recommendation from Davie Gibson), though his top-flight experience was brief. Lammie found it impossible to settle in a City line-up then changing shape almost weekly, and faced a sceptical crowd who had got hold of the rumour that McLintock had originally bid for his Exeter team-mate Alan Beer, and hadn't wished to come away empty-handed. Accordingly, his occasionally delicate ball skills were exhibited largely in a reserve context until he resumed his travels.

Appearances:
FL: 6 (1) apps. 0 gls.
Total: *6 (1) apps. 0 gls.*

ROBERTSON, Hugh

Role: Centre forward
b. (Scotland)

CAREER: Partick Thistle/cs 1890:Everton/ cs 1894:Millwall Athletic/June 1895:Burnley/ June 1897:Lincoln City/May 1899:Millwall/ cs 1900:Dundee/(Nov 1900-trials-FOSSE).
Debut v Burton Swifts (H) 1.12.1900
(scored once)

An experienced Scottish centre-forward deemed not to fit the bill for Fosse at the end of his month's trial, Hugh previously had top-scored both at First Division level at Turf Moor, and in two Second Division seasons as an ever-present at Sincil Bank, and had fitted in two Southern League spells with Millwall. (There is contradictory evidence about his early contribution to Everton's cause, for he is often confused with his contemporary there, a wing-half named Hope-Robertson who moved on to Bootle).

Hugh Robertson

Appearances:
FL: 5 apps. 1 gl.
Total: *5 apps. 1 gl.*

ROBINS, Mark Gordon

Role: Striker
b. Ashton-under-Lyme, 22nd December 1969

CAREER: YT July 1986/pro Sept 1986: Manchester United/Aug 1992:Norwich City/ Jan 1995:CITY.

Debut v Manchester City (A) 25.1.95 (scored once)

Mark McGhee's second capture for rock-bottom City, and the club's second £1 million import, nippy striker Mark scored the debut header which secured the only away win of the Premiership campaign at a waterlogged Maine Road, and signed off his first Leicester term with a fine last-minute equaliser at The Dell. In the interim, he'd shown characteristic mobility around the edge of the box, and a few more glimpses of a predatory nature within it, though his confidence was clearly affected by the generally downbeat context in which relegation-booked City were performing. A graduate of the FA School of Excellence at Lilleshall, Mark became a prolific reserve scorer at Old Trafford, and made his debut in January 1989 in an FA Cup tie. It was his crucial contribution to the Reds' next Cup campaign which first brought him headlines, though; when his three strikes on the way to Wembley (including the extra-time semi-final winner against Oldham) earned him an entry from the bench during the first drawn Final against Crystal Palace. However, despite a fine haul of representative honours (following England Youth caps with six appearances for the Under-21 side, and a personal five-goal tally from one such game against France), Mark was far too regularly confined to the subs' bench with United, making 42 late entries into League and Cup action, yet only 27 starts. Listed at his own request, he declined an offer from Dynamo Dresden, but £800,000 took him to Carrow Road, and his 15 goals in 1992/3 helped the Canaries into Europe. Mark was injured in the famous away win over Bayern Munich, and two subsequent knee operations ruined his second Norwich term, though he had proven his fitness again in sporadic outings during the first half of 1994/5, before McGhee swooped, and before Norwich began their own slide to join City in the relegation frame.

Appearances (to end 1994/5):
PL: 16 (1) apps. 5 gls.
FAC: 2 apps. 0 gls.
Total: *18 (1) apps. 5 gls.*

Mark Robins

ROBINSON, Walter L.

Role: Defender
b. Irthlingborough, Northants

CAREER: Finedon/Irthlingborough Town/
Aug 1898:FOSSE/Aug 1905:Burton United.
Debut v Newton Heath (H) 17.12.1898

Walter Robinson

A dogged, hard-tackling defender, Walter inherited the Fosse pivot's role from Jimmy Brown and over seven seasons turned out in all five full- and half-back positions, battling his way back past countless interim signings after several times appearing to have dropped out of the senior reckoning. His loyalty was rewarded, and his popularity acknowledged, with a benefit game in 1903 (a Christmas friendly against Clapton), and his fighting spirit was recognised by Burton United, who he skippered through their final two seasons in the Football League, and whose player/manager he became in the summer of 1908.

Appearances:
FL: 177 apps. 3 gls.
FAC: 17 apps. 0 gls.
Total: *194 apps. 3 gls.*

ROBSON, Keith

Role: Striker
b. Hetton-le-Hole, Co.Durham,
15th November 1953

CAREER: May 1971:Newcastle United/
Sept 1974:West Ham United/(May 1977-loan-
Team Hawaii)/Aug 1977:Cardiff City/
Feb 1978:Norwich City/Sept 1981:CITY/
(Mar 1983-loan-Carlisle United)/Sept 1983:
(Hong Kong)/Wroxham/Norwich Busmen/
Corinthians/Wroxham.
Debut v Derby County (A) 12.9.81

The luckless understudy to Malcolm MacDonald on Tyneside, Keith exhibited some of his rival's bustling aggression, and became something of a Cup-tie specialist at Upton Park after a £60,000 move: missing out on the 1975 FA Cup Final, but scoring one of the Hammers' consolation goals in the 1976 European Cup Winners' Cup Final defeat by Anderlecht, and briefly forming a twin striking partnership with his namesake and fellow North-Easterner, 'Pop'. Two moves later, Jock Wallace bought him for a small fee to inject some extra experience and weight into City's youthful promotion challenge, but his first-team tenure as a left-sided attacker was brief. He returned to East Anglia after a short spell in Hong Kong football, and for some time remained active in local football in the Norwich area. Keith's semi-idyllic summer of '77 came about when four Hammers assisted Team Hawaii in their only North American Soccer League campaign: the club franchise had simply shifted from San Antonio to mid-Pacific, and gates at the Aloha Stadium, Honolulu ranged from 1,800 up to almost 13,000.

Appearances:
FL: 8 (1) apps. 0 gls.
FAC: 1 (1) apps. 0 gls.
LC: 1 app. 1 gl.
Total: *10 (2) apps. 1 gl.*

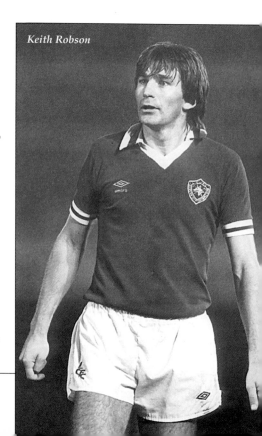

Keith Robson

RODRIGUES, Peter Joseph

Role: Right back
b. Cardiff, 21st January 1944

CAREER: May 1961:Cardiff City/Dec 1965:
CITY/Oct 1970:Sheffield Wednesday/July
1975:Southampton/1977:Romsey Town.
Debut v Stoke City (H) 1.1.66

At his peak the undisputed master of the sliding tackle, Peter was already an established
Welsh international right-back, with additional
experience in Cardiff's initial Cup Winners'
Cup forays, when he
became a New Year's
Eve signing for City
at the new record fee
of £42,500. Thereafter,
his pace, overlapping
inclinations and that
trademark method
of dispossession
brought a new
dimension to
received notions of
Filbert Street full-
back play, and his
City career would
surely have
stretched much
further had it not
been for the
exciting emergence of
Steve Whitworth.

Peter Rodrigues

Only one sad incident - a missed close-range
goal chance in the 1969 FA Cup Final -
remotely shadowed Peter's stay at Leicester,
but he firmly obliterated that particular
Wembley memory when, after being freed by
the Owls and having won the last of his 40
caps, he skippered underdogs Southampton to
Cup victory over Manchester United in 1976.
Peter has subsequently busied himself as the
landlord of pubs in Hampshire and
Carmarthen, and with coaching such local
outfits as Telephone Sports, Braishfield,
Romsey Town and Blackfield & Langley, as
well as holidaying schoolkids at Tenby Soccer
Schools.

Appearances:
FL: 139 (1) apps. 6 gls.
FAC: 18 (1) apps. 0 gls.
LC: 11 (1) apps. 0 gls.
Total: *168 (3) apps. 6 gls.*

ROFE, Dennis

Role: Left back
b. Epping, Essex, 1st June 1950

CAREER: app Sept 1965/pro Feb 1968:
Orient/Aug 1972:CITY/Feb 1980:Chelsea/
July 1982:Southampton.
Debut v Coventry City (H) 26.8.72

Lined up to rejoin his former manager
Jimmy Bloomfield at Leicester on the very
day David Nish left, Dennis cost about half
the £250,000 fee City received.

Comparisons between the left-backs,
if invidious, were inevitable, but
sound judgement saw that what City
had lost in sheer elegance, they'd
gained in cheery enthusiasm and
whole-hearted vigour. Dennis
justifiably became a fixture in City's
No.3 shirt, quick into the tackle and
quick to augment the attack, and was
unlucky to win only one Under-23 cap.
The dressing room joker among City's
Cockney colony of the mid-70s, he
faced his on-field responsibilities with
determined seriousness, and took the
team captaincy when Frank McLintock
arrived. The majority of his small tally
of goals remain utterly memorable: a
last-minute solo waltz from the halfway
line to clinch a 4-3 away win over
Birmingham; a flukey free kick from his

Dennis Rofe

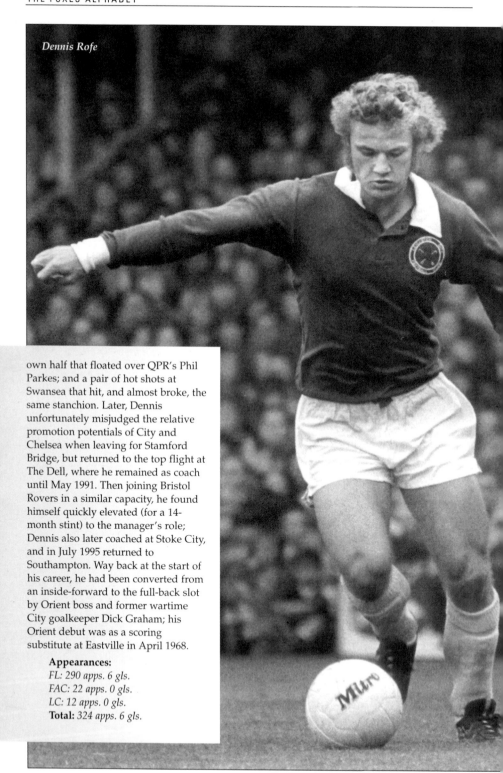

Dennis Rofe

own half that floated over QPR's Phil Parkes; and a pair of hot shots at Swansea that hit, and almost broke, the same stanchion. Later, Dennis unfortunately misjudged the relative promotion potentials of City and Chelsea when leaving for Stamford Bridge, but returned to the top flight at The Dell, where he remained as coach until May 1991. Then joining Bristol Rovers in a similar capacity, he found himself quickly elevated (for a 14-month stint) to the manager's role; Dennis also later coached at Stoke City, and in July 1995 returned to Southampton. Way back at the start of his career, he had been converted from an inside-forward to the full-back slot by Orient boss and former wartime City goalkeeper Dick Graham; his Orient debut was as a scoring substitute at Eastville in April 1968.

Appearances:
FL: 290 apps. 6 gls.
FAC: 22 apps. 0 gls.
LC: 12 apps. 0 gls.
Total: *324 apps. 6 gls.*

ROLLINSON, Frank

Role: Inside left
b. Sheffield

CAREER: Heeley/1906:Sheffield Wednesday/ Aug 1911:FOSSE/Feb 1912:Portsmouth/ Sept 1913:Luton Town.

Debut v Gainsborough Trinity (A) 2.9.11

An inside-left with a 15-goal First Division tally for for the Owls, Frank rather lost his scoring touch at Leicester and, after leaving the field in the notorious weather-beaten match at Grimsby in January 1912, which ended with only five Fossils on the pitch, and stretched the Second Division run to ten games without a win, he promptly departed for pastures new. He helped both of his subsequent Southern League clubs to promotion, and got back to some serious scoring form at Luton, with 26 strikes across two pre-war seasons.

Frank Rollinson

Appearances:
FL: 17 apps. 2 gls.
Total: *17 apps. 2 gls.*

ROSEVEAR, C.

Role: Centre forward

CAREER: Mar 1900:FOSSE.

Debut v Newton Heath (A) 29.3.02

One of three local centre-forwards tried out at the tail end of the goal-drought season of 1901/2, Rosevear had earlier entered the Fosse record books as the club's first (albeit unofficial) substitute, when replacing the injured Billy Wragg during Johnny McMillan's benefit friendly against Notts County on Christmas Eve 1900, and scoring the third goal.

Appearances:
FL: 3 apps. 0 gls.
Total: *3 apps. 0 gls.*

ROULSTON, Arthur

Arthur Roulston

Role: Left half
b. Castle Donington, Leics

CAREER: Jan 1896: Loughborough/ cs 1900:Kettering/ May 1901:FOSSE/ cs 1903:Whitwick White Cross.

Debut v Woolwich Arsenal (A) 7.9.01

The only player to serve the Luffs in each of their five seasons in the Football League (and their record-holder for most appearances - 123 - in that competition), Arthur made his breakthrough as a winger, but soon converted to the left-half position he was to hold until the end of his career. With Fosse he proved a consistently sound, steady defender as an ever-present throughout two fairly nondescript Second Division seasons, ending in placings of 14th and 15th.

Appearances:
FL: 68 apps. 1 gl.
FAC: 3 apps. 0 gls.
Total: *71 apps. 1 gl.*

ROWELL, Thomas

Role: Defender
b. Birtley, Co.Durham, c 1875

CAREER: Hedley Harriers/Dipton Wanderers/Birtley/Aug 1897:FOSSE.

Debut v Walsall (H) 16.10.1897

A tough right-back from Northern Alliance football (and the Durham county team), Tom briefly covered absences in four different defensive positions during his single Fosse season after finding Jack Walker virtually immovable from his favoured berth. Like many fringe players of his era, he fared better in the club's then-heavy programme of friendlies and minor cup games, playing in eleven of the season's 20 such matches, and scoring once in the Burford Cup semi-final victory over Notts County.

Appearances:
FL: 5 apps. 0 gls.
Total: *5 apps. 0 gls.*

ROWLEY, George Arthur

Role: Inside left
b. Wolverhampton, 21st April 1926

CAREER: Blackhall St.Lukes/
am:Wolverhampton Wanderers/Apr 1944:
West Bromwich Albion/Dec 1948:Fulham/
June 1950:CITY/June 1958:Shrewsbury Town
(p/mgr).

Debut v Bury (A) 19.8.50 (scored once)

The most prolific scorer the Football League
has known, and second only to Arthur
Chandler in City's aggregate scoring stakes,
Arthur clearly gave early promise of feats to
come despite Wolves' failure to sign him on
professional forms. He made his senior debut,
alongside his brother Jack and only five
days after his 15th birthday, in a wartime
Manchester United fixture at Anfield; and
also turned out as a guest player for
Middlesbrough, Brighton and Lincoln before
military service in Germany and Palestine. His
introduction to League combat, however, was
a slow process at the Hawthorns (4 goals in 24
apps; including one 60-minute stint as stand-in
goalkeeper against Leicester in February 1948),
and it wasn't until he reached Craven Cottage,
and gunned Fulham into the First Division,
that his reputation began to rise. There was
still much disquiet among City fans, though,
when Arthur arrived as an instant, cheaper
replacement for the well-liked Jack Lee; but
the imminent event of the first of his sixteen
Leicester hat-tricks and a first seasonal total of
28 goals rather smoothed his integration, and
his smashing of Arthur Chandler's seasonal
scoring record with 38 the following term duly
conferred on him heroic status. Arthur went
one goal better in 1953, rifled home thirty in
the 1954 promotion campaign, 23 more in the
First Division, then was actually toppled from
the peak of the club's League goals chart for
one season by Willie Gardiner's 34 (Arthur
following with 29). The Second Division
championship year of 1957 was a matter of
numerous club records for City, so Arthur just
had to help himself to one that would last: 44
strikes in an ever-present season. A haul of
only (!) 20 counters back in the top flight was
considered such a lapse from his standards
that the club rather crazily allowed Arthur to
slip away to Shrewsbury, there to continue his
path towards a career total of 434 League
goals from 619 games. At the risk of
representing the burly, lion-hearted inside-left
as a merely statistical construct, it can be
added that he scored in all four Divisions (50
in One; 232 in Two; 114 in Three; and 38 in the
basement, from which he lifted the Shrews at
the first attempt); that he was the League's top
individual scorer in both 1953 and 1957; and
that he incidentally holds the City record for
most penalties converted (41 in League and
Cup). That he never added full England
honours to his single appearances for each of
the 'B' team and the Football League (both in
1956) was a clear injustice (his less prolific
brother Jack won 6 caps); and that City will
probably never again see a forward with quite
such an appetite for hitting the back of the net
is an inescapable inference. Arthur's
managerial career after hanging up his
shooting boots was comparatively
unremarkable, taking him from Gay Meadow
to spells at Sheffield United, Southend United
and Oswestry Town; and it was sad that his
second, belated testimonial game in 1977 was
such a low-key affair between Southend and
City. (Twelve years earlier the celebratory
participants had been Shrewsbury and
Wolves, and these two clubs would meet again
in May 1995 for Arthur's benefit, when a
Filbert Street collection also helped towards
the financing of a knee operation). But nothing
could dim the Leicester folk memory of 'The
Gunner' rampaging through helplessly flailing
defenders, bringing his thunderbolt left peg
into lethal action, and giving the Goalkeeper's
Union a collective backache. A district
manager for Vernons Pools after his football
ties were severed, Arthur now lives in
retirement in Shrewsbury.

Appearances:
FL: 303 apps. 251 gls.
FAC: 18 apps. 14 gls.
Total: *321 apps. 265 gls.*

❑ FOX FACT: *Of the six City players to surpass
the 100-goal mark for the club in peacetime
football, Arthur Rowley achieved the feat quickest -
his ton-up coming in the April 1953 home game
against Rotherham which represented his 122nd
City appearance. Arthur Chandler took 140 games,
Ernie Hine 185 starts, Gary Lineker 207 (7)
outings, Derek Hines 259 matches and Arthur
Lochhead 267 appearances.*

Arthur Rowley

ROWLEY, William Spencer

Role: Goalkeeper
b. Hanley, Staffs, 1865
d. USA, c 1939

CAREER: Hanley Orion/1883:Stoke/
Apr 1884:Burslem Port Vale/cs 1886:Stoke/
Aug 1898:FOSSE.
Debut v Lincoln City (H) 3.9.1898

Billy Rowley

Fosse just couldn't escape controversy with their newly-signed goalkeeping choices for the start of the 1898/9 season. Not only did the 'poaching' of Godfrey Beardsley land them in deep trouble, but their engagement of this former England and Football League custodian also had them carpeted before the football establishment. Billy, who had been in Stoke's inaugural League team of 1888, had played his final game for them in 1896, while serving them as, successively, secretary/manager and general secretary, and in fact had reverted to amateur status back in 1891. Yet Fosse paid him a signing-on fee after he'd negotiated his own transfer, and prior to his single appearance in a 3-2 win, and it was only a month later that the FA's wrath descended upon all parties concerned: with Fosse fined £10, and Rowley and Fosse secretary/manager W.D.Clark each suspended for 12 months for such unethical practice. Curiously, there had been legalistic shenanigans when Stoke re-signed Billy back in 1886, with Vale winning a courtroom argument that their already-illustrious keeper had been 'seduced' by their rivals, and accepting a 'player-plus-cash' deal in compensation. After his Fosse move had soured, Billy was successively a postman and a licensee in the Potteries, then emigrated to the USA.

Appearances.
FL: 1 app. 0 gls.
Total: *1 app. 0 gls.*

ROWSON, Samuel

Role: Right back

CAREER:
1889: FOSSE/1892:
Leicester YMCA.

*Debut (competitive) v
Burton Wanderers (H)
FAC 4.10.1890*

Sammy Rowson

Another of the pioneer Ancients (as Fosse were nicknamed in their early years), Sammy was a right-back who turned out in each of the club's first two ill-fated stabs at FA Cup glory, then faded from the scene during the initial Midland League season. He did, however, play in both of Fosse's Leicestershire Senior Cup-winning teams of 1890 and 1891, and represented Leicestershire against Birmingham Association in 1890.

Appearances:
FAC: 2 apps. 0 gls.
ML: 6 apps. 0 gls.
Total: *8 apps. 0 gls.*

ROXBURGH, Andrew

Role: Inside forward
b. Granton, Edinburgh, 1900

CAREER: Rugby Town/June 1920:CITY/
Leicester Nomads/Rugby Town.
Debut v Clapton Orient (A) 28.8.20

The elder of two Scottish-born, Rugby-educated brothers who contemporaneously assisted City as amateurs, Andy was a ball-playing inside forward and remains (along with Alfred Barratt) one of only two men to have played at first-team level for both of Leicester's senior football clubs during peacetime, having also turned out as a fly-half for the Tigers in several fixtures during 1922. Indeed, while playing the oval ball game for Old Laurentians around this time, he also won County

Andy Roxburgh

representative honours for Warwickshire. Andy did continue his soccer, however, for well over a decade with the all-amateur Nomads, and also occasionally resumed his association with Rugby Town in the early 30s. In 1936, he was noted as treasurer of both Nomads and of the competition they then played in, the Central Amateur League.

Appearances:
FL: 19 apps. 2 gls.
Total: *19 apps. 2 gls.*

❏ FOX FACT: *Apart from Messrs. Roxburgh and Barratt mentioned above, and WW1 Fossil F R Broadley (see Appendix 1), there have been a few other two-code men connected to the club. Former City reserve winger Richard Pell was, in the mid-1980s with the Tigers, the most recent successful convert to Rugby Union, while early-50s City reserve Ken Armstrong actually became an Irish rugger international in 1961. Additionally, several City players over the years (like Gary Mills and Russell Osman) won junior recognition at the 15-a-side game prior to turning to soccer professionally.*

ROXBURGH, John A.

Role: Outside right
b. Granton, Edinburgh, 10th November 1901

CAREER: Edinburgh Emmett/Rugby Town/ June 1920:CITY/ Oct 1922:Aston Villa/ Feb 1924:Stoke/Aug 1925:Sheffield United/ Sheffield FC.

Debut v West Ham United (H) 9.10.20

Initially more single-minded about a senior soccer career than his brother Andy, Jack was once actually selected for an England amateur international (the March 1926 game against Wales) before his birthplace was made known to the FA. After making a teenage League debut for City, but then missing half a season following an industrial accident at the BTH Engineering works in Rugby, where a heavy trolley ran over both his feet, this jinky outside-right went on to tot up around 80

League appearances for his four senior clubs. A pen picture during his City days dubbed him 'fast and clever, and an ornament to the game both on and off the field'. The Roxburgh brothers appeared in the same City side together on only five occasions, and it was somewhat ironic that each should have effectively surrendered their positions to one of the Duncan brothers. A third Roxburgh sibling, Walter, played in City's pre-season trials of 1921, and for the Tigers in 1924.

Appearances:
FL: 48 apps. 2 gls.
FAC: 2 apps. 1 gl.
Total: *50 apps. 3 gls.*

RUSSELL, Andrew

Role: Right half
b. Airdrie, Lanarkshire

CAREER: Harthill Athletic/Airdrieonians/ Dec 1927:CITY/Sept 1928:Falkirk/cs 1930: Morton/July 1931:Queen of the South/July 1934:Coleraine.

Debut v Birmingham (H) 14.4.28

Jack Roxburgh

Brought South to bolster City's reserve half-back strength during the push for the First Division title, Andy got just the one chance to deputise for Billy Findlay in a 3-0 home win, and was soon heading back over the border (in the company of fellow reserve George Wyness) in the part-exchange deal that brought George Ritchie to Leicester. As a regular for Queen of the South, he assisted them to their first-ever promotion in 1932/3, and to their highest-ever Division One placing of 4th a year later, before trying his luck in Ireland. Andy had originally qualified as an engineer during his days with Airdrie; for whom he had faced City in a Filbert Street friendly in April 1925.

Appearances:
FL: 1 app. 0 gls.
Total: *1 app. 0 gls.*

RUSSELL, Edward Thomas

Role: Left half
b. Cranwell, Lincs, 15th July 1928

CAREER: St.Chad's College/Apr 1946:
Wolverhampton Wanderers/Dec 1951:
Middlesbrough/Oct 1953:CITY/Aug 1958:
Notts County.
Debut v Notts County (A) 14.11.53

Eddie Russell

One of several City players over the years to
have simultaneously followed a
schoolteaching career, Eddie was a tall wing-
half, hard-tackling yet constructive. He wore
the Old Gold in the 1949 Charity Shield game,
and toured Canada with the FA party in 1950,
but was certain of a first-team place at neither
Molineux nor Ayresome. An £8,000 fee gave
him the chance, however, to contribute to
City's 1954 promotion push, and he was the
regular No.6 in the ensuing top-flight
campaign. Eddie missed out entirely on the
1957 championship effort, but bounced back
again in the First Division before having a
brief spell at Meadow Lane.

Appearances:
FL: 90 apps. 5 gls.
FAC: 11 apps. 0 gls.
Total: *101 apps. 5 gls.*

RUSSELL, Kevin John

Role: Striker
b. Portsmouth, 6th December 1966

CAREER: app 1983:Brighton & Hove Albion/
Oct 1985:Portsmouth/July 1987:Wrexham/
June 1989:CITY/(Sept 1990-loan-Peterborough
United)/(Jan 1991-loan-Cardiff City)/(Nov
1991-loan-Hereford United)/(Jan 1992-loan-
Stoke City)/June 1992:Stoke City/June 1993:
Burnley/Mar 1994:Bournemouth/Feb
1995:Notts County/cs 1995:Wrexham.
Debut v Hull City (A) 19.8.89

A major Filbert Street cult hero for his
inspirational interventions in the closing
stages of two contrasting Second Division
campaigns, 'Rooster' in fact had to quarry his
limited chances to shine from what was
otherwise a mass of ill-fortune at Leicester.
Fitness problems hit the prematurely-balding
but extremely pacy frontman almost as soon
as he arrived, and even when loaned out
Kevin fared little better: his Posh period
embraced a severe shaking in a car crash and
ended with a stress fracture, while Cardiff
faced winding-up proceedings during his spell
there. Eventually Gordon Lee brought Kevin
back from the wilderness as City strove to stay
up in 1991, and his impact (and goals) over the
final thirteen games proved crucial to the last-
gasp escape. The advent of Brian Little's
reshaped line-up meant that once more Kevin
dropped out of the picture, but his late-season

return (in a slightly deeper-lying role) again turned out to be a substantial fillip to City's ambitions, this time ending in Play Off qualification. Kevin's willingness to chase and to run at defenders with the ball marked him out for many, but his keenness to make himself available to hemmed-in providers was every bit as useful: there was genuine regret that the out-of-contract player moved on to Stoke, closer to the Wrexham base he had maintained as a hedge against Filbert Street uncertainties. Kevin's last games for both Wrexham and City, therefore, turned out to be in Play Off Finals, for David Pleat had originally laid out £175,000 to the Welsh club after their defeat at Orient in the 1989 version, and after Kevin had scored 50 goals in just two seasons for the Robins. Originally a midfielder when released from his Brighton apprenticeship without a senior chance (despite England youth honours), Kevin laid the foundations of his striking career with his hometown club, making a May 1986 Second Division debut, and intermittently deputising for Paul Mariner in Pompey's 1987 promotion side before the lure of regular first-team fare (and a £10,000 fee) drew him to the Racecourse Ground. In 1993 he was a member of Stoke's Second Division championship squad, but in 1995 suffered in Notts County's drop from the First alongside Gary Mills and Phil Turner.

Appearances:
FL: 24 (19) apps. 10 gls.
FAC: 1 app. 0 gls.
LC: 0 (1) app. 0 gls.
FMC: 2 apps. 0 gls.
P/O: 3 apps. 2 gls.
Total: *30 (20) apps. 12 gls.*

Kevin 'Rooster' Russell

RUSSELL, Martin Christopher

Role: Midfield
b. Dublin, 27th April 1967

CAREER: Belvedere YC/1983:Manchester United/(Oct 1986-loan-Birmingham City)/(Jan 1987-loan-Norwich City)/Mar 1987:CITY/Feb 1989:Scarborough/Mar 1990:Middlesbrough/Aug 1991:Portadown.

Debut v West Ham United (H) 18.4.87

Honoured at Under-21 level by the Republic of Ireland both before and after his £25,000 move to Filbert Street, Martin built a fair reputation in the Old Trafford reserves as an attacking midfielder, but left United without a senior game to his credit. In fact, his only League experience had come during his brief St.Andrews loan spell, and it hadn't really equipped him with sufficient assertiveness for the left-flank role which Bryan Hamilton initially asked him to fill for City's relegation-bound side. Martin's neat footwork and silky changes of direction were put briefly to better use in the midfield department of David Pleat's Second Division squad, though a tendency to get too easily hustled out of his stride still limited his senior chances. The valuation of his outward move at £105,000 raised a few eyebrows, and represented by some margin Scarborough's record fee, but was soon overtaken by the amount paid by Colin Todd to take Martin to

Martin Russell

Ayresome. Martin still failed to become a Second Division regular, yet he won an initial 'B' cap for the Republic a few months after being freed to join Northern Irish champions Portadown.

Appearances:
FL: 13 (7) apps. 0 gls.
LC: 3 (1) apps. 0 gls.
FMC: 1 app. 0 gls.
Total: *17 (8) apps. 0 gls.*

RUSSELL, William

Role: Outside right

CAREER: West Norwood/Dec 1913:FOSSE.
Debut v Huddersfield Town (A) 20.12.13

An amateur outside-right, noted as 'a sprinter' at the time of signing, William was elevated from Isthmian League football to cover briefly for the injured George Douglas, but found himself on the losing side in every game after his debut two-pointer. He had also played representative matches for both Surrey and London, and in fact turned out for London against Southern Counties on New Year's Day 1914, when Fosse were without a fixture.

Appearances:
FL: 5 apps. 0 gls.
Total: *5 apps. 0 gls.*

William Russell

SAER, Charles

Role: Goalkeeper
b. West Carmarthenshire, c 1871

CAREER: Fleetwood Rangers/Feb
1897:Blackburn Rovers/Sept 1897:FOSSE/cs
1898:Stockport County.
Debut v Grimsby Town (A) 18.9.1897

A cheerfully
charismatic but
ultra-competent
goalkeeper, Charlie
earned much due
credit for helping
Fosse to create their
best defensive record
during his single
season with the club;
but not, apparently,
all his pay - for he
was said to be still in
dispute with Fosse

Charlie Saer

over back wages when injury cut short his
subsequent Lancashire League career after
only two games. In fact, shortly after joining
Stockport, Charlie became centrally
involved in early activism among professional players, being voted secretary
of the first Players' Union during 1898,
and leading the initial attempt to reform
the transfer system. His scheme for
tying transfer fees to wages met with
haughty disdain from both the League
and the FA, however, and Charlie soon
resigned to concentrate on his career as
a schoolmaster in Fleetwood.

Appearances:
FL: 28 apps. 0 gls.
FAC: 1 app. 0 gls.
Total: *29 apps. 0 gls.*

SALMONS, Geoffrey

Role: Midfield
b. Mexborough, Yorks, 14th January 1948

CAREER: Feb 1966:Sheffield United/
July 1974:Stoke City/(Sept 1977-loan-
Sheffield United)/Oct 1977:CITY/
Aug 1978:Chesterfield/cs 1982:
Gainsborough Trinity.
Debut v Coventry City (H) 15.10.77

A regular alongside
Tony Currie in the
exciting Blades
midfield which
helped them to
promotion behind
City in 1971, Geoff cost Stoke a hefty £180,000
fee as he continued his top-flight progress.
Three seasons later, though, with the Potters
relegated, he commenced successive loan
spells at Bramall Lane and Filbert Street,
where his thrusting displays in Frank
McLintock's struggling side soon earned him a
£40,000 transfer. Though it was an all-too-
typical reflection on a disastrous season that
Geoff's four goals made him the club's joint
top scorer, it was surprising that Jock Wallace
deemed him surplus to City's revivalist
requirements at the start of the following term.
Geoff later starred alongside John Ridley for
the Chesterfield team which became the last
winners of the Anglo-Scottish Cup in 1981.

Appearances:
FL: 25 (1) apps. 4 gls.
FAC: 2 apps. 0 gls.
Total: *27 (1) apps. 4 gls.*

Geoff Salmons

SAMMELS, Jonathan Charles

Role: Midfield
b. Ipswich, 23rd July 1945

CAREER: app/pro Aug 1962:Arsenal/July 1971:CITY/Mar 1978:Vancouver Whitecaps/ Nuneaton Borough (p/coach)/Trowbridge Town.
Debut v Huddersfield Town (A) 14.8.71

Though having gained immense top-level experience at Highbury, and having shared in some of Arsenal's greatest glory days, Jon had also suffered a rare measure of disappointment before arriving at Leicester for £100,000 as Jimmy Bloomfield's first purchase. To set against his winning of one Football League honour and nine England Under-23 caps, his Wembley League Cup trips had both ended in defeat, while his winning goal in Arsenal's 1970 Fairs Cup Final triumph had seemed to herald a brighter future for Jon than the fate of being sidelined for much of the following Double season. The elegant midfielder soon shrugged off any ill-effects on his morale, though, as he set about helping re-establish City as a First Division force, and in fact, in his first senior game, prompting them to capture the FA Charity Shield. Adept at slowing the pace of a game, Jon didn't always endear himself to an impatient crowd, but he was blessed with a sharp eye for a telling long pass and could also unleash a fair long-distance shot, as well as showing a willingness to play guinea-pig at the centre of some of Bloomfield's more extrovert tactical experiments. (Remember the short lived 'S Plan' with Jon cast in a Beckenbauer-like sweeper's role)? His consistency over

six and a half seasons in the top flight was admirable, and it was notable that the team's precipitate decline in 1977/8 coincided with the waning influence of Jon on the City attack. After spells in the NASL and in senior non-league football, Jon returned to Leicestershire to open a driving school.

Appearances:
FL: 236 (5) apps. 21 gls.
FAC: 17 (1) apps. 1 gl.
LC: 12 apps. 3 gls.
Total: *265 (6) apps. 25 gls.*

❏ FOX FACT: *Jon Sammels was one of seven City players - but the only ex-Gunner - to have faced Arsenal no less than seven times during 1974/5. Two First Division encounters were supplemented by three FA Cup meetings and two League Cup ties - a club record for matches against one club in one season. The other City 'ever-presents' in this little series were Steve Whitworth, Keith Weller, Steve Earle, Frank Worthington, Alan Birchenall and Len Glover.*

Jon Sammels

Ken Sandercock

SANDERCOCK, Kenneth Leslie

Role: Midfield
b. Plymouth, 31st January 1951

CAREER: app/pro Jan 1969:Torquay United/
Nov 1969:CITY/Nov 1971:Torquay United.
Debut v Blackpool (A) 8.11.69 (sub)

A youth-team player under Frank O'Farrell at
Plainmoor, Ken followed his former manager
to Filbert Street and found an early senior
squad place for his compact midfield skills
and tenacity. His Bloomfield Road bow as
substitute gave him more time to impress than
did his first 'full' match, however - for Ken
was carried off only moments into the next
game at Bolton. Thereafter he alternated
between the half-back line and the bench for a
while, but failed to get a look-in during the
following promotion push, and eventually
returned to Torquay, where he often played
alongside his brother Phil, until his contract
was cancelled in January 1975.

Appearances:
FL: 5 (5) apps. 0 gls.
Total: *5 (5) apps. 0 gls.*

SCOTT, Alex MacNaughton

Role: Outside left / Left back
b. Kingsbarns, Fife, 17th November 1922
d. Glenrothes, Fife, 27th August 1995

CAREER: Lochgelly Albert/Mar 1947:CITY/
Jan 1950:Carlisle United/July 1956:South
Shields.
Debut v Fulham (A) 3.1.48

A strongly-built inside- or outside-left when
signed from Scottish junior football, Sandy
was soon converted to left-back by Johnny
Duncan, and then went through his forward to
defender transformation all over again in the
course of City's 1949 Cup run, during which
he was notably successful in the Highbury
semi-final against Portsmouth. In the interim,
he had been a scorer in the 1948 Combination
Cup Final victory over Bournemouth. New
manager Norman Bullock let him go for £1,500
halfway through 1950/51, though, after
signing Ron Jackson for the No.3 berth, and it
was left to Bill Shankly to recognise Sandy's
fighting qualities by taking him to Brunton
Park, where he totted up 203 League
appearances in six years.

Appearances:
FL: 31 apps. 1 gl.
FAC: 10 apps. 0 gls.
Total: *41 apps. 1 gl.*

Sandy Scott

SCOTT, Geoffrey Samuel

Role: Defender
b. Birmingham, 31st October 1956

CAREER: app:Aston Villa/Kings Heath/
Solihull Borough/Highgate United/Apr 1977:
Stoke City/Feb 1980:CITY/Feb 1982:
Birmingham City/Oct 1982:Charlton Athletic/
Aug 1984-trials-Middlesbrough/Sept 1984:
Northampton Town/July 1985:Cambridge
United.

Debut v Swansea City (H) 20.2.80

The regular left-back in Stoke's 1979
promotion side, Geoff replaced the departed
Dennis Rofe for the run-in to City's Second
Division championship the following season.
His form, though, was far from convincing,
and it was as an emergency central defender
that he played his best games for City in their
subsequent attempts to retain top-flight status.
Almost exclusively a one-footed player, Geoff
could appear ungainly, but his new-found
effectiveness in the middle of the back four
earned him a £50,000 move back into the First
Division with Birmingham. Later, serious

Geoff Scott

injury marred his Charlton spell and
threatened his career, finally forcing him to
retire midway through his first season as
Cambridge skipper. Geoff eventually returned
to Midland Combination minnows Highgate
United as manager.

Appearances:
FL: 39 apps. 0 gls.
FAC: 2 apps. 0 gls.
LC: 3 apps. 0 gls.
Total: 44 apps. 0 gls.

SEALY, Anthony John

Role: Striker
b. Hackney, London, 7th May 1959

CAREER: app/pro May 1977:Southampton/
Mar 1979:Crystal Palace/(Feb 1980-loan-Port
Vale)/Mar 1981:Queen's Park Rangers/
(Feb 1982-loan-Port Vale)/(Dec 1983-loan-
Fulham)/cs 1984:Fulham/Sept 1985:CITY/
(Feb 1987-loan-Bournemouth)/July 1987:
Sporting Lisbon/Aug 1988:SC Braga/
Mar 1989:Brentford/Aug 1989:Bristol Rovers/
May 1991:MYPA Myllykosken/Oct 1991:
Brentford/(Aug 1992-trials-Merthyr Tydfil)/
Sept 1992:Michelotti (Hong Kong)/July 1993:
Eastern (Hong Kong).

Debut v Birmingham City (A) 21.9.85
(scored once)

A well-travelled striker, neat and speedy, Tony
too often found that his lack of height and
weight in the box made him a likely candidate
to step down from the frontline; at least to the
sub's bench. Indeed, it was in short bursts of
energetic and enthusiastic harrying that Tony
proved most effective for each of his clubs,
and rather symptomatic of his stop-start career
that for long his most treasured moment
should remain his brief Wembley appearance
as Southampton's No.12 in their 1979 League
Cup Final defeat. He did, though, play important roles in promotion pushes at both QPR
and Bournemouth, and impressed sufficiently
with both City and the Cherries for Keith
Burkinshaw to whisk him off to Portugal,
where he formed a useful striking partnership
with the Brazilian Cascavel. Tony twice broke
his fibula while with Bristol Rovers, but made
sufficient appearances to receive a Third
Division championship medal in 1990; and he
also helped his Finnish club to a long-awaited
promotion (again as champions) to the

Premier Division a year later. As he played out the twilight of his career in Hong Kong, Tony also trained for qualification as a physiotherapist.

Appearances:
FL: 28 (11) apps. 7 gls.
LC: 2 (2) apps. 0 gls.
Total:
30 (13) apps. 7 gls.

SEED, Angus Cameron

Role: Right back
b. Whitburn, Co.Durham,
6th February 1893
d. Barnsley,
7th March 1953

CAREER:
Seaham Harbour/
(Dec 1913-trials-
Everton)/Jan 1914:
FOSSE/July 1914:
Reading/Nov 1916:
St.Bernards/Dec
1919:Mid-Rhondda/
cs 1921:Workington/
cs 1922:Broxburn
United/cs 1923:
Workington.

Debut v Glossop (H) 21.2.14

Tony Sealy

Briefly tried out as a right-back replacement for the Tottenham-bound Tommy Clay, Angus was destined to follow a career at both playing and managerial levels that was largely over-shadowed by the achievements of his brother Jimmy. Angus's glory was to come during WW1, when, after a season as a Southern League reserve at Elm Park, he joined the Footballers' Battalion and was decorated with the Military Medal for valorous service at Vimy Ridge. But while he was making a return to football in, successively, Scottish wartime fare, the Southern League and the North Eastern League (eventually becoming trainer, then manager, at Workington), Jimmy was winning England caps as a Spurs schemer, and then skippering the Sheffield Wednesday side which pipped City to the League title in 1929. Even when Angus moved on for lengthy spells in the boss's chair at Aldershot and Barnsley, Jimmy was taking the limelight in a similar capacity at, first, Clapton Orient and then, for a record 23 years, at Charlton Athletic.

Appearances:
FL: 3 apps. 0 gls.
Total: *3 apps. 0 gls.*

SEYMOUR, Thomas

Role: Right half
b. Paisley, Renfrewshire

CAREER: 1886:Arthurlie/Dec 1889:
Middlesbrough Ironopolis/cs 1893:FOSSE/
May 1895:Arthurlie.

Debut v Burton Wanderers (H) ML 9.9.1893

A right-half who served Fosse throughout the final season of Midland League football and

Tom Seymour

into the initial Second Division season, Tom had left the 'Nops' (the first professional club on Teesside) just before their own one and only League campaign, despite having scored a hat-trick in the game which sealed their third successive Northern League title. He was badly injured at Burton in February 1895, and thereafter made his recuperative return to Scotland permanent. Tom represented Renfrewshire both before and after his English experience; was a runner-up in the Renfrewshire Cup Final of 1887 (a riot-interrupted game against Abercorn); and a beaten Finalist again in the Scottish Qualifying Cup of 1898/9 when, as captain, he scored Arthurlie's consolation against East Stirlingshire. He had retired, however, prior to Arthurlie's 1901 election to the Scottish League.

Appearances:
FL: 19 apps. 1 gl.
FAC: 13 apps. 1 gl.
ML: 20 apps. 1 gl.
Total: *52 apps. 3 gls.*

Tommy Shanks

SHANKS, Thomas

Role: Inside forward
b. New Ross, Co.Wexford, 1880

CAREER: Wexford/Derby West End/ Apr 1898:Derby County/Oct 1901:Brentford/ Dec 1902:Woolwich Arsenal/May 1904: Brentford/Oct 1906:FOSSE/cs 1909:Leyton/ cs 1912:York City.
Debut v Clapton Orient (A) 13.10.06

Best remembered as the man who schemed Fosse into the First Division, and as scorer of the winning goal in the crucial promotion decider at Stoke in April 1908, Tommy was an Irish international inside-forward (capped three times between 1903-5) who had played his first League football alongside Steve Bloomer for the Rams, and had also shot Arsenal to promotion in 1904 - as top scorer and penalty expert - between his two spells with Southern League Brentford. He later played alongside Jamie Durrant at Southern League Leyton, then joined the first professional York City side, which competed in the Midland League for three years from 1912 before folding.

Appearances:
FL: 57 apps. 16 gls.
FAC: 2 apps. 0 gls.
Total: *59 apps. 16 gls.*

SHARKEY, Dominic

Role: Striker
b. Helensburgh, Dunbartonshire, 4th May 1943

CAREER: May 1958:Sunderland/ Oct 1966:CITY/Mar 1968:Mansfield Town/ July 1970:Hartlepool/cs 1972:South Shields.
Debut v Manchester United (H) 30.11.66

A diminutive striker who inherited Brian Clough's No.9 shirt at Roker and helped shoot Sunderland back into Division One in 1964, earning for himself two Scottish Under-23 selections, Nick arrived at Filbert Street with better than a goal-every-other-game scoring ratio to his credit. Initially, it was intended that he would take some of the attacking weight from Derek Dougan, but the pair played together only once, and it was the end of the 1966/7 season before Nick grabbed another chance with characteristic goal flair. He soon

Debut v Liverpool (H) 1.2.34

The son of a former Notts County and Grimsby player, whose turn-of-the-century League experience had amounted to only two senior games for the Magpies, Fred was a versatile and muscular stalwart of City's up-and-down struggles of the 30s. Primarily a defender, standing in for and then displacing Roger Heywood at centre-half, he also took the right-back spot from time to time, and had one lengthy spell at centre-forward during 1935/6, with no mean success as a bustling goalscorer. Fred won a Second Division championship medal as pivot in 1937, and was still going strong when war broke out, making a further 54 appearances during the hostilities and also guesting for Notts County and his old Brush Sports side, but retiring in 1944. He later returned briefly to Filbert Street as reserve-team trainer. One curiosity adheres to Fred's City record: while it was partly inevitable that a player so determined to intervene in every dangerous defensive situation would find himself credited with a fair few own goals against his name, it was less so that three of Fred's half-dozen were notched in three separate games against Birmingham at St.Andrews!

Nick Sharkey

lost his place the following term, though, and it was his prolific reserve-team partnership with Jimmy Goodfellow, later continued at League level after both had moved to Field Mill, which most memorably marked his City career.

Appearances:
FL: 6 apps. 5 gls.
Total: *6 apps. 5 gls.*

SHARMAN, Frederick

Role: Defender / Centre forward
b. Loughborough, Leics,
19th November 1912
d. 1976

CAREER: Loughborough Red Triangle/Brush Sports/ Loughborough Corinthians/ May 1933:CITY.

Appearances:
FL: 190 apps. 18 gls.
FAC: 10 apps. 0 gls.
WW2: 54 apps. 1 gl.
Total:
254 apps. 19 gls.

Fred
Sharman

SHARP, Buchanan

Role: Inside forward
*b. Alexandria, Dunbartonshire,
2nd November 1894
d. Bolton, 11th January 1956*

CAREER: Vale of Leven/Clydebank Jnrs/
Nov 1919: Chelsea/Mar 1923:Tottenham
Hotspur/Jan 1925:CITY/June 1926:Nelson/
Sept 1928:Southport.
Debut v Coventry City (H) 24.1.25 (scored once)

A tricky Scottish inside-forward who was just
getting into his goalscoring stride at Stamford
Bridge when Spurs leapt in for his signature,
Buchanan then found his progress somewhat
stymied at White Hart Lane, where he only
managed three League appearances. Peter
Hodge recruited him as an experienced back-
up to Johnny Duncan during City's 1925
promotion push, but after a few games in the
top flight during the following campaign he
moved on to complete his League career in
Lancashire, netting 23 goals in his first season
at Nelson in the Third Division (North). The
most intriguing aspect of his City stay
occurred over the weekend following his
scoring debut: for the Leicester rumour
machine sent wildfire whispers through the
clubs and pubs that Buchanan had been killed

Buchanan Sharp

in a motorcycle accident on his way home, and
it took an official City statement of denial on
the Monday to quash the idea.

Appearances:
FL: 12 apps. 2 gls.
Total: *12 apps. 2 gls.*

SHARP, W.A.

Role: Outside right
b. Leicester

CAREER: Leicester Imperial/Apr 1902:FOSSE.
Debut v Chesterfield (H) 10.1.03

There's a time-honoured tradition in football
journalism that even a disastrous debut by a
player is usually commented on with an
indulgent epithet of the order of 'promising',
or some such. 'Observer' of the Leicester *Daily
Post* well and truly broke ranks, though, in
summing up this outside-right on his sole
senior run-out: 'a total failure' and 'very weak'
constituted his assessment on the local lad
after a particularly dispiriting 0-2 home defeat.

Appearances:
FL: 1 app. 0 gls.
Total: *1 app. 0 gls.*

SHARPLEY, William

Role: Left back

CAREER: Army football/(Mar 1912-trials-
FOSSE).
Debut v Leeds City (H) 27.4.12

An Army corporal given the briefest of League
breaks in the final game of the 1911/12 season
(a 2-1 win which lifted Fosse to 10th in the
table), at left-back behind fellow squaddie and
trialist J. Mitchell, at a point when he still had
two years to serve in the Essex Regiment.

Appearances:
FL: 1 app. 0 gls.
Total: *1 app. 0 gls.*

SHAW, H.

Role: Inside forward

CAREER: London Road/Aug 1893:FOSSE.
Debut v Burton Wanderers (H) ML 9.9.1893

A local inside-forward who played under the
pseudonym 'Archer' in pre-season trial games,

then hid his talent on his only Midland League outing - the 1-2 home defeat on the opening day of 1893/4 which nonetheless effectively made the difference between Fosse and Burton taking that campaign's championship.

Appearances:
ML: 1 app. 0 gls.
Total: 1 app. 0 gls.

SHEARD, Frank

Role: Centre half
b. Spilsby, Lincs,
29th January 1922
d. Leicester, 11th July 1990

CAREER: Skegness Town/am Nov 1940/ pro Aug 1941:CITY/ May 1946:Southend United/Aug 1956: Gravesend & Northfleet.

Frank Sheard

Debut (WW2) v Mansfield Town (A) 22.3.41; (postwar) v Chelsea (A) FAC 5.1.46

A hefty young centre-half signed on during the second season of wartime football, whilst working at Whitwick colliery, Frank held the senior pivot's position for both legs of the first postwar FA Cup-tie, but had moved on to Southend before the resumption of Football League action. There totting up 180 games over seven seasons, he gained a reputation for the classic virtues of a stopper: uncompromising robustness and bravery.

Appearances:
FAC: 2 apps. 0 gls.
WW2: 84 apps. 2 gls.
Total: 86 apps. 2 gls.

SHEFFIELD, John Davenport

Role: Outside right
b. Coalville, Leics, c 1879
d. Neuve Chapelle, France,
10th March 1915

CAREER: Coalville Albion/ Whitwick White Cross/ Oct 1902:Burton United/ cs 1903:Coalville Town/July 1904:FOSSE/cs 1905:Ibstock

Jack Sheffield

Albion/Coalville Town/Coalville Excelsior/ Coalville Swifts/Coalville Wednesday.
Debut v Liverpool (A) 1.10.04

Outside-right Jack clearly didn't fancy taking his football talents far from home (his father ran the Railway Hotel, Coalville), as his list of clubs in the North Leicestershire area testifies, though he also managed to fit a spell of far-flung military service during the Boer War into the above chronology. He totalled twelve Second Division appearances for the Brewers, but was effectively debarred from greatly extending his experience at that level with Fosse by the consistency of Jamie Durrant - and the fact that the 0-4 Anfield defeat above was followed by a 0-3 home loss to Manchester United. He took runners-up medals from the County Cup Finals of 1904 (with Coalville Town) and 1905 (with Fosse reserves). Jack's second stint in his country's colours unfortunately heralded his death in the trenches.

Appearances:
FL: 2 apps. 0 gls.
Total: 2 apps. 0 gls.

SHEPHERD, John

Role: Inside left

CAREER: Apr 1912:FOSSE.

Debut v Stockport County (A) 20.4.12

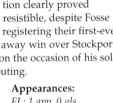

A trialist inside-left of so-far untraced origin; though John was stated at the time of arrival to be 'well recommended from the South'. The recommendation clearly proved resistible, despite Fosse registering their first-ever away win over Stockport on the occasion of his sole outing.

Appearances:
FL: 1 app. 0 gls.
Total: 1 app. 0 gls.

SHILTON, Peter Leslie

Role: Goalkeeper
b. Leicester, 18th September 1949

CAREER: app June 1965/pro Sept 1966:
CITY/Nov 1974:Stoke City/Sept 1977:
Nottingham Forest/Aug 1982:Southampton/
June 1987:Derby County/Mar 1992:
Plymouth Argyle (p/mgr)/Feb 1995:
Wimbledon/Mar 1995:Bolton Wanderers/
June 1995:Coventry City.

Debut v Everton (H) 4.5.66

It's almost the case that however far back
into Peter's superb goalkeeping career one
delves for perspective, one could have safely
predicted the heights it would reach. A
schoolboy prodigy, his dedication to working

*Peter Shilton leads the England under-23 team
out against West Germany at Filbert Street in
October 1970. England won 3-1 in front of
24,752 fans.*

on the practice and psychology of his
destined profession (and even on building
the correct physique for it) was evident
while he was helping Leicester Boys to their
1965 Trophy win, and picking up his first
international recognition with England
Schools. At Filbert Street there was
immediate acknowledgement of Peter's
precocious talent, and he became City's
youngest-ever First Division debutant at 16
when characteristically keeping a clean sheet
against Cup-winners-to-be Everton. Barely
another year had elapsed before a queue of
top clubs was forming, ready to snatch Peter
(now an automatic choice for England
Youth) from the Filbert Street shadow of
Gordon Banks, and an unenviable choice
soon faced Matt Gillies over which of his
top-rank keepers to part with. He elected to
invest in the younger man's ability and
ambition, and it was not too long before his
judgement was substantiated by Peter's
assumption of Banks's place in the
international arena. In the interim, City
experienced a Cup Final, a relegation and a
promotion (with Peter's shot-stopping
solidity, aerial agility, uncanny sense of
positioning and absolute command of his
area in large part responsible for the club
creating its best-ever defensive record during
1970/1, when he kept a record 23 clean
sheets). Rarely out of the public eye - his
adoption of an all-white playing kit and his
long-distance scoring success at
Southampton at various times assuring that -
Peter was inevitably now adding full
international mementos to his thirteen
England Under-23 caps, but also becoming
less than enchanted with City's trophy-
winning prospects. Jimmy Bloomfield
accepted a £325,000 cheque from Stoke for
the unsettled star, and the move ironically
threatened to rebound on Peter as the Potters
themselves struggled, and he found himself
only sharing the yellow jersey of England
with Ray Clemence. But when Stoke
dropped into Division Two, Peter was the
subject of a typically shrewd bit of Brian
Clough business, and in five years of almost
uninterrupted success in domestic and
European competitions with Forest, he once
more re-established himself as the country's
undisputed No.1. Maintaining his
impeccable, highly self-critical standards at

management. Initially successful as Argyle's player/manager (though content to sideline himself from action on a career total of 995 League appearances), Peter soon proved unable to juggle the pressures of a relegation scrap with those of his well-publicised personal financial difficulties, and resigned from Home Park in January 1995, after being suspended by his chairman; but not before giving his 16-year-old son Sam a League break. He then signed on a non-contract basis as goalkeeping cover at Selhurst and Burnden, and almost 29 years to the day after his City debut, appeared once more at League level for Bolton as a substitute at Stoke. A fine Play-off semi-final performance at Molineux then assisted the Trotters to Wembley and promotion. There would be few even now willing to bet against Peter - whose uncle Fred was a City reserve keeper during 1935/6, on loan from Leicester Nomads - soon reaching the magic 1,000 League outings.

The Dell (after another £325,000 move), Peter became the most-capped England keeper of all time, skippering the national side on occasion, and earning the civil honour of the MBE in 1986. Then, following a final big-money transfer to the Baseball Ground, he set about creating a further series of career landmarks: passing Terry Paine's all-time record for the highest number of League appearances with his 825th such game in April 1988, and overtaking Bobby Moore's record haul of England caps with his 109th selection against Denmark in June 1989. In July 1990, Peter finally retired from the international scene with a world record 125 caps to his name, bowing out at the very top of his profession. He was up-graded to an OBE in 1991, and later took the plunge into

Appearances:
FL: 286 apps. 1 gl.
FAC: 33 apps. 0 gls.
LC: 20 apps. 0 gls.
Total: *339 apps. 1 gl.*

❏ FOX FACT: *Peter Shilton is statistically the safest keeper the club have ever had. Of those goalies who made sufficient (100+) appearances in League and Cups to render the figures meaningful, Shilton conceded an average of only 1.118 goals per game for City. Higher averages accrue to George Hebden (1.135), Mark Wallington (1.319), Herbert Bown (1.370), Jimmy Thraves (1.453), Gordon Banks (1.486), Kevin Poole (1.500 to date), Sandy McLaren (1.750), Johnny Anderson (1.762) and Jim McLaren (1.805).*

SHINTON, Frederick

Role: Centre forward
b. Wednesbury, Staffs, March 1883
d. West Bromwich, 11th April 1923

CAREER: Hawthorn Villa/Moxley White
Star/Wednesbury Old Athletic/Hednesford
Town/Apr 1905:West Bromwich Albion/
Nov 1907:FOSSE/June 1910:Bolton
Wanderers/Jan 1911:FOSSE.

Debut v Lincoln City (A) 30.11.07 (scored once)

Fosse decidedly got the best
of the bargain from the
part-exchange deal which
took Harry Wilcox and
£125 to The Hawthorns
and brought inside-
forward Fred to Leicester
part-way through what
turned out to be the club's
first promotion season; for
the latter also went on to
become Fosse's first true
goalscoring hero. His strike

Fred Shinton

rate at West Brom was already mightily
impressive (46 goals in 64 League games), and
ten goals towards the promotion target did
much to endear the enthusiastic bustler to his
new supporters. Strangely, Fred got fewer
chances to enliven Fosse's struggling front-line
in the top flight, but when they tried to
bounce straight back up again in 1909/10,
Fred weighed in with a 32-goal haul from the
centre-forward berth that remained a club
record until the days of Arthur Chandler. His
brave, almost reckless style of headlong
assault earned him the Filbert Street nickname
of 'Nutty', while it was often remarked at the
time how much of an attraction his fair-haired,
handsome looks seemed to Fosse's fairly
substantial female support. A brief, unhappy
spell at Bolton interrupted Fred's progress and
seemed to take the gloss off his game, for
despite a scoring comeback for Fosse, he failed
to earn a new contract for the following
season. He was, nonetheless, the only Fossil
ever to break the 50-goal barrier. A younger
brother, Arthur, signed for City in 1919, but
never made the grade.

Appearances:
FL: 92 apps. 55 gls.
FAC: 9 apps. 3 gls.
Total: *101 apps. 58 gls.*

SILVESTER, Edward Ernest

Role: Centre half
b. c 1869

CAREER:
1889:Kidderminster
Harriers/West
Bromwich Albion/
Dec 1891:Walsall
Town Swifts/
cs 1892:FOSSE.

Edward Silvester

*Debut v Mansfield
Town (A) ML 19.9.1892*

A centre-half taken on to add creative wit to
Fosse's middle line after the embarrassments
of the initial Midland League season, and
handed the captaincy in Snooks Nuttall's
absence, Edward had previously graduated
from assisting the Harriers to victory in the
Kidderminster Weavers' Cup, through a
reserve stint at West Brom, to Football Alliance
service for Walsall. He at least aided Fosse to a
respectable 4th place, and scored himself in
the club's record Midland League victory, 7-1
over Newark, but was not retained on the
expiry of his contract. (Several sources render
Edward's surname as Sylvester; the local press
in Leicester unhelpfully alternated the
spellings during his stay).

Appearances:
FAC: 4 apps. 0 gls.
ML: 11 apps. 1 gl.
Total: *15 apps. 1 gl.*

SIMMS, Samuel

Role: Centre forward
b. Atherton, Lancs, January qtr 1888
d. Swindon, Wilts, 25th May 1952

CAREER: Tyldesley College/cs 1910:Ton
Pentre/Dec 1912:Everton/June 1913:Swindon
Town/June 1914:FOSSE/July 1919:Swindon
Town/June 1921:Gillingham.

Debut v Lincoln City (H) 2.9.14 (scored twice)

Essentially a reserve centre-forward at each of
his previous clubs, Sam had scored on the first
of his two First Division appearances for
Everton, and had thrice stepped in as understudy leader for Swindon during their

Southern League championship season of 1914. He got off on the right foot with Fosse, but then had to vie with near-namesake Stephen Sims for a regular forward berth (eventually making emergency excursions to left-back and centre-half) in what proved the worst season ever for the club, ending in rock-bottom position and re-election. After the war, during which he briefly guested for Stockport County, Sam retreated to the right-half berth with Swindon and the Gills.

Sam Simms

Appearances:
FL: 16 apps. 5 gls.
FAC: 1 app. 0 gls.
Total: 17 apps. 5 gls.

SIMPSON, Frank L.

Role: Outside left

CAREER: Syston Victoria/(Oct 1902-trials-FOSSE)/Leicester Imperial/Aug 1903:FOSSE/cs 1904:Leicester Imperial/cs 1907:Leicester Nomads.

Debut v Burton United (at Derby) FAC 7.12.03

A local amateur outside-left who came back from a dispiriting setback during his first spell with the club - he broke his collarbone in a rough-house reserve match at Whitwick, after which Fosse director Tom Collins was suspended for a month by the FA for his incautious comments and behaviour. Familiarly known as Sandy, he eventually had only a brief brush with the senior game after his bow in a Cup second replay, and was later alongside ex-Fossil Ernest Vickerstaffe in helping found Leicester Nomads as the town's first-class amateur combination. In 1910 he was noted as residing in Exeter, but appears to have had no connection with the Grecians.

Appearances:
FL: 2 apps. 0 gls.
FAC: 1 app. 0 gls.
Total: 3 apps. 0 gls.

SIMPSON, Henry C.

Role: Inside right
b. Aberdeenshire

CAREER: Peterhead/Oct 1907: St.Bernards/Mar 1910:FOSSE/July 1910:St.Bernards.

Debut v Oldham Athletic (A) 2.4.10

A member of St.Bernards' 1907/8 Qualifying Cup-winning side, and well experienced in Scottish Second Division football (playing alongside Harry Graham on occasion), Harry joined Fosse as an inside-right partner to Fred Shinton just at the unfortunate point when their efforts to bounce straight back into the First Division were beginning to founder, leaving them a frustrated 5th at the end of 1909/10. In fact the tiny forward failed to appear in a winning Fosse side during his brief stay, and returned to Edinburgh for a fee of £45.

Appearances:
FL: 7 apps. 1 gl.
Total: 7 apps. 1 gl.

SIMPSON, Thomas

Role: Outside left
b. Keyworth, Notts, 13th August 1879
d. Oldham, 19th December 1961

CAREER: 1899:Notts County/Oct 1902: FOSSE/May 1903:Everton.

Debut v Barnsley (A) 18.10.02

An outside-left who only really came into his own while at Leicester, Tom had totted up only seven League appearances for the Magpies prior to his Fosse stint, and would play but one senior game for the Toffees while understudying the noted amateur and England international, Harold Hardman. Yet his left-wing thrusts and his brief scoring burst did much to save Fosse from the embarrassment of a re-election application in 1902/3 (albeit only for one year), and earned him at least the promise of elevation from the League's basement to its heights. His goal tally should have been one higher: for during a 3-1 Fosse win at Burnley in January 1903, his goalbound shot was stopped on the line by a stray dog! Tom was also a Nottinghamshire cricketer.

Appearances:
FL: 27 apps. 5 gls.
FAC: 1 app. 0 gls.
Total: *28 apps. 5 gls.*

SIMS, Stephen

Role: Inside forward
b. Bedminster, Bristol,
11th December 1895
d. Weston-super-Mare,
January qtr 1973

CAREER:
1913:Bath City/
Aug 1914:FOSSE/
July 1919:Bristol
Rovers/July 1922:
Burnley/July 1924:
Weymouth/Sept 1925:
Bristol City/Sept
1926:Bristol Rovers/
July 1927:Newport
County.
Debut v Lincoln City
(H) 2.9.14

Stephen Sims

A prolific scorer for 1914 Western League runners-up Bath, Stephen unfortunately proved to be another of Louis Ford's signings for the final pre-war League season who could do little to halt the Fosse's disastrous decline, despite his clear promise as a 19-year-old. By the time his career resumed after the war, however, Stephen was alternating between the front line and the centre-half berth, and impressed sufficiently in Bristol Rovers' first two seasons in Division Three (after top-scoring in their final Southern League term) to attract a £2,000 bid from top-flight Burnley. His career aggregate of League games eventually amounted to 105; and he subsequently became a Bristol publican.

Appearances:
FL: 11 apps. 2 gls.
Total: *11 apps. 2 gls.*

SIMS, Steven Frank

Role: Centre back
b. Lincoln, 2nd July 1957

CAREER: Lincoln United/app Aug 1973/ pro July 1974:CITY/Dec 1978:Watford/ Sept 1984:Notts County/Oct 1986:Watford/ June 1987:Aston Villa/June 1990:Burton Albion/Oct 1990:Lincoln City/(Feb 1991-trials-Bournemouth)/1991:Boston FC/1991:Stafford Rangers/ Dec 1991:Shepshed Albion.

Debut v Manchester City (A) 20.8.75

Like Fred Sharman before him and Russell Osman more recently, Steve was a City centre-half with a footballing father: in his case, Frank, a good Lincoln City clubman for seven years in the 50s. After a rapid rise through the City junior ranks, Steve made his League bow as replacement for the injured Jeff Blockley, and established himself during the last year of Jimmy Bloomfield's managership as a central defender of some class, whose evident

Steve Sims

brawn was simply a highly useful adjunct to his astute intelligence. He became an England Under-21 regular (10 caps; 1 goal) and appeared once for England 'B', and even came out of the 1978 relegation farrago with some credit. Yet he didn't last long into the Jock Wallace era, moving on to Vicarage Road at a fee of £175,000: a then-record outlay by a Third Division club. Watford were, though, in the middle of their meteoric rise up the League and, as an unfussily effective exponent of their long-ball tactics, Steve eventually had two seasons in the top flight with them, plus a taste of European competition, until transferring to Meadow Lane after a series of injuries. He again tasted relegation with the Magpies, but was soon reunited with his former manager and mentor, Graham Taylor, both in the First Division with Watford, and in Villa's successful 1988 promotion drive. Steve then remained in Birmingham as part of a 'Football in the Community' scheme, part-timing for various non-league setups after breaking his jaw five games into a non-contract spell with his hometown Red Imps.

Appearances:
FL: 78 (1) apps. 3 gls.
FAC: 3 apps. 0 gls.
LC: 5 apps. 0 gls.
Total: *86 (1) apps. 3 gls.*

SINCLAIR, Harvey Patrick

Role: Goalkeeper
b. Bournemouth, 30th November 1933

CAREER: am:Bournemouth & Boscombe Athletic/Dec 1950:Fulham/cs 1954:Cambridge United/Aug 1956:CITY/July 1957:Yeovil Town/Sept 1958:Bristol Rovers/July 1959: Fulham.

Debut v Grimsby Town (H) 26.1.57

More familiarly known as Harry, this luckless goalkeeper must have been heartily sick of reserve-team football by the time he finished his wanderings. His belated League debut was for City, replacing injury victim Johnny Anderson in a crucial 4-3 home victory, but within days the club had bought Dave MacLaren to see out the rest of the 1957 promotion season. Some eighteen months later, he ended his League career with a solitary appearance for Bristol Rovers, two days after signing for them, in a 2-3 defeat at Derby.

Appearances:
FL: 1 app. 0 gls.
Total: *1 app. 0 gls.*

'Harry'
Sinclair

SINCLAIR, John Evens Wright

Role: Winger
b. Culross, Fife, 21st July 1943

CAREER: Blairhall Colliery/cs 1960:
Dunfermline Athletic/May 1965:CITY/Dec
1967:Newcastle United/Dec 1969:Sheffield
Wednesday/(Mar 1973-loan-Chesterfield)/
cs 1973:Durban (SA)/Aug 1973:Dunfermline
Athletic/cs 1975:Stenhousemuir.

Debut v Liverpool (H) 21.8.65 (scored once)

A Jock Stein signing for Dunfermline, Jackie
was a nippy, goalscoring winger who had
already come close to glory in both European
competition and the 1965 Scottish Cup Final
when Matt Gillies brought him to Filbert Street
for £25,000 to forge an instantly successful
little-and-large striking partnership with
Derek Dougan. The adjective 'dynamic'
seemed coined for Jackie as he adapted
his killing pace and shooting instincts to
service on either flank, and it was no
surprise that he won a full Scotland
cap at the end of his first City season
(making up for the earlier
disappointment of being chosen for
a postponed Scottish League
representative game). After two
years in the First Division, Jackie
was still bettering the classic
striker's average of a goal-every-
other-game, and though his
scoring ratio dropped off a little
during 1967/8, it seemed he
was being jettisoned with
undue haste at the wave of a
Newcastle cheque for
£67,500. He met less overall
success on Tyneside, despite
contributing crucially to the
Geordies' 1969 Fairs Cup
victory, and was eventually
exchanged for Sheffield
Wednesday's David Ford,
linking up again at
Hillsborough with former
City team-mate Peter
Rodrigues. Later Jackie found
his way back to East End
Park, and ended his career
with an aggregate of 115
League goals to his name. His
older brother Willie played
for Falkirk, Huddersfield,

Tranmere and Halifax; his uncle was Tommy
Wright, Sunderland's Scottish international of
the 50s; his cousin was City's 90's winger
Tommy Wright; and his son, Chris, played for
Dunfermline in the Scottish League Cup Final
of October 1991.

Appearances:
FL: 103 apps. 50 gls.
FAC: 5 apps. 2 gls.
LC: 5 apps. 1 gl.
Total: *113 apps. 53 gls.*

*Jackie
Sinclair*

SJOBERG, John

Role: Right back / Centre back
b. Aberdeen, 12th June 1941

CAREER: Banks O'Dee/Aug 1958:CITY/
June 1973:Rotherham United.

Debut v Cardiff City (A) 28.10.60

A teenage centre-half when he followed
Jack Lornie's route to Filbert Street, John
made his initial impact for City's first team
as a right-back, taking over from Len
Chalmers just prior to the start of the 1963
Cup run, and climaxing his first season as a
regular with a Wembley appearance against
Manchester United. He was a stalwart of
the League Cup campaigns of the next two
years (scoring the decisive semi-final goal at
Home Park in 1965), and was still shuttling
between the Nos. 2 and 5 shirts with
effective ease until the arrival of Peter
Rodrigues to hold down the former
position. Settling thereafter to a memorable
central defensive partnership with Graham
Cross, John displayed a craggy consistency
and imposed his aerial mastery on many a
First Division game. This quality tempted
Matt Gillies into giving him one spell at
centre-forward during 1967/8, but John's
back-four abilities were more vital to City's
strength and shape, and it was notable that
the club's 1969 relegation occurred in a
season when niggling injuries severely
limited John's appearances, and indeed
kept him out of the Cup Final line-up. Two
years later, he was a key
member of the Second
Division promotion side,
and took his testimonial
game against Derby after
the championship had been
secured, attracting a crowd
of around 24,000. During
his latter Leicester days, he
had started a printing
business, and it was to this
that John returned after a
very brief spell of six
League games at Millmoor.

John Sjoberg

Appearances:
FL: 334 (1) apps. 15 gls.
FAC: 44 apps. 1 gl.
LC: 34 apps. 3 gls.
Total: *412 (1) apps. 19 gls.*

❏ FOX FACT: *John Sjoberg is
the only City player to have
contributed two own goals to
the opposition in one game:
having achieved this luckless
feat at West Brom in April
1966 during a 1-5 defeat.
Aston Villa's Chris Nicholl
did the same on City's behalf
at Filbert Street in March
1976, but compensated by also
scoring twice at the right end
in a 2-2 draw.*

SKEA, David Frederick

Role: Inside left
b. Arbroath, Angus, 1871

CAREER: 1888:Arbroath/cs 1892:Aston Villa/ Apr 1893:Dundee Thistle/July 1893:Darwen/ Dec 1893:Bury/Aug 1894:FOSSE/cs 1896: Swindon Town/Dec 1896:New Brompton/ cs 1898:Cowes.

Debut v Grimsby Town (A) 1.9.1894 (scored twice)

A skilful hotshot of an inside-left to whom a number of the club Football League 'firsts' attach, David notched Fosse's initial goal in the competition, and became the scorer of each of the club's first hat-tricks and penalties at this level. Unsurprisingly, his marksmanship granted him the honour of being the Fosse's first seasonal top scorer (with a creditable 23 goals from a maximum 30 games), and his tally stood as a record until Fred Shinton's goalrush in 1909/10. Clearly, he suffered closer attentions from Second Division defences the following term, and his goal rate dropped accordingly, but David could still accept limited opportunities with a rare alacrity, as his 5 goals from only 6 Southern League games for Swindon would indicate. His original bow in English football (after an international trial during 1890/1) had been a scoring one, but one game and one goal represented the extent of his Villa Park career, and a single appearance at League level (owing to injury) was his lot with Darwen; while his promising spell with Swindon was actually cut short as a disciplinary measure after he had arrived for training 'in an intoxicated condition'.

Appearances:
FL: 45 apps. 29 gls.
FAC: 7 apps. 8 gls.
Total:
52 apps. 37 gls.

David Skea

SLACK, Alfred

Role: Centre forward
b. c 1871

CAREER: cs 1890: Mansfield Town/ cs 1892:FOSSE.

Debut v Mansfield Town (A) ML 17.9.1892

Alf Slack

Fosse's ever-present centre-forward during 1892/3, but an irregular reserve the following season, Alf claimed the club's first hat-trick at Midland League level, during the 7-1 demolition of Newark which constituted Fosse's best win in that competition. His second personal triple came in the 6-0 win over Derby Junction that same season which was later declared void (the scheduled away fixture having played at Filbert Street), and was thus stricken from the record. Previously, Alf had picked up medals from two Mansfield Challenge Cup wins, and as a runner-up from the Newark Cup.

Appearances:
FAC: 4 apps. 1 gl.
ML: 26 apps. 11 gls.
Total: *30 apps. 12 gls.*

SLACK, Rodney

Role: Goalkeeper
b. Farcet, nr.Peterborough, 11th April 1940

CAREER: Fletton YC/ Sept 1958:CITY/ Mar 1961:Queen's Park Rangers/cs 1962: Cambridge United.

Debut v Mansfield Town (H) LC 12.10.60

Standing in for Gordon Banks in City's first-ever Football League Cup tie, Rodney kept a clean sheet on what proved to be his only senior outing, but was soon back in third-team football behind Banks

Rodney Slack

on the left flank and contributed the bulk of his City goals, that he was able to make a substantial breakthrough, and even this run was soon curtailed by the pressing claims of young Derek Hogg. Peter was somewhat luckier in his three years on Trentside (87 apps; 20 gls), and was a squad member for Forest when they accompanied City back into the First Division in 1956/7. The following term, he contributed 3 goals in 8 outings towards Brighton's Division Three championship-winning effort.

Appearances:
FL: 65 apps. 16 gls.
FAC: 7 apps. 4 gls.
Total: *72 apps. 20 gls.*

Peter Small

and George Heyes. In fact, he'd managed a shut-out, too, a year previously against Charlton Athletic, in the club's initial game in the Southern Professional Floodlit Cup - an invitational forerunner of the League Cup in which City played but one term, going out at the second hurdle to Arsenal. His spell with QPR resulted in only one League appearance (in a 1-1 draw at Halifax), but he served Cambridge consistently well in their Southern League battles, culminating in a 1969 Double win.

Appearances:
LC: 1 app. 0 gls.
Total: *1 app. 0 gls.*

SMALL, Peter Victor

Role: Winger
b. Horsham, Sussex, 23rd October 1924

CAREER: Horsham Town/Aug 1947:Luton Town/Mar 1950:CITY/Sept 1954:Nottingham Forest/July 1957:Brighton & Hove Albion.

Debut v Sheffield United (A) 18.3.50

A compact, strong winger who was nick-named 'The Horsham Flier', and had faced City for Luton in the epic Cup ties of 1949, prior to switching clubs for £6,000, Peter had to be content to spend the majority of his Filbert Street days in the shadow of Mal Griffiths. It was only during the 1954 promotion season, when he starred mainly

SMITH, Alan Martin

Role: Striker
b. Birmingham, 21st November 1962

CAREER: Alvechurch/June 1982:CITY/ Mar 1987:Arsenal/(Mar-May 1987:loan back to CITY).

Debut v Charlton Athletic (H) 28.8.82

Capped by England at semi-pro level while playing as a left-sided striker for Alvechurch's successful Southern League side, Alan became the final signing of the Jock Wallace era at City, and a bargain inheritance for Gordon Milne, who immediately paired the tall, elegant attacker with Gary Lineker. Though the latter initially hogged the headlines for his scoring exploits as City returned to the First Division and set about their battle for consolidation, Alan soon proved an unselfish foil, creating numerous chances with his excellent ball control and vision, and snapping up a fair quotient himself. Displaying a rare combination of stylishness and ready willingness to chase and harry, and posing an effective striking threat both in the air and on the ground, Alan also stood out for that even rarer commodity of sportsmanship: for while neither his bravery nor commitment could be questioned, his record of a single booking over five seasons was positively remarkable in a context of so much 'professional' niggling. On Lineker's departure, Alan determinedly shouldered the responsibility as City's primary goalgetter, and after he finally shrugged off his reputation as a sluggish seasonal starter in 1986/7, there was as much inevitability in the upsurge of million-pound transfer rumours as there was credit in the player's modestly-expressed desire to honour his Leicester contract. Indeed, when his £800,000 move to Highbury was finally negotiated, he agreed on an instant loan-back to City, to aid their eventually futile fight to stay in the top rank. Alan's initial season with the Gunners brought mixed fortunes under intense scrutiny, though he scored one of their consolation goals in the Littlewoods Cup Final of 1988 and finished as the club's top scorer; but it was his goal burst at the start of 1988/9 which elevated him into the England squad. He won his first cap as a substitute in Saudi Arabia, heralding a brief international renewal of his old Filbert Street partnership with Lineker; then scored one and made one of the goals at Anfield which brought Arsenal the 1989 championship by the narrowest possible of margins. Alan's 23 First Division strikes also earned him the Golden Boot for 1989. He similarly led the Highbury scoring list in the 1991 championship win; with England again was noted as the innocent party in the controversy surrounding Lineker's final international substitution; shared in Arsenal's 1993 FA Cup win; and then volleyed the winning goal in the 1994 European Cup Winners' Cup Final against Parma. A knee injury wrecked his 1994/5 campaign, and medical advice sadly led to his retirement, at the age of only 32, in July 1995, at a point where he had amassed an aggregate tally of 199 League and Cup goals.

Appearances:
FL: 190 (10) apps. 76 gls.
FAC: 8 apps. 4 gls.
LC: 8 (1) apps. 4 gls.
Total: *206 (11) apps. 84 gls.*

Alan Smith

Arthur E. Smith

SMITH, Arthur Eric

Role: Inside left
b. Whetstone, Leics, 5th September 1921

CAREER: Whetstone Athletic/am 1939:
Wolverhampton Wanderers/am:Nov 1940/
pro Feb 1941:CITY/June 1948:West Bromwich
Albion/Aug 1952:Plymouth Argyle/
June 1954:Crewe Alexandra.
Debut (WW2) v Walsall (H) 30.11.40;
(postwar) v Brentford (A) FAC 25.1.47

Arthur was a locally-born inside-left who
impressed City with some convincingly crafty
performances in wartime football after his step
up from the then-inoperative Wolves' juniors
(a move which cost City a small Football
League fine, for they had in fact fielded him in
ignorance of his Wolves registration). Despite
gaining additional senior experience with
Linfield and Derry City while serving as a
military PT instructor in Ireland, he
nonetheless found his first-team chances
limited by the partnership of Dewis and Lee
when League football resumed (though he
scored the reserves' winning goal when they
lifted the 1948 Combination Cup with a 2-1
victory over Bournemouth); and then at the
Hawthorns briefly found his way barred by

Jack Haines, who had preceded him from
Leicester to West Brom a few months earlier.
Arthur did, however, tot up 49 League
appearances (12 goals) there before moving to
Plymouth (28 games; 8 goals) and ending his
career with a four-game spell at Gresty Road.
His younger brother Jack (also a WW2 player
for City) was an eleven-year stalwart for
Northampton Town from 1949.

Appearances:
FL: 17 apps. 3 gls.
FAC: 5 apps. 2 gls.
WW2: 74 apps. 32 gls.
Total: *96 apps. 37 gls.*

SMITH, Arthur Hugh

Role: Outside right
b. Bury

CAREER: Bury Co-Op FC/May 1935:Bury/
May 1938:CITY.
Debut v Stoke City (H) 27.8.38

A right-winger signed on a free transfer on the
eve of the final pre-war League season, Arthur
soon lost his place to newcomer Mal Griffiths,
and barely got a look-in thereafter. He claimed
two goals in the first match of the 1939/40
season, but promptly
'lost' them from
official records when
that campaign was
abandoned, and soon
he disappeared from
senior football
entirely, with City
frankly admitting in
late 1942 that they
had no idea of his
whereabouts: a
position they were
still in when they
formally freed him in
1946. (Incidentally, a

Arthur H. Smith

third Arthur Smith, a Sileby-born wing-half,
was a 1935 City signing, but never rose above
reserve-team football before a move to
Southern League Gillingham in 1938).

Appearances:
FL: 8 apps. 0 gls.
WW2: 2 apps. 2 gls.
Total: *10 apps. 2 gls.*

SMITH, Dean

Role: Striker
b. Leicester, 28th November 1958

CAREER: app Apr 1975/pro Dec 1976:CITY/ (Apr 1978-loan-Houston Hurricane)/Oct 1978: Brentford/Feb 1981:Nuneaton Borough/ Enderby Town/Corby Town/Shepshed Charterhouse/St.Andrews/Aug 1990: Houghton Rangers/1992:Lutterworth Town/ Hinckley Town/Thurnby Rangers/Oadby Town.

Debut v Everton (H) 10.9.77 (sub)

Another of the several City teenagers unlucky enough to be thrown into the deep mire of the 1977/8 relegation farce, and then find themselves either at odds with, or superfluous to the plans of, incoming manager Jock Wallace. Dean was a strong, combative and mobile striker who got off the scoring mark in a home defeat by Manchester United, but nonetheless failed to bear out his high promise after a £20,000 move to Griffin Park, and returned to the local non-league arena after scoring 16 goals in 54 League games for the Bees, mainly played in front of Pat Kruse.

Appearances:
FL: 8 (2) apps. 1 gl.
Total: *8 (2) apps. 1 gl.*

Dean Smith

SMITH, Eric Thomas Henry

Role: Centre half
*b. Tamworth, Staffs,
3rd November 1921*

CAREER: Castle Bromwich/am 1942/ pro 1945:CITY/ Jan 1947:Bath City.

Eric Smith

Debut (WW2) v Newport County (A) 3.11.45; (postwar) v Manchester City (H) 31.8.46

A young pivot whose promise, shown during the transitional season of 1945/6, tempted City into releasing Frank Sheard on the resumption of peacetime football. Eric held the No.5 berth for the initial postwar quintet of Second Division matches, but soon dropped out of the senior game altogether. He had been loaned to Walsall for one wartime game at Filbert Street, in September 1944.

Appearances:
FL: 5 apps. 0 gls.
WW2: 13 apps. 0 gls.
Total: *18 apps. 0 gls.*

SMITH, George H.

Role: Right back
b. Nottingham

CAREER: Mapperley/ Sneinton/Bulwell/ Hinckley Athletic/ Dec 1892:FOSSE/(Aug 1895-trials-Preston North End)/Aug 1895: Ilkeston Town.

George Smith

Debut v Grantham Rovers (H) ML 26.11.1892

A sure-footed stalwart right-back for Fosse in the last two Midland League seasons, plus the initial campaign in the Second Division, George failed to earn a Deepdale contract after his release, and returned to Midland League fare. For some unfathomable reason, his first Fosse appearance saw him adopting the pseudonym 'Thompson': surely one of very few instances of a man named Smith seeking anonymity!

Appearances:
FL: 24 apps. 0 gls.
FAC: 12 apps. 0 gls.
ML: 36 apps. 0 gls.
Total: *72 apps. 0 gls.*

SMITH, Harry

Role: Centre forward

CAREER: Worcester Rovers/Dec 1887:
Kidderminster Olympic/
cs 1891:Kidderminster Harriers/
cs 1893:Berwick Rangers/Aug 1897:FOSSE/
cs 1898:Bedminster (p/mgr).

Debut v Luton Town (H) 4.9.1897

Harry led the Fosse attack during the early
stages of 1897/8 without conspicuous success,
after joining as a veteran from the Birmingham
& District League club who would later
become Worcester City (i.e. not the current
Scottish League club of the same name).
Elevated to team management at his
subsequent Southern League club, he decided
against picking himself for any senior game
with the Bristol-based outfit.

    Appearances:
    FL: 15 apps. 4 gls.
    Total: *15 apps. 4 gls.*

SMITH, Isaac

Role: Left half
b. Wednesbury, Staffs

CAREER: Wednesbury/
Darlaston/Oldbury Town/
June 1919:CITY.

*Debut (WW1) v Notts County (H)
22.3.19; (postwar) v Wolverhampton
Wanderers (H) 30.8.19*

A young left-half who failed to live
up to the demands of post-WW1
League football, Ike at least makes
the record books as a member of
Leicester City's first side to play
under that title. He had previously
played half-a-dozen wartime games
for Fosse during 1918/19, when so
much of the club's player recruitment drive was focused on the West
Midlands.

    Appearances:
    FL: 2 apps. 0 gls.
    WW1: 6 apps. 0 gls.
    Total: *8 apps. 0 gls.*

SMITH, Richard Geoffrey

Role: Centre back
b. Leicester, 3rd October 1970

CAREER: Oadby Town/YT 1987/pro Dec
1988:CITY/(Sept 1989-loan-Cambridge
United)/(Dec 1990-loan-Nuneaton
Borough)/(Sept 1995-loan-Grimsby Town).

Debut v Oldham Athletic (H) 3.4.90 (sub)

One of the very few locally-born players to
have held anything like a regular senior spot
with City over the past five years, Richard
must have wondered initially whether his
Filbert Street career would ever truly take off.
His Cambridge stint brought him the
experience of five League and Cup games, but
even when he made the City bench, it seemed
an age until he got a taste of the action; and it
was ten months, five sub appearances and a
taste of non-league football later that he finally
started a City game - the home defeat by
Blackburn that proved to be David Pleat's last
in charge at Leicester! Gordon Lee barely
called on Richard at all, but Brian Little eased
the tall central defender into regular
contention, and he responded with some
classy performances under pressure. He hit his
first League goal just after Christmas 1991,
and precisely seven days later volleyed home

Richard
Smith

from close range at the far post the late winner against Crystal Palace which secured for City their first FA Cup victory in seven years. Richard missed only two games during 1992/3, took over Tony James' long-throw role, did a stint as stand-in goalkeeper for the injured Carl Muggleton in a crucial home win over Oxford, and was in the Wembley side which suffered ultimate frustration at the hands of Swindon Town. Injuries then cut severely into Richard's progress, and his senior breaks became more intermittent as his pace and concentration seemed to slip a notch. Occasional excursions to full-back did little either to build or inspire confidence, and he won but a handful of selections from Mark McGhee before being listed in May 1995.

Appearances (to end 1994/5):
PL: 10 (2) apps. 0 gls.
FL: 71 (14) apps. 1 gl.
FAC: 5 apps. 1 gl.
LC: 4 apps. 0 gls.
FMC: 5 apps. 0 gls.
AIC: 4 apps. 0 gls.
P/O: 3 apps. 0 gls.
Total: *102 (16) apps. 2 gls.*

SMITH, Robert Nisbet

Role: Utility
b. Dalkeith, Mid Lothian, 21st December 1953

CAREER: 1970:Hibernian/Dec 1978:CITY/ (Feb 1982-loan-Peterborough United)/(Nov 1982-loan-Hibernian)/Oct 1986:Hibernian/ Sept 1987:Dunfermline Athletic/cs 1989: Partick Thistle/Aug 1990:Berwick Rangers.

Debut v Oldham Athletic (H) 1.1.79 (scored once)

Basically an attacking midfielder, Bobby had proven his versatility at Easter Road by leading Hibs' seasonal scoring list and then converting to left-back in the course of a year, and Jock Wallace chased his signature for some six months before an £85,000 deal was struck in time for Bobby to share a League bow with both Gary Lineker and David Buchanan. He settled well at Filbert Street as an aggressive prompter, opportunist and penalty expert, and was second-top scorer in the 1980 promotion campaign. Yet a lean spell followed, when City seemed willing to off-load Bobby at the end of either of his loan-outs, and it was at full-back that he surprisingly re-established himself, contributing to the 1983 promotion effort,

and holding his place in Gordon Milne's line-ups for much of the next three seasons. Eventually, another Easter Road loan did lead to Bobby rejoining his first club on a free transfer; though Hibs pocketed a decent fee when he shifted Premier Division bases. Dunfermline made a presentation to Bobby midway through their 1988/9 promotion season to mark his 500th senior game. By the time he made a flying return to Leicester in 1993 to play in Nev Hamilton's benefit game, Bobby was installed as a pub landlord back in Dalkeith.

Appearances:
FL; 175 (6) apps. 21 gls.
FAC: 10 apps. 1 gl.
LC: 8 (1) apps. 0 gls.
Total: *193 (7) apps. 22 gls.*

Bobby Smith

SMITH, Septimus Charles

See pages 390/1

SMITH, Thomas Gable

Role: Forward
b. Whitburn, Co.Durham, 18th October 1900
d. Whitburn, 21st February 1934

CAREER: Marsden Villa/Whitburn/May 1919:South Shields/Dec 1919:CITY/Jan 1924: Manchester United/June 1927:Northampton Town/May 1930:Norwich City/Feb 1931: Whitburn.

Debut v Stoke (H) 20.12.19

Another of the Whitburn clan of footballing Smiths, and the first to taste League football with South Shields (as did Jack and Willie, but not Sep or Joe), Tom was an inside-forward purchase by Peter Hodge whose attacking versatility ironically militated against him holding down a regular first-team berth with City across the first five postwar seasons. He turned out in each of the forward positions except outside-left as City sought a promotion-worthy blend, yet he had to move to Old Trafford to win a rise in status, as United accompanied City out of the lower sphere in 1925. Indeed, Tom's United debut in the inside-right slot he held for 83 matches (12 goals) was against City; and he also appeared in that berth in the all-Mancunian FA Cup

Tom Smith

semi-final of 1926. Then as a Cobbler he totted up another 112 League appearances (22 goals), before finishing his career with a single game for Norwich. It was widely (but erroneously) credited in Leicester that it had been during the reception following a Northampton v. City friendly in 1929 that Tom in fact 'sold' Willie Orr on the idea of signing young Sep, but at least he was able to see the 'babe' of the family become a First Division regular before his own tragically early death. Tom also had a few games for Durham in Minor Counties cricket.

Appearances:
FL: 72 apps. 12 gls.
FAC: 9 apps. 3 gls.
Total: *81 apps. 15 gls.*

SMITH, Wallace

Role: Forward
b. Allerton, Yorks, 1883
d. Worksop, Notts, 3rd July 1917

CAREER: Rothwell/1901:Kettering Town/cs 1904:Northampton Town/May 1905:Bradford City/Jan 1909:FOSSE/Mar 1909:Hull City.
Debut v Bristol City (A) 9.1.09

A Yorkshireman whose first senior experience came in the Southern League with two Northamptonshire clubs, Wally was a gutsy inside- or centre-forward who scored a hat-trick at Filbert Street for Bradford City in March 1906, and won a Division Two championship medal with the Bantams in 1908, when they just pipped Fosse for the title. He cost the latter club a hefty £625 fee when enlisted to the ensuing, vain relegation struggle, but failed either to shine or score. After less than two months as a Fossil, Wally was on his way again for the reduced sum of £500, and managed 33 goals in 90 League games for Hull before injury put paid to his playing career in early 1912. He still made one further appearance at Filbert Street, though: as emergency linesman for the first half of the Fosse v. Hull fixture of March 1912, when the appointed whistler arrived late. Wally had become a Worksop licensee when he died, aged only 33.

Appearances:
FL: 5 apps. 0 gls.
FAC: 1 app. 0 gls.
Total: *6 apps. 0 gls.*

SMITH, Septimus Charles

Role: Inside forward / Half back
b. Whitburn, Co.Durham, 13th March 1912

CAREER: Whitburn/am 1928/pro Mar 1929:CITY.

Debut v Huddersfield Town (A) 31.8.29

Still many veteran followers' notion of the best all-round City player ever, Sep was unarguably one of the club's most loyal servants, ending his magnificent twenty-year playing span with a brief spell as coach. As his name implies, the seventh son of a fanatical footballing family (of whom five played at League level, with Tom also turning out for Leicester, Joe moving from City reserves to Watford, and Jack and Willie both spending the bulk of lengthy careers at Portsmouth), Sep was an England Schoolboys star in 1926 (after playing in the North/South trial at Filbert Street that March) and clearly destined to join the top echelon of creative midfielders. His early games as a City teenager were at inside-forward, where he exhibited a fair scoring prowess to supplement his cool distributive skills, but it was at right-half that Sep truly made his mark throughout the club's turbulent times of the mid- and late-30s. His repute was national, yet his representative honours tally looks comparatively derisory: only one full cap (against Northern Ireland in 1935/6), one appearance as second-half substitute in the 1935 Jubilee international against Scotland, and one game for the Football League. For club honours, too, Sep had to make do with only meagre reward for his inspirational captaincy, by way of a Second Division championship medal in 1937.

He managed a City appearance record during WW2 that was second only to Billy Frame's, despite sitting out a year's suspension, and was still holding together City's postwar efforts as a veritable veteran of a pivot, constantly taking younger players like Don Revie under his tutelary wing, aiding Johnny Duncan's tactical preparations for City's 1949 Wembley trip, and finally hanging up his boots after seeing the club's Second Division future assured in the crucially drawn last-match tussle at Cardiff.

Appearances:
FL: 350 apps. 35 gls.
FAC: 23 apps. 2 gls.
WW2: 213 apps. 48 gls.
Total: *586 apps. 85 gls.*

SMITH, Walter Ernest

Role: Goalkeeper
b. Leicester, 25th March 1884

CAREER: Leicester Imperial/
Feb 1904: FOSSE/May 1906:
Manchester City/Oct 1920:
Port Vale/June 1922:Plymouth
Argyle/Nov 1922:Grimsby Town.

Debut v Bristol City (H) 25.2.04

The first of Leicester's star-quality
goalkeepers to be generally recognised as
such, Walter initially joined Fosse as an
amateur, but turned pro in September 1904,
and missed only three games thereafter
until his £600 move to Hyde Road. In the
interim he had helped restore defensive
confidence to Fosse's re-elected side and
shift them several notches up the Second
Division table, gaining a reputation as the
Division's best keeper for his agility and
resilience, with his lack of height (5ft.8ins)
proving no handicap, but his hefty frame
presenting an awkward barrier for
rampaging, charge-happy forwards. Walter
saved two penalties at Anfield during
Fosse's 1906 Cup exit (when Billy Bannister
also missed a spot-kick during the 1-2
defeat), while a year later the *Athletic News*
correspondent was dubbing him 'the only
first-class goalkeeper in the country who
disdains training', with his subject opting

to follow his plumbing business
rather than indulge in such
unnecessary practice. Walter
totted up 233 League games for
the Mancunians (bracketing
wartime spells when he
returned to assist Fosse during
1915/16, and also guested for
Fulham), was honoured once for
the Football League against the
Scots in 1915, and was still
exhibiting a clean pair of hands in
senior football until the close season of
1923. There was only one (temporary) blot
on Walter's record: he was actually arrested
on the very morning of his Port Vale debut
at South Shields, falsely accused of
assaulting a hotel chambermaid, then bailed
in time to play, nervily, in front of a crowd
augmented by a watching detective!
Something of an all-round sportsman
himself (a schoolboy rugby star, and a
wicket-keeper for both Leicester
Temperance and the County seconds), this
non-smoker and complete teetotaller had a
son, Walter A.Smith, who captained
Combined Universities at both rugby and
cricket and also played both sports for
Leicestershire.

Appearances:
FL: 79 apps. 0 gls.
FAC: 8 apps. 0 gls.
WW1: 24 apps. 0 gls.
Total: *111 apps. 0 gls.*

SOO, Frank

Role: Left half / Inside left
b. Buxton, Derbyshire,
8th March 1914
d. Cheadle, Cheshire,
25th January 1991

CAREER: West Derby BC/Prescot
Cables/Jan 1933:Stoke City/
Sept 1945:CITY/July 1946:Luton
Town/cs 1948:Chelmsford City.

Debut (WW2) v Plymouth Argyle (H) 29.9.45;
(competitive) v Chelsea (A) FAC 5.1.46

The first player of Chinese extraction to play
League football when he made his breakthrough as a First Division professional with

Frank Soo

Stoke, Frank was a midfield ball-
artist whose skills both
complemented and contrasted
with those of his great pre-war
team-mate, Stanley Matthews.
He was on the verge of full
international recognition in 1939,
and indeed won a total of eight
wartime and Victory caps, the
last (against Wales in October
1945) being gained shortly after
he signed for an all-too-brief spell
on City's books. Frank also
played in numerous RAF and FA
representative games, and had guested for
Everton, Blackburn, Burnley, Crewe, Millwall,
Norwich City, Reading, Shrewsbury, Chelsea
and Brentford while hostilities continued, but

it was to join his former Stoke boss Tom Mather that he accepted a £4,600 move to less fashionable City a few games into the transitional postwar campaign. Frank impressed City supporters immensely with his craft and trickery, but RAF duties and representative honours (and an unsanctioned guest outing for Port Vale) cut into his availability, and he failed to settle to the prospect of a new regime after Mather left, so the club rather gratefully recouped £3,000 of its outlay in banking Luton's cheque for his services. After 71 League games for Luton (4 goals) and some Southern League success, Frank had spells as manager of both Scunthorpe United and St.Albans City, and coached extensively abroad (in Italy with Padova; in Sweden with Eskilstuna, Orebro, Djurgardens, Oddevold, Kopings IS, AIK, IFK and Hoganas; and in Denmark with AB Copenhagen amongst other clubs).

Appearances:
FAC: 2 apps. 0 gls.
WW2: 14 apps. 3 gls.
Total: *16 apps. 3 gls.*

SPARROW, F. Henry

Role: Centre forward
b. Faversham, Kent,
13th June 1889
d. Lincoln, 13th June 1973

CAREER:
Faversham Thursday/
Dec 1909: Portsmouth/
cs 1911:Sittingbourne/
Oct 1911:Croydon Common/
Feb 1912:FOSSE/
Jan 1914:Tottenham Hotspur.

Debut v Bristol City (A)
10.2.12 (scored once)

Clearly a player for whom Cup exits brought on itchy feet, centre-forward Harry was a £90 signing for Fosse immediately after they had removed Croydon Common from the 1911/12 competition, and two seasons later moved with Tommy Clay to Spurs the

Harry Sparrow

day after that club had k.o.'d Fosse at the second attempt. Harry had struggled to find a Southern League place with Pompey, making only five scoreless appearances over two seasons, but flourished at Croydon under manager Jack Bartlett, who rejoined him at Leicester only a month after selling him and oversaw his immediate rise to the top of the Fosse scoring chart. Harry maintained his excellent goal ratio in a struggling side until whisked off to White Hart Lane, where he got fewer opportunities to shine (18 games, 7 goals) before the outbreak of war. Two days after Harry's Fosse debut noted above, he scored all four goals in a friendly at Merthyr.

Appearances:
FL: 48 apps. 29 gls.
FAC: 3 apps. 0 gls.
Total: *51 apps. 29 gls.*

SPEARING, Anthony

Role: Left back
b. Romford, Essex, 7th October 1964

CAREER: Oulton Broad Eagles/ app 1980/pro Oct 1982:Norwich City/(Nov 1984-loan-Stoke City)/ (Feb 1985-loan-Oxford United)/ July 1988:CITY/June 1991:Plymouth Argyle/Jan 1993:Peterborough United.

Debut v West Bromwich Albion (H)
27.8.88

A former England Youth skipper and a graduate of Norwich's 1983 FA Youth Cup win, Tony had become a Carrow Road regular at left-back in the First Division (despite a debut own goal, and a broken leg suffered shortly afterwards), and surprised many observers when electing to step down a grade to join City for £100,000 and challenge Simon Morgan for the No.3 shirt. Initially exhibiting tenacious tackling and jockeying skills, and an infectious cheeriness, he became a regular choice for one season only, after which injuries, inconsistencies and occasional impetuosity saw him follow a stop-start course across two more years of lowly Second Division football. Indeed, David Pleat put him on the

Tony Spearing celebrates what proved to be his only goal for City, against Newcastle in 1989/90.

open-to-offers list at the end of the 1989/90 campaign, only to reinstate him later that summer; but a year on there was no new contract forthcoming from the club, and Tony moved to Home Park as a free agent. He then suffered relegation campaigns with Argyle in 1992 and Posh in 1994.

Appearances:
FL: 71 (2) apps. 1 gl.
FAC: 1 app. 0 gls.
LC: 2 (1) apps. 0 gls.
FMC: 2 apps. 0 gls.
Total: *76 (3) apps. 1 gl.*

SPEEDIE, David Robert

Role: Striker
b. Glenrothes, Fife, 20th February 1960

CAREER: app July 1977/pro Feb 1978: Barnsley/June 1980:Darlington/June 1982: Chelsea/July 1987:Coventry City/Feb 1991: Liverpool/Aug 1991:Blackburn Rovers/ July 1992:Southampton/(Oct 1992-loan-Birmingham City)/(Jan 1993-loan-West Bromwich Albion)/(Mar 1993-loan-West Ham United)/July 1993:CITY/Aug 1995:Crawley Town.

David Speedie

Debut v Peterborough United (H) 14.8.93

A demonised hate-figure to City fans at one juncture of his regularly controversial career, David had become something of a cult hero to the Filbert Street faithful by the time his playing days were sadly curtailed by injury. The man whose graceless 'dive' at Wembley in 1992 had apparently cheated Leicester out of promotion-via-Play Off to the inaugural Premiership campaign, whose two goals for West Ham a year later did much to derail another upward push, and whose free-transfer signing by Brian Little was therefore instantly adjudged a potential PR disaster, ended up with the scorer's credit for giving the club their third-time-lucky chance at Wembley glory in 1994. His late nudged (?) goal in the Play Off semi-final second leg against Tranmere, and his subsequent (rather unfair) dismissal in that game, unfortunately proved to be David's last acts in a senior City shirt, for a summer knee injury then prompted an enforced retirement in January 1995. City thus had the final season from this former Scottish international striker, and one in which his full repertoire was demonstrably still in play: a bustling predatory sense at close range, a speciality of controlled chip shots, a ready willingness to forage deep, a fine heading ability for a small man, and a distinctly volatile temperament. Scots-born, but Yorkshire-raised, this former Brodsworth Colliery miner was initially a midfielder at Oakwell (where he was overshadowed by Ian Banks), but graduated at Feethams to a secondary striker's role (one which he most memorably incarnated while playing off Kerry Dixon at Chelsea). David's five caps came while he was a Stamford Bridge regular, and a Wembley hat-trick (from the 1986 Full Members' Cup victory over Manchester City) was another highlight of his Blues stint. His career scoring record in League games alone aggregated 148; and a hat-trick for a City XI in the relaxed circumstances of Gordon Banks' benefit game in April 1995 showed just what City had been missing in their Premiership struggles.

Appearances:
FL: 37 apps. 12 gls.
FAC: 1 app. 0 gls.
LC: 3 apps. 1 gl.
P/O: 0 (1) app. 1 gl.
Total: *41 (1) apps. 14 gls.*

SPITTLE, William Arthur

Role: Inside right
b. Southfields, London, April qtr 1893

CAREER: Southfields Juniors/Sept 1912: Woolwich Arsenal/Oct 1919:CITY/May 1921: Nuneaton Town/Jan 1922:Tamworth Castle.

Debut v Huddersfield Town (A) 18.10.19

Billy Spittle

Partnering Harry King in a joint move from Highbury, Billy was a scheming forward who had totalled only seven Second Division games for Arsenal in the two seasons before the war, and unfortunately failed to establish himself to Peter Hodge's satisfaction in several shots at holding down City's inside-right position in the two campaigns after it. He wasn't helped, though, by either the after-effects of wounds received while serving in France in the Footballers' Battalion (17th Middlesex Regt) or the need to undergo a cartilage operation in April 1920. Billy effectively disappeared from the football record books shortly after leaving Filbert Street, though one source credits him with a few comeback outings for Brentford's reserves during 1925/6.

Appearances:
FL: 26 apps. 3 gls.
Total: *26 apps. 3 gls.*

SPRIGGS, F.

Role: Centre forward

CAREER:
Leicester Imperial/
Apr 1902: FOSSE.

*Debut v Lincoln City (H)
19.4.02 (scored twice)*

F Spriggs

A local young centre-forward who made quite an impact in the final game of 1901/2, yet thereafter only got one more first-team chance, in a near-embarrassing Cup qualifying tie at Irthlingborough, before being released in 1904. (The difficulty of researching players of this era, however, leaves open the outside possibility that this Fossil and his namesake below were in fact one and the same person. The only other F Spriggs we have tracked down in senior football at this time was a New Brompton forward of 1907/8, reputedly signed from Hitchin Town).

Appearances:
FL: 1 app. 2 gls.
FAC: 1 app. 0 gls.
Total: *2 apps. 2 gls.*

SPRIGGS, Frank

Role: Centre forward

CAREER: Sept 1909:FOSSE/cs 1910:Merthyr Town/cs 1911:Rochdale.

Debut v Blackpool (A) 2.10.09

A centre-forward who partnered Fred Shinton in the above 1-0 away win, but played the rest of his senior football in, successively, the lower reaches of the Southern League and (for a trio of games under ex-Fossil and 'Dale player/ manager Joe Blackett) the Lancashire Combination. (The notes of confusion and caution sounded for the previous entry are now echoed here; for one isolated source cites *this* player as the former New Brompton man...)

Appearances:
FL: 1 app. 0 gls.
Total: *1 app. 0 gls.*

STAPLES, John William

Role: Outside left

CAREER: Whitwick White Cross/May 1902: FOSSE/1903: Whitwick White Cross.

John Staples

Debut v Small Heath (H) 6.9.02

A left-winger whose brief elevation from the Midland League was already being judged a failure at the time Fosse were forced to pay a £10 fine for having made an illegal transfer approach to him the previous April. Four of John's quintet of Second Division games ended in defeat for Fosse.

Appearances:
FL: 5 apps. 0 gls.
Total: *5 apps. 0 gls.*

Jonty Starbuck

STARBUCK, Jonathan

Role: Goalkeeper
b. Measham, Leics, 1884
d. Burton-on-Trent, 18th April 1939

CAREER: Measham/cs 1905:Burton United/ June 1907:FOSSE/cs 1912:Ilkeston United.

Debut v Leeds City (H) 7.9.07

A tall 'keeper who joined Fosse after Burton's demise as a League club, 'Jonty' gave five seasons of loyal service despite regularly being cast in the role of reserve to H.P. Bailey and Fred Mearns. His safe handling helped Fosse through several tricky encounters on the route to promotion in 1908, and he was hardly to blame for either their immediate return to the lower Division or any failure to bounce back. He finished his playing days in the Central Alliance; while at the time of his death he was licensee of the Plough Inn, Burton.

Appearances:
FL: 77 apps. 0 gls.
FAC: 12 apps. 0 gls.
Total: *89 apps. 0 gls.*

STARKEY, A.E.

Role: Outside right
b. Coalville, Leics

CAREER: Shepshed Albion/Mar 1911:FOSSE/
1911:Coalville Swifts.

Debut v Fulham (H) 25.3.11

A local outside-right who had an extended
first-team trial at the end of 1910/11,
inheriting Fred Threlfall's role, but failed to
win a contract for the next season. He did
briefly reappear, though, for a single wartime
runout in Fosse colours against Nottingham
Forest six years later.

> **Appearances:**
> *FL: 8 apps. 0 gls.*
> *WW1: 1 app. 0 gls.*
> **Total:** *9 apps. 0 gls.*

STEPHENSON, Roy

Role: Outside right
b. Crook, Co.Durham, 27th May 1932

CAREER: Sunnyside Jnrs/June 1949:Burnley/
Sept 1956:Rotherham United/Nov 1957:
Blackburn Rovers/Mar 1959:CITY/July 1960:
Ipswich Town/June 1965:Lowestoft Town.

Debut v Chelsea (H) 14.3.59

Though he had racked up a fair number of
League games as a utility forward in the top
flight, had picked up some good habits at Turf
Moor from the likes of Jimmy McIlroy and
Jimmy Adamson, and had been a regular for
the Millers in the Second Division, Roy
appeared to be facing something of a late
career crisis when he found himself sidelined
for all but two games of his second season at
Filbert Street. Matt Gillies, in his first
managerial deal, had paid £8,000 to add Roy's
prompting skills to City's successful attempt
to ward off relegation, but he was then edged
out of the reckoning for his favoured No.7
shirt by Tommy McDonald and Howard Riley.
One move, though, revived Roy's enthusiasm
and effectiveness at a stroke; with Alf Ramsey
adding him to the Ipswich team-building
jigsaw as the right-wing provider for the
Crawford/Phillips goal combine which
sensationally saw the East Anglians to the

Roy Stephenson

championships of Division Two and One in successive seasons, and into the European Cup. Roy had, while still a young Burnley part-timer, qualified as a mining engineer.

Appearances:
FL: 12 apps. 0 gls.
Total: *12 apps. 0 gls.*

STEVENS, Gregor

Role: Centre back
b. Glasgow, 13th January 1955

CAREER: 1974:Motherwell/May 1979:CITY/ Sept 1979:Rangers/(Jan 1984-loan-Heart of Midlothian)/cs 1984:Motherwell/Nov 1984: Partick Thistle/Aug 1986:Brechin City/ Oct 1989:Dumbarton.

Debut v Rotherham United (H) LC 11.8.79

All too evidently ill-at-ease with English football, Gregor struggled through only a handful of shaky performances as a City central defender before Jock Wallace somehow shrewdly contrived to recoup his £125,000 investment in a second cross-border deal.

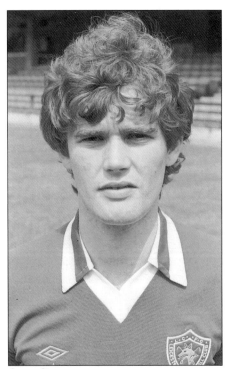

Gregor Stevens

Gregor had begun his Motherwell career as a midfielder, but had developed as a tough-tackling sweeper to win Scottish League and Under-21 honours; though he was definitely to overdo the toughness when he got to Ibrox, where he revelled in the nickname 'Igor' and, in February 1982, received a shaming six months suspension after his fifth sending-off in two years. He also picked up Scottish Cup medals from the Finals of 1980 (loser's) and 1981 (winner's) but, sadly, was still showing the less salubrious side of his playing nature even as an 'old head': taking early baths both on the first day of 1989/90 and again, shortly afterwards, on his Dumbarton debut.

Appearances:
FL: 4 apps. 0 gls.
LC: 2 apps. 0 gls.
Total: *6 apps. 0 gls.*

STEVENSON, James

Role: Inside left
b. Paisley, Renfrewshire, 1876

CAREER: Clyde/Jan 1895:Derby County/ Oct 1898:Newcastle United/cs 1900:Bristol City/Sept 1901:Grimsby Town/Jan 1902: FOSSE/Oct 1902:Clyde.

Debut v Burton United (A) 18.1.02

A Cup Finalist with Derby in 1898, and described before that 1-3 defeat by Nottingham Forest as 'a wizard of the leather', James was a noted dribbler as an inside-left, as well as a fair marksman (31 goals in 73 League games for the Rams), and fetched the handsome transfer fee of £225 from newly-promoted Newcastle. He began his wanderings as his goal touch waned, though, and his brief spell at Leicester ended in acrimony, with James one of several Fosse players suspended as an internal disciplinary measure within two months of signing on. (He should not be confused with the James Stevenson who played for Morton, Nottingham Forest and New Brompton in the early years of the century).

Appearances:
FL: 7 apps. 1 gl.
Total: *7 apps. 1 gl.*

STEWART, Alexander

Role: Inside left
b. Greenock, Renfrewshire, 1869

CAREER: Morton/ Dec 1889: Burnley/ Dec 1892: Everton/ cs 1893: Nottingham Forest/Mar 1897: Notts County/ cs 1898:Bedminster/ cs 1899:Northampton Town/Aug 1901: Burnley/Aug 1902:FOSSE.

Alick Stewart

Debut v Glossop (A) 10.4.03 (scored once)

The scorer of both Burnley's goals when they beat FA Cup-holders Blackburn in the 1890 Final of the prestigious Lancashire Cup, and an Evertonian FA Cup Finalist in 1893 as a wing-half, Alick had a full and successful playing career which was supposed to be over when he signed on as Fosse's trainer in 1902. Yet injury crises conspired to force him to don his boots again in the above match, and his goal from inside-left pointed the way to a welcome away win that did much to avert the threat of an enforced application for re-election. Alick also turned out in three friendly fixtures to demonstrate his own fitness to his charges, and remained at Filbert Street until 1905.

Appearances:
FL: 1 app. 1 gl.
Total: *1 app. 1 gl.*

STIRLING, James

Role: Forward

CAREER: Third Lanark/Oct 1894:FOSSE/May 1895:Partick Thistle.

Debut v Newton Heath (A) 27.10.1894

A utility forward, James could never command a regular spot during Fosse's initial Second Division campaign, despite never being in a beaten side, and scoring in his final senior game (a 4-0 win over Crewe in February 1895). He had been signed in a joint deal with Thirds' inside-forward James Milliken, whose own Fosse career was restricted to friendlies and games in the short-lived United Counties League competition, in which Stirling also managed a record of four games and one goal. James barely made any subsequent impact with Partick, either.

Appearances:
FL: 4 apps. 1 gl.
Total: *4 apps. 1 gl.*

STOODLEY, Claude Henry

Role: Inside right

CAREER: Walthamstow Grange/Mar 1912: Glossop/Aug 1913:FOSSE/May 1914:Merthyr Town.

Debut v Birmingham (A) 20.9.13

Hardly a prolific scorer during his Fosse season at inside-right, Claude must have rather startled himself by belatedly opening his goal account with a hat-trick in the classic 5-5 Cup tie draw with Tottenham. This was very much his only moment of glory, however as Fosse bowed out of the knock-out competition in the replay and then barely kept their heads above the re-election zone.

Appearances:
FL: 25 apps. 3 gls.
FAC: 2 apps. 3 gls.
Total: *27 apps. 6 gls.*

Claude Stoodley

STOTT, -.

Role: Centre forward

CAREER: Feb 1893:FOSSE.

Debut v Burton Wanderers (A) ML 25.2.1893

Barely commented upon at the time of either his appearance (he 'failed to shine' in the 0-3 defeat which represented his only Midland League game) or disappearance (after a further handful of reserve games), this centre-forward has unfortunately proven utterly resistant to further research.

Appearances:
ML: 1 app. 0 gls.
Total: *1 app. 0 gls.*

STRAUGHTON, James H.

Role: Centre forward
b. Workington, c 1889

CAREER: Army football/Sept 1912:FOSSE/ Aug 1914:Pontypridd/Jan 1915:Leicester Imperial/cs 1919:Flimby Rangers.

Debut v Wolverhampton Wanderers (H) 16.11.12

Derek Strickland

A Cumbrian centre-forward whose football prowess was noted while he was soldiering in the Border Regiment, James turned out to be something of a goal-shy attack leader for Fosse, and was regarded as very much third choice behind Sparrow and Mortimer. Indeed, the whole team failed to score on the five occasions he played during 1913/14. James was later 'borrowed' by Lincoln City for a wartime game at Filbert Street in September 1918. His brother Joe also had a few games for Fosse reserves in 1912/13 before joining Workington Central and dying only months later in an industrial accident.

James Straughton

Appearances:
FL: 15 apps. 2 gls.
Total: *15 apps. 2 gls.*

STRICKLAND, Derek

Role: Winger
b. Stoneyburn, West Lothian, 7th November 1959

CAREER: 1976:Rangers/Sept 1979:CITY/ May 1981:Heart of Midlothian/Feb 1983:East Stirlingshire.

Debut v Fulham (H) 22.9.79 (sub)

A Scottish schoolboy international, and a youth-team forward at Ibrox under Jock Wallace, Derek came to Filbert Street as part of the deal which returned Gregor Stevens north of the border. He'd had only two senior games for Rangers, and found his City opportunities limited, but acted as a virtual lucky mascot for the promotion-bound side of 1980: scoring against Wrexham on his first start, never appearing on a losing side, and contributing the only goal of a crucial win at Notts County. Derek moved to Hearts alongside Pat Byrne, but managed only one substitute appearance for the Tynecastle club's first team. He stayed active in Scottish non-league football, however, after leaving Firs Park: being noted in 1994 as manager of Whitburn Juniors.

Appearances:
FL: 4 (3) apps. 2 gls.
Total: *4 (3) apps. 2 gls.*

STRINGFELLOW, Michael David

Role: Outside left
b. Kirkby in Ashfield, Notts, 27th January 1943

CAREER: Feb 1960:Mansfield Town/Jan 1962:CITY/cs 1975:Nuneaton Borough.

Debut v Everton (A) 20.1.62

To attempt to characterise Mike's fourteen seasons with City is to risk an unfortunately not overly glib analogy with the footballing cliche: 'It's a game of two halves'. For seven years after his £25,000 move from Mansfield the lanky outside-left was one of the most feared attackers in the country, forming a lethal left-wing partnership with Davie Gibson and racking up a healthy goal tally. He was also taking a disproportionate amount of 'stick', though, from defenders otherwise at a loss to curb his pace and strength; and the legacy was a further seven years of courageous struggle and determination as Mike fought off a succession of near-crippling injuries (and a sometimes sadly unsympathetic crowd) to continue to give his all for City. Mike had developed at Field Mill under Raich Carter, making his League bow at 17 alongside Ken Wagstaffe, playing at Filbert Street in the inaugural Football League Cup tie, and soon impressing Matt Gillies as a likely successor to Gordon Wills. He hit 19 League and Cup goals in his first full season at Leicester, including the looping header past Liverpool's Tommy Lawrence which assured City of a 1963 Wembley appearance, and for five years thereafter his seasonal goal tally never dropped below double figures, while the number of strikes attributable to his crosses was countless. Mike was a scorer in the 1964 League Cup Final second leg against Stoke, took a runners-up memento from the next year's Final, and is still, with eight goals, City's all-time leading scorer in that competition. Injury problems (which had previously cost Mike an England Under-23 cap) really began to bite, however, during the 1968/9 relegation/Cup Final campaign, and a catalogue of operations, comebacks, breakdowns and sheer frustrations ensued. Yet all this time even a semi-fit 'Stringy' was a valuable squad member, and his April 1975 testimonial game against Wolves was barely adequate recognition of the club's debt to his early excellence and later against-the-odds example. He remains only the second player after Arthur Chandler to figure in the club's top-ten records for both appearances and goalscoring. Mike's spell with Nuneaton was brief, and he subsequently ran pubs in Narborough and Littlethorpe before moving into the newsagents business, latterly in Enderby. His nephew, Ian, began a senior footballing career with Mansfield Town in 1986.

Appearances:
FL: 292 (23) apps. 82 gls.
FAC: 26 (2) apps. 7 gls.
LC: 26 (1) apps. 8 gls.
Total: *344 (26) apps. 97 gls.*

Eric Stubbs

but only once turned out for City again after war had caused the 1939/40 season to be abandoned; often guesting for Wrexham (with whom he'd originally made his League bow) and Chester (for whom he signed during the transitional 1945/6 season), while working as a Cheshire fruit farmer.

Appearances:
FL: 74 apps. 14 gls.
FAC: 4 apps. 1 gl.
WW2: 4 apps. 1 gl.
Total: *82 apps. 16 gls.*

SUMMERS, John Lawrence

Role: Outside right
b. Manchester, 8th February 1915
d. Southampton, 12th April 1991

CAREER: 1931:Manchester North End/(Feb 1932-trials-Burnley)/Fleetwood/(1932-trials-Preston North End)/June 1933:Tunbridge Wells Rangers/Apr 1934:CITY/May 1935: Derby County/Oct 1936:Southampton/ 1938: Southampton Police.

Debut v Chelsea (A) 1.9.34 (scored once)

A young right-winger who was given two spells during City's 1935 relegation season in which to lay claim to the place of the ageing Hughie Adcock, Jack much impressed George Jobey with a goalscoring performance against the latter's Derby side, and

STUBBS, Philip Eric Gordon

Role: Outside left
b. Chester, 10th September 1912

CAREER: Jan 1934:Bolton Wanderers/ Sept 1934:Wrexham/June 1935: Nottingham Forest/Nov 1936: CITY/Dec 1945:Chester.

Debut v Southampton (H) 14.11.36

Something of a prototype for Mike Stringfellow in terms of physical stature and playing style, Eric was also an outside-left who had a dramatic impact on City's fortunes on arrival. Again it was a matter of a 'natural' partnership, for where Mike preceded Davie Gibson into the City side by a week, so Eric had become Frank Womack's first major signing a week before Jack Bowers joined the club, and the powerful pair set about transforming a mundane Second Division season into a convincing championship win. Eric held his place for much of the following two top-flight campaigns,

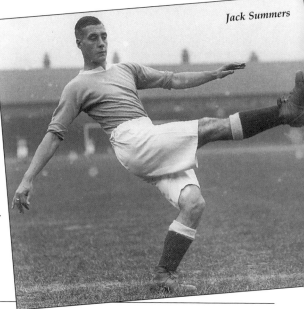

Jack Summers

moved on a few months later to learn more of the tricks of his trade in the shadow of another international, Sammy Crooks, at the Baseball Ground. Such high-class tutelage at least bore a modicum of fruit at The Dell, where Jack notched seven League goals in 31 outings after a £250 move partly underwritten by the Saints Supporters Club. He retired prematurely from the professional game in 1938 to join the police force, but continued to represent his cup-winning constabulary side until 1954, and eventually reached the rank of Chief Inspector.

Appearances:
FL: 11 apps. 2 gls.
Total: *11 apps. 2 gls.*

SVARC, Robert Louis

Role: Striker
b. Leicester, 8th February 1946

CAREER: app Oct 1961/pro Mar 1963:CITY/ Dec 1968:Lincoln City/(Sept 1970-loan-Barrow)/Oct 1971:Boston United/Dec 1972: Colchester United/Oct 1975:Blackburn Rovers/(Sept 1977-loan-Watford).

Debut v Peterborough United (H) LC 23.9.64

A free-scoring reserve striker of Czech descent, Bobby initially got a chance to take over the City centre-forward slot from Ken Keyworth, but then had to wait another three seasons for his next few opportunities to impress. A tough forager rather than a target man, he always looked likelier to make the grade at a lower League level, and Boston manager Jim Smith certainly seemed to agree with that assessment: subsequently signing Bobby again for both Colchester and Blackburn. With the U's, who he assisted to promotion in 1974, he claimed 59 strikes from 116 games, and eventually finished his senior career only four goals short of his League century, after suffering injury in his sole game for Watford. A Jehovah's Witness, Bobby went into the burglar alarm business in the Blackburn area.

Appearances:
FL: 13 apps. 2 gls.
FAC: 1 app. 0 gls.
LC: 4 apps. 0 gls.
Total: *18 apps. 2 gls.*

Bobby Svarc

SWEENIE, Thomas Thornton

Role: Inside forward
b. Paisley, Renfrewshire, 15th July 1945

CAREER: Johnstone Burgh/June 1963:CITY/(July 1968-trials-Arsenal)/(Aug 1968-trials-Huddersfield Town)/Oct 1968:York City/cs 1969:Burton Albion.

Debut v Gillingham (H) LC 27.11.63

A teenage inside-forward of unbounded promise, possessing a firecracker left-foot shot which at one point drew earnest, if exaggerated, comparisons with Puskas from the football press, Tom sadly had his top-class career cut short by injury. Matt Gillies was determined to nurture Tom's career slowly after his senior bow in City's only competitive meeting with the Gills, and subsequent explosive two-goal League bow at Blackpool (and after Liverpool had been pipped for his signature), but a lengthy career as a deep-lying attacker seemed assured until a bad tackle at Forest in February 1967 caused severe damage to his knee, which remained weakened thereafter. In the interim Tom had won two League

Cup tankards (appearing in the second-leg victory over Stoke in 1964, and in the Stamford Bridge leg of the following year's Final) and also put himself in the records as City's first-ever scoring substitute (against Blackburn in April 1966). He was also the second-leg scorer who levelled the aggregate in the Final against Spurs when City's reserves took a share of the Combination Cup in 1967. Released from Filbert Street in June 1968, he was offered a short-term contract by Arsenal, but after testing his fitness with Billy Hodgson's York, sadly gave up the senior game. Tom later set up a carpet fitting business in the county.

Appearances:
FL: 50 (1) apps. 11 gls.
FAC: 1 app. 1 gl.
LC: 4 apps. 0 gls.
Total: 55 (1) apps. 12 gls.

SWIFT,
George Harold

Role: Left back
b. Oakengates, Shropshire, 3rd February 1870

CAREER: St.Georges Swifts/1885:Wellington Town/(1886-trials-Stoke)/Wellington St.Georges/1888:Crewe Alexandra/cs 1891: Wolverhampton Wanderers/cs 1894: Loughborough/Aug 1896:FOSSE/

George Swift

June 1902: Notts County/cs 1904: Leeds City.

Debut v Darwen (H)
5.9.1896

A fine left-back who showed early promise in Shropshire football, played in the Football Alliance for Crewe, and stepped up to the

Tom Sweenie

top flight with Wolves, George appeared for the latter club in the Cup Final of 1893 (when they beat Everton 1-0), then became the only Loughborough player ever to win senior representative honours when selected for the Football League against the Irish League in 1895. He proved an inspirationally consistent captain for Fosse, being ever-present in four of his six seasons, and almost leading them into the First Division in 1899, when they finished third. His goals tended to be either penalties or spectacularly long-range efforts: George scored from the half-way line against Walsall in March 1901, and was not much closer to goal when he won the home game with Blackpool a year later with a shot past the visitors' secretary, Tom Barcroft, who was forced to play between the sticks that afternoon and remained otherwise unbeaten. George took a well-earned benefit from an October 1900 friendly against Wolves, and eventually moved on to Notts County, where the promise of the trainer's role awaited his eventual retirement. He then took on the trainer's duties at newly-founded Leeds City, yet had to don playing kit once more in an emergency when Leeds played at Chelsea in March 1906. George became manager of Chesterfield in 1908, and of Southampton in 1911. When City reached the Cup Final in 1949, a press snippet identified George as a Wembley resident, having just celebrated his golden wedding anniversary.

Appearances:
FL: 186 apps. 4 gls.
FAC: 14 apps. 2 gls.
Total: 200 apps. 6 gls.

TAYLOR, H.A.

Role: Left back
b. Earl Shilton, Leics

CAREER: Earl Shilton/Jan 1914:FOSSE.
Debut v Huddersfield Town (H) 19.9.14

A local left-back ('a sturdily-built youth') who initially had trials with Fosse in January 1914, then vied with Sam Currie for a first-team place during the disastrous final pre-war season. He also had the unfortunate experience of seeing three Derby County goals whizzing past him in 15 minutes after he'd replaced the injured Herbert Bown between the sticks during that term's 0-6 Filbert Street defeat. In April 1917, he suffered six wounds to an arm and both legs in fighting at Arras, and was taken prisoner by the Germans.

Appearances:
FL: 14 apps. 0 gls.
Total: *14 apps. 0 gls.*

TAYLOR, Henry

Role: Defender
b. Birmingham, c 1870

CAREER: Saltley Gas Works FC/Small Heath/cs 1891:FOSSE/cs 1894:Hinckley Town.
Debut v Long Eaton Rangers (A)
ML 23.1.1892

Harry
Taylor

A versatile reserve defender for Fosse in both the first and third Midland League campaigns, Harry was an inter-im ever-present in the half-back line in 1892/3. He had previously failed to make a senior breakthrough at Small Heath, then playing at Football Alliance level, but had nonetheless represented Warwickshire in inter-county fare.

Appearances:
FAC: 4 apps. 0 gls.
ML: 30 apps. 1 gl.
Total: *34 apps. 1 gl.*

TEARSE, David James

Role: Striker
b. Newcastle-on-Tyne, 11th August 1951

CAREER: North Kenton Boys Club/May 1969:CITY/Nov 1971:Torquay United/(Jan 1975-loan-Reading).
Debut v Preston North End (A) 11.10.69 (sub)

A teenage Geordie striker given an early chance by Frank O'Farrell, David played his first full game for City as an emergency right-back at Ewood Park, and then had a brief run in competition with Ally Brown and Murray Brodie as a candidate for Andy Lochhead's target-man role. After two further isolated appearances, he made an

David Tearse

early departure when Jimmy Bloomfield started applying the chequebook to rebuilding his First Division forward line. David, whose £15,000 fee was a Torquay record, scored 23 goals in 77 League games across four seasons at Plainmoor until freed in 1975.

Appearances:
FL: 7 (1) apps. 1 gl.
FAC: 1 (2) apps. 0 gls.
LC: 0 (1) app. 0 gls.
Total: *8 (4) apps. 1 gl.*

TEWLEY, Alan Bernard

Role: Winger
b. Leicester, 22nd January 1945

CAREER: app/pro July 1962:CITY/(Aug 1964-loan-Rugby Town)/Nov 1969:Bradford Park Avenue/Oct 1970:Crewe Alexandra/ cs 1973:Boston United.

Debut v Newcastle United (H) 6.5.67 (sub)

A patient reserve winger, effective on either flank, Alan picked up some useful goals after his belated City

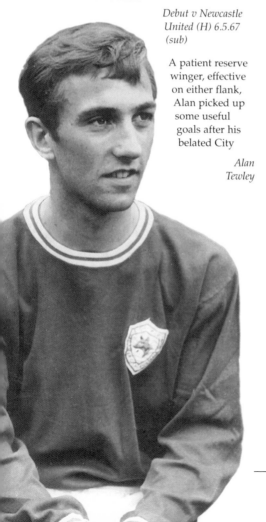

Alan Tewley

breakthrough (scoring on his first start, in the 5-1 win at The Dell in October 1967 which still represents City's only victory on that ground). But he suffered badly from the shift in tactical thinking that saw the employment of even one orthodox flanker as something of a luxury; for City already had Len Glover operating on the left and Rodney Fern emerging as a versatile attacker in the No.7 shirt. Alan's sense of a rather cruel fate must have been compounded when Park Avenue dropped out of the bottom of the Fourth Division: he played in both their last-ever League game and their first at Northern Premier level. But at least he got a decent run of League outings at Gresty Road (scoring 13 times in 68 games), and was part of the Boston side which fought its way to the Third Round of the Cup in 1974 and almost embarrassed the then-mighty Derby, leaving the Baseball Ground with a scoreless draw after Alan's header had hit the post and run along the line.

Appearances:
FL: 15 (3) apps. 5 gls.
LC: 1 (1) apps. 0 gls.
Total: *16 (4) apps. 5 gls.*

THOMAS, Barrie Ernest

Role: Inside forward
b. Measham, Leics, 19th May 1937

CAREER: Measham Imperial/July 1954:CITY/ June 1957:Mansfield Town/Sept 1959: Scunthorpe United/Jan 1962:Newcastle United/Nov 1964:Scunthorpe United/ Nov 1966:Barnsley.

Debut v Sheffield United (A) 25.12.54

A precocious former pit-boy who made a First Division breakthrough at 17 as deputy for Johnny Morris, became an England Youth international, and signed off the 1954/5 season with a hat-trick against Bolton, Barrie was clearly jettisoned inadvisedly early by City after his return from National Service, for he went on to build a substantial striking reputation until injury curtailed his career in 1968. There were few frills to his game, but a brave, direct style brought him a phenomenal haul of League goals, and he was once called up for an England training squad while at Newcastle. He was first noticed claiming 48 goals from 72 centre-forward games with the Stags, then grabbing 67 in 88 games for

Barrie Thomas

Arthur Thompson

reserve team (Fosse Rovers, as they were for some time known) and regularly turning out in the more prestigious friendly games, especially if the opposition themselves were amateurs. He also played for Leicestershire in inter-county competition. (Arthur was previously credited with a Midland League debut in 1892, when his surname was in fact adopted as a pseudonym by George Smith; but there now remains no doubt about the credit for the last of his isolated League appearances, despite Fosse having signed another full-back named Arthur Thompson from Castle Donington in April 1899. We are now certain that it was this veteran who took his final senior bow in the game against Small Heath that month).

Appearances:
FL: 4 apps. 0 gls.
Total: *4 apps. 0 gls.*

Second Division Scunthorpe. A fee of over £40,000 took him to Tyneside (48 goals in 73 apps), and half that amount constituted Scunthorpe's transfer record when he returned there. A nagging knee problem brought his exploits to a halt at Oakwell with a career League aggregate of 210 goals from 335 games, and Barnsley met Newcastle in a testimonial for Barrie in November 1968, by which time he was back at Measham SW, in the Leicestershire Senior League, as manager.

Appearances:
FL: 7 apps. 3 gls.
Total: *7 apps. 3 gls.*

THOMPSON, R. Arthur

Role: Right back
b. Derby, c 1876

CAREER: 1894:FOSSE.
Debut v Burslem Port Vale (H) 23.3.1895

An amateur to the core, this right-back was on Fosse's books until the turn of the century, captaining the

THOMPSON, Robert

Role: Full back
b. Bells Close, Newcastle on Tyne, 1890
d. Liverpool, 1958

CAREER: 1909:Scotswood/May 1911:FOSSE/ Apr 1913:Everton/cs 1921:Millwall/cs 1922: Tranmere Rovers.
Debut v Nottingham Forest (A) 16.9.11

A Geordie full-back who vied with both Tommy Clay and Sam Currie for a first-team berth during his two Leicester seasons, Bob was snapped up by Everton in a joint transfer deal with winger George Harrison, and went on to serve at Goodison throughout the WW1 period, making 83 League appearances on either side of the conflict, and winning a First Division

Bob Thompson

championship medal in 1915. Five goals eventually accrued to Bob's career record: all coming for Tranmere during his final season of League football.

Appearances:
FL: 27 apps. 0 gls.
FAC: 1 app. 0 gls.
Total: *28 apps. 0 gls.*

THOMPSON, Stephen James

Role: Midfield
b. Oldham, 2nd November 1964

CAREER: Poulton Victoria/app/pro Nov 1982:Bolton Wanderers/Sept 1991:Luton Town/Oct 1991:CITY/Feb 1995:Burnley.

Debut v Oxford United (A) 26.10.90 (sub) (scored once)

The creative fulcrum of Brian Little's persistent promotion seekers, midfielder Steve was nearly lost to City entirely, for David Pleat beat Little to the Bolton playmaker's signature, only to use him, six weeks and five League starts later, as barter material in the transfer of Scott Oakes and Des Linton to top-flight Luton. Previously a fixture for almost nine years in the Burnden Park midfield (totalling 421 League and Cup games there), Steve had played in all three lower Divisions (twice suffering relegation, and enjoying a 1988 promotion from the basement) and had three times turned out at Wembley for the Trotters (on the losing side in the 1986 Freight/Rover Final and the 1991 Play Offs, and as a victor in the 1989 Sherpa Van Trophy). After a 45-minute City debut at the Manor Ground which featured one peach of a through-ball for Paul Kitson and an amazing chipped goal as welcome auguries of his vision, Steve soon settled as the distributive hub of the Filbert Street middle-line, and would return thrice to Wembley with the club in successive Play Off Finals: coolly sliding home the third comeback goal against

Swindon, and coming on as sub in the climactic victory over Derby. Sadly, Steve did not shine so brightly in the Premiership: record signing Mark Draper inherited his key prompting role; he wasted two important penalties over the Christmas/New Year period, after a valuable run of nine without a miss; and looked generally below the pace, even if his passing accuracy was still a pleasure to behold. Steve had talks with Port Vale in February 1995, and a week later joined struggling Burnley for £200,000, only to go down to Division Two with them at season's end. Steve's father Jimmy also had a lengthy League career, with Oldham, Exeter, Rochdale and Bradford City.

Appearances:
PL: 16 (3) apps. 0 gls.
FL: 105 (3) apps. 18 gls.
FAC: 8 apps. 1 gl.
LC: 6 apps. 2 gls.
FMC: 3 (1) apps. 1 gl.
AIC: 2 apps. 0 gls.
P/O: 6 (2) apps. 3 gls.
Total: *146 (9) apps. 25 gls.*

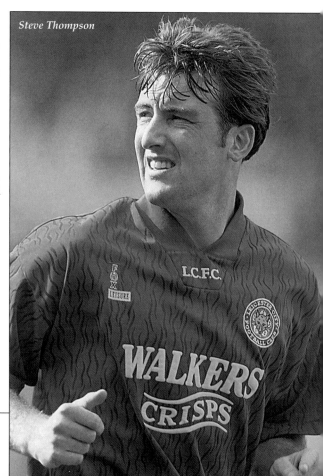
Steve Thompson

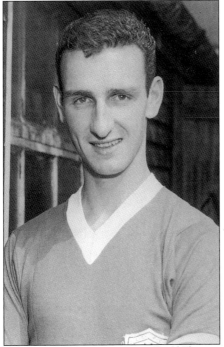

David Thomson

THOMSON, David L.

Role: Inside left
b. Bothkennar, 2nd February 1938

CAREER: Bo'ness United/cs 1959:
Dunfermline Athletic/Aug 1961:CITY/
cs 1963:Queen of the South.
Debut v Tottenham Hotspur (H) 30.4.62
(scored once)

The hero of Dunfermline's 1961 Scottish Cup
win - as an unexpected selection for the Final
replay against Celtic, he scored the first goal
with a diving header - centre-forward David
was snapped up by Matt Gillies as a possible
replacement for Ken Leek, but in two
seasons managed only
the one senior outing
(and that at inside-left)
while the City No.9 shirt
was being swapped
around with some
abandon.

Appearances:
FL: 1 app. 1 gl.
Total: *1 app. 1 gl.*

THOMSON, William

Role: Wing half
b. Glasgow, c 1895

CAREER: Blantyre Victoria/cs 1912:Clyde/
Sept 1914:FOSSE/1915:Arthurlie/cs 1919:
CITY/Oct 1924:Bristol Rovers.
Debut v Grimsby Town (A) 12.9.14

By the time he left for Eastville, Billy was the
last of the pre-war Fossils still to be active for
the reconstructed City. Having originally
signed from Shawfield as a tough wing-half,
and suffered Fosse's plunge to the nadir of
their fortunes, he returned from Scotland (and
wartime work on naval repairs) for City's
reinvigorated assault on the Second Division,
and became a strong defensive anchor for
Peter Hodge's predominantly attack-minded
team-building efforts, partnering Jim Harrold
and Mick O'Brien in succession until displaced
by John Bamber. Billy's single season with
Bristol Rovers brought him a further 25
League and Cup selections (plus a sending-off
in the Ashton Gate League derby), then in
November 1925 he took up the position of
coach at Highland League club Inverness
Citadel.

Appearances:
FL: 197 apps. 3 gls.
FAC: 12 apps. 0 gls.
Total: *209 apps. 3 gls.*

THORNTON, William

Role: Inside right
b. Birmingham

CAREER: Bathurst Works/ May 1919:CITY/
cs 1920:Wellington Town.
Debut v Wolverhampton Wanderers (H) 30.8.19

Signed from a Birmingham factory team in
time for City's first match under their new
title, but dropped immediately after
that 1-2 home defeat, William was an
inside-right who also failed
subsequently to satisfy Peter Hodge's
rigorous standards, and moved on
after one season to contribute to
Wellington's 1920/1 Birmingham &
District League championship win.

Appearances:
FL: 11 apps. 2 gls.
Total: *11 apps. 2 gls.*

THORPE, Harold Cheetham

Role: Left back
b. New Whittington, Chesterfield, 1880
d. New Whittington, 16th September 1908

CAREER: 1900:Chesterfield/May 1903:
Woolwich Arsenal/cs 1904:Fulham/
Aug 1907: FOSSE.

Debut v Leeds City (H) 7.9.07

A left-back of some skill and power, Harry had built up a solid body of top-class experience before joining Fosse, playing Second Division football for his hometown club, helping Arsenal gain promotion from that sphere in 1904, and assisting Fulham to two Southern League championships in 1906 and 1907. His defensive capabilities were a major boost to Fosse's successful promotion effort, but Harry

Harry Thorpe

sadly failed to finish the season, having contracted a debilitating strain of influenza after a game at Glossop in March 1908. Tragically, he never recovered, and died at his family home within months. Several Fosse players acted as pall-bearers at his funeral.

Appearances:
FL: 26 apps. 0 gls.
FAC: 2 apps. 0 gls.
Total: 28 apps. 0 gls.

THORPE, John

Role: Right half
b. Skegby, Mansfield

CAREER: Mansfield Mechanics/
May 1911: FOSSE/cs 1912:
Mansfield Mechanics.

*Debut v Huddersfield Town (H)
21.10.11*

A young right-half who failed to make the transition from Notts & Derbyshire League football to the demands of Second Division fare when deputising for Arthur Randle, and

played in only a pair of defeats during a campaign Fosse finished in 10th place. John arrived at Leicester in a straight swap for George King.

Appearances:
FL: 2 apps. 0 gls.
Total: 2 apps. 0 gls.

THRAVES, James

Role: Goalkeeper
b. Nottinghamshire, 1870
d. Bramcote, Notts, 29th May 1936

CAREER: Notts St.Johns/1889:Notts County/
cs 1892:FOSSE/Sept 1897:Long Eaton Rangers.

Debut v Mansfield Town (A) ML 17.9.1892

Notts County's FA Cup Final goalkeeper in 1891, at a time when he had only two previous League games to his credit, Jimmy even ended his stint with the Magpies having played in more Cup combat than First Division fare! He then got off to a strange start with Fosse, missing a train connection and turning up 35 minutes late for his Midland League debut at Mansfield; but rather compensated by being an ever-present between the sticks for the next four and a half seasons. A measure of his ability as much as his consistency was that his frustrated understudy during the first League season, former Buxton keeper Tom Chappell, was good enough to win himself an eventual move to Manchester City; while the man in his

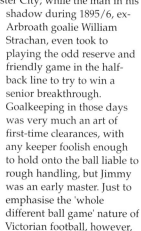

shadow during 1895/6, ex-Arbroath goalie William Strachan, even took to playing the odd reserve and friendly game in the half-back line to try to win a senior breakthrough. Goalkeeping in those days was very much an art of first-time clearances, with any keeper foolish enough to hold onto the ball liable to rough handling, but Jimmy was an early master. Just to emphasise the 'whole

Jimmy Thraves

different ball game' nature of Victorian football, however, one could instance the fact that Jimmy actually played through the eventually-abandoned Midland League fixture against Doncaster at a snowbound Filbert Street in November 1893 wearing his overcoat. For a couple of years he also pursued a unique parallel career as Fosse groundsman. He benefited from a friendly against Luton in September 1896, and played his last competitive Fosse game in the 1897 Burford Cup Final victory over Notts County, who he rejoined in the 20s for an eleven-year spell as a director. At this time Jimmy was a successful Stapleford businessman.

Appearances:
FL: 80 apps. 0 gls.
FAC: 24 apps. 0 gls.
ML: 44 apps. 0 gls.
Total: *148 apps. 0 gls.*

THRELFALL, Frederick

Role: Winger
b. Preston, 1879

CAREER: June 1898: Manchester City/cs 1905: Fulham/July 1909:FOSSE.
Debut v Wolverhampton Wanderers (H) 1.9.09 (scored once)

A deft, speedy winger whose Manchester City mentor was the great Billy Meredith, Fred was one of the few 'innocents' on the Hyde Road payroll when the FA uncovered a mesh of financial irregularities there and slapped massive fines and suspensions on a majority of the players and management, almost causing the club to fold. His move to Craven Cottage brought him immediate success, as Fulham raced to the Southern League championship in 1906 and 1907, and won election to the League. Fred played in the Professionals v. Amateurs international trial (alongside Arthur Collins) in 1906, and was regarded a prize capture by Fosse as they attempted to bounce straight back into Division One. He turned in some scintillating displays on either flank until February 1911 (his goal at Leyton putting the club into the FA Cup quarter-finals for the first time in 1910), and off the field was a member of the management committee of the Players Union. He later became trainer to the Irish team Cliftonville.

Appearances:
FL: 50 apps. 6 gls.
FAC: 6 apps. 4 gls.
Total: *56 apps. 10 gls.*

TIMSON, David Youles

Role: Goalkeeper
b. Leicester, 24th August 1947

CAREER: app Dec 1962/pro Sept 1964:CITY/ Aug 1967:Newport County.
Debut v Blackpool (H) 11.4.64

Until fellow goalkeeper Peter Shilton broke his record two years later, David was the youngest peacetime City debutant, having made a single stand-in appearance at the age of sixteen (in a 2-3 home defeat) when Gordon Banks was on England duty and regular reserve George Heyes was injured. Ironically, David was not to don the first-team green jersey again until Shilton had become the established No.1; playing in the final two games of 1966/7 (both home wins) while Shilton was on an England Youth tour. He then managed 27 League and Cup games at Somerton Park before departing the senior game.

Appearances:
FL: 3 apps. 0 gls.
Total: *3 apps. 0 gls.*

Fred Threlfall

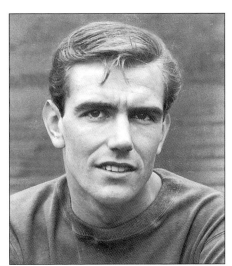

David Timson

David Tomlin (left) with Jimmy Bloomfield.

TOMLIN, David

Role: Winger
b. Nuneaton, Warks, 9th February 1953

CAREER: app Aug 1970/pro Oct 1971:CITY/ Apr 1977:Torquay United/Aug 1978: Aldershot/cs1981:Andover/Godalming.
Debut v Huddersfield Town (H) 16.10.71

A young winger who persistently fringed Jimmy Bloomfield's squads of the early 70s, and regularly warmed the sub's bench, David is chiefly remembered for one inspired performance in his first season, when he ran England full-back Terry Cooper ragged in a home game against Leeds. It was the sort of form David could not maintain consistently, however, and his role became that of occasional stand-in for Len Glover. He managed 38 games at Torquay and 30 at Aldershot, scoring twice for each club.

Appearances:
FL: 19 (7) apps. 2 gls.
FAC: 1 (2) apps. 0 gls.
LC: 1 app. 0 gls.
Total: 21 (9) apps. 2 gls.

TOMPKIN, Maurice

Role: Outside right
b. Countesthorpe, Leics,
17th February 1919
d. Leicester, 27th September 1956

CAREER: Countesthorpe United/Mar 1938: CITY/ Dec 1945:Bury/Sept 1946: Huddersfield Town/ 1947:Kettering Town.

Maurice Tompkin

Debut v Birmingham (H) 7.5.38

The son of former City winger Percy, and an outside-right himself, Maurice made a pre-war teenage debut, replacing Tony Carroll in a final fixture 1-4 home defeat. But service with the RAMC in India meant that he played no more senior football until appearing in 20 games for Bury during the transitional 1945/6 season, and going on to make ten First Division starts at Huddersfield. Maurice was always happier as a cricketer, though; starring as a prolific, stylish batsman for Leicestershire from 1938 to the time of his early death, and amassing 29 centuries amongst his 18,590 runs.

Appearances:
FL: 1 app. 0 gls.
Total: 1 app. 0 gls.

TOMPKIN, Percy Lord

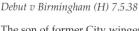

Role: Outside left
b. Salford, Lancs,
28th January 1894
d. Countesthorpe,
Leics, 25th February
1948

CAREER:
Countesthorpe United/Leicester Imperial/(Apr 1913-trials-FOSSE)/Sutton Junction/Hinckley United/cs 1914:Nuneaton Town/Army football/June 1919:Huddersfield Town/June 1920:CITY/ cs 1925:Nuneaton Town.

Debut v Bury (H) 2.9.20 (scored once)

The pacy, left-sided, senior member of the Tompkin family duo, Percy rejoiced in the non-derogatory nickname of 'Fairy', and battled for four Second Division seasons with Sandy Trotter for the City's outside-left spot, with honours roughly even between them until both were eclipsed by the advent of Harold Wadsworth. Percy had previously played but a single League game for the powerful Terriers side which in 1919/20 both won promotion and reached the Cup Final.

Appearances:
FL: 87 apps. 4 gls.
FAC: 3 apps. 0 gls.
Total: *90 apps. 4 gls.*

TOWERS, William Harry

Role: Left half
b. Leicester, 13th July 1920

CAREER: Bentley Engineering Co FC/am Mar 1940/pro Jan 1945: CITY/Oct 1946:Torquay United/ Sept 1956:Minehead.

Debut (WW2) v Coventry City (H) 7.9.40;
(competitive) v Chelsea (A) FAC 5.1.46

A local left-half who had played a handful of Regional League games for City in 1940/1, before returning to local Senior League football with Bentley's, Bill eventually proved himself worthy of a professional contract from wartime boss Tom Bromilow. He briefly shared in the return to Second Division football under Johnny Duncan, but was soon

Harry Trainer

allowed to join former City trainer/coach Jack Butler, by then Torquay manager, at Plainmoor. He stayed with Torquay for 10 years, making 274 League appearances, and prompting City to visit Devon for his 1952 benefit match.

Appearances:
FL: 4 apps. 0 gls.
FAC: 2 apps. 0 gls.
WW2: 44 apps. 2 gls.
Total: *50 apps. 2 gls.*

TRAINER, Harry

Role: Centre forward
b. Wrexham, 1872
d. Wrexham, 1924

CAREER: 1890:Wrexham Victoria/1891:Wrexham Grosvenor/ 1893:Westminster Rovers/cs 1894:Wrexham/ (Feb 1895-trials-West Bromwich Albion)/ Aug 1895:FOSSE/cs 1897:Sheppey United/ cs 1899:Wrexham.

Debut v Burton Swifts (H) 7.9.1895

International centre-forward Harry first cropped up in the Fosse annals in November 1894, when the club received an FA censure for illegally approaching and registering him. But they got their man eventually, after he had led Wales in all three home internationals of March 1895 (scoring twice against Ireland), had spearheaded Wrexham to the Welsh League title, and had picked up his second successive Welsh Cup consolation medal. Harry nonetheless proved an inconsistent marksman in the Second Division, and a nap hand of goals in an 8-0 demolition of Rotherham Town provided precisely half his first seasonal League tally. Unable thereafter to command a regular attacking role, he moved on for a couple of seasons to Sheppey, then enjoying an elevated status in the Southern League's top echelon, and bowed out of the game when 'knee failure' aborted his second Wrexham stint. He was a cousin of the oft-capped Welsh keeper Jim Trainer.

Appearances:
FL: 31 apps. 12 gls.
FAC: 4 apps. 4 gls.
Total: *35 apps. 16 gls.*

Bill Towers

TRAVERS, James Edward (George)

Role: Inside forward
b. Newtown, Birmingham, 4th November 1888 (?)
d. Smethwick, Worcs, 31st August 1946 (?)

CAREER: 1904:Bilston United/1905:Rowley United/July 1906:Wolverhampton Wanderers/ Aug 1907:Birmingham/Dec 1908:Aston Villa/ May 1909:Queen's Park Rangers/Aug 1910: FOSSE/Jan 1911:Barnsley/Feb 1914: Manchester United.

Debut v Bolton Wanderers (H) 3.9.10 (scored twice)

George Travers

Essentially a youthful reserve for his West Midlands clubs, inside-forward George was best known prior to his brief Fosse spell for having notched a hat-trick on his Villa debut against Bury on Boxing Day 1908. As deputy to future England international Harry Hampton, however, he found few chances at Villa Park and, curiously, it was his Southern League record with QPR (of only 7 goals in 34 games) which recommended him to Leicester player/manager Andy Aitken. After a fine start to 1910/11 (six wins in nine fixtures), however, Fosse slumped, and both George and new centre-forward Jack Hall were soon jettisoned. George was involved in a straight swap with Barnsley 'keeper Fred Mearns, and in fact went on to appear in the Tykes' victorious 1912 FA Cup Final team before switching to First Division fare at Old Trafford in the final pre-war season, and then enlisting for Army service. (Possessors of the original *Of Fossils & Foxes* - and those who broaden their football-history reading across tomes devoted to several other clubs - will note that the above career chronology has been virtually halved from that originally/usually published for this player. Indefatigable researchers Mike Davage and Jim Creasey have only recently discovered that the lengthy active career path hitherto attributed to a single player most probably related in actuality to two men. Their valid contention is that a different forward {born in Bow, London, in 1901} featured in several post-WW1 club line-ups - notably those of Swindon, Millwall, Norwich and Gillingham - and in as many colourful off-field scrapes; culminating in a Gillingham jail sentence in 1933. However, as the age given for this ex-footballing George Travers in court reports (49) corresponds with neither of those above, we hope readers will appreciate the problems and pitfalls of all such biographical research. As ever, the current authors would be sincerely pleased to receive any additional information on 'our' George's life or career).

Appearances:
FL: 12 apps. 5 gls.
Total: *12 apps. 5 gls.*

TROTTER, Alexander E.

Role: Outside left
b. Jarrow, Co.Durham

CAREER: Jarrow/Dec 1916:Leeds City/Apr 1917:Raith Rovers/Dumbarton/Ashington/ June 1920:CITY/May 1924:South Shields/ May 1927:Port Vale/July 1928:Manchester Central/Oct 1929:Bedlington United.

Debut v Bury (H) 2.9.20 (scored once)

Essentially an outside-left, Sandy made his City bow in the centre-forward berth after stepping up from North Eastern League football, and managed quite a few more games as a makeshift leader while attempting to shrug off Percy Tompkin's challenge for the flank position. He exhibited flair and dash in City's attempts to rise from the Second Division, but by the time they achieved that feat he was in the middle of a three-season spell with South Shields, which ended with relegation to the Third Division (North) and presaged that club's later lock, stock and barrel uprooting to Gateshead. Sandy's prior wartime experience was not only on Northern and Scottish football fields: he also lost a finger in military action.

Appearances:
FL: 96 apps. 10 gls.
FAC: 4 apps. 1 gl.
Total: *100 apps. 11 gls.*

TROTTER, Michael

Role: Utility
b. Hartlepool, 27th October 1969

CAREER: YT/pro 1987:Middlesbrough/ (Nov 1988-loan-Doncaster Rovers)/ cs 1990:Darlington/Dec 1991:CITY/ Nov 1993:Chesterfield/(1994-trials-Walsall)/ Dec 1994:Buxton/Jan 1995:Halifax Town.

Debut v Bristol Rovers (A) 1.1.92 (sub)

A Brian Little protege at both Ayresome and Feethams, defensive midfielder Michael was given a further chance to live up to his early promise when brought to City by his mentor as something of a wild card in the Jimmy Willis purchase deal. But his isolated senior appearances tended to emphasise willingness

Michael Trotter

and workrate rather than technical acumen, and a limited future in the Central League seemed to beckon until a loan spell at Saltergate (marked by a debut goal) developed into a further free transfer. Nonetheless, Michael dropped out of the senior game in 1994.

Appearances:
FL: 1 (2) apps. 0 gls.
LC: 1 app. 0 gls.
AIC: 0 (1) app. 0 gls.
Total: *2 (3) apps. 0 gls.*

TROUGHEAR, William B.

Role: Right back
b. Workington, 1885

CAREER:
Workington/May 1909:Sunderland/May 1914:FOSSE/cs 1919:Flimby Rangers.
Debut v Lincoln City (H) 2.9.14

Billy Troughear

Right-back Billy made exactly a century of League appearances for Sunderland, but only the final six of them had been in the year of their 1912/13 First Division title win. An England trialist in 1910/11 (Whites v. Stripes), he was approaching the veteran stage when he brought his dour defensive qualities to Leicester, and proved no better equipped than his team-mates to stem the tide of humiliating results which left Fosse clutching at the re-election straw before the abandonment of League football. After wartime munitions work, and guest appearances for Preston North End, Billy played out his postwar career in the North West Cumberland League, in the company of another former Fossil, James Straughton.

Appearances:
FL: 15 apps. 0 gls.
FAC: 1 app. 0 gls.
Total: *16 apps. 0 gls.*

TRUEMAN, Albert Harry

Role: Left half
b. Leicester, April qtr 1882
d. Leicester, 24th February 1961

CAREER: Grasmere Swifts/am Aug 1899:
FOSSE/cs 1902:Hinckley Town/1903:Coalville
Town/Aug 1905:FOSSE/May 1908:
Southampton/Mar 1911:Sheffield United/
cs 1913:Darlington/1914:Leicester Imperial.
Debut v Clapton Orient (H) 2.9.05

Inexplicably known to all and sundry
throughout his career as 'Nigger', this local
left-half was on Fosse's books as an amateur
from an early age, represented the county at
juvenile level, and faced Notts County in a
benefit friendly at Christmas 1900, but also
played for several local sides before settling to
a regular challenging role as a Filbert Street
professional. Albert wrestled for three seasons
with Bob Pollock for a first-team place, and
also patiently captained the reserves as Fosse
headed for promotion. He flourished with
Southampton, though, winning representative
honours for the Southern League and scoring
the winning goal for that combination when
they beat the Football League in November
1910 at White Hart Lane, on the way to a clean

Albert Trueman

sweep of that season's Inter-League tournament. After further travels (including a 55-
game First Division stint at Bramall Lane), he
made a nostalgic return to Filbert Street action
in September 1916, when persuaded from the
stands to make up the numbers in a wartime
game against Grimsby Town. It is believed he
also later assisted Clydebank in WW1 football.

Appearances:
FL: 43 apps. 2 gls.
FAC: 1 app. 0 gls.
WW1: 1 app. 0 gls.
Total: *45 apps. 2 gls.*

TURNER, Philip

Role: Midfield
b. Sheffield, 12th February 1962

CAREER: Sheffield Rangers/app July 1978/
pro Feb 1980:Lincoln City/Aug 1986:Grimsby
Town/Feb 1988:CITY/Mar 1989:Notts County.
Debut v Blackburn Rovers (A) 19.3.88 (sub)

Arriving in the part-exchange deal that took
Kevin Jobling to Blundell Park, and departing
in the two-way transaction that brought Gary
Mills to Leicester, Phil also found in the
interim his tactical role in David Pleat's
Second Division side being swapped around
on a fairly regular basis. Stints at full-back, in
midfield and as an auxiliary winger hardly
allowed him to settle, but his neat skills on the
ball were unfortunately supplemented neither
by exceptional pace nor a great deal of
penetration - though a magnificent 30-yard
strike against Blackburn at Filbert Street,
bringing him his first City goal, will live long
in the memory. Phil had totted up 242 League
appearances for Lincoln, and built a fine playmaking reputation in his season and a half at
Grimsby. He later skippered the Magpies back
into the First Division via Wembley victories
in both the 1990 and 1991 Play-offs; appeared
twice more at the national stadium in Anglo-
Italian Cup Finals in 1994 (as a runner-up) and
1995 (as a victor); and suffered two Meadow
Lane relegation terms in 1992 and 1995. Phil
finished the most recent campaign on a career
total of 551 League appearances.

Appearances:
FL: 18 (6) apps. 2 gls.
FAC: 1 app. 0 gls.
LC: 1 (1) apps. 0 gls.
Total: *20 (7) apps. 2 gls.*

TURNER, Richard William

Role: *Inside left*
b. *Leicester*

CAREER: Leicester Imperial/Feb 1906: FOSSE/Aug 1910: Portsmouth/Aug 1911:Leyton.

Debut v Bradford City (H) 24.3.06

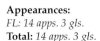

Billy Turner

Despite making an earlier first-team breakthrough than his brother Bob, inside-left Billy then had to spend a rather longer apprenticeship in Fosse's reserves, and barely got a game until Bob moved on. Indeed, the only occasion on which the pair turned out together (after their joint introduction as trialists in an April 1905 friendly against Forest) was when they formed the left flank in the 2-2 draw at Chesterfield in the promotion season of 1907/8. Billy later had a none-too-successful spell in Southern League football, making 34 appearances in a relegated Pompey side (claiming six goals) after a £25 move, and starting only twice (scoring once) for Leyton.

Appearances:
FL: 14 apps. 3 gls.
Total: *14 apps. 3 gls.*

TURNER, Robert Frewin

Role: Outside left
b. *Leicester, 15th July 1885*
d. *Darlington, 15th February 1959*

CAREER: Leicester Imperial/Mar 1905: FOSSE/Apr 1909:Everton/July 1911:Preston North End/cs 1912:Darlington/June 1914: Coventry City/Dec 1919:Durham City.

Debut v Barnsley (H) 22.9.06

The younger and more successful of the Turner brothers, Bob - or 'Leggy' as he was usually known - also led the more colourful career. Not only was he a speedy outside-left with Fosse, good enough to take over from Frank Middleton halfway through the 1908 promotion season and hold his place in the top flight, but he also emulated his father Frew as a cricketing all-rounder for Leicestershire (1909-11). His transfer to Everton, when Fosse's relegation fate was already settled, was a truly controversial affair, with Bob's new club reporting him to the FA for demanding an illicit £100 signing-on fee, and the player finding himself suddenly somewhat worse off after a £50 fine. Undaunted, however, he made a scoring Goodison debut in the Liverpool derby and set about making final preparations for his impending marriage: the notoriously celebrated affair attended by most of the Fosse team on the eve of their record 0-12 defeat at Nottingham Forest. As if Bob hadn't wrought enough havoc for one month, he then assisted Everton to a 4-2 win over a rather more sober Fosse only three days later. His later efforts for a relegated Preston side, for North Eastern League champions Darlington, and for Coventry in the Southern League's Second Division inevitably seem mundane by comparison!

Bob Turner

Appearances:
FL: 56 apps. 7 gls.
FAC: 3 apps. 1 gl.
Total: *59 apps. 8 gls.*

Phil Turner

VENUS, Mark

Role: Left back
b. Hartlepool, 6th April 1967

CAREER: YT cs 1984:Hartlepool United/
Aug 1985:CITY/Mar 1988:Wolverhampton
Wanderers.
Debut v Aston Villa (A) 31.3.86

Recruited as a trainee by his hometown club
after he'd spurned approaches by Barnsley
and Coventry, left-back Mark made four

Mark Venus

League appearances as a non-contract player,
and came to Leicester as a free agent when
United wanted him to continue on that basis.
Reserve-team 'Player of the Year' by the end
of his first season, Mark had also made a
single appearance in Simon Morgan's stead
prior to finding himself the regular senior
No.3 from the start of 1986/7. Though he
understandably betrayed occasional defensive
naïveté in City's First Division struggles, he
also demonstrated commendable accuracy
with his crosses from advanced positions, and
laid on several of the goals which lifted the
club to an unaccustomed early mid-table slot.
Thereafter suffering as something of a regular
scapegoat for a frustrated crowd, Mark
nonetheless stuck doggedly to his defensive
tasks, and his single goal for City was a
memorable last-minute volley that won the
home game against Swindon in 1987/8. David
Pleat allowed Mark to move on for £40,000 to
Fourth Division leaders Wolves for their
championship run-in, and he was a Third
Division medallist a year later, too, before
graduating to the Molineux captaincy. Mark
scored the last senior goal to date conceded by
Peter Shilton, in the first leg of the Play-off
semi-finals of May 1995, but Wolves'
Premiership ambitions were thwarted once
more on aggregate scores.

> **Appearances:**
> *FL: 58 (3) apps. 1 gl.*
> *FAC: 2 apps. 0 gls.*
> *LC: 3 apps. 0 gls.*
> *FMC: 2 (1) apps. 0 gls.*
> **Total:** *65 (4) apps. 1 gl.*

VICKERS, A.

Role: Left half

CAREER: 1889:FOSSE.

*Debut (competitive) v
Loughborough (A)
ML 14.11.91*

Left-half throughout Fosse's   *A. Vickers*
initial County Cup-winning
run of 1889/90, this Fosse amateur maintained
his attachment to the club into the Midland
League era, and was still turning out in
occasional friendly fixtures in 1892/3.

> **Appearances:**
> *ML: 4 apps. 0 gls.*
> **Total:** *4 apps. 0 gls.*

VICKERSTAFFE, Ernest B.

Role: Right back
b. Hanley, Staffs

CAREER: Cheltenham Town/Eastville Athletic/(trials-Bristol City)/Leicester Old Boys/Dec 1902:FOSSE/1904:Leicester Old Boys/cs 1907:Leicester Nomads/ cs 1909:Hinckley United.

Debut v Burslem Port Vale (A) 27.2.04

A well respected amateur full-back, raised in Leicester, and then showing a belated homing instinct after starting his football career in the West, Ernest suffered the cruellest of luck on his senior debut, breaking his leg in two places during a 2-6 defeat. Fortunately he eventually recovered ('guesting' for Fosse in an April 1906 friendly against Notts County, as well as for the reserves in such games as the 1905 and 1909 County Cup Finals), and became captain of the all-amateur Leicester Nomads in their inaugural season. His affinity for the Leicestershire Senior Cup continued with Hinckley, for whom he turned out in the Finals of 1910 (won against Market Harborough Town) and 1911 (lost to Leicester Imperial).

Appearances:
FL: 1 app. 0 gls.
Total: *1 app. 0 gls.*

VILLIERS, Henry George

Role: Wing half
b. Faversham, Kent, 29th June 1892
d. Leicester, 28th August 1972

CAREER: Bedford Town/ Army/cs 1919:Rugby Town/ July 1920:CITY/cs 1922: Mansfield Town/cs 1923: Nuneaton Town/ Oct 1923:Rugby Town/ Hinckley United.

Debut v Clapton Orient (A) 28.8.20

A wing-half in whom high hopes were invested at the start of 1920/1, Henry failed to bridge the considerable gulf between the Birmingham Combination and the Second Division, and was released after two seasons of understudying Teddy King and Billy Thomson, having made considerably less impact than his former Rugby teammates, the Roxburghs. Mansfield finished tenth in the Midland League with Henry in their side, and he claimed a single FA Cup goal from that campaign.

Appearances:
FL: 5 apps. 0 gls.
Total: *5 apps. 0 gls.*

VINCETT, John Herbert

Role: Left back
b. Hastings, Sussex, 24th May 1883
d. Lambeth, London, 28th December 1953

CAREER: Hastings & St.Leonards/ Aug 1907:Grimsby Town/Aug 1908:FOSSE/ Jan 1909:Barnsley/cs 1909:not known/ Dec 1910:Tottenham Hotspur.

Debut v Manchester United (A) 12.12.08

Noted for his powerful, lengthy kicking, John was a tall, weighty full-back who had been a regular in his Mariners season, but his essentially unsophisticated defensive style was deemed not to be up to the First Division mark after his £100 transfer, and he was allowed to move on within a month of his sole senior game. Indeed, that 2-4 Old Trafford defeat proved to be John's final League outing, for he appeared at first-team level for neither Tykes nor Spurs. For twelve summers from 1907 he was a professional medium-pace bowler with Sussex, and also turned out twice for Surrey in 1921.

Appearances:
FL: 1 app. 0 gls.
Total: *1 app. 0 gls.*

Henry Villiers

WADDLE, Alan

Role: Striker
b. Wallsend, Northumberland, 9th June 1954

CAREER: Nov 1971:Halifax Town/July 1973:
Liverpool/Sept 1977:CITY/May 1978:Swansea
City/Dec 1980:Newport County/Aug 1982:
Mansfield Town/cs 1983:(Hong Kong)/
Aug 1983:Hartlepool United/Oct 1983:
Peterborough United/Jan 1985:Hartlepool
United/Mar 1985:Swansea City/cs 1986:Barry
Town/Dec 1986:Wakrah Sports (Qatar)/
Feb 1987:Barry Town/Jan 1988:Llanelli/
Port Talbot/Maesteg Park/Nov 1989:Bridgend
Town/Dec 1989:Llanelli.

Debut v Nottingham Forest (H) 24.9.77

A tall striker who had only scored 4 goals in
40 games when added to the Anfield
investment collection for £45,000, Alan failed
to make the grade on Merseyside despite

Alan Waddle

scoring the winning goal in his first Goodison
derby, and had become accustomed to Central
League football when Frank McLintock asked
him to help turn around City's atrocious start
to the 1977/8 season. Within a couple of
months, though, it was evident that neither
Alan's confidence nor mobility were up to the
task at hand, and it was only during his first
spell at Swansea, under John Toshack, that
Alan began to score with any regularity. He
assisted the Swans up to the Second Division
(on their whirlwind rise from Fourth to First),
then cost Newport their all-time record outlay
of £80,000. His subsequent wanderings
brought mixed fortunes; perhaps best summed
up in Alan's experience in the Mansfield v.
Crewe fixture of October 1982, when he scored
for both sides and was then sent off! His
return to the Vetch sparked a successful
fight-back against relegation on the part of the
Swans, and though Alan joined Barry Town
for the 1986/7 season, he also held a post running Swansea's commercial operations. He is a
cousin of England international Chris Waddle.

Appearances:
FL: 11 apps. 1 gl.
Total: *11 apps. 1 gl.*

WADSWORTH, Harold

Role: Outside left
b. Bootle, Lancs, 1st October 1898
d. Chesterfield, 2nd November 1975

CAREER: Bootle St.Matthews/Tranmere
Rovers/Aug 1918:Liverpool/Jun 1924:CITY/
Apr 1927:Nottingham Forest/June 1928:
Millwall.

Debut v Manchester United (A) 30.8.24

Harold joined his older brother, long-serving
centre-half Walter, at Anfield during the final
season of WW1 football, and soon etched a
reputation as a raiding winger, but was then
relegated to reserve status for the bulk of both
Liverpool championship seasons of 1922 and
1923. The move to Filbert Street, however,
brought him immediate recompense (albeit in
a lower key), as his ever-present record on
City's left wing immeasurably aided the 1925
promotion success, and his continuing
consistency as partner to George Carr or
Arthur Lochhead contributed sturdily to First
Division consolidation. Harold's rather lowly
goal ratio picked up appreciably during his

Harold Wadsworth

Scottish League goals in a rapid burst, George was a centre-forward who relied more on speed than brawny bustling. But in attempting to fill Jock Paterson's boots at Leicester, he was always aware of the persistent challenge of Albert Pynegar for City's chief scoring mantle. Subsequently George set aside the marksman's role for that of provider, accomplishing a shift towards the right-wing position across three Second Division seasons at Orient, a basement spell at Hartlepools, and a Midland League term with York. His postwar career had started with six First Division outings for Bradford.

Appearances:
FL: 28 apps. 12 gls.
FAC: 2 apps. 0 gls.
Total: *30 apps. 12 gls.*

Forest season (10 in 35 League and Cup games), and he then helped establish newly-promoted Millwall as a Second Division force over the following three campaigns.

Appearances:
FL: 98 apps. 7 gls.
FAC: 8 apps. 0 gls.
Total: *106 apps. 7 gls.*

WAITE, George

Role: Centre forward
b. Bradford, 1st March 1894
d. Bradford, April qtr 1972

CAREER: Royal Artillery/ June 1915:Bradford Park Avenue/May 1920:Raith Rovers/(Aug 1920-loan-Heart of Midlothian)/ Jan 1921: Clydebank/ cs 1921:Pontypridd/May 1922:CITY/ Mar 1923:Clapton Orient/July 1926: Hartlepools United/cs 1927:York City.

Debut v Sheffield Wednesday (A) 6.5.22

Briefly a team-mate of Davie Moyes and the Duncans at Raith, where he scored eleven

George Waite

WALKER, Charles J.

Role: Goalkeeper

CAREER: 1889:FOSSE/ Mar 1892:Leicester Hornets.

Debut (competitive) v Burton Wanderers (H)
FAC 4.10.1890

Charlie Walker

One of the Fosse pioneers from the pre-Midland League days, Charlie was the goalkeeper in both the first victorious County Cup campaign and the club's initial FA Cup encounter. He was also the embarrassed centre of the 'lost in the fog' incident, when belatedly discovered still guarding his goal some time after the end of a mist-enshrouded Fosse v. Loughborough friendly in December 1890. Charlie's three first-class games, all defeats, resulted in his conceding eleven goals.

Appearances:
FAC: 1 app. 0 gls.
ML: 2 apps. 0 gls.
Total: *3 apps. 0 gls.*

WALKER, David

Role: Forward
b. Walsall, 1884
d. Walsall, 30th October 1935

CAREER: Walsall White Star/Birchfield Villa/1904:Wolverhampton Wanderers/cs 1905:Bristol Rovers/Apr 1907:West Bromwich Albion/May 1908:FOSSE/June 1911:Bristol Rovers/1912:Willenhall Swifts/ Dec 1913:Walsall.

Debut v Sheffield Wednesday (H) 1.9.08

A new signing (jointly with Randle for £700) for Fosse's inaugural campaign in the First Division, Davie held one of the three inside-forward positions for almost three seasons at Leicester, without quite replicating the scoring form which had first brought him to the directorate's attention. He had briefly tasted top flight fare at Molineux (2 apps), had scored 25 Southern League goals in 61 games during his first Eastville spell, and claimed 15 strikes in his Second Division season with West Brom; while the irony of his Fosse scoring record was that his third and least prolific season (when he was also sent off after scoring in a rough encounter with Clapton Orient) nonetheless saw him as the club's top marksman with only seven counters. Davie's later travels took him back via the Southern League to the Birmingham & District League, where in fact Walsall were then playing on par status with Willenhall.

Davie Walker

Appearances:
FL: 73 apps. 27 gls.
FAC: 9 apps. 2 gls.
Total: *82 apps. 29 gls.*

WALKER, David Clive Allan

Role: Right back
b. Watford, 24th October 1945

CAREER: app/pro Nov 1962:CITY/Oct 1966:Northampton Town/July 1969:Mansfield Town/cs 1975:Chelmsford City/Gravesend.

Debut v Aston Villa (A) 18.4.64

A youthful understudy at right-back to John Sjoberg and Len Chalmers, Clive was a quick-tackling defender who had to follow the rather well-worn trails to both the County Ground and Field Mill to really establish his League name. He turned out in 72 games during the Cobblers' vertiginous plummet to the Fourth Division, but made sufficient impression as an influentially cool strategist to be recalled there later for successive spells as coach, manager and assistant manager (until the summer of 1990) after a lengthy interim 229-game stint with Mansfield. His backroom career continued at Maidstone United, with elevation from the assistant's role to the manager's chair in January 1992, but he was a helpless onlooker, with only two registered players to manage, when the Stones folded on the eve of the following season. Thereafter he became assistant boss at Kettering until early 1995. Clive's solitary League Cup appearance for City earned him a runners-up tankard from the second leg of the 1965 Final against Chelsea.

Appearances:
FL:
17 apps. 0 gls.
LC: 1 app. 0 gls.
Total:
18 apps. 0 gls.

Clive Walker

Don Walker

WALKER, Donald Hunter

Role: Wing half / Inside forward
b. Edinburgh, 10th September 1935

CAREER: Tranent Juniors/Nov 1955:CITY/
Oct 1959:Middlesbrough/Sept 1963:Grimsby
Town/(July 1964-trials-Workington).
Debut v Nottingham Forest (H) 19.10.57

A nephew of Hearts, Chelsea and Scotland
star Tommy Walker, Don helped City re-
establish themselves in the First Division with
a series of playmaking midfield performances
at both wing-half and inside-forward, but his
claim to the No.6 shirt soon crumpled against
the vigorous competition of Ken Keyworth
and Colin Appleton. His occasionally
fastidious style subsequently guaranteed him
a first-team place at neither Ayresome nor
Blundell Park, but he totalled 23 League
games with Boro' and 15 with Grimsby,
scoring once for each club, before breaking a
leg with the latter.

Appearances:
FL: 32 apps. 1 gl.
FAC: 2 apps. 0 gls.
Total: *34 apps. 1 gl.*

WALKER, Ernest Edwin

Role: Forward / Left back
b. Hinckley, Leics, 24th November 1889

CAREER: Hinckley United/Oct 1919:CITY/
cs 1924:Hinckley United.
Debut v Huddersfield Town (A) 18.10.19

Quite what a second stint
of military discipline did
to Ernie's sense of
attacking adventure is
hard to discern, but after
this hefty Army reservist
was briefly called up
again in April 1921, with
over thirty games as an
inside-forward or
outside-left already to his
credit, he re-emerged as

Ernie Walker

a left-back challenger to Adam Black, and won
selection in an equivalent number of games as
an out-and-out defender. During his first spell
in the uniform of the Leicestershire Regiment,
before and during the war, he was better
known as a successful rugby player, chosen for
numerous representative fifteens; though he
had, in fact, previously undergone trials with
Arsenal. In later years Ernie (sadly partially
disabled) returned to Filbert Street as a
gateman.

Appearances:
FL: 64 apps. 3 gls.
FAC: 9 apps. 2 gls.
Total: *73 apps. 5 gls.*

WALKER, John

Role: Defender
b. Alexandria,
Dunbartonshire, c 1869

Jack Walker

CAREER: Vale of Leven/
1891:Grimsby Town/cs 1893:Everton/
Oct 1894:Manchester City/May 1895:FOSSE.
Debut v Burton Swifts (H) 7.9.1895

A versatile Scottish defender who joined
Grimsby during their Football Alliance days
and stayed with them into the League, Jack
scored on his First Division debut for Everton,
but played only two further games for them at
centre-half before joining the newly-formed
Manchester City (that club being reconstructed

from the debris of Ardwick). Moving on again to Leicester, Jack settled as an ever-present pivot in Fosse's second League season, and indeed missed few games over four seasons - the latter two at right-back - until he suffered a broken shin in an April 1899 fixture against Grimsby which ended his career. He was awarded a benefit friendly against Everton in October of that year, which not only raised about £75 but also a storm of protest about Fosse's unpublicised decision to field an under strength side, by all accounts flattered by only a 1-4 reverse.

Appearances:
FL: 113 apps. 1 gl.
FAC: 12 apps. 0 gls.
Total: *125 apps. 1 gl.*

WALKER, Joseph Nicol

Role: Goalkeeper
b. Aberdeen, 29th September 1962

CAREER: Elgin BC/Elgin City/(1979-loan-Keith)/(1980-loan-Inverness Caledonian)/ July 1980:CITY/Jan 1983:Motherwell/ Dec 1983:Rangers/(Dec 1986-loan-Falkirk)/ (Dec 1987-loan-Dunfermline Athletic)/ Aug 1989:Heart of Midlothian/(Feb 1992-loan-Burnley)/Dec 1994:Partick Thistle.
Debut v Chelsea (A) 9.3.82

Another of Jock Wallace's recruits from the Highland League, tall goalkeeper Nicky had once toured Holland in the same Caley youth team as Kevin MacDonald, and was soon

WALLINGTON, Francis Mark

Role: Goalkeeper
b. Sleaford, Lincs, 17th September 1952

CAREER: Heckington United/am cs 1971/ pro Oct 1971:Walsall/Mar 1972:CITY/July 1985:Derby County/Aug 1988:Lincoln City (- May 1991)/Sept 1994:Grantham.
Debut v West Ham United (H) 11.3.72

Faced with the initially daunting and thankless task of succeeding Banks and Shilton between the Leicester posts, Mark more than made up for a comparative lack of charismatic flair by dint of a dogged consistency and willingness to work at the raw edges of his game, eventually building a monumental club record for consecutive appearances as testament to his awesome reliability. He was very much a goalkeeping tyro when bought for £30,000 by Jimmy Bloomfield as cover for Shilton, having made only eleven League appearances as a Fellows Park discovery, but having impressed mightily with a spectacular televised performance in a Cup-tie at Everton. Indeed, for several seasons he continued to learn his trade while very much in the England keeper's shadow, only

stepping up for an extended first-team run at the beginning of 1974/5 when Shilton's determination to move was becoming irresistible. It was ironic that Mark should suffer injury only weeks after his predecessor's sale to Stoke, for his return to the fray in the Third Round FA Cup-tie with Oxford in January 1975 became the start of a run in which he was never again absent until March 1982: a spell of 294 League games, 22 FA Cup encounters, and 15 League Cup ties (331 senior games in all). During this time he had added two England Under-23 caps to his haul of schools and amateur youth honours, experienced two relegation seasons and one Second Division championship, and become one of the select band of goalkeeper-captains in League football; while one of the more remarkable aspects of his unbroken run of appearances was that he'd actually been prevented from training for several years in the middle of his career by a skin affliction. Even after a sickening collision with Shrewsbury's Chic Bates had sidelined Mark for the first time in years, he came back to tot up another invaluable ever-present contribution to City's 1983 promotion season (picking up a deserved testimonial on the way), to see off the imported challenge of Mark Grew whilst briefly in contract dispute with the club, and finally to be displaced from the City six-yard box only by the youthful promise of Ian Andrews. Mutterings about the veteran's apparent loss of sharpness - prompted as much by superficial judgements winning Scottish caps at that level after his move to Filbert Street. He briefly stepped up for Second Division action after Mark Wallington's record-breaking run of consecutive appearances came to an end through injury, and impressed with his confidence and clean handling after a shaky start at Stamford Bridge. Nicky was then signed twice more by Jock Wallace, developing into an Ibrox regular until displaced by England international Chris Woods. He later competed with Henry Smith for the No.1 jersey at Hearts, winning a surprise Scotland call-up in March 1993, at the age of 30, for a cap from a home encounter with Germany.

Appearances:
FL: 6 apps. 0 gls.
Total: *6 apps. 0 gls.*

Nicky Walker

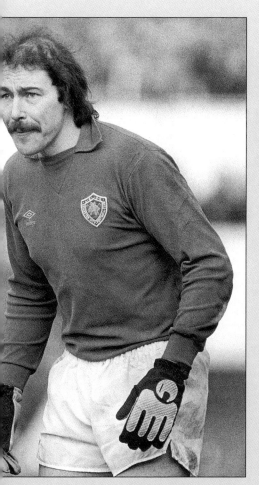

about thinning hair and a widening girth as by genuine signs of creakiness - were still proven somewhat premature, though, as his rearguard experience materially assisted new club Derby to successive promotions from the Third to the First Division in the two years following his £25,000 transfer. It was hardly apt reward, then, when Mark subsequently found himself once more stuck in reserve behind Peter Shilton at the Baseball Ground. A return to his native county coincided with the Red Imps' return to League football, following their one-year exile in the GM Vauxhall Conference; and retirement, three years later, only came after a career total of 577 League games. Mark briefly acted as a specialist goalkeeping coach at Everton; then took up a coaching appointment with the Lincolnshire FA. A week after his 42nd birthday, he answered an emergency call to turn out in the Beazer Homes League for Grantham.

Appearances:
FL: 412 apps. 0 gls.
FAC: 25 apps. 0 gls.
LC: 23 apps. 0 gls.
Total: *460 apps. 0 gls.*

❏ FOX FACT: *Mark Wallington was an ever-present for City in seven campaigns (1975/6-1980/1 inclusive, plus 1982/3). His nearest rivals for such consistency, with four ever-present seasons apiece, have been Jimmy Thraves, George Swift, Adam Black, Richie Norman and Steve Whitworth. The last-named player held the club record for consecutive appearances, at 198, prior to Wallington.*

WALSH, James

Role: Inside right
b. Glasgow, 3rd December 1930

CAREER: Valleyfield Colliery/Bo'ness United/
Oct 1949:Celtic/Nov 1956:CITY/cs 1964:
Rugby Town.

Debut v Fulham (H) 23.3.57

A scorer in the Finals of both the 1953
Coronation Cup and the 1955 Scottish Cup,
and capped once for Scotland Under-23s,
Jimmy was yet never quite assured of his
inside-forward place for Celtic at a time when
the likes of Fernie, Tully, Mochan and Bobby
Collins were also in front-line contention. He
became the subject of one of David Halliday's
regular cross-border transfer raids, but played
only his debut game in the 1957 Second
Division championship effort, reserving his
substantial striking energies for the next six
years of top flight combat, during
which he was twice City's top
scorer. Jimmy claimed a hat-trick
against Mansfield in the club's first-
ever League Cup-tie (indeed, the
first registered in that competition),
and later that season led his team
out at Wembley as skipper, having
contributed the breakthrough goal
in the drawn-out FA Cup semi-final
series against Sheffield United.
Another scoring milestone was
Jimmy's opening of City's account
in European competition, but his
quick-witted, darting elegance was
later offset by a diminishing
effectiveness in front of goal, and
through a combination of problems
with injuries and eyesight (Jimmy
was one of the first footballers to
play regularly in contact lenses), he
had lost his place by the time the
1963 Wembley return was achieved.
On leaving Rugby, Jimmy moved
into the newsagent's business in
Leicester city centre.

Appearances:
FL: 176 apps. 79 gls.
FAC: 18 apps. 5 gls.
LC: 4 apps. 5 gls.
Eur: 1 app. 2 gls.
Total: *199 apps. 91 gls.*

WALSH, Steven

Role: Centre back / Striker
b. Fulwood, Lancs, 3rd November 1964

CAREER: 1982:Wigan Athletic/June 1986:
CITY.

Debut v Luton Town (H) 23.8.86

The longest-serving player on the current City
staff, Steve has also proved himself one of the
most enigmatic across his nine years at Filbert
Street; to the extent that it is difficult to decide
precisely *which* Steve Walsh to attempt to
describe. The rugged stopper or the swashbuckling striker? The coolly commanding
captain or the reckless recipient of seven red
cards between October 1986 and November
1992? The red rag to Steve Bull, or the man
who led the Rams to slaughter...? Steve
followed Bryan Hamilton from Wigan as the
new manager's initial City purchase, justifying

Jimmy Walsh leads City out in 1961.

his £100,000 fee as a strapping central defender by deposing the unsettled John O'Neill in the First Division line-up. But even in his first term he was alternating the promise of becoming an aerially dominant influence with moments of naive impetuosity which cost his relegation-bound side dearly. Steve's first Second Division game for City ended with his (second) dismissal, for a vicious assault on Shrewsbury's David Geddis which eventually earned him an eleven-game ban, but he returned with an apparently much more mature outlook, developing his defensive timing and positioning, and began to show himself additionally as a useful goalscorer. Indeed, Steve took the Player of the Year award in 1988 to index his rehabilitation, but ill-luck with injuries hampered his progress the following term. He remained at the heart of the defensive formations of each of David Pleat, Gordon Lee and Brian Little (skippering the side under the latter boss despite three dismissals in 1990/91 and two more early in 1992/3), until Little then gambled on shifting him forward into a muscular target-man role, to which he adapted with enthusiasm and no little effectiveness. Steve became the 15-goal top marksman of 1993 (at one point scoring in five successive victories) as a second Play-off Final came into view, and he contributed an additional Wembley goal to the exciting fightback against Swindon, to help ease memories of the penalty he'd unluckily conceded against Blackburn's David Speedie the year before. It was a further year on at Wembley, though, that Steve's true glory would come, with the two goals against Derby that finally lifted City into the Premiership coming after he'd missed the bulk of the season following a horrendous cruciate knee ligament injury at Middlesbrough. Further knee trouble completely ruined Steve's top-flight campaign; but with fitness regained there are now further question marks for Steve and Mark McGhee to juggle with - not least attaching to the genuine dilemma of whether he is of most use to the side as a rugged defensive cornerstone or an inspirational attacking totem (By May 1995, City had lost on only five occasions when Steve has scored, albeit three against Newcastle!).

Appearances (to end 1994/5):
PL: 5 apps. 0 gls.
FL: 243 (2) apps. 41 gls.
FAC: 7 apps. 0 gls.
LC: 21 apps. 3 gls.
FMC: 10 apps. 1 gl.
AIC: 1 app. 0 gls.
P/O: 8 apps. 3 gls.
Total: *295 (2) apps. 48 gls.*

Steve Walsh celebrates his Wembley winner against Derby.

WALTERS, Victor

Role: Outside left

CAREER: Gravesend/Walthamstow Grange/Oct 1913:FOSSE/Oct 1914:Abertillery.
Debut v Huddersfield Town (A) 20.12.13

Fosse manager Jack Bartlett was almost as partial as his later City counterpart Jimmy Bloomfield to players with London or South East footballing credentials: this amateur left-winger being another of his signings to attempt to make the leap from London League fare to Second Division struggles. In common with such exact or near contemporaries as Russell, Ridley and Legge, though, Victor failed to register with sufficient impact at the higher level.

> **Appearances:**
> *FL: 11 apps. 2 gls.*
> **Total:** *11 apps. 2 gls.*

WARD, Ashley Stuart

Role: Striker
b. Middleton, Lancs, 24th November 1970

CAREER: Cheadle Town/YT/pro Aug 1989: Manchester City/(Jan 1991-loan-Wrexham)/ July 1991: CITY/(Nov 1992-loan-Blackpool)/ Dec 1992: Crewe Alexandra/Dec 1994: Norwich City.

Debut v Swindon Town (A) 17.8.91

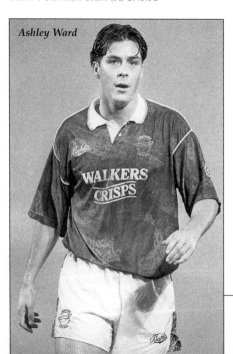

Ashley Ward

A highly-regarded graduate of the Maine Road youth set-up, who had overcome injury worries and had scored twice on his Wrexham debut, Ashley was the most expensive (at £80,000) of Brian Little's initial batch of City purchases. The tall striker seemed, however, to suffer a severe lack of confidence (not to mention luck) on his senior outings, and had to be content with heading the scoring list for the promoted Central League side of 1991/2 during his only full term with the club. He scored again on his Blackpool bow; then only weeks later became the subject of Crewe's record transfer payment as City recouped their original outlay. Sent off halfway through his Alex debut, Ashley nonetheless assisted them to the 1993 Wembley Play-off Final (where his own successful spot-kick was not enough to see them through a penalty shoot-out against York City), and to guaranteed promotion a year later. His move to Norwich was at a fee rising in steps to £500,000, and he scored twice against Chelsea on his Premiership bow. The Canaries were to join City in the relegation zone, however, and Ashley's Filbert Street jinx continued when he had a 'goal' disallowed during the April 1995 fixture finally settled by Garry Parker's strike for City.

> **Appearances:**
> *FL: 2 (8) apps. 0 gls.*
> *FAC: 0 (1) app. 0 gls.*
> *LC: 2 (1) apps. 0 gls.*
> *FMC: 0 (1) app. 0 gls.*
> **Total:** *4 (11) apps. 0 gls.*

WARD, Gavin John

Role: Goalkeeper
b. Sutton Coldfield, 30th June 1970

CAREER: YT:Aston Villa/1988:Shrewsbury Town/(1989-trials-West Bromwich Albion)/ Sept 1989:Cardiff City/July 1993:CITY/ July 1995:Bradford City.

Debut v Peterborough United (H) 14.8.93

A 6ft 4in keeper who made his belated senior breakthrough with Cardiff in October 1989, and later displaced Mark Grew to help seal the 1993 Division Three championship (under Eddie May's managership, and alongside Paul Ramsey and Robbie James), Gavin was a Brian Little purchase at an appearance-related fee of between £175,000 and £250,000. Kept busy during a debut game City were fortunate to

Gavin Ward

WARD, Patrick

Role: Left half
b. Dumbarton, 28th December 1926

CAREER: Renton Guild/Glasgow Perthshire/
1948:Hibernian/Sept 1955:CITY/June 1958:
Crewe Alexandra/Sept 1960:Rugby Town.
Debut v Fulham (A) 22.10.55

An early purchase by David Halliday as City
regrouped for a fresh assault on the Second
Division, Pat was a sturdy, fair-haired left-half
whose Easter Road experience had largely

win (the first fixture played in the eerie
atmosphere of a three-sided Filbert Street,
while the Carling Stand was still under
construction), and exhibiting fine agility to
add to his natural shot-stopping advantage of
reach, he held the first-team jersey on merit for
much of the promotion season, though
occasionally showing poor judgement on
when to leave his line for high balls. His
performance in the Prenton Park leg of the
Play-off semi-finals was inspirational, and a
Wembley selection against Derby his reward.
Gavin started the Premiership term in
possession, but was sidelined by Kevin Poole
for the majority of the campaign: during
which he became the first substitute
goalkeeper used by City, replacing the groggy
Poole at half-time in the FA Cup exit at
Molineux. New manager Mark McGhee was,
however, clearly not convinced about Gavin's
all-round reliability and he departed for
£175,000 to join the growing ex-City
contingent at Bradford in summer 1995.

Appearances:
PL: 6 apps. 0 gls.
FL: 32 apps. 0 gls.
FAC: 0 (1) app. 0 gls.
LC: 3 apps. 0 gls.
AIC: 1 app. 0 gls.
P/O: 3 apps. 0 gls.
Total: *45 (1) apps. 0 gls.*

Pat Ward

been gained in the central defensive berth. Signed for £3,500, he took the City No.6 shirt from Eddie Russell, and for some time thwarted the first-team progress of the teenage Colin Appleton; yet after contributing some fine tight-marking performances to the 1957 promotion success, Pat only got an isolated trio of opportunities to impress at the top level in England. His stay at Gresty Road brought him 31 Fourth Division appearances and one goal.

Appearances:
FL: 57 app. 0 gls.
FAC: 1 app. 0 gls.
Total: *58 apps. 0 gls.*

WARNER, Reginald Owen

Role: Defender
b. Anstey, Leics, 1st March 1931

CAREER: Anstey Methodists/Apr 1949:CITY/ Mar 1955:Mansfield Town/cs 1957:Hinckley Athletic.

Debut v Swansea Town (A) 8.11.52

An England Youth international centre-forward, Reg became a versatile utility defender as he struggled to fulfil his potential at League level. At wing-half he was used as an occasional deputy for either Johnny King or Jimmy Baldwin, and made a small

Reg Warner

contribution to the 1954 promotion drive before hitting the well-worn Field Mill trail for a run of 33 games in the Third Division (North), several of them at centre-half.

Appearances:
FL: 7 apps. 0 gls.
FAC: 1 app. 0 gls.
Total: *8 apps. 0 gls.*

WARREN, George

Role: Centre forward
b. Hinckley, Leics

CAREER: Hinckley Town/Dec 1903:FOSSE/ cs 1904:Gresley Rovers/ cs 1906:Nuneaton Town/ cs 1907:Coventry City/Sept 1911: Willenhall Swifts/Oct 1911:Stockport County/ cs 1912:Nuneaton Town/Hinckley United.

Debut v Glossop (H) 12.12.03

George Warren

As would the on-loan Peter Eastoe precisely eighty years later, George had the curiously frustrating experience of making his club debut in a match which was abandoned: in this centre-forward's case the disappointment was doubled by the fact that he'd already notched a goal in the fog-halted away fixture against Manchester United in December 1903. He was, however, to hold his line-leading position for most of the rest of the humbling 1903/4 season, despite appearing in a winning side only five times. George picked up the nickname 'Tubby' at Coventry (who he joined in their Birmingham & District League days, and starred for in their early Southern League campaigns), and later made a brief three-game return to League soccer at Edgeley Park. A recent Coventry history asserts that he was killed in action during WW1.

Appearances:
FL: 21 apps. 7 gls.
Total: *21apps. 7 gls.*

❏ FOX FACT: *Apart from George Warren, nine other Fosse and City players have had a single goal deleted from their records following the abandonment of games in which they had scored. In chronological order, they are Tommy Brown, Ike Evenson, Billy Jackson (his only City strike), Danny Liddle, George Dewis (his first League goal), Arthur Chandler, Gene O'Callaghan, Willie Muncie and Frank Large.*

WATERALL, Thomas William

Role: Outside left
b. Radford, Nottingham, October qtr 1884
d. Nottingham, 8th November 1951

CAREER: 1904:Radford Institute/1905:
Eleanor United/Apr 1906:Notts County/
June 1908:Bradford Park Avenue/cs 1909:
Mansfield Mechanics/July 1913:FOSSE/
July 1914: Watford/Feb 1921:Gillingham/
May 1922:Sheppey United/Sittingbourne.

Debut v Nottingham Forest (A) 3.9.13
(scored once)

Tom Waterall

An outside-left who cost Fosse a £10 transfer fee, and kept bouncing back into first-team contention despite manager Bartlett's several attempts to replace him, Tom was one of a trio of brothers to play as top-level forwards, with Ike following him into the Notts County side and later moving to Millwall, and Albert leaving Meadow Lane to build a substantial reputation with Stockport County. Tom himself found his moment of glory in the final pre-war season of Southern League football, assisting Watford to the championship; and the one-time miner was still there, alongside Ernest Bacon, in Watford's first-ever Football League line-up in 1920. In the interim, he had made 87 wartime appearances for Stockport County in the company of brother Albert.

Appearances:
FL: 31 apps. 6 gls.
FAC: 2 apps. 0 gls.
Total: *33 apps. 6 gls.*

Joe Waters scoring on his debut at QPR in the FA Cup.

Joe Waters

WATERS, Joseph J.W.

Role: Midfield
b. Limerick, 20th September 1953

CAREER: app Apr 1969/pro Sept 1970:CITY/
Jan 1976:Grimsby Town/cs 1984:Tacoma Stars.

Debut v Queen's Park Rangers (A) FAC 9.3.74
(scored twice)

Joe's explosive entry into the City annals - joining the 1974 Cup fray as a last-minute replacement for Alan Birchenall, and ensuring the club a semi-final place with two cracking goals past Phil Parkes before a national television audience - perhaps inevitably

overshadowed all his subsequent efforts on Leicester's behalf. The little midfielder, already capped at schools and youth level, earned himself a near-immediate call-up to the full Republic of Ireland squad for a South American tour, and then showed himself to be an astute and energetic prompter on his sporadic returns to the City first team after Birchenall's recovery. But Jimmy Bloomfield's side was at its most settled when Joe was ready for regular senior football, and the apparent backslide to Blundell Park was in fact a shrewd move. In eight years with Grimsby, Joe established himself as an inspirational skipper, eventually leading his team back into Division Two from the basement depths, and was limited to a mere couple of full caps mainly by the competing claims of Johnny Giles and Liam Brady. In 357 League games for the Mariners, he also claimed 65 goals, before moving into a player/coaching role in America in 1984. Eight years later Joe was still there, assisting Keith Weller with Tacoma Stars in the Major Soccer League.

Appearances:
FL: 11 (2) apps. 1 gl.
FAC: 2 apps. 2 gls.
LC: 1 app. 0 gls.
Total: *14 (2) apps. 3 gls.*

WATKIN, Frank H.

Role: Outside left

CAREER: Leeds City/Newark Castle Rovers/ Oct 1910:FOSSE/Aug 1912:Notts County.

Debut v Clapton Orient (H) 28.1.11

A left-wing understudy to Sydney Owen, Frank had no sooner laid claim to the amateur international's flank position than he was himself displaced by a fellow capture from Nottinghamshire junior football, Paul Haig. He played no senior football for either Leeds or the Magpies.

Appearances:
FL: 4 apps. 1 gl.
Total: *4 apps. 1 gl.*

WATKINS, Alfred Ernest

Role: Forward
b. Llanwnnog, Montgomeryshire, June 1878
d. Barking, Essex, 7th December 1957

CAREER: Caersws/1895:Oswestry United/ Oct 1897:FOSSE/Apr 1899:Aston Villa/ Feb 1901:Grimsby Town/cs 1901:Millwall/ cs 1906:Southend United.

Debut v Darwen (H) 5.2.1898

Alfred Watkins

Holding jointly with Dick Jones the record of being the first player to win a full cap while on Fosse's books, Alfred had, by the time of the Welsh international against Scotland on 19th March 1898, played only a single senior game for the club! Indeed, by the time the close season came round, his appearances for club and country evened out at two apiece. At least the inside- or outside-left became a Fosse regular in the near-miss promotion effort of 1898/9, showing a useful goal touch, turning down further Welsh honours to help the League cause, and attracting an unrefusable offer from Villa at season's end. With the First Division giants, however, his internationals-to-League-games ratio looked even more disproportionate - Alfred twice representing Wales, but only once turning out for Villa's seniors. He was in Millwall's 1903 FA Cup semi-final team (having got them that far with a 40-yard strike against Everton in the previous round); gained the last of his five caps in 1904, playing alongside his brother Walter Martin Watkins, of Stoke, Villa and Sunderland fame; and in September 1906 was in the newly-formed Southend United's first-ever competitive line-up. After leaving the game, Alfred was an assistant station-master, and then a cemetery caretaker. He died in a fire at his home.

Appearances:
FL: 31 apps. 12 gls.
FAC: 4 apps. 2 gls.
Total: *35 apps. 14 gls.*

WATKINS, Alfred W.

Role: Inside right

CAREER: 1901:Accrington Stanley/Nelson/ May 1904:FOSSE/ Nov 1904:Blackburn Rovers.

Debut v Blackpool (A) 3.9.04

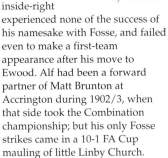

Alf Watkins

Joining Fosse after building a high-scoring reputation in the Lancashire Combination, this inside-right experienced none of the success of his namesake with Fosse, and failed even to make a first-team appearance after his move to Ewood. Alf had been a forward partner of Matt Brunton at Accrington during 1902/3, when that side took the Combination championship; but his only Fosse strikes came in a 10-1 FA Cup mauling of little Linby Church.

Appearances:
FL: 4 apps. 0 gls.
FAC: 1 app. 2 gls.
Total: *5 apps. 2 gls.*

WATSON, Norman

Role: Half back
b. Chester-le-Street, Co.Durham, 21st December 1899

CAREER: Southwick/Chester-le-Street/May 1922:CITY/June 1932: Notts County/cs 1933:Workington/ Aug 1934:Wigan Athletic.
Debut v Manchester United (H) 14.4.23

A sturdy half-back who exhibited versatility and patience in equal measure when sporadically backing up City's early-20s promotion efforts, Norman was rewarded with a lengthy run in the pivot's role as

Norman Watson

soon as Division One was reached, and thereafter shuttled left and right across the middle line (with odd excursions to outside-right and full-back) for another seven top-flight seasons as a semi-regular. Ironically, his only League goal came in a 2-8 defeat at Grimsby in November 1930. Eventually moving to Meadow Lane as a veteran, he made only five League starts before dropping into non-league football. Norman became both skipper and penalty-kick expert at Wigan.

Appearances:
FL: 173 apps. 1 gl.
FAC: 5 apps. 0 gls.
Total: *178 apps. 1 gl.*

WEBB, Charles

Role: Outside right
b. *Higham Ferrers,
Northants, 4th March
1879*
d. *Wellingborough,
Northants, January
1939*

CAREER:
Chesham Grenadiers/
Higham Ferrers/
1898:Rushden/cs 1900:
Kettering/May 1901:FOSSE/
cs 1902: Wellingborough/cs 1903:Kettering/
May 1904:Southampton/July 1905:Dundee/
Mar 1908: Manchester City/June 1909:
Airdrieonians.

Charles Webb

Debut v Woolwich Arsenal (A) 7.9.01

The regular outside-right in Fosse's somewhat
goal-shy attack of 1901/2, Charles exhibited a
marked affinity for playing alongside that
other Northamptonshire-born soccer
wanderer, Herbert Dainty - the pair appearing
together for both Southampton (Southern
League) and Dundee (Scottish League) as well
as for Fosse in the Second Division. Charles
faced Fosse in the First Division in October
1908, but Manchester City were booked for the
same relegation frame as Leicester that term.
He was originally a harness-maker by trade,
but on retirement from the game became a
bakery manager in Rushden.

Appearances:
FL: *32 apps. 3 gls.*
FAC: *1 app. 0 gls.*
Total: *33 apps. 3 gls.*

WEBB, David James

Role: Centre back
b. *East Ham, London, 9th April 1946*

CAREER: am:West Ham United/May 1963:
Leyton Orient/Mar 1966:Southampton/
Feb 1968:Chelsea/July 1974:Queen's Park
Rangers/Sept 1977:CITY/Dec 1978:Derby
County/May 1980:Bournemouth (p/coach;
then mgr)/Feb 1984:Torquay United (p/mgr).

Debut v Wolverhampton Wanderers (A) 1.10.77

Best remembered as a chunkily piratical figure
at the heart of Chelsea's defence, whose

occasional forward rampages brought about
such magic moments as the winning goal in
the replayed 1970 FA Cup Final against Leeds,
and whose try-anything enthusiasm even saw
him chosen as goalkeeper for a League game
against Ipswich in December 1971, Dave
started his lengthy career as a crew-cut full-
back at Brisbane Road and The Dell, and only
later developed into such a swashbuckling
stopper. Dave's first move helped seal
Southampton's 1966 promotion to the First
Division, but most of his club honours accrued
while he was on the Stamford Bridge books,
including a victor's medal from the 1971
European Cup Winners' Cup. A six-figure
transfer to Loftus Road saw him partnering
Frank McLintock at the back as QPR came
within a whisker of championship success,
and the pair were reunited at Filbert Street as
manager McLintock attempted to shore up
City's hard-pressed defence with Dave's
combative experience. The disappointment of
relegation was part of his lot at both Leicester
and Derby, but Dave was back on the
promotion trail at Bournemouth during his
first stint of management. His final
appearances as a player came at Torquay,
some time after his nominal retirement and
before his brief elevation to Managing
Director, and he has subsequently also

David Webb

occupied the managerial chairs at Southend (taking his charges from Division Four to Two in successive seasons in the early 90s), Chelsea and Brentford (1995 Play-off qualifiers).

Appearances:
FL: 32 (1) apps. 0 gls.
FAC: 2 apps. 0 gls.
Total: *34 (1) apps. 0 gls.*

WEBB, Harry

Role: Forward
b. c 1870

CAREER: Stafford Wanderers/Stafford Rangers/Oct 1888: FOSSE.

Debut (competitive) v Burton Wanderers (H) FAC 4.10.1890

Harry Webb

Fosse's first professional player, initially engaged at the princely sum of 2s.6d per week, Harry was a versatile forward who drew particular plaudits for his heading prowess (despite standing less than 5ft.4ins tall), and remained a loyal leading attacker for the club until the end of the second Midland League season. He had scored six times on his County Cup debut in November 1888 (against Syston Wreake Valley on Victoria Park), and was a Final scorer when Fosse won that trophy for the second time in 1891, with a 2-0 win over Gresley Rovers at Loughborough. He and Billy Dorrell also claimed Fosse's first hat-tricks in the FA Cup: from the 7-0 win over Rushden in October 1892 which was Fosse's first game in the senior competition actually to take place at Filbert Street. Previously, Harry had picked up a winner's medal from the Staffordshire Junior Cup, and featured in the Final of the Senior Cup in that county: he had also appeared in court there during 1884, for playing street football with rolled-up paper as a ball 'to the annoyance of foot passengers', and was levied the costs of the case.

Appearances:
FAC: 6 apps. 5 gls.
ML: 26 apps. 8 gls.
Total: *32 apps. 13 gls.*

WEBB, William

Role: Left back / Outside left
b. Mexborough, Yorks, 7th March 1932

CAREER: Wath/May 1951:Rochdale/June 1951:CITY/June 1957:Stockport County/July 1963:Hyde United.

Debut v Sheffield Wednesday (A) 27.8.51

A teenage first-teamer at Leicester within months of his surprise £1,250 elevation from Rochdale (where he played only a single senior friendly in his brief stay), Bill assumed Ron Jackson's No.3 shirt for what proved to be the longest run of appearances in his six-year City sojourn. National Service soon beckoned, and Bill represented the Army alongside Derek Hines, but following his return to full-time football he could never quite shake the tag of reliable stand-in. His main asset was pace, and a couple of his intermittent senior run-outs were in the outside-left spot, but it was back in defence that Bill later clocked up 243 League games in an admirably consistent Stockport stint (which incidentally still left him goalless).

Appearances:
FL: 47 apps. 0 gls.
FAC: 2 apps. 0 gls.
Total: *49 apps. 0 gls.*

Bill Webb

WEBB, William George

Role: Outside left
b. Shettleston, Glasgow,
12th July 1906

CAREER: Cambuslang
Rangers/Sept 1925: CITY/
cs 1927:St.Johnstone/
May 1930: Bournemouth and
Boscombe Athletic/May
1933:Ramsgate/1936:Bo'ness/
Aug 1937: Hinckley United.

Debut v Bolton Wanderers (A) 6.2.26

Willie Webb

Born in Scotland of English parents,
Willie spent most of his professional
career shuttling across the Tweed. The young
outside-left was unlucky enough to find
himself third in line for a City first-team slot
behind Wadsworth and Bell (and to suffer a
first-half injury on his sole senior appearance),
so had to move to Perth for an effective re-
launch of his career. He then managed three
seasons in the Third Division (South) at Dean
Court after a further cross-border move,
scoring 7 times in 57 League appearances.

Appearances:
FL: 1 app. 0 gls.
Total: *1 app. 0 gls.*

WEBSTER, Francis R.

Role: Centre half

CAREER: Shepshed Albion/
Dec 1908:FOSSE.

Debut v Manchester United (A) 12.12.08

A local centre-half who
understandably struggled to make
the quickfire transition from the
Leicestershire Senior League to the
First Division when flung into the
midst of Fosse's fateful season of top-
flight struggle; briefly holding the
pressurised pivotal role - for three draws and
four defeats - after England international
Bannister and before Scottish cap Aitken.
(Some sources place Francis with Everton from
1909; but if he did indeed move to Goodison,
he failed to break through at senior level).

Appearances:
FL: 7 apps. 0 gls.
FAC: 3 apps. 0 gls.
Total: *10 apps. 0 gls.*

WEIR, Peter Russell

Role: Winger
b. Johnstone, Renfrewshire,
18th January 1958

CAREER: Neilston Juniors/
1978:St.Mirren/May 1981:
Aberdeen/Jan 1988:CITY/
Nov 1988:St.Mirren/
June 1990:Ayr United.

Debut v Shrewsbury Town (A) 16.1.88

A tall, deceptively shuffling left-flank
forward with notable dead-ball skills
and crossing acumen, Peter won the
first four of his six Scottish caps while
dazzling the Love Street faithful, and was
soon involved in a part-exchange deal which
valued him at £330,000 and set a new transfer
record between two Scottish clubs. With the
Dons he hit occasionally devastating form and
shared in most of the glories of their '80s
renaissance, earning medals from two Premier
Division championship campaigns, three
Scottish Cup wins, and the classic European
Cup Winners' Cup Final triumph over Real
Madrid in 1983.

Becoming at £70,000
David Pleat's first sign-
ing for Leicester a week
before his 30th birthday,
Peter quickly slotted into
a re-organised midfield,
linking elegantly with
Gary McAllister and
occasionally delighting
those nostalgic for the
intricacies of the touch-
line dribbling art.
Unfortunately, Peter's
family found it difficult
to settle in the South;
but his £135,000
homeward move was
profitable recognition of

Peter Weir

the significance of his role in City's Second
Division revival. He retired in 1992 with an
ankle injury, after performing player/coach
duties at Ayr.

Appearances:
FL: 26 (2) apps. 2 gls.
LC: 1 app. 0 gls.
FMC: 1 app. 0 gls.
Total: *28 (2) apps. 2 gls.*

WELLER, Keith

Role: Forward
b. Islington, London, 11th June 1946

CAREER: Jnr 1961:Arsenal/am Aug 1963/
pro Jan 1964:Tottenham Hotspur/June 1967:Millwall/
May 1970:Chelsea/Sept 1971: CITY/(Apr 1978-loan-
New England Tea Men)/Feb 1979:New England
Tea Men/July 1980:Fort Lauderdale Strikers/
1984:Fort Lauderdale Sun (p/coach)/South Florida
Sun (p/coach)/1986:Houston Dynamo (p/coach)/
Dallas Sidekicks (p/coach)/San Diego Sockers
(p/coach)/1990:Tacoma Stars (p/coach).

Debut v Crystal Palace (H) 2.10.71

A marvellously talented, sometimes
temperamental individualist who lent £100,000
worth of forceful right-flank panache to Jimmy
Bloomfield's elegant teams of the early 70s, Keith
could usually be relied upon to deliver a tellingly
spectacular contribution to the most mundane of
games. City fans were treated to regular displays of
both his midfield and striking skills, while national
television audiences also gasped at some of his
exploits: a mazy 'Goal of the Season' at Luton in the
Cup (and a long-range own goal on the same
ground a year later!), a thunderbolt volley against
Newcastle, and Keith's final City goal - when he
dazzled Norwich defenders with his white tights -
among them. Keith won four England caps (scoring
once with a rare header) and once represented the
Football League while with City - and he had
previously toured New Zealand and the Far East with
an FA party during his Millwall days - yet his sole
honour at club level remained his medal from
Chelsea's European Cup Winners' Cup victory of 1971.
His occasional frustrations at Leicester peaked in the
notorious incident when he refused to take the field for
the second half of a League game against Ipswich in
December 1974, and his last couple of Filbert Street
seasons were marred by knee injuries that sadly cut short
his top-class career, but memories of his cool brilliance
predominate. Keith settled longer than most in Stateside
football, moving into club management and coaching roles
in both the conventional and indoor games, and
forming an early-90s partnership with Joe Waters
at Tacoma Stars. After retirement in 1993, he
remained in Seattle, driving an outside-broadcast
rig for a local TV station.

Appearances:
FL: 260 (2) apps. 37 gls.
FAC: 24 apps. 3 gls.
LC: 11 apps. 3 gls.
Total: *295 (2) apps. 43 gls.*

WELSH, Peter Martin

Role: Utility
b. Coatbridge, Lanarkshire, 19th July 1959

CAREER: Caldervale YC/Aug 1976:CITY/ (Apr 1978-loan-Houston Hurricane)/July 1982:Hibernian/Nov 1983:Falkirk/Mar 1984: Alloa Athletic/(1984/85-trials-Charlton Athletic, Port Vale, Northampton Town)/ Wigston Town/Lutterworth Town/cs 1990: Houghton Rangers (p/mgr)/cs 1992: Lutterworth Town/Nov 1992:North Kilworth (p/mgr)/Sept 1993:Anstey Nomads/Oct 1993: Houghton Rangers.

Debut v Tottenham Hotspur (A) 14.5.77

'Blooded' as a teenage midfielder in Jimmy Bloomfield's penultimate game in charge at City, Peter had to wait patiently for a call-up from Jock Wallace for further League experience. A versatile reserve, he employed his strong build best in defensive situations, filling in at various stages in all the back-four positions, yet could also move forward with effective purpose, making him a useful choice for the sub's bench. A late burst of goalscoring

unfortunately failed either to gain City promotion in 1982 or indeed to win Peter a renewed contract, and his subsequent experiences in Scottish football were not of the happiest, comprising only a total of thirty senior games for his three clubs. Injury then stymied his attempt at a League comeback, but he returned to Leicester and became a well known figure in local Senior League circles, while working in the glazing trade. In July 1995, Peter became manager of Senior League side Narborough and Littlethorpe.

Appearances:
FL: 24 (17) apps. 4 gls.
Total: 24 (17) apps. 4 gls.

WESLEY, George Thomas

Role: Centre forward

CAREER: (Army football)/Leicester Imperial/ (Jan 1907-trials-FOSSE).

Debut v Barnsley (A) 26.1.07

An amateur centre-forward, still attached to the Army officers' mess at Portsmouth when given a brief trial by Fosse after starring for the local Imps. A 2-2 draw at Oakwell proved to be his sole selection.

Appearances:
FL: 1 app. 0 gls.
Total: 1 app. 0 gls.

WEST, Alfred

Role: Full back

CAREER: Feb 1903:FOSSE.

Debut v Bristol City (H) 25.2.04

A stand-in full-back whose individual potential was somewhat overwhelmed by the collective malaise of a Fosse side bound for the re-election zone. Alfred's trio of home games produced a win, a defeat and a draw.

Appearances:
FL: 3 apps. 0 gls.
Total: 3 apps. 0 gls.

Peter Welsh

WEST, James (Jack)

Role: Outside left
b. Enderby, Leics

CAREER: Enderby Town/Aug 1908:FOSSE/
Aug 1910:Leyton.

Debut v Notts County (A) 9.4.09

Jack West

A local outside-left who played his initial first-team game in Fosse's first-ever floodlit friendly (against Blackburn at Burton-on-Trent in October 1908), and then took the First Division flank position after the departure of Leggy Turner. Unable to hold his place against the challenge of Fred Threlfall, however, Jack made less than a handful of appearances the following season before re-uniting with Jamie Durrant and Tommy Shanks at Southern League Leyton.

Appearances:
FL: 10 apps. 2 gls.
Total: *10 apps. 2 gls.*

Winston White

WHITE, Eric Winston

Role: Winger
b. Leicester, 26th October 1958

CAREER: app July 1975/pro Oct 1976:CITY/
Mar 1979:Hereford United/Apr 1983:(Hong Kong)/Sept 1983:Chesterfield/Oct 1983:Port Vale/Nov 1983:Stockport County/Dec 1983: Bury/(Oct 1986-loan-Rochdale)/Mar 1987: Colchester United/Oct 1988:Burnley/Mar 1991:West Bromwich Albion/Oct 1992: Bury/Jan 1993:Doncaster Rovers/Feb 1993: Carlisle United/Mar 1993:Wigan Athletic.

Debut v Stoke City (A) 19.3.77

A speedy orthodox winger whose dozen City games encompassed selection by three different managers and gave notice of genuine potential, Winston exhibited remarkable resilience in extending his career past several stiff setbacks. General upheavals at Filbert Street meant he had few chances to consolidate the promise of a debut in which he laid on Frank Worthington's winning goal, though a fine performance at Anfield shone through the relegation-haunted gloom of the following season, a year before Jock Wallace accepted Hereford's £15,000 bid. Then, after 175 League games at Edgar Street (21 goals), Winston was freed for a summer of Far East football, but fixed himself up with a series of trials on his return; the fourth of which paid off in the form of a contract offer from Bury. He was ever-present in the Shakers' successful 1985 promotion push from the Fourth Division; later strengthened the Colchester squad which narrowly failed to repeat that feat in 1987, when they reached the Play Offs; and was still deemed worth a five-figure fee when moving on to Turf Moor with over 400 senior games already under his belt. Winston's mature midfield displays there eventually attracted a £35,000 bid from struggling West Brom, returning him to the Second Division sphere over 12 years after his last City outing at that level. His goal in City's Hawthorns defeat a few weeks later threatened to help seal his hometown club's relegation to the Third, but after final-game traumas it was in fact Albion who made the drop in Leicester's stead.

Appearances:
FL: 10 (2) apps. 1 gl.
Total: *10 (2) apps. 1 gl.*

WHITE, Ian Samuel

Role: Right half
b. Glasgow, 20th December 1935

CAREER: Port Glasgow Hibs/St.Anthony's/
Petershill/Apr 1956:Celtic/July 1958:CITY/
June 1962:Southampton/July 1967:Hillingdon
Borough/June 1968:Portals (p/mgr).
Debut v Sheffield Wednesday (H) 7.11.59

Never given a senior break at Parkhead,
despite a fine playing record in Junior football,
Ian initially found himself similarly stuck in
City's reserve team, albeit the 1959
Combination championship side, as Johnny
Newman held on to the first-team No.4 shirt.
Then, even though he grasped every
opportunity to display his wing-half skills, the
unassuming redhead was unfortunate enough
to be vying for his place with the younger and
more flamboyantly talented Frank McLintock,
and it was not really until he resumed his
occasional partnership with Tony Knapp
down at The Dell that Ian could claim a
regular League selection. He later ran a sports
goods shop in Southampton. Ian's

early career had peaked, incidentally, with a
victor's medal from the Scottish Junior Cup
Final of 1956, when Petershill beat Lugar
Boswell Thistle in front of a Hampden crowd
of 64,702.

Appearances:
FL: 47 apps. 1 gl.
FAC: 3 apps. 0 gls.
Eur: 4 apps. 0 gls.
Total: 54 apps. 1 gl.

WHITEHEAD, Harry

Role: Right back
b. Barlestone, Leics, 19th September 1874
d. Leicester, 14th September 1944

CAREER: Aug 1896:
Loughborough/
cs 1897:Hinckley
Town/May 1902:
FOSSE/cs 1903:
Hinckley Town.

*Debut v Small Heath
(H) 6.9.02*

COUNTY CRICKETERS.

H. WHITEHEAD,
LEICESTERSHIRE.

Harry's trio of right-
back appearances
for Fosse (each in a
losing side, as had
been his pair of
League outings
for the Luffs)
were rather
emphatically
overshadowed
by his cricketing
record of 380 first-class matches
for Leicestershire between 1898 and 1922.
His prowess as an opening batsman and
medium-pace bowler was recognised by
selection for the Players v. Gentlemen
fixture at the Oval in 1907, and it was the
opinion of County historian E.E.Snow that
only Harry's 'lighthearted' and somewhat
'impetuous' approach to the game
prevented him gaining higher honours. He
scored over 15,000 runs and took over 100
wickets for Leicestershire.

Appearances:
FL: 3 apps. 0 gls.
Total: 3 apps. 0 gls.

Ian White

WHITELAW, Andrew

Role: Left back
b. Jamestown, Dunbartonshire, 19th May 1865
d. Mansfield, 1938

CAREER: Vale of Leven/cs 1891:Notts County/cs 1893:Heanor Town/Aug 1894: FOSSE/cs 1895:Heanor Town.

Debut v Rotherham Town (H) 8.9.1894

Twice capped for Scotland while with Vale of Leven (in 1887 and 1890), and a Scottish Cup Finalist with that team in 1890 (when they lost after a replay to Queen's Park), Andrew was a rather more mobile exponent of full-back play than many of his hefty peers, and apparently more thoughtful about his distribution. His 42-game League experience with Notts recommended him to the Fosse for their first assault on the Second Division, but afterwards he played out the rest of his career in the Midland League.

Appearances:
FL: 16 apps. 0 gls.
FAC: 5 apps. 0 gls.
Total: *21 apps. 0 gls.*

WHITFIELD, Norman

Role: Inside forward
b. Prudhoe, Northumberland, 3rd April 1896
d. 1970

CAREER: Prudhoe Celtic Jnrs/1912:Jarrow Croft/cs 1913:FOSSE/cs 1920:Hednesford Town/May 1922:Chesterfield/cs 1927: Nuneaton Town.

Debut v Stockport County (A) 28.2.14

A Geordie inside-forward signed as a 17-year-old, Norman was a scorer in Fosse reserves' 1914 County Cup Final victory over Holwell Works, and at senior level sporadically served

Norman Whitfield

Fosse before and during WW1 and City afterwards, though he was lucky to do so: being twice wounded and hospitalised while serving with the RGA in France. He was primarily a schemer, though occasionally pressed into the central attacking role as the club sought desperately for firepower; yet it was not until later, at Saltergate, that he delivered the goods in this respect, with 57 goals over five seasons.

Appearances:
FL: 24 apps. 6 gls.
WW1: 7 apps. 0 gls.
Total: *31 apps. 6 gls.*

WHITLOW, Michael William

Role: Left back
b. Northwich, Cheshire, 13th January 1968

CAREER: Rudheath YC/app 1985:Bolton Wanderers/1987:Witton Albion/(trials-Sheffield Wednesday)/Nov 1988:Leeds United/Mar 1992:CITY.

Debut v Middlesbrough (H) 1.4.92

The only ever-present in City's three-year, nine-game series of Play-off ties, Mike soon added an aggressive bite to the left flank (and occasionally the centre) of the defence when he arrived from Elland Road for £250,000 a

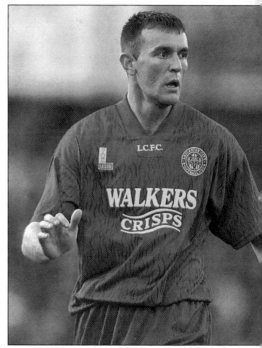

Mike Whitlow

Steve Whitworth

fortnight after Simon Grayson. Mike, who was treated as something of a utility man by Leeds before settling to the No.3 berth, had just failed to make sufficient appearances in their 1992 Championship side to gain a medal, but he brought to Filbert Street a determination to get among the honours that finally bore fruit with the Wembley victory over Derby. Strong in the tackle and in the air, if sometimes a little too markedly one-footed, he is also forceful in assisting the attack, and usually among the first to volunteer for shot-worthy free-kick duties. Mike's Premiership season, interrupted by injury, also featured City's equalising goal at Old Trafford, and a red card at Anfield.

Appearances (to end 1994/5):
PL: 28 apps. 2 gls.
FL: 58 (2) apps. 3 gls.
FAC: 5 apps. 0 gls.
LC: 4 apps. 1 gl.
AIC: 2 apps. 0 gls.
P/O: 9 apps. 0 gls.
Total: *106 (2) apps. 6 gls.*

WHITWORTH, Stephen

Role: Right back
b. Ellistown, Leics, 20th March 1952

CAREER: app July 1968/pro May 1969:CITY/ Mar 1979:Sunderland/Oct 1981:Bolton Wanderers/July 1983:Mansfield Town/ cs 1985:Barnet.

Debut v Bristol City (H) 2.9.70

An immaculately cool and perceptive right-back, perfectly suited in his adventurous adaptability to a game in which tactical developments meant he was only rarely in direct opposition to an orthodox winger, Steve won his first-team spurs as an early-season stand-in for the injured Peter Rodrigues in Frank O'Farrell's promotion-bound side, and missed only three games throughout the entire span of Jimmy Bloomfield's subsequent managerial reign. His consistently classy performances (one run of 198 consecutive appearances at the time creating a club record) made international selection look inevitable, and Steve duly won seven full caps to add to six at Under-23 level and complete his English representative set, following numerous schools and youth selections. A temporary loss of form during his testimonial season preceded Steve's £120,000 move to Roker, but the carrot-

haired defender continued to display his pace and tackling ability at League level for another six years, when also finally laying to rest the idiosyncratic jinx that may have earned him one of the most unwanted records in football. For while Steve's close-range goal against Liverpool had won for City the FA Charity Shield in 1971, and he had also got on the scoresheet for England Under-23s, he had never registered a strike in League or Cup football until converting a penalty for Mansfield against Hereford in March 1985 - in his 570th League game, and over fourteen and a half years after his debut! The irony here is that it was as an overlapping auxiliary attacker that Steve had first made his name! He was in promoted sides at Leicester and Sunderland, and experienced relegation with both City and Bolton; then, at Barnet, was player/coach in the near-miss attempt to become the first club to gain automatic elevation from the Vauxhall Conference to the Fourth Division.

Appearances:
FL: 352 (1) apps. 0 gls.
FAC: 29 apps. 0 gls.
LC: 18 apps. 0 gls.
Total: *399 (1) apps. 0 gls.*

WIGGINS, Joseph Albert

Role: Centre forward / Left back
b. Wembley, Middlesex, April qtr 1909

CAREER: Grays-Thurrock/Aug 1927: Brentford/May 1928:CITY/July 1934: Gillingham/July 1935:Rochdale/May 1936: Oldham Athletic/Feb 1937:Stalybridge Celtic/ Apr 1937:Hurst.

Debut v Liverpool (H) 21.3.31

A promising Griffin Park reserve who had scored twice in his four Brentford League games, Joe was recruited at £1,400 as centre-forward cover for Arthur Chandler, but spent a frustrating six years at Filbert Street, finally converting to the left-back berth in an attempt to claim a first-team place. It was at right-back that Gillingham then employed him, while Rochdale got 13 goals out of Joe to make him their top scorer during his single Spotland season.

Appearances:
FL: 9 apps. 0 gls.
Total: *9 apps. 0 gls.*

Harry Wilcox

WILCOX, Harry Melbourne

Role: Centre forward
b. Dalston, London, 7th January 1878
d. Plymouth, 21st July 1937

CAREER: Bromsgrove Rovers/(1897-trials-West Herts)/Aug 1898:Small Heath/July 1900:Watford/cs 1901:Preston North End/cs 1905:Plymouth Argyle/May 1906:FOSSE/Nov 1907:West Bromwich Albion/July 1908:Plymouth Argyle.

Debut v Burslem Port Vale (A) 1.9.06
(scored once)

Fosse's 14-goal top scorer in 1906/7, when utilised mainly at centre-forward, Harry had first made his mark as a prolific inside-right and penalty expert with Preston (15 of his 42 goals there were from the spot), helping shoot them back into Division One in 1904. He missed out on a further promotion success at Leicester when Fosse and West Brom agreed to exchange attackers, and Fred Shinton arrived as the bargain half of the deal, to score twice as many goals for the elevated Fosse as Harry did for fifth-placed Albion. Harry then made his final move, back to Southern League Plymouth, where he converted into a masterful centre-half and went on to complete a club aggregate of 325 games (41 goals) before retirement in 1920. He captained the Argyle championship side of 1913, and won representative honours for the Southern League against the Irish League in 1911, playing alongside fellow ex-Fossils Trueman and Moody and scoring the first goal in a 4-0 win.

Appearances:
FL: 44 apps. 16 gls.
FAC: 1 app. 0 gls.
Total: *45 apps. 16 gls.*

WILD, Arthur

Role: Inside left

CAREER: Feb 1903:FOSSE.

Debut v Stockport County (H) 26.3.03

The eighth of nine occupants of the Fosse inside-left berth during 1902/3, and another so-far untraceable one-shot player, Arthur featured only in a 0-2 reverse at Edgeley Park.

Appearances:
FL: 1 app. 0 gls.
Total: *1 app. 0 gls.*

WILKINS, E.

Role: Centre forward

CAREER: Apr 1892:FOSSE

Debut v Doncaster Rovers (A) ML 30.4.1892

A trialist of unknown club origin (although identified as an Essex County player), fielded at centre-forward in the final, goalless, Midland League fixture of Fosse's first season at that level.

Appearances:
ML: 1 app. 0 gls.
Total: *1 app. 0 gls.*

WILKINSON, Stephen John

Role: Striker
b. Lincoln, 1st September 1968

CAREER: app July 1985/pro Sept 1986:CITY/(Aug 1988-loan-Rochdale)/(Sept 1988-loan-Crewe Alexandra)/Sept 1989:Mansfield Town/June 1995:Preston North End.

Debut v Manchester City (H) 28.3.87 (sub)

Working his way through the City ranks as a prolific teenage goalscorer, Steve took early

Steve Wilkinson

WILLIAMS, Darren

Role: Midfield
b. Birmingham, 15th December 1968

CAREER: app July 1985/pro Dec 1986:CITY/(Nov 1989-loan-Lincoln City)/(Mar 1990-loan-Lincoln City)/(Sept 1990-loan-Chesterfield)/Dec 1990:Worcester City/Mar 1992:Tamworth/cs 1993:Brierley Hill/Hinckley Athletic/Redditch United.

Debut v Hull City (A) 4.10.88 (scored once)

A bracingly honest and mature self-assessment, rare in a business in which starry eyes and inflated egos often predominate, encouraged Darren to sever connections with both the club and League football as a whole at the age of 21, immediately after he had returned to Filbert Street from his third lower-division loan-out spell. The lightweight midfielder, originally acquired by way of youth coach Dave Richardson's extensive Brummie scouting network, had made an instant impact on his surprise introduction to senior football with City, claiming a fine scoring strike at Boothferry Park, but had generally failed to

encouragement from a brief taste of First Division action, and assumed Mark Bright's mantle as chief Central League striker, topping the Reserves' goal charts in each of 1987/8 and 1988/9. His intermittent senior appearances nonetheless brought him little joy in the finishing stakes (though he scored twice in a five-game spell at Gresty Road) and, after a brief luckless breakthrough in David Pleat's struggling Second Division side, Steve's promise was deemed not to match that of the younger Paul Kitson, and he was allowed to move to Field Mill for an £80,000 fee. There, in a lowly Stags side, he nonetheless equalled the Third Division scoring record (shared, amongst others, by Barrie Thomas and Steve Earle) with a nap-hand return from the 5-2 win over Birmingham during his first season. Relegation for Mansfield followed in 1991, despite Steve forming a twin spearhead with the veteran Trevor Christie, and Divisional yo-yo-ing continued over the next two terms, with Steve building a substantial goal aggregate. In fact his 90th senior goal for the club was notched at the unsuccessful semi-final stage of their attempt to rise again via the Play Offs in 1995.

Appearances:
FL: 5 (4) apps. 1 gl.
FAC: 1 app. 0 gls.
Total: *6 (4) apps. 1 gl.*

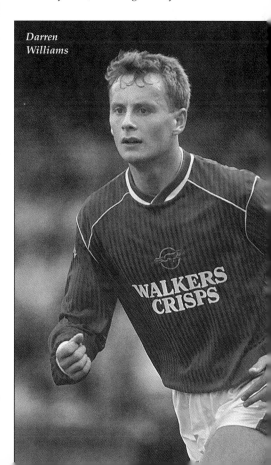

Darren Williams

consolidate his progress in subsequent Division Two outings, where a tidy workman-like application was more evident than a distinguishing spark. Both his utilisation in the Central League (occasionally as a full-back or winger) and on loan produced hints of a talent truncated in its development, and the phrase 'by mutual consent' for once seemed genuine when applied to the cancellation of Darren's City contract; at which point he evinced an ambition to qualify for an HGV driver's licence. A few months later, he was noted in the less pressured environment of the Southern League, playing in front of former City youth keeper Mark Gayle.

Appearances:
FL: 7 (3) apps. 2 gls.
LC: 3 apps. 0 gls.
FMC: 1 app. 0 gls.
Total: *11 (3) apps. 2 gls.*

WILLIAMS, Thomas Edward

Role: Utility
b. Winchburgh, West Lothian,
18th December 1957

CAREER: app July 1974/pro Dec 1975:CITY/ July 1986:Birmingham City/cs 1988:Grimsby Town/Aug 1990:Leicester Constabulary.
Debut v Chelsea (A) 5.10.77

Born in Scotland but raised in Leicester, Tommy often had to call on his reserves of native grit to see him through a lengthy City spell as one of the club's most versatile yet most ill-fated players of recent years. Pitched into the senior game in the midst of the 1977/8 relegation struggle, and asked to play in central defence, at full-back and in midfield during his first few months as a first-teamer, Tommy responded with boundless enthusiasm and no little skill, going on to establish himself as a regular utility player under Jock Wallace, and eventually settling to the right-back role. Having experienced a Second Division championship and a second relegation term, Tommy was at the heart of City's bid to secure a promotion/Cup double in 1982 when he suffered a broken leg during the Villa Park semi-final against Spurs, and the cost to the club was inestimable as both targets disappeared in his absence. Worse, however, was to follow, for after a comeback of only four senior games, Tommy broke the same leg again in training, and faced another gruelling period of recovery. It was characteristic that he bounced back into First Division football with full-blooded fervour, and his efforts in the centre-back role in 1984/5 did much to secure City's continued top-flight status. Despite Tommy's move to St.Andrews, he enjoyed a deservedly profitable testimonial at Filbert Street in December 1986, when City Present met a team of former Leicester stars. His senior playing career over, he returned to Leicester to join the police.

Appearances:
FL: 236 (5) apps. 10 gls.
FAC: 18 apps. 0 gls.
LC: 12 apps. 0 gls.
Total: *266 (5) apps. 10 gls.*

Tommy Williams

Brian Williamson

WILLIAMSON, Brian William

Role: Goalkeeper
b. Blyth, Northumberland, 6th October 1939

CAREER: Seaton Delaval/Oct 1958:
Gateshead/July 1960:Crewe Alexandra/
Dec 1962:Leeds United/Feb 1966:
Nottingham Forest/(Aug 1967-loan-
CITY)/Dec 1968: Fulham.

Debut v Sheffield Wednesday (H)
30.8.67

Borrowed by City from Forest
after Peter Shilton had suffered an
injury at Old Trafford and the club
were caught without senior cover,
Brian was an experienced keeper who
had nonetheless spent some five years
in the reserve teams of both Leeds and
Forest, understudying Gary Sprake and
Peter Grummitt. He didn't endear
himself to City supporters with his habit of
punching almost every aerial ball, but
otherwise performed adequately during his
short spell between the Filbert Street sticks, to
which he returned the following May as the
Forest goalie past whom City uncharitably put
four. Earlier, Brian had racked up 55 League
games for each of Gateshead and Crewe; later

he would manage only a dozen for Fulham
before retiring to go into the security business.

Appearances:
FL: 6 apps. 0 gl.
LC: 1 app. 0 gls.
Total: *7 apps. 0 gls.*

WILLIAMSON, William M.

Role: Outside right
b. Longton, Staffs, c 1884

CAREER: Stoke Nomads/
Sept 1905:Stoke/cs 1908:Crewe
Alexandra/May 1910:FOSSE/
June 1911:Stoke.

Debut v Barnsley (H) 27.12.10

Billy
Williamson

An outside-right who barely got a
look-in over Fred Threlfall's shoulder
during his Fosse season. At Stoke,
where his father was a director, Billy had twice
appeared alongside Syd Owen in his
eight-game, scoreless League stint; but he
made no further senior appearances there on
his nominal return.

Appearances:
FL: 2 apps. 0 gls.
Total: *2 apps. 0 gls.*

WILLIS, James Anthony

Role: Centre back
b. Liverpool, 12th July 1968

CAREER: YT 1985:Blackburn Rovers/1986:
Halifax Town/Dec 1987:Stockport County/
Mar 1988:Darlington/Dec 1991:CITY/
(Mar 1992-loan-Bradford City).
Debut v Bristol Rovers (A) 1.1.92

Originally a teenage forward, but denied a
senior outing until he arrived at Stockport for
a defensive debut behind Frank Worthington,
Jimmy then played for Brian Little at
Darlington as they first suffered relegation to
the Conference, then shot through two
successive promotion campaigns. Little added
him to the City squad in a £200,000 deal
(which also landed free-transfer man Michael
Trotter at Filbert Street), but the tall centre-
back's integration to the Play-off-bound side
was comprehensively derailed by a nightmare
performance in the first half of a home defeat
by Watford, and only days later Jimmy was off
to Valley Parade to rebuild his confidence. He
was a debut scorer for the Bantams, and well-
regarded by their fans, but he spent the whole
of the following term in City's reserves, and
his October 1993 comeback was stymied by
injury. Nonetheless, two operations later, he
returned to the fray to perform heroically in
the run-in to promotion, deservedly winning
the Man of the Match award from the Play-off
Final victory over Derby. In the Premiership,
too, Jimmy was the most consistent and
reliable defender in the City ranks; undaunted
even by conceding own goals in successive
fixtures against QPR and Wimbledon, or his
ludicrous dismissal in the home game with
Coventry. His tackling shows as much finesse
in its timing as it does bite, and his energetic
commitment is exemplary. As a result of a
childhood injury, one of Jimmy's legs is
slightly shorter than the other, but this has
never represented a handicap on the field.

Jimmy Willis

Appearances (to end 1994/5):
PL: 29 apps. 2 gls.
FL: 18 (1) apps. 1 gl.
FAC: 4 apps. 0 gls.
LC: 3 apps. 0 gls.
FMC: 1 (1) apps. 0 gls.
AIC: 1 app. 0 gls.
P/O: 3 apps. 0 gls.
Total: *59 (2) apps. 3 gls.*

WILLS, Gordon Francis

Role: Outside left
b. West Bromwich, 24th April 1934

CAREER: am:West Bromwich Albion/
Dec 1951:Wolverhampton Wanderers/
Aug 1953:Notts County/May 1958:CITY/
June 1962:Walsall/cs 1964:Sankeys.
Debut v Arsenal (A) 30.8.58

A National Serviceman in the RAF who had
been unable to break through the ranks at
Molineux, Gordon had made his League bow
with the Magpies and notched 47 goals in 154
Second Division games before Matt Gillies
plucked him from a relegated side for £9,000
and installed him on City's top-flight left
flank. The tall winger helped City through the
panics which attended their first few seasons
back in Division One, and contributed a lot to
the 1961 Cup run with his willingness to

augment the attacking spearhead as well as maintain pressure on his full-back. Occasionally injury-prone, Gordon picked up a severe knock in the first semi-final tie of 1961, yet insisted on continuing until the whistle despite the eventually-realised danger that he would miss the Final. The advent of Mike Stringfellow spelled the end of Gordon's days with City, and the residual toll of his injuries then restricted him to only two seasons at Fellows Park (35 games; 1 goal).

Appearances:
FL: 111 apps. 30 gls.
FAC: 10 apps. 2 gls.
LC: 3 apps. 0 gls.
Eur: 4 apps. 1 gl.
Total: *128 apps. 33 gls.*

Gordon Wills

WILSON, Ian G.

Role: Outside left
b. Fife, 11th February 1923

CAREER: Sept 1946:Forfar Athletic/Nov 1946:Preston North End/June 1948:Burnley/ Mar 1950:CITY/Oct 1951:Chesterfield/May 1953:Rotherham United/July 1956:Boston United/1957:Vancouver St.Andrews.
Debut v Sheffield United (A) 18.3.50

Ian G. Wilson

One of the objects of Norman Bullock's pre-deadline spending spree of 16th March 1950 (along with Jack Marsh and Peter Small), £7,000 buy Ian was a calculating outside-left who had never quite borne out the promise Preston had discerned during his brief introduction to the senior game with Forfar. Six goals in 16 League games had been his lot at Deepdale, while Ian's Turf Moor memories focused more on the way his goals had won Burnley a last-gasp Central League championship than on his 19 games in their first team. Ian was soon deemed below par at Leicester, too; succumbing to the joint challenge of the veteran No.11 Charlie Adam and newcomer Tom Dryburgh. Yet he turned out in 77 League matches for Chesterfield (19 goals), and became a great favourite at Millmoor, where he helped knock City out of the Cup in 1955, and where he contributed four goals to the final League game of that season in a bold attempt to push Rotherham to the double-figure score they needed to gain promotion to Division One on goal average. (In fact they beat Liverpool 6-1 and stayed down). After 108 games and 44 goals for the Millers, and a brief spell with Boston, Ian emigrated to Canada, where he continued playing and coaching into the 60s.

Appearances:
FL: 12 apps. 2 gls.
Total: *12 apps. 2 gls.*

WILSON, Ian William

Role: Midfield
b. Aberdeen, 27th March 1958

CAREER: jnr:Aberdeen/jnr:Dundee/Elgin
City/Apr 1979:CITY/Sept 1987:Everton/
Aug 1989:Besiktas/Feb 1991:Derby
County/Aug 1991:Bury (p/coach)/
Aug 1992:Wigan Athletic/Nov 1992:Peterhead.
Debut v Rotherham United (H) LC 11.8.79

Blending constructive and combative play in
the middle of the park, Ian caught Jock
Wallace's eye in Highland League football,
and arrived for a £30,000 fee, which he repaid
many times over with his influential prompting and playmaking skills. A key member of
both Wallace's and Gordon Milne's promotion
sides, Ian impressed most in the latter,
adopting an advanced role which saw him
coming in late behind Lineker and Smith and
claiming a fair tally of eight goals, including
the crucial winner at Craven Cottage. He fell
victim to the recent City habit of selecting
midfielders in full-back positions during the
next two seasons, but re-emerged as a mature
motivator and anchor-man, long forgiven by
even his most grudging critics for his
unfortunate own-
goal contribution
to City's 1982 Cup
semi-final defeat.
Belated but
deserved interna-
tional recognition
came Ian's way at
the age of 29,
when he followed
his call-up at 'B'
level in April 1987
with two full
Scottish caps a
month later; but
the combined
experience of this
personal elevation
and City's
relegation
unsettled him, and
a transfer became
inevitable.
Nonetheless, Ian

saved one of his finest performances for his
final Filbert Street game: scoring once and
laying on two more goals against Plymouth on
the day before his £300,000 move to Goodison.
He picked up an FA Cup runners-up medal as
a Wembley substitute for Everton in 1989, then
rejoined Gordon Milne in Turkey, where he
qualified for both League and Cup medals as
Besiktas achieved the domestic Double for the
first time ever in 1990 (though Ian actually sat
out the Cup Final against Trabzonspor as an
unused substitute following recovery from
injury). Unfortunately, on his return to
England, Ian could turn around the fortunes of
neither the Rams nor the Shakers, both of
whom proved relegation-bound within
months. A brief non-contract spell under
Bryan Hamilton at Wigan then pointed to a
full-circle return to the Highland scene, where
Ian himself took over management duties at
Peterhead before another call from Milne in
February 1994: landing Ian the assistant's job
at Nagoya Grampus Eight in Japan.

Appearances:
FL: 276 (9) apps. 17 gls.
FAC: 15 apps. 1 gl.
LC: 18 apps. 1 gl.
Total: *309 (9) apps. 19 gls.*

Ian Wilson

WILSON, W.T.

Role: Goalkeeper

CAREER: Alfreton/
Aug 1901:FOSSE.

*Debut v Barnsley (H)
14.9.01*

Fosse's reserve
goalkeeper for two
seasons, understudy-
ing Teddy Daw and
Archie Ling in suc-
cession. He kept a
clean sheet on his
debut, was on the
losing side only once, and conceded only
seven Second Division goals in total.

W.T. Wilson

Appearances:
FL: 5 apps. 0 gls.
Total: *5 apps. 0 gls.*

WINTER, R.E.

Role: Outside left

CAREER: Notts County Rovers/Nottingham
Forest reserves/(Apr 1892-trials-FOSSE).

Debut v Burslem Port Vale (H) ML 19.4.1892

One of Fosse's Midland League amateur
trialists, Winter took the left flank spot in the
above match and in two subsequent friendlies
against Loughborough and Bolton Wanderers:
all ended in home defeats.

Appearances:
ML: 1 app. 0 gls.
Total: *1 app. 0 gls.*

WISE, Harold A.

Role: Inside forward
b. London

CAREER: Custom House/July 1914:FOSSE/
cs 1915:Croydon Common.

Debut v Huddersfield Town (A) 21.9.14

Another Fosse signing of the immediate pre-
war days from the London League; a teenage
amateur inside-forward whose patent
inexperience was less than useful to the club's
scrabbling necessity to haul themselves out of
the re-election zone. Harold (whose
moves were both made in tandem
with centre-forward Legge) played
in Croydon's pre-season public
practice games, but made no
competitive appearances thereafter.

Appearances:
FL: 11 apps. 1 gl.
Total: *11 apps. 1 gl.*

WOOD, A.

Role: Left back

CAREER: Finedon/Nov 1891:
FOSSE.

Debut v Loughborough (H) ML 28.11.1891

A Northamptonshire left-back given a brief
trial during Fosse's initial Midland League
season, in the above home defeat and the
following game, the only away win of that
embarrassing term, 4-3 at Wednesbury Old
Athletic.

Appearances:
ML: 2 apps. 0 gls.
Total: *2 apps. 0 gls.*

WOOD, Alexander Lochian

Role: Left back
b. Lochgelly, Fife, 12th June 1907
d. Gary, Indiana, USA, 20th July 1987

CAREER: c 1927:Chicago Bricklayers/
Holley Carburetors (Detroit)/Nov 1930:
Brooklyn Wanderers/Feb 1933:CITY/May
1936:Nottingham Forest/cs 1937:Colchester
United/cs 1938:Chelmsford City.

Debut v Blackpool (H) 30.3.33

A distinctly well-travelled full-back, Sandy
had won a Scottish schoolboy cap (against
Wales in May 1921), just before his family
sailed to try their fortune in the United States;
settling in Gary, Indiana. He became a
naturalised American (1922) and, having
starred in such Stateside soccer showpieces as
the 1928 US Open Cup Final (when Chicago
Bricklayers lost on aggregate to New York
Nationals), was chosen to appear in each of
the three games the USA played in reaching
the semi-final of the inaugural World Cup in
Uruguay in 1930. Having eventually earned

four caps in total for his adopted country, Sandy found full-time work difficult to obtain in Depression-hit America, and sailed for England. After trials for City, Sandy signed League forms - only to become entangled in the combined red tape of the FA and the Home Office. For some time he had to turn out as an amateur on a short-term permit; but was then officially repatriated. For just over three seasons at Filbert Street he vied principally with Dai Jones for the left-back spot, assisting City to their first-ever Cup semi-final in 1934, and breaking his collar-bone at Hillsborough in April 1935, and was then allowed to move on to Trentside for £750. Sandy was later a member of Colchester

Sandy Wood

United's newly-formed professional side in the Southern League, and represented that combination in Inter-League competition alongside team-mate George Ritchie. He briefly worked in a Marconi Radio plant on the outbreak of war, then sailed once more for the States in October 1939; settling back in Gary, and working for the US Steel Corporation (where he helped start up a soccer club) until retirement in 1970. Four years before that, he assisted his son William in inaugurating a youth soccer league in Northwest Indiana; while back in 1958 he had been elected to the local Sports Hall of Fame alongside his niece Jean Stunyo, an Olympic silver-medallist diver.

Appearances:
FL: 52 apps. 0 gls.
FAC: 5 apps. 0 gls.
Total: *57 apps. 0 gls.*

WOOD, Cecil John Burdett

Role: Inside right / Right half
b. Northampton, 21st November 1875
d. Leicester, 5th June 1960

CAREER: Leicester YMCA/Oct 1896:FOSSE.

Debut v Walsall (A) 20.3.1897 (scored once)

Yet another Fossil better known for his prowess at the summer game, 'Cis' was a Leicestershire stalwart between 1896 and 1923, captaining the County in 1914, 1919 and 1920, having also played for London County (opening the batting with W.G.Grace) and, four times, for the Gentlemen v. Players. He carried his bat through an innings on 17 occasions for Leics, including the time he managed the feat in both innings in a 1911 game against Yorkshire. He also, in later life, had a spell as secretary to the club during the Second World War. Next to all this, his amateur football exploits seem rather a sideshow, with his second and third senior Fosse appearances being made some three years apart. Yet 'Cis' also scored in the annual Christmas fixture against the powerful Corinthians in 1899, and occasionally deserted his favoured positions of inside-forward or wing-half to assist Fosse reserves in goal.

Appearances:
FL: 3 apps. 1 gl.
Total: *3 apps. 1 gl.*

❏ FOX FACT: *Fosse and City have, over the years, fielded a remarkable number of footballer/cricketers who have played both games at senior level. Aside from C.J.B.Wood, the senior roster reads: Tommy Allsopp, Jimmy Atter, Harry Bailey, Ewart Benskin, Graham Cross, Ernest Gill, Teddy King, Jack Lee, John Mitten, Arthur Mounteney, Fred Osborn, Maurice Tompkin, Bob Turner and Harry Whitehead (all Leicestershire); Fred Bracey and Tom Fletcher (Derbyshire); Jim Harrold (Essex); Tom Simpson (Nottinghamshire); Tal Lewis*

(Somerset); and John Vincett (Sussex & Surrey). Additionally, Gary Lineker featured in MCC sides; Reg Halton played Minor Counties cricket for Staffordshire, Tom Smith for Durham, and Archie Ling for Cambridgeshire; Steve Yates was an England choice at schoolboy level; while City trainer David Jones was a Notts cricketer. City's WW2 guests included Bill Barron (Lancashire & Northamptonshire), Maurice Dunkley (Northants) and Eric Houghton (Warwickshire). Among Leicestershire players to have turned out at reserve-team level with Fosse or City were Les Berry, George Dawkes, Tom Jayes, Albert Matthews, Billy Odell, Harold Riley, George Shingler and Laurie Thursting. Finally, mention must be made of the events of 12th August 1937, when Arthur Chandler was summoned from Filbert Street to Aylestone Road to act as 12th man for both Leics and Notts, and contrived to field for both sides during three spells on the pitch!

WOODVINE, Albert

Role: Outside right
b. Kirk Sandall, Yorks, 16th June 1917
d. 1972

CAREER: Pilkington Recreational/ Nov 1937:CITY.
Debut v Brentford (A) 5.2.38

A City junior whose prospects were wrecked by the coincidence of a broken leg and the eruption of WW2, this winger made a brief comeback in the last two seasons of regional fare after impressing in RAF football, but was

'Cis' Wood

Albert Woodvine

formally freed in 1946. At least one other appearance should have been Albert's, for he was chosen for his senior debut at home to Chelsea only three weeks after signing, but had to cry off through injury from his home near Doncaster.

Appearances:
FL: 1 app. 0 gls.
WW2: 4 apps. 0 gls.
Total: *5 apps. 0 gls.*

WOODWARD, Maurice

Role: Wing half
b. Enderby, Leics, 23rd February 1892

CAREER: Enderby Town/Aug 1912:FOSSE/June 1914:Southend United/Apr 1920:Wolverhampton Wanderers/June 1922:Bristol Rovers.

Debut v Stockport County (A) 28.2.14

A young local wing-half who turned out in a pair of Fosse defeats towards the end of his two years at Filbert Street, and had to move into Southern League football on either side of WW1 (in which he was an early Middlesex Regiment volunteer) to gain more substantial experience. Maurice then made a return to Second Division fare at Molineux, and represented Wolves at right-back in their 1921 FA Cup Final defeat by Spurs. He was later kept out of the League side at Eastville by ex-City man Walter Currie.

Appearances:
FL: 2 apps. 0 gls.
Total: *2 apps. 0 gls.*

Maurice Woodward

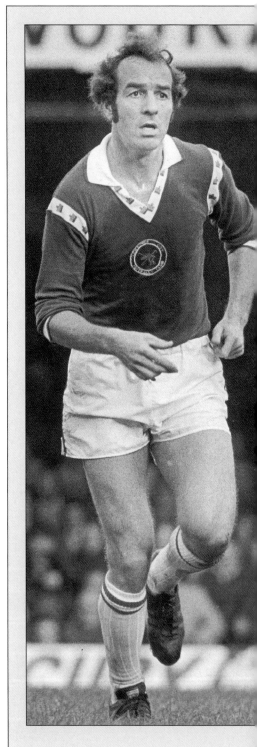

WOOLLETT, Alan Howard

Role: Defender
b. Wigston, Leics, 4th March 1947

CAREER: app Aug 1963/pro Aug 1964: CITY/July 1978:Northampton Town/ cs 1979:Corby Town.
Debut v Sheffield United (H) 22.4.67 (sub)

All too often in his early days the scapegoat of an impatient City crowd, Alan was a tenacious central defender and a resilient character, belying his almost diffident appearance with a steely determination both in tackling opponents and in building a more amicable rapport with his vociferous critics. A single off-colour game, albeit in a vital Sixth Round Cup-tie with Everton in 1968, set the crowd on Alan's back (and some even went so far as to blame him for Manchester City's goal in the 1969 Cup Final, when he stood in for injury victim John Sjoberg), yet subsequently there were countless occasions when the central defender earned much more than grudging cheers for his sterling back-line performances. Over the course of several seasons Alan looked as if he'd have to settle for becoming merely a fringe utility member of the first-team squad, but each time he bounced back to reclaim a senior berth, and he was probably at his peak almost ten years after his debut, when regularly partnering Jeff Blockley during 1975/6. The loyal clubman took a deserved testimonial from a friendly against Chelsea in May 1977, and eventually closed his career with a season at Northampton, in the familiar company of coach Clive Walker and on-loan Paul Matthews. Alan is now a prison officer.

Appearances:
FL: 213 (15) apps. 0 gls.
FAC: 15 apps. 0 gls.
LC: 17 apps. 0 gls.
Total: *245 (15) apps. 0 gls.*

Left: Alan Woollett

WOOLLISCROFT, Arthur

Role: Inside right
b. Salford, Lancs, 17th February 1904
d. 1977

CAREER: Salford/Manchester Docks/Sept 1926:Manchester City/cs 1928:Caernarvon Athletic/Mar 1929:CITY/Jan 1930:Watford/ Sept 1933:Newport County/July 1934: Northwich Victoria.
Debut v Sheffield Wednesday (A) 2.11.29

A junior at Maine Road who made no first-team breakthrough, Arthur was simultaneously employed as a cargo hand on the Manchester Ship Canal, then moved into the Welsh National League with his former manager David Ashworth, to play alongside former City reserve Chris Hackett. After one season City paid £400 for Arthur's inside-forward services (denying him the honour of representing the Welsh League against the Cheshire League a week later), but he only got a single chance to stand in for Ernie Hine - in a 0-4 Hillsborough defeat - before being off-loaded. He netted 14 League goals for Watford, but failed to score in 15 appearances for Newport.

Appearances:
FL: 1 app. 0 gls.
Total: *1 app. 0 gls.*

Arthur Woolliscroft

WOOLRIDGE, John

Role: Outside left

CAREER: Hanley Swifts/May 1900:FOSSE.

Debut v Small Heath (A) 8.9.1900

A winger from the Potteries given a brief run-out on the Fosse left flank and soon jettisoned, after appearances in Birmingham, Burton and Glossop, without appearing before the home crowd.

Appearances:
FL: 3 apps. 0 gls.
Total: *3 apps. 0 gls.*

WORRALL, Arthur

Role: Centre forward

CAREER: Aug 1889:Wolverhampton Wanderers/cs 1891:Burton Swifts/ Apr 1893:FOSSE/Jan 1894:Woolwich Arsenal/ cs 1894:Nelson/cs 1897:Stockport County/ Mar 1899:Barnsley.

Arthur Worrall

Debut v Mansfield Town (H) ML 22.4.1893 (scored once)

A scoring debut on trial was enough to convince Fosse to sign Arthur for the coming (final) Midland League campaign, but this prolific centre-forward could hardly be kept at that level for long (his whirlwind start to 1893/4 included 6 goals in four friendlies), and Arsenal soon paid Burton for his signature and League registration. He had initially also made a scoring bow for Wolves, helping them to 4th place in the League in consecutive seasons, and would do later for Stockport, at Lancashire League level. (It has yet to be confirmed, but we strongly suspect that Arthur moved to Ireland after his Barnsley stint, to win two Irish League representative selections while with Distillery in 1900; and there is a possibility that he returned to play briefly for Kettering in the Southern League during 1901/2).

Appearances:
ML: 4 apps. 3 gls.
Total: *4 apps. 3 gls.*

WORTHINGTON, Frank Stewart

Role: Striker
b. Halifax, 23rd November 1948

CAREER: app/pro Nov 1966:Huddersfield Town/Aug 1972:CITY/Sept 1977:Bolton Wanderers/(May 1979-loan-Philadelphia Fury)/Nov 1979:Birmingham City/ (Apr 1981-loan-Tampa Bay Rowdies)/ Mar 1982:Leeds United/Dec 1982: Sunderland/June 1983: Southampton/ May 1984:Brighton & Hove Albion/ July 1985:Tranmere Rovers (p/mgr)/ Feb 1987:Preston North End/Nov 1987: Stockport County/Apr 1988:Cape Town Spurs/Oct 1988:Chorley/Dec 1988: Stalybridge Celtic/Feb 1989:Galway United/Sept 1989:Weymouth/ Oct 1989:Radcliffe Borough/Nov 1989: Guiseley (p/coach)/1990:Preston North End (p/t coach)/Sept 1990:Hinckley Town (p/mgr)/1991:Cemaes Bay/Aug 1991: Halifax Town (p/coach).

Debut v Manchester United (A) 23.8.72 (scored once)

At a time when the concepts of 'personality' and 'charisma' first underwent their continuing devaluation in the hands of a 'build 'em up; shoot 'em down' media, and when sports

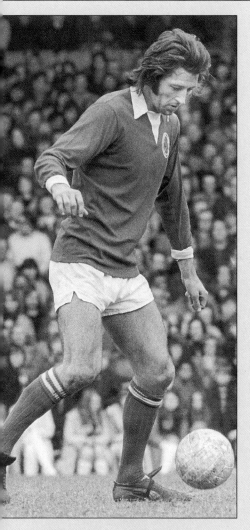

alternately subtle and spectacular, was an integral part of his repertoire - along with the incisive flick, the arrogant ball control and the deceptively lazy stride - from the time he helped Huddersfield into the First Division in 1970. City made an early move for 'Wortho' as the Terriers began to slide, but an England Under-23 tour intervened, pushing up the likely fee and alerting Liverpool to Frank's quality. A failed medical test quashed Anfield interest, though, and Jimmy Bloomfield jumped at the second chance, watching with glee as his six-figure investment accrued compound interest over five seasons of entertaining 'total football' (or thereabouts) from City. Frank was a popular choice for the national side, winning eight England caps (2 goals) while at his most prolific with City, yet his best single season as a scorer came at Burnden, after Frank McLintock had allowed him to slip away, when he headed the 1979 First Division list with 24. His St.Andrews debut came against City, and then in the 80s Frank's wanderings began in earnest, with his disdain for the predictable spicing the rather bland tactical recipes of a host of aspiring clubs, and the personal 200-goal landmark being easily surpassed. He briefly shouldered managerial responsibility, too, at Prenton Park until balance-sheet politics edged him onwards into Preston's 1987 promotion run-in, and Frank left Stockport for South Africa with the record of having scored League goals in each of 21 successive seasons. The PFA backed his 1991/2 benefit season, which included games at St.Andrews, Leeds Road and Filbert Street; while the Elvis obsession has entered popular legend, and the contents of the idiosyncratic autobiography, 'One Hump Or Two?' have further fed the folkloric memory. Frank's father Eric played during WW2 for Halifax Town and Lincoln City; brothers Dave and Bob each had lengthy League careers after launching off from Halifax as hefty defenders; and nephew Gary became another peripatetic striker, most notably with Wigan Athletic.

commentators in particular seemed desperate to assign 'character' status to random workhorses, Frank remained an original: mainly because his outsize image was always harnessed to an outsize talent. Off-field flamboyance ever had its footballing concomitant as Frank's consistent practice of the attacking arts graced the League sphere for over two decades, and one has to reach for a paradoxical construct to try to sum up his striker's impact for City and his numerous other clubs: something like 'casually lethal' might do the trick. The elegant thrust,

Appearances:
FL: 209 (1) apps. 72 gls.
FAC: 18 apps. 4 gls.
LC: 10 (1) apps. 2 gls.
Total: *237 (2) apps. 78 gls.*

WORTHINGTON, Fred

Role: Inside right
b. Manchester, 6th January 1924

CAREER: July 1947:Bury/Mar 1951:CITY/
July 1955:Exeter City/July 1956:Oldham
Athletic/cs 1957:Chorley (p/coach)/June
1958:Mossley.

Debut v Leeds United (A) 31.3.51

Belatedly following manager Norman Bullock
from Gigg Lane to complete a City inside trio
with Hines and Rowley (and to renew
acquaintance with other former Bury
acquaintances in Reg Halton and trainer
David Jones), Fred became the thoughtful,
deeper-lying prompter of the forward line for
some eighteen months, until the arrival of the
classier Johnny Morris consigned him to a
regular diet of reserve football. As something
of a veteran following his brief contribution to
City's 1954/5 First Division campaign, he
subsequently found his opportunities limited
in each of his seasons at Exeter (one goal in 16
games) and Oldham (one in ten).

Appearances:
FL: 55 apps. 9 gls.
FAC: 2 apps. 0 gls.
Total: *57 apps. 9 gls.*

*Fred
Worthington*

WRAGG, William

Role: Defender
b. Bradford, 1875 (?)

CAREER: Notts Olympic/Newstead Byron/
Mar 1895:Hucknall Portland/May 1896:
Nottingham Forest/Mar 1899:FOSSE/Jan
1901:Small Heath/Aug 1901:Watford/Aug
1902:Hinckley Town/Aug 1903:Chesterfield/
cs 1904:Accrington Stanley/Sept 1905:
Brighton & Hove Albion/(poss: July 1906:
Wombwell Main/Jan 1907:Grantham Avenue/
Apr 1907:Wombwell Main).

Debut v Blackpool (A) 1.4.1899

The left-half in
Forest's FA Cup-
winning side of 1898
(and creator of the
first goal of the
Final against Derby
despite the
handicap of a leg
injury), Billy joined
Fosse just as they
were about to suffer
the disappointment
of missing
promotion by one
place and one point.

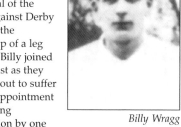

Billy Wragg

Fosse used his versatile talents primarily in the
right-back berth, but before he moved on he
had served in all five of the defensive
positions, and proved himself a genuine
hot-shot of a free-kick specialist. He made but
a single appearance in Birmingham's 1901
promotion push, but the previous season had
got on their scoresheet with a Fosse own goal.
At least one segment of Billy's post-football
career retains major retrospective interest: as a
hand-bill for the Nottingham Empire music-
hall from January 1910 indicates. For not only
did Billy tread the theatrical boards with three
other former pro's in Fred Karno's Colossal
Production 'The Football Match (A Struggle
for Supremacy between Midnight Wanderers
and Middleton Pie-Cans)', but he did so in the
co-starring company of no less than Charlie
Chaplin and Stan Laurel, in their pre-
Hollywood days!

Appearances:
FL: 49 apps. 5 gls.
FAC: 4 apps. 0 gls.
Total: *53 apps. 5 gls.*

WRIGHT, Joseph

Role: Goalkeeper
b. Gateshead, 1907
d. Newton Abbott, Devon, 20th November 1936

CAREER: Birtley/Apr 1929:CITY/July 1930:
Torquay United/July 1932:Brighton & Hove
Albion.

Debut v Manchester United (H) 2.9.29

A Geordie goalkeeper who made a remarkably
rapid vault from the Second Division of the
NorthEastern League into the top flight, Joe
became Jim McLaren's 'occasionally
impetuous' stand-in during the early days of
the 1929/30 season, and accumulated an
unexpected amount of experience. Much of it,
however, was backbending, despite City's
reasonable League position. He was the first
City keeper to face a penalty (by Newcastle's
Hughie Gallacher) under the revised (and still
current) 'no movement' ruling, while his final
game was the exhilarating 6-6 draw with Cup
Finalists Arsenal. Two seasons as first choice at
each of Plainmoor and the Goldstone Ground
ensued, but ill-health cut short Joe's
career, and he died at the age of 29.

Appearances:
FL: 15 apps. 0 gls.
Total:
15 apps. 0 gls.

Joe Wright

WRIGHT, Thomas Elliott

Role: Winger
b. Dunfermline, Fife,
10th January 1966

CAREER: Hutchisonvale/app Apr 1982/
pro Jan 1983:Leeds United/Oct 1986:Oldham
Athletic/Aug 1989:CITY/July 1992:
Middlesbrough/July 1995:Bradford City.

Debut v Hull City (A) 19.8.89

The son of a Scottish international forward
(also Tommy), and a cousin of former City
favourite Jackie Sinclair, Tommy earned an
Under-21 squad call-up shortly after breaking
through as a nippy teenage striker at Elland
Road. But he had to wait for his first Scottish
cap at that level until after his £80,000 move to
Boundary Park, where he made his mark
playing wide on the left; especially enjoying
the discomfiture of visiting defenders
uncertain of how to deal with the combination
of his pace and the 'plastic' home pitch. With
City he enjoyed (and occasionally suffered) the
reception accorded many orthodox wingers,
effectively polarising terrace opinion during

Tommy Wright

his three-year Second Division stint. Certainly there were infuriating aspects to Tommy's game, with the ratio of useful to wasted crosses (often delivered head-down) coming in for most criticism. But the scampering flair of his flank play engendered high excitement levels on a fairly regular basis, and he certainly hit a decent quota of telling strikes, eventually becoming top scorer in his final Filbert Street season. Indeed, his exploits by then had made him something of a cult hero to sections of the crowd, and his last home game, in the Play-off demolition of Cambridge, was a true virtuoso performance, worthy of attracting the sort of Premier League attention that soon led to his £650,000 move northwards. Boro, however, were relegated in 1993, and Tommy lost first-choice status soon afterwards; being freed in May 1995 after barely getting a chance to contribute to that year's championship effort under Bryan Robson. In the summer he joined Lennie Lawrence's growing contingent of ex-City players at Bradford.

Appearances:
FL: 122 (7) apps. 22 gls.
FAC: 4 apps. 0 gls.
LC: 7 (1) apps. 0 gls.
FMC: 7 apps. 5 gls.
P/O: 3 apps. 2 gls.
Total: *143 (8) apps. 29 gls.*

❏ FOX FACT: *Tommy Wright's five-goal haul from Full Member's Cup ties made him the club's leading scorer in that unloved competition, which City initially disdained to enter, but which provided a modicum of entertainment under its various Simod and Zenith Data Systems sponsorships, until the Premier League breakaway split its constituency and spelt its demise.*

WRIGHT, William John

Role: Winger
b. Blackpool, 4th March 1931

CAREER: May 1950:Blackpool/Aug 1955: CITY/July 1958:Newcastle United/Aug 1959: Plymouth Argyle/Aug 1961:Hull City/ Aug 1961:Millwall/cs 1962:Tonbridge.

Debut v Barnsley (H) 10.9.55

Understandably frustrated as understudy to Stanley Matthews at Bloomfield Road, where

he had managed only 15 League games and two goals over four seasons, Billy then found his high hopes of a regular place with City (after a £1,500 move) soon looking bleak against the challenge of the club's mid-50s superabundance of wingers. He could hardly be accused of not grasping the main chance when it presented itself, though: entering the 1956/7 promotion fray on Christmas Day, and contributing ten goals to the championship success from 17 games on either flank. It was somewhat surprising that Billy did not start the following campaign as an automatic choice; less so, in this light, that Newcastle soon jumped in with £7,500 for his signature. He suffered cruelly from injuries while on Tyneside, though, and moved south with a record of only five games; three goals. A full season at Home Park (in the company of Dave MacLaren, Gordon Fincham and John Newman) fuelled his wanderlust, but his spell at The Den ended a League career marked more by might-have-been's and if-only's than by potential fulfilled.

Appearances:
FL: 27 apps. 10 gls.
FAC: 2 apps. 0 gls.
Total: *29 apps. 10 gls.*

Billy Wright

YATES, Stephen

Role: Left back
b. Measham, Leics, 8th December 1953

CAREER: app July 1970/pro Mar 1972:CITY/
Nov 1977:Southend United/Dec 1983:
Doncaster Rovers/(Feb 1985-loan-
Darlington)/(Mar 1985-loan-Chesterfield)/
Aug 1985:Stockport County/(Sept 1985-trials-
Burnley)/Oct 1985:Shepshed Charterhouse.

Debut v Newcastle United (A) 23.3.74 (sub)

A second cousin of David Nish who had
shown all-round sporting ability as a
schoolboy - representing England at cricket,
and holding the national record for discus-
throwing - Steve was a heftily built full-back
who made the majority of his City
appearances as a competent stand-in for
Dennis Rofe, but stood little chance of
displacing the ebullient No.3 on a regular
basis. At Southend, however, he gradually
converted into a central defender during the
course of a run of
exactly 250 League
and Cup games,
and contributed
immense solidity to
their 1981 Fourth
Division championship side. At left-back
again, he also assisted Doncaster to promotion
from the League basement in 1984; while his
final two senior games came during a non-
contract spell at Stockport.

Appearances:
FL: 12 (7) apps. 0 gls.
FAC: 1 app. 0 gls.
LC: 1 app. 0 gls.
Total: *14 (7) apps. 0 gls.*

YOUNG, Alexander Forbes (Alan)

Role: Striker
b. Kirkcaldy, Fife, 26th October 1955

CAREER: Kirkcaldy YMCA/July 1974:
Oldham Athletic/May 1979:CITY/Aug 1982:
Sheffield United/Aug 1983:Brighton & Hove
Albion/Sept 1984:Notts County/Aug 1986:
Rochdale/Mar 1988:Shepshed Charterhouse
(p/coach)/1989:Lutterworth Town.

Debut v Rotherham United (H) LC 11.8.79
(scored once)

Scorer of the hat-trick by which Oldham
removed City from the FA Cup in 1979, Alan
became one of the first players to be
transferred under the new freedom-of-contract
regulations and have his transfer fee set by an
independent tribunal. The £250,000 move
upset Oldham while still equalling City's then-
record fee, but appeared more of a bargain as
Alan led the club's charge towards Division
One with a fair goalscoring verve and no little
delicacy of skill for a forward so apparently
forceful. His scoring touch deserted him
somewhat thereafter, though, and it
occasionally looked as if he was more intent
on back-chatting his way through a game than
getting on and playing it. Fitness problems
also marred the picture, though Jock Wallace
stood by Alan despite the striking challenge of
Jim Melrose, and it was not until the very eve
of the next season, by which time Gordon
Milne had taken over, that Alan was on his
way to Bramall Lane for £200,000. Seven
League goals for the Blades, twelve for the
Seagulls and thirteen for the Magpies

Steve Yates

Alan Young

YOUNG, Archibald Wishart

Role: Inside left / Left half
b. Kirkintilloch, Dunbartonshire,
10th December 1906

CAREER: Kilsyth Rangers/Dunipace/(trials-
Preston North End)/Dunfermline Athletic/
Apr 1932:CITY/July 1935:Bristol Rovers/
June 1936:Exeter City/May 1937:Gillingham/
Sept 1938:Rochdale.
Debut v Arsenal (A) 29.10.32

A creative inside-left or wing-half, Archie
didn't make the happiest of entries to English
senior football: standing in for Arthur
Lochhead in a crushing 2-8 Highbury defeat
by Herbert Chapman's champions-to-be.
Undaunted, however, he proved a useful
reserve for three First Division seasons. His
subsequent Third Division wanderings still
left him goalless after a further 64 League
outings, and he faced further embarrassments,
too: he was in the Bristol Rovers side beaten
0-12 at Luton in April 1936 (when Joe Payne
claimed his League record ten goals), while
the Gills failed to win re-election at the end of
Archie's season there. He made only a single
appearance at Spotland.

Appearances:
FL: 14 apps. 0 gls.
FAC: 1 app. 0 gls.
Total: *15 apps. 0 gls.*

subsequently represented a one-in-three
scoring ratio, but Alan's spells on the
treatment table, especially for a nagging back
ailment, were becoming more frequent, and
severely limited his contribution to Rochdale's
Fourth Division struggles. He returned to
Leicestershire as player/coach at Shepshed,
and to help run the indoor cricket and soccer
centre at Thurmaston, and was later organiser
of Notts County's 'Football in the Community'
scheme.

Appearances:
FL: 102 (2) apps. 26 gls.
FAC: 10 apps. 2 gls.
LC: 5 apps. 1 gl.
Total: *117 (2) apps. 29 gls.*

Archie Young

A Armstrong is alphabetically the first of the several mystery men amongst Fosse's WW1 roster of one-shot players; though there is some circumstantial evidence to suggest the outside-right who faced Bradford Park Avenue (A) in April 1919 (in Fosse's penultimate wartime fixture) was a pre-war Loughborough Corinthians winger. (1 app)

Tom Bailey was a Gresley Rovers right-half who turned out for Fosse in each of the wartime seasons except 1917/18. (36 apps; 1 goal)

Four otherwise totally unknown players assisted Fosse at Grimsby Town in October 1918 (not an unusual occurrence at that ground during the war, with rail connections often disrupted): inside-left **J Barber** was one, though he did not join the fray until Fosse had completed 40 minutes with only 10 men. (1 app)

Joe Barratt (Josiah; b. Bulkington, 21.2.1895; d. Coventry, April 1968) was an outside-right with Nuneaton Town at the time he guested for Fosse in 1916/17. While hostilities (and service with the 3rd Royal Berkshire Regiment) continued, he also guested once for Birmingham, and occasionally for Coventry City in friendlies. In May 1919, Joe signed for Southampton (featuring in their first-ever Football League game in 1920), and in February 1922 transferred to Birmingham. He moved to Pontypridd in June 1923, Lincoln City in June 1924, and Bristol Rovers in May 1926; and rejoined Nuneaton Town a year later; before becoming a Coventry youth coach. His son Harry was a City guest during WW2. (4 apps)

A Bradford Park Avenue reserve, who never played for them in League football before or after his seven wartime games, **G Barrett** was picked up by an under-strength Fosse on their way to Sheffield United in February 1918, and played at outside-right in a 2-6 defeat. (1 app)

Private **C H Barrow**, 'a Leicester lad stationed near Hull', was fielded at outside-right in a 1-2 defeat at Hull in March 1917. (1 app)

Balmoral United right-half **T Bee** made his sole Fosse appearance at Barnsley in a 0-5 defeat in December 1916. (1 app)

Corporal **F Bennett** was reputed to be on the books of Queens Park Rangers when selected for Fosse at inside-right in the December 1916 home game with Leeds City; but no records exist of him playing any peacetime or wartime games for them. (1 app)

Chelsea right-back **Walter Bettridge** (b. Oakthorpe, 1886; d. Ashby-de-la-Zouch, 23.12.1931) was in Fosse's initial WW1 line-up and was an ever-present until November 1915; afterwards joining up with the Flying Corps. A former Measham and Worksop Town player, he'd signed for Chelsea from Burton United in May 1909, and served them in 224 League games on either side of the war until a November 1922 move to Gillingham. (9 apps)

Inside-right **Walter Smith Bird** (b. Hugglescote, 1891; d. Coalville, 2.3.1965), who was a Fosse regular for a year from March 1917, had previously gained a little League experience as an amateur with Notts County, following an April 1911 move from Coalville Swifts. Coalville once more transferred his registration to a League club in February 1920, when he joined Grimsby Town, and subsequent senior moves saw him at Bristol Rovers (May 1920; figuring in their initial League line-up, and later registering their first hat-trick at that level), Dundee (June 1921), Hearts (January 1924) and Kilmarnock (June 1924). (22 apps; 8 goals)

Borrowed from home club Sheffield United in February 1919 after Herbert Bown had missed his train, goalkeeper **Ernest Blackwell** (b. Sheffield, 19.7.1894; d. Sheffield, 16.10.1964) had joined the Blades in May 1914 from Scunthorpe & Lindsey United, and continued to serve them until retirement through injury and illness in November 1924. He also assisted Sheffield Wednesday in one WW1 game. (1 app)

Chosen at inside-right for Fosse's 0-5 defeat at Barnsley in December 1916, **C Botterill**, from an unnamed local Leicester club, won no subsequent senior chances. (1 app)

Another local one-shot during this period was **V H Bowden**, the Balmoral United right winger, who featured in a 0-4 defeat at Leeds City in January 1918. (1 app)

D. DONALD
QUEENS PARK RANGERS

H. EDGLEY
QUEEN'S PARK RANGERS

J. LEACH
ASTON VILLA

J. PENNINGTON
W. B. ALBION

Born in Leeds (October 1891), but raised in New Zealand, **Reginald Boyne** joined Aston Villa in December 1913, and played eight times in Division One before the outbreak of war. He became a Fosse regular during 1916/17, despite a less-than-prolific scoring record for a centre- or inside-forward, but found his shooting boots for Brentford after his 1919 signing, and claimed the Bees' first-ever League goal a year later. (23 apps; 2 goals)

Chelsea inside-right **Harry Brittain** (Harold Pemberton; b. Derby, 1894) had a couple of Fosse outings in March 1919. Originally signed from Ilkeston United in December 1913, he left Stamford Bridge in 1920 and emigrated to the United States, playing there for Bethlemen Steel (May 1920), Philadelphia (September 1921), Fall River Marksmen (October 1922), New Bedford Whalers (September 1926) and Boston Fall River (March 1927). (2 apps)

Oadby man **F R Broadley** played at outside-right for Fosse against Rotherham County in October 1916, and was excused his unremarkable performance by the '*Daily Post*' reporter on the unlikely grounds that he was 'playing his first Association game'! However, he had been an occasional Tigers player between 1911-15, scoring 8 tries in 13 games as a wing-threequarter; and, in correspondence with the local press in 1939, claimed to have played cricket for the County Seconds as well. (1 app)

A Brown, who turned out at outside-right in the January 1917 away game with Rotherham County, was a Gresley Rovers player who had previously served Shirebrook. (1 app)

A Bradford Park Avenue amateur, **Tommy Brown** (b. Sheffield, 27.3.1897) was picked up by a depleted Fosse on their way to play Sheffield United in February 1918, and played at centre-half in a 2-6 defeat. Postwar, he played 19 games in the top two Divisions for Avenue, before joining Rotherham Town in May 1923. (1 app)

Coalville Swifts winger **T Brownlow** took the left flank for Fosse against Notts County and Bradford City on successive afternoons at Easter 1917. (2 apps)

Sgt-Major **J E C Buckley** volunteered from his local Army camp to turn out for a distinctly under-strength Fosse when they nonetheless ground out a 1-1 draw at Grimsby in December 1917. (1 app)

In the same game, which featured a pair of off-duty soldiers and an on-leave sailor in Fosse's makeshift line-up, an otherwise unknown player named **Burton** held the right-half position. (1 app)

A winger from the Birmingham area, **E Burton** first took the Fosse right flank on a trial basis in the March 1917 game at Nottingham Forest, and appeared once more a year later for the final fixture of 1917/18 at Birmingham. (2 apps)

A son of the Chelsea (and former Lincoln City) manager of the same name, **David Calderhead** (b. Dumfries, ca.1891) was a centre-half who had signed on at Stamford Bridge directly from Lincoln schools football in September 1907, and had not left the paternal orbit until transferring to Motherwell in April 1914. He was in Fosse's initial WW1 line-up in September 1915, staying for three months, and also guested for Notts County and, once more, Chelsea. Postwar, David signed for Clapton Orient in 1919, and then himself became manager at Lincoln from 1921-24. He was later licensee of the Newmarket Hotel in Sincil Street, Lincoln. (8 apps)

A free-scoring centre-forward in the pre-war years (and again as a veteran afterwards), **James Cantrell** (b.Sheepbridge, 7.5.1882; d. Basford, 31.7.1960) played for Fosse in the home defeat by Bradford City on Easter Tuesday 1917, having scored against them for Notts County in each of the previous Saturday and Monday holiday games. Having learned his football with Bulwell Red Rose, Bulwell White Star and Hucknall Constitutionals, Jimmy had joined Aston Villa in July 1904, moved to Notts County in March 1908, and to Tottenham Hotspur in October 1912. Most of his WW1 football was played back at Meadow Lane, but he continued with Spurs after the war, earning a 1921 FA Cup-winners medal, until released to Sutton United in October 1923. (1 app)

Barnsley's young centre-forward **G Chapman** was borrowed by Fosse (along with team-mate Jack Gittins) to make up the numbers for their fixture at Leeds City in January 1918. (1 app)

Otherwise unidentified by the local press at the time, **W Clarke** featured on Fosse's left flank at Bradford Park Avenue in February 1917. (1 app)

T Cope, a friend of regular guest Richard Gibson's from a Birmingham junior team, played ('ineffectively') at outside-left for Fosse at Bradford Park Avenue in October 1915; having been called in after George Harrison missed his train. (1 app)

Frank R Crowe (b. Birmingham, 1893), an inside-forward who made 14 wartime appearances for Birmingham following his April 1917 signing from Apollo Works FC, assisted Fosse against his own club in April 1918. Curiously, after an August 1919 move to Coventry City, both his League appearances for his new team were as a 'vigorous' wing-half against Leicester. Frank then moved on to Merthyr Town in 1920, to Chesterfield in May 1922, Rochdale in June 1923, and back to Merthyr in 1924; finishing his career with Penrhiwceiber after 1925. (1 app)

Another Brummie from junior football tried out by Fosse was **J Crutchley**, who played in two November 1916 defeats at right-half. (2 apps)

Chesterfield full-back **Percy H Cullin** featured in a 1-5 defeat at Notts County in October 1916, and also guested for Nottingham Forest in this period. Prior to his Saltergate signing, Percy had been on the books of Belper Town, Ilkeston United and Derby County. (1 app)

Another of the many to briefly swap military khaki for Fosse's blue and white stripes was Sapper **Dalton**, fielded at outside-right at Hull City in December 1917. (1 app)

A former Birmingham St.Georges and Evesham player, **Arthur G Davis** (b. Birmingham, ca.1900) had an extended trial with Fosse at inside-right in December 1918 and January 1919, and also played wartime football for Coventry City and Aston Villa. It was the latter club, however, which signed him up for peacetime action (in July 1919), and his subsequent career took him on to Queens Park Rangers (May 1922), Notts County (February 1924) -- where he formed a left-wing partnership with Len Barry -- and Crystal Palace (May 1928. He ended his playing days with Kidderminster Harriers after a 1929 move. (6 apps; 4 goals)

A previous occupant of the inside-right berth in that final WW1 season was Asfordby's **George Davis**, a scorer on his October 1918 debut in a 5-3 home win over Grimsby Town. (3 apps; 1 goal)

Lieutenant **Day** of the Leicestershire Regiment featured as Fosse's right-back at Hull in March 1917, and then skippered his regimental team against Fosse in a friendly two months later. (1 app)

Though he made a pair of consecutive forward appearances for Fosse in November 1916, **T Day** was confusingly described in successive weeks as hailing from a junior Birmingham club, and as 'a local man living in Derby'. (2 apps)

Local winger **George Thomas Dennis** (b. Moira, 12.9.1897; d. Burton-on-Trent, 13.10.1969) made his Fosse bow in friendly games in March 1917, but didn't break through to competitive wartime football until December 1918. His roster of junior clubs included Stanton, Coalville Swifts and Newhall Swifts; while his career took off in the League sphere when peace returned. George took the opposite Nottingham Forest flank to Sid Harrold from February 1921; moved to Luton Town (where he claimed 42 goals in the 1924 close season; to Norwich City in May 1929; and to Bristol Rovers for the 1930/1 season, throughout which he played at leftback. At both Kenilworth Road and Eastville, he was regarded as a penalty expert. (5 apps; 1 goal)

Borrowed by Fosse from home club Coventry City in March 1919, when Jack Parker failed to turn up, inside-left **Harry Dobson** (b. Newcastle, ca 1891) had joined Coventry in May 1913 from North Shields Athletic and starred in their pre-war Southern League line-up. Within months of his Fosse outing, 'Dobbin' was on his way to Newport County, and in

February 1922 moved to Southend United for a three-year stint, before finishing his career with Rugby Town. (1 app)

A Fosse regular on the left wing throughout 1917/18, and again at the start of the following season, **David Morgan Donald** (b. Coatbridge, 21.7.1885; d. Derby, 19.1.1932) had begun his career with Albion Rovers (July 1905) before successive moves to Bradford Park Avenue (June 1908), Derby County (March 1910), Chesterfield (June 1912), Watford (June 1913), and Queens Park Rangers (in the 1914 close season). He assisted Derby again during WW1, and in July 1922 moved briefly homeward with Hamilton Academical. (42 apps; 3 goals)

Raised in Leicester from the age of 10, **Alec Donaldson** (Alexander Pollock; b. Barrhead, 4.12.1892) played local football for Belgrave Primitive Methodists, Balmoral United and Ripley Athletic, and had trials with Sheffield United in March 1911, but was snapped up by Bolton Wanderers in December of that year, and went on to win six Scottish caps and appear in an additional trio of Victory internationals. The skilful outside-right was brought back to Leicester by wartime munitions factory work and turned out for Fosse in every WW1 season but 1916/17. He also assisted Arthurlie during this period, then picked up his Burnden Park career until a March 1922 move to Sunderland. Alec signed for Manchester City in May 1923, then later served Chorley (for six seasons) and Ashton National. While with Fosse, he once scored direct from a corner, but before such skill (or fortune!) was recognised by the laws of the game. (51 apps; 6 goals)

A youthful Bradford City reserve full-back, **George Draycott** was working at Church Gresley when given a break by Fosse in December 1916, and went on to give consistent service until the end of the following season. Tragically, though, he was killed in action in France in November 1918. (44 apps)

Twice borrowed by Fosse from their Lincoln City hosts, in November 1915 and February 1917, left-sided defender **John Dunne** (b. Donnybrook, ca.1890) had been at Sincil Bank since June

1914, when he signed from Shelbourne. With that club he had won an Irish Cup-winner's medal in 1911, and in 1913 had represented the Irish League against the Scottish League. John also played wartime football for Rustons Aircraftmen and RAF Cranwell, and his postwar moves took in Mid-Rhondda (June 1919), Boston Town (1921) and Horncastle Town. (2 apps)

A guesting Fossil for a year from December 1915, **Harold Edgley** (b. Crewe, 1892; d. Birmingham, 1966) was an Aston Villa outside-left who'd signed up from Whitchurch in February 1911, and had briefly been loaned to Stourbridge during 1913. He additionally assisted Birmingham, West Brom and Port Vale during WW1 before resuming his Villa Park career, which hit its nadir when Harold broke his leg a week before the 1920 FA Cup Final, after he had played in every round and scored the semi-final winner. He moved on to Queens Park Rangers in June 1921, and signed for Stockport County in August 1923; dropping down a year later into Cheshire non-league football. Harold subsequently acted as a Notts County director. (32 apps; 2 goals)

N Edwards was 'a Birmingham lad' given a trial at outside-left by Fosse on the same day as Tommy Roberts, in a 3-2 away win over Notts County in April 1917. (1 app)

Another unheralded and unsuccessful right-wing trialist was **A Ellis**, who faced Nottingham Forest in a 1-0 home win in March 1918. (1 app)

One of the quartet of unknowns recruited by Fosse at Grimsby in October 1918 was outside-left **A Faulconer**. The emergency was created when four selected men (Davis, Donald, Price and Underwood) all missed the train. (1 app)

A local journalist on Bradford City's books as an amateur, **E Fearnley** was twice borrowed by Fosse for away games at Bradford Park Avenue, playing at inside-right in February and December 1917. He also assisted Park Avenue themselves, and Huddersfield Town, during the war years. (2 apps)

On leave from service as a stoker on a minesweeper, **G A Foreman** volunteered to make up Fosse's depleted numbers at Grimsby in December 1917, and took the right-wing berth in the 1-1 draw. (1 app)

A former Leeds City reserve, **N Fox** was recruited at the last minute by Fosse to complete their weakened eleven at Leeds in January 1916; forming an eccentric right-wing partnership with long-retired ex-Burnley goalkeeper Billy Green! (1 app)

At inside-left in Fosse's first fistful of WW1 fixtures was **Charlie Freeman** (Charles Redfern; b. Overseal, 17.3.1956), who had graduated via Overseal Swifts and Burton United to Chelsea in 1907, and had scored 22 goals in 95 League games for them before war broke out. He added 21 wartime goals to his Stamford Bridge haul before a move to Gillingham in June 1921, then joined Maidstone United in June 1923. On ceasing playing, Charlie returned to Chelsea for the rest of his working life: initially as trainer, then as groundsman until 1953. (5 apps)

Alongside his near-namesake in Fosse's inaugural wartime line-up was **Neddy Freeman** (Edwin; b. Northampton, 1886; d. Northampton, 7.12.1945), a centre-forward whose career had false-started with trials for Stoke in 1904, but who then served his hometown club from 1906 to 1921 (and nearly made the County Ground a full-time workplace, appearing there additionally as an occasional Northants cricketer between 1908 and 1920). Neddy stuck with Fosse until November 1917, and also turned out for Spurs later in the war. (35 apps; 10 goals)

Corporal **Billy George** (William Samuel; b. Aston, 1895), who had been playing for Austin Motor Works, and had made one friendly appearance for Aston Villa during 1916/17, assisted Fosse at right-half at Coventry in March 1919. For the 1919/20 season, he was on Merthyr Town's books, then transferred to Sunderland in August 1920, but only made two First Division appearances prior to joining Shildon in the following close season. (1 app)

An outside- or inside-right who had been on Birmingham's books since signing from Sultan FC in

September 1911, **Richard Samuel Gibson** (b. Holborn, 1889) made most of his Fosse wartime appearances during 1915/16, when his own club had shut down; though he later briefly reappeared in January 1919 when an army Private stationed at Bradford. After the war, he remained at St.Andrews until a £250 move in June 1921 to Manchester United. (19 apps; 7 goals)

A Barnsley full-back from 1914, when signed from Bentley Colliery, to October 1926, when he moved to Chesterfield, **Jack Gittins** (John Henry; b. Stanton Hill, 11.11.1893; d. Bentley, 8.10.1956) amassed a 259-game peacetime record for the Tykes. He was borrowed by Fosse in January 1918 as an emergency fill-in for the game at Leeds City. (1 app)

On trial from a Mansfield club in January 1917 was **J W Goddard**, who featured as a right-sided forward in successive games at Grimsby and at home to Notts County. (2 apps)

The unrelated **Sidney H Goddard** (d. Leicester, 18.5.1970) was a Leicester Imperial forward who made sporadic entries into the Fosse line-up in the first three wartime seasons, but never in a winning side. (4 apps)

A familiar tale: "With Vlaminck having to go to London for medical examination, King down with influenza, Donald unfit, Bailey unable to play, and Nottingham out of bounds to soldiers, Fosse had to make drastic changes ..." for their game at Notts County in November 1918. One otherwise unidentified draftee was inside-right **Green**. (1 app)

Coaxed from the crowd awaiting the game at Leeds City in January 1916, **Billy Green** (William John; b. Gravesend, 1882) was given the Fosse right-wing berth for the day -- despite the fact that he was a long-retired goalkeeper! Billy had started his career with Gravesend, moved to Brentford in 1910, and to Burnley in 1903. After 147 League games between their sticks, he transferred for the last time in December 1908 to Bradford Park Avenue, retiring in 1910. (1 app)

Uncommented upon by the local press despite his trio of Fosse

outings during March and April 1917 was full-back **G.Hampton**, who we presume to have been a local trialist. (3 apps)

Fosse were still picking up obscure talent to make up their numbers at Leeds in September 1916, when local lad **H Hawden** featured at outside-right. (1 app)

Chesterfield left-half **Henry Crookes Hibbert** was another emergency stand-in for Fosse, at Sheffield United in April 1916. He had started his career with Hathersage, and moved on to Sheffield Wednesday (cs 1907), Stockport County (March 1908), Lincoln City (July 1909), Rotherham County (cs 1911), and Sheffield United (April 1913); in each case predominantly as a reserve player. He also guested for Rotherham during WW1. (1 app)

Fosse's centre-forward at Nottingham Forest in January 1919 was **Leonard G Hopkins**, who also guested for Coventry City during WW1, but who had been on Cardiff City's books since a November 1913 move from Brierley Hill Alliance. (1 app)

Overseal outside-left **G Jordan** was deemed 'not clever enough' by the local *Post* after his Fosse outing at Bradford City in October 1918. He was useful enough, however, to be borrowed by the Bantams when they paid the return visit to Filbert Street a week later. (1 app)

A youngster on Aston Villa's books who failed to beak through to their senior side in either wartime or peacetime football, **J H Joyce** turned out at inside-right for Fosse at Huddersfield Town in October 1916. (1 app)

Fosse's centre-forward in home and away fixtures with Leeds City in 1918/19 was **Frank Bernard Kirrage** (b. Bromley, 3.3.1893; d. Fiskerton, 25.1.1933), who also guested for Blackpool as well as making a wartime breakthrough with his own club, Nottingham Forest. He failed, though, to make more than a single subsequent League appearance for Forest (who he had originally joined after stints with Mapperley and Bulwell), and moved on to Ilkeston United in 1920. (2 apps; 1 goal)

J W Lambert was the outside-right of local club Belvoir S.S.

when given a Fosse trial at Lincoln City in November 1915. (1 app)

Harry William Lane (b. Stoney Stanton, 23.10.1894) was a part-time player and schoolmaster before the war but had still to make a League bow when Fosse gave him a senior break in December 1915, playing him in both wing-half spots as well as at inside-right and centre-forward. The former Hinckley United player had spent 1912/13 on Forest's books and the following term with Notts County, but was by then with Sutton Town. Only days after his final Fosse outing in January 1916, Harry signed up with the Royal Flying Corps. Finally, after the war, he made a minor splash in London football: with West Ham United from May 1919, Charlton Athletic from May 1921, and Queens Park Rangers from June 1922. His Fosse debut match against Bradford City lasted only 73 minutes due to bad weather, and was played without a half-time break. (4 apps; 1 goal)

A Fosse stalwart at left-half throughout the entire WW1 period, despite never officially switching his registration from Aston Villa, **Jimmy Leach** (James McIntyre; b. Spennymoor, 1890) had originally signed up at Villa Park in August 1912 from North-Eastern football, and remained there until a July 1922 move to Queens Park Rangers, who he represented only once. (102 apps; 1 goal)

Fosse's inside-right in a handful of successive games from September 1916, **Syd Leigh** (Alfred Sydney; b. Shardlow, 1893) had been a Derby County signing from local club Osmaston in June 1914, but he managed only a couple of League games for the Rams before joining Bristol Rovers in July 1920, and going on to become that club's top scorer in each of their first two seasons in the League. He also guested for Bradford City during WW1. (5 apps; 2 goals)

Another Ram to assist Fosse was **Harry Leonard** (Henry Doxford; b. Sunderland, 1886; d. Derby, 3.11.1951), who took the centre-forward shirt in the home defeat by Nottingham Forest in January 1919. He'd joined Newcastle United from Sunderland North End in November 1907, then transferred to Grimsby Town in

May 1908, Middlesbrough in March 1911, and Derby in October 1911. After 72 League goals in 144 games (and another 25 in 34 wartime appearances) for Derby, Harry moved to Manchester United in September 1920, and Heanor Town in June 1921. (1 app)

A Leyland, whose parent club affiliations -- if any -- remain unknown, guested at right-half for Fosse at Lincoln City in February 1917. (1 app)

Balmoral United centre-forward **J Longlands** (who'd also served Belgrave Athletic and Hinckley United before the war) got a couple of isolated run-outs for Fosse in heavy defeats -- 0-5 at Barnsley on Boxing Day 1916, and 2-4 at home to Leeds City in January 1918. The next month he was lent to Barnsley when they arrived at Filbert Street a man short: Fosse won 5-1! (2 apps)

W R Lowe was the mystery man at left-back when Fosse recruited four unknowns to their depleted ranks at Grimsby in October 1918. (1 app)

Described simply as 'a Birmingham youth', **J Machin** took the Fosse inside-left position in the 2-1 home win over Sheffield United in February 1919. (1 app)

E Marriott of Pinxton made a quartet of appearances as Fosse's outside-left from December 1916. (4 apps)

A Huddersfield Town reserve, **R May** was borrowed by Fosse to complete their line-up at Barnsley in December 1918, playing right half in a 2-3 defeat. (1 app)

A veteran whose first-class career was behind him, **Charles J H Millington** (b. Lincoln, 25.4.1884; d. Lincoln, 13.6.1955) assisted Fosse to a goalless draw at Birmingham in December 1917, taking the inside-right berth. His pre-war wanderings had taken him from Grantham to Ripley Athletic (Jan 1905), Aston Villa (Sept 1905), Fulham (Oct 1907), Birmingham (cs 1909), Wellington Town (1912), Brierley Hill (March 1913) and Stourbridge (April 1914). (1 app)

Seaman **H Minney**, a local player with Victoria Athletic and Standard Engineering Co FC prior to his Naval service, featured on the right wing in Fosse's December 1918 home defeat by Bradford Park Avenue. (1 app)

W Montgomery, an inside-forward from Birmingham works team Bellis & Morcom, spent three weeks as a Fossil in March 1916, scoring on his debut in a 5-2 away win at Derby. (3 apps; 1 goal)

Whitwick Imperial right winger **A Moore** had his sole Fosse outing on the opening day of season 1917/18, in a 1-2 defeat at Notts County. (1 app)

T Morrell, from Birmingham Suburban League side Redditch, was Fosse's inside-right trialist in a 2-2 home draw with Barnsley in February 1916. (1 app)

Drafted in as cover for the recently-bereaved Sam Currie in the home game with Hull City in February 1919, Coalville Swifts right-back **E Mugglestone** earned from the local *Post* the archaically unselfconscious comment that his performance was 'rather ragged'. (1 app)

Shirebrook outside-left **E Mullins** assisted Fosse at Nottingham Forest in March 1917, and also turned out in four games for Forest the following term, including their fixture at Filbert Street. (1 app)

T Murray was drafted into the Fosse team at outside-left when they arrived at Bradford Park Avenue in December 1917 extremely late and three men short. Indeed, the game kicked off with only eight Fossils on the pitch, and was severely foreshortened, so Murray's sole appearance lasted a mere 52 minutes. (1 app)

On the verge of a promising Aston Villa career when called a halt to League football, **Harry Nash** (Harold Edward; b. Fishponds, Bristol, 10.4.1892) had scored a hat-trick on his debut against Liverpool only two months after his February 1915 signing from Pontypridd. During the following term, however, he was playing for Bellis & Morcom in the Birmingham Suburban League; and a season later (from February 1917) guesting for Fosse. He failed to settle with Villa after the war, moving on to Coventry City in July 1920, to Cardiff City in February 1921, and Merthyr Town in May 1923; later finishing his career with Aberbargoed and Ystradmynach. Indeed, he had first started his wanderings in Wales, moving from Mardy to Aberdare in 1910, and to Pontypridd in 1913. (4 apps)

Only once during WW1 did Fosse resort to using in their line-up that most transparent of pseudonyms, **A Newman**. The identity of the outside-right in the home game with Lincoln City in October 1916 will ever remain a mystery: there is no mention of him in any of the local press reports; and the fact that Football League records credit Tommy Benfield with this appearance would seem misleading: Benfield played both before and afterwards under his own name and military rank, and would certainly have been recognised in a home game if subterfuge were intended. (1 app)

Stourbridge-born **Jack Nock** was a wartime discovery by Millwall, who signed him in October 1915 from his hometown club. A prolific centre-forward, he returned to the Midlands in 1919, and featured in Fosse's last eleven regional games, as well as scoring the last goal the club ever registered under that name (in a 1-1 friendly draw with the BEF [France] XI), before being resurrected as Leicester City. Nonetheless, Jack failed to gain a Filbert Street contract, and signed instead for Merthyr Town during the 1919 close season. Spells with Nuneaton Town, Tamworth Castle and Cradley Heath followed, until Cardiff City introduced him to the League sphere in March 1922. For Wrexham from November 1924 he bagged 22 goals in 65 League games, and later served Flint Town. (11 apps; 5 goals)

The brother of pre-war Fossil Fred, Lieutenant **G Osborn** was a former Hinckley United player who featured at inside-right in a trio of Fosse games in December 1917 and January 1918. He also assisted Hull City during WW1. (3 apps)

There is a possibility that the same man also played in the home and away fixtures with Nottingham Forest in April 1919, for the local press somewhat clouded the identity of Fosse's inside-right in these games. The consensus seems to be that Lieutenant **F Osborne**, an amateur on Lincoln City's books, was the player in question; but at least one paper gave his initial as 'G'. Just to add to the potential confusion, there have been claims advanced that Fosse's Fred Osborn was a Lincoln guest during this period..! (2 apps)

Borrowed from home team Hull City to face them as Fosse's centre-forward in March 1917, **Arthur Pace** (b. Newcastle, 1885; d. Hull, 1968) was a former wing-half who had initially signed for the Tigers from Hebburn Argyle in November 1907, and had subsequently moved to Rotherham Town (cs 1910) and Croydon Common (September 1911) before returning on the outbreak of war. He also assisted Sheffield United and Southport Central during WW1. (1 app)

Another to face his own club in Fosse colours was **George Padley** (b. Grimsby, 1882; d. 2.11.1965), a forward better known by his nickname, 'Punch'. Fosse were several men short when arriving at Grimsby in January 1917, and shocked the home team by romping home 3-1 winners with a distinctly makeshift lineup: Padley claiming one of the goals. Having first signed for Grimsby Town in 1904 from Grimsby St.Johns, he had made his final League appearance in 1906, spending the interim years until the war largely with Worksop Town. 'Punch' was also a Lincolnshire cricketer. (1 app; 1 goal)

No details at all adhered to the right-half appearance of **G H Parker** in the September 1918 home win over Rotherham County: it is merely assumed that he was a local trialist. (1 app)

Few more bits of background information were forthcoming when Private **P Parker** featured at centre-forward in a handful of Fosse games in April 1916, beyond the fact that he'd recently impressed in an otherwise unrecorded friendly for the Pioneers against Fosse. (5 apps; 2 goals)

Harry Parsonage, who'd tasted League fare with Wolverhampton Wanderers between 1911 and 1913, moved into the Birmingham League with Shrewsbury Town, and would feature postwar at that level with Walsall, was a regular forward for Fosse during their generally goal-shy 1916/17 campaign. (17 apps; 5 goals)

A Peel, a right-back from 'a Northern club', 'made a moderate start' (according to the *Daily Post*) in a goalless home draw with Leeds City in February 1919, but never played again. (1 app)

A rather more famous full-back, who featured for Fosse in the Christmas Day and Boxing Day games against Birmingham in 1918, was **Jesse Pennington** (b. West Bromwich, 23.8.1883; d. Stourbridge, 5.9.1970). The eventual winner of 25 England caps between 1907 and 1920, he had signed for West Bromwich Albion from Dudley Town in March 1903, and remained, in peacetime at least, a one-club man until retirement in 1922. During WW1, however, his services were also lent to Birmingham, Coventry City, Notts County, Manchester United and Oldbury Town. (2 apps)

A local given a chance after a Fosse trial appearance at Belvoir S.S., inside-right **Cecil Harry Phipps** (b. Leicester 25.10.1896; d. Leicester, 24.9.1968) faced Coventry City away in March 1919, played in the final Fosse friendly against the BEF (France) XI the following month, and was offered an amateur contract by City for 1919/20. [One source traces him as then turning up in West Ham United colours for a single senior outing in September 1919 and, after an August 1921 move, appearing at outside-left in Halifax Town's first-ever League line-up. Other West Ham sources, though, identify their man by the initial 'R']. (1 app)

One of the players recruited at the ground when Fosse arrived three men short at Bradford Park Avenue in December 1917, **S Pollard** took the outside-right position. He also played a single WW1 game for Park Avenue on the left wing. (1 app)

A former Southern League representative player, **Harry Pullen** (b. Wellingborough, 1888) featured at right-back for Fosse at Lincoln City in November 1915. He'd joined Queens Park Rangers from Kettering in June 1910, and amassed a 187-game record in the Southern League before a transfer to Newport County exactly ten years later. A further move, to Hartlepools United in June 1921, was stymied when Harry contracted appendicitis. (1 app)

A wartime player for Notts County, **B Pykett** was another to answer Fosse's emergency call for the game at Grimsby Town in January 1917, when he held the centre-forward spot. (1 app)

Formerly a winger with Colne, Sunderland (April 1910), Chelsea (May 1911) and Dundee (March 1913), **William H Read** figured on Fosse's right flank at Hull City in March 1919, in one of eleven jerseys borrowed from the home club after Fosse's kit skip went astray en route. (1 app)

A centre-forward named **Roach** was one of Fosse's otherwise anonymous foursome of temporary recruits at Grimsby in October 1918. (1 app)

The only genuine Fosse discovery of the WW1 era to go on to full international honours was future England centre-forward **Tommy Roberts** (William Thomas; b. Handsworth, 29.11.1898; d. Preston, 13.10.1965). Previously experienced only in Birmingham area junior football (with Kentish Rovers, Boyce Engineers, Lord Street and Soho Villa), Tommy threw in his lot with Fosse in April 1917, and soon hit the goal trail. Disappointingly, in late 1918, his war work enforced a change of residence to Lancashire, and Southport Vulcan utilised his playing services for much of the final WW1 season; while Preston North End leapt in for his professional signature in the following close season. He was twice capped in 1924, and moved to Burnley in October of that year (scoring a hat-trick against City in September 1925, shortly after recovery from a broken pelvis), but was back for a second stint at Preston from July 1926. After an aggregate total of 179 League and Cup goals for the Deepdale club, he had a brief stint with Tottenham Hotspur (May 1928), then finished his career back in Lancashire with Dick Kerr's FC (August 1929) and Chorley (October 1930). (32 apps; 24 goals)

Left-half **Joseph Roulson** (b. Sheffield, 7.10.1891) was on Birmingham's books (having signed from Cammell Laird FC in August 1912) at the time of his single Fosse outing, but was playing much of his wartime football in his home town. He guested occasionally for Sheffield Wednesday, but it was at Bramall Lane that Fosse borrowed him for their December 1916 meeting with United. Birmingham eventually transferred Joe to Swansea Town in August 1922, and he moved again in August 1924 to Clapton Orient. (1 app)

Corporal **H Sarson** was a bandsman in the Leicestershire Regiment when he appeared as a right-sided forward for Fosse in February and March 1918. (4 apps; 1 goal)

Chesterfield winger **G Sharp** helped out Fosse at Sheffield United in April 1916, and then appeared several times the following season after a December outing for Fosse against his own team. (9 apps; 1 goal)

A single pre-war League outing for Aston Villa (plus a trio of wartime games) was the sole top-level experience of **Herbert Horace Smart** when he took Fosse's spearhead role in the February 1919 home win over Sheffield United. He'd originally signed up at Villa Park from Bilston United in January 1914. (1 app)

Borrowed from Rotherham County when Fosse faced them in November 1917, and positioned on the right wing, **Jack Smelt** (John William) was a versatile clubman who even occasionally turned out in goal for the club which also regularly featured his brother Len at full-back. Previously experienced with Mansfield Mechanics and Chesterfield Municipals before his Millmoor stint, Jack later served Portsmouth (both as goalkeeper and forward from October 1919), Sheffield Wednesday (from January 1921) and Barrow (from 1922). He also guested for Leeds City and Bradford City during WW1. Brother Len became a noted postwar Burnley player, and another brother, Tom, kicked off a lengthy, multi-club centre-forward career with Accrington Stanley in 1922. (1 app)

Whitwick Imperial right-half **F Smith** appeared in a trio of Fosse defeats from December 1916. (3 apps)

Recently demobbed, and reputed to have once been a junior on Notts County's books, **George R Smith** settled into Fosse's right-back position for three months at the tail end of 1918/19. (9 apps)

S Smith had a handful of outings at outside-right and right-half after December 1916, when his local club was Newhall Swifts; and added a further right-wing selection in October 1918, when identified as a Stanton player. (6 apps; 1 goal)

T Smith was a Mansfield defender, recommended by former Army football colleague Charlie Storer, who got a Fosse break at right-back in a 2-4 defeat at Leeds City in January 1919. (1 app)

A trialist right winger from Birmingham junior football, **J Southwell** played in the home defeat by Hull City in November 1916. (1 app)

The surprise 3-1 win at Grimsby achieved by Fosse's patchwork eleven in January 1917 was materially aided by a goalscoring contribution from **Colin Stainsby**, borrowed on the day from the home club (who used him themselves only under wartime conditions). Fosse also had to borrow a magenta strip on this day, with their own lost in transit. (1 app; 1 goal)

Balmoral United and former Hinckley United forward **A M Stanton** figured in Fosse's front line in both home and away fixtures with Sheffield United in February 1919, scoring in the initial home win. (2 apps; 1 goal)

Former Mexborough right-back **J Stern** was a late addition to the Fosse line-up at Barnsley in December 1916 which went down 0-5. (1 app)

A centre-forward turned centre-half who had moved from Gresley Rovers to Bradford City in February 1913, **Charles Storer** (b. Ibstock, 29.3.1891) spent much of the war back in Leicestershire when not on Army service, and became a regular for both Fosse and Coalville Swifts from late 1916, usually in the pivotal position. By the time Bradford City let him move on to Hartlepools United in September 1924, Charlie had amassed a record of 208 League appearances (13 goals) for them. (71 apps; 2 goals)

Sid Storer was Charlie's brother, a Coalville Swifts right-half, who made exactly half of his sporadic Fosse appearances between January 1917 and January 1918 in Charlie's company. He later played for Ibstock Colliery. (8 apps)

One of two youths borrowed for the first game of the 1916/17 season at Elland Road was Leeds City reserve **E F Sturdy**, who managed a goal for Fosse in the

2-2 draw, yet never forced his way into the reckoning for his own club. (1 app; 1 goal)

Aaron Swain, the Coalville Swifts right-winger, signed amateur forms for Fosse in April 1917, but faded from the first-team picture after his final game the following September. (9 apps; 2 goals)

Loughborough Corinthians forward **A Thurman** filled in for Fosse at inside-left in their away game with Sheffield Wednesday in November 1916. The previous January he had guested for Notts County. (1 app)

Left-sided half-back or forward **W Timmins** was borrowed from Nottingham Forest for the City Ground fixture in December 1916. He made 27 wartime appearances for Forest after 8 for Derby County; it remains unclear at present, however, if he was the same player of this name who turned out during WW1 for Lincoln City and Chesterfield. (1 app)

More regularly a wartime player for Notts County, **A Turner** was Fosse's inside-left in their game at Birmingham on Christmas Day 1917. (1 app)

Originally a pre-war reserve, unlucky enough to have broken his leg before gaining a senior try-out, **Joe Tyler** held the army rank of sergeant when belatedly handed the Fosse inside-right berth at Barnsley in February 1918. Only recently recovered from a long bout of trench fever, he was nonetheless deemed to look overweight by the *Post's* match reporter. (1 app)

A Coalville right-back who signed on for Fosse prior to the final WW1 season of 1918/19, **J Underwood** became a regular only until the following January, and failed to win a peacetime contract. (21 apps)

Belgian soldier **Honore Vlaminck**, wounded in 1914, recuperated in Leicester with a number of his compatriots, and was well enough to turn out for Leicester Imperial from March 1915. Fosse gave him a chance at a higher level in November 1918, just before his repatriation, and he showed signs of real class in the centre-forward shirt. In his second game, a 7-3 home win over Sheffield Wednesday, he claimed two scoring headers and missed a

penalty, and he was also on the mark against Huddersfield a fortnight later. Back in Brussels, he played for Daring (champions in 1921) and won four full caps for Belgium between 1919 and 1923, scoring four times. (4 apps; 3 goals)

Sergeant-Major **L Wale** was one of several military volunteers from a local camp to help Fosse fulfil their fixture at Grimsby in December 1917; taking the centre-half role in a 1-1 draw. (1 app)

Gunner **G H Walker**, otherwise a Notts County reserve left-back, joined his Meadow Lane club-mate Jimmy Cantrell in guesting for Fosse in their home game against Bradford City in April 1917. (1 app)

Fosse's top scorer in 1915/16 -- when his own club, Birmingham, were not playing competitive football -- centre-forward **Billy Walker** (William Baird; b. New Cumnock, 5.5.1893) also claimed Fosse's first two hat-tricks of the wartime period from home games with Leeds City and Hull City. Having started his career in his native Scotland with New Cumnock and Lugar Boswell, Billy had a spell with Bradford City between August 1911 and March 1913, then returned north to minor club Lanemark. Birmingham reintroduced him to the League game in November 1913 and held his registration until the close season of 1919, when he transferred to Coventry City. A year later he moved to Merthyr Town, claiming that club's first-ever League goal; then transferred successively to Bristol City (October 1922; helping seal their Third Division South championship) and Sheffield Wednesday (October 1923) before taking the player/manager's role at Weymouth from 1924. During WW1 Billy also turned out briefly for Aston Villa and Bradford City, scoring against Fosse for the latter in April 1917, when serving as a Sapper in the Royal Engineers. (26 apps; 13 goals)

The pre-war full-back partner to Walter Essom with Leicester Imperial, **Bert Waterfield** had just become an army Private when Fosse briefly utilised his services in April 1916. Soon, after only a month at the front in France and a promotion to Lance-Corporal, he was dead, killed in action on 27.7.1916, aged 23. (2 apps)

J Watson, a right-back from a Nottingham works team, played in Fosse's last competitive WW1 fixture, a 2-4 home defeat by Birmingham in April 1919. (1 app)

Despite playing in every game of Fosse's June 1913 tour of Sweden, Croydon-born centre-half **George A Webber** never got another senior outing in his year at Filbert Street; and it was only under wartime conditions that he played competitive football for Fosse. A 1912 signing by Southern League Croydon Common from Croydon Gas Co FC, he had followed his former manager Jack Bartlett to Leicester, and moved on with his boss in 1914 to Swansea Town. At the start of the following season, George was back with Croydon Common (soon to fold), and then featured with Balmoral United in local Leicester circles. Strangely, of his sporadic Fosse appearances between April 1916 and April 1917, two were on the left wing. In 1919, George was with Atherstone Town. (4 apps)

'A local youth' with some wartime experience with Barnsley, **A Whiteman** was borrowed by Fosse to play as their right-half in the February 1918 game at Oakwell. (1 app)

A Rotherham soldier already honoured with the DCM, Private **G W Whitworth** assisted Fosse at inside-left against his own club in the clash with Rotherham County in January 1917. (1 app)

Lance-Corporal **A Willmott** made up the Fosse numbers at Lincoln City in February 1917, playing on the right wing in a 0-1 defeat. (1 app)

Recommended to Fosse by then-regular guest G Sharp, Sheffield-based inside-right **G Willoughby** was tried out in the match at Hull City in March 1917, when Fosse's goal in a 1-2 defeat came from goalkeeper Herbert Bown's penalty kick. (1 app)

The most exotic of City's WW2 guests, **Emilio G Aldecoa** (b. Bilbao, 30.11.1922) was a refugee from the Spanish Civil War who signed for Wolves in 1943 (scoring for them against City in September 1944), guested in City's front line in four games during September and October 1945, then transferred to Coventry City, where he continued to play in postwar League football. Eventually returning to Spain in 1947 to join Athletic Bilbao, he later played for Valladolid and Barcelona, winning League and Cup honours with the latter. Emilio also won one Spanish cap (as substitute against the Republic of Ireland in May 1948). He was on the Barcelona coaching staff in the 50s and, briefly, chief coach at Birmingham City under Gil Merrick from 1960. (4 apps; 1 goal)

Primarily remembered for scoring in Walsall's celebrated 1933 giant-killing of Arsenal, **Gilbert Arthur Alsop** (b. Frampton Cotterell, 22.9.1908, d. Walsall, 16.4.1992) turned out eight times for City during 1943/4, though only twice in his accustomed centre-forward role. Gilbert joined Coventry City in December 1929 from Bath City, moved to Walsall in October 1931, to West Brom in November 1935, to Ipswich Town in June 1937, and back to Walsall in November 1938, playing until 1947. Of his 157 League goals, 151 were for the Saddlers; but his 106 wartime goals were accrued for a host of clubs, including Coventry, Bristol Rovers, Mansfield, Luton and Northampton. On Walsall's groundstaff for twenty years after his playing retirement, Gilbert had the honour of having a stand at the new Bescot Stadium named after him. (8 apps; 3 goals)

Tom Ansell was an 18-year-old amateur whose sole City appearance was at outside-left away to Northampton in February 1940. His local clubs had been Humberstone St.Mary's and Petronians. (1 app)

Derek O Ashton (b. Worksop, 4.7.1922) had already figured on the City scoresheet (with an own goal for Wolves in March 1945) by the time he became a City guest (the only such in Johnny Duncan's first managerial selection) at right-back in the home game with Coventry in March 1946. Derek never made a peacetime appearance for Wolves, who he

joined in 1941, but got eight League outings for Aston Villa after a May 1946 transfer, and before a 1949 move to Wellington Town. (1 app)

When both Sep Smith and Fred Kilshaw missed their train to join City's party at Charlton Athletic in September 1945, **Arthur Attwood** was recruited as an emergency guest at outside-right. An old RAF colleague of Dai Jones, who had intended spectating, Arthur was also reported to have been an old Bristol Rovers player: if so, he was definitely at the veteran stage, as records show 43-year-old Arthur Albert Attwood (b. Walsall, 1.12.1901; d. Hove, 6.12.1974) to have retired almost ten years previously after a career at centre-forward which had taken in Walsall (January 1928), Everton (March 1929), Bristol Rovers (May 1930), Brighton & Hove Albion (November 1931) and Northfleet (August 1935). (1 app)

A City Colt during 1941/2, signed as an amateur after being spotted in Hinckley ATC football, **William P Barnes** played twice at left-half in home and away fixtures against Bristol City in May 1942. (2 apps)

A City regular on the right wing during 1941/2 and 1942/3, **Harry Barratt** (b. Headington, 25.12.1918, d. Coventry, 23.9.1989) was the son of Fosse's WW1 player Josiah Barratt. On Coventry City's books from December 1935 (when signed from Herbert's Athletic) to 1952, Harry was a sergeant in the Royal Warwickshire Regiment during the retreat from Dunkirk, then engaged in industrial war work. He also guested for Nottingham Forest and Walsall. After cutting his football links following spells as manager of Rugby Town, Snowdown Colliery, Gillingham (1957-62) and Tunbridge Wells, and an interim stint as Coventry's chief scout, Harry became national coach and secretary to the British Crown Green Bowls Association. (45 apps; 16 goals)

One of two guests in City's first competitive WW2 game, Northampton's **Bill Barron** (William; b. Herrington, 26.10.1917) scored the final goal in a 6-1 win over Walsall from the outside-left position,

R. IVERSON (ASTON VILLA)

FREDERICK STEELE, Stoke City F.C. Topical Times

and continued to feature occasionally throughout 1939/40. An October 1937 Charlton Athletic signing from Annfield Plain (after having been an unsuccessful Wolves trialist in November 1936), Bill moved to Northampton in May 1938, and stayed thirteen years before joining Kettering. A pre-war cricketer for Durham, he turned out in the County Championship afterwards for Lancashire and Northants. His son Roger was a Cobblers goalkeeper in the 60s. (7 apps; 1 goal)

Nottingham Forest centre-half **Bill Baxter** (William Amelius; b. Nottingham, 6.9.1917; d. Nottingham, 21.2.1992) assisted City twice in March 1945, in home and away Cup games against Derby, and also guested for Notts County, Mansfield and Derby during the war. A professional with Forest from December 1936, Bill crossed the Trent to Meadow Lane in October 1946, and finished his career with Grantham after a 1954 move. (2 apps)

Briefly stationed at Old Dalby, at the RAOC's Central Ordnance Depot (and playing Leicestershire Senior League football for his unit), Scottish international full-back **Andy Beattie** (b. Kintore, 11.8.1913, d. Nottingham, 20.9.1983) was recruited for a quartet of City games in December 1939 and January 1940. A Preston North End signing from Inverurie Loco in March 1935, Andy had appeared in two Wembley Cup Finals and won seven caps before the war, and retired in 1947 as essentially a one-club man. During WW2, however, he also guested for Notts County, Aldershot, Northampton, Derby, Manchester City, Clapton Orient, and Bradford City, and played four wartime internationals; while on retirement he commenced a managerial merry-go-round which encompassed stints with Barrow, Stockport, Huddersfield, Carlisle, Nottingham Forest, Plymouth and Wolves; as well as two spells as boss of Scotland's international team, and other backroom roles at Notts County and Sheffield United. Andy had scored an own goal for City to settle the home game with Preston in November 1937. (4 apps)

Noted for his all-action enthusiasm at full-back, Arbroath

stalwart **Attilio Becci** guested for City during 1943/4. A 1932 signing for his Scottish club, where he was familiarly known as 'Teel', he also turned out for Notts County during WW2, and represented a high-quality British Army XI in Naples in 1945. (8 apps)

Mick Betteridge (Raymond Michael; b. Redditch, 11.8.1924) was a Loughborough College student when he made his sole City appearance (as inside-right at Aston Villa in December 1942), and had previously played for Leicester Nomads. It was some time later, however, before he made his senior mark, signing for West Bromwich Albion in November 1948, for Swindon Town in January 1951, and for Chester in March 1954. With the latter club he was a Welsh Cup medallist as runner-up in the 1954 Final. (1 app)

Struggling to raise eleven men for the final fixture of 1942/3, at Stoke, City borrowed amateur winger **W J Birks** from the then-inactive Port Vale to help make up the side. Birks made but a trio of wartime appearances for Vale in 44/5, and then faded into obscurity. (1 app)

An 18-year-old amateur on Arsenal's books when he burst into City's seniors in October 1943, **Norman H Bowden** (b. Glossop, ca.1925) made such an immediate impact that the Gunners took the insurance-policy step of signing him professionally the next month. The prolific centre-forward had his City stint (in which he was 1943/4's top scorer) interrupted by RAF aircrew training in Florida, and before the war was out had survived baling out of his burning aircraft at 10,000 feet. Norman also guested for Burnley, Wolves, Blackburn and Manchester United, yet curiously made no peacetime League appearances for Arsenal or anyone else. (23 apps; 14 goals)

'Sailor' Brown (Robert Albert John; b. Great Yarmouth, 7.11.1915) was known as such because of his rolling gait, for he served with the Auxiliary Police and then the RAF during the war. His single City outing (as inside-right in a defeat at West Brom in October 1944) was but one of many guest appearances for the Charlton schemer, who also

turned out briefly for Wolves, Manchester City, Millwall, Luton, Newcastle, West Ham, Chelsea, Aldershot, York, Huddersfield and East Fife during wartime. Previously, he had signed on at The Valley from Gorleston in August 1934. He had toured South Africa with the FA in 1939, and won seven wartime caps for England, but moved on to Forest in May 1946, to Aston Villa in October 1947, and back to Gorleston (as player/manager) in June 1949. (1 app)

J H Browne was a military policeman and unblooded Aston Villa junior when he turned out at inside-left for City at home to Stoke in April 1943. (1 app)

A Scottish League representative while on Celtic's books (signed January 1933 from Grange Rovers), **Willie Buchan** (William Ralston Murray; b. Grangemouth, 17.10.1914) had been since November 1937 a Blackpool inside-forward, and was in the RAF when he made a quintet of City appearances from March 1942. Also winning one Scottish wartime cap, Willie similarly turned out during the hostilities for Manchester United, Aberaman, Bristol City, Fulham, Bath City, Hamilton Academical and Stenhousemuir. Postwar, he moved to Hull City in January 1948, to Gateshead in November 1949, to Coleraine (as player/manager) in July 1953, and to East Stirling in January 1954. Pre-war, when he'd scored the winner in the 1937 Scottish Cup Final, it had been before a British record crowd at Hampden of 146,433. (5 apps; 2 goals)

A teenaged Wigston winger, **Maurice C Buckby** had already had one 1943/4 outing for the youth-oriented Wolves when he signed amateur forms for City in December 1944, going on to play one game on either flank for City in the two months thereafter. (2 apps)

Aptly christened, **Charles Guest Bulger** (b. Manchester, 19.1.1915, d. Ipswich, 18.6.1976) was a Walsall forward who turned out once for City in April 1942, and several times in 1943/4, usually at outside-left. Signed by Birmingham from Congleton Town in May 1934, he had moved to Lincoln City in June 1935, and to Fellows Park in May 1936. He played no senior football postwar;

though was reported to be coaching in Trinidad in 1947. (10 apps; 1 goal)

A Leicestershire talent City had missed, **Ken Burditt** (Frederick Charles Kendall; b. Ibstock, 12.11.1906, d. Ibstock, 27.10.1977) was at the end of his career when called for a quartet of inside-forward outings in 1940/1, and one as emergency centre-half in the final game of 1942/3. A product of Ibstock Penistone Rovers and Gresley Rovers, Ken had joined Norwich City in November 1930, Millwall in August 1936, Notts County in January 1938, and Southern League Colchester United in May 1939. The war years also saw him turning out for Ibstock Colliery and Pegsons (and once, at Filbert Street, for an under-strength Spurs), before he became player/manager back at Ibstock PR. Ken's brother Les had been a City trialist in March 1933; while his brother George played League football for Millwall, Forest and Wrexham. (5 apps)

Sergeant **W Carver**, a forward on Arbroath's books, was based in Leicester as a PT instructor, and playing for his unit, 23rd PTC, in the Senior League, when chosen by City at inside-left for their trip to Notts County in October 1942. He scored in a 1-1 draw. (1 app; 1 goal)

A Lincoln-born teenager promoted from the Colts after a hat-trick display, **George Chapman** made a couple of senior appearances at centre-forward (home and away to Birmingham) in September 1943. (2 apps)

Goalkeeper **Arthur Chesters** (b. Salford, 14.2.1910) assisted City's run in the 1940/1 League War Cup - eventually to end at the semi-final stage. A pre-war mover between Sedgley Park, Manchester United (May 1929), Exeter City (July 1933) and Crystal Palace (April 1937), Arthur had featured in the Grecians' FA Cup giant-killing of City in 1937, and had been under City boss Tom Bromilow's management at Palace. He additionally guested during the war for Brighton and Fulham, and transferred from Palace to Rochdale in October 1945. (4 apps)

A wartime member of the National Fire Service, Lincoln

winger **Joseph Clare** (b. Westhoughton, 4.2.1910, d. Christchurch, 23.9.1987) guested for City at outside-left at Derby in March 1945, and also briefly lent his skills to Nottingham Forest. His pre-war career path led from Westhoughton Town to Manchester City (August 1930), Wigan Borough (August 1931), Westhoughton again (October 1931), Accrington Stanley (November 1933), Arsenal (December 1934), Margate (1935, on loan), Norwich City (May 1936), and to Lincoln (June 1937), where he was top scorer in 1938/9. Joe was later on the Bournemouth coaching staff from 1946-1960; then worked for that town's Water Company. (1 app)

A former Leicester Schools full-back, Countesthorpe-based **William Arthur Cobley** (b. Blaby, 31.12.1913; d. Leicester, April 1989) had signed for Aston Villa in September 1935, and made 45 League appearances during his three years there. Back with Leicester club Solus on the outbreak of war, William served in the RAF, and then worked and played for Mellor Bromleys until City called on him during September and October 1944. He also guested for Northampton and Fulham, and in 1946 signed for Notts County, but played no senior football for them. (3 apps)

Primarily a centre-half, but the scorer of eight goals in one wartime game between Coventry and West Brom, **Thomas Crawley** (b. Blantyre, 10.11.1911) also played one of his four City games in March and April 1942 at centre-forward. Having started his career with Blantyre Victoria, he successively signed for Hamilton Academical (cs 1932), Motherwell (March 1934) and Preston North End (May 1935) before starting an eleven-year stier with Coventry in February 1936. (4 apps)

Signed on amateur forms by City in May 1941, young Welshman **David L Cronin** continued to turn out at outside-right for BTH Sports (Rugby) until getting a senior Filbert Street call-up in September 1943. He continued to win sporadic selections until August 1945. (18 apps; 4 goals)

Burnley reserve **Ben Crossland** never got a chance in peacetime League football, but his outside-left outing for City at Stoke in

March 1944 was supplemented by extra wartime appearances for Blackburn, Luton and Southampton, as well as back at Turf Moor. (1 app)

Edwin Cunningham (b. Jarrow, 20.9.1919) was a pre-war Luton Town junior who had officially moved to Bristol City by the time City recruited him from the Luton crowd to play on the right wing in October 1940, on a day when four selected players missed the train. Also a wartime guest for Brentford, he made but a single postwar League appearance for Bristol City. (1 app)

The outbreak of war stymied the Norwich City career of **Fred Cutting** (Frederick C; b. North Walsham, 4.12.1921), who had signed professionally only months previously and had yet to make his debut. Apparently having guested for a so-far unidentified Scottish League club while on Army posting (and having earned the Military Medal), he was recruited by City in January 1946, but released after a trio of forward outings. Fred spent the next term in Norwich's reserves, then joined Colchester United who, as a Southern League club, reached the last 16 in the 1948 FA Cup with his inside-left assistance. Fred was still in the side on its election to the League in 1950, then joined Great Yarmouth Town in 1952. (3 apps)

Unfortunately badly injured during his only City game - at Nottingham Forest in February 1944 - **David Davidson** (b. Lanark, 25.3.1920; d. Hackney, 1954) was a left- or centre-half who had joined Bradford Park Avenue in May 1938 from Douglas Water Thistle, but had to wait for postwar football for his League debut. He became a Leyton Orient stalwart after January 1947, until joining Headington (now Oxford) United in April 1950 for the finale of their inaugural professional campaign in the Southern League. (1 app)

Forest centre-half **Bob Davies** (Robert Griffith; b. Blaenau Ffestiniog, 19.10.1913, d. Nottingham, 10.5.1978) had decidedly mixed fortunes during the war: having luckily survived an incident of his 'chute failing to open while acting as a paratroop instructor in 1941, he recovered sufficiently from having both legs in plaster to add to his Welsh wartime cap tally. A Forest signing from his hometown club when he was on the verge of amateur international honours in November 1936, he remained at the City Ground as a player until 1947, and on the training staff until 1974, when he became Walsall's physio. During wartime, however, he also turned out for Blackpool, Rochdale, Notts County and Leicester - assisting in home and away fixtures against Portsmouth in October 1945. (2 apps)

Aberdonian **Percy Dickie** (b. 11.12.1907) became a City regular at wing-half or inside-forward for 15 months from the opening game of 1943/4, and additionally made wartime appearances for Lincoln City, Manchester City, Walsall and Bradford PA. He was officially a Blackburn Rovers player; having signed on at Ewood in September 1937 following stints with Mugiemoss, Aberdeen (1929) and St.Johnstone (1932). (31 apps; 1 goal)

On Manchester United's books during wartime, but never a League player for them, **Stuart Dimond** (b. Chorlton, 3.1.1920) became a typically peripatetic centre-forward in regionalised football, briefly turning out for Notts County, Newcastle United, Stockport County and both Bradford clubs as well as for City (at inside-left in home and away games with Villa in December 1943). Eventually he got a November 1945 move to Bradford City, but experienced only nine League outings before a January 1948 stepdown to Winsford United. (2 apps)

Selby-born outside-left **David N Douglas** was in the RAF when signed by City in October 1944. He got only a trio of chances at senior level (plus two guest outings for Wrexham during the same season), and was formally freed in May 1946. (3 apps; 1 goal)

A defeat at Walsall in November 1941 marked the sole City appearance of England centre-forward **Ted Drake** (Edward Joseph; b. Southampton, 16.8.1912; d. Wimbledon, 30.5.1995). A Hampshire cricketer and prolific Southampton striker from 1931 (joining from Winchester City), Ted had transferred to Arsenal in March 1934 for a sizeable £6,500 fee, and won two Championship

medals on either side of a Cup-winning performance in 1936. His seven-goal haul from a December 1935 game at Aston Villa remains a top-flight record; and his 42 strikes in 1934/5 a Highbury benchmark. An RAF Flight Lieutenant during the war, he also guested for West Ham, Fulham and Portsmouth before a back injury ended his playing career; later he took managerial responsibilities at Hendon, Reading and Chelsea (leading them to the 1955 championship), assistant's posts at Fulham and Barcelona and, eventually, a director-cum-life-president's role at Craven Cottage. (1 app)

A tricky, speedy outside-right who had two spells as a City guest during 1942/3 and 1944/5, **Maurice Dunkley** (Maurice Edward Frank; b. Kettering, 19.2.1914, d. Rutland, 27.12.1989) also served both Kettering Town and Northampton Town twice; each side of a stint with Manchester City that started in March 1938 and ended in 1947. Also a pre-war Northants cricketer, Maurice turned out additionally during the war for West Ham, Millwall, West Brom and Walsall; and finished his career with Corby Town after 1950. (20 apps; 4 goals)

A City guest at inside-forward for three months from November 1939, **Harry Eastham** (Henry; b. Blackpool, 30.6.1917) was a former Bloomfield Road discovery (am September 1933, pro May 1934) who had signed for Liverpool in February 1936, would go on to win a Championship medal with them in 1946/7, before moving on to Tranmere Rovers (May 1948) and Accrington Stanley (July 1953). His wartime wanderings would also take him briefly to the assistance of each of New Brighton, Leeds, Southport, Brighton, Bolton, Newcastle and Irish club Distillery. (6 apps)

One of two guests making their sole City appearances in the club's final game of wartime football, at home to Brentford on 4.5.46, **George Robert Edwards** (b. Great Yarmouth, 1.4.1918; d. Hockley Heath, 21.1.1993) was in fact Aston Villa's top scorer during WW2. He'd joined Norwich City as a professional in April 1936 and moved to Villa Park in June 1938, and would stay until 1951, when

linking up with Bilston United. Norwich, Notts County, Northampton, Forest, Wrexham and Walsall also utilised his services during the war. (1 app)

Bryn Elliott (Bernard Harry; b. Beeston, 3.5.1925) was a Forest reserve at the time he made his trio of appearances in March and May 1945: each of them in cup ties against Derby! The wing-half had signed on at the City Ground in October 1942, and made a postwar League bow prior to being released to Boston United in 1948. In October 1949, however, Southampton restored Bryn to the League sphere, and he turned out in 235 games for them at that level before a July 1959 move to Poole Town. In September 1952 he got on the City scoresheet with an own goal at The Dell. (3 apps)

City were only one step from Wembley when they drafted in Liverpool's **William Fagan** (b. Musselburgh, 20.2.1917; d. Wellingborough, 29.2.1992) at inside-left to face Arsenal in the second leg of the 1941 War Cup semi-final, though it proved one step too far, with a 1-2 home reverse sealing aggregate defeat. Willie, who won wartime caps for Scotland, began his career with Wellesley Juniors before signing for Celtic in June 1934, and moving south to Preston North End in October 1936. He served at Anfield from October 1937 to January 1952, amassing 161 League appearances, then wound down with Distillery and, as player/manager from July 1952, Weymouth. He played in three defeated Wembley teams (Preston and Liverpool in the 1937 and 1950 FA Cup Finals, and as a Chelsea guest in the 1944 League South Cup Final). He also guested while on RAF service for Aldershot, Celtic, Northampton, Reading and Crystal Palace. (1 app)

Kenneth Flint (b. Selston, 12.11.1923) first had his promise noted by City as a 19-year-old left-winger during 1942/3, and played a few wartime games for Notts County the following term, but his professional career was very much a slow-burn affair until 1950. His first postwar club was Bedford Town, who sold Ken to Tottenham Hotspur in July 1947; but his senior record of one goal in five Spurs matches was then dwarfed by his service to

Aldershot, amounting to 70 goals in 324 games. He spent season 1958/9 with Leyton Orient, then joined Bath City. (4 apps)

February 1941 was a busy month for **Walter L Foster** (b. Coalville, 1920; d. Leicester, Dec 1992). The former Coalville Town and Western Athletic outside-left signed as a City amateur, played once for the Colts, made his senior debut a week later (scoring in a 3-3 home draw with Birmingham) and two days later joined the Navy. Becoming a Chief Petty Officer, and playing in the odd friendly game for Plymouth Argyle during 1944/5, he returned to Filbert Street to sign pro forms in December 1945, showed further goalscoring ability, but was freed in the following May; later serving Kettering Town and (from 1951) Burton Albion. (10 apps; 5 goals)

Signed as an amateur in August 1939, **William H Freer** was a local youngster who had played for Syston St.Peters and Syston Imperial, and who got but one chance to shine in senior wartime football with City, at outside-left in the May 1941 home defeat against Spurs. During 1942/3, though, Billy assisted Bath City in the Football League West. (1 app)

Better remembered now as a manager (with Port Vale, Rugby Town, Hinckley Athletic, Stafford Rangers and, particularly, for two spells at Coventry City), **Billy Frith** (b. Sheffield, 9.6.1912) was a defensive half-back who'd begun his playing career in 1929 with Worksop Town, and moved successively to Mansfield Town (April 1930), Chesterfield (May 1931) and Coventry (May 1932). City regularly utilised his experience between January 1941 and May 1942, while Coventry's Highfield Road was out of commission owing to bomb damage. (42 apps)

Stanley D Frost (b. Northampton, 19.10.1922) had made but a single wartime appearance for the Cobblers before being involved in one of the few permanent transfer deals City undertook during the war, albeit a straight exchange for George Bedford in March 1941. The outside-right then made isolated City appearances across each season until 1944/5 (his last such coming while on leave from Germany), and was retained for postwar football; only to be

offloaded, untried at League level, back to Northampton in January 1947. Stan later assisted Rugby Town. (12 apps; 2 goals)

Capped once by Scotland in 1935, while in the middle of a 101-gaol stint at Sunderland (signed from Bridge of Weir in September 1928), inside-forward **Patsy Gallacher** (Patrick; b. Bridge of Weir, 21.8.1909; d. Greenock, 4.1.1992) joined Stoke City in November 1938 and almost immediately hit injury trouble, but was still on their books when briefly guesting for City (in two goalless draws in September 1942), as well as for Newcastle United, Crewe Alexandra and several other clubs. He also later became Weymouth player/manager. (2 apps)

A degree of mystery still surrounds the club affiliations of the **C Gardiner** who briefly assisted City in October and December 1942. The inside-forward, who scored on his debut in an away win at Mansfield, was serving (and playing) with COD (Old Dalby) at the time, when he was variously described as being on Portsmouth's books, an ex-Forest player, and a Montrose man! [Charlie Gardiner (b. Glasgow, 17.3.1913; d. North Africa, WW2), a forward whom Nottingham Forest signed from Roselea in 1935, and released to Mansfield in 1938, seems a potential, if unconfirmed, suspect.] (2 apps; 1 goal)

Jimmy Gemmell (b. Sunderland, 17.11.1911; d. Birmingham, May 1952) first played at Filbert Street in the same schoolboy international trial side as Sep Smith, but was very much a Bury stalwart by the time he returned, having joined the Gigg Lane side from West Stanley in March 1930, and having accumulated 255 League games for them as either full-back or centre-half. While temporarily based in Hinckley, Jimmy became a City regular between November 1942 and September 1944, and also assisted Rochdale, Manchester United and Southport during the war, signing officially for the latter club in August 1945. (53 apps)

A two-footed winger, **Billy Goffin** (William Charles; b. Tamworth, 12.12.1920; d. Tamworth, 15.9.1987) had joined Aston Villa from his home town club in December 1937, but

was still awaiting a League blooding at the time he guested for City (from January 1944). He similarly built wartime experience with Birmingham, Forest and Swansea before his 156-game, 36-goal Villa Park record began in earnest. Billy then spent 1954/5 with Walsall before returning to Tamworth. (5 apps)

City really called on the veterans for their September 1945 fixture at Charlton, when Sep Smith and Fred Kilshaw missed their trains. Arthur Attwood was one such hastily recruited, and the other was **Jim Graham** (James Arthur; b. Rothwell, 13.1.1911; d. Bath, 28.11.1987), who had last played League football in 1937, and had merely one emergency appearance for Charlton during 1944/5 as subsequent recommendation! He was, however, City goalkeeper Dick's older brother, and he lasted the 90 minutes at right-half. As a forward, he had joined Nottingham Forest from Desborough Town in 1932, and moved to York City in 1935. (1 app)

Though he later proved himself a fine goalkeeper in both City's wartime side and Crystal Palace's postwar League teams, **Dick Graham** (Richard Douglas; b. Corby, 6.5.1922) had a torrid introduction to net-minding at Filbert Street. Signed in December 1941 (after representing Corby Town and Northampton Town's juniors), Dick was within days lent to Norwich City for their game against City, and conceded five goals before being stretchered off during a 6-1 win. The following May, he was similarly lent to Bristol City, and again conceded five, while two days after that he was at last on City's side for the fixture with Northampton: a 1-4 home defeat! It was April 1945 before he reclaimed a City place (having guested for Southport, Notts County and Crewe in the interim), but competition for the green jersey was fierce, and Dick moved permanently to Selhurst Park in December 1945. After retirement, he built a lengthy off-field career: as coach to West Brom, then as manager of Palace, Leyton Orient, Walsall, Colchester and Wimbledon. (18 apps)

Originally signed as a professional from local football in the close season of 1939, centre-forward **Ron Grant** (Ronald A) spent much of his war on Navy service (being rescued when the cruiser 'Fiji' was sunk off Crete), and was usually restricted to Colts or Reserve appearances when home on leave. He did make a senior bow, however, on Christmas Day 1943 in an away match against Aston Villa. He had a fine record in Leicestershire Senior Cup Finals: scoring twice for City in the 5-1 defeat of Coalville in 1945/6; a hat-trick against City for Brush Sports a year later; and two more in Brush's 1948 win over Whitwick. (1 app)

The only WW2 City guest to masquerade (initially) under the name of 'Newman', Preston's **Willie Hamilton** (b. Hamilton, 1.9.1918) played in four victories off the reel during February and March 1943. Having signed on at Deepdale in September 1937 from Blantyre Victoria, left-half Willie stayed until 1948, when joining Queen of the South; he also guested for Bury, Arsenal, Fulham, Millwall and Oldham. (4 apps)

Norman Hanford signed for City from Quorn Methodists in August 1944, and was briefly tried in each full-back berth in March 1945. As a City reserve, he was successively a Senior Cup winner and runner-up in 1946 and 1947, while with Brush Sports he earned another loser's medal in 1950. (2 apps)

One of four Aston Villa players to assist City during 1939/40, **Fred Haycock** (Frederick Joseph; b. Bootle, 19.4.1912; d. Great Barr, 10.4.1989) was an inside-left who'd started his senior career in Ireland, with Waterford, in 1928, joined Prescot Cables in 1932, and signed on at Villa Park in February 1934. He was certainly a traveller for the rest of the war; additionally guesting for Plymouth, Liverpool, Wolves, Northampton, Notts County, Forest, Walsall and Kidderminster Harriers before signing for Wrexham in December 1945, and Stourbridge in 1947. (13 apps; 3 goals)

The scorer of City's final goal in WW2 competition was **Wilfred Heathcote** (b. Hemsworth, 29.6.1911; d. Lambeth, 15.6.1991), one of three guests appearing in the 1-3 home defeat by Brentford in May 1946. An Army sergeant, and very much a late entrant to senior football in early 1943, Wilf was best known for scoring 89 goals in 100 wartime appearances for Queens Park Rangers, though he could only manage a single score in five games thereafter, and only briefly served Millwall from December 1946. Millwall had also been one of the other clubs he guested for, as had Wolves, Reading and Southampton. (1 app; 1 goal)

Jock Hillard (John Gordon, b. Aberdeen, 3.9.1916) was an amateur with Leicester Nomads and Coalville Town prior to signing for City in a joint deal with Stan Baines in November 1937. He made little immediate progress, however, and had been released by the time he popped up in the early wartime teams of Grimsby Town and Mansfield Town. Jock was also with Anstey Methodists during 1940/1, then re-signed for City during 1942/3; making appearances in both wing berths as well as at left-half, and additionally guesting for Northampton that term. During 1944/5 he guested for Lovell's Athletic in the Football League West; then in September 1946 City transferred him to Torquay United for a 6-game League career. (8 apps)

Seven times capped for England as a Villa player after joining them from Boston United in August 1927, **William Eric Houghton** (b. Billingsborough, 29.6.1910) amassed a Villa Park peacetime career record of 360 games and 160 goals, while also representing Warwickshire as a cricketer. City borrowed his left-wing services between March and June 1940, and he also turned out in wartime for Coventry, Hereford United, Brentford, Forest and Notts County; eventually being transferred to Meadow Lane in December 1946. He retired in 1949 straight into the Notts manager's chair, and later managed Villa and Rugby Town. He additionally scouted for Forest and Walsall, became general secretary of the Fellows Park club, and served as a Villa director in the 70s. In December 1942, Eric scored a hat-trick against City. (15 apps; 2 goals)

A left-back turned left-winger who never got a break in League football before or after the war, **Leonard Hubble** was a Newcastle United reserve signed from Horden Colliery, who briefly turned out for City during November and December 1944. Elsewhere, he got two WW2 outings for the Magpies, one for Middlesbrough, and a trio for Charlton Athletic, scoring once. (3 apps)

A young outside- or inside-right when captured by City on amateur forms from BTH (Rugby) in October 1942, **Gwyn Hughes** (Thomas Gwynfor; b. Blaenau Ffestiniog, 7.5.1922) had converted to a wing-half role by the time he signed for Northampton Town in August 1944, though he still scored against City in November of that year. He stayed with the Cobblers until a May 1956 move to Bedford Town, having played 281 postwar games, scoring 26 times. (10 apps; 1 goal)

A City guest at inside-left from December 1944 to May 1945, Preston North End's **Harry Iddon** (b. Preston, 20.2.1921) never made the senior grade with his home town club. For someone whose postwar career (with Barrow from October 1946 and Southport from June 1947) was so essentially modest, however, he was much in demand during wartime, with Manchester City, Wolves, Aldershot, Reading York, Chester, Chesterfield and Notts County the other clubs to utilise his temporary services. (11 apps; 2 goals)

Another of City's 1939/40 Villains, **Bob Iverson** (Robert Thomas James, b. Folkestone, 17.10.1910; d. Birmingham, 19.6.1953) was a left-half who had first been noted by Spurs while playing for Folkestone, and had signed on at White Hart Lane in May 1932, but didn't make a League breakthrough until switching to Lincoln City in September 1933. His travels thereafter took him via Wolves (February 1935) to Villa Park (December 1936), where he would remain as a player until 1949, before becoming coach to their juniors. During the war, Bob also assisted Birmingham, Forest, Notts County, Northampton and Sutton Town. (11 apps)

A genuine prodigy -- an England schoolboy international, and a 14-year-old scorer in City's senior pre-season public practice game in 1938 -- **Gordon Jayes** (Alfred Gordon; b. Leicester, 26.9.1923) had his footballing development almost totally wrecked by the

Gordon Jayes

war's intervention. Signed as an amateur, he was briefly loaned to Nuneaton Borough in April 1939; then made his competitive City debut (as inside-right at West Brom on 11.11.1939) at the age of 16 years, 46 days. Soon afterwards he was declared by the Football League investigation of City's books to be a professional (despite not being eligible to sign pro forms until his 17th birthday), and suspended until a successful appeal. Gordon later signed up as an Army PT instructor, and in fact played his last senior City game in February 1944, when still only twenty. In October 1946, he was allowed to join Notts County, for whom he scored 7 times in 27 League games. (59 apps; 22 goals)

A pre-war England international, capped five times in 1936/7, **Joe Johnson** (Joseph Alfred; b. Grimsby, 4.4.1911; d. West Bromwich, 8.8.1983) turned out just once for City, on the left wing at Wolves in November 1945. He'd moved from Scunthorpe United to Bristol City in May 1931, to Tom Mather's Stoke City in April 1932, and to West Brom in November 1937. As a Baggie, he also guested during wartime for Crewe, Walsall, Notts County and Northampton; then dropped into non-league football in 1946 with Northwich Victoria and Hereford United. (1 app)

Harry Johnston (b. Droylsden, 26.9.1919; d. Blackpool, 12.10.1973) was essentially a one-club player, starring for Blackpool from June 1935 to 1955, but briefly assisted both Reading and City

during the war. Now remembered as much for having been Stanley Matthews' skipper in the 1953 Cup Final as for his ten England caps at half-back, Harry made (or, more accurately, delayed) his Leicester bow under faintly farcical circumstances: he'd no sooner promised to turn out, on leave, for City against Stoke at home in September 1940, than he discovered his fiancée had arranged her wedding for that very day. Nonetheless, he was in the City team for the following week's return fixture at the Victoria Ground! Harry later managed Reading for eight years, and was twice caretaker boss at Blackpool. (4 apps)

A Hearts discovery, left-sided forward **Tom Johnston** (Thomas Deans; b. Berwick-on-Tweed, 30.12.1918) played almost all his senior football in the Midlands. He signed for Northampton Town from Peterborough United in 1942, joined City in February 1943, and was on Forest's books later that year. He also guested for Derby and City during this period, and in August 1948 his transfer from the City Ground only took him across the Trent to Notts County. (12 apps; 3 goals)

Eleven times capped by Wales before the war, and a wartime international on five occasions, **Les Jones** (Leslie Jenkin; b. Aberdare, 1.7.1911; d. Llanfyrnach, 11.1.1981) was a much-travelled inside-forward or wing-half who made an isolated guest appearance for City in October 1941, and then returned as a regular between March and December 1944. His career had started with Aberdare Athletic before an August 1929 signing for Cardiff City, and he had gone on to star for Coventry City (from January 1934) and Arsenal (from November 1937). During WW2 he also guested for West Ham, Coventry, Forest, Fulham, Notts County, Lincoln, Manchester City, Southampton, Swansea, Mansfield and Colchester; then was released in June 1946 to become player/ coach at Swansea. For 1947/8 he was player/manager of Barry Town, and the following term wound down his playing career at Brighton. Les was later manager of Scunthorpe United for their initial, 1950/51 Football League season. (18 apps; 2 goals)

Leslie O Jones was a City player for little more than a year after his March 1943 signing. A local left-half, he hobbled on the wing as a passenger throughout most of his debut at Derby that month, and got only sporadic chances afterwards, despite switching his role to the forward flank position. (3 apps)

A former Rugby Union player with Caerau, **Ralph Jones** (b. Maesteg, 19.5.1921) was a City signing as an amateur in May 1944 and as a pro in the following December. A couple of February 1945 outings at wing-half (in successive 4-1 wins over Notts County) were his only City chances, however, and he was released to Newport County in May 1946. Nineteen League games later, in December 1947, he became a Bristol Rovers player, but injuries there led to him dropping down to non-league level with Bath City in 1952 and Trowbridge Town from 1955. At this point of his life, Ralph was also noted as an operatic baritone at Glyndebourne. (2 apps)

Tommy Jones was on Derby's books at the time he guested for City, as outside-right in a handful of fixtures during September and October 1944, and he totted up 33 wartime appearances for the Rams. Yet he got League opportunities at neither the Baseball Ground nor after a 1948 move to Rochdale. (5 apps)

An amateur signing for both Coventry and City during the war, **Don Kelly** (Donald J; b. Market Harborough, 2.7.1922) managed a quartet of outings for each club, mainly in the centre-forward berth: in fact his scoring debut for City came in a November 1944 game at Highfield Road! After the war, he had a brief League career with Torquay United, scoring three goals in five games, but then returned to Harborough to play for Symington's FC. (4 apps; 1 goal)

Another to serve both City and Coventry at this time was **Jack Kendall** (John T; b. Rugby), a young left-half who signed on at Filbert Street in January 1942, and shifted allegiance to Highfield Road in 1944. He also turned out regularly for the Coventry factory team, Riley FC. (6 apps)

Like several of his Army comrades stationed at the Central

Ordnance Depot in Old Dalby, **Fred Kilshaw** (b. Wrexham, 24.8.1916) already had a League club connection before his call-up. In his case, he'd been an Everton junior; but it was his exploits with his unit team in the Leicestershire Senior League and Senior Cup which brought him to City's attention. Fred appeared in each of the 1943, 1944 and 1945 Finals of the Senior Cup: and scored twice against City's Colts in the 1944 Final, only a week after his City debut. By the time of the 1945 Final, Sgt.Kilshaw was in fact a City professional, having signed in January. Released in July 1946, he joined Third Division New Brighton, scoring once in eight games, and then moved to Prescot Cables. (6 apps; 1 goal)

One of two guests from Northampton Town in City's first competitive WW2 fixture, in October 1939, **Bobby King** (Frederick A Robert; b. Hardingstone, 19.9.1919) notched the first goal in a 6-1 victory over Walsall. A month later he became the first player in England to be conventionally transferred under wartime conditions, signing for Wolves, and a further month later scored for them against City! Bobby also guested for Manchester City during the war. He was transferred back to Northampton in December 1947, and joined Rushden in 1950. (2 apps; 1 goal)

Sid King (Sidney Harvey; b. Bordesley Green, 1914) was reserve goalkeeper at Birmingham to Gil Merrick, having joined the Blues from Cradley Heath in October 1936. He assisted City in a quartet of games during March 1943, and also lent his wartime services to Coventry and Northampton. Two FA Cup appearances in 1945/6 constituted the entirety of his 'official' Birmingham record, and he joined Hereford United in 1946. (4 apps)

A Scottish amateur international who had moved from Queens Park to Liverpool in April 1938, **Bill Kinghorn** (William John Darroch; b. Strathblane, 27.2.1912) briefly guested for City at outside-left in December 1939, and also turned out during wartime for Brighton, Newcastle, Blackburn, Manchester City, Leeds and Burnley. He was released from Anfield in 1946. (2 apps; 1 goal)

Outside-right **Jack Kirkaldie** (John; b. Coventry, 2.8.1917; d. Coventry, July 1985) started his career with Nuneaton Town, and moved successively to Southend United (February 1936), West Ham United (February 1937) and Doncaster Rovers (April 1939, staying until 1948). He assisted City during August and September 1942, and similarly guested for Port Vale two years later. (3 apps)

There was a remarkable disparity in the peacetime and wartime scoring records of **Herbert Knott** (b. Goole, 5.12.1914). A 17-year-old Arsenal signing from Goole Town in October 1932, released without a game at senior level, he stepped up again at Walsall in August 1937, and managed but two strikes for the Saddlers, and a loan spell at Stourbridge, before being offloaded to Brierley Hill in the summer of 1939. Postwar, he would notch but a solitary goal for Hull City. In the interim, however, he was very much an in-demand wanderer, totalling 67 goals in 80 games for a host of clubs, with City included in a list that stretched across Derby, Sheffield United, Lincoln, Notts County, York, Millwall, Hull, Forest, Halifax, Norwich, and Bradford Park Avenue. A sergeant at the time of his City stint (from January to March 1944), he claimed a hat-trick from an away win at Stoke in the Midland Cup as the highlight of his stay. (8 apps; 6 goals)

Also claiming a City hat-trick during a guest stint was **Tommy Lawton** (b. Bolton, 6.10.1919), who scored in each of his trio of games during November and December 1939, but was on the losing side at Walsall with his threesome. The scoring prodigy who had been nurtured at Burnley by City boss Tom Bromilow (he'd signed as a 15-year-old amateur from Rossendale United in May 1935), and by then was an Everton and England star (transferred to Goodison in January 1937), Tommy also guested for Chelsea, Aldershot, Millwall, Notts County, Charlton and Morton. In November 1945 he signed for Chelsea, and exactly two years later for Notts County, before moving to Brentford (March 1952), Arsenal (September 1953) and Kettering Town (February 1956, as player/manager). Tommy's peacetime England record was 22

goals and 23 caps, while his return from 22 wartime and victory internationals was 24 goals. He later managed Notts County. (3 apps; 5 goals)

Bill Leitch, signed from Wishaw High School by Motherwell in May 1942, was regarded primarily as a reserve centre-half by the Fir Park club. Yet he was mainly played by City, during the January to April 1945 period, at centre-forward; claiming a hat-trick on his debut in an 8-3 win over Mansfield Town, and finishing 1944/5 as the club's joint top scorer. (12 apps; 12 goals)

An 18-year-old on Rangers' books, **W J Letters** partnered his fellow Scottish amateur, Ken Chisholm, at outside-left in a home defeat by Southampton in February 1946. (1 app)

Glyn Lewis (b. Abertillery, 3.7.1921) was in the RAF when signing for Crystal Palace in 1941, and continued to play at Selhurst until a July 1948 move to Bristol City. He briefly assisted both City (at inside-left at Derby in March 1943) and Lincoln City during WW2. (1 app)

Though he didn't make a League breakthrough until 1947/8, **Maurice Lindley** (William Maurice; b. Keighley, 5.12.1915) had joined Everton from his home town club in February 1936. He did make wartime appearances at Goodison, however, as well as guest outings for Bradford City, Leeds, Walsall, Bournemouth and City (at left-half in January 1945). After retiring in 1952, he became manager of Swindon Town and Barry Town, and then a long-serving Leeds coach. (2 apps)

George Little (b. Newcastle, 30.6.1915) was an August 1936 signing for Doncaster Rovers from Throckley Welfare. He guested at outside-right for City from November 1943 to April 1944, and similarly assisted York City, Aldershot, Brentford, QPR and Chelsea. Rovers transferred him to York in December 1947. (11 apps; 1 goal)

A trialist from the Highfields area, **S Logan** was chosen at inside-left for the final game of the 1939/40 season, against Northampton at home, and scored after 30 seconds in a 2-0 win. It proved to be his only outing, and he was back in local football with Wellington Vics the following term. (1 app; 1 goal)

Another unsuccessful amateur trialist, this time from Nottinghamshire, was **Danny Long**, who took the outside-left berth at Northampton in November 1944. A month later, Danny was in the makeshift Nottingham Forest side beaten 1-9 on the same ground. (1 app)

Borrowed from the home team to complete the City line-up at Stoke for the final game of 1942/3 was **Eric Longland**, who made the odd appearance for the Potters during wartime, but never got a League break. (1 app)

Tamworth-born **Tim Lycett** was a City signing in August 1943 from a Castle Bromwich works team, and turned out at inside-left in several games during 1943/4 and 1945/6. In the interim season, he was a four-game guest for Walsall. Tim scored twice for City in the 1946 Senior Cup Final win over Coalville, but was not retained thereafter. (19 apps; 4 goals)

A left-winger whose City appearances came during February and March 1941, in the War Cup, **Colin Chad Lyman** (b. Northampton, 9.3.1914; d. Cambridge, 9.5.1986) had started his career with Rushden before signing amateur forms for Southend United in July 1933. He moved to Northampton in July 1934, and to Spurs in June 1937. His wartime services were spread between City, Port Vale, Derby, Chesterfield, Forest, Northampton, Notts County, Aldershot and Coventry; then Spurs released him to Port Vale in May 1946. Forest signed Colin in October 1946, and let him go to Notts County in August 1947. After 1948 he was successively player/manager of Long Eaton Town and Nuneaton Borough. (4 apps)

A COD (Old Dalby) player reputed to be attached to Third Lanark, **A McAskill** twice turned out at outside-right for City during October and November 1942. He additionally represented the Northern Command military select side with COD teammate Gardiner. (2 apps)

Topping and tailing his playing career with stints for Worksop Town, **Bob McCall** (Robert Henry; b. Whitwell, 29.12.1915) was a Nottingham Forest full-back (February 1935 to 1952; 162 Lge apps) who aided City in home and away fixtures against Derby in March 1945, and also played wartime games for Mansfield and Lincoln. (2 apps)

James McCormick (b. Rotherham, 26.4.1912; d. Marbella, 4.1.1968) was on Spurs' books during the WW2 period, but additionally fitted in guest appearances for each of Fulham, Crystal Palace, Lincoln, Southend, Derby, Birmingham, Bolton, Reading, Liverpool, Crewe, West Brom, Chelmsford City, Chester, Shrewsbury, Rochdale, Tranmere, Walsall and Leicester (March/April 1943). A local signing by Rotherham United in March 1931, the versatile forward had joined Chesterfield in August 1932, and Spurs in March 1933. Postwar, he transferred to Fulham in May 1946, to Lincoln in August 1947 (champions of Div. 3N in 1948), and to Palace in February 1949. His subsequent coaching career took him to Norway, Malta, Turkey, Wycombe Wanderers and Sheffield United; and he was York City manager in 1953/4. Later a licensee, he had run a North London sports outfitters during his playing career. (3 apps)

Motherwell's **John McInally** (b. Blantyre, 17.5.1915) briefly appeared in City colours at inside-right for a pair of away fixtures in London (at Fulham and Tottenham) in September 1945. This RAF physical training instructor had been a pre-war star with Celtic (signed from Wishaw in April 1934) and Arbroath (September 1937), and also played as a guest with Albion Rovers and Inverness Clachnacuddin. Postwar he had brief stints with Arbroath, Queen of the South, Cowdenbeath, Ballymena United and Albion Rovers. (2 apps)

An NCO in the Military Police, **Bobby McNeil** was a Hamilton Academicals player (as had been his father Bob, better known as an inter-war Chelsea star) when he turned out at outside-right for City in the first game of 1943/4, away to Mansfield Town. (1 app)

Signed by City as an 18-year-old amateur in December 1940, and given a break during 1941/2, **Reg Mansfield** (Reginald Frederick) had previously played for Gresley Rovers. Later in the war, he was noted (with the rank of Lance-Corporal) in the COD (Old Dalby) side in the 1944 County Cup Final. (4 apps)

Reg Mansfield

A pair of isolated inside-left appearances (in April 1944 and October 1945) marked local lad **William Middleton**'s contribution to City's wartime efforts. More often he was to be found in the playing ranks of Pegson's Athletic, and he also served Whitwick Colliery. (2 apps)

Reportedly 'overwhelmed' on his sole City outing, at centre-half in a 2-5 defeat at Stoke in December 1944, **John H Morby** (b. Wednesfield, August 1920) had been a year earlier a wartime Aston Villa recruit from Hednesford Town. Though he also guested for Notts County, Portsmouth and Wolves, and played in three FA Cup ties for Villa in 1945/6, he was released at war's end to Worcester City. (1 app)

Geordie goalkeeper **Bill Morgan** (William; b. Ryton-on-Tyne, 1914; d. Coventry, February 1993) had joined Coventry City from Chopwell Institute in March 1932 (having a month previously been on amateur forms at Wolves), and built a pre-war record of 150 League games. He guested for Northampton and both Nottingham clubs as well as turning out for City for much of 1941/2, but it was at Filbert Street in September 1942, playing for Coventry against City, that he suffered the severe shoulder injury which eventually enforced his retirement. (17 apps)

An RAF representative and a Derby County signing from Ross County in October 1944, **Angus Cameron Morrison** (b. Dingwall,

26.4.1924) assisted City at outside-left in home and away fixtures with Aston Villa in April 1945; a month in which he also guested for Stockport County. Postwar, he totalled 95 League goals in 329 games with Derby, Preston North End (November 1948) and Millwall (October 1957), and won one Scotland 'B' cap. In 1958, he became player manager of Nuneaton Borough, and later performed similar functions with Belper Town. (2 apps)

Working at, and playing for, Morris Motors, **Alex Morton** signed amateur forms for City in February 1944, and made his sole appearance three days later, on the right wing against Sheffield Wednesday at Filbert Street. He also featured once in a Coventry City line-up the following season, but that seems to have been the extent of his senior experience. (1 app)

Jimmy Mullen (James; b. Newcastle, 6.1.1923; d. Wolverhampton, October 1987) had barely turned 16 when he made his League debut for Wolves in February 1939, and had to wait another 11 months before being able to sign professionally for the Molineux club. In 1940/1, when Wolves did not compete at all in regional competition, he and Billy Wright became regular guests for City; both having major roles in the capture of the Midland Cup, and indeed both scoring in the Final win over Walsall. Apart from other brief guest stints with Newcastle, Darlington, Middlesbrough, Walsall and Reading, the left-winger then returned to Wolves for the remainder of his career, which stretched to 1960, and brought him 98 League goals from 445 games, as well as eleven England caps. (25 apps; 15 goals)

Very much a wanderer, **Ambrose 'Jock' Mulraney** (b. Wishaw, 18.5.1916) was as active before and after the war in terms of his club connections as he was during it. Starting in Scottish junior football with Wishaw White Rose and Carluke Rovers, he had trials or reserve spells with each of Hearts, Celtic, Hamilton, Sligo Rovers, Blackpool, and Clapton Orient in a three-year spell from 1933-36. He briefly settled at Dartford, then joined Ipswich Town in November 1936, featuring in that club's initial

Jimmy Mullen

League season two years later. During the war, he guested for Birmingham, Manchester City, Charlton, Northampton, Clapton Orient, Brentford, Wolves, Brighton, Norwich, Blackburn and Sheffield Wednesday; as well as once, in November 1941, for City (at inside-right at Northampton). Then Jock was on the move 'officially' again: to Birmingham (September 1945), Shrewsbury Town (July 1947), Kidderminster Harriers (July 1948), Aston Villa (September 1948) and Cradley Heath (August 1949, as player/ manager). He later managed Brierley Hill from 1952-54. (1 app)

Having built a solid local reputation with Leicester Nomads and Brush Sports (for whom he claimed a hat-trick in the 1941 Senior Cup Final), inside-forward **Tom North** (Thomas W; b. Barrow on Soar, 31.10.1919) signed for City in July 1943, but won only one selection, at Birmingham in September of that year. In December 1944, Nottingham Forest signed him in time to make

his debut against City, and he went on to score eleven times in 46 wartime games for them, though only appearing once after the resumption of League football. (1 app)

A goalkeeper with Gresley Rovers and Holwell Works, **Harry Parker** signed forms for City in September 1941, as cover for Joe Calvert, but conceded six goals in home and away fixtures with West Bromwich Albion that month. (2 apps)

Capped by Scotland in 1938, and with a typical medal haul (two League championships, one Scottish Cup) under his belt after signing for Celtic from Dunipace Juniors in March 1932, **George Denholm Paterson** (b. Denny, 26.9.1914; d. New Zealand, 1985) was a fine left-half who substantially lifted City's efforts between April 1941 and October 1942. He also guested for Arsenal, Wolves, Tranmere, Shrewsbury and Blackpool, represented the RAF, and played in three Victory internationals. In October 1946 he transferred from Parkhead to Brentford, and ended his playing career with Yeovil Town from October 1949. George was briefly manager of Stirling Albion from October 1951, and then on the Celtic coaching staff from 1952-56. (32 apps; 2 goals)

Described as 'a North Wales lad' (and by one source as an ex-Rhyl Athletic player), **George Pearce** was an RAF sergeant stationed at Market Harborough when he turned out at left-half for City at Newport in October 1945, and was unfortunately injured on this debut. He had played one wartime game for Walsall previously. (1 app)

A pre-war Plymouth Argyle amateur, **Russell G T Phillips** (b. Exeter, 22.6.1916) was an Army corporal when registered at Filbert Street in March 1943. He turned out occasionally for City at inside-forward until September 1944, then switched allegiance to Millwall (for whom he scored in a 1945/6 FA Cup tie) and Torquay United, who continued to represent into the first postwar League season. (18 apps; 7 goals)

A former Stourbridge forward, rediscovered as an army sergeant playing in Nottinghamshire football for RAOC Chilwell, **Doug Pimbley** (Douglas William; b. Kings Norton, 19.6.1917) had played two wartime games for Manchester City when City signed him in December 1945. A debut scorer against West Brom that month, he stayed only until the end of that 'transitional' term, also guesting twice for Forest;

then signed professionally for Birmingham City in July 1946, and moved to Notts County in March 1948. (8 apps; 4 goals)

Also a Stourbridge product, but on Stoke City's books since 1938, **Wallace Poulton** had been playing Leicestershire Senior League football for RAF (Melton) when he won his sole City selection, at outside-left in a home game with Forest in October 1945. He made no peacetime appearances for Stoke. (1 app)

An occasional City guest on either wing during 1939/40, **Jack Pritchard** (Harvey John; b. Meriden, 30.1.1918) was an August 1935 signing by Coventry City from Exhall Colliery, who had moved to Crystal Palace in June 1937, and on to Manchester City in March 1938. He additionally guested for Northampton, Coventry, Aldershot and West Ham during the war years; then left Maine Road for Southend United in February 1947, and finished his career with Folkestone from August 1952. (10 apps; 1 goal)

A local goalkeeper who had represented Leicester Boys in 1928, **Arthur Queenborough** twice stood in for Sandy McLaren during May 1940; having signed three months previously from Wigston COB. (2 apps)

'Tex' Rickards (Charles Thomas; b. Giltbrook, 19.2.1915; d. Peterborough, 10.7.1980) was a versatile forward who guested once for City in March 1944, and more regularly from September to December of that year; notching one hat-trick against Port Vale. Originally a Notts County signing in September 1933 from local works team Johnson & Barnes, he had transferred to Cardiff City for a season from May 1938. He was reported as signing for Scunthorpe United the following summer, but was playing regularly for Mansfield Town from the earliest days of wartime football, and additionally guesting for Notts County, Crewe Alexandra, Stockport County, Derby County and Chesterfield. (13 apps; 7 goals)

An inside-left or left-half, **Dick Riley** (Richard J; b. Northampton) signed for City as an amateur in December 1944, and professionally a month later, but his final senior game came only a year

afterwards. He was never on a winning City side. (5 apps)

A Wolves teenager who guested for City on the left wing at Coventry in September 1943, and also briefly assisted Notts County, **Douglas Gordon Roberts** (b. Foleshill, 30.5.1925) signed for Northampton Town in August 1944, and subsequently served Brighton & Hove Albion (from March 1949), Accrington Stanley (from July 1951), Rugby Town (from 1952) and Cheltenham Town. (1 app)

The scorer of 75 pre-war goals for both Bradford clubs, **Jimmy Robertson** (James Henry; b. Berwick, 22.3.1913; d. Bradford, 1973) was a wartime guest for both Nottingham Forest and Mansfield Town, and it was at the latter's ground in October 1942 that he volunteered to turn out at left-half for a reshuffled City when George Dewis didn't arrive in time. Bradford Park Avenue had signed Jimmy from Welbeck Colliery in August 1932, and he had crossed the city to Valley Parade in February 1938. (1 app)

Manchester City prospect **Peter Robinson** (b. Manchester, 29.1.1922) had a host of wartime opportunities to develop his game at, and away from, Maine Road, with guest outings for Manchester United, QPR, Luton, Aldershot, Clapton Orient and Crystal Palace, as well as for City. Though primarily a full-back, he turned out at left-half in a pair of London away games for City in September 1945. (2 apps)

A Geordie from Hexham who had played pre-war for Hexham United and Durham University, **Alan Rochester** made a May 1940 debut for City, and signed for the club in November of that year, going on to make sporadic appearances at outside-right or right-half across the first four wartime seasons, latterly when on leave from aircraft-carrier services with the Fleet Air Arm. (27 apps)

A December 1940 signing from Gresley Rovers, **Robert G Roome** got but a single senior chance: at outside-left in a home win over Forest in June 1941. (1 app)

A former Airdrieonians wing-half whose 85 wartime games for Chelsea after a 1942 signing included two Wembley appearances in the League (South) Cup, **Robert Russell**

Harry Parker

(b. Aberdour, 27.12.1919) guested once at left-half for City, at Brentford in September 1945, and also for Crystal Palace. Postwar, he played only twice more for Chelsea, and twice for Notts County after an August 1948 move. The following October, he returned to London, with Leyton Orient, but failed to gain a first-team place. (1 app)

Bill Rutherford was a Londoner on Army service locally when signed as an amateur outside-left in April 1943. He made a scoring bow at Northampton that month, but a week later had finished his senior career. (2 apps; 1 goal)

Described as a 'diminutive livewire', **Don Sanderson** cost City a 10s 6d fine from the League when they signed him four days after his February 1941 scoring debut against Lincoln City. A former Hugglescote United and Coalville Town centre-forward, Don notched 31 goals for the Colts in 1940/1, and continued to play the occasional first-team game until December 1944. He was also lent to Luton Town at Filbert Street in October 1941, scoring the opening goal for them in a game City eventually won 7-2. After the war, Don played for Whitwick Colliery under Hughie Adcock's management. (22 apps; 9 goals)

A 20-year-old bricklayer from Fleckney, **Fred Sansome** signed for City in April 1940 from Oadby Imperial, and had a brief run as senior outside-right. (4 apps)

An Aston Villa centre-forward who had claimed a hat-trick from his pre-war debut, **Frank Shell** (Francis Henry; b. Hackney, 2.1.1912; d. Axminster, July 1988) turned out at inside-left for City at Northampton in November 1939. A former amateur with Barking and Ford Sports (Dagenham), he had joined Villa in May 1937, and he also guested for Northampton, Walsall and Notts County during the war. From September 1946 he was briefly a Birmingham City reserve, soon released to Hereford United, though he spent 1947/8 with Mansfield Town. (1 app)

A Bolton Wanderers first-teamer in the final pre-war season, **Tommy Sinclair** (Thomas M; b. Ince, 13.10.1921) additionally assisted Norwich City, Reading, Gainsborough Trinity, Aldershot and City (on the right wing at

Brentford in September 1945) during the war years. Subsequently, from 1946, Aldershot picked up his League registration, before moves to Brentford (August 1950) and Bradford City (August 1951). (1 app)

The winner in the 1940 War Cup Final was one of 80 wartime goals centre-forward **Sam Small** (Samuel John; b. Birmingham, 15.5.1912) scored for West Ham United, to add to his 39-goal League record. A Birmingham signing from Bromsgrove Rovers in March 1934, he had moved to Upton Park in January 1937, and would stay until a March 1948 transfer to Brighton. As well as his City outing in a home defeat by Fulham in September 1945, Sam guested for Birmingham and Coventry. (1 app)

Dundee United winger **I S Smart** had his only City outing on the left flank at Walsall in September 1944. (1 app)

Also a one-shot winger was **Charlie Smith** (Charles J; b. Cardiff, 26.8.1915), who appeared at outside-right for City at Derby in February 1945. A pre-war player with Exeter City (August 1936), Yeovil & Petters United (1937) and Aberdeen (January 1938), he briefly served Torquay United from 1946. (1 app)

At one stage during the war, City actually had no less than nine players with the surname 'Smith' simultaneously on their books. One of that ilk was **Jack Smith** (John D; b. Whetstone), the younger brother of Arthur E Smith. An April 1940 signing from Fairfax United, he was an occasional senior choice at inside-right until 1942/3. He guested once for Forest in that term, and once for Southampton a season later, and also assisted Portsmouth's reserves. (18 apps; 3 goals)

Leslie G Smith was a local signing in August 1940 who made a quartet of inside-forward appearances in the following campaign. He was unfortunately later a prisoner-of-war in Japanese hands. (4 apps)

The better-known **Les Smith** (Leslie George Frederick; b. Ealing, 13.3.1918; d. Lichfield 20.5.1995) had become an England international a couple of years before he briefly assisted City in

October 1941, scoring on his debut against Luton, at a time when he was taking refereeing exams at Loughborough. An inside-left whose teenage talent developed with Petersham, Wimbledon and Hayes, he signed for Brentford in March 1936. He won further wartime caps while on RAF service; also guested for Chelsea and Fulham; and played in one Victory international after moving officially to Aston Villa in October 1945. In June 1952 he moved back to Brentford, and in August 1953 became player/manager at Kidderminster Harriers. (2 apps; 1 goal)

A versatile defender for City from October to December 1942, and also briefly a wartime guest for Falkirk, **John Snape** (b. Birmingham, 2.7.1917) was a Coventry City stalwart from 1935 to 1951. He'd previously been spotted with Shirley Town and Solihull Town, and would afterwards serve Bedworth Town. (6 apps)

Terry Sparrow was a young defender signed as an amateur in February 1942 after a few outings with Bristol City's 'A' team. Joining the professional ranks in March 1944, he filled in once at right-half and once at right-back before the end of 1943/4. Terry also turned out twice for Notts County during the following term. (2 apps)

Just turned 17 when appearing as a stand-in left-back in a 5-4 win at West Brom in December 1940, **Terry Springthorpe** (Terrance Alfred; b. Draycott, 4.12.1923) had already faced City as a 15-year-old for Wolves during the previous season. A 1939 Molineux signing from Sedgeley Rovers, who also guested for Cardiff and Wrexham during the war, he would make a League bow in the Old Gold in 1947/8, and oppose City again in the 1949 FA Cup Final. A December 1950 transfer to Coventry City didn't work out happily, and in 1951 Terry emigrated to the States; though he didn't give up football, for he featured in the USA team against England in June 1953. (1 app)

A former captain of Leicester Boys, and an England schools international, **Len Staples** (Leonard Eric; b. Leicester, 23.1.1926) got a few chances as a 17-year-old amateur forward with City in the final game of 1942/3 and the early months of 1943/4, but spent most of his war on Navy service, occasionally representing the Mediterranean Fleet XI. He was a Torquay United trialist during 1946/7, but signed professional forms for City in July 1947, by which time he was regarded as a right-half. Lucklessly, he was the only member of the 1948 Combination Cup-winning side not to taste first-team action with City, but he built a fine 164-game record as a Newport County full-back after an August 1949 move. In July 1957, Len signed for Weymouth, and in June 1958 for Nuneaton Borough. (5 apps; 1 goal)

An outside-left who had wandered far and wide before the war, **Ernest Steele** (b. Middleton, 18.6.1908; d. Farnworth, 1972) finished his career as a City guest, forced to retire through injury after a quintet of appearances between November 1942 and January 1943: a period which also saw him hit by the death of his wife. A Rochdale professional from August 1931, he moved exactly a year later to Oldham Athletic, in May 1933 to Torquay United, in October 1934 to Notts County, in July 1936 to Bath City, and in December 1936 to Millwall. Tom Bromilow signed him for Crystal Palace in September 1938, and he moved back to Rochdale on the eve of war. Also a wartime guest for Chesterfield, Stockport and Palace, he was playing in Army football when re-signed by Bromilow. (5 apps; 1 goal)

On three occasions in the same City line-up was the unrelated **Freddie Steele** (Frederick Charles; b. Hanley, 6.5.1916; d. Newcastle-under-Lyme, 23.4.1976), who averaged a goal-a-game for City across two guest stints, in 1940/1 and 1942/3. A six-cap England international centre-forward who had signed for Stoke City in 1931 from Downings Tileries, Freddie eventually totalled 140 League goals and 88 wartime counters for the Potteries club; the latter haul remarkable for a man who also guested for Fulham, Doncaster, Leeds, Northampton, Forest, Bradford Park Avenue, Notts County and Sheffield United. In June 1949 he became player/manager at Mansfield Town, and performed similar dual duties for Port Vale from December 1951. He concentrated on managerial duties for the Valiants from 1953 to 1957,

and had a further spell as their boss from 1962 to 1965. (18 apps; 18 goals)

A creative inside-forward who'd signed for Blackburn Rovers in September 1942, **Harry W Stephan** (b. Farnworth, 24.2.1924) guested briefly for City during the winter of 1944/5, and also turned out in wartime football for Bolton Wanderers. He made 13 postwar appearances at Ewood, but following unsuccessful trials with Accrington Stanley in September 1948, soon dropped into the non-league sphere with Mossley. (4 apps; 1 goal)

Unfortunately unblessed with so much as an identifying initial by any of the local press at the time, centre-forward **Steward** featured in a goalless draw at Mansfield in September 1943, a week after claiming five goals from the Colts' 15-1 Senior League win at Melton. (1 app)

Two months later, Third Lanark's **A Sutton** wore the City spearhead's shirt at Derby. A Military Policeman, he had been assisting the Colts from the beginning of 1943/4. (1 app)

Another from that same Colts team was **Len Sutton**, a former Quorn Methodists team-mate of Jack Lee; though his only centre-forward outing for City came shortly after his military demob, when he led the line in a 1-7 home defeat by Chelsea in January 1946. Back with Quorn after the war, he appeared in the County Cup Finals of 1952, 1953 and 1954. (1 app)

Blackpool's **Fred Tapping** (Frederick H; b. Derby, 29.7.1921) numbered several Midlands clubs for whom he guested. His City spell was at right-half or inside-right between March and May 1945, and he also had wartime outings for Derby, Chesterfield, Mansfield and Notts County. He left Bloomfield Road for Chesterfield in November 1947, and in 1949 found himself in the initial Southern League line-up of the newly-professionalised Headington United (now Oxford United). (7 apps; 2 goals)

George Thomas Taylor (b. Walsall, 1908) was at the veteran stage when he briefly assisted City in March 1942: indeed the Coventry City winger retired from the game entirely a year later. A former England

schoolboy international, George had joined Notts County from Stourbridge back in May 1925, transferring to Bolton Wanderers in December 1933, and to Coventry in September 1937. He additionally returned to each of his previous clubs as a wartime guest. (2 apps; 1 goal)

A corporal in the RAF when he turned out at inside-left for City in March and April 1945, **Ron Thompson** (b. Sheffield, 24.12.1921) had been a 1942 Sheffield Wednesday signing from Wadsley Colliery. He remained at Hillsborough until a May 1947 move to Rotherham United, then joined York City in June 1949. (3 apps)

Tommy Thompson became Tom Bromilow's first signing as City manager when he joined from Tunbridge Wells Rangers in August 1939. The young outside-right got a fair bit of senior experience in the initial season of wartime football, but was soon posted to Ireland with his Army unit. There he represented the Army in Ulster XI and guested regularly for Linfield: in fact scoring twice in their 1942 Irish Cup Final win over Glentoran. He managed a couple more appearances for City in December 1942, but was unheard of again until officially freed in May 1946. (17 apps; 1 goal)

Offering his services to City along with Mullen and Wright when Wolves ceased operations for the 1940/41 season, **Dennis Thornhill** (b. Draycott, 5.7.1923; d. Southend, Aug 1992) had only a short spell as senior left-half at the beginning of that term. He failed to make a postwar break-through at Molineux, and was unfortunate to have his career cut short by injury after only eleven games for Southend United, following a March 1948 move. (3 apps)

A former member of the *Leicester Evening Mail* staff, who had played occasionally for City's Colts during 1941/2, **Harry Walton** (b. Manchester 1.4.1924) signed professional forms in September 1942: ironically, only two days after his sole senior outing in a goalless draw with West Brom. Harry made one post-war Third Division appearance for Southend United in October 1946, and later served Nuneaton Borough. (1 app.)

Primarily a right-back, but occasionally utilised at centre-forward, **Dick Walton** (Richard; b. Hull, 12.9.1924) signed as an amateur for City in June 1942, and stepped up to the senior ranks in January 1943, when partway through a run of 25 consecutive appearances. The following term, he was also a guest for Chester, Middlesbrough and Third Lanark. Dick was discharged from the Army in early 1944, but immediately signed up with the Palestine Police for the duration of the war. City released his registration to Leyton Orient in July 1948, and he moved to Exeter City in December 1951. After 199 League games for these two clubs, he joined Tonbridge in 1956. (31 apps)

Gresley Rovers 'keeper **E Ward** was a local stand-in for Joe Calvert against Spurs in May 1941, and earned praise despite a 1-2 home defeat. Later with Pegsons Athletic, he also represented the Combined Services locally, and was with Coalville Town in 1945/6. (1 app)

Forward **John H Wattie** was climbing the status ladder of Scottish football when war broke out, having moved from Inverurie Loco Works to Forfar in the 1937 close season, and having signed for Dundee two years later. He came to City's notice (rather inevitably) in 1942/3, when playing locally for COD (Old Dalby) and breaking scoring records with ease: in fact he scored a hat-trick or better in seven successive Senior League games from September to November that season. His City outings came in successive matches in April 1944 (in the outside-left berth), and a week after the third, he helped COD beat City in the Final of the Senior Cup. John was still on Dundee's initial postwar roll-call, but his subsequent moves are unknown to us. (3 apps; 1 goal)

Ray Watts was described as a 20-year-old Chesterfield lad, working as an engineer, when signing for City in April 1945. He had a single outing in each full-back spot during the 'transitional' season of 1945/6. (2 apps)

A pre-war Scottish schoolboy international, playing in junior football prior to joining the RAF in 1940, **Andy Weatherston** had attained the rank of Flight

Lieutenant by the time he joined City (am in cs 1945, pro in December 1945). His subsequent trio of senior games came on the left wing; but he won his 1946 Senior Cup medal as Don Revie's right-flank partner. We are as yet unable to confirm whether Andy forged a postwar career in Scottish football. (3 apps)

Playing in borrowed boots a couple of sizes too small, **Fred C Wilson** (b. Nottingham, 10.11.1918; d. January 1994) gamely helped City out in October 1940 when they arrived at Luton minus Mullen and Wright. A tall centre-half, ironically nicknamed 'Shorty', he was a former Wolves reserve who had joined Bournemouth & Boscombe Athletic in February 1939, and who went on to serve the Cherries until a June 1951 move to Weymouth. (1 app)

A local miner who had been assisting Derby County's Colts, **Eric Windle** (one source gives his forename as Ronald) was drafted into City's under-strength line-up at the Baseball Ground in April 1944, and scored from the inside-left berth in a 2-0 victory. He also had a couple of run-outs with City Reserves at the beginning of 1944/5. (1 app; 1 goal)

Capped by Wales both during and after the war, **Doug Witcomb** (Douglas Frederick; b. Ebbw Vale, 18.4.1918) made a single guest appearance for City at inside-left at Spurs in May 1941. He'd actually started his senior career as a Spurs amateur in the mid-30s, but found himself farmed out to Northfleet and Enfield before moving to West Bromwich Albion in October 1937 and establishing himself. Newport County, Swansea Town, Lovells Athletic and Grimsby Town also benefited from Doug's wartime services; while postwar he moved to Sheffield Wednesday (March 1947), Newport (November 1953), Llandudno Town (August 1954) and, in October 1955, to Redditch. (1 app)

Dennis Wright (b. Chesterfield, 19.12.1919; d. Chesterfield, July 1993) was a reserve goalkeeper for Mansfield Town (signed in March 1939 from Clay Lane Rangers) when he was recruited by City to make up the numbers at Field Mill in November 1940, and surprisingly claimed both goals from the right wing berth in a 2-4

defeat. Dennis also assisted Glentoran while on military service in Ireland, but didn't make Mansfield's senior line-up until peacetime football returned. He went on to play 380 League games for the Stags, and later became their groundsman. (1 app; 2 goals)

While everyone now remembers **Billy Wright** (William Ambrose; b. Ironbridge, 6.2.1924; d. Barnet, 3.9.1994) as the man who won 105 England caps as a centre-half, it was as a teenage forward that City fans first knew him. A 15-year-old when he opposed City for Wolves during 1939/40, he came to Filbert Street less than a year later (upon Wolves' playing shutdown) to star throughout 1940/1 primarily as a goalscoring right-winger. He scored in the Midland Cup Final win over Walsall, and also helped City to within one step of Wembley in the League War Cup. He would, of course, later skipper Wolves to FA Cup victory over City in 1949: he had signed initially as an amateur for them in June 1938 (from Cradley Heath), and only as a pro in February 1941 (partway through his Leicester sojourn), and would serve them through three Championship campaigns until retirement in 1959. A spell managing Arsenal and a later career in television would follow, and the civil honour of a CBE also accrued to this legendary sporting gentleman. (33 apps; 12 goals)

Harold Wyles (b. Melton Mowbray, 28.10.1922) first signed for City as an amateur in August 1939, made his debut in April 1941, and signed professional forms a year later. Usually a full-back or centre-half (who also enjoyed occasional excursions to centre-forward), he continued to split his playing time between City and his RAOC unit team, COD (Old Dalby), who he represented in successive Senior Cup Finals from 1942-44; and once guested for Nottingham Forest during 1943/4. In February 1948, Harold moved from City to Gateshead, going on to play 235 League games for them, scoring seven times. (24 apps)

Scottish full-back **David Agnew** (b. Kilwinning, 4.8.1939) left City in 1961, played once for Scunthorpe, then carved out an 85-game career at Notts County. He has been most recently noted back in Leicester in 1995, helping run a football scheme for people with learning disabilities. Inside-forward **John Allen**, who claimed City's opening goal in their first-ever London Combination game against West Ham reserves in August 1926, was a 1925 recruit from Scottish juniors Parkhead, who then made 8 appearances for Manchester City after Peter Hodge signed him for a second time in March 1927; while near-namesake striker **Johnny Allen** (b. Coventry, 24.4.1955) was a modest Jock Wallace purchase from Hinckley Athletic who was freed in 1980 for a season at Port Vale, and then returned to Hinckley. Belfast-born **Ken Armstrong** was an early-50s defender at Filbert Street whose subsequent soccer career we have been unable to trace: he became, however, an Irish Rugby Union international in 1961.

A noteworthy Fosse pioneer, **T S Ashmole** (b. Winshill, Derbys, 1863) joined the club in 1886 after previous experience with Stapenhill, Burton Swifts and Leicester Town, and soon took the captaincy, which he held when Fosse fought out their first-ever competitive matches, in the Leicestershire Senior Cup in 1887/8 (exiting in a Round Two second replay to inaugural winners Shepshed). He left for Loughborough (with goalkeeper Tom DeVille) in the 1888 close season when Fosse were forced to switch their fixtures from the Belgrave Road Grounds back to Victoria Park. A former Burton Harriers athlete (specialising at 440 yards) and Burton St.Marks cricketer, who had worked for Bass from the age of 14, he was also behind the scenes the Honorary Secretary of the County FA from 1887-94, and a leading referee (taking an FA Cup semi-final in 1893). He moved away from the area in 1894 to work in Edinburgh.

Bob Atkins (b. Leicester, 16.10.1962) failed to win a professional contract after his City apprenticeship, but the defensive midfielder soon stepped up from Enderby Town to Sheffield United in 1981, and moved to Preston North End in 1985 for a 200-game back-line stint. **Geoff Aunger** (b. Red Deer, Alberta, 4.2.1968) was a Canadian international winger when he arrived from Vancouver 86ers for Central League trials in February 1992; he has gained a little subsequent League experience with Luton Town and Chester City while adding to his cap tally.

Forward **Mick Balmer** (b. Hexham, 25.5.1946) managed 28 games for Halifax Town (9 gls) after being released in 1965, and then moved to Derry City. Another to make a mark in Ireland was **Arthur Leonard Bamford**. A Wigston-born forward who played several senior Fosse friendlies during 1896/7 and 1897/8 (scoring, for instance, against Glasgow Rangers, Derby County and Burton Wanderers), he then walked out on the club and was next discovered, playing under the name Arthur Leonard, winning Irish League representative selections while starring for Glentoran. He signed for Small Heath in 1901 (with both Fosse and Glentoran claiming fees), and later success-fully served Stoke, St.Bernards, Clapton Orient and Plymouth Argyle.

Northumbrian centre-forward **Fred Baron** (Frederick John; b. Prudhoe, 29.12.1901) utilised the pseudonym 'Charles' when claiming three goals from City's first two public practice matches of August 1922. Immediately signing on, he nonetheless soon departed for Mid-Rhondda, then

THE NEARLY MEN

Over the years, the club has been served, of course, by numerous reserve players who failed to make a single breakthrough into senior competitive football at Leicester. A few of these have been players with prior experience at senior level; a greater number have gone on to build variably lengthy careers with subsequent clubs. A small percentage of 'those who got away' have proved sufficiently successful elsewhere to embarrass or haunt the club which discarded them. Below we index alphabetically a representative cross-section of Fosse and City players whose careers peaked, statistically at least, away from Filbert Street; and a handful more whose roles in the club's history demand acknowledgement.

JIMMY DICKSON

CHARLES GELLATLY

stepped up to join Liverpool in February 1925. After 7 goals in 20 games, he claimed 42 from 62 outings for Southend United. Right-winger **Harry J Bates** (b. Sutton Coldfield, 1890) was a reserve Fossil for barely a month, signing from Birmingham in September 1913 after thrice representing their League side the previous season, and moving on to Birmingham League side Walsall in October.

Full-back **Peter Bebbington** (b. Oswestry, 13.10.1946), signed from Oswestry Town in 1965, later made 52 League appearances for Barrow (where he faced City in the Cup in 1968) and 17 more for Stockport. County cricketer **Les Berry** (Leslie George; b. Dorking, 28.4.1906; d. Great Glen, 15.2.1985) played in goal for both City reserves and Market Harborough club Symington's during 1926/7. He was later a Sheffield Wednesday reserve, but went on to play an aggregate of 56 League games for Bristol Rovers and Swindon Town between 1930-33. **Brian Billington** (b. Leicester, 28.4.1951) had a brief spell with Notts County in 1969/70, and then joined Enderby Town.

City's goalkeeper for the 1975/6 FA Youth Cup campaign was trialist **Pat Bonner** (Patrick Joseph; b. Clochglas, Donegal, 24.5.1960) of Keadue Rovers, later to win considerable fame with both Celtic and the Republic of Ireland. An April 1894 trialist from Castle Donington, **Samuel Bosworth** featured at outside-right in a senior friendly against Rotherham Town that month, then joined Long Eaton Rangers. During 1898/9, he figured at League level for each of Loughborough, Derby County and Sheffield Wednesday. **Ken Brandon** (b. Birmingham, 8.2.1934) was already experienced in League football with Swindon Town and Chester (and had scored in the 1955 Welsh Cup Final for the latter club) before supplementing City's squad in 1956: he had to wait two years for a move to Darlington, however, before adding to his senior appearance tally. Young Irish forward **Bobby Bruce** (b. Belfast, 14.10.1928) arrived from Larne in March 1950, but his sole League game came after a move to Leyton Orient in November 1951.

A goalkeeper very close to a senior breakthrough with City was **John B Bunting**, who had trials in April 1922 (featuring in two friendlies against Northampton), and was chosen for that month's Second Division away game at Rotherham County. The day before the match, however, it was discovered he was ineligible: though playing for Sneinton, he was still officially on Nottingham Forest's amateur roster, and in fact City were later fined for mis-registering him. John did, though, later step up from Boston Town in 1924 to win eight League selections for Brighton & Hove Albion before once more joining the non-league ranks at Mansfield Town.

Released from Filbert Street in 1985, Edinburgh-born defender **Scott Burnside** later had brief spells with each of Berwick Rangers, East Stirlingshire and Cowdenbeath. Full-back **Jimmy Burt** (James H L; b. Harthill, 5.4.1950) moved to Aldershot along with Murray Brodie in 1970: he had 24 League outings there, followed by spells at Northampton Town and Rochdale.

John Cairns (b. Glasgow, 1902; d. Shooters Hill, 24.6.1965) was an experienced forward who could not add to his senior record following his May 1928 signing from Brentford (though he did pop up again briefly at Rochdale during 1933/4, after interim stints with Kettering, Margate and Portsmouth reserves). He'd moved from St.Bernards to play in Broxburn United's initial Scottish League fixture in 1921, and for Dunfermline, Kettering and Charlton Athletic before scoring on his sole Brentford outing. A player of higher calibre who City rejected after 1930 trials was **Raich Carter** (Horatio Stratton; b. Sunderland, 21.12.1913), who went on to win 13 England caps in a marvellous inside-forward career with Sunderland, Derby County and Hull City, and later managed Hull, Leeds United, Mansfield Town and Middlesbrough.

Young centre-forward **David Cartlidge** (b. Leicester, 9.4.1940) left Filbert Street in 1961 after four years on the books, and played briefly for both Bradford City and Chester within a season. **Mervyn Cawston** (b. Norwich, 4.5.1952)

was a much-travelled goalkeeper who had a brief loan spell with City in 1975/6, and served each of Norwich City, Southend United, Newport County, Gillingham, Chicago Sting and Maidstone United at first-team level.

Winger **Peter Chamberlain** (b. Liverpool, 30.6.1935) was a City reserve during 1956/7, but made 78 senior appearances in five years at Swindon Town, and then served Aldershot for 46 games. **Thomas Chappell** was a goalkeeping understudy to the ever-present Jimmy Thraves: he signed from Buxton in 1894 (having starred in the side which removed Fosse from the FA Cup in 1892/3), moved on to non-league West Manchester in 1895, and then joined Manchester City, for whom his eight League outings included two against Fosse. Given December 1984 trials by Gordon Milne, but allowed to return to Brondby, defensive midfielder **Kim Christofte** (b. 24.8.1960) won his 16th Danish cap in the victorious European Championship side of 1992. His other clubs have included Lokeren, OB Odense and 1FC Koln.

Goalkeeper **Trevor Churchill** (b. Barnsley, 20.11.1923) started his career with Yorkshire Amateurs, played during WW2 for Sheffield United, and featured in ten games for Reading during 1946/7 before joining City for a two-year reserve stint. He went on to play 110 times for Rochdale and on eleven more occasions for Swindon Town. Current Wimbledon winger **Andy Clarke** (b. London, 22.7.1967), then with Barnet, tried out for David Pleat in a City friendly at Andover in November 1989, and scored in a 10-1 win. A reserve forward, **Willie Clarke** (William Henry; b. Leicester, 1916), joined City in February 1936 from Leicester Nomads, then played for Exeter City during 1937/8, and fleetingly for Southampton the following term. He returned to local fare with Hinckley United and Anstey Methodists. On the City bench at Tranmere in August 1993, as stand-by substitute goalkeeper, **Richard Clay** (b. Leicester, 24.3.1976) was released in 1994, joining Hinckley Town, and linking with Oadby Town and VS Rugby for 1995/6.

City changed their mind about releasing forward **Barry Cliff** (b. Motherwell, 10.9.1964) in 1984, but he was still on his way a year later without senior experience; and it wasn't until he reached Stranraer for the 1986/7 season that he found first-team football, despite an interim spell with Hibernian. Forward-cum-midfielder **Robert Codner** (b. Walthamstow, 23.1.1965) played in Spurs' youth teams and City's reserves in the early 80s, then made his reputation with Barnet in the Conference, earning a £115,000 move to Brighton & Hove Albion in September 1988. He was loaned to Reading in September 1995. Forward **Robert Cooper** (b. Sutton Coldfield, 3.9.1966) was loaned out for a five-game spell with Preston North End during 1985/6, but released by City at the end of that term. **Billy Coventry** was a goalkeeper who joined Fosse from Chester in 1906: his League outings, though, came both before and afterwards with Crewe Alexandra.

Full-back **Paul Crawford** (b. Edinburgh, 14.7.1964) won Scottish Youth honours while at Filbert Street, but had to move back north of the border in 1982 for first-team football with Dunfermline Athletic and East Stirlingshire. Outside-right **Jack Crisp** (John; b. Hamstead, Birmingham, 27.11.1894) was a Fosse reserve in 1913/14, but his best days were after the war and elsewhere. He won a 1920 League championship medal with West Bromwich Albion, and also played for Blackburn Rovers (from March 1923) and Coventry City (from February 1927). **Paul Culpin** (b. Kirby Muxloe, 8.2.1962) was City's reserve Player of the Year and top scorer during 1981/2, but was released to pick up his career with Nuneaton Borough. This he did with a vengeance, smashing scoring records at the top of the non-league pyramid with 131 goals in 150 appearances, and earning a £50,000 move to Coventry City in June 1985. Capped at semi-professional level for England, he later played for each of Peterborough United, Barnet, Telford United, Kettering Town, Hereford United, Nuneaton again, and Racing Club Warwick.

William James Cummings (b. Newcastle on Tyne, 1883) was a reserve half-back for Fosse in 1907/8: a former Newcastle United reserve and a senior player with Ashington, Reading and Norwich City, he moved on to Chelsea, but failed to make a first-team breakthrough there, either. **John G Currie** (b. Dumfries, 7.4.1939) came to Leicester in 1957 with Scottish schoolboy caps to his name, but was unable to claim a senior wing-half position until moving to Workington in 1961. He also turned out later for Chester.

Finishing his career with a 1907/8 reserve season at Filbert Street was left-back **Harry Davies**, who had played previously for Wolves (from March 1898), Shrewsbury Town, Gainsborough Trinity, Doncaster Rovers (1904) and Grimsby Town. Creative inside-forward **Jimmy Dickson** (James Whitford; b. Glasgow) was a £200 buy from Dunfermline Athletic in August 1930, though he had spent the previous term playing in the Irish Free State League with Fordson's. He returned to that club for 1931/2 after finding no senior joy at Leicester, then spent successive seasons with Partick Thistle and Cowdenbeath. Another City man to enjoy his best days in Ireland was **Gavin Drummond**, a Derry-born young striker released in 1982 to play for Athlone Town, Longford Town and Monaghan United.

Outside-left **Stan Duff** (Stanley Douglas; b. Liverpool, 1919), a former schoolboy international, picked up appearances with Tranmere Rovers, Waterford, Chester and New Brighton after leaving City's professional ranks in 1937, while still only in his teens. **Tommy Dutton** (b. Southport, 7.12.1906) signed for City from Chorley in 1931, but left unrewarded for his reserve-team forward-line efforts in 1934; going on to score six times for Queens Park Rangers, ten for Doncaster Rovers, and twelve for Mansfield Town. He also made one appearance for Rochdale during 1939/40.

Of a somewhat different pedigree was **Helge Ekroth** (b. 26.2.1892; d. 29.11.1950), who came to Filbert Street on extended trial following Fosse's 1913 tour of Sweden: he represented

Stockholm club AIK for the bulk of his career, and scored ten goals in 18 international appearances between 1911 and 1922. A striker elevated to the professional ranks at Darlington by Brian Little in 1990, **Lee Ellison** (Anthony Lee; b. Bishop Auckland, 13.1.1973) rejoined his former boss at Leicester on a year's contract in August 1994, after the contrasting experiences of a March 1993 loan to Hartlepool United and July 1994 trials with Kenny Dalglish's Blackburn Rovers. Only a handful of Central League goals accrued, however, and Lee was freed in May 1995; subsequently linking with Crewe Alexandra.

Alexander Farmer (b. Lochgelly, 1909) was a wing-half who'd moved from Kettering to Nottingham Forest in April 1930, and won 16 League selections there until signing on at Filbert Street in August 1932. He left, untried, for Yeovil & Petters United, but returned to the senior sphere with Queens Park Rangers in January 1934 (80 games, 10 goals), and later was trainer there until the 50s. One of his charges there was **Des Farrow** (b. Peterborough, 11.2.1926), a City amateur during WW2, who moved on to QPR in 1944, and then had a brief spell with Stoke City from October 1952. Former Scottish international goalkeeper **Bobby Ferguson** (b. Ardrossan, 1.3.1945) briefly helped out City's reserves during a loan spell from West Ham United in March 1974. He'd been a Kilmarnock discovery who'd signed up at Upton Park for a £65,000 fee in May 1967, and also had a brief spell on loan with Sheffield Wednesday in 1974.

Michael Ford (b. Bristol, 9.2.1966; a son of former Bristol City and Bristol Rovers stalwart Tony) drifted away to Devizes Town after completing his City apprenticeship, but joined Cardiff City in 1984 as a utility player, and earned himself a £150,000 transfer to Oxford United in June 1988. Striker **Mark Forster** was on home-town club Middlesbrough's books as an amateur until signed by City in 1983, but playing for Darlington's League side before the season was out, and eventually notching 13 goals in 38 games after his loan move was made permanent. He later joined Guisborough. **Mike Foster** (b. Leicester, 3.2.1939) was also a forward, on City's roster from 1959: he played his League football subsequently for Colchester United and Millwall.

Herbert Galloway, a left-half signed from Wombwell in April 1928, did not fulfil expectations with City: he had, however, tasted one game of League football with Halifax Town during 1926/7. Also with prior League experience before a City reserve stint was full-back **Herbert A Garner** (b. Mexborough, c.1899), whose up-and-down career had taken him from Mexborough GC Loco, via Denaby United, Lincoln City (1921-24; 6 apps) and Rotherham Town to Mansfield Town; from whom City signed him in a February 1926 joint deal with Billy Bell. It was 1930 before he again briefly enjoyed the League limelight (with two games for Stockport County), and after October trials with Torquay United he rejoined Mansfield.

Young winger **Jason Garwood** (b. Birmingham, 23.3.1969) was loaned out from Filbert Street for League experience at Northampton Town during the early months of 1988/9, and made seven senior appearances. After a further loan spell at Southern League Leicester United, however, he was released by David Pleat to Burton Albion in March 1989. Goalkeeper **Ted Gaskell** (Edward; b. Bedbury, 19.12.1916) sought first-team football with a move from City to Brentford in 1937, yet had to wait no less than ten years for his League bow - ironically against City! He went on to top up 34 senior starts, and shared in a Griffin Park testimonial in 1954.

Youth-team keeper **Mark Gayle** (b. Bromsgrove, 21.10.1969) was freed in 1989 for a term with Blackpool in which he made but one League Cup start. He dropped down to Worcester City, but a £15,000 move to Walsall in May 1991 heralded the start of his League career. A loan spell with Cheltenham Town and a £35,000 move to Crewe Alexandra followed, and Mark was also briefly on loan with Liverpool in February 1994. Paisley-born brothers **Andy Geddes** and **Paul Geddes** both joined City in 1979 from Scottish Junior football. Midfielder Andy won a £20,000 move to Dundee in November 1980, and within a month was appearing in the Scottish League

Cup Final. He left Dens Park in 1984 to play in South Africa, for Wits University and Kaiser Chiefs. Defender Paul meanwhile had also returned to Scotland, but found no more joy with Hibernian than he had at Filbert Street. He did, however, play two League games while on trial at Wimbledon in November 1981. He, too, then tried his luck in South Africa; both brothers later featured on the Leicestershire non-league scene.

Full-back **Charles T Gellatly** (b. Brodworth), a signing from Shirebrook in May 1930 (on the same day as Jim Bulling), moved on a year later for a three-season, 61-game stint at Gillingham. Former schools international winger **George Gibbs** (b. Chester-le-Street, c.1907), an August 1924 City signing, had two spells with Barnsley after leaving Filbert Street in 1928, and also represented Worcester City in 1931. Attacking left-back **Michael Gilkes** (b. Hackney, 20.7.1965) had youth and reserve outings with City in 1983/4 as a non-contract trialist, but has subsequently built a lengthy career of over 300 games with Reading (incorporating loan-outs to Chelsea and Southampton during 1991/2).

Midfielder **Adie Green** (b. Leicester, 22.10.1957) had a loan spell with Rochdale in 1977/8 to prepare him for the step up to City's senior squad, but was released to Aldershot shortly after Jock Wallace's arrival. Little forward **Bobby Greig** (b. Sunderland, 13.9.1949) got a brief League run at Workington after leaving City in February 1968. The first foreign international to represent the club, **Karl Gustafsson** (b. 16.9.1888; d. 20.2.1960) was a regular for Fosse reserves during 1912/13, prior to the summer tour of Sweden, and turned out in senior friendlies against both Gillingham and Barrow. He played for IFK Koping until 1910, then Kopings IS, to whom he returned after his Fosse spell. The inside-forward or wing-half's tally of caps between 1908 (Sweden's first-ever international, against Norway) and 1924 amounted to 32 (22 goals), and in 1926 he joined Vikings of Chicago.

On City's books from December 1924 to the 1928 close season, outside-right **Chris**

Hackett (Christopher Edward; b. Mansfield, 9.2.1903; d. Leicester, 1983) eventually got a brief taste of League fare at Bristol Rovers and Accrington Stanley in the early 30s. His wandering career, which had seen him representing Mansfield Town, Langwith Colliery, Newark Town and Grantham before his City stint, also took in spells with Caernarfon Town, Bury reserves, Scunthorpe United and Loughborough Corinthians. Scottish full-back **Steve Hamilton** had to return home for senior football: with Hearts from 1980, East Fife from 1981 and East Stirlingshire from 1983.

Central defender **Nigel Hart** (b. Golborne, 1.10.1958; a son of ex-Manchester City star Johnny, and a brother of Leeds, Forest and Sheffield Wednesday centre-back Paul) had played one League game for Wigan Athletic before joining City in 1979, but it wasn't until two years later, after a move to Blackpool, that he extended his senior career. Spells with Crewe Alexandra, Bury, Stockport County, Chesterfield (where his brother was boss), York City and Droylsden followed. Inside-forward **Tom Hartley** (Thomas William; b. Gateshead, 7.5.1817; d. Chesterfield, January 1984) had only a month with City's reserves from his signing from North Shields just after Christmas 1947 until his involvement in the five-man move to Watford at the end of January 1948. He had started his career at Gateshead in 1935/6, and also had a wartime spell with Chesterfield.

An August 1937 signing from Scottish juniors Benburb, wing-half **Willie Hay** (b. Blantyre) moved on a year later to Irish club Sligo Rovers and, alongside the veteran Dixie Dean, won a runners-up medal from the replayed 1939 FAI Cup Final against Shelbourne. Chesterfield gave a 5-game break during 1983/4 to Sheffield-born midfielder **Mike Higginbottom**, whom City had freed in 1981. Former miner **Stanley High** (b. Hetton-le-Hole, 18.2.1908; d. Horden, 13.4.1982) spent the 1928/9 season at City as a reserve wing-half, having been signed from Easington Colliery, then played at League level for each of Torquay United, Accrington Stanley and Gillingham.

Ian Hill (b. Dublin, 9.5.1965), a full-back signed from his home-town junior side Cherry Orchard, moved on to League of Ireland fare with Shelbourne after a September 1988 release. **Richard Hill** (b. Hinckley, 20.9.1963) was for some time the record-holder for the largest fee paid for a former City reserve. The strongly-built attacking midfielder was released to Nuneaton Borough in 1983 (after a brief stint in New Zealand), and two years later joined Northampton Town, becoming the Fourth Division's top scorer in 1986/7 before a £240,000 move to Watford. His subsequent travels have taken him to Oxford United, Kettering Town, Worcester City, Racing Club Warwick, Witney Town, back to Nuneaton and in August 1995 to Hinckley Athletic.

A Hodges was a former Croydon Common forward with Southern League experience who was briefly a Fosse trialist during 1913/14, but settled later that term at Pontypridd. **William Hogan** (b. Aldershot, c.1872) was a Fosse signing as a winger from Fleetwood Rangers in 1895, who turned out once in the League for Grimsby Town during 1896/7: he was nonetheless more famous at the time as a baseball pitcher with both Preston North End and British champions Derby.

Another City reserve forward to wander was **Mick Hollis** (b. Loughborough, 14.11.1949). After three years of frustration at Filbert Street, he joined Barrow in 1969, and subsequently also served Chester, Stockport County and Reading in an almost 250-game League career. A prolific reserve scorer, and former schools international, **Alan J Hoult** (b. Burbage, 7.10.1957) made the City sub's bench at Hull for the FA Cup tie of 1978, but was not called on. Yet months later he was turning out for Hull on loan. He also played on loan at Lincoln, but managed only one League Cup outing after a transfer to Bristol Rovers the following close season, and later served Nuneaton Borough and Bedworth United.

Goalkeeper **Steve Humphries** (b. Hull, 29.5.1961) had two spells with City in the shadow of the immovable Mark Wallington. His League experience came, though, at Doncaster Rovers, Cardiff City and Wrexham in the early 80s;

and he also turned out for Kettering Town (again in two stints), Vancouver Whitecaps, Barnet (where he won England semi-pro recognition), Welling United, Telford United and Solihull Borough before briefly becoming assistant manager to Brendan Phillips at Stafford Rangers in 1993/4. **Mark Hutchinson** (Colin Mark; b. Stoke on Trent, 12.11.1963) was a 1983 City signing, after being released from his Aston Villa apprentice-ship. The midfielder, however, had to wait for a loan a year later to Carlisle United before making his League bow. He also featured briefly for Northampton Town before joining the colony of one-time City men at Nuneaton Borough.

A David Pleat signing from Brian Little, **Gary Hyde** (b. Wolverhampton, 28.12.1969) was a speedy attacking midfielder at Darlington who initially came to Leicester on loan in April 1990, scored twice for the reserves, and signed permanently a month later. He was then loaned to Finnish side Kumu Kuusankoski for the summer, and broke his collarbone in his fourth game. Gary made the City bench at Millwall on Boxing Day 1990, but got no further before a May 1990 release to Scunthorpe United. He has subsequently served Bishop Auckland. David Pleat gave a month's City trial in September 1989 to his former Luton striker **Godfrey Ingram** (b. Luton, 26.10.1959), who by that stage had also appeared in the colours of Northampton Town, Cardiff City, New York Cosmos, San Jose Earthquakes, Golden Bay Earthquakes and Minnesota Strikers. Godfrey subsequently had a brief spell in Holland with Haarlem, then joined St.Albans City.

Peter Jackson was top scorer for City reserves in 1975/6: despite trials with Cardiff City, he never made the League game, but had a helping of near-glory in assisting St.Patrick's Athletic to the semi-final of the FAI Cup while on loan in Ireland during 1974/5. **Andy Jeffrey** (b. Bellshill, 15.1.1972; a son of former Celtic winger Bob) was a trainee full-back at Leicester until his 1992 release to Cambridge City, and since 1993 has been a regular League player for Cambridge United.

A 19-year-old centre-forward signed in August 1937, **William Thomas Johnson** (b. Brantford, Ontario) had a Barwell upbringing after his Canadian birth. He stayed only a year at Filbert Street before signing for Gillingham, who had just been replaced in the Third Division (South) by Ipswich Town, and for whom he claimed 14 goals in 36 Southern League outings in 1938/9. **David D Johnston** (b. Scothern, 17.9.1941; a son of former Sunderland and Scotland player Robert) joined City in February 1960 from Bishop Auckland, but was freed in 1962 to spend one League campaign with each of Exeter City and Stockport County.

Inside-left **Syd Kearney** (Sydney Francis; b. Liverpool, 28.3.1917; d. Chelsea, 1982) had a lengthy career after leaving City for Tranmere Rovers in 1937; going on to play for Accrington Stanley on both sides of the war, guesting for Sunderland, and becoming a left-half regular at Bristol City. **Francis Keith** was a City reserve inside-forward for 1935/6: signed from Dunipace, he moved on to Falkirk.

Some might dispute that **Tom Kilkelly** (b. Galway, 22.8.1955) ought to qualify for inclusion in the main Alphabet of senior players: but his only first-team run-out for City was in the 3rd/4th place consolation game of the 1973/4 FA Cup, a game we haven't counted towards any other player's official statistics. The midfielder won Irish youth caps while with City, and played for Northampton Town on loan during 1974/5, but was freed the following summer. He subsequently played for Burton Albion, Shamrock Rovers and in South Africa before returning to the Midlands non-league scene. Also released from City to Burton Albion, in 1980, was winger **David Kirk**, an 18-year-old Jock Wallace signing from Bulwell Forest Villa in November 1978. David would most notably be regarded, however, for his efforts in helping Napier City Rovers lift the 1989 New Zealand National Soccer League Championship.

William Lavery (b. Fleetwood, c.1887) was a trialist full-back with Fosse in 1907/8: the previous season he had played 14 First Division games for Preston North

End, and indeed went on to extend his senior career at Deepdale after his Leicester sojourn, and before moves to West Ham United (1909) and Belfast Celtic (1911). **Edward J Leahy** was a goalkeeper signed by Jack Bartlett from Walthamstow Grange, who went on to serve Southend United (1914/15), West Ham (during WW1) and Aberdare Athletic, where he became player/manager. **Tony Lee** (b. Middlesbrough, 26.11.1947) was a prolific youth and reserve scorer for City between 1965 and 1967, but notched only three goals in a subsequent brief League career at Bradford City and Darlington. His later days in management saw him bossing Billingham Synthonia, Gateshead and Bishop Auckland.

Well-travelled blond striker **Mark Lillis** (b. Manchester, 17.1.1960) had a Central League spell as a non-contract player in September 1991, but City turned out to be the only one of his clubs not to offer first-team football. Having previously played for Huddersfield Town, Manchester City, Derby County, Aston Villa and Scunthorpe United, he was soon on his way to Stockport County. **Gordon Livie** (b. Billingham, 10.6.1932) was a full-back who moved in 1952 to Mansfield Town, and made 53 appearances for the Stags. Half-back **Matt Lockhead** signed for Fosse in 1909 from Swindon Town: he had earlier served St. Mirren, and would subsequently have a reserve spell at Manchester City before moving back south to Swindon, Bath City and Reading.

An instance of father and son being united in their frustrations at Leicester is provided by the case of **John Loughlan** and **Tony Loughlan**. Full-back John (b. Coatbridge, 12.6.1943) waited patiently but in vain for a City breakthrough in the early 60s, but starred for Morton, Crystal Palace and Wrexham thereafter. At Selhurst he shared in the 1969 promotion campaign which lifted Palace to Division One for the first time; while after returning to Leicester he was for a while landlord of 'The Turnstile', the pub closest to Filbert Street. His son Tony (Anthony John; b. Croydon, 19.1.1970) was a trainee striker with City from 1986-88,

and a year later stepped up from Leicester United to Nottingham Forest, scoring on his League debut in March 1991. He has had subsequent stints with Kettering Town, Lincoln City and Dundalk.

Another former trainee, defender **Des Lyttle** (b. Wolverhampton, 24.9.1971) signed professionally for City in 1990, but had his contract cancelled after a brief loan spell at Burton Albion. He rebuilt his career with Worcester City, and moved in 1992 to Swansea City. In July 1993 Nottingham Forest paid £375,000 for Des, making him currently the most expensive of City's 'Nearly Men', and he has been their regular right-back since.

Jack McAlpin, who played at centre-half in Fosse's final United Counties League fixture of 1894/5 (the only time the club entered a supplementary senior league competition), was from a local sporting family primarily connected to the Tigers, though his amateur soccer loyalty was usually due to Leicester YMCA. Inside-forward **Gerry McCaffrey** won an Irish Under-23 cap while on City's books in 1962/3, and was later honoured with four appearances for the Irish League after picking up his senior career with Distillery (IFA Cup Finalists in 1969), Glentoran and Drogheda. Defensive midfielder **Owen McGee** (b. Teesside, 20.4.1970) had played 21 League games for Middlesbrough (scoring once - against City), and had featured in the 1990 ZDS Cup Final at Wembley, when he came to Leicester for a Central League stint stretching from November 1991 to March 1992. He then moved on to Scarborough. Derry City full-back **Ray McGuinness** had a two-game reserve trial with City in December 1988 (after having played in the previous term's FAI Cup Final), and contrived to get himself sent off on his debut at Old Trafford.

Edwin Rolland MacLachlan (b. Glasgow, 24.9.1903; d. Leicester, 16.3.1970) had been on the books of Vale of Leven, Queens Park, Third Lanark and Hibernian as an amateur before signing similar forms for City in August 1926. After scoring 7 times in 11 reserve games, the outside-left turned pro in January 1927, though it wasn't until he moved

to Nottingham Forest in the following close season that he got a League debut. He later played for Mansfield Town (scoring the goal by which the non-leaguers KO'd Wolves from the Cup in 1929) and Northampton Town, but it was in football administration that 'Mac' made his biggest mark locally, as a long-serving secretary to the Leicestershire Senior League and, between 1963 and 1970, as chairman of the County FA.

Young Glaswegian forward **John Hamilton McNeil** signed for City from Parkhead Juniors in March 1935, but was allowed to move on to Ayr United in May 1936, shortly after being sent off playing for the reserves at Reading. Further transfers saw him become a decent goalscorer at both Hull City and Bury before the outbreak of war. Striker **Dixie McNeil** (b. Melton Mowbray, 16.1.1947) became something of a goalscoring legend after his Filbert Street seconds' days. Signed from Holwell Works in November 1964, he was released in 1966, to claim an aggregate of 239 League goals from a wandering career that took in Exeter City, Northampton Town, Lincoln City, Hereford United (twice) and Wrexham. He was manager of the latter club from April 1985 to November 1989, and later joined the Coventry City coaching staff.

Winger **Dick Marshall** (b. Leicester, 23.11.1945) notched seven goals in 31 League outings for Southport after a 1965 move. Former youth-team goalkeeper **Keith Mason** (b. Leicester, 19.7.1958) got 30 League chances in five years at Huddersfield Town from 1982, and won an FA Vase winners' medal with Colne Dynamos in 1988; later serving Witton Albion. Half-back **Ken Mellor** (b. Leicester, 22.8.1934) managed two seasons at each of Mansfield Town and Swindon Town after his 1957 release. Yugoslavian international full-back **Branko Miljus** tried out for David Pleat in City's friendly at Exeter City in August 1990, but was not taken on. His club affiliations were to Hajduk Split and Spanish outfit Real Valladolid.

Scottish forward **James Milliken** played in six of the seven United Counties League games of 1894/5, scoring once, and also claimed two goals from his four senior friendlies of that term. He had arrived from Third Lanark, and moved on to St.Mirren, Tottenham Hotspur and Clyde. Ending a distinguished career as a City reserve in 1926/7, after taking up an appointment locally with Stead & Simpson in October 1926, was bespectacled amateur international goalkeeper **James Frederick Mitchell** (b. Manchester, 1897). A Manchester University graduate, and son of a famous billiards player, he had represented Preston North End in the 1922 FA Cup Final, and in the interim served Manchester City.

Striker **Christian Moore** (b. Derby, 4.11.1972) was a Filbert Street trainee from 1989-91, whose subsequent senior record at Stockport County amounted only to one substitute outing at League level, and a start in an Associate Members Cup tie. He has subsequently played for Nuneaton Borough, Gresley Rovers, Sandiacre and Leicester United. Tragically deprived of any sort of senior career was **Paul Moss**, a 19-year-old winger of high promise, signed from Chorley in the 1930 close season. He collapsed in a midweek practice match at Filbert Street and days later, on 22.3.1931, died of meningitis. Dundonian forward **R Mullaney** (signed in 1936 from Clepington Juniors) knocked in a couple of League goals for Barrow after a 1937 move.

Jon Narbett (b. Birmingham, 21.11.1968), a former Shrewsbury Town midfielder, came on loan to City from Hereford United in November 1991 (as Kevin Russell made the reverse trip). A year later he was with Oxford United, then played in Swedish football, and for Chesterfield and Merthyr Tydfil. Inside-left in two of the 1894/5 United Counties League fixtures, and a scorer against Notts County, the otherwise unidentified **Narraway** left Fosse for Hinckley Town in 1895. Central defender **David Needham** (b. Leicester, 21.5.1949) and goalkeeper-turned-full-back **Gordon Nisbet** (b. Wallsend, 18.9.1951) were both City trialists in the mid-60s: the former went on to star for Notts County, QPR and Nottingham Forest and won England B caps; while the latter

was capped at Under-23 level while with West Bromwich Albion and before moves to Hull City, Plymouth Argyle and Exeter City. **George Norton** (b. Stockton, 18.11.1916) lost his senior career to the war: on the heels of his City release, his sole appearance at inside-left for Bradford Park Avenue was in the second game of the abandoned 1939/40 League season, and he later featured at lower levels with West Hartlepool.

Pat O'Toole (b. Dublin, 2.1.1965) was a midfielder signed by David Pleat in February 1990, after he'd faced City in a friendly against Pat Byrne's Shelbourne side. He'd previously served Shamrock Rovers, Drogheda United, Galway United and Sligo Rovers; and twice made the City subs' bench during 1989/90 (at West Brom and Sunderland). Pat was loaned in December 1990 to Exeter City, then sold in March 1991 to Shrewsbury Town. He has since turned out for Shamrock again, and for Cobh Ramblers, Halifax Town (briefly replacing Jason Peake) and Stafford Rangers.

Young forward **Tom Paterson** (b. Newcastle on Tyne, 30.3.1954) won League selections for Middlesbrough, Bournemouth and Darlington between 1974 and 1979 following a City apprenticeship; while defender **Jess Payne** (b. London, 7.3.1958) had a 25-game stint with Torquay United from December 1977, and then gave long service to Yeovil Town. Barnet winger **Lee Payne** (b. Luton, 12.12.1966) commenced a City trial in September 1988 with a Central League outing against Newcastle United: it was the visitors, however, who immediately snapped him up on a League contract at a substantial fee. He moved on to Reading in March 1989, and has played most of his football since 1990 in Holland, for Veendam and Emmen, bracketing a brief 1993 Conference spell with Gateshead.

Full-back **Jon Pearson** (b. Birmingham, 12.10.1966) didn't taste League football after his City release but within twelve months he was appearing at Wembley as a substitute for Kidderminster Harriers on their way to eventual FA Trophy triumph, and he later played in the 1989 Welsh Cup Final. In

November 1989, along with Robbie Jones, he joined the opponents from the Wembley draw, Burton Albion, and has subsequently served Stafford Rangers and Solihull Borough. **Ernest 'Dick' Pegg** (b. Leicester, 1878; d. Leicester, 11.6.1916) was an amateur forward with Fosse's second string in 1895 and 1896, but first signed professional for Loughborough in June 1897. After two terms as the Luffs' top scorer, he became part of Kettering's 1899/1900 Midland League championship side, then served Reading, Preston North End, Manchester United, Fulham and Barnsley before retiring with knee trouble and taking over the Vine Tavern in Leicester.

Petur Petursson appeared twice in the Football Combination for Frank McLintock's reserves during 1977/8, and went on to win 41 Icelandic caps (11 goals). He scored twice in Feyenoord's Dutch Cup Final win over Ajax in 1980; also played for Antwerp; and was later top scorer under Gordon Lee for KR Reykjavik. Winger **Brendan Phillips** (b. West Indies, 16.7.1954) got only a single League chance with Peterborough after moving from Leicester in 1973, but after joining Kettering Town and winning England semi-professional caps while at Boston United, he cost Mansfield Town a £15,000 fee in 1980. After 23 League and Cup games, he was back at Boston; while in the early 90s he had a stint as manager of Stafford Rangers, and in summer 1995 took the reins at Nuneaton Borough.

Goalkeeper **Gary Plumley** (b. Birmingham, 24.3.1956), son of former City secretary Eddie, and with City from 1972-76, got his break with Newport County, for whom he played European soccer, and to whom he returned twice on loan and twice on a non-contract basis after interim spells with Hereford United, Cardiff City, Ebbw Vale, Caerleon and Hong Kong's Happy Valley. Gary came out of virtual retirement in 1987 to play for injury-hit Watford in their FA Cup semi-final against Spurs at Villa Park, but was beaten four times. Luton Town midfielder **Neil Poutch** (b. Dublin, 27.11.1969) had an unsuccessful loan spell with City during 1989/90, then gained Republic of Ireland Under-21 recognition and moved on to Shamrock Rovers, Athlone Town and Drogheda. He was an FAI Cup Finalist in 1991 with Shamrock.

Outside-right **Jimmy Prew** (b. Coventry, 1914), a Hinckley United star, featured in City's reserves in September 1936, but a month later was in West Bromwich Albion's first team. He got a few outings for Walsall during 1937/8, yet was back with Hinckley for the next term. Enjoying a slightly longer spell at League level was **Jack Price** (John William; b. Ibstock, 9.6.1900; d. Coalville, 3.11.1984), brother of first-teamer Fred and nephew of Cliff, who played as a full-back for Bristol Rovers, Swindon Town and Torquay United for several years (and an aggregate 38 Third Division appearances) after his 1923 release from Filbert Street. Former England Youth international **Brian Punter** (b. Bromsgrove, 16.8.1935) had been on Wolves' and Kidderminster Harriers' books before joining City as a reserve winger from Bromsgrove Rovers in 1958, but it was at Lincoln City a year later that he made his League bow as a centre-forward, going on to score 21 goals in 75 games. During the later of two spells with Hereford United, he played in the Welsh Cup Final of 1968; and also served South African team Arcadia and Nuneaton Borough.

Sean Rafter (b. Rochford, 20.5.1957) was another goalkeeper to suffer a frustrating spell as cover to Mark Wallington, from January 1978 to July 1979: he had built his reputation with Southend United, and later got a few chances with Orient. **Richard Reader** was briefly a Fosse reserve, but joined Derby County in 1913 from Ripley Athletic. A year later, he moved to Bristol City and served them at outside-right until a 1922 move to Luton Town. Full-back **Barry Reed** (b. Huntingdon, 24.11.1937) was for four years on City's roster as an amateur, and two as a professional, but his release in 1961 earned him only a single League game at Luton Town.

W Roberts, a reserve trialist in November 1907, had played twice at inside-forward for Preston North End's First Division side the season before. Wing-half **Peter**

Rushworth (b. Bristol, 12.4.1927) signed in 1951 from Cheltenham Town, and moved on in 1953 for 88 games with Bournemouth & Boscombe Athletic. Forward **Alan Russell** (b. Aberdeen, 16.11.1953) featured in 14 games for Peterborough United after his 1971 release, then moved on to Stamford.

Already a Swedish Under-21 international when he made two Combination appearances under Jock Wallace in November 1980, **Haakan Sandberg** later graduated to win full caps during a career played all across Europe, including a stint with Olympiakos in Greece. Bank clerk **Keith Scott** (b. Westminster, 10.6.1967) scored on his City reserves trial outing, but was then soon on the move from Leicester United to Lincoln City in March 1990. Loan spells with Gateshead and Boston United preceded a £30,000 transfer to Wycombe Wanderers in March 1991, and Keith was a Wembley scorer in the 1991 FA Trophy Final against Kidderminster Harriers. In November 1993, he signed on for Swindon Town at a £300,000 fee, and then moved on at equivalent cost to Stoke City in December 1994.

Hefty defender **Malcolm Shotton** (b. Newcastle on Tyne, 16.2.1957) was another City cast-off to rebuild his confidence at Nuneaton Borough. He moved on to skipper Oxford United in their rise from the Third to the First Division, and in 1986 received the Milk Cup at Wembley for them. Rapid moves thereafter took him to Portsmouth, Huddersfield Town, Barnsley and Hull City, and following a two-year spell with Ayr United, Malcolm returned to Oakwell as player-coach in 1994/5. Goalkeeper **Albert Smith** joined City from Wombwell in 1928 and left a year later, playing five League games during a month's trial at Watford, but declining the preferred contract and favouring a northerly move to Denaby United. Full-back **Joe Smith** was a contemporary, but this member of the Whitburn brotherhood failed to emulate Tom or Sep with a senior career at Filbert Street, and instead made his mark with two seasons at Watford after a 1930 move; later joining Market Harborough Town.

Banik Ostrava goalkeeper **Pavel Srnicek** (b. Ostrava, Czechoslovakia, 10.3.1968) had trials with City in October 1990, and was due to return, but Newcastle United stepped in for his signature in the interim. He was sent off at Filbert Street in the opening Premiership game of 1994/5. Striker **John Stalker** (b. Musselburgh, 12.3.1959) was sold by Jock Wallace to Darlington in October 1979 and went on to score 36 League goals in 116 games there, though he had less success in subsequent short spells with Hartlepool United, Meadowbank Thistle and East Fife. Eventually capped by Scotland on 30 occasions, inside-left **Billy Steel** (b. Denny, 1.5.1923; d. 13.5.1982) was on City's groundstaff for five months from January 1939, but made his substantial name in postwar football with Morton, Derby County and Dundee. The £15,500 fee which took him to the Baseball Ground in June 1947 was at the time a British record.

Northern Ireland international winger **Ian Stewart** (b. Belfast, 10.9.1961), previously with QPR and Newcastle United, had a couple of games with City's Central League side in December 1988, following his release by Portsmouth, but failed to earn a contract. Goalkeeper **William Strachan** (b. Arbroath, c.1874) had featured for his home-town club before joining Fosse for the 1895/6 campaign, when he occasionally also turned out in the second string's half-back line in an attempt to win the senior selection which Jimmy Thraves' consistency otherwise denied him. **Arni Sveinsson** accompanied Petursson on trial with City during 1977/8, having three Combination outings as a defender. He eventually amassed 50 caps for Iceland, scoring four times.

Former Sheffield Wednesday left-half **J Taylor** was a Fosse trialist in 1910/11. Midfielder **Robin Taylor** (b. Rinteln, Germany, 14.1.1971) played seven times for City reserves in September and October 1989, but was released by David Pleat to join Bryan Hamilton at Wigan Athletic. An Associate Members Cup outing and a League substitution accrued before Robin left for Loughborough University.

He represented British Universities in the World Student Games, and has subsequently played for Kettering Town, and on trial at both West Ham United and Sheffield United.

The vastly experienced **Steve Thompson** (Steven Paul; b. Sheffield, 28.7.1955) was bought by David Pleat in June 1988 as a likely replacement for the departing Russell Osman, but the hefty central defender, who had skippered Lincoln City and had been instrumental in helping keep Charlton Athletic in the top flight, wore a senior City shirt only in a pre-season friendly at Cambridge United, and was allowed to move to Sheffield United after only five months at Filbert Street. He returned to Sincil Bank in 1989, and succeeded Allan Clarke as Lincoln manager from November 1990 to May 1993. From February 1994 Steve was part of the management team at Southend United, and in June 1995 appointed team manager of Notts County.

Tony Thorpe (b. Leicester, 10.4.1974), a City trainee forward from 1990-92, scored on his FA Cup debut for Luton Town in January 1994. **Aaron Tighe** (b. Banbury, 11.7.1969) was a Luton midfielder who had a short loan spell with City during 1989/90; then joined Shamrock Rovers. Reserve 'keeper **George Syme Torrance** (b. Glasgow, 27.11.1935) left Filbert Street in 1956, and collected a handful of senior appearances with Oldham Athletic, Rochdale and Albion Rovers.

Geordie full-back **John W Traynor** (a May 1931 signing from South Bank) was unable at either Leicester or Crystal Palace to win a first-team place, but he finally made League appearances for Gateshead in 1934/5. Inside-forward **William Lee Tuckley** similarly had to wait until his third League club before he got a senior call-up. A former England schools cap, he had played for Wellington St.Georges and Leamington Town prior to joining City in December 1924, but he had also been on Wolves' books. Soon City were fined £75 for an improper registration, but Wolves also had to cough up £25 for having him on their retained list rather than their transfer list! After leaving City for Hinckley United, Billy finally got on

Chesterfield's scoresheet during 1927/8, and later served Nuneaton Town and Loughborough Corinthians.

Birmingham-born full-back **Harry Turner** was with Fosse in 1903, having previously had two spells with Portsmouth and a League stint with New Brighton Tower. Apart from the earlier-mentioned Narraway, the only Fossil to play in the United Counties League supplementary matches of 1894/5 who we have not been able to definitely identify is **Tyler**, the outside-right in the final fixture, at home to Nottingham Forest. However, he was either Herbert or Maurice of that ilk, both brothers being regulars for Leicester YMCA.

Ted Udall (Edward William; b. Atherstone, 1912) took a regular full-back berth in the City reserve side after signing from Atherstone Town in November 1931, and also had a stint as a goalscoring winger, but left in 1934 to play 81 League games in defence for a Derby County side which he helped to runners-up spot in Division One in 1935/6, before suffering recurrent shoulder problems. (His brother Sid also joined City from Atherstone in October 1935, but spent a fruitless two years at Filbert Street).

Amateur centre-forward **Bernard William Vann** (b. 9.7.1887; d. Ramicourt, 3.10.1918) was a Fosse reserve unable to break into the senior promotion line-up of 1907/8. He had the season previously assisted each of Northampton Town, Burton United and Derby County, but his fame would come in another sphere, when he was posthumously awarded the Victoria Cross in 1918. He graduated from Jesus College, Cambridge in 1910; became successively curate at St.Barnabas' Church, Leicester, and chaplain and senior master at Wellingborough Grammar School; and was commissioned in the Sherwood Foresters in 1914. Awarded the Military Cross in April 1915, Bernard had risen to the rank of Lieutenant-Colonel when killed in valorous action in France.

Percy Vials, a mid-20s City reserve trialist at centre-forward when with Little Bowden Albion, gained elevation via Kettering and

Market Harborough Town to join Bristol City in 1928, and became joint top scorer there in his first term. **Ron Viner** (Ronald Jesse; b. Reading) cost City £850 when signing from Kettering in December 1925, but the centre-half moved on to Guildford City in July 1927. Accrington Stanley returned him to the League sphere in September 1930, and after 96 games (2 goals) he had brief spells with Chester, Barrow and Nelson.

Abraham Wales (b. Kilwinning, 1909), the elder brother of Motherwell and Scotland star Hugh, had several clubs under his belt before joining City for the start of 1932/3: he'd already featured in the forward lines of Kilwinning Rangers, Kilmarnock, Galston, Montrose and Luton Town; and a year later would be on his way to Queen of the South. **Ralph Arthur Ward** (b. Oadby, 5.2.1911) was an England schools international who had played for Hinckley United when signed on amateur forms by City in 1928, but it was Bradford Park Avenue who secured the full-back on a professional contract a year later, and who sold him to Tottenham Hotspur in March 1936. After ten years at White Hart Lane, Ralph moved to Crewe Alexandra and, following an interim playing spell with Oadby Town, eventually returned to Gresty Road as manager from 1953-55.

Archie Waterston (Archibald Rutherford; b. Musselburgh, 13.10.1902; d. Edinburgh, 13.5.1982) was a wanderer of an inside-forward. City became his first senior club after he'd starred alongside Billy Findlay in Musselburgh Bruntonians' 1923 Scottish Junior Cup win (scoring twice in the Final against Arniston Rangers), but he returned north to Cowdenbeath in 1926 without a first-team outing to his credit. A subsequent aggregate 128-goal haul at League level, from stints with Newport County, Southampton, Tranmere Rovers, Southport, Doncaster Rovers and Aldershot, at least bore out the promise City had initially discerned.

Striker **Derek Watts** (b. Leicester, 30.6.1952), who made the City sub's bench during 1971/2 but failed to get into the action, managed a single appearance as No.12 for Northampton Town while on loan during 1973/4, then was released the following summer for a successful campaign with Miami Toros in the NASL, scoring twice in the semi-final to lift his team into the League Championship Play-off Final, lost on penalties to Los Angeles Aztecs. Goalkeeper **J Watts** was a December 1900 signing whose only senior outing was in a Christmas friendly against the respected amateur Corinthians; earlier in the season he had played two League games for Burton Swifts, with his debut having come against Fosse.

Capped at youth level by the Republic of Ireland while a trainee at Leicester, striker **Alan Weldrick** (b. Dublin, 8.10.1971) signed pro in February 1990, but was released only three months later to pursue a career in the League of Ireland with St.Patrick's Athletic, Longford Town and Drogheda United. A full-back who failed to make a Fosse

breakthrough was Galston-born **John White**, who had played 50 times for Newcastle United, and had previous spells with Kilmarnock, St.Mirren, Clyde and Dundee before his frustrating 1899/1900 term at Leicester.

Martin Williams (b. Luton, 12.7.1973), a two-year trainee from 1989-91, signed as a pro with Luton Town the following season, and made sporadic League appearances thereafter. He went on loan to Colchester United in March 1995, and in July 1995 joined Reading. Winger **Paul Williams** (b. Leicester, 11.9.1969), the first City signing from the FA School of Excellence at Lilleshall, was freed in 1989 to Stockport County, becoming the regular left-back in their 1990/1 promotion campaign. In 1993 he moved to Coventry City; then had loan spells with West Bromwich Albion and Huddersfield Town; and in summer 1995 joined Plymouth Argyle.

Jimmy Wilson (b. Glasgow, 19.12.1929) was a close-season signing in 1954 from Alloa Athletic, but he moved on untried to Mansfield Town in March 1955, for an 18-game spell in which he claimed one goal. England youth international forward **Brian Wright** (b. Leicester, 9.1.1937) has occasionally been erroneously credited elsewhere with two senior appearances for City that were in fact made by his contemporary, winger Billy Wright; but at least he won a brief (22-game, 3-goal) breakthrough with Lincoln City after a January 1959 move, and before a July 1961 transfer to Bedford Town. **George Wyness**, a defender from Jarrow who joined City from Houghton CW and then moved on to Falkirk with Andy Russell in the September 1928 part-exchange deal which brought George Ritchie south, later returned to Football League action in the 30s half-back lines of Southport, Chester, Rochdale, Notts County and Gateshead.

1995 UPDATE

City's trialists so far in 1995/6 have been a cosmopolitan bunch.

Dariusz Adamczuk (b. 21.10.1969) played at right back, and scored City's consolation, in the August friendly at Notts County. Having started his career with Pogon Szczecin (Polish Second Division champs in 1991/2), won his first cap in May 1992 and got himself sent off in the Olympic Games semi-final of that summer, he has in the interim served each of Eintracht Frankfurt, Dundee and Udinese.

Vladimir Kinder featured as a left-sided attacking midfielder for City in three games of their pre-season German tour, but the impressive Slovakian international, available from Slovan Bratislava at a reported £500,000, spoke almost no English, and was deemed too risky an investment.

Markus Kranz (b. 4.8.1969) turned out for City reserves in their August Central League

Zeljko Kalac

fixture against Preston North End, but was not retained. The defensive midfielder had been a 1986 signing for Kaiserslautern from minor club FSV Schifferstadt, and featured prominently in the 1991 Bundesliga winning squad. He moved to Bayern 05 Uerdingen in 1992, and subsequently to Dynamo Dresden.

Franck Rolling (b. Colmar, France, 23.8.1968) signed on a month's loan from Ayr United after a trial outing for the reserves in September 1995 then found himself on the first team bench at Port Vale. Central defender Franck had previously been with FC Pau in his home country.

... there is also the real possibility that City's biggest signing of the summer of 1995 may yet still become merely a 'nearly man':

At deadline time, the Department of Employment have still to rule on City's appeal against their denial of a work permit for giant goalkeeper **Zeljko Kalac** (b. Sydney, Australia, 16.12.1972), who remains set to become, at a fee to Sydney United of £760,000, the most expensive Australian export ever, and by some margin City's most expensive 'keeper. The Croatian-descended 6ft 7in international (13 caps) was plucked by City from under the noses of Leeds United, and had previously interested Norwich City.

BARTLETT, John William

Born in Forest Gate, London, in 1878, Jack Bartlett had joined junior minnows Croydon Common as a player in 1898, and taken the role of secretary/manager there in 1903. Something of a visionary, he proposed setting up an entirely new professional club called Croydon Town in 1907, but settled instead for professionalising the existing club on its election to the Southern League that summer. The Robins would have some success in that sphere until their disbandment during the First World War, with Jack at their helm until Fosse tempted him to the Midlands a few months after the two teams had met twice in the 1912 FA Cup.

With a cash-strapped Fosse he was mainly noted for a policy of recruiting a motley collection of southern-based amateur players to supplement the local youngsters; and indeed helped build some useful publicity (if not a successful combination) out of what was dubbed, on the eve of 1913/14, 'the £105 team' - this being the aggregate cost of the only three players in the senior squad for whom any fee had been paid at all! Fosse's precarious playing position (they would escape that term's re-election zone only on goal average) combined with a rap from authority (for employing an agent, and through him making an illegal approach to yet another London-based amateur) prompted Jack's resignation; but, after turning down a coaching offer from Germany, he took over as Swansea Town manager in May 1914, and piloted the Southern League Swans to FA Cup victory over Fosse during the next season.

BLOOMFIELD, James Henry

If, under David Halliday and Matt Gillies, the predominant dressing-room accent was Scottish, then under Jimmy it became Cockney. Expensive exiles from London clubs abounded as Jimmy waved the City cheque-book around with effective abandon and built a superbly entertaining First Division side in the early and mid-70s. Leicester at that time were essentially a 'nearly' team: always threatening to gain a place in European competition yet, somehow, finding 7th to be their highest end-of-season ranking, and a semi-final replay defeat

MANAGERS & COACHES

MANAGERS

1884 - 1892:	FRANK GARDNER
1892 - 1894:	ERNEST MARSON
1894 - Nov 1895:	J LEE
Nov 1895 - July 1897:	HENRY JACKSON
July 1897 - Sept 1898:	WILLIAM CLARK
Sept 1898 - Jan 1912:	GEORGE JOHNSON
Mar 1912 - Mar 1914:	JACK BARTLETT
Apr 1914 - Jan 1915:	LOUIS FORD
Jan 1915 - Sept 1919:	HARRY LINNEY
Sept 1919 - May 1926:	PETER HODGE
July 1926 - Jan 1932:	WILLIE ORR
Feb 1932 - Aug 1934:	PETER HODGE
Oct 1934 - Oct 1936:	ARTHUR LOCHHEAD
Oct 1936 - May 1939:	FRANK WOMACK
July 1939 - May 1945:	TOM BROMILOW
June 1945 - Mar 1946:	TOM MATHER
Mar 1946 - Oct 1949:	JOHN DUNCAN
Nov 1949 - Feb 1955:	NORMAN BULLOCK
June 1955 - Oct 1958:	DAVID HALLIDAY
Nov 1958 - Nov 1968:	MATT GILLIES
Dec 1968 - June 1971:	FRANK O'FARRELL
July 1971 - May 1977:	JIMMY BLOOMFIELD
July 1977 - Apr 1978:	FRANK McLINTOCK
June 1978 - July 1982:	JOCK WALLACE
Aug 1982 - May 1987:	GORDON MILNE
June 1986 - Dec 1987:	BRYAN HAMILTON
Dec 1987 - Jan 1991:	DAVID PLEAT
Jan 1991 - May 1991:	GORDON LEE
May 1991 - Nov 1994:	BRIAN LITTLE
Dec 1994 - date:	MARK McGHEE

Note 1: All incumbents prior to the appointment of Arthur Lochhead bore the title Secretary/Manager, and all up to Willie Orr carried out those joint responsibilities alone.

Note 2: During George Johnson's tenure, Fosse gave player **Jimmy Blessington** the title of Team Manager between January 1907 and April 1909, and **Andy Aitken** the title of Player/Manager from April 1909 to May 1911.

Note 3: Fosse director **S Scattergood** was honorary secretary for the brief period between the departure of George Johnson and the arrival of Jack Bartlett; and fellow board member **J M Hawkes** did similar duty between Bartlett's departure and Louis Ford's appointment.

Note 4: Head coach **Bert Johnson** was acting manager for several months during 1967/8 while Matt Gillies was on medically-prescribed leave of absence.

Note 5: Former assistant manager **Ian MacFarlane** took over in a caretaker role to complete the 1977/8 season following Frank McLintock's resignation.

Note 6: From June 1986 to May 1987, Gordon Milne was designated as General Manager and Bryan Hamilton as Team Manager.

Note 7: Coach **Peter Morris** was briefly caretaker boss between the departure of Bryan Hamilton and the arrival of David Pleat.

Note 8: Following the departure of Brian Little, the caretaker role was in the hands of coach **Allan Evans** for one game, and then passed to the youth-team coaching partnership of **Kevin MacDonald** and **Tony McAndrew** for three more Premiership fixtures before Mark McGhee's arrival.

Jimmy Bloomfield

their best FA Cup performance. Jimmy's oft-expressed penchant for attacking football was nonetheless interpreted with some intriguing and genuinely aesthetic variations by his adventurous teams, and regular (if inconsistent) displays of pace and improvisatory skill were almost ample compensation for the lack of tangible success in the eyes of City fans. His man-management abilities were always going to be tested by the blend of quicksilver and occasionally temperamental stars under his wing at Filbert Street, but Jimmy usually coped admirably; and while his occasional tactical experiments were usually progressively intended, he generally seemed less inclined to impose formations than to invest in sheer flair.

Jimmy (b. Kensington, 15.2.1934; d. London, 3.4.1983) started his playing career as a constructive inside-forward with Hayes, and went on to give fine service between 1952 and 1969 with Brentford (twice), Arsenal, Birmingham City, West Ham United, Plymouth Argyle and Orient, amassing 496 League appearances and claiming 93 goals from them, and even managing to play in two Fairs Cup Finals (for London and Birmingham). Graduating to the managerial office at Orient in 1969, he pointed his team to the Third Division championship, and a year later found himself preparing Leicester for their FA Charity Shield win and their return to the top flight. Following his six seasons' tenure at Filbert

Street, Jimmy returned to Orient as boss, but ill-health forced him to resign prematurely, and he was acting as a part-time Luton scout at the time of his tragically early death.

BROMILOW, Thomas George

Tom prepared newly-relegated City for a Second Division campaign throughout the summer of 1939, saw the official season abandoned after only three games on the declaration of war, and stayed at the helm throughout the difficult days of regionalised wartime competition until May 1945. To him fell the twin tasks of keeping the club going as a morale booster on the home front and coping with the vicissitudes of fielding eleven recognised footballers each week; and it was to his credit that sufficient attractive 'guest' players (with a vital supporting cast of old hands and youthful colts) turned out in the blue and white during that period to fulfil both functions. Given also that the spine of his team (plus a majority of his Board!) was subject to a year's suspension from the start of 1940/1 for the previous regime's financial misdemeanours, Tom earns a fair share of retrospective kudos for keeping the club alive through one of its darkest hours.

Tom (b. Liverpool, 7.10.1894; d. Nuneaton, 4.3.1959) had an eleven-year, 341-game playing career as a constructive left-half at Anfield during the immediate post-WW1 seasons, and was recognised as the brains behind Liverpool's championship wins of

Tom Bromilow

1922 and 1923. He won five England caps and represented the Football League on six occasions, then turned to management: with Burnley, in Holland, and then twice at Crystal Palace. He joined City from Selhurst, and was later manager at Newport County for four years until 1950. Later still, Tom returned to Filbert Street as an 'A' team trainer and as chief scout, in which capacity he was acting for City when he died while returning from a talent-spotting mission at a Welsh Cup tie. His son George was an England amateur international forward who played League football for Southport in the mid-50s.

BULLOCK, Norman

The man who bought Arthur Rowley, and who pointed City to their first postwar promotion, as champions in 1954 (right on course for the five-year plan of progress he had initially delineated to his Board and the press), Norman rather lost control of his charges as the First Division adventure turned sour, and was ushered out of his post in February 1955.

It was September 1920 when a £10 signing-on fee to Sedgely Park landed young centre-forward Norman (b. Monkton, Manchester, 8.9.1900; d. 27.10.1970) at Bury, and eighteen years before he left the Gigg Lane club whose League appearance record (506 games) he still holds, and whose aggregate scoring record he held until the 1980s, with 124 goals. Three times capped by England, he led the Shakers to promotion in 1924, and to fourth position in Division One two years later; briefly held the player/manager's dual responsibility; and then opted for management as a full-time activity in June 1935. His bid for complete control over the team, however, brought him into conflict with certain Bury directors in 1938, and he promptly shifted allegiance to Chesterfield.

Norman had nonetheless been back with Bury for four years when he succeeded John Duncan at Leicester in November 1949, and he soon created something of a whirlwind of activity on the arrivals and departures front as he re-ordered both the playing and backroom staffs. His scouting net was cast far and wide (Matt Gillies, Johnny Morris and Jack

Froggatt were among his other successful purchases after Rowley; Andy Graver the last of several conspicuously less so), but his style of man-management was becoming worrying to the Board, who had already given him notice that his contract would be terminated at the end of 1954/5, when incidents of indiscipline at a Whitley Bay hotel brought matters to a premature head. Norman's accordingly rolled. He never again sought a similar job.

CLARK, William D

William had been associated with Derby County before becoming secretary/manager with Burton Wanderers in 1894. Appointed to the Fosse post when the club became a Limited Company, he evinced both an eye for gimmickry, and a rather more worrying blind eye for League and FA rules. He arranged baseball games at Filbert Street, plus a series of 100-yard handicap races for footballers; and even pitched the club's champion sprinter, Billy Dorrell, into a 440-yard challenge with a visiting American athlete prior to the kick-off of the February 1898 home game with Darwen. He saw no less than six of his players given their cards by the Fosse directorate that same month for undisclosed (but almost certainly alcohol-related) disciplinary reasons, but then capped his own slightly anarchic approach to authority by getting himself suspended indefinitely from all football involvement by the FA, after having been found guilty of poaching Loughborough goalkeeper Godfrey Beardsley, and conspiring with William Rowley, Stoke's secretary and former goalkeeper, to pay the latter (a re-registered amateur) a signing-on fee to play for Fosse. When his ban was later rescinded, at his second petitioning, William found himself back in Burton, with the reins of the amalgamated United, between 1901 and 1904.

DUNCAN, John

See main Players' Alphabet.

FORD, Louis

A real veteran of football administration by the time he found himself at Leicester, Louis had been honorary financial secretary of West Bromwich

Albion from 1887, their general secretary from 1890-92, and then a director until 1896. In that year he joined Walsall as secretary, but by 1900 was acting as a League referee. He was an FA councillor from 1890-93, served on the Football League Management Committee, and was Vice-President of that body between 1894-97; though ironically it was a League commission's assessment of Fosse's internal problems (they claimed to have adjusted 'difficulties' between the club and its players, but damningly noted that here was 'a club shrouded in an atmosphere of pessimism, lacking vitality and confidence'), which led directly to his early resignation in 1915, before Fosse were confirmed as re-election candidates. Louis had much earlier distinguished himself, at the very foundation of League football in 1888, by proposing the motion that only victories counted towards the League table, and opposing the granting of one point for a draw!

GARDNER, Frank

See main Players' Alphabet.

GILLIES, Matthew Muirhead

See main Players' Alphabet

HALLIDAY, David

Stirring a few more Scots into the playing blend inherited from Norman Bullock, and keeping a much firmer grip on them, David took two seasons to get City back into the top flight after their tumble in 1955 - and his championship-winning side of 1957 proved a record-breaking one as well, as they piled on the goals and considerably heightened the Filbert Street entertainment quotient. That David clearly cared more to see his team going forward than defending with any particular security was, perhaps inevitably, his downfall when First Division attacks began exploiting the gaps his tactical plans simply didn't cover.

The origins of his attacking inclinations are not hard to pin down. As a player, David (b. Dumfries, 11.12.1897; d. Aberdeen, January 1970) was a centre-forward who scorched his way goalwards with admirable regularity. His football in the immediate post-WW1 era was

played with Queen of the South, St.Mirren and Dundee, and he won selection for the Scottish League against the Football League in 1924. Then he came south of the border, claiming 153 League goals for Sunderland at a ratio of only a little under one-per-game, and winning a £6,000 move to Arsenal. He could not, however, get a regular place at Highbury, and exactly half of his League goals as a Gunner came in one match against City: the remarkable 6-6 Filbert Street draw of 1930 in which he netted four, and which proved to be his final outing before a move to Manchester City. For them he notched 47 goals, and for Clapton Orient a further 33, until taking the player/manager post at Yeovil & Petters United in 1935. He became boss at Aberdeen in January 1938, and took over at Leicester in July 1955. Several of his former Pittodrie charges joined him at Filbert Street over the next few years, and he also introduced Scottish surprise packages like Willie Gardiner to the Leicester scene. David took much due credit for his marshalling of the 1957 promotion side, and at least ensured last-gasp First Division survival the following term (with bold team changes securing an essential final-game win at Birmingham); but his days were numbered as soon as 1958/9 started shaping as a similar uphill struggle. David's younger brother John played League football for Lincoln City and Doncaster Rovers in the early 30s.

HAMILTON, Bryan

Brought in by City to work in tandem with Gordon Milne and attempt to reverse the mid-80s pattern of First Division brinkmanship, Bryan got off to a fine start as his infectious enthusiasm caught the imagination of both the Leicester crowd and, unfortunately less sustainedly, his playing staff. His initial months in the Team Manager's post saw City move into the top half of the First Division table for the first time in a decade, yet by the end of that switchback 1986/7 campaign the club found itself relegated; and Bryan, then working solo, proved unable to halt a slide which threatened to lead to the ignominy of the Third Division.

Twice he broke the club transfer record, in signing Steve Moran and Mike Newell, but there was otherwise little conviction evident in either his team-building dealings or his attempts at morale-lifting motivation.

Bryan (b. Belfast, 21.12.1946) started his playing career with Distillery, and earned the first of his 50 Northern Ireland caps while starring for Linfield, before Ipswich Town won the race for his in-demand attacking midfield services in August 1971. Over four years and 153 League games later, Everton paid a substantial fee to take him to Goodison, and he appeared in the 1977 League Cup Final before moving on to Millwall, and then to Swindon Town, where he entertained thoughts of retirement to concentrate on coaching. In October 1980, however, Bryan assumed the player/manager's job at Tranmere Rovers, and clocked up another 109 League games before hanging up his boots. Working on the proverbial shoestring, Bryan saw several crises through at Prenton Park before leaving in February 1985, and taking up the manager's role at Wigan Athletic. A Freight/ Rover Trophy win at Wembley in May 1985 was a highlight of his stay there, and in June 1986, after impressing on a World Cup TV panel with his easy manner and analytical shrewdness, he topped the shortlist for the City manager's position.

Questions over the precise division of responsibilities between the new man and General Manager Gordon Milne

Bryan Hamilton

were temporarily shelved as City made their best start to a campaign for years, but the rapport Bryan built with the fans was not matched by that with his players as City tumbled. He survived a boardroom vote of confidence following relegation and Milne's departure, but thereafter dissension in the ranks soon became evident, and there was visible distaste from several players over the positional and tactical roles they were being asked to perform. City were in desperate straits when, unsurprisingly, the axe fell on Bryan in December 1987. Shortly afterwards, he seemed to have tacitly acknowledged his limitations as a track-suited boss when returning to Wigan as chief executive, before he later re-assumed control of team matters at Springfield Park until March 1993. Eleven months out of the game followed, until Bryan became a surprise choice to succeed Billy Bingham as Northern Ireland's national manager.

HODGE, Peter

Rightly regarded as the primary architect of City's rise to First Division respectability in the 20s, Peter clearly commanded greater respect from his Board than his Fosse predecessors had done in the same nominal joint role of secretary/manager; and equally clearly exercised a greater degree of autonomy in his involvement with matters of recruitment, selection and tactics. Though he was not actually at the helm for the pinnacle years of City's championship pursuit, he had gradually built up many of the systems and much of the side which saw the club go so close to its grail.

Entering football administration in his home town of Dunfermline with a juvenile team in 1890, he then combined the role of secretary for Dunfermline Juniors with refereeing duties in the Scottish League's Second Division, which he carried out from 1897 to 1906. Peter was honorary secretary to Dunfermline Athletic when Raith Rovers appointed him as their first manager in April 1907, and he remained at Starks Park until October 1912, when an ambitious director ousted him only two years after he'd taken Raith into the top flight. In June 1914 he took

Peter Hodge

over at Stoke, and led them to the top of the Southern League's Second Division. They promptly applied for re-election to the Football League, and were successful runners-up to Leicester Fosse in the voting, though the wartime break meant that they then could not take their place until 1919. By this time, Peter was back in Kirkcaldy, as both a local military recruiting officer and, once more, as manager of Raith, who he rebuilt towards peacetime football from 1916 onwards.

After the reconstruction of Leicester City, the new Board began negotiations for Peter to take over at Filbert Street almost immediately, and the formalities of his resignation from Raith and his official appointment at City's helm took place during the first two weeks of September 1919. Not surprisingly, the new boss returned north of the border for a fair proportion of his key signings; several of whom (like the Duncan brothers) had experienced his guidance at Raith. Peter experimented and dabbled shrewdly in the bargain end of the market (for Arthur Chandler, for instance) with a single-minded aim to get City into Division One; yet his appreciation of football artistry never left him. He finally turned out a side of Second Division champions in 1925, and altered it only slightly into one which consolidated its new, elevated status. Then, however, in May 1926, Peter was tempted away by Manchester City, who had reached the previous term's FA Cup Final, but had also been relegated. His new charges missed out by one place on an instant return, but were promoted as champions next time out, and Peter also led them to a third-place finish in the top flight during a Maine Road stint further distinguished by his signing of the young Matt Busby. But in March 1932, with City perilously close to the drop, he returned to Filbert Street.

The stars of City's recent heyday were now ageing, and replacements of a similar calibre were hard to come by on a limited budget. Peter helped them stay up by the skin of their teeth in 1932 and 1933, lifted them two places to 17th in 1934, and also gave Leicester its first taste of an FA Cup semi-final during that latter term. Tragically, however, he suffered illness during preparations for 1934/5, and died in August 1934, still in office.

JACKSON, Henry S

'Swin' Jackson was a hard-working pioneer of West Bromwich Albion's rise to prominence. A clerk to the local magistrates and a Staffordshire cricketer, he chaired the West Brom committee from 1885-88, was on their initial Board of Directors from 1891-93, and was their general secretary from 1892-94. With Fosse he was also the servant to a committee (one damningly described as 'hamstrung by cliques'), for it was not until the end of his second term at Filbert Street that the club took the step of becoming a Limited Company, after he'd only nominally presided over two fairly nondescript Second Division campaigns. 'Swin' then became secretary to Luton Town, and later emigrated to Canada, where he became a parish registrar and postmaster.

JOHNSON, George

The longest-serving of Fosse's secretary/managers, George had originally been a rugby follower, and a former honorary secretary of the Leicester branch of the National Cyclists' Union. Even his initial attachment to the Fosse came about obliquely via other sporting interests, for he had run their then-annual fund-raising Sports Days for a few years before he took on the task of steadying Fosse's football fortunes (and restoring their administrative respectability) after the damaging

scrapes of the William Clark management. George clearly left the bulk of responsibility for on-field matters to his trainers and senior pro's (and Fosse experimented during his almost fourteen-year tenure with both Jimmy Blessington and Andy Aitken in nominal managerial roles); while team selection was still then seen essentially as the province of the directorate. The respect in which he was held within the game, however, was instanced when, upon George's retirement to concentrate on his printing business partnership, Bradford City and a Steve Bloomer XI met in a Filbert Street friendly for his benefit in March 1913.

LEE, Gordon F

A short-term appointment with a far-reaching effect on the club, Gordon presided over the 'Great Escape' of 1991, when the final day's results at Filbert Street and Twerton Park (where rivals-in-distress West Brom only drew with Bristol Rovers) combined to keep City out of Division Three, and bought time for the subsequent assaults on top-flight status. David Pleat's coach since January 1988, Gordon was handed a caretaker role in January 1991, was named as manager in March, was replaced by Brian Little at the end of May, and departed a week later. He bought no-one, and gave no player a debut: but he gave a distinctly demoralised team a sufficient extra boost in self-belief, and enough extra space for self-expression, to get them to halt what could so easily have been the most damaging decline in all the club's history; right on the precipice.

Gordon (b. Hednesford, 13.7.1934) was for eleven years and 118 League games an Aston Villa defender, his 1955 signing after National Service with the RAF, and featured in the League Cup Finals of both 1961 and 1963. He took a player/coach role at Shrewsbury Town in July 1966 (briefly guiding winger David Pleat a year later), and commenced his managerial career with Port Vale in June 1968, taking them to the championship of Division Three in 1971. His one term at Blackburn Rovers (1974/5) also ended in a Third Division promotion campaign; while Newcastle United reached

the League Cup Final under his management in the following season. One year on, and it was Everton he was leading out at Wembley in the same competition; and Gordon remained at Goodison until 1981. He was Preston North End boss from 1981-83, then coached and managed abroad in climes as disparate as those of Saudi Arabia and Iceland. Indeed, he had been managing KR Reykjavik when re-united with Pleat at Filbert Street. On leaving Leicester, he stated with dignity that he'd never had to apply for a job in football in his life, and wasn't about to start.

LEE, J

Ludicrously, we have still been unable to discover any biographical details whatsoever for the first 'professional' secretary/manager Fosse ever appointed from outside the ranks of their own committee, and the man who oversaw the club's crucial first season in the Football League. We know he had the respect of his players, who clubbed together to buy him a commemorative gold medal on his departure; but no amount of scouring the local and sporting press of the time has brought forth even so much as a forename for the gentleman - let alone details of his footballing provenance or his fate.

LINNEY, Harry

In managerial terms, Harry was almost as much an unknown quantity: he was the Fosse director who took over the secretary/manager's role on Louis Ford's departure, and led the successful petition to the League for re-election to Division Two at the end of 1914/15; only to find that his nominal *pro tem* appointment actually stretched four years, throughout the entire period of WW1 football. On the club's 1919 reconstruction, Harry - self-described on registration documents as a cotton manufacturer - became a founder director of Leicester City and gladly gave up his figurehead responsibilities to Peter Hodge. He was still on the City board when he died on 15.3.1924, reportedly at the age of only 41. At this point, he was described as a financier and partner in the Leicester firm of Arthur Geary & Co.

Brian Little

LITTLE, Brian

The boss whose Blue Army thrice stormed Wembley in search of promotion-by-Play Off, and who finally gave City their first taste of Premiership football, Brian deadpanned his way through an incredibly turbulent period of City's history; and it is possibly still too early to judge with adequately balanced perspective just what his contribution means. The sense of betrayal felt by City fans on his defection to Aston Villa was genuine (fed by inadvised contrary statements in the days beforehand as much as by residual hero-worship), but that move was little short of inevitable in the circumstances. It was the contradictions of his success, really, which still puzzle: for one has to ask how many previous City managers would still have been in post to savour the third-time-lucky glory of the elevating win over Derby if they'd previously finished Second Division campaigns with placings of 4th, 6th and 4th and there had been no Play Off safety net? Which other managers would have seemed so reticent to buttress their squads with players they hadn't previously coached or managed? Which would have so often watched their admittedly classy midfield swamped in numbers for the sake of fielding a flat back-five? On the other hand, was it luck or judgement which oversaw the emergence of Julian Joachim, the conversion of Steve Walsh, the eventually or instantly justified acquisitions of Jimmy Willis or Mark Draper? And was

it just wretched fortune with injuries (Speedie, Walsh, Joachim) that derailed the Premiership challenge?

Brian (b. Durham, 25.11.1953) was a Villa apprentice from July 1969, and then had ten years there as a pro from March 1971 until his injury-enforced premature retirement from the striking line. He'd been in their Youth Cup-winning side of 1972, their League Cup-winning teams of 1975 and 1977, and had top-scored in their 1975 promotion campaign. His England career had unluckily amounted to only one outing as an 80th-minute substitute against Wales in May 1975, but it was greater mischance that knee injuries effectively wrecked his advancement only a few years later, when he was stuck on a career tally of 82 senior goals. He became a coach with Wolves in January 1986, and managed them from August to October of that year before being unceremoniously dumped when they recruited Graham Turner. He then coached Middlesbrough's reserve and youth teams before becoming boss at Darlington in February 1989. Brian couldn't save the Quakers from relegation to the Conference a matter of months later, but chivvied them straight back into the League in 1990, and to the Division Four championship in 1991; at which point City chairman Martin George tempted him to Filbert Street.

For some time after Brian's mid-season move back to Villa Park, it looked as though his new charges might accompany City into the Premiership drop zone, but they survived and Brian is at the time of writing flourishing Doug Ellis's cheque-book with some fervour, and has included Mark Draper amongst his expensive purchases. Brian's brother Alan is also in club management, having helmed York City since March 1993, after a 70s and 80s playing career with Villa, Southend United, Barnsley, Doncaster Rovers, Torquay United and Halifax Town.

LOCHHEAD, Arthur William

See main Players' Alphabet.

McGHEE, Mark Edward

The current incumbent of the Filbert Street hot seat, Mark could barely conceal his disappointment at precisely how ill-equipped

were the City side (and squad) he inherited in mid-fall during the Premiership misadventure. Having arrived from Reading and a background of purist passing football to find such basics beyond too many of his new charges, he was clearly gambling on a backs-to-the-wall revivalism permeating the side, but received only intermittent encouragement before the relegation fate was sealed. He easily retained the fans' sympathy and support, however, with general approval attending his signings of Jamie Lawrence, Mark Robins, Mike Galloway and Garry Parker; and he has stated his rapport with the consensus that a major turnaround in playing personnel is required for the 1995/6 campaign.

Mark (b. Glasgow, 20.5.1957) was a teenage Bristol City apprentice who had to move to Morton in 1975 for his first senior action. A sturdy but skilful striker, he had the first of two spells with Newcastle United from December 1977 to March 1979, then joined Aberdeen for five glory years, during which they won the European Cup Winners Cup in 1983, the Scottish League in 1980 and 1984, and a hat-trick of Scottish Cups from 1982-84; and were Scottish League Cup runners-up in 1980. In May 1984 he joined Hamburger SV for a 30-game, 7-goal Bundesliga stint, then returned to another major Scottish medal-haul with Celtic (champions in 1986 and 1988, Cup-winners in 1988 and 1989, and League Cup runners-up in 1987). In August 1989 Mark returned to St.James's Park, and in

Mark McGhee

May 1991 took over as player/ manager at Reading: only hanging up his boots in May 1993, a year before the Division Two championship was secured. Mark's four Scottish caps were won in 1983/4, and he closed his active career on 170 senior goals.

McLINTOCK, Francis
See main Players' Alphabet.

MARSON, Ernest A
Elected from the Fosse committee to succeed inaugural secretary Frank Gardner, Ernest saw Fosse through the second and third Midland League campaigns before his honorary position became professionalised with the appointment of J Lee. Also a founder committee member of the Leicestershire FA, Ernest later briefly acted as a League referee, and became a Fosse director following their assumption of Limited Company status in 1897.

MATHER, Thomas
City's boss for most of the transitional postwar season of 1945/6, Tom never so much as selected a team for League duty, was frustrated (predominantly by financial constraints) in attempting to rebuild a City side in the stylish image of his pre-war club teams, and resigned after only nine months in March 1946. His signing of classy playmaker Frank Soo indicated the sort of football he would wish a postwar City to play; but it was John Duncan who would lead the club into resumed Second Division combat.

Tom Mather

Tom (b. Chorley, 1888; d. Stoke-on-Trent, 29.3.1957) had entered football administration in 1910, as secretary of Bolton Wanderers, and remained in post there throughout WW1, despite an interim spell in the Navy. A brief stint in the Manchester City office preceded his appointment as Southend United manager in May 1920, upon the mass elevation of Southern League sides into the new Division Three, and he stayed at their home of the time, the Kursaal, until January 1922. Tom assumed the managerial position at Stoke in October 1923 (there giving Stanley Matthews his senior break); and was in charge of Newcastle United from June 1935 to the outbreak of WW2, during one of their Second Division slump periods. After leaving Leicester, he helmed Kilmarnock for most of the 1947/8 season, and then returned to the Potteries to work in the catering industry.

MILNE, Gordon
Decidedly less charismatic than his predecessor Jock Wallace, Gordon quietly edged City into the promotion frame at the end of his first campaign in charge, and somehow contrived to keep them in the top flight against the odds for three seasons, before closing the Leicester chapter of his career with a year as General Manager, working in harness with new team boss Bryan Hamilton. Gordon's public image through-out his stay was of a man whose first priority was to perform the increasingly difficult task of balancing the City books. His essentially safety-first approach to club management may well have been the most appropriate response to the shifting economic structure of modern top-flight football; but it also appeared to many supporters that perhaps Gordon gained rather more respect from the boardroom than he did from the dressing room, and certainly more than he did from the terraces. Nonetheless, he marshalled his on-field resources with relative success, and rode with dignity the storms of criticism which met decisions like the Melrose/English swap, the failure to retain Gerry Daly, or the attempted conversion to full-back of seemingly the entire midfield complement.
A man with football in his

Gordon Milne

blood, Gordon (b. Preston, 29.3.1937) started his senior playing career at Morecambe, but soon signed up at Deepdale, where his father Jimmy had been a pre-war star and was then manager. After 81 League games for Preston as a right-half, he moved to Anfield and took a regular berth in Bill Shankly's first great Liverpool side, helping them to promotion and on to two League championships, winning 14 England caps, and only moving on to Blackpool in 1967 after 236 League outings (18 goals). His managerial career started a couple of years later at then-non-league Wigan Athletic, and he took up the reins at Coventry City in June 1972: initially in partnership with Joe Mercer, then as solo manager, and eventually as chief executive when Dave Sexton arrived to assume team manager duties. He was as well used, therefore, to the system of dual responsibility which operated for the first time at Leicester in his final season, as he was to keeping a club of limited means in the First Division.

Some two months after his contract with City expired in May 1987, Gordon surprised many by accepting an offer to manage the Turkish club Besiktas, who finished as League runners-up in his first season there. They won the Turkish Cup in 1989, did the Double in 1990 (with Ian Wilson in their line-up), and took further League championships in 1991 and 1992, when they remained unbeaten all term. Besiktas were runners-up on goal difference in 1993, but a new contract for Gordon cemented his record as the longest-serving foreign coach ever in Turkey. He left Ankara in November 1993; and next took an even more far-flung posting, managing Nagoya Grampus Eight in the J-League throughout most of 1994 (with Ian Wilson as coach), before departing at the same time as Gary Lineker. In June 1995, Gordon was appointed Chief Executive of the League Managers' Association.

O'FARRELL, Frank

Narrowly winning the board's vote over Allan Brown of Luton as City quickly sought a successor to Matt Gillies, Frank took over a relegation-bound team, yet led them to Wembley as a distinctly consoling diversion. The softly-spoken Irishman then remoulded the club for a rapid return to the top flight, achieved after two seasons on the basis of intelligent pragmatism (and a quick-break style based on defensive tightness), when his management methods even justified the close scrutiny of a series of educational documentary TV programmes. Perhaps unfortunately for City, Manchester United may have watched the latter, for they spirited Frank away with the proverbial offer he couldn't refuse.

Frank (b. Cork, 9.10.1927) was introduced to English football by West Ham United, who signed him as a wing-half from Cork United in January 1948. He soon became a Republic of Ireland international and, presciently, joined the unofficial Hammers

Frank O'Farrell

'Academy' then being informally tutored by Malcolm Allison, and including such future managerial luminaries as Noel Cantwell, John Bond and Ken Brown. After 197 League games, Frank moved on in November 1956 to Preston North End for 118 more, and then assumed the player/manager's role at Weymouth, who he eventually helmed to the Southern League championship in 1964/5. Torquay United then stepped in with an offer of the manager's chair, and it was from Plainmoor that Frank moved to Leicester. Several of his early City purchases were of questionable value, but the signings of Bobby Kellard and Willie Carlin to energise and motivate the push to the 1971 Second Division championship were masterstrokes. Frank and his coach Malcolm Musgrove (another ex-Hammer) were less happily employed at Old Trafford, though, where the shadow of Matt Busby and the insistence on instant success from a transitional team weighed heavily upon them. Frank later took over at Cardiff City for a crucial four months of anti-relegation struggle during 1973/4, had a spell coaching in Iran, and returned for a couple of stints back at Torquay as general and caretaker manager in the early 80s.

ORR, William

The man who inherited Peter Hodge's First Division side, Willie fine-tuned it to the extent that it sat for two seasons proudly, if slightly frustratedly, in its highest ever top-flight placings: third in 1927/8 and second (to Sheffield Wednesday) in the following campaign.

Willie (b. Shotts, Lanarkshire, 20.6.1873; d. 26.2.1946) was in his playing days a fine defender with Airdrieonians, Preston North End and, for ten years from 1897, with Celtic. He won three full Scottish caps, four Scottish League championship medals, and five Scottish Cup medals; three as a winner. In 1909 he became a director back at Airdrie, and served as such until 1921, when he took over the manager's chair there. His side took the Scottish Cup in 1924, missing the Double by one League placing, and his reputation was high enough for City to take him on a month after Hodge's departure to Manchester City. Jim McLaren, Sid Bishop and

Willie Orr

Len Barry were among his Filbert Street purchases who contributed to the championship pursuit; while Sep Smith was a later junior recruit. As City began to struggle for First Division survival, however, things began to sour for Willie. He left Leicester in March 1932 as distress signals were being transmitted north for the return of Peter Hodge, and while he soon found new employment as secretary/manager of Falkirk, it was not long before he was definitively disgraced. For in April 1935, the Scottish League banned him for life after he had been charged with bribery, and found guilty of paying £3 to Ayr United player Robert Russell to miss a crucial relegation fixture against Falkirk. (The game in question was ordered to be replayed). Though the suspension was actually lifted as early as February 1937, Willie was by then a traffic superintendant for a bus company in Crieff, and evinced no desire to return to football.

PLEAT, David John

Both City and David Pleat were at a low ebb when the latter inherited Bryan Hamilton's managerial duties at Filbert Street. City were nudging the bottom of the Second Division, and were in the midst of their record run of seven League matches without a goal, while David was still suffering from the fall-out following a gutter-press smear campaign which led to his departure from Tottenham. By the end of his first term in charge, though, both club and boss were very much rehabilitated, for

David had rapidly turned around both tactics and fortunes, and soon had his team playing the most attractive football seen from a Leicester side in some time. Unfortunately, however, neither David nor his charges were able to maintain this progressive momentum; and for all his media-friendly punditry, it became intensely frustrating for the fans to see such an evident mismatch between tactics and skills as spoken about, and as expressed on the Filbert Street pitch. David's transfer record was distinctly patchy, too, with the likes of Peter Weir, Gary Mills, Tommy Wright and David Kelly settling in the bonus column, but such purchases as Jimmy Quinn, Mick Kennedy, Wayne Clarke, Billy Davies, Pat Gavin, Rob Johnson and Ricky Hill contributing little to the cause. Indeed, by the time of David's sacking in January 1991, City were pretty much back where they were at the time he arrived, and once more in danger of the unthinkable drop to Division Three.

David (b. Nottingham, 15.1.1945) won England honours at schools and youth level as a speedy winger, but found it hard to sustain a first-team challenge at Nottingham Forest, and moved on while still only 19 to Luton Town. There, a series of injuries cut down his reliance on sheer pace, and forced him into a more studiously constructive game, which served him well through subsequent moves to Shrewsbury Town, Exeter City and Peterborough United. David became player/manager at Nuneaton Borough for a spell,

David Pleat

then took on a succession of backroom jobs with Luton, which saw him through the coaching heirarchy and into the manager's chair in early 1978. He returned the Hatters to the top flight in 1982, kept them there the following term (when his delight at a last-gasp reprieve was evident to the TV millions who saw him jig across the Maine Road pitch), and had them established as an entertaining playing force when he left to meet the challenge of raising Spurs to the heights coveted by their ambitious board. David saw Tottenham to the 1987 FA Cup Final, but his future became unsure when press agitation mounted for the return of Terry Venables, and the coincidental appearance of tabloid allegations about David's private life effectively enforced his resignation. In these difficult circumstances, there was courage evident on the parts of both the City board and David himself when his Leicester appointment was made, but vindication came early where it mattered: on the pitch.

It may have been true thereafter that David was as irked as the City support by the comparative paucity of financial resources at his disposal, but whether he confused his players or merely overburdened them with tactical formulae, he could not seem to imbue much cohesive spirit in his sides, who looked particularly forlorn in away matches for the greater part of his stay. David rejoined Luton Town as manager in June 1991, gave senior chances to a number of his former City juniors, was almost tempted back to Spurs in November 1994, and in June 1995 left Kenilworth Road (amid much acrimony over compensation) for Sheffield Wednesday.

WALLACE, John Martin Bokas

Deserving of heartfelt thanks for taking a dispirited club by the scruff of the neck, shaking it back to self-respect and infusing its representative teams with a battling swagger, Jock quickly built his own potent mythology at Leicester; but in many ways became unproductively trapped within it before he left. It might justifiably be argued that his feat in stopping the side falling into Division Three in 1978/9 (which seemed likely given the

Jock Wallace

downward momentum of the Frank McLintock disaster) was a greater triumph than the Second Division championship success he prompted the following season; and there is a case to be made for his embarrassment when City dropped straight back as primarily a consequence of the club's belt-tightening priorities starving him of cash. But in that top-flight term, and the subsequent unsuccessful attempt to bounce straight back up again, the conflicting strengths and weaknesses of the patented Wallace approach became more and more obvious. A great motivator, a shrewd judge of a player's hunger and commitment, and always one to encourage youthful talent, Jock could nonetheless often appear a rather naive tactician; and it did not help on this score that his assistant, Ian MacFarlane, seemed cut from the same craggy rock. The abiding memory of the latter years of the Wallace regime, which would end in legalistic acrimony when Jock broke his contract to join Motherwell in August 1982, was of Jock and Ian rising together from the City bench, snarling and shaking their fists to demand more frenetic effort, rather than conveying any subtler shift in playing pattern.

Jock (b. Wallyford, 6.9.1935) was the son of a goalkeeper, also Jock, who played for Raith Rovers, Blackpool and Derby County on either side of WW2. He began his own peripatetic goalkeeping career while on National Service, performing for a motley collection of clubs during and after army action. Initially a young amateur with Blackpool, he joined Workington in 1952, and then played for Ashton United and Airdrieonians until joining West Bromwich Albion in 1959. After 69 League games at The Hawthorns, Jock moved on again, to Bedford Town, Hereford United and, as player/manager, to Berwick Rangers, where he appeared in the celebrated giant-killing of their Glasgow namesakes. He had a spell coaching at Hearts, and then took over the Ibrox manager's office in June 1972. Remarkable success for Rangers ensued, with the pinnacles of Jock's career coming in 1976 and 1978, when the domestic Treble was clinched. Almost deified by the Ibrox faithful, Jock genuinely shocked British football when joining City, where the contrast in recent fortunes could not have been more extreme. Instituting a famously rigorous fitness-training routine (including the sandhill), and savagely reducing the average age of his senior squad, he made an instant impact. And it is worth reiterating that, although Jock left City in the same nominal Second Division grade as when he joined them, his gruffly populist, up-and-at-'em approach had in the interim given the club back its pride.

The row over Jock's 'poaching' by Motherwell had barely died down when he left Fir Park to return to Ibrox. Success in his second spell at his spiritual home was, however, harder to come by, and in April 1986 he again bade farewell to Glasgow. A couple of months later, Jock was installed as boss at Spanish League club Seville, but was somewhat out of his element during this brief continental sojourn. He then remained in semi-retirement in Spain until answering an SOS to return to management in January 1989 at Colchester United, then 92nd in the League and apparently Conference-bound. Predictably, Jock roused them to survival by an eight-point margin. He resigned in the following December, and briefly took a seat on the Layer Road board; but in

February 1990 announced he had Parkinson's Disease and was retiring from football. Still living in Fuengerola, Jock returned to Filbert Street in November 1994 for a star-studded testimonial dinner.

WOMACK, Frank

Remembered mainly for his success in turning around City's fortunes in his first season at the helm with one decisive flurry of transfer-market activity, Frank pushed the club from the Second Division depths to its 1937 championship within a matter of months on the heels of his purchases of Eric Stubbs and, especially, Jack Bowers.

Frank Womack

A Sheffielder by upbringing (b. Wortley, 16.9.1888; d. Caistor, 8.10.1968), and originally apprenticed in the cutlery business, Frank spent the entirety of a 515-game, 20-year playing career (1908-28) as a Birmingham full-back, and figured in an England trial match in 1913. He won his managerial spurs with Worcester City, taking them to the 1929 title of the Birmingham League, and then bossed Torquay United (1929-32) and Grimsby Town (1932-36; Second Division champs in 1934) before succeeding Arthur Lochhead at Filbert Street and tasting instant glory. His perception in recognising what it took to get out of Division Two, however, did not extend to any brilliant insights as to how to keep City in the top flight thereafter, and he resigned in May 1939 after the club tumbled back down again on the eve of war. A sad epilogue to his Leicester career was provided in 1940 by the FA, who handed him a one year suspension from football for his implication in the payment irregularities then found in City's pre-war books; but Frank bounced back to take charge of Notts County from July 1942 to March 1944, and of Oldham Athletic from February 1945 until April 1947. In 1951, he returned for a few months as caretaker manager at Grimsby Town.

TRAINERS & COACHES

Biographical notes for those men who served Fosse and City in the above roles after having played for the club are found elsewhere. Thus entries for Arthur Chandler, George Dewis, Allan Evans, Matt Gillies, Derek Hines, Teddy King, Billy Leech, Kevin MacDonald, Ian MacFarlane, David Nish, George Ritchie, Bobby Roberts, Fred Sharman, Sep Smith and Alick Stewart are to be found in the main Players' Alphabet; while Gordon Lee may be found in the Managers' appendix.

Charlie Brown was Fosse's trainer throughout the final Midland League season of 1893/4. Almost as anonymous as his immediate predecessor Mr. Smith, he was merely noted in the local press as being 'well known amongst the athletes of Leicester'.

Jack Butler (John Dennis; b. Colombo, Ceylon, 14.8.1894; d. London 5.1.1961) coached City throughout most of the WW2 era, from November 1940 to May 1946. His sixteen-year stint as an Arsenal centre-half had earned him one England cap in 1924, and he had finished his playing career with Torquay United before joining Daring FC of Belgium as coach, and running the Belgian national side from 1935-40. On leaving Filbert Street, where he and manager Tom Bromilow instituted a useful Colts policy that linked football and civilian employment, he became successively manager of Torquay, Crystal Palace, Daring again, and Colchester United, and also contrived an interim spell coaching for the Danish FA.

David Coates (b. Newcastle on Tyne, 11.4.1935) joined the City coaching staff under Frank O'Farrell and stayed throughout the Bloomfield and McLintock managements. A former player with Hull City, Mansfield Town and Notts County, he later worked with David Pleat at Luton, as youth coach at Oxford United and as chief scout for Sunderland.

Bill Dodgin Jr (b. Durham, 4.11.1931) was a City coach under Jimmy Bloomfield from 1972-73.

A former Under-23 cap who had played for Fulham and Arsenal, coached Millwall and QPR, and returned to Craven Cottage as both coach and manager. Less than a year after arriving at Filbert Street, though, he was off for the first of two spells managing Northampton Town; and also fitted in an interim stint as Brentford boss.

Alex Dowdells (b. Slamannan, Lanarkshire) came in to head the City training staff under David Halliday in 1956, after 16 years in a similar role with Celtic, and nine years as trainer to the Scottish national side. To mark his retirement in May 1966, after he'd become a familiar sight as sponge-man through the bulk of the Matt Gillies era, a strong Scotland XI (the first chosen by new boss John Prentice) came to Filbert Street for his testimonial game, and drew 1-1. Alex, who had been a Wishaw centre-forward in Scottish junior football, and studied medicine at Glasgow University from 1933, had held training posts with both Shettleston and the Scottish junior international team prior to joining up at Parkhead. He retired to live in Norfolk.

Bob Dunmore was in charge of Fosse's fitness from 1898-1900, and later moved to perform similar functions for Woolwich Arsenal. His son Horace was a Loughborough Corinthians goalkeeper, and a Bristol Rovers trialist in 1929.

Laurie Edwards joined City as trainer in 1933, and stayed until 1939. A former half-mile champion athlete (Powderhall,

John Gregory

1919), and coach at Shrewsbury School and Liverpool University, he'd toured Canada with the FA XI in 1926, acted as trainer to the full England side for their games in France and Belgium in 1931, and had been an official athletics trainer to the South African team competing in the 1932 Los Angeles Olympic Games. He'd also served under George Jobey at Derby County; and on leaving Filbert Street set up in a private electrical therapy practice in Leicester.

Mike Everitt (Michael Dennis; b.Clacton, 16.1.1941) was another coach to serve Jimmy Bloomfield, staying with City from 1975-77. He had been a player with Arsenal, Northampton Town, Plymouth Argyle and Brighton & Hove Albion; player-manager at non-league Wimbledon; and boss at Brentford. He was last heard of coaching in Kuwait in 1992.

Bill Fox (b. Islington, ca.1874; d. Leicester, 21.3.1935) was part of the Filbert Street scene for over 20 years. He'd become a masseur before Army service in the Boer War and in India, when his duties as a Seaforth Highlanders signaller using heliographs contributed to him going blind. He occasionally assisted Fosse, as well as county cricketers and other local sportsmen, and then was employed full-time by City throughout the 20s and early 30s. He cut his own throat after returning from a lengthy hospital stay, and Filbert Street hosted a Boxers v. Police benefit game which raised £85 for his widow in April 1935.

Dave Gardner (David Richmond; b. Glasgow, 31.3.1873; d. Longcliffe, 5.11.1931) was City's head trainer from 1919-31, serving under Peter Hodge and Willie Orr throughout the club's First Division heyday. Capped for Scotland as a Third Lanark defender in 1897, Dave had in the interim been a solid left-back for Newcastle United, Grimsby Town, West Ham United and Croydon Common, where he had been signed by Jack Bartlett and where he first took up training duties.

John Charles Gregory (b. Scunthorpe, 11.5.1954) followed Brian Little into Filbert Street after a matter of weeks, and followed him again to Villa Park after a matter of days, having coached both the reserves and first-team during his Leicester stay (and having turned out on occasion in the Central League). A former midfielder with Northampton Town, Aston Villa, Brighton, QPR, Derby County and England; he had been Portsmouth manager before re-uniting with Little and Allan Evans. His father, also John, had played for West Ham, Scunthorpe United and Aldershot.

Mike Hickman (Michael Frederick Thomas; b. Elstead, 2.10.1946) came from Reading with Mark McGhee and Colin Lee in December 1994, and immediately took responsibility for the midweek Central League side as well as helping coach the first team. He'd been an inside-forward with Brighton, Grimsby Town, Blackburn Rovers and Torquay United in the 60s and 70s; and had established his coaching credentials in Australia, working with the national side there.

Steve Hunt (Stephen K; b. Witton, Birmingham, 4.8.1956) was Brian Little's youth coach from 1991-93. The former Aston Villa, New York Cosmos, Coventry City, West Bromwich Albion and England striker had previously managed Willenhall Town and from 1989 looked after Port Vale's youth set-up.

John Jackson (b. Aston, Birmingham, 1861) was Fosse's trainer from 1896-98. He'd been assistant trainer to Wolves when they'd won the Cup in 1893, had guided Loughborough between 1893-95, culminating in a Midland League championship, and trained Liverpool throughout

Alex Dowdells

1895/6, when they were Division Two champions. He moved on from Leicester to become inaugural trainer/manager of Brighton United in 1898, and commenced a long tenure of pubs in that locality (The Farm Tavern and The Running Horse) when that club collapsed in 1900. Only a year later, though, he was back as a prime mover in the formation of Brighton & Hove Albion, and remained with them as secretary/manager until 1905. His pub duties then occupied him, apart from one brief return to football in a backroom role at Blackpool in 1907, until his death in June 1931.

Bert Johnson (William Herbert; b. Stockton-on-Tees, 4.6.1916) was Matt Gillies' coaching No.2 for much of his stay with Leicester, though he initially joined the club in 1959 as head scout. Often given a share in the credit for the tactical innovations that helped City to four Cup Finals in the early 60s, he took over as acting manager during Gillies' absence through illness in 1968, and it was his sacking later that year which prompted Gillies' immediate resignation. A devout churchman, Bert had begun his playing career in the Northern League with South Bank, Stockton and Spennymoor United before signing for Charlton Athletic as a wing-half in March 1939. He guested for Bolton Wanderers alongside Gillies during the war, played in two Victory internationals for England, and took successive runners-up and winners' medals from the FA Cup Finals of 1946 and 1947. From 1953, he had been player/manager at each of Bexleyheath & Welling and Cambridge United prior to his Filbert Street recruitment; and he was chief scout for each of Nottingham Forest and Derby County after leaving.

David Jones (b. Whitwell, 9.4.1914), a former Bury wing-half under Norman Bullock, followed his boss to Leicester as head trainer in 1950, and stayed in this role until 1956. He then returned as assistant trainer from 1958-78. He was also a former Nottinghamshire CCC batsman.

Frank King (Francis Oliver; b. Alnwick, 13.3.1917), a former pre-war Blyth Spartans, Everton and Derby County goalkeeper, was assistant trainer to David

Jones from 1954, and left City in 1958 to take the senior trainer's role at Luton Town.

Cyril Lea (b. Moss, nr.Wrexham, 5.8.1934) assumed the youth development role with Bryan Hamilton's City set-up in 1987, and later performed similar duties for West Bromwich Albion from 1989. His playing career had started with Leyton Orient in 1957, and peaked with two Welsh caps in 1965, while he was with Ipswich Town. He had coached at Ipswich, Stoke City and Hull City before becoming Colchester United manager from 1983-86.

Colin Lee (b. Torquay, 12.6.1956) became City's assistant manager when moving from Reading with Mark McGhee and Mike Hickman in December 1994. Primarily remembered as a player for scoring four times on his Spurs debut against Bristol Rovers, and twice for Chelsea in the Full Members Cup Final of 1986, he had commenced his senior career at Bristol City, and also featured for Hereford United and Torquay United before his 1977 move to White Hart Lane. At Stamford Bridge from 1980, the striker also occasionally figured at right-back and in central defence. Colin was player/youth coach at Brentford from 1987; youth coach and then briefly full manager at Watford; and coach at Elm Park from July 1991.

Tony McAndrew (b. Glasgow, 11.4.1956) joined City as youth coach in July 1993, having previously performed the same role with Darlington. He was part of the 'Two Macs' caretaker management partnership with Kevin MacDonald in November 1994, in the wake of Brian Little's departure, and resigned in January 1995. His playing career as a defender had encompassed two spells with Middlesbrough between 1971 and 1986, a season with Vancouver Whitecaps, and two with Chelsea.

Willie McLean arrived at Leicester in the summer of 1932, assisted Laurie Edwards with City's training duties through most of the 30s, and returned to Filbert Street for almost four years after the war, accompanying John Duncan's side to Wembley in 1949. A former Powderhall sprinter who had played professional football in the United States, he held training roles with

St.Mirren and Doncaster Rovers before coming to Leicester. His brother Walter was a hugely influential Scottish scout for City in the 40s, 50s and 60s.

Eddie May (b. Epping, 19.5.1943) was brought in by Jock Wallace as reserve-team coach in 1978, and stayed four years. A former rock-solid centre-half with Southend United, Wrexham, Swansea City and Chicago Sting, he moved on to coach Charlton Athletic after leaving Leicester. He became manager of Newport County in July 1988, after their relegation to the Conference, but stayed less than a month at the crisis-racked club before being recruited as coach by the side who'd taken their League place, Lincoln City. He has been boss at Cardiff City since 1991, except for a brief spell during 1994/5 when he helmed Barry in the Konica League before returning to Ninian Park.

Jim Metcalfe had two spells as City trainer: initially arriving from Preston North End on the eve of war in 1939, he was released in October 1940 to look after his sick wife and undertake munitions work in Lancashire, and then returned in 1949/50 to briefly succeed Willie McLean. He had originally played League football for South Shields in the 20s.

John Moore (b. Harthill, 21.12.1943) had only one season, 1989/90, with David Pleat's City as youth team boss before returning to Luton as reserve manager. He'd previously been a player, coach and manager at Kenilworth Road, and had also played briefly in the 60s and 70s for Motherwell, Brighton and Northampton Town.

Peter Morris (b. North Houghton, 8.11.1943) was brought in on the 1987 break-up of the Milne/ Hamilton tandem to work as assistant to the latter manager, and found himself in a caretaker role at senior level in December, before the arrival of David Pleat. He took the Kettering manager's job in July 1988, switched to Boston United in June 1992, became assistant at Northampton in June 1994, and boss of Kings Lynn in summer 1995. Peter's playing career encompassed lengthy stints with Mansfield and Ipswich, a couple of seasons with Norwich, and a graduation to player/manager status in a second Mansfield spell. He'd also been assistant at Newcastle United, and had managed Peterborough United and Crewe Alexandra before arriving at Filbert Street.

Colin Victor Murphy (b. Croydon, 21.1.1944) was youth coach with City from August 1990 to May 1991; and has elsewhere gained as much recognition for his often surreal programme notes as for his lengthy list of clubs served in managerial and coaching roles. A relatively undistinguished and injury-hit playing career never brought him a League breakthrough, but he has made a compensatory circuit since concentrating on backroom and training ground activity. He started on the coaching staffs of Charlton Athletic and Nottingham Forest, became assistant boss to Dave Mackay at both Forest and Derby County, and then managed Derby himself from November 1976 to September 1977. He had subsequently completed two stints at the helm of each of Lincoln City and Stockport County, and coaching posts at Notts County and Ittihad (Saudi Arabia) when taken on by David Pleat, and he rejoined Pleat in June 1991 as assistant at Luton. Colin managed Southend United in 1992/3, briefly bossed Irish club Shelbourne from December 1994, and was appointed general manager at Notts County in June 1995, with former City reserve Steve Thompson as his team manager.

Malcolm Musgrove (b. Durham, 8.7.1933) arrived from a coaching role at Aston Villa to become assistant to Frank O'Farrell in

1969, and departed with the boss for Old Trafford. The former West Ham United and Leyton Orient winger, who had substantially helped dump City out of the Cup in 1964 with the latter club, and who had been chairman of the PFA from 1963-66, followed his Manchester United spell with jobs as manager at Torquay United and as coach with Connecticut Bi-Centennials, Chicago Sting, Exeter City, Plymouth Argyle and, most recently, Shrewsbury Town (where he has also assumed physiotherapy duties).

Joe Newton was Fosse's trainer for 1895/6. He'd been Hearts' trainer when they won the Scottish Cup in 1891, and two years later was being used to endorse the beneficial effects of Bovril in press advertisements. On departure from Filbert Street, he joined Dundee.

Ernest Nixon was an assistant trainer to Dave Gardner, and assumed the senior role on Gardner's death in late 1931, until being replaced by Laurie Edwards in 1933.

Dave Richardson was a Jock Wallace appointment at Filbert Street, his second home became Belvoir Drive as he completely reorganised City's junior coaching, scouting, and recruitment network over a successful six-year period. Bryan Hamilton passed the Youth Development Officer over for promotion in 1987, and he moved on immediately to assist Graham Taylor at Aston Villa. In fact Villa Park had been the previous base, too, for this former Middlesbrough schoolteacher, who'd played part-time for Northern League clubs Whitby Town and South Bank, and managed Whitby for two years from 1974.

Bob Roberts (b. Penycae, July 1864; d. Wrexham, 15.3.1932) was a former Welsh international who trained Fosse for and through their inaugural Football League campaign of 1894/5. He'd played in two Welsh Cup Finals (1883, 1884) with his first club, Druids, before signing for Bolton Wanderers in April 1884. Capped nine times as a wing-half, he also briefly served Preston North End and Lincoln City, though he was twice suspended for drink offences during his 1892/3 stint with the latter.

Dave Richardson

Gerry Summers (b. Birmingham, 4.10.1933) was Gordon Milne's assistant for four years from 1982. A former West Bromwich Albion, Sheffield United, Hull City and Walsall player, he had coached at Wolves and West Brom, and had six-year spells as manager at each of Oxford United and Gillingham. On leaving City, he took up a youth coaching role at Derby County.

Harley Thompson, the trainer accused of 'enticing' six Fossils from the Grimsby pitch during the last 15 minutes of the notoriously weatherbeaten match at Grimsby Town in January 1912, and suspended for two months by the League, had been with Fosse since 1905. He remained with the club as assistant when Billy Leech became the first Fossil to be elevated from the playing ranks to the senior trainer's role.

Chris Turner (Christopher Robert; b. Sheffield, 15.9.1958) joined the City backroom staff in the summer of 1995 to assist David Nish with the youth team, and was soon called upon to turn out in goal for the Reserves as the Zeljko Kalac work-permit saga dragged on. Most recently the joint manager of Leyton Orient, Chris had previously starred between the sticks for Sheffield Wednesday (in two spells), Sunderland, Manchester United and Orient, as well as on loan with Lincoln and Leeds.

Malcolm Musgrove

APPENDIX FIVE

STOP PRESS

The data and records in this book are complete up to the end of the 1994/5 season, though a majority of subsequent close-season transfer moves have also been incorporated. Our absolute deadline, though, has fallen after the commencement of 1995/6; and in this section we log both City's latest senior debutants and brief supplementary updates to our main text.

CORICA, Stephen Christopher

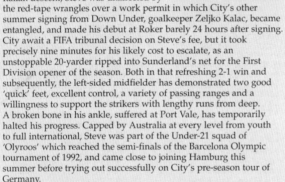

Role: Midfield
b. Innisfail, Queensland, Australia,
24th March 1973

CAREER: Marconi Fairfield (Sydney)/
(July 1995-trials-Hamburger SV)/
Aug 1995:CITY.

Debut v Sunderland (a) 12.8.95 (scored once)

An EC passport holder on account of his Italian descent, Steve was unaffected by the red-tape wrangles over a work permit in which City's other summer signing from Down Under, goalkeeper Zeljko Kalac, became entangled, and made his debut at Roker barely 24 hours after signing. City await a FIFA tribunal decision on Steve's fee, but it took precisely nine minutes for his likely cost to escalate, as an unstoppable 20-yarder ripped into Sunderland's net for the First Division opener of the season. Both in that refreshing 2-1 win and subsequently, the left-sided midfielder has demonstrated two good 'quick' feet, excellent control, a variety of passing ranges and a willingness to support the strikers with lengthy runs from deep. A broken bone in his ankle, suffered at Port Vale, has temporarily halted his progress. Capped by Australia at every level from youth to full international, Steve was part of the Under-21 squad of 'Olyroos' which reached the semi-finals of the Barcelona Olympic tournament of 1992, and came close to joining Hamburg this summer before trying out successfully on City's pre-season tour of Germany.

TAYLOR, Scott Dean

Role: Midfield
b. Portsmouth, 23rd November 1970

CAREER: YT/pro June 1989:Reading/
July 1995:CITY.

Debut v Sunderland (a) 12.8.95

Reunited with former Reading boss Mark McGhee at a cost to City of £500,000, midfielder Scott made a quiet start to the First Division term, but is beginning to gel effectively with Garry Parker and Steve Corica in the new-look Leicester middle line, where both harrying and prompting duties now seem more democratically shared around. Often played as an orthodox winger at Elm Park, Scott made his senior debut there in September 1988 while still a trainee, and his 207 League games for the Royals (24 goals) earned him both a 1994 Division Two championship medal and a stab at the 1995 Play-offs; with his final Reading outing coming in their 3-4 Wembley defeat by Bolton.

ADDENDUM

■ Omitted from career details in the main text were Tony Brien's June 1995 loan to Sheffield Wednesday, for a one-game outing at Millmoor against Basle in the Inter-Toto Cup, prior to his signing for West Brom; and Trevor Christie's March 1995 move to Arnold Town. Peter Eccles starts 1995/6 in Northern Ireland with Crusaders. David Kelly moved from Wolves to Sunderland in September 1995 for a £950,000 fee; while Eddie Kelly is now managing Western League side Barnstaple Town. Russell Osman has signed a short-term playing contract with Brighton & Hove Albion following September 1995 trials; and Nicky Platnauer has left Lincoln City to sign for Bedworth United. Tony Sealy has returned to action with Hong Kong FC after an interim stint as a TV pundit in the Colony; and Alan Smith has been offered a part-time ICIS League contract by St. Albans City.

■ As we went to press, City publicly unveiled £840,000 signing Pontus Kamark (b. 5.4.1969, Västerås). The

Swedish international defender began his career with Västerås SK, before joining IFK Göteborg in 1989. He was expected to remain with his present club until the Swedish season ends in October.

■ As referred to in the introduction, at the time of going to press, Mike Galloway was still in hospital, having suffered serious injuries in a head-on car crash in Leicestershire just days after agreeing to join Portsmouth on loan. Needless to say, everyone associated with this book wishes Mike a speedy recovery.

1 MARTIN GEORGE (Chairman)
2 MARK McGHEE (Manager)
3 BARRIE PIERPOINT (Chief Executive)
4 KEN BRIGSTOCK (President)
5 TOM SMEATON (Vice-Chairman)
6 JOHN ELSOM FCA (Vice-Chairman)
7 ROY PARKER (Director)
8 JOHN SHARP (Director)
9 TERRY SHIPMAN (Director)
10 BILL SHOOTER FCA (Director)
11 GARY LINEKER (Hon. Vice-President)
12 GORDON BANKS (Hon. Vice-President)
13 IAN SILVESTER (Football Secretary)
14 PAUL MACE (Head of Publicity)
15 ALAN BIRCHENALL (Public Relations Officer)
16 DAVID NISH (Youth Team manager)
17 NEVILLE HAMILTON (Community Football)
18 JACK CURTIS (Youth Liaison)
19 ALAN BENNETT, Leire, Leics
20 CLARICE LAXTON, Burnmoor Street, Leicester
21 DANNY McKEOWN, Leicester Forest East
22 GERALD TOON, Leicester
23 'ASHY', Clarendon Park, Leicester
24 JOHN HARRIS, Southgate, London
25 ALEX KINNAIRD, Aylestone Park, Leicester
26 EUGENE A. MACBRIDE, Grantham, Lincs
27 ANDY & ALISON ABBOTT, Leicester
28 STEVE AKERS, Brixton, London
29 In Memory of SID ROBINSON of Burbage
30 HENRYK CYNKAR, Leicester
31 ARTHUR J. HANDS, Hinckley, Leics
32 ANDY WINDRAM, Anstey, Leics
33 GRAEME MALCOLM NORRIS, Rothwell, Northants
34 FRED J. NORMAN, Praze an Beeble, Cornwall
35 IAN PARKER, Wigston Magna, Leics
36 GARRY McCREADIE, Corby, Northants
37 MARK O'NEILL, Skillington, Grantham
38 PETER BRYAN WREN, Countesthorpe, Leics
39 LEE BALDWIN, Wigston, Leicester
40 Mrs KAREN CROSSLEY, Whetstone, Leicester
41 PAUL RUSSELL, Market Harborough, Leics
42 PHILIP CHARLES PLOWRIGHT, Market Harboro'
43 JOHN PATRICK, Thurnby, Leics
44 GARY PATRICK, Thurnby, Leics
45 JILL BOCOCK, Rothley, Leics
46 GEORGINA DEXTER, Rothley, Leics
47 PETER & JANE KINAL, Oakham, Rutland
48 DAVE MARCH, Orpington, Kent
49 DAMON PATRICK BOYLE, Grantham, Lincs
50 ADRIAN GARNER, West Bridgford, Nottingham
51 PHIL ARNOLD, Winchmore Hill, London
52 BARRY LOUNT, Oadby, Leicester
53 MARK STOCKER, Leicester
54 GLEN McGRAW, Rushey Mead, Leicester
55 RICHARD 'Moggy' MORRIS, Oadby, Leicester
56 ASHLEY DAVIDSON, Lyppard Kettleby, Worcester
57 CHRISTOPHER MORRIS, Redditch, Worcester
58 DAVID WALLWORK, Leicester
59 JONATHAN HURST, Thurnby, Leicester
60 ANDY SIMMONS, Hinckley, Leics
61 DAVID B. MOORE, Leicester
62 IAN PAGET, Ibstock, Leics
63 A. SMITH, Countesthorpe, Leics
64 ROBERT HOWLING, Rugby, Warwicks
65 DAVID KENNELL, Leicester
66 MICHAEL SMITH, Leicester
67 CARL DARBY, East Hunsbury, Northampton
68 ADRIAN WILTSHIRE, Mountsorrel, Leics
69 DAVID REILLY, Wigston Harcourt, Leics
70 ALAN DIGBY, Melton Mowbray, Leics
71 MICHAEL PEARMAN, Loughborough, Leics
72 ROB GAHAN, Broughton Astley, Leics
73 ANDY INGALL, Leicester
74 SHARRON EVANS, Oakham
    (Happy 16th from Melanie!)
75 ALUN JONES HUGHES, Eldwick, Bingley, Yorks

76 JEREMY PAGE, Oadby, Leicester
77 DOREEN DALE, Wigston Magna, Leicester
78 RICHARD DALE, Orton Malbourne, P'Boro
79 ANTHONY CHARLES HAYES, Rugby, Warwicks
80 GORDON LESLIE SMITH, Sth Wigston, Leicester
81 DAVID R. LEAKE, Countesthorpe, Leicester
82 PAUL PRESTON, Huncote, Leics
83 DAVID HEATHCOTE, Ibstock, Leics
84 I. SHARMAN, Burbage, Leics
85 D. BOWLCOTT, Leicester
86 PETE ROSEN, Oadby, Leicester
87 MAUREEN TAYLOR, Leicester
88 IAN MATTHAMS, Hathern, Leics
89 DAVID ASKHAM, Whetstone, Leicester
90 SOPHIE BROOKES, Bournville, Birmingham
91 Lord RICHARD ATTENBOROUGH, Surrey
92 KERRY CHAMBERLAIN, Earl Shilton, Leics
93 D. FEARN, Bilton, Rugby, Warwicks
94 DAVID HORNBUCKLE, Whitwick, Leicester
95 JOHN DESMOND BRYSON, Sawbridgeworth, Herts
96 N.S.G. WAKELY, Loughborough, Leics
97 GORDON SMITH, Glenfield, Leicester
98 MARK & MARY BLOCKLEY, Cambridge
99 Miss C.L. & Mrs I. JONES, Oadby, Leicester
100 BRIAN LEE, Market Harborough, Leics
101 NICHOLAS HANGER, Kettering, Northants
102 RONALD JOHNSON, Wellingborough, Northants
103 NIGEL WATTAM, Werrington, Peterboro'
104 J. KAY, Southwick, Sunderland, Tyne & Wear
105 GARETH SMITH, Market Harborough, Leics
106 TREVOR NUNN, Spondon, Derbyshire
107 A.C. JUDSON, Asfordby, Leics
108 DENNIS GRAHAM JUDSON, Asfordby, Leics
109 STEVEN PHILIP BROWN, Wigston, Leicester
110 DON KENDALL, Birstall, Leicester
111 TRINA M. CLARKE, Sileby, Leicester
112 PAUL DESMOND, Cosby, Leics
113 JOHN KEIGHTLEY, Melton Mowbray, Leics
114 DAVID & PETER JOHNSON, Markfield, Leics
115 DAVID LONG, West Knighton, Leicester
116 C.J. WELLMAN, Littlehampton, West Sussex
117 A.W.C. TAYLOR, Spalding, Lincs
118 DAVID N. LUMB, Leicester
119 ADAM JAMES GASK, Rushey Mead, Leicester
120 ROBERT DAVID GASK, Rushey Mead, Leicester
121 PAUL SMITH, Barlestone, Nuneaton, Warwicks
122 JONATHAN ANDREW MILES, Tooting, London
123 L.B. CROSS, Leicester
124 TIM SANDERS, Doncaster, South Yorkshire
125 RICHARD J. COOK, Cosby, Leicester
126 JONATHAN HAYES, Earl Shilton, Leics
127 MATTHEW HAYES, Earl Shilton, Leics
128 PAUL ORTON, Wigston, Leicester
129 STEPHEN BRADLEY, Oadby, Leicester
130 MARK CAIN, Singapore
131 TIM HICKMAN, Market Overton, Nr. Oakham
132 GRAHAM PARKER, Market Overton, Nr. Oakham
133 JEREMY SILVER, Hertford, Herts
134 NIGEL PETER WILBY, Twerton, Bath
135 CHRIS JINKS, Wigston Harcourt, Leicester
136 SIMON HODGETT, Desborough, Northants
137 ALEC STENSON, Aylestone, Leicester
138 TERRY POTTER, Leicester
139 STUART ILIFFE, Accra, Ghana
140 BRYAN PLANT, Leicester
141 LEE HARRIS, Hinckley, Leics
142 CLIVE BRIGGS, Countesthorpe, Leics
143 PHILIP YORK, Hinckley, Leics
144 CLIVE GARRY CREASEY, Grantham, Lincs
145 JOHN PULLEN, Broughton Astley, Leics
146 PRITEN, PRAJY & NALINKUMAR PANCHOLI, Leicester
147 RICHARD PYATT, Leicester
148 A.R. OWEN, Birstall, Leicester
149 ANDREW THOMAS STAFFORD, Mountsorrel, Leicester

150 JAMES A. HATTON, Wigston, Leicester
151 PATRICIA ARNOLD, Oadby, Leicester
152 ROBERT FARMER STANIFORTH, Anstey, Leics
153 JOHN KASPEREK, Kelvedon, Colchester
154 STEPHEN WALKER, Norwich
155 GILLIAN CHENEY, Market Harborough, Leics
156 GEOFFREY LOVETT, Burbage, Leics
157 PAUL R. HATTON, Milton Ernest, Bedfordshire
158 JIM OSBORNE, Kegworth, Derbyshire
159 L.C.F.C. Supporters' Club, Notodden, Norway
160 PER ARNE HANSEN, Notodden, Norway
161 DAVID WILLIAM KIRKHAM, Sonning Common, Oxon
162 JAMES McGREGOR, Rugby, Warwicks
163 JOHN PAGE, Abbey Rise, Leicester
164 ANNE C. NEWBERY, Reading, Berkshire
165 D.E. SCOTT, Sennelager, BFPO 16
166 IAN MICHAEL GILLARD, Loughborough, Leics
167 ADAM GREENWAY, Desford, Leicester
168 DAVID & GARY MARTIN, Cuckfield, W. Sussex
169 JAMES E.G. JOHNSON, Bradford, W. Yorks.
170 PAUL MATTHEWS, Wigston, Leicester
171 RICHARD CODD, Leicester
172 NICK DUGGAN, Leicester
173 NEIL MILLER, Beaumont Leys, Leicester
174 LOUISE MARIE WATCHORN, Melton Mowbray
175 DAVID BUTCHER, Moulton, Northampton
176 ALEX BURNIP, Woodhouse Eaves, Leics
177 IAN PARKER, Woodhouse Eaves, Leics
178 PETE BELTON, Hitchin, Herts
179 DAVID LAYHE, Worksop, Notts
180 KJETIL KVALEN, Lillehammer, Norway
181 DANIEL COTTERELL, Hinckley, Leics
182 SIMON KING, Long Lawford, Warwickshire
183 R.P. WRIGHT, Cranfield, Bedford
184 R.F. BEAUMONT, Merrimac, Massachusetts, USA
185 PHILIP SWALES, Stoneygate, Leicester
186 EDWARD HOLMES, Glen Parva, Leicester
187 BARRIE PARKER, Hinckley, Leics
188 STEWART, ANDY & CATHY VEASEY, Burbage
189 CHRISTOPHER JOHN HARRISON, Earl Shilton
190 STUART CONOPO, Kilsby, Warwickshire
191 CHRIS KERSLAKE, Grange Park, Swindon
192 The FAULKES FAMILY, Thurmaston, Leicester
193 MICHAEL MILLS, Glenfield, Leicester
194 MICHAEL IAN TURNER, Littlethorpe, Leics
195 SIMON KIMBER, Cosby, Leics
196 GAVIN JACKLIN, Huncote, Leics
197 TONY ROE, Nottingham
198 The HENRY FAMILY, Walthamstow, London
199 DENNIS & HILDA HENRY, Torquay, Devon
200 CAROLINE NEALE, Market Harborough, Leics
201 DAVID ANTHONY PANTHER, Belgrave, Leicester
202 PHILIP HAWTIN, Broughton Astley, Leics
203 COLIN BAINES, Mountsorrel, Leics
204 PETER & SAMMI GREGORY, Leicester
205 C.W. HOPPER, Ravenshead, Notts
206 MARK J.C. HOLMES, Glen Parva, Leicester
207 MARK EASON, Wigston Meadows, Leicester
208 PETE SHARP, Humberstone, Leicester
209 PHIL & STEVE BROWN, Leicester Forest East
210 P.W. KEIGHTLEY, Melton Mowbray, Leics
211 AMY & DAVID KING, Stoney Stanton, Leics
212 NOEL BOWE, West Hampstead, London
213 PETER CHARLES CARNALL, Barkby, Leicester
214 JOHN CHECKETTS, Melton Mowbray, Leics
215 STEPHEN KEENAN, Stoney Stanton, Leics
216 DOUGLAS TREVOR HIRD, Leicester
217 MARK DAULBY, Maidenhead, Berkshire
218 RICHARD TERRY, Hampton, Evesham, Worcs
219 PETER GILBERT (The Filbert), Buxton, Derbys
220 MICHAEL WILBUR, Addiscombe, Surrey
221 DOUG KEMP, Wellingborough, Northants
222 ANDREW EATON, Thorpe End, Norwich
223 PETER J.S. WILFORD, Aylestone, Leicester
224 STUART GEORGE, Nuneaton, Warwickshire
225 STEPHEN ROSS, Leicester
226 MAVIS GOODFELLOW, Leicester

227 PHILIP GOODFELLOW, Leicester
228 IAN HARRIS, Stoughton, Leicester
229 JOHN McCARTHY, Duncormick, Co. Wexford
230 MARK OSBORNE, Sutton, Surrey
231 JIM HAWKES, Oadby, Leicester
232 MARK JOHNSON, Skipton, N. Yorkshire
233 STEVEN R. BOTTING, Stanton-under-Bardon
234 PAMELA HOLMES, Lincoln
235 JIM PURDIE, Coventry
236 JOHN PURDIE, Coventry
237 E.B. RICHARDSON, Harlaxton, Grantham, Lincs
238 ADHEV BHARAT PANKHANIA, Birstall, Leicester
239 ANDREW PHILIP KNIGHT, Irthlingborough
240 IAN LEONARD VINCENT,
    Clarendon Park, Leicester
241 STEPHEN PAUL VINCENT,
    Clarendon Park, Leicester
242 TROWNI ANSTEY, Coalville, Leics
243 MARTIN CONNOR, Oxhey, Hertfordshire
244 T.J. GRANT, Saffron Walden, Essex
245 Dr. R.J. SHERRIFF, Yate, Bristol
246 THOMAS MATTHEWS, Leicester
247 TONY HALL, Yaxley, Peterborough
248 MATTHEW EDWARD KNOTT, Chilwell, Notts
249 A. & I. WILLETT, Leicester
250 DAVID & ALISON LENTON, Blaby, Leicester
251 NEDDY NEEDHAM, Coalville, Leics
252 RICHARD PIERRE MALCOLM,
    Leicester Forest East
253 THOMAS J. DAWSON, Leicester
254 Dr. J. STUART HORNER, Samlesbury, Preston
255 SERBIA FOOTBALL CLUB, Evington, Leicester
256 VICTORIA LESLEY AUSTIN, Sileby, Leics
257 GRAHAM M. VERBY, Chigwell, Essex
258 J. RINGROSE, Romford, Essex
259 GORDON SMALL, Penwortham, Preston, Lancs
260 L.A. ZAMMIT, Fareham, Hampshire
261 DAVID KEATS, Thornton Heath, Surrey
262 DEREK HYDE, Llanishen, Cardiff
263 DAVID DOWNS, Tilehurst, Reading
264 FRED LEE, Ford, Plymouth, Devon
265 JONNY STOKKELAND, Kvinesdal, Norway
266 ROB O'DONNELL, Wigston Fields, Leicester
267 SIMON CHALLANDS, Ryehill, Newcastle
268 SYLVIA HIRONS, Lutterworth, Leics
269 ÖRJAN HANSSON, Helsingborg, Sweden
270 DAVID ILIFFE, Leytonstone, London
271 Dr. JOHN E. BATTERBEE, Zwijndrecht, Holland
272 ANNALISE BATTERBEE, Seaford, Sussex
273 CHRISTOPHER BATTERBEE, Brighton, Sussex
274 SIMON J. BATTERBEE, Naperville, Chicago, USA
275 ANNA McDERMOTT, Stoneygate, Leicester
276 NIGEL I. SPIERS, Llanbedr, Crickhowell, Powys
277 CHRISTOPHER JAMES STEVENS, Burbage, Leics
278 PETER JOHN STEVENS, Wellingboro', Northants
279 JOHN ALAN JOHNSON, Burton on Trent, Staffs
280 DAVE McPHERSON, Colchester, Essex
281 ADAM LEWIS, Newbold Verdon, Leicester
282 NICHOLAS HILL,
    May Bank, Newcastle under Lyme, Staffs
283 CHRISTOPHER JAMES ROBINSON,
    Burbage, Leics
284 CAITLIN RUTH EVANS, Loughborough, Leics
285 S. WHITEHOUSE, Western Park, Leicester
286 MICHAEL GRAYSON, Handsworth, Sheffield
287 DAVID BUCKLEY, Eltham Park, London
288 GARETH MILLER, Knighton, Leicester
289 DUNCAN WATT, Sleaford, Lincs
290 TOMMY COTTRELL, Rugby, Warwickshire
291 GILL DONALDSON, Stoneygate, Leicester
292 FAY DONALDSON, Stoneygate, Leicester
293 KEVAN ALBRIGHTON, Hong Kong
294 B. SPIERS, Leicester
295 PETER BURDETT, Kirton in Lindsey, Lincs
296 BILL COOK, Telford, Shropshire
297 GEOFFREY MOSES, Lightcliffe, Halifax
298 J. GARNER, Leicester

299 ROBERT HAMPSON, Oadby, Leicester
300 JAMES SMITH, Wigston, Leicester
301 M.W. STANLEY, Erdington, Birmingham
302 JEFFREY HURLEY, Abertillery, Gwent
303 THE EARL FAMILY, Oadby, Leicester
304 STEPHEN MARK PORT, Surbiton, Surrey
305 STUART COE, Leicester
306 SHAUN MICHAEL JONES, Broughton Astley
307 ROBERT & RUTH COX, Shepshed, Leics
308 RICHARD RAWLINSON, Wigston, Leicester
309 JOHN DAVID HAMILTON, Enderby, Leicester
310 ROSEMARY A. HARVEY, Nuneaton, Warwicks
311 DAVID M. MILES, Scunthorpe, Humberside
312 IAN ALLARD, Normanton-on-Soar, Leics
313 KEN HERTS, Ossett, West Yorkshire
314 ADRIAN PETER WOOD, Duston, Northampton
315 H. BAKER, Leicester
316 MARK HAYWARD, Burbage, Leics
317 ANDY ROBINSON, Burbage, Leics
318 TIM ROBINSON. Glen Parva, Leicester
319 JOHN C. ROBINSON, Melbourne, Australia
320 JOHN ROBINSON, Hinckley, Leics
321 ANGELA BROWN, Syston, Leicester
322 STEWART FELL, Radcliffe, Manchester
323 PAUL TOMPKINS, Kettering, Northamptonshire
324 RICHARD WELLS, Surbiton, Surrey
325 PAUL STEVEN KANIA, Bulphan, Upminster
326 STEVE EMMS, Evesham, Worcs
327 WALTER HIGGINS, OBE, JP, Great Glen, Leics
328 JOHN GREW, Oadby, Leicester
329 ANDY GROOM, Oadby, Leicester
330 MARK NORTON, Glenfield, Leicester
331 WAYNE D. MURBY, Hugglescote, Leics
332 A.W. BAXTER, Leicester
333 DAVID SULLIVAN, Bethnal Green, London
334 CHRIS WIGGINTON, London SW1
335 P. FERGUSON, Whitwick, Leics
336 DEREK PRICE, Wigston, Leicester
337 JOHN WALLAM, Shepshed, Leics
338 BARRIE E. UNDERWOOD, Rugby, Warwicks
339 DARREN BALE, Market Harborough, Leics
340 PETER SMITH, Wigston, Leicester
341 REID ANDERSON, Halifax, West Yorkshire
342 LEE TURNER, Great Gonerby, Grantham, Lincs
343 MICK HARVEY, Thurmaston, Leicester
344 RAYMOND SHAW, Sutton-in-Ashfield, Notts
345 TIMOTHY JAMES LONGMAN,
    Glastonbury, Somerset
346 PHIL STOCKER, Weymouth, Dorset
347 B.W. HUDSON, Sileby, Leics
348 ROY K. SHOESMITH, Cranham, Upminster
349 GARRY STOKES, Loughborough, Leics
350 TIM JEWITT, Oadby, Leicester
351 P.R. WATTS, Kettering, Northamptonshire
352 CHRISTINE HUDSON, Loughborough, Leics
353 PAUL ANTHONY STACEY, Thatcham, Berkshire
354 M.G. MORLEY, Market Harborough, Leics
355 D.J. MILLER, Loughborough, Leics
356 TIM HAYES, Wigston, Leicester
357 N. HOPKIN, Loddon, Norwich, Norfolk
358 ROGER ELKINGTON, Witham, Essex
359 C. BROWN, Bognor Regis, West Sussex
360 MARTIN SPENCER, Desborough, Northants
361 REGINALD WARD, Braunstone, Leicester
362 ANDREW CARL PEARSON,
    Thorpe Acre, Loughborough
363 MARTIN SIMONS, Bekkevoort, Belgium
364 STEVE MATTHEWS, Calverton, Nottingham
365 ANDREW GARNER, Leicester
366 JAMES AUGUSTUS, Groby, Leicester
367 CHRIS SWISTAK, Grimston, Leics
368 ALAN DAVIES, Worcester
369 RICHARD PRESTON, Trowbridge, Wiltshire
370 R. HUTCHINSON, Loughborough, Leics
371 MATTHEW SOADY, Brackley, Northants
372 DANIEL SOADY, Brackley, Northants
373 PAUL SOADY, Brackley, Northants

374 TIMOTHY STEPHEN MAWBY, Lockeridge,
    Marlborough, Wilts
375 DARRELL JOHN QUINN,
    Wigston Fields, Leicester
376 RICHARD HALL, R.A.F. Waddington, Lincs
377 PHIL PASSINGHAM, Market Harborough, Leics
378 PINA MAZZOTTI, Loughborough, Leics
379 SIMON LISSER, Oadby, Leicester
380 SIMON MEASURES, Shepshed, Leics
381 MICHAEL SKELHAM, Uttoxeter, Staffs
382 BRIAN MOORE, Glenfield, Leicester
383 JOHN RAYNS, Wymans Brooke, Cheltenham
384 DAVID RAYNS, Islington, London
385 RICHARD "CLAUDE" RAYNS,
    Farnborough, Hants
386 SHANE HULL, Castle Bytham, Grantham, Lincs
387 DAVE WINDROSS, Barlby, Selby, N. Yorks
388 GEOFFREY HADDON, Hinckley, Leics
389 ROBIN HADDON, Hinckley, Leics
390 NEVILLE CAMPBELL, Leamington Spa
391 DAVID BARRADELL, Sandiacre, Notts
392 MARTIN TOONE, Weston-on-Trent, Derbyshire
393 ANDREW WILFORD, Broughton Astley, Leics
394 SARAH J. WEST, Pitstone, Leighton Buzzard
395 ANDREW ROSE, Grantham, Lincs
396 ALBERT ROSE, Queniborough, Leics
397 ANDY BAILEY, Leicester
398 DAVE SQUIRES, Stamford Hill, London
399 MICK HARDY, Norwich, Norfolk
400 MICK HARDY, Norwich, Norfolk
401 ROGER WATSON, Wigston, Leicester
402 IAN C. THOMPSON, Newtown Linford, Leicester
403 S.R. BAUM, Cosby, Leicester
404 DAVID STEPHEN HUMBERSTON, Leicester
405 STEVE WALTON, Melton Mowbray, Leics
406 PHILL WALTON, Belgrave, Leicester
407 ROBERT PRATT, Syston, Leicester
408 MALWYN DAVEY, Bradgate Ridge, Leicester
409 COLIN BEWLEY, Bardwell, Suffolk
410 MATT CUNDY, Fleckney, Leicestershire
411 IAN D. SMITH, Corby, Northamptonshire
412 CHRISTER SVENSSON, Ödeshög, Sweden
413 STANLEY GRANT, Mowmacre Hill, Leicester
414 HOWARD F. WATMORE, Kingsway, Leicester
415 J.C. JAQUES, Ramsden Bellhouse, Essex
416 PHILIP BIRD, Colchester, Essex
417 IAN HUNTER, Melton Mowbray, Leics
418 GERALD JOHN HUTCHINSON, Leicester
419 J.S. TAYLOR, Tockwith, York
420 R.W. TAYLOR, Beaumont Lodge, Leicester
421 P.A. SHARRATT, Markfield, Leics
422 STEVE ANSTEE, Hanwell, London
423 PAUL JACKSON, Clanfield, Hampshire
424 A.N. OTHER, West Cheshunt, Herts
425 MOIRA & FREDERICK FURNESS,
    North Shields, Tyne & Wear
426 JANICE M. DRUCE, Fleckney, Leicester
427 ANDREW M. BURNHAM,
    South Wigston, Leicester
428 GARY JOHN HUNT, Portishead, Bristol
429 MARK FRENCH, Nuneaton, Warwickshire
430 RICHARD IAN CLARKE, Market Harborough
431 STEVEN BOURNE,
    Woodville, Swadlincote, Derbys
432 NIGEL SHIER, Swinderby, Lincoln
433 STEPHEN ANDREW,
    Rothwell, Northamptonshire
434 ROGER BRAY, Ashby-de-la-Zouch, Leics
435 MICHAEL, DIANA & DAVID CARR,
    Whitehouses, New Jersey, USA
436 DAVID L. SMITH, Glen Rock, New Jersey, U.S.A.
437 CLIVE K. ORMONDE,
    Emmer Green, Reading, Berkshire
438 JOHN T. BROWN, South Wigston, Leicester
439 PETER BAXTER, Tilehurst, Reading
440 GEOFF ALLMAN, Essington, Wolverhampton
441 ROGER EMBURY, Wyre Piddle, Worcestershire

442 ARTHUR J. AYRES, Camberley, Surrey
443 ROBERT H. AYRES, Carshalton, Surrey
444 ARTHUR SHAW, Amesbury, Salisbury, Wilts
445 CAMPBELL CAIRNS, Leicester
446 S.A. FERROW, Grouville, Jersey
447 S.W. BUCKLEY, Penn, Buckinghamshire
448 SIMON JOSEPH MESSENGER,
Woburn Sands, Bucks
449 GRAHAME WOODROFFE, Loughborough, Leics
450 S. DREWERY, Belgrave, Leicester
451 ELIZABETH BAUM, Mountsorrel, Leics
452 ELIZABETH BAUM, Mountsorrel, Leics
453 CARL & GORDON HARRISON,
Mountsorrel, Leics
454 ROB YOUNG, Stoney Stanton, Leics
455 SIMON BOOR, Whetstone, Leicester
456 J.R. CHAMBERLAIN, Nottingham
457 LINDA & ROBERT WORTLEY,
Leicester Forest East
458 R.G. JONES, Market Bosworth, Warwickshire
459 ANDREW WHITTLE,
Ross-on-Wye, Herefordshire
460 TIMOTHY J. VESTY, Barnstaple, Devon
461 STEPHEN KIERAN BYRNE,
Iwerne Minster, Dorset
462 WILLIAM JOHN SHERWOOD, Gosport, Hants
463 PAUL HARRIS, Altrincham, Cheshire
464 SIMON C. WEST, Wigston Harcourt, Leicester
465 JOHN & IAN WILLARS, Over, Cambridge
466 PAUL GUNBY, Wigston Fields, Leicester
467 DEREK NEWTON, Northborough, Peterborough
468 GAVIN PUGH, Hinckley, Leics
469 GAVIN CHARLES POYNTON, Syston, Leicester
470 MATTHEW KENNETH POYNTON, Syston, Leics
471 DAVID HUTCHINSON, Markfield, Leics
472 MARK HICKENBOTHAM, Rothley, Leics
473 JOHN HICKENBOTHAM, Glenfield, Leicester
474 RICHARD & JOSEPH FREARSON,
Ashby-de-la-Zouch, Leics
475 NIGEL & DEBBIE ROBINSON,
Bromham, Bedford
476 JOHN CASEY, Hinckley, Leics
477 MURRAY WARNER, Pimlico, London
478 KELVIN & JOHN KNIGHT, Earl Shilton, Leics
479 DAVE COBLEY, Leicester
480 DAVID MOODIE, Ipswich, Suffolk
481 ALAN P. CRAFT, Kingston upon Thames, Surrey
482 ROBERT A. CRAFT, Pinner, Middlesex
483 JONATHAN C. DUCKWORTH, Oadby, Leicester
484 MALCOLM, BEN & TOM SNELL,
Thrussington, Leics
485 MARTIN JARRED, York
486 JAMES McCLELLAND, Farnborough, Hampshire
487 P. STONES, Leicester
488 DALE TONKS, Leicester
489 ANDREW JOHN WYNN, Banbury, Oxon
490 GERALD MORTIMER, Ilkeston, Derbyshire
491 DENNIS A. LAMBERT, Noctorum, Birkenhead
492 KEN PRIOR, Bitterne, Southampton
493 CHARLES GUY FRENCH, Hillmorton, Rugby
494 MIROSLAW OLSZEWSKI,
West Knighton, Leicester
495 TERRY MORGAN, Glen Parva, Leicester
496 GEOFF SHARP, Loughborough, Leics
497 STEVE HITCHCOX, Banbury, Oxon
498 CHRIS HORNER, Chiswick, London
499 WILLIAM DAVID WILKINS,
South Wigston, Leicester
500 ROBERT LEE, Leicester
501 WAYNE PYCROFT, Swadlincote, Derbyshire
502 MICK HORN, Knighton, Leicester
503 TOM LOGUE, Belgrave, Leicester
504 COLIN GRANBY, Haworth, West Yorkshire
505 KEVIN BONSER, Hinckley, Leics
506 ANDREW NEALE, Norwich, Norfolk
507 JONATHAN HALL, Henleaze, Bristol
508 DEREK SEATON, Botcheston, Leics

509 ANDY, SARAH & DONNA BARTON, Banbury
510 TONY WARD, Burley-in-Wharfdale, W. Yorks
511 DAVID NORTON, Gloucester
512 ANDY RICHMOND, Beccles, Suffolk
513 A. CLAYTON, Christchurch, Dorset
514 J. CLAYTON, Braunstone, Leicester
515 JOHN PASIECZNIK, Hadfield, Glossop, Derbys
516 ALAN & STEVEN RAY,
Newport, Brough, N. Humberside
517 DAVID ARCH, Bourne, Lincs
518 JOHN MUSGROVE, Gateshead, Tyne & Wear
519 M.J. BAXTER, North Walsham, Norfolk
520 DAVID PAYNE, Thornton Cleveleys, Lancs
521 DEAN HENFREY, Melton Mowbray, Leics
522 TONY HUMBERSTON, Thurnby, Leicester
523 R.C. STEADMAN, Barrow upon Soar, Leics
524 ANDREW WELLS, Hathern, Leics
525 TIM ENGLISH, Stratton, Bude, Cornwall
526 TONY WORN, Quorn, Leicestershire
527 ROBERT GREGORY & DIANE,
Stockton Brook,Staffs
528 JOHN ALDRIDGE, Leicester
529 NICK CARTER, Leicester
530 PETER HOLLINS, Leicester
531 PETER, GRAHAM & MATTHEW JEPSON,
Narborough, Leics
532 DAVE CHRISTIAN, Melton Mowbray, Leics
533 ADRIAN JOHN CALVERT, Leicester
534 Dr. ROBERT GARNER, Leicester
535 ANDREW MOUTREY, Gunthorpe, Peterborough
536 PHILIP DAVID CLARKE, Shepshed, Leics
537 KEN McGUINNESS, Toronto, Canada
538 KEVIN VERNON, Hinckley, Leics
539 DAVID RICHENS, Exeter, Devon
540 CRAIG BREWIN, Bounds Green, London
541 NIGEL WALKER, Bakersfield, Nottingham
542 JOHN KING, Leicester
543 SYD & SHEILA BOWERS, Stamford, Lincs
544 T.I.S. BURNS, Broughton Astley, Leics
545 LESLIE EXTON, Bedford
546 SIMON RANDON, Fritton Common, Norwich
547 TONY McMAHON,
Addlestone, Weybridge, Surrey
548 SIMON CHRISTOPHER MAXFIELD,
Gainsboro', Lincs
549 DEREK JOHN COOKE, Countesthorpe, Leics
550 DAVID STANHOPE, Leicester
551 ANDY PATEMAN, Leicester
552 Mr DAVID K.B. SMITH, Prestbury, Cheltenham
553 JOHN SPIERS, Oadby, Leicester
554 NEAL REEVE, Syston, Leicester
555 PETER W. JONES, Great Barton, Suffolk
556 ANDREW JOYCE, Kirby Muxloe, Leicester
557 PAUL LEATHERLAND, Syston, Leicester
558 IAN CASSIE, Twickenham, Middlesex
559 ANDY CASSIE, East Molesey, Surrey
560 LANCE WELLS, Colchester, Essex
561 STEPHEN J. SHERWOOD, Colchester, Essex
562 LAURENCE FORD, King's Heath, Birmingham
563 CHRISTOPHER DAVIS, Dorchester
564 MARK BEECROFT, London SW20
565 D.J. GOODACRE, Heywood, Lancashire
566 STEPHEN PEARS, Castle View, Nottingham
567 STEPHEN PEARS, Castle View, Nottingham
568 D. CARRUTHERS, Burbage, Leics
569 ALEXANDER DALGLEISH, Sauchie, Clacks
570 MALCOLM CHARLES CLAPHAM,
Wigston, Leicester
571 TIM WORMLEIGHTON, Glen Parva, Leicester
572 GERARD BOLAND, Southcourt, Aylesbury
573 JANICE BENFIELD, Abbey Lane, Leicester
574 BEN ATKINS, Little Harrowden, Northants
575 MICHAEL SCHLAPHOFF, Leicester
576 ALAN HINDLEY, Maghull, Merseyside
577 ROBERT SMITH, Enderby, Leicester
578 JOHN & SOPHIE HUTCHINSON, Leicester
579 STEPHEN INGALL, Cosby, Leics

580 CHRISTOPHER J.M. DEWEY,
Thurmaston, Leicester
581 KIERAN & CLINT BLACKSHAW,
Stocking Farm, Leicester
582 NORMAN KINCAID, Hayes, Bromley, Kent
583 K. PINK, Salisbury, Wiltshire
584 W.S.C. WORSWICK, Desborough, Northants
585 DAVID ANDREW BENNETT, Scraptoft, Leicester
586 ANDREW WATERFIELD, Teddington, Middlesex
587 MARK FISH, Ealing, London
588 ROGER PETTITT, Walsall, West Midlands
589 RICHARD PATRICK WHITTINGTON,
Wigston, Leics
590 ANDRW JOHN BRAKER, Syston, Leicester
591 THOMAS & EMILY MILES, Houghton on the Hill
592 M.K. NEWELL, Doncaster, Yorkshire
593 JAMES CLARKE, Brighton
594 DANTE CLARKE, London SW6
595 STEVE WEAVER, Petham, Canterbury
596 A.P. WHITE, Barrow-in-Furness, Cumbria
597 CONNOR MARK ANDERSON,
Hamilton, Leicester
598 DAVE METCALF, Leicester
599 BRIAN R.M. PLAYFAIR, Blantyre, Scotland
600 ALAN THOMAS
601 NATHAN THOMAS
602 MICHAEL CONIBEAR, Ashby-de-la-Zouch, Leics
603 KEN & ROSS McSEVENEY, Market Harborough
604 ANDREW MARK WELLS, London SW12
605 GRAHAM & ARTHUR PROSSER, Leicester
606 DEAN A. GALE, Loughborough, Leics
607 A.F. PEARSON Jnr, Stapenhill, Burton-on-Trent
608 A.F. PEARSON Jnr, Stapenhill, Burton-on-Trent
609 PAUL KIRWAN, Hamilton, Leicester
610 TONY SMITH, Leicester
611 DAVE SMITH, Orpington, Kent
612 STUART & NATALIE FRETTER,
Market Harborough
613 MICHAEL J. TAYLOR,
Mark, Highbridge, Somerset
614 JULIE KIRK, Burton Lazars, Leics
615 OLLIE PARDO, Spital, Chesterfield, Derbys
616 DAVID STEPHEN KENDALL,
Wigston Meadows, Leics
617 IAN HAFFORD, BFPO 140
618 TIM GOSS, Leicester
619 NICK NOVAKOVIC, Aylestone Meadows, Leicester
620 DAVID JOHN SHELTON, Bishopsworth, Bristol
621 DONALD SIMPSON, Queniborough, Leics
622 PAUL V. SYKES, Great Glen, Leicester
623 S., L., I.J. & R. PEARS,
Newbold Verdon, Leicester
624 BEN BERRY, Ashley
625 The FOX FANZINE, Cosby, Leicester
626 The HOLMES FAMILY, Church Gresley, Derbys
627 JONATHAN LEIGH, Moseley, Birmingham
628 A.J. ELLIOTT, Fleckney, Leicester
629 NEIL M. WHITE, Thurmaston, Leicester
630 STEPHANIE JASTRZEBSKI, Elmesthorpe, Leics
631 STEVE MARRIOTT, Burnley, Lancashire
632 COLIN CAMERON, Sidcup, Kent
633 PETER WARRINGTON, Woodville, Derbyshire
634 TIM HEMS, Lyddington, Rutland
635 HANNAH FAIRGRIEVE, Stoney Stanton, Leics
636 JAMES E. BRIND, Pawlett, Somerset
637 STUART J. ALLCOCK, Exeter, Devon
638 M.F. DOWNIE, Chilwell, Nottingham
639 KEITH HUBBARD, Barlestone, Warwickshire
640 NIGEL DOWNES, Wigston, Leicester
641 ALAN SOLE, Ferndown, Dorset
642 CHRISTOPHER F. GRIFFIN,
Holmes Chapel, Cheshire
643 JASON BOWERS, Stamford, Lincs
644 STEPHEN L. MARTIN, Bleasby, Notts
645 DONALD M.L. MARTIN, Bleasby, Notts
646 MICHAEL & SYLVIA COSGROVE,
Horncastle, Lincs

647 PETER WILSON, Clarendon Park, Leicester
648 MAL COXON, Measham, Swadlincote, Derbys
649 BENJAMIN P. SCANLAN, Mountsorrel, Leics
650 STUART CLARKE, Gainsborough, Lincs
651 JOSHUA RYLATT, Leicester
652 PAUL WELCH, Barlestone, Warwickshire
653 MARK WAGSTAFF, Whitwick, Leics
654 COLIN WOODFORD, Chiswick, London
655 DAVID PITCHER, Market Harborough, Leics
656 JOHN HUNT, Whitwick, Leics
657 ASTLEY V. SHARPLES, Medbourne, Leics
658 RAJESH KUMAR, Evington, Leicester
659 NEIL T. BROOKES, Melton Mowbray, Leics
660 T.G. LORAN, Stevenage, Herts
661 DAVID HART, Weymouth, Dorset
662 RICHARD HART, Weymouth, Dorset
663 BRIAN CROUCH, Ratby, Leicester
664 HENRY HAMMOND, Oadby, Leicester
665 JAMES STORER, Barwell, Leics
666 IAN BURCHNALL, Enderby, Leicester
667 TERRY WOMACK, Starcross, Exeter
668 T.H. HARRIS, Oadby, Leicester
669 P. LOWE, Whitwick, Leicester
670 G.S. WHITE, Braunstone, Leicester
671 ANDREW HARTY, Thurmaston, Leicester
672 NIK BOWERS, Stamford, Lincs
673 CEL PERONE, Bishops Itchington, Warwicks
674 ROBERT KNIGHT, Cuffley, Potters Bar, Herts
675 DENIS BREWIN, East Leake, Leics
676 DAVE JOHNSON, Oadby, Leicester
677 ROY JOHNSON, Oadby, Leicester
678 PAUL J. DANIELS, Markfield, Leics
679 NICHOLAS SMART, Leicester
680 COLIN HALL, Belgrave, Leicester
681 MARKAS MARRIOTT, Hugglescote, Leics
682 PAUL NICHALAS GREWCOCK,
    Stoney Stanton, Leics
683 MARK TOTTMAN, Cotesbach, Lutterworth
684 KEITH ANDREW MORLEY, Wigston, Leicester
685 JOHN & PATRICIA BENNETT, Syston, Leicester
686 DEREK M. CURTIS, Market Harborough, Leics
687 DAVID HARDY, Anstey, Leicester
688 JUSTIN PAVEY, Glen Parva, Leicester
689 JOHN CHARLES OSBORNE, Hinckley, Leics
690 RICHARD I. BOOKER,
    Water Orton, Birmingham
691 GARY EDEN, East Goscote, Leics
692 CARL McDERMOTT, Barwell, Leics
693 STEWART G. CARTER, Harborne, Birmingham
694 CLIFF GARNER, Nuneaton, Warwicks
695 NORMAN PESSIO, Stonavaill, Birmingham
696 MICHAEL TAYLOR,
    Bancroft Park, Milton Keynes
697 ANDY WILKINSON, Braunstone, Leicester
698 PAUL WISDISH, Groby, Leicester
699 MICHAEL KEITH HARTLAND, Hinckley, Leics
700 IAN JAMES DAVIS, Ratby, Leicester
701 AIVARS T. KING, Radlett, Herts
702 CHRISTOPHER LEWITT, Leicester
703 DAVID KNIGHT, Chilwell, Nottingham
704 BOB BUTLIN, Market Harborough, Leics
705 ROBERT TINSLEY, Long Clawson, Leics
706 KEITH CLAYSON, South Wigston, Leics
707 KEVIN W. BRANT, Evington, Leicester
708 SEAMUS GOGAN, Corby, Northamptonshire
709 NICOLA GOGAN, Corby, Northamptonshire
710 MARK ANTHONY SHAW, Coalville, Leics
711 TIMOTHY ROBERT CARVELL, Hinckley, Leics
712 DAVID FAWCETT, Aylestone, Leicester
713 C.J. FREER, Saxilby, Lincoln
714 ROGER REVELL, Thurmaston, Leicester
715 MARK HOOK, Aylestone, Leicester
716 MARK ERNEST CAIN, Leicester
717 C.H. HANDLEY, Loughborough, Leics
718 STEPHEN N. PETCHER, Barlestone, Warwicks
719 JOHN WILLIAM DIAMOND, Fleckney, Leics
720 DAVID BAILEY, Leicester

721 BRETT LYNES, Narborough, Leics
722 COLIN JOHNSON, Atherstone, Warwicks
723 DAVID G. BENTLEY, Abbotts Bromley, Staffs
724 MARY CHESTER, Coalville, Leics
725 DAVE CATTLE, Leicester Forest East
726 CHARLES KENT, Anstey, Leics
727 DAVID K. LEWIS, Whetstone, Leicester
728 COLIN LEE, Whetstone, Leicester
729 HELEN WALLIS, Leicester
730 BOB LAMBERT, Rugby, Warwicks
731 ANDREW MICHAEL GREATOREX,
    Glenfield, Leicester
732 RUSSELL CARR, Braunstone, Leicester
733 MARK ORTON, Burbage, Leics
734 MARK J. BOYCE, Gilmorton, Leics
735 ANDREW JOHN BUNCHER, Oadby, Leicester
736 KEITH HOLLIS, Leicester
737 CHERYL BOULTON, Knighton, Leicester
738 LEIGH SPENCER, Kirby Muxloe, Leicester
739 PHILLIP BRADLEY, Whitwick, Leics
740 NEIL PARTRIDGE, Barby, Rugby, Warks
741 DAVID WRIGHT, Burbage, Leics
742 ALEX GRIFFITHS, Broughton Astley, Leics
743 MARTIN JARVIS, Wellingborough, Northants
744 BARRY N. CLAYTON, Oadby, Leicester
745 Miss STELLA SWANN, Leicester
746 PAT MANNION, Hinckley, Leics
747 GUY COOPER, Ibstock, Leics
748 MATHEW DAVIES, Enderby, Leicester
749 P.J. MANSHIP, Leicester
750 EDWIN STRAW, Hungarton, Leics
751 STEPHEN RENNOCKS, Hinckley, Leics
752 NEIL HUBBARD, Hinckley, Leics
753 ROB AUCOTT, Knighton, Leicester
754 ASHLEY DAVIS, Ratby, Leicester
755 ROGER GANDY, Rozelle, Sydney, Australia
756 CHARLES HILL, Deeping St James, P'boro
757 MARK WALLEY, Nuneaton, Warwicks
758 GARY & CHRIS SMITH, Wigston, Leicester
759 RAY KIRBY, Wigston Magna, Leics
760 RUSSELL J. MATCHETT, Whitwick, Leics
761 GLYN JONES, Shepshed, Leics
762 GRAHAM R. JOHNSON, Oadby, Leicester
763 MICHAEL SMITH, R.A.F. Bruggen
764 JOHN CAWLEY, Leicester
765 RICHIE CUMBERLIDGE, Countesthorpe, Leics
766 GARY DAVI MacFARLANE, Leicester
767 BARRY VINIKER, Loughton, Essex
768 BRETT D. WAIN, Oadby, Leicester
769 RICHARD BILSKI, Blaby, Leicester
770 R.C. STANIFORTH, Melksham, Wiltshire
771 ROBERT MARK TOMLINSON,
    Kingston upon Thames
772 STEVE ORAM, Broughton Astley, Leics
773 MATTHEW REED, Ibstock, Leics
774 GRAHAM & STEPHEN PICKERING,
    Market Harborough
775 GARY BOND, Leicester
776 CHRISTOPHER PAUL CARTER, Loughborough
777 DAVID GAYTON, Maltby, South Yorkshire
778 IAN HOOPER, Dagenham, Essex
779 CLIVE RICHARDS, Wigston, Leicester
780 CHRIS EYRE, Wendover, Bucks
781 TIM EDSON, Oadby Leicester
782 BARRY CROUCH, Western Park, Leicester
783 DAVID HARDBATTLE, East Goscote, Leics
784 STEPHEN BEIGHTON, Markfield, Leicester
785 SHARON COE, Whetstone, Leicester
786 TONY OLIVER, Loughborough, Leics
787 ANTHONY SHARMAN, Leicester
788 MICK, JULIE, KATIE & EMMA ANDREWS,
    Wilbarston, Leics
789 ANDREA, Love, Mum and Dad
790 ADRIAN TAYLOR, West Ealing, London
791 MATTHEW GANDY, Mayfair, London
792 PER PERSSON, Borlange, Sweden
793 PETER NAYLOR, Melton Mowbray, Leics

794 AMANDA INGAMELLS, Beaumont Leys
    Leicester
795 DAVID NURSE, Thurcaston, Leicester
796 M.G. LIMBERT, Melton Mowbray, Leics
797 M. FISHER, Glenfield, Leicester
798 E.R. DAGLEY, Coalville, Leics
799 GLENN RICHARDSON, Goose Bay, BFPO 9
800 MARTYN BULMAN, Blaby, Leicester
801 HAYLEY THOMPSON, Holts Close, Leicester
802 BARBARA TAYLOR, Littlethorpe, Leicester
803 KATE TAYLOR, London N22
804 HELEN TAYLOR, London N22
805 LINDA CARRUTHERS-WATT,
    Muswell Hill, London
806 PAUL TAYLOR, London
807 JENNY & ALEX (Leicester Grill)
808 COLIN BOULTER, Barwell Leics
809 NEIL BULLOUS, Wigston, Leicester
810 NATHAN OSWIN, Oadby, Leicester
811 MIKE DAVAGE, Old Catton, Norwich
812 STEPHEN BALL, Grange, South Australia
813 CHRISTOPHER JOHN EASTWOOD,
    Groby, Leicester
814 JIM BURTON, Breedon on the Hill, Derbys
815 RICHARD S. WELLS, Stratton St Margaret, Wilts
816 NICK COE, Little Bowden, Leics
817 JONATHAN CHARLTON, Evington, Leicester
818 PAUL ADDISON, Rugby, Warwicks
819 ANTHONY G. HUNKIN, Tuffley, Glos
820 DAVID J. SMITH, South Wigston, Leicester
821 BAS FORGHAM, Hugglescote, Coalville, Leics
822 STEPHEN R. BOOT, Thurmaston, Leicester
823 NEILL, HARRY & JOANNE STANIFORTH
    LCFC Premier Fans
824 BALBI MURRELL, Maidstone, Kent
825 GLENN MURRELL, Maidstone, Kent
826 PETE NUNWA, Plumstead, London
827 SHELLEY PABLA, Swavesey, Cambs
828 KIERON PABLA, Swavesey, Cambs
829 LEE PAYNE, Cropston, Leicester
830 NIGEL A. RILEY, Dudley, Northumberland
831 PETE WORRALL, Kirby Muxloe, Leics
832 GEORGE TOON, Rowlatts Hill, Leicester
833 DAVE SMITH, Oadby, Leicester
834 HELEN SMITH, Oadby, Leicester
835 TOM SMITH, Oadby, Leicester
836 JENNIE SMITH, Oadby, Leicester
837 PAUL SMITH, Oadby, Leicester
838 SALLY SMITH, Oadby, Leicester
839 IAIN STURCH, Acocks Green, Birmingham
840 JANE MANSELL, Morden, Surrey
841 JAMES HUNT, Withington, Manchester
842 KEITH WATHEY, Stoney Stanton, Leicester
843 ROMAN SCUPLAK, Leicester
844 AMANDA JAYNE BONSELL, Aylestone, Leicester
845 STEVE WELLS, Clapham, London
846 JON HOLMES, Park Associates, Nottingham
847 STEVE ARSCOTT, Belgrave St Peters Super-Blue
848 DAVID GASK, Rothley, Leicester
849 STEVE LAMBDEN, Central TV, Nottingham
850 LEE RIGBY, Thurmaston, Leicester
851 RICHARD GRAVES, Loughborough, Leics
852 GARETH M. DAVIES, Holyhead, Gwynedd
853 BOBBY BASKCOMB, Worth Matravers, Dorset
854 JULIAN BASKCOMB, Leicester